Encyclopedia of Asylum Therapeutics, 1750–1950s

ALSO BY MARY DE YOUNG
AND FROM MCFARLAND

―――――――――――――――――――

*Madness: An American History of
Mental Illness and Its Treatment* (2010)

*The Day Care Ritual Abuse Moral Panic* (2004)

*The Ritual Abuse Controversy:
An Annotated Bibliography* (2002)

*Child Molestation: An Annotated Bibliography* (1987)

*Incest: An Annotated Bibliography* (1985)

*The Sexual Victimization of Children* (1982)

# Encyclopedia of Asylum Therapeutics, 1750–1950s

Mary de Young

McFarland & Company, Inc., Publishers
*Jefferson, North Carolina*

LIBRARY OF CONGRESS CATALOGUING-IN-PUBLICATION DATA

de Young, Mary, 1949– , author.
Encyclopedia of asylum therapeutics, 1750–1950s / Mary de Young.
    p.    cm.
Includes bibliographical references and index.

ISBN 978-0-7864-6897-3 (softcover : acid free paper) ∞
ISBN 978-1-4766-1788-6 (ebook)

I. Title.
[DNLM: 1. Mental Disorders—therapy—Encyclopedias—English.
2. Commitment of Mentally Ill—history—Encyclopedias—English.
3. History, 18th Century—Encyclopedias—English.
4. History, 19th Century—Encyclopedias—English.
5. History, 20th Century—Encyclopedias—English.
6. Hospitals, Psychiatric—history—Encyclopedias—English.
7. Mental Disorders—history—Encyclopedias—English.    WM 13]

RC437        616.89003—dc23        2014050024

BRITISH LIBRARY CATALOGUING DATA ARE AVAILABLE

© 2015 Mary de Young. All rights reserved

*No part of this book may be reproduced or transmitted in any form
or by any means, electronic or mechanical, including photocopying
or recording, or by any information storage and retrieval system,
without permission in writing from the publisher.*

On the cover: Patient undergoing hydrotherapy treatment
(The National Library of Medicine)

Printed in the United States of America

*McFarland & Company, Inc., Publishers
Box 611, Jefferson, North Carolina 28640
www.mcfarlandpub.com*

To Joe Verschaeve ... because he knows why it matters.

# Acknowledgments

I would like to offer a sincere thanks to colleagues and friends who offered advice and support during the writing of this book. I am particularly indebted to Bob Hendersen, Joe Verschaeve, Michael and Mary Louise Ott, Jennifer Stewart, and Erika King and Robert Beasecker.

The librarians at Grand Valley State University are owed a special thanks for hunting down and retrieving often obscure reference material, and then never raising an eyebrow about the sometimes, shall we say, "unsettling" content.

I learned so much from my visits to the *Het Dolhuys,* the national museum of psychiatry, in Haarlem, Netherlands, and to the *Medicinsk Museion* in Copenhagen, Denmark, which has an interesting exhibit on therapeutic interventions used in the country's asylums. The Glore Psychiatric Museum in St. Joseph, Missouri, was a wonderful place to spend a long, rainy afternoon, and I want to thank Sarah Elder, curator of collections, for allowing me to take photographs and publish them in this book.

# Table of Contents

*Acknowledgments* — vi
*Preface* — 1

## The Entries

| | |
|---|---:|
| Awakenings | 5 |
| Bed Therapy | 7 |
| Cerebral Stimulation (Psychic Stimulation) | 13 |
| Color Cure (Chromotherapy, Colorology) | 22 |
| Counterirritation | 26 |
| Deep Sleep Therapy (Prolonged Narcosis, Prolonged Sleep, Continuous Sleep) | 44 |
| Depletive Therapy ("Heroic Therapy," Antiphlogistic Therapy, "Rush's System") | 52 |
| Diet | 71 |
| Electrotherapy | 82 |
| Etherization | 96 |
| Exodontia | 98 |
| Expressive Therapy | 101 |
| Fever Therapy (Pyrotherapy, Pyretotherapy) | 120 |
| Fixing (The Eye, Catching the Eye, the Gaze, the Clinical Gaze) | 137 |
| Forced Feeding (Forced Alimentation, Gavage) | 141 |
| Genital Surgery | 152 |
| Hydrotherapy (Hydropathy) | 164 |
| Hypothermia (Cold Narcosis, Refrigeration Therapy, Frozen Sleep) | 188 |
| Isolation | 191 |
| Masks, Gags and Toggles | 205 |
| Mechanical Restraints | 208 |

| | |
|---|---:|
| Metallotherapy (Metalloscopy, Burquism) | 239 |
| Moral Treatment (Moral Management, Moral Therapy) | 242 |
| Organotherapy (Opotherapy, Séquardotherapy, Histotherapy, Zootherapy, *Materia Medica Animalis*) | 254 |
| Orthomolecular Therapy | 261 |
| Ovarian Compression | 264 |
| Phototherapy (Light Therapy) | 267 |
| Pious Frauds (Salutary Demonstrations, Innocent Ruses, Curative Ruses, Suggestive Therapies) | 270 |
| Psychic Driving, Accelerated Psychotherapy, or Automated Psychotherapy | 275 |
| Psychosurgery | 277 |
| Rotation, Oscillation and Vibration | 295 |
| Salutary Fear | 306 |
| Shock Therapy (Convulsive Therapy) | 322 |
| Surgery | 346 |
| Total Push | 351 |
| *Index* | 355 |

# Preface

"A book or a set of books giving information on many subjects or on many aspects of one subject and typically arranged alphabetically." That venerable screed *The Oxford Dictionary* so defines "encyclopedia."

The *Encyclopedia of Asylum Therapeutics, 1750–1950s,* meets all of those definitional standards. It is a book, although nearly verbose enough to be a set of books; it contains multiple perspectives on a single topic, in this case two centuries of the treatment of the insane; and it is alphabetically arranged, first by each primary therapeutic and then by any subentries that further elaborate upon it. Readers will find a list of references after each major therapeutic entry that is relevant to it, as well as to any and all of its subentries.

The book aspires to also capture the essence, the spirit, of "encyclopedia." The term is from the Greek, meaning a "circle of learning" that can opened, indeed must be opened, by new knowledge. The question here is, whose knowledge? This encyclopedia is predicated on the recognition that there are multiple sources of knowledge about asylum therapeutics, and multiple ways in which knowledge has been, and is still, derived from wisdom and socially constructed from information and experience. At the same time it recognizes that certain types of knowledge, and certain sources of it, have been and are still privileged over others. Thus historical archives are filled with papers and reports authored by asylum physicians who, with various degrees of clarity and reflexivity, discuss therapeutic interventions with their patients. Had this book collected, organized, synthesized and presented only that privileged body of knowledge, a deceptively progressive metanarrative would have emerged: to cure insanity things were tried, mistakes were made, lessons were learned, different and better things were then tried, mistakes were made, more lessons were then learned, *ad infinitum*.

Privileged knowledge often maintains its privilege by muting, if not silencing, challenges to its hegemony. A deeper spelunking of the historical archives was necessary to recover and then synthesize these quieted bodies of knowledge. The memoirs and memories of treated asylum patients, the reports of investigating and oversight committees, local newspaper reportage, and other subaltern sources were synthesized into the encyclopedic entries of this book, thus inviting readers to read not just along the grain of the metanarrative, but against it.

That is the intent, but what is the content of this book? It is an encyclopedia of asylum therapeutics, a curious topic, perhaps, but one for which a case can be made. Therapeutics are best thought of as interventions through which abstract knowledge is made practicable. Therapeutics link medical knowledge with practitioner skill and with the personal expectations of embodied patients who experience and understand their own maladies in different ways. It is curious, then, that such an important endeavor has not been granted its due of scholarly attention. The present book seeks to redress that oversight.

And it does it in an encyclopedic form. Perhaps a case for that has to be made as well. Despite the appeal of a metanarrative of steady progress in the treatment of asylum patients, therapeutics have proceeded over history in fits, starts and turns. They often have neither a clear beginning nor a definitive end, and certainly not an even spread over the geographic landscape. The inherent urge to impose order was resisted in the compilation of this book in the hope that the discontinuities, disappearances and reappearances, and recycles of therapeutics opens the encyclopedia's "circle of learning" to critical inquiry.

To that end also, the entries herein are narrative in form rather than consisting of a cold recitation of facts. Central to many of those narratives are individuals, more often asylum physicians than not, who loom large. Some of them may have been compassionate, others inquisitive, others simply zealous in their desire to treat insanity, but in the encyclopedic narratives, and to the extent possible, their ulterior motives have been bracketed off. This, too, is in service of opening up the "circle of learning" to critical inquiry about the various contexts—from social to professional to institutional—that influenced the practice of therapeutics, their administration, and the assessment of their effects and efficacy. The bracketing off serves another purpose as well. It goes a little way towards explaining why some therapeutics that should not have worked, seemed to have worked in aiding recovery. If society, science, institution and interaction share a system of beliefs about the nature of insanity, and if the therapeutic intervention is appreciated as a reflection of those beliefs and is expected by all parties to be effective, it very well may be. That is more than a placebo effect. It is, instead, the intimate relationship between structure and agency, contexts and individuals. The encyclopedic entries are intended to invite consideration of that relationship.

The *Encyclopedia of Asylum Therapeutics, 1750–1950,* limits its scope in time and place. The first purpose-built asylum for the insane was constructed in the fifteenth century for the purpose of containment, not treatment. By the mid-eighteenth century, though, and in reaction to changing social and ideological contexts, asylums began to earnestly carry out the dual, and perhaps somewhat contradictory, goals of containment *and* treatment. By the mid-twentieth century most of the therapeutic innovations those goals had spawned had given way to pharmaceutical innovations, and the steady decanting of asylum patients into the community soon followed. Within those two historical markers can be found the entries in this encyclopedia. Place is also limited. The entries tend to focus on asylum therapeutics in the Western world, about which there are rich and accessible sources of information.

The language of therapeutics has always been somewhat idiosyncratic, if not sloppy. There are terms such as "mechanical restraints" that always have had wide usage throughout history and might even be said to be universally understood. But that certainly was not so of the term "straightjacket." As one example of mechanical restraints, it variously has been referred to as a "camisole de force," or a "strait-waistcoat," or a "madd-shirt," or even a "polka," depending of course on the time and place of its reference. The language of therapeutics had a considerable influence on the organization of this book. Herein readers will find that many of the primary entries include a variety of synonymous terms, in parentheses, that were used in different times and places to identify them. Readers will open the book to the entry on "Pious frauds," for example, and find that they also were known as "salutary demonstrations," "innocent ruses," "curative ruses," and "suggestive therapies." While the inclusion of all of these terms might seem unnecessary, the intent here is to open the circle of learning by building a vocabulary of therapeutics that aids critical inquiry and discussion. For cross-referencing purposes only the first term of each primary entry is noted in the text in brackets. The subentries that further elaborate upon each primary entry also list various synonymous terms, although they are not cross-referenced in the text.

Finally, it is important to clarify the terminology used. "Asylum" sounds like an old-fashioned term and, in fact, it is. There is probably no other institution that has gone through so many attempts to rebrand itself—from lunatic asylum, to insane asylum, to state hospital, to mental institution, to mental hospital, to psychiatric hospital, to psychiatric campus—than the asylum. But what has remained consistent is that the institution has always been a separate place, a place intended for refuge and assistance. And because that is the very definition of asylum, it seems appropriate to use the term. A bit of rebranding has also occurred for the professionals charged with the responsibility of treating the insane. They originally were referred to as mad-doctors, a moniker that inevitably called into question the difference between the healers and those being healed, then alienists, and then much later psychiatrists. Since the historical scope of this book is inclusive of all of those titles, the term "asylum physician" is used for the sake of consistency.

And then there is the object of therapeutic interventions by asylum physicians. Insanity is the settled-upon term. Affliction, distraction and lunacy were rejected as too archaic; madness as too protean; mental illness as too modern. The challenge with using insanity as a term, as well as the specific diagnoses that are referred to, was to use them in a person-first manner: the patient labeled as insane, versus the insane patient, for example, or the patient diagnosed with schizophrenia, as opposed to the schizophrenic patient, as another example. The cumbersomeness of the language is itself sad testimony as to how much mental disorder is considered identity, how much the disorder is thought to have the patient, rather than the other way around.

There is a great deal of original source material, often quoted at length, in this book. These original materials are presented as is, and with the purpose of offering knowledges, in the plural, about asylum therapeutics that are both particular and contrasting. No attempts have been made to achieve some kind of *post hoc* political correctness by correcting misspellings, adding "she" to the persistent male pronouns in order to achieve gender equity, or [*sic*] to call attention to an inaccurate expression or an unconventional spelling. And speaking of spelling, the occasional references in the book to the essential fluids of health are spelled "humours," with a "u," in the British fashion, a spelling that will greatly facilitate any research endeavor that their mention might prompt.

The working title of this book was originally "*To a Mind Diseased*," an homage to that great observer of the human condition, William Shakespeare. In his dark and powerful play *Macbeth*, insanity is the leitmotif and the desire, indeed the desperation, to remedy it is palpable. Even with its final title, *Encyclopedia of Asylum Therapeutics, 1750–1950s*, this book reflects on centuries of attempts to answer Macbeth's most pressing question:

Canst thou not minister to a mind diseased,
Pluck from the memory a rooted sorrow,
Raze out the written troubles of the brain,
And with some sweet oblivious antidote
 Cleanse the stuffed bosom of that perilous stuff
Which weighs upon the heart?

# The Entries

## Awakenings

*Techniques to startle insane patients from senselessness into reason.*

"Invasion by wakefulness," as the eminent social theorist and philosopher Michel Foucault referred to it (Foucault, p. 185), was one of the earliest asylum therapeutics on record. And, it could be convincingly argued, its lingering influence is evident in other early therapeutics such as salutary fear [see **Salutary Fear**], pious frauds [see **Pious Frauds**], and even in the much more recent and familiar therapeutic of shock therapy [see **Shock Therapy**].

Each early nineteenth century asylum physician on record had a preferred strategy for "gathering up the senses" and forcing them to "hie back to their confine," as John Conolly, medical superintendent of Bethlem Asylum in London, England, once referred to awakenings (Conolly, p. 96). At the Vadstena Asylum, the first of its kind in Sweden, for example, medical director Georg Engström tied up patients in sacks of ants to awaken their senses, and at the private asylum he managed near Berlin, Germany, J.H. Lehmann submerged distracted patients in tubs of writhing eels to get their attention.

While credit certainly has to be given to imagination, the inspiration for awakenings surely must belong to Johann Christian Reil, a German physician who, despite having had little interaction with the insane himself, coined the word "psychiatry" and founded two journals devoted to it, and launched what has come to be known as the Romantic Psychiatry movement in Germany. The term "Romantic" requires clarification, since, in the early nineteenth century, it was meant not so much as a compliment but as a criticism. Romanticism was a reaction against the hegemony of biological theories about the cause of insanity and, to a lesser but still significant extent, to somatic methods in treating it. It entwined psychiatry with philosophy and even poetry to set out what it proposed were the moral causes of insanity and the harmonizing "psychic" therapies aimed at the feelings, desires and ideas that had gone astray. Although the Romantic movement could not hold its own against the biological juggernaut, its historical significance can be found in its introduction of psychological thinking into the emerging discipline of psychiatry.

Reil unabashedly identified with the movement. The title of his widely read text, *Rhapsodies on the Use of Psychological Therapies for the Mentally Disturbed*, might be considered sufficient evidence, in and of itself, of that identification. But within it, and in homage to the philosophers Immanuel Kant and Friedrich Wilhelm Joseph Schelling, he laid out a complex theory of the mind and of its disturbances. In Reil's romantic idealism, insanity was a failure in self-consciousness. The self, he argued was fractured by the steady progress of civilization that in equal measures propelled the human race forward and pushed it backwards and "ever nearer to the madhouse" (Reil, p. 12). That fracturing of the self, or soul in his philosophy, resulted in impairments of prudential awareness, attention and self-consciousness. It is the latter that "synthesizes the mental man, with his different qualities, into the unity of a person" (p. 55); thus when self-consciousness was impaired, the world of the person was rendered incoherent.

Reil's psychological strategies for treating the incoherence of insanity were influenced by experts such as Philippe Pinel in France, Francis Willis in England, and Johann Langermann in Germany. Thus, he advocated good diet, outdoor activities, exercise, sexual intercourse, dancing, music, and education—all progressive treatments of insanity in the early nineteenth century. But some of his therapeutic strategies were distinctly and recognizably his own. Crusting the soles of a patient's feet with salt that was then licked off by a goat was promoted as a wise therapeutic intervention for restoring self-consciousness, as was submersing a patient in a tub of live eels, and placing an open-bottomed glass dome filled with mice on the patient's bare skin. All of these "awakened" self-consciousness, drew attention and stimulated awareness, as did the startling cannon shots fired on the asylum grounds, the sudden rat-a-tat of a drumroll and blast of a firecracker disturbing the relative quiescence of the asylum, the unexpected appearance of staff costumed as "furmen" and skeletons, and the discordant sound of Reil's most innovative awakening therapeutic, the cat-piano.

The cat-piano, or *katzenclavier,* was described by Reil as such:

> [Cats] be arranged in a row with their tails stretched behind them. And a key board fitted out with sharpened nails would be set over them. The struck cats would provide the sound. A fugue played on this instrument—when the ill person is so placed that he cannot miss the expressions of their faces and the play of these animals—must bring Lot's wife herself from her fixed state into conscious awareness [Reil, p. 205].

Katzenclavier. Johann Christian Reil's appalling "cat-piano." The wailing of the cats when the sharpened nails struck their tails was sure to "bring Lot's wife herself from her fixed state into conscious awareness." Rumors to the contrary, the cat-piano most likely was never used as an awakening therapeutic (*La Natura* [1883], v.2.)

Although Reil lamented that the "voice of a jackass [would be] even more heartbreaking" he admitted that the animal suffered from a certain "artistic caprice" (p. 205) and therefore was unsuitable to the task of awakening the insane. In truth, the cat-piano was not Reil's invention. Its origination was attributed, but not without contention, to Athanasius Kircher in his 1650 text, *Musurgia Universalis*, and represented in a late sixteenth century woodcut by Theodor deBry. And, in truth once again, Reil's suggestion that it be used as an awakening therapeutic may never have been more or different than that—a suggestion. Although a few early European and British asylum physicians sometimes mentioned it, there was no indisputable historical evidence that it ever was in use.

The cat-piano, in the end, may be more interesting as an object lesson in how tales of asylum therapeutics circulate and detach from their historical referents, and then take on the mantle of truth. The same could be said of another of Reil's innovative strategies for awakening patients as they first arrived at the asylum, and that was to attach them to a catapult that would sweep them up into the tower of the asylum and then precipitously drop them into a dark cavern filled with snakes. The Bethlem Asylum superintendent John Conolly was the first to translate this suggestion into English, and he did so with fidelity to Reil's original assertion that this was something he "wished" were possible, but did not recommend or suggest as an awakening therapeutic. As time went on, "wished" having long since disappeared from the narrative, the now apocryphal account was presented as historical truth.

The euphemism "snake pit" predates Reil's wistful idea by centuries. The term most likely was derived from the medieval practice of throwing convicts and other undesirables into such pits as punishment for their offenses. The wide circulation of Reil's fanciful awakening account, however, more strongly linked the euphemism with asylums than with other total institutions.

REFERENCES

Beam, A. (2001). *Gracefully insane: The rise and fall of America's premier mental hospital.* New York: PublicAffairs.
Conolly, J. (1850). *Familiar views of lunacy and lunatic life.* London: John W. Parker.
Deutsch, A. (1945). *The mentally ill in America: A history of their care and treatment from Colonial times.* New York: Columbia University Press.
Foucault, M. (1965). *Madness and civilization.* New York: Pantheon.
Greenfeld, L. (2013). Mind, modernity, madness: The impact of culture on human experience. Cambridge, MA: Harvard University Press.
Hankins, T.L. (1994). The ocular harpsichord of Louis-Bertrand Castel; or, The instrument that wasn't. *Osiris, 9,* 141–156.
Kircher, A. (1650/1970). *Musurgia universalis.* Rome: Francesco Corbelletti.
Lehmann, J.F. (1837). *Remarks on the conduct to be observed towards lunatics by those who are in charge of them.* Berlin: Author.
Marx. O.M. (2008). German Romantic psychiatry. In E.R. Wallace and J. Gach (eds.), *History of psychiatry and medical psychology: With an epilogue on psychiatry,* pp. 313–334. New York: Springer.
Qvarsell, R. (1985). Locked-up or put to bed: Psychiatry and the treatment of the mentally ill in Sweden, 1800–1920. In W.F. Bynum, R. Porter, and M. Shepherd (eds.), *The anatomy of madness,* Vol. 2, pp. 86–97. London: Tavistock.
Reil, J.C. (1803/2010). *Rhapsodieen Uber Die Anwendung Der Psychischen Curmethode Auf Geisteszerruttungen* [*Rhapsodies on the Use of Psychological Therapies for the Mentally Disturbed*]. Whitefish, MT: Kessinger Publishing.
Richards, R.J. (1998). Rhapsodies on a cat piano, or Johann Christian Reil and the foundations of Romantic psychiatry. *Critical Inquiry, 24,* 700–736.

# Bed Therapy

*The strict confinement of insane patients in beds.*

This therapeutic was carried out either inside asylum wards, outside in tents or on specially built verandas and patios, or in private clinic rooms. One form or another of this therapeutic was popular in asylums around the world during the mid-nineteenth to the early twentieth century.

## References

Beard, G.M. (1894). *A practical treatise on nervous exhaustion (neurasthenia), its symptoms, nature, sequences, treatment.* 3rd ed. New York: E.B. Treat.

Boschma, G. (2003). *The rise of mental health nursing: A history of psychiatric care in Dutch asylums, 1890–1920.* Amsterdam: Amsterdam University Press.

Campbell, B. (2007). The making of "American": Race and nation in neurasthenic discourse. *History of Psychiatry, 18,* 157–178.

Clouston, T.S. (1863). Tuberculosis and insanity. *Journal of Mental Science, 9,* 56–57.

Dickens, C. (1907). *The life and adventures of Nicholas Nickelby.* London: Chapman and Hall.

Dumas, A. (1848/2013). *The lady of the camellias.* Trans. S. Schillinger. New York: Penguin Classics.

Easterbrook, C.C. (1907). The sanatorium treatment of active insanity by rest in bed in the open air. *British Journal of Psychiatry, 53,* 723–750.

Engstrom, E.J. (2003). *Clinical psychiatry in Imperial Germany.* Ithaca, NY: Cornell University Press.

Gijswijt-Hofstra, M., and Porter, R. (eds.). (2001). *Cultures of neurasthenia: From Beard to the First World War.* Amsterdam: Rodopi.

Gilman, C.P. (1899). *The yellow wallpaper.* Boston: Small, Maynard.

Haviland, C., and Carlisle, C. (1905). Extension of tent therapy to additional classes of the insane. *American Journal of Insanity, 62,* 95–115.

Kirkbride, T.S. (1890). *On the construction, organization, and general arrangements of hospitals for the insane.* Philadelphia: J.B. Lippincott.

Madsen, J. (1966). Some pages from the history of Sankt Hans Hospital. *Acta Psychiatrica Scandinavica, 41,* 13–56.

Mann, T. (1924). *The magic mountain.* [*Der zauerberg*]. Berlin: S. Fischer Verlag.

Mitchell, S.W. (1877). *Fat and blood: An essay on the treatment of certain forms of neurasthenia and hysteria.* Philadelphia: J.B. Lippincott Company.

Mitchell, S.W. (1888). *Doctor and patient.* 3rd ed. Philadelphia: J.B. Lippincott Company.

Mitchell, S.W. (1894). Address before the fiftieth annual meeting of the American Medico-Psychological Association. *Journal of Nervous and Mental Disease, 21,* 413–437.

Neissen, C. (1900). Rest in bed in the treatment of acute forms of insanity, and the modifications which would be necessary in the organization of the insane asylums if this method of treatment were carried out. *St. Louis Medical Review, 42,* 291–292.

Oppenheim, J. (1991). *Shattered nerves.* New York: Oxford University Press.

Qvarsell, R. (1985). Locked up or put to bed: Psychiatry and the treatment of the mentally ill in Sweden, 1800–1920. In W.F. Bynum, R. Porter, and M. Shepherd (eds.), *The anatomy of madness,* Vol. 2, pp. 86–97. London: Tavistock.

Serieux, P. (1899). The treatment of acute psychoses by rest in bed. *Medical Press and Circular, 119,* 500–502.

Van Deusen, E.H. (1869). *Observations on a form of nervous prostration (neurasthenia) culminating in insanity.* Lansing, MI: W.S. George.

Wiglesworth, J. (1908). On the treatment of cases of acute insanity by rest in bed in the open air. *British Journal of Psychiatry, 54,* 105–106.

Wright, A.B., and Haviland, F. (1903–1904). Additional notes upon tent treatment for the insane at the Manhattan State Hospital, East. *American Journal of Psychiatry, 60,* 53–59.

## Bed Therapy, or Bed Treatment, or Clinotherapy

Strict confinement in bed in order to reduce external stimuli, calm agitation and, most importantly, to convince patients of their own insanity in a setting that optimized physician and staff observations. Bed therapy most likely originated in Germany. In the mid-nineteenth century the psychiatric reformer Wilhelm Griesinger had urged the development of scientific observatories within asylums; over ensuing decades these *Wachabteilung,* or surveillance wards, as they came to be known, became a feature of many asylums, general hospitals and university-based psychiatric clinics around the country.

Bed therapy was perfectly suited to both surveillance and the new era of scientific psychiatry in Germany. It allowed for the constant scrutinizing of patient behavior as well as the continual monitoring and charting of pulse, blood pressure and temperature. It had other important implications as well. German asylum physicians had been somewhat reluctant to embrace a policy of non-restraint, and had suffered more than a little criticism by their international colleagues for it. Bed therapy allowed them to take Griesenger's advice and replace "mechanical surveillance with live observation and care," (Engstrom, p. 64), thus bringing German psychiatry into the mainstream of the international non-restraint movement [see **Mechanical Restraints**].

Bed therapy and the surveillance it required also served the purpose of keeping order in the bedlamic setting of the asylum, and it was orderliness, methodical regulation, and regimented control that finally erased the distinction between the asylum and the hospital, as well as between mental and physical illness. Although scientific psychiatry implicated the brain and the central nervous system as the seats of insanity, the successful treatment of it required that patients acknowledge they indeed were insane, and bed therapy was a convincing therapeutic for doing just that. Confined to bed and monitored, the patients assumed the sick role, and took the asylum physician's interpretation and diagnosis of "sick" as their own. These contributions of bed therapy to scientific psychiatry were summarized by Clemens Neissen, assistant physician at the Leubus Asylum in Silesia:

> The introduction of treatment in bed in cases of insanity is the last and definite step towards regarding the insane as sick people. Through this the hospital character will become impressed on the insane asylum absolutely; a true and positive care of the sick will follow, and the therapy (especially in the acute psychoses) will be based upon a physiologic conception of the subject [Neissen, p. 291].

Scientific psychiatry required that bed therapy be tightly regimented. The patients first were bathed, then medically examined before being placed in beds; very restless and agitated patients often were consigned to mattresses with three feet high padded sides until calm enough to lie down in beds. As improvement progressed the patients were allowed to sit up and even to take a short stroll outside, but with that exception and one more of a single toilet break, they were not allowed to leave the bed. Any resistance to staying in bed was met with a kind but firm reminder that the patients' sickness required it; distractions in the form of food, newspapers, or holding hands with a nurse or attendant were recommended to overcome any opposition. The typical patients remained in bed for up to two months; any longer risked creating what was known as the "bed urge," that is, a refusal to ever leave it.

Bed therapy also required augmented skills for attendants and nurses alike. Not only were they expected to maintain order by keeping patients in their beds, but to prevent bed sores and assist patients with bed pans. German asylum physicians, who had enjoyed a rather high and mighty status that kept them aloof from staff, now found themselves having to educate and supervise their underlings.

Outside of Germany, bed therapy was adopted in Sweden; in Buenos Aires, Argentina by Domingo Cabred at the Lujan Lunatic Asylum; in Denmark by August Wimmer who, upon taking the position of medical superintendent of Sankt Hans Hospital in Copenhagen confined most of the patients to bed; in Russia by Sergei Korsakoff at the Preobrazhenski mental hospital; and in the Netherlands by Jacob vanDeventer at the Meerenberg Asylum when he assumed his position as medical superintendent in the late nineteenth century. Because of vanDeventer's reported success with bed therapy, other Dutch asylums adopted it as well, but only after architectural changes had been made. Bed therapy required large wards with attached observation rooms, and it is most likely that these architectural demands were behind the unwillingness of American asylum physicians to try it. In the late nineteenth century state asylums were still being built across the country, most of them on the "Kirkbride Plan," a minutely detailed plan of "moral architecture" which was much more conducive to the activities and independence of moral treatment [see **Moral Treatment**] than the passivity and dependence of bed therapy.

## *Open Air Rest, or Tent Treatment, or Sanatorium Treatment*

Strict confinement in a bed placed on an open veranda or in a tent on the grounds of an asylum. The open air treatment was predicated on observations regarding the successful treatment of the contagious bacterial infection of tuberculosis. Although it is likely that tuberculosis, also known as consumption, has a history almost as old as the human race, it was not recognized as a unified disease until the early nineteenth century, and not considered curable until a few decades later when the German physician, Hermann Brehmner, himself a tuberculosis patient, introduced the sanatorium cure that featured good nutrition, rest, and fresh air.

The ravages of tuberculosis were all too familiar to physicians and lay people alike. The English novelist and social critic Charles Dickens described it in this manner:

> There is a dread disease which so prepares its victim, as it were, for death; which so refines it of its grosser aspect, and throws around familiar looks, unearthly indications of the coming change; a dread disease, in which the struggle between soul and body is so gradual, quiet, and solemn, and the result so sure, that day by day, and grain by grain, the mortal part wastes and withers away, so that the spirit grows light and sanguine with its lightening load, and, feeling immortality at hand, deems it but a new term of mortal life; a disease in which death and life are so strangely blended, that death takes the glow and hue of life, and life the gaunt and grisly form of death; a disease which medicine never cured, wealth never warded off, or poverty could boast exemption from; which sometimes moves in giant strides, and sometimes at a tardy sluggish pace, but, slow or quick, is ever sure and certain [Dickens, p. 734].

This "dread disease" was represented in popular novels, such as Thomas Mann's *The Magic Mountain*, stage plays such as Alexandre Dumas's *The Lady of the Camellias*, and operas such as Giacomo Puccini's *La Bohème*, but its relationship to insanity was first conjectured in the mid-nineteenth century by Thomas Clouston, superintendent of the Scottish Royal Edinburgh Asylum, also known as Morningside. Based on comparative autopsy data, he found that tuberculosis was more frequently assigned as the cause of the death of asylum patients than of the general population, and that the number of asylum deaths from tuberculosis had increased signifi-

Tent therapy at the Manhattan State Hospital in New York, circa 1902. Twenty patients diagnosed as "demented" and "filthy," that is, unable to tend to their bodily needs, spent the summer in a large tent on the asylum grounds. The experiment was deemed an unqualified success. All of the patients gained weight, participated in exercise, and improved their personal self care (A.B. Wright [1902]. Tent therapy for the demented and uncleanly. *American Journal of Insanity, 59,* Plate XI).

cantly over just the previous three years. Based on these data, Clouston asked two questions that influenced the practice of open air rest: did tuberculosis cause insanity, and/or do the conditions of asylum life cause insanity? In answer to his first question, Clouston proposed that tuberculosis indeed caused a particular type of insanity which he termed phthisical insanity, characterized by morbid suspicion, withdrawal, irritability, food refusal, and adolescent onset. Open air rest, in so far that it replicated the therapeutically successful sanitaria cures, was established in many asylums to treat the phthisical patient.

The contagious nature of tuberculosis answered Clouston's second question. In crowded, and often unsanitary asylums, the transmission of tuberculosis was a considerable risk for patients and staff alike. Thus open air rest for non-phthisical patients was used as a prophylactic against the disease. At the Ayr District Asylum in Scotland, for example, all newly admitted patients as well as those who had recently relapsed, were confined to beds, separated by wooden screens, on one of the large specially constructed verandas. They remained there from seven in the morning until seven in the evening. as much of the year as possible. In the absence of long-term data on the effects of open air rest, superintendent Charles Easterbrook nonetheless concluded that "it is a more satisfactory method of treating those who are actively insane than either outdoor exercise or indoor rest" (Easterbrook, p. 724). He cited the "rapid subsidence of the active mental and nervous symptoms...[the] rapid amelioration of mania, melancholia, delirium, confusion, stupor, vivid hallucinatory and delusional manifestations, impulsiveness and mental excitement" (p. 737) as evidence of its therapeutic success. Joseph Wiglesworth reported similar success at the asylum in Rainhill, England, where he was superintendent. Although he advised against using open air rest as a panacea, his experience led him to the conclusion that

> certain patients get well under this treatment who would not otherwise have recovered, and that the convalescence of many others is appreciably hastened. Even if no more could be said than this, the treatment would more than repay the little extra trouble involved in carrying it out [Wiglesworth, p. 106].

In the United States, open air rest often took the form of what was called tent treatment. At asylums such as the Manhattan State Hospital East, formerly known as Wards Island Asylum in New York City, large tents replete with coal stoves were pitched on the asylum grounds. There both the tubercular insane, the term preferred over "phthisical" by American asylum physicians, and the "dirty" insane, a term used worldwide to label patients who urinated and defecated on themselves, were confined to bed throughout the year. In many American asylums in the early twentieth century, tents were replaced with wooden pavilions, expansive porches or large sun rooms, and the therapeutic value of bed rest gradually took second place to the therapeutic value of fresh air, as patients were increasingly encouraged to actively engage with their surrounding environment.

## *Rest Cure, or Mitchell's Cure, or Rest/Fattening Cure*

A strictly enforced regime of six to eight continuous weeks of bed rest, isolation, intellectual and creative inactivity, a diet rich in milk and meat, massage and electrotherapy. The rest cure was devised by the American neurologist Silas Weir Mitchell in the late nineteenth century as a cure for neurasthenia, or nervous collapse.

The term "neurasthenia" was not coined by Mitchell, with whom it was so intimately associated, but by Edwin Holmes Van Deusen, medical superintendent of the Michigan Asylum for the Insane in Kalamazoo, Michigan. Van Deusen had used the term to describe a kind of nervous prostration that had culminated in insanity for some of his patients, most of them hard-working, rurally isolated farmers and, even more likely, farmers' wives. Lonely, bored, depressed and often overburdened with the demands of child care and housekeeping, the wives were particularly prone to the irritability, insomnia, indigestion and general malaise that were the early warning signs of neurasthenia and that, in Van Deusen's assessment, developed into insanity if ignored. The treatment of neurasthenia, though, made no special demands on physicians or on the asylums in which they practiced. Gentle exercise, sponge baths, improved nutrition and nerve tonics such as quinine were all indicated and Van Desuen confidently reported that once convalescence commenced there was no tendency to relapse.

Coincidentally, the term "neurasthenia" was being used at the same time by George Miller Beard, a New York neurologist, to describe a chronic functional disease of the nervous system brought on by the hectic pace of urban life, which was made even more so by American "civilization itself," with its "railways, telegraphs, telephones and periodical press" (Beard, p. 255). Just as Van Deusen had, Beard considered neurasthenia not just treatable but curable. He prescribed exercise, exposure to air and sunlight, a change in diet and, most importantly, electrotherapy that toned up nerves, revitalized nervous energy and repaired nerve tissue.

The fact that Van Deusen attributed the cause of neurasthenia to rural isolation and boredom, and Beard to urban crowding and overstimulation, "aptly illustrated neurasthenia's capacity to be all things to all medical men" (Oppenheim, p. 93). So to another of those medical men, neurologist Silas Weir Mitchell, it was imagined to be a depletion of nerve force that irritated the brain, the digestive organs and the reproductive system—the latter more so, and with greater debilitating consequences, for women than men. The rest cure was particularly suited to treat women, he argued, if only because the fairer sex better tolerated the ennui of repose and seclusion.

If the rest cure was gendered, it also was classed. Increasingly, physicians in the United States and Europe, where neurasthenia had migrated as a diagnosis, recognized that nervous exhaustion had no economic or social class boundaries, but the rest cure typically was administered to well-heeled women, and occasionally men, to ready them for their highly gendered roles in rapidly modernizing Western society. By enforcing intellectual and creative inactivity, the rest cure assured that neurasthenic women abandoned the pursuits and desires that Mitchell believed undermined their health and reproductive functions. With its combination of high protein diet and bed rest, the rest cure also packed on pounds, sometimes as much as thirty to fifty pounds during a six to eight week course of treatment, thus women patients gained "flesh and color, which means gain in quality and quantity of blood" (Mitchell, 1888, p. 137) and with it, a renewed vigor "to make [them] as a mother more capable, as a wife more helpful" (Mitchell, 1888, p. 150). For men, the rest cure revitalized the nervous system and energized them for their important role as the "brainworkers" who assured the steady progress of commerce and culture.

Public asylums, however, were not filled with these educated, skilled and moneyed kinds of patients. Rather, they were teeming with lower and working class women and men whose insanity did not so much exhaust as disorientate, baffle and delude; they were packed with patients who had little prospect of ever being discharged, let alone being remade into productive citizens. The rest cure *ala* Mitchell, then, was more likely to be administered in the homes of the neurasthenic patients, or in private asylums, sanitaria or nervine clinics, the latter of which were specially designed for its administration.

Mitchell nonetheless excoriated the physicians of public asylums for not providing at least a semblance of the rest cure, not just for the neurasthenic patients who could be found on their rolls, but for insane patients in general:

> Have you people in your asylums trained to use massage? I see plenty of folks in your wards who need this potent blood-stirring tonic. In how many [asylums] is there an electric room and an electrician? ... [S]ome of us think hy-

drotherapeutics of great value. How many [asylums] are provided with the appliances for such treatment? How many of you employ it at all? [Mitchell, 1894 p. 433].

Indeed, some pastiche of the rest cure was patched together in many public asylums towards the end of the nineteenth century; hydrotherapy suites were constructed [see **Hydrotherapy**], nutritional standards were raised, blood tonics and restoratives were routinely administered, and bed rest sometimes was prescribed. But by the early twentieth century what variously had been called the "fashionable disease" and the "distinguished malady" of neurasthenia had all but disappeared. In many ways it was a victim of its own popularity. The claims that had been made about it "were too vast; the novelty and convenience of the label prompted [physicians] to apply it too sweepingly, so that it covered everything from extreme fatigue to temporary insanity" (Oppenheim, p. 109). Neurasthenia had become everything and, at the same time, nothing. And with its disappearance, the rest cure disappeared as well.

# Cerebral Stimulation (Psychic Stimulation)

*The alteration of respiration and brain metabolism by inducing temporary anoxia.*

In the late eighteenth century a well-educated and well-traveled physician by the name of Caleb Hillier Parry set up practice in the fashionable spa town of Bath, England. Many well-to-do people were in the habit of "taking the waters" at the spa, either for relaxation or restoration. One of them was a young woman who suffered from fainting spells that were preceded by throbbing in the head, flushing and hypersensitivity to light and sound. She was referred to Parry when conventional medical treatments had failed. Theorizing that many diseases, most particularly those of a "nervous" origin, as he assumed hers was, were due to a "determination of the blood" due to its excessive flow to and through the brain, he pressed on her carotid artery and immediately terminated the prodromal phase of her fainting spell.

In a presentation to the Medical Society of London, Parry discussed his experiments with slowing the heartbeat through carotid compression and proposed that it should be considered an effective therapeutic for the treatment of nervous disorders, mania, paroxysms of occasional insanity, and even "permanent insanity," all of which he attributed to the increased impetus of blood that irritated the brain. Parry's promotion of carotid compression to remediate the symptoms of insanity drew the attention of asylum physicians. Among them was John Gideon Millingen, medical superintendent of the County of Middlesex Pauper Lunatic Asylum, more often known simply as Hanwell, after its location just outside of London. Hanwell was the first purpose-built asylum in England, accommodating nearly 500 patients and had quickly developed a reputation for therapeutic innovation. Millingen used carotid compression to relieve the "excitement" of the brain, although there is no indication he did so frequently or, for that matter, with enthusiasm. He mused that perhaps a yoke of some kind could be constructed and placed around the patient's neck to free asylum physicians from the somewhat risky intervention of placing their hands on, or around, the necks of their patients. Carotid compression also was advocated by George Mann Burrows, who boasted he was able to calm a violent manic fit with a single finger pressed on the carotid artery. Although Parry had asserted that pressure on both carotid arteries would do the same in a case of violent insensibility and even restore the senses in the bargain, Burrows could not replicate the result with the patients he cared for at his small private asylum near London.

It was not so much carotid compression as a therapeutic that was controversial as it was the theory of insanity that justified its use in the first place. Perhaps it was not the "determination of blood" in the brain that was the cause of insanity, some asylum physicians began arguing in the early twentieth century, but brain metabolism. If that were the case, the purported efficacy of carotid compression could be better explained: the brief anoxia it produced stimulated not only post-compression respirations but brain metabolism as well. Two propositions supported this emerging theory. First, schizophrenia, inarguably the most frustratingly intractable type of insanity, was caused by deficient oxidative processes. Second, the purported success of shock therapies [see **Shock Therapy**] in ameliorating the symptoms of schizophrenia was due to the alterations they produced in brain metabolism—metrazol, for example, deprived the brain of oxygen; insulin deprived it of sugar. Thus the possibility emerged of treating schizophrenia and other types of debilitating insanity by stimulating respiration and altering brain metabolism with a variety of different chemical agents.

"Cerebral stimulation" was appropriate as a label for these therapeutics; their actions were hypothesized to be directed to the brain. But their influence on the mind was a matter of increasing interest, a consequence, no doubt, of the growing influence of psychoanalysis in the early twentieth century. Psychoanalysis was the brainchild of the Viennese neurologist Sigmund Freud. As a set of techniques for accessing and treating the mind, it was regarded as much more suitable for the treatment of neurosis than psychosis or more particularly, for the outpatients of private practices than the inpatients of asylums. Freud himself had expressed doubt that psychoanalysis would ever be effective as an asylum therapeutic, a doubt not only shared by most asylum physicians but amplified by their concern that it actually might be harmful.

Psychoanalysis was not just a set of techniques, however, it also was a structural and dynamic theory of the mind. It was that facet of it that exercised considerable sway over asylum physicians, so much so that the term "cerebral stimulation" gradually, and without apparent comment, was replaced with "psychic stimulation." The effects of the administration of these anoxic chemicals, then, were increasingly described in psychoanalytic terms: they were said to activate the unconscious, loosen repressive controls, encourage insight and expression. It was the putative psychic stimulation, in fact, that accounted for the use of anoxic chemicals for several decades after their cerebral stimulation had been discredited. By the mid-twentieth century, however, cerebral or psychic stimulation was no longer in use as an asylum therapeutic.

## References

Alexander, F.A.D., and Himwich, H.E. (1939). Nitrogen inhalation therapy for schizophrenia. *American Journal of Psychiatry, 94,* 643–655.

Atoynatan, T.H., Goldstone, S., Goldsmith, J., and Cohen, L.D. (1954). The differential effects of carbon dioxide and nitrous oxide inhalation therapies upon anxiety symptoms under permissive and nonpermissive conditions. *Psychiatric Quarterly, 28,* 641–649.

Burrows, G.M. (1828). *Commentaries on the causes, forms, symptoms, and treatment, moral and medical, of insanity.* London: Thomas and George Underwood.

Clark, D.H. (1954). Carbon dioxide therapy of the neuroses. *British Journal of Psychiatry, 100,* 722–726.

El-Hai, J. (2005). *The lobotomist.* New York: John Wiley and Sons.

Fogel, E.J., and Gray, L.P. (1940). Nitrous oxide anoxia in the treatment of schizophrenia: Report of 24 cases. *American Journal of Psychiatry, 97,* 677–685.

Frazer, R., and Reitmann, F. (1939). A clinical study of the effects of short periods of severe anoxia with special reference to the mechanism of action in cardiazol "shock." *Journal of Neurology, Neurosurgery & Psychiatry, 2,* 125–136.

Gasser, H.S. (1929). Arthur S. Loevenhart. *Science, 70,* 317–321.

Hawkings, J.M., and Tibbetts, R.W. (1956). Carbon dioxide inhalation therapy in neurosis. *British Journal of Psychiatry, 102,* 52–59.

Hinsie, L.E., Barach, A.L., Harris, M.M., Brand, E., and McFarland, R.A. (1934). The treatment of dementia praecox by continuous oxygen administration in chambers and oxygen and carbon dioxide inhalations. *Psychiatric Quarterly, 8,* 34–71.

Hull, G. (1998). Caleb Hillier Parry, 1755–1822: A notable provincial physician. *Journal of the Royal Society of Medicine, 91,* 335–338.
Lehmann, H., and Bos, C. (1947). The advantages of nitrous oxide inhalation in psychiatric treatment. *American Journal of Psychiatry, 104,* 164–170.
Levine, A., and Schilder, P. (1940). Motor phenomena during nitrogen inhalation. *Archives of Neurology and Psychiatry, 44,* 1009–1017.
Lipetz, B. (1940). Preliminary report on the results of the treatment of schizophrenia by nitrogen inhalation. *Psychiatric Quarterly, 14,* 496–503.
Loevenhart, A.S., Lorenz, F.W., Martin, H.G., and Malone, J.Y. (1918). Stimulation of the respiration by sodium cyanide and its clinical application. *Archives of Internal Medicine, 21,* 109–129.
Loevenhart, A.S., Lorenz, W.F., and Waters, R.M. (1929). Cerebral stimulation. *Journal of the American Medical Association, 92,* 880–883.
McCulloch, W.S. (1950). Nature of processes in the central nervous system in the psychoneuroses. *Archives of Neurology and Psychiatry, 64,* 305–306.
Meduna, L.J. (1950). *Carbon dioxide therapy: A neurophysiological treatment of nervous disorders.* Springfield, Il., Charles C Thomas.
Meduna, L.J. (1985). Autobiography of L.J. Meduna, Part 2. *Convulsive Therapy, 1,* 121–135.
Millingen, J.G. (1842). *Aphorisms on the treatment and management of the insane.* Philadelphia: Ed. Barrington and Geo. D. Haswell.
Moriarty, J.D. (1954). Evaluation of carbon dioxide inhalation therapy. *American Journal of Psychiatry, 110,* 765–769.
Parry, C.H. (1815). *Elements of pathology therapeutics, being the outlines of a work intended to ascertain the nature, causes, and most efficacious modes of prevention and cure of the greater number of the disease incidental to the human frame.* Bath, U.K.: R. Cruttwell.
Roth, M. (ed.). (1998). *Freud: Conflict and culture.* New York: Knopf.
Sillman, L.R., and Terrence, C. (1963). An analysis of shock therapy in schizophrenia on the basis of a nitrogen inhalation control series. *Psychiatric Quarterly, 17,* 241–245.
Valenstein, E.S. (1986). *Great and desperate cures.* New York: Basic Books.
Wolpe, J. (1987). Carbon dioxide inhalation treatments of neurotic anxiety. *Journal of Nervous and Mental Disease, 175,* 129–133.
Yacorzynski, G.K. (1962). *Investigation of carbon dioxide therapy.* Springfield, IL; Charles C. Thomas.

## *Air Pressure*

The manipulation of the oxygen level of the bloodstream by the alteration of air pressure. Upon his arrival at St. Elizabeths Hospital in Washington, D.C., Walter Freeman was determined to find a cure for schizophrenia. In the mid–1920s the federal asylum, located on a bluff overlooking the confluence of the Potomac and Anacostia rivers, held thousands of patients. Most of those diagnosed with schizophrenia were considered incurable and had been consigned to languish in the back wards. Freeman, whose name would later become synonymous with the controversial surgical procedure of the lobotomy [see **Psychosurgery**], was an unabashed somatist and as director of the asylum's laboratory had free reign to examine the bodies and brains of deceased patients. To his consternation he was unable to discover anything that differentiated patients with schizophrenia from patients with other disorders or, for that matter, from persons with no history of insanity whatsoever.

Although stalled in his own research, Freeman was impressed by the methods of what was variously referred to as "cerebral stimulation" or "psychic stimulation" that were being used to treat patients with schizophrenia in various asylums in the United States. At St. Elizabeths he tried to replicate their purported success. He treated schizophrenic patients with carbon dioxide and with sodium amytal, and although he was unimpressed with the results, he remained intrigued by the underlying theory that altering brain metabolism would remediate schizophrenia. Hypothesizing that doing so by non-chemical means may be more efficacious, he sought a way to improve brain metabolism by altering the level of oxygen in the bloodstream. This hypothesis brought him to the Washington navy yard where he subjected himself to sessions in a hyperbaric chamber. He noted that low pressure resulted in headaches and mental dullness; a pressure of forty-five pounds per square inch, or three atmospheres, resulted in hypomania. For patients who had been rendered unresponsive, mute and dazed by catatonic schizophrenia, he reasoned, this hypomanic state would constitute an improvement, not to mention an opportunity for psychotherapeutic intervention.

When administered to patients at St. Elizabeths, however, the manipulation of air pressure failed to live up to expectations. The only observable effect, Freeman wryly noted, was that one catatonic patient who spent time in a hyperbaric chamber was stimulated enough to eat a sandwich instead of being tube-fed. Freeman concluded that air pressure variation was not a viable method of producing cerebral stimulation. Other asylum physicians who experimented with it concurred.

## Carbon Dioxide Inhalation Therapy, or Meduna's Mixture Inhalation Therapy, or Carbogen Inhalation Therapy

The inhalation of a mix of 30 percent carbon dioxide (the average atmospheric amount is .03 percent) and 70 percent oxygen. The therapeutic caused rapid and deep breathing, heart rate increase, anxiety, panic and eventually unconsciousness. Developed in the late 1920s by Arthur Solomon Loevenhart and colleagues at the University of Wisconsin during their investigation into the metabolic processes of the respiration center in the brainstem, the therapeutic was found in small scale experiments to alleviate the symptoms of catatonic schizophrenia as well as manic-depression and involutional melancholia.

Loevenhart's experiments with carbon dioxide inhalation came to the attention of László Meduna. The Hungarian born physician, who already had made his name as "the father of shock therapy" for his development of metrazol shock therapy [see **Shock Therapy**], became intensely interested in the potential of this therapeutic. In his brief autobiography, written for the first issue of the journal *Convulsive Therapy,* Meduna offered the backstory to this interest. While still in Hungary, he had heard from a German colleague that "some Americans," presumably Loevenhart and his colleagues, were using "some gas" to resolve the symptoms of catatonic schizophrenia (Meduna, 1985, p. 133). After making inquiries, he heard the Americans were injecting pure oxygen into the subarachnoid space between the cerebellum and the medulla of the brain, known as the cerebellar cistern. Because he could not read English, Meduna was unable to confirm this information against the published report. Nonetheless, he enthusiastically began injecting pure oxygen into the cerebellar cisterns of asylum patients diagnosed with catatonic schizophrenic. "Naturally," he wrote with neither irony nor regret, "I did not succeed" (p. 133). It was only later that he learned that the gas being used was carbon dioxide, not oxygen, and that the method of administration was inhalation, not injection.

Armed with these facts, Meduna then attempted to replicate the findings of Loevenhart and colleagues, but with generally poor results. Some of the catatonic schizophrenic patients he treated did seem to benefit from the inhalation of carbon dioxide; they became more responsive, communicative and mobile, just as Loevenhart and his colleagues had found. These effects, however, were short-lived. Every patient Meduna treated slipped back into the catatonic condition within half-an-hour of inhaling the gas. Meduna, for a time, discontinued administering the therapeutic—at least to schizophrenics.

Reasoning that schizophrenia was the result of a biochemical disturbance that was largely unaffected by carbon dioxide inhalation, Meduna considered its use for psychoneurotic asylum patients. This relatively new diagnostic category contained a broad range of anxieties, phobias, compulsions and disturbances of everyday life that were thought to be psychological, rather than neurological, in origin. It was with some of these patients that Meduna boasted success. Giving them the standard mix of 30 percent carbon dioxide and 70 percent oxygen over sixty to one hundred separate sessions, Meduna noted improvement for sixty-eight of his first one hundred patients. The most resistant to improvement were the patients who had been diagnosed with obsessive-compulsive neurosis, but significant successes were noted for patients whose complaints ranged from tension, frustration, anxiety, maladjustment, phobias, nervous tics, homosexuality to stuttering. It was, in fact, in regards to stuttering that the positive results of carbon dioxide inhalation therapy were most remarkable.

Following Meduna's protocol, D.H. Clark also treated psychoneurotic patients at the Maudsley Hospital in south London. He was particularly struck by the abreactions that Meduna also had noticed, but had not discussed in great detail. Some of the forty-two patients reacted violently to the administration of the carbon dioxide, screaming and fighting with the doctors and nurses; a few engaged in sexualized behaviors, and one had orgasmic spasms. Her case, which reveals as much about the nature of psychoneurosis as it does about the risks of the administration of carbon dioxide inhalation therapy, was discussed in some detail:

> *Case 4:* An unmarried woman of 32 complained of lassitude, dyspepsia, and difficulties in social relationships. She had a disturbed unhappy childhood and lifelong personal difficulties; despite good intelligence and an adequate education she had failed various careers, including nursing; she had several close women friends, but had always showed a marked dislike of men. She had 18 administrations.... She always showed a marked reaction, and on five occasions exhibited body arching and thigh flexing of an unmistakably sexual nature. On recovery she usually wept bitterly, but expressed a desire to carry on with the treatment, claiming that she was better. Two days after her 18th administration, however, she had to be admitted to hospital in a dissociated state which rapidly developed into a state of terror and hallucinations, during which she heard voices accusing her of being a sex maniac and a beast. This state has persisted with brief intermissions for over a year, with only transient improvements over a course of electroconvulsive therapy and later a planned psychotherapeutic approach over two months; she remains a patient in a disturbed ward and ... was being considered for leucotomy. In her clearer periods she says she has no doubt that the carbon dioxide treatment made her worse [Clark, p. 724].

The woman was one of nine patients whose condition worsened after the administration of carbon dioxide inhalation therapy. Twenty of the treated patients, however, improved, some of the significantly. And that begged the question: why did the therapeutic work at all? On this point, Meduna had borrowed heavily from the theory of Warren Sturgis McCulloch, a distinguished American physician, neurophysiologist and cybernetician, who had hypothesized that the psychoneuroses were, in essence, a perversion of the reflex circuits. Impulses were diverted from their usual circuit, he argued, into recurrent nervous circuits where they reverberated indefinitely, forming a kind of "repetitive core" that was the diagnostic hallmark of the psychoneuroses. Meduna suggested that this inappropriate circuiting was due to a low threshold, that is, a reduced capacity to conduct nerve impulses, of the component neurons. Carbon dioxide inhalation, he concluded, increased that threshold.

Meduna's *post hoc* neurological explanation for the efficacy of carbon dioxide inhalation therapy with psychoneurosis was hardly compatible with the reigning psychological explanation of its cause. As a result, the theory of Joseph Wolpe of the Medical College of Pennsylvania, quickly eclipsed that of Meduna. Wolpe theorized that the maladaptive anxiety that was at the core of all of the various psychoneuroses was the result of learning, that is, it was a conditioned response to the conflict or noxious stimulation that produced it in the first place. Reasoning that the inhalation of carbon dioxide would inhibit free-floating, or pervasive, anxiety by creating intense respiratory excitation and/or by creating later reactive relaxation, he administered the therapeutic to five patients, without significant benefit for four of them. But it worked well for the fifth, a patient who had been diagnosed with "war neurosis," and who was extremely anxious and had startle responses to loud noises and thunder. Taking one full breath at a time of the carbon dioxide mixture twice a week, the war veteran was cured of his anxiety. So was a scientist Wople had treated for the free-floating anxiety he had suffered for a decade. The scientist described the administration and the effects of the carbon dioxide inhalation therapy in the following manner:

> Having emptied my lungs, I put the mask on and inhaled the gas through my mouth as deeply as I could. For a second or two nothing happened. Then I noticed rapid breathing, and for a moment everything became brilliant and detailed. I remember shutting my eyes and holding the cover of the sofa as the gasping for breath became more intense. Then I felt a tingling in my arms and legs and a very odd feeling of being affected all through. When my breathing returned to normal, I felt somewhat more calm and relaxed than usual...[I] discovered that I was already more relaxed than I could ever remember having been before [Wolpe, p. 130].

Wolpe had less success in treating patients with phobias. To desensitize them to the object of their fear, he administered the carbon dioxide mixture and when moderate hyperpnea (deep and rapid breathing) was evident, he asked them to imagine or verbalize a scene from an anxiety hierarchy. This procedure was repeated, using a scene one higher rung up in the hierarchy until the scene ceased to be disturbing. Carbon dioxide inhalation facilitated desensitization; however, it worked well with patients suffering from panic attacks. Theorizing that these patients were reacting to a fearful symptom and that their reaction increased the likelihood they would experience the feared symptom, and on and on in a viciously escalating circle, he administered carbon dioxide inhalation therapy at a time of relative calm until they demonstrated a reduced anxiety in relation to the feared symptom.

While Wolpe recommended the therapeutic, especially for patients with free-floating anxiety, not all asylum physicians had similarly positive results. J.R. Hawkins at the Midland Hospital for Nervous Disease in Birmingham, England, for example, found that patients administered carbon dioxide inhalation therapy fared no better or worse than those administered compressed air under identical conditions. Results like this reinforced for Wolpe and other practitioners of the therapeutic that its effects may be due to nothing more than suggestion, and/or the fear that the sensation of suffocation produced. Indeed, many of the physicians who entered asylum practice in the 1950s through 1970s were more psychologically than somatically orientated and would not use carbon dioxide inhalation therapy without intensive adjunctive psychotherapy, a time-consuming and, on the bottom line, expensive treatment modality for crowded and understaffed asylums.

Carbon dioxide inhalation therapy was used for some time in asylums. Despite the fact that Meduna's initial use of it was largely ineffective in treating psychosis, and that his neurological theory of what limited success it did have had been discredited, the therapeutic remained so strongly associated with him that the standard mix of 30 percent carbon dioxide and 70 percent oxygen was known as Meduna's Mixture.

## *Continuous Oxygen Therapy*

The continuous exposure of patients to an atmosphere containing between 45 and 50 percent oxygen, and between 3 and 4 percent carbon dioxide. The treatment was designed by Leland Hinsie of the New York State Psychiatric Institute and Hospital in the early 1930s. Reflecting that era's trend to consider schizophrenia as caused by a deficiency in the oxidative processes in the cerebral cortex of the brain, Hinsie and his colleagues placed five catatonic schizophrenic patients in a small portable Barach oxygen chamber where they remained for eighty-seven continuous days. None, however, showed improvement.

Theorizing that the presence of carbon dioxide would make more oxygen available for the cortical brain cells, Hinsie and his colleagues modified their approach. They placed ten catatonic schizophrenic patients in oxygen chambers for ten continuous weeks, however, once a day for six days of the week they were removed from the chamber and placed in an oxygen tent and given inhalations of a mixture of 15 to 20 percent carbon dioxide and 80 percent oxygen via a hood placed over their heads. Before being placed back into the chamber, attempts were made to engage the patients in conversation; when conversations could be sustained, they continued for one to two hours. Two of the patients in this modified procedure improved to the point of remission. The clinical abstract of one of them in particular offers an interesting glimpse into what was understood as the nature of catatonic schizophrenia, as well as into the mediated interaction between patient and therapeutic.

> E. Ha, age 23, single.... The onset of his psychiatric disorder was in part at least associated with his effort to develop a love affair with a girl. It was a relatively acute onset, characterized by confusion, anxiety, ideas of reference, insomnia. He subsequently became stuporous, mute, inactive when left alone and negativistic under stimulation.... Treatments were started on April 18, 1931. He protested with great vigor against the administration of carbon dioxide and it was necessary to take such measure as would prevent him from destroying the hood that was placed over his head while carbon dioxide was being given. Treatments were discontinued on June 6, 1931. He began to show improvement during the first week in May, 1931. The improvement continued steadily and he was discharged from the hospital on November 10, 1931, as recovered [Hinsie, Barach, Harris, Brand & McFarland, p. 45].

Seven of the patients in the modified treatment showed partial improvement, and the remaining showed no improvement whatsoever. The clinical abstract of one of those unimproved patients was especially revealing of the complicated family dynamics that just a few decades after brain metabolism theories fell out of vogue, would be considered a possible cause of his catatonic schizophrenia:

> E. We., age 19, single. A quiet, seclusive home boy, who was described by his mother as always having been "like a girl." He was slow, deliberate and disinterested. His only consistent activity was observed in school work. He was bashful, a day-dreamer and never had any companions. What little emotions he exhibited were toward his father. "He was all for his father." But there were times when he showed antagonisms and these were ordinarily toward his mother. From the age of 4 until 6 (when his father died) he slept with his father. The onset of the psychiatric disorder was insidious; character changes were observed at the age of 14; he became more seclusive at 16 when his father died. He complained of inability to think, insomnia and restlessness. His symptoms became progressively worse; at the age of 19 he began to attitudinize and at times developed periods of excitement during which he assaulted his mother.... From March 15, 1932, until June 10, 1932, he resided continuously in the oxygen chamber. During this time he also received short daily inhalations of carbon dioxide. There were no essential changes during this period, save for the great resistance to carbon dioxide administration. Subsequent to treatment his condition has remained the same—mutism, rigidity, immobility, apathy, unkemptness [p. 47].

Hinsie and his colleagues found the results of the modified continuous oxygen therapy to be promising and decided to carry it out on a larger scale. To that end, they converted a dormitory into an oxygen chamber so that patients could reside in a familiar environment. The dormitory was made leak-tight by heavy coats of paint on the floors and ceiling, and a rubber-gasketed door was put into place. A motor-blower unit delivered the ventilation and the temperature of the room was maintained between 60° and 70° F. Most importantly, the atmosphere of 45 to 50 percent oxygen and 3 to 4 percent carbon dioxide was maintained through carefully calibrated regulators.

Ten patients lived in this dormitory for ten weeks; half of them had no other treatment while the other half had inhalations of carbon dioxide and oxygen six days each week and for ten to fifteen minutes duration each time. For those who had no other treatment than the oxygenated dorm room, no clinical alterations were noted during the period of their confinement. For those who had the adjunctive carbon dioxide inhalation therapy, however, the changes were unexpected and, in Hinsie's opinion, directly related to the treatment. The changes comprised of:

> (1) a distinct and often overwhelming fear of death or injury, followed by vigorous resistance to the inhalation of high concentrations of carbon dioxide. When it appeared that consciousness was about to be lost, the patients protested with great fervor. (2) The strenuous objections were manifested by physical resistance, or by verbal resistance, or by both. Not infrequently the patient beseeched the physician to release him from the impending fearful experience and he promised to speak if the treatment were not given [p. 42].

When the entire procedure had finished, Hinsie and his colleagues further noted, the patients tended to "return to the condition that prevailed before treatment was instituted" (p. 42). Such startling and disappointing results left Hinsie and his colleagues to call into question whether the improvement they had noted in a few of the patients in the earlier version of continuous oxygen therapy had, in the end, anything at all to do with the treatment. On the basis of their findings, Hinsie and his colleagues could not advocate continuous oxygen therapy as a treatment for catatonic schizophrenia.

## Nitrogen Inhalation Therapy

The replacement of inhaled oxygen with approximately six liters of nitrogen per minute through a tight fitting face mask. Developed by Frederick Alexander and Harold Himwich at the Albany Medical College in New York as a safer and more manageable alternative to metrazol and insulin shock treatments [see **Shock Therapy**], nitrogen inhalation therapy produced short periods of cerebral anoxia with transient facial twitching, clonic contractions of the muscles and unconsciousness. Lasting only five to six minutes, the treatment was immediately terminated by the administration of oxygen. Nitrogen inhalation therapy typically was administered three times per week and because it did not produce confusion, stiffness or soreness, patients required little post-treatment nursing or supervisory care.

In 1938 Alexander and Himwich administered more than 300 nitrogen inhalation therapy treatments to twelve schizophrenic patients at the Albany Hospital without serious complications. Four of the patients went into "full remission, although one had a "mild relapse"; one "greatly improved"; one "definitely improved" and showed "better adjustment"; three "improved," one with "better adjustment" and one not; two "somewhat improved" and one of them "left of own accord"; and one remained "unimproved" (Alexander & Himwich, p. 646). Although these evaluative terms were not defined, Alexander and Himwich concluded that the ease of administration of nitrogen inhalation therapy and its low risks to patients constituted convincing evidence for its further use.

But how did it work? Basile Lipetz, who had been involved in the pioneering use of the therapeutic at the Albany Hospital, demonstrated that nitrogen inhalation therapy not only deprived the brain of oxygen, a critical metabolic factor, but carried the resulting cerebral anoxia further by reducing the saturation of hemoglobin to a mere 15 percent, one-third the saturation rate produced by metrazol shock treatment [see **Shock Therapy**]. It was this severe, albeit short-termed, cerebral anoxia, he argued, that was responsible for the effectiveness of the treatment.

Lipetz brought a somewhat more critical evaluative eye to the outcomes of nitrogen inhalation therapy for the seventeen schizophrenic patients he had treated. He defined the outcome for each with a very brief clinical vignette that provided a glimpse into how improvement was envisioned, if not measured. For the five patients who went into remission, for example, he described changes in behavior and mood that were indicative of cure, such as "more cheerful, less seclusive," the number of treatments after which the changes were noted, the length of remission, and the current mental status of the discharged patient. Similar details were noted for the five patients who showed no improvement. For the remaining seven patients, however, the differences between the evaluations of "greatly improved," "improved," and "slightly improved" were perplexing. The "great improvement" of one patient, for example, was based on her developing doubts about her delusions; the "slight improvement" of another was rather redundantly based on "some improvement noted" (Lipetz, p. 499).

The imprecision in evaluative language both problematized the replication of the findings of these early reports on the effectiveness of nitrogen inhalation therapy, as well as dampened the enthusiasm for its widespread use. At Brooklyn State Hospital, for example, Leonard Sillman and Christopher Terrence found that when they used more rigorous evaluative definitions their nitrogen inhalation therapy patients had an improvement rate equal to the 20 percent spontaneous remission rate of schizophrenia. They saw no reason to recommend it.

## Nitrous Oxide Inhalation Therapy

The administration via a well-fitting rubber mask of nitrous oxide, colloquially known as "laughing gas." The colorless, odorless gas was hypothesized to increase the oxygen-carrying capacity of the blood vessels.

At the Warren Sate Hospital in Pennsylvania, E.J. Fogel and his colleagues administered nitrous oxide to twelve patients experiencing an acute episode of schizophrenia, as well as to twelve patients whose schizophrenia had been chronic for longer than two continuous years. All of the patients reported having experienced pleasant dreams during the five minute treatment sessions, and looked forward to continued treatments over several subsequent days. Only the acute patients, however, experienced any amelioration of their symptoms, and those changes were transitory. Fogel, nonetheless, argued that because nitrous oxide inhalation therapy was both easy to administer and well-tolerated by patients, it might be considered in some cases a viable alternative to insulin shock therapy [see **Shock Therapy**], or at least as a preparation for it.

Frederick Alexander and Harold Himwich at the Albany Medical College in New York disagreed. They found that the brief amelioration of symptoms post-nitrous oxide inhalation for the twenty schizophrenic patients they treated was often followed by an increase in cognitive confusion. In addition, reports of nausea and findings of cardiac arrhythmias for some of the patients argued against its use as an asylum therapeutic.

## Sodium Cyanide Therapy

The injection of small doses of sodium cyanide, a highly toxic asphyxiant, to alter respiration and thus brain metabolism. The therapeutic was first experimentally used by Arthur Solomon Loevenhart who was conducting research at the University of Wisconsin on metabolic processes in the respiratory center located in the medulla oblongata, the lowermost part of the brainstem. In experiments on dogs, he attempted to stimulate the respiratory center with lactic acid, atropine sulphate, caffeine and strychnine sulphate, but discovered that sodium cyanide was particularly effective to the task while not simultaneously raising blood pressure. Further experiments showed that the continuous, as opposed to intermittent, administration of the drug produced continuing stimulation of the respiratory center.

In this dawning era of biological psychiatry, one emerging area of inquiry was on metabolic theories of insanity. Because respiration was considered a key element in both brain blood flow and metabolism, the respiration patterns of asylum patients was of some interest. It was noted that neurotic patients tended to have shallow respirations, irregular inhalations and exhalations, and sighing, while psychotic patients variously had low, irregular or rapid respirations. Thus the brain flow and metabolism were compromised in both groups.

The prospect of producing continuous respiratory center stimulation of almost any intensity and duration through the administration of sodium cyanide to these patients enticed Loevenhart to focus further research on asylum patients diagnosed with catatonic schizophrenia. Their inert, often silent and even motionless state, allowed for the easy observation and measurement of their breathing; it also obviated the concern about obtaining informed consent. He administered sodium cyanide to ten asylum patients and produced results that fully supported the earlier animal experiments. Each patient showed marked and almost immediate improvement. The most dramatic recovery was noted in a twenty-one-year-old patient. Institutionalized for a year, he had never spoken a word, but after receiving a continuous drip of sodium cyanide over sixty-four minutes, he "conversed, answered questions and attempted to explain his prolonged silence" (Loevenhart, Lorenz, Martin & Malone, p. 128). To Loevenhart and his colleagues, the sodium cyanide had done more than stimulate the respiration center—it had stimulated the cerebrum of the brain in its entirety, and most especially its "psychic centers" (p. 129).

At the advent of World War I, Loevenhart's laboratories at the University of Wisconsin were seconded to the Chemical Warfare Service of the United States Army. It was his experience working with a team of chemists, pharmacologists and others on organic arsenic compounds that convinced Loevenhart that a collaborative effort towards therapeutics, whether psychiatric or medical, would most benefit patients. Upon his return to civilian life, he put that ideal into practice and turned his team's attention once again to the treatment of psychosis. He administered sodium cyanide to patients in a catatonic depression, and found that it animated them, making conversation and insight possible, but that the salutary effects could not be maintained for more than a half-an-hour.

Loevenhart died in 1929, but the Chemical Warfare Service had a continuing interest in sodium cyanide. At the start of World War II, it contacted the Hungarian physician László Meduna who already had achieved considerable notoriety for his development of metrazol shock treatment [see **Shock Therapy**] and asked him to experiment with its use. Meduna injected forty schizophrenic patients at the Illinois Neuropsychiatric Institute with sodium cyanide, took electroencephalographic readings during the resulting convulsions and compared them to those taken during convulsions produced by metrazol and electroconvulsive shock treatment. He found that metrazol and electroconvulsive shocks increased the activity of the cortex of the brain, while sodium cyanide reduced it to "almost complete inactivity and silence" (Meduna, p. 132), even while it stimulated the deep motor structures of the brain. In the end, however, the sodium cyanide induced convulsions were of no lasting benefits to the patients.

Sodium cyanide treatment was cautiously used in some asylums until the mid-twentieth century.

## Color Cure (Chromotherapy, Colorology)

*The treatment of insanity through the use of color.*

In the late nineteenth century G.L. Ponza, superintendent of the insane asylum in Alessandria, Italy, speculated that solar rays might have a therapeutic effect on the insane. Influenced by observations being made in Europe and the United States that sunlight filtered through colored glass had an invigorating effect on plant and animal life and, perhaps, on human health and well-being as well, he consulted Father Pietro Angelo Secchi, director of the Roman College Astronomical Observatory, and an expert on astronomical spectroscopy. He encouraged Ponza to experiment in treating insane patients by replacing clear window panes with violet colored panes—violet being, in his opinion, the color of insanity—and painting the walls of the room the same color. A furious maniac placed in that room, he hypothesized, would be calmed and soothed by the color. Ponza reported an excellent outcome with a single patient who, after passing the day in the violet room, asked to be sent home because he believed himself cured. Buoyed by the result, Ponza immediately began experimenting with other colors: red to stimulate the melancholic, blue to calm the manic, and all with good results which he explained as follows:

> The violet rays are of all others, those that possess the most intense electro-chemical power; the red light is also very rich in calorific rays; blue light, on the contrary, is quite devoid of them as well as of chemical and electric ones. Its beneficent influence is hard to explain; as it is the absolute negation of all excitement, it succeeds admirably in calming the furious excitement of maniacs ["Colored Light," p. 451].

What quite quickly became known as the "color cure" prompted a variety of experiments in asylums around the world, but with decidedly mixed results. Henri Taguet, painted the walls and floor of a south-facing room blue in the Asylum of Ville-Evrard in a suburb of Paris, France, and fitted it with a blue window. The first patient placed in the room was in the early stages of general paresis (neurosyphilis) and was in the throes of maniacal excitement so severe that he had to be restrained on the bed. He remained in the blue room three hours, his eyes closed the entire time, leading Taguet to hypothesize that the blue light seemed to fatigue him. The following day, however, it had no effect, nor did it on the second patient who was in the throes of acute mania, nor with a hysterical patient whose only response to several hours in the blue room was the exclamation, "How very strange that blue room is!" (Aldridge, p. 117). Although Taguet found some reason to agree with Ponza that blue light produced a slight fatigue, he was forced to conclude that it did not have the therapeutic effect that Ponza had observed.

The findings of Ludwig Schager at the Vienna Asylum in Austria were more encouraging. He, too, observed the effects of several hours in a blue room on sixty patients over a three year period and found, as Ponza had, that the color had a calming, albeit not a curing, effect. His experiments with a red room to stir melancholic patients out of their torpor also had reassuring consequences. Experiments with other colors soon followed in asylums around the world. The violent patient was housed in a violet or yellow room; since either color was believed to dampen the spirits of a sane person to the point of depression, its inhibiting effect on someone violent was fully anticipated. The irritated and restless patient was housed in a brown room or made to wear brown clothing. The choice of that color may have been influenced by the idiom "in a brown study," a phrase that can be traced back to the sixteenth century and that referred to a kind of daydreamy tranquility.

Asylum physicians argued about the effect of the absence of color, i.e., black, on the insane patient, but none seemed willing to experiment until George Zeller was appointed superintendent of the Peoria Asylum in Illinois in at the start of the twentieth century. Zeller was an ardent devotee of the color cure. Influenced not only by reports on its use from asylums physicians in France, Russia, Spain and all the way from Uruguay where a blue glass roof was constructed over the first asylum ever built there, Zeller also was inspired by the "blue glass craze" that briefly took hold in the United States. A retired Civil War general, Augustus J. Pleasonton had published a book in 1876, on blue paper and in blue ink, titled *The Influence of the Blue Ray of the Sunlight and of the Blue Color of the Sky*, in which he argued on the basis of his experiments that sunlight filtered through blue panes of glass increased the growth and vigor of plants, the weight and health of animals, and most certainly would have health benefits for humans as well. As a result of the "blue glass craze" his findings set off, many farmers began growing crops under blue lights, people started replacing the clear glass of their spectacles with blue-tinted glass, and asylum physicians, who may or may not have even heard of Ponza's findings in Italy, began painting some of their rooms blue.

On his arrival at the Peoria Asylum, Zeller had seven cottages on the grounds painted blue and immediately observed its restful effect on the patients. Having heard that female workers at a film developing business where they had to work under red light were so giddy as to be non-productive, he painted one cottage red and placed melancholy female patients there. Two years later, he was pleased to report that there was a "growing cheerfulness" among them (Lisman & Parr, p. 75). Zeller then experimented with black. He placed a very violent, manic female patient in a black room, completely devoid of light, where she remained for three days, checked every half hour by a nurse, and with a physician nearby the entire time. The patient slept a great deal, and upon awakening on the third day, appeared so calm and docile that she was returned, without further violent incidents, to her regular ward. From that point on, the black room was used to quiet female patients diagnosed with hysterical insanity.

Zeller then traveled to Denmark to visit the laboratories of the late Niels Finsen, a physician and Nobel Prize Laureate who had experimented with the "light cure" of skin diseases, small pox, tuberculosis and lupus. Impressed with the results of what Finsen had called "phototherapy," he returned to the Peoria Asylum and had red incandescent bulbs installed in an operating room to reduce inflammatory conditions, blue panes of glass in the solarium to enhance the healing of tubercular patients, and painted the walls yellow in the epileptic ward to reduce the likelihood of seizures.

About these experiments with the color cure, Zeller wrote:

> I have been exceedingly reticent in claiming beneficial results. The whole subject of phototherapy is yet in its infancy and even the literature is meager. I do not wish to add to it unpreparedly, but I do wish to say that something has benefited these patients beyond the power of the pen to describe. They have been brought here in many instance in the wildest of maniacal excitement and with no other treatment than exposure to violet or amber ray of the leucodescent lamp have speedily recovered and always and invariably without narcotics, without imprisonment and without mechanical restraint. Not only the acute but the chronic patients have improved beyond measure and our institution partakes of the nature of a village with its two thousand inmates contented and happy and engaged in a variety of labor extensive as to bring our per capita cost of maintenance far below the allowance. Some influence has calmed these excited minds and perhaps the same influence has cheered up the depressed and changed despondency into contentedness [Lisman & Parr, p. 76].

Anecdotal evidence of the curative power of color also came from the Wards Island Asylum in New York City where physicians used the standard blue to calm, red to stimulate, black to soothe, and added a bright white room for the patient who was "practically well" and almost ready to be released. A newspaper report explained how the asylum's various colors cured by relating the case of a recently admitted melancholic woman who was being led down the hall:

> First come the black rooms; these she passed without evincing any difference in her state of observation. The violet, green, and blue rooms had the same effect; before each door she paused, but did not raise her eyes. Then came the brilliant orange room. For a moment she raised her eyes, then lowered them again. Three of these rooms she passed, and was then brought abruptly in front of the room with the red walls. She raised her head instantly, looked into the room, and then about her. The vibrations produced by this color had evidently been felt by her, while the others had no effect ["Use Colors," p. 25].

Whether it was by "vibrations," or "electrochemical power," the color cure was used extensively in the early twentieth century in asylums around the world, even as experiments and controlled observations called into question the promising reports of some asylum physicians. "I am satisfied that colored light has no greater power in the cure of insanity," wrote one asylum physician who had experimented with its use, "than colored water has in the treatment and cure of the diseased stomach of the inebriate" (Reed, p. 554). All skepticism aside, the color cure was built into asylums, from specifically colored rooms, to tinted panes of glass, to the hallways so universally painted the same calming color that the hue has come to be known as "institutional green."

At the Salpêtrière Asylum in Paris, France, however, color was used in a particularly creative way. It was there that physician Albert Pitres cured a patient of hysteria by having her put on red-tinted spectacles every time she felt the aura of an imminent hysterical attack. In one month, she was completely cured. Although Pitres and his colleagues were investigating what they referred to as the "ocular stigmata" of hysteria, including color-blindness, tubular vision, and such a predominance of the red color field that a physician once declared that "it may be affirmed that red is the hysterical color" (Thompson, p. 88), he only occasionally prescribed the use of the red-tinted spectacles to prevent a hysterical attack, all the while warning that certain colors also could set one off.

Yet red also was considered the "schizophrenic color" by D. Ewen Cameron, then a newly appointed physician at the Brandon Hospital for Mental Diseases. Located on the prairie of Manitoba, Canada, "the Hill," as the asylum was known to locals, had ambitions to be at the forefront of North American psychiatry, an ambition shared by Cameron who would go on to become president of the both the Canadian and the American Psychiatric Associations, as well as the World Psychiatric Association. Like other asylums around the world, however, the Hill's back wards were filled with schizophrenic patients who seemed to stifle both institutional and personal ambitions. Because none of them had been responsive to the shock treatments that were all the vogue in the early twentieth century [see **Shock Therapy**], Cameron tried red light treatment. He had read how red light stimulated the growth of plants and animals, and had a salutary effect on the fertility of humans. Drawing on received medical wisdom of the era that schizophrenia was often accompanied by endocrine disorders, especially those involving the sex glands, he improvised a red-light cage, fitted with fifteen 200-watt lamps, filtered by an inch of running water and a layer of sodium salt of sulfuric acid infused into cellophane, in order to transmit the light at the appropriate wave length.

The Hill's schizophrenic patients were then made to lie naked below the filters for as long as eight continuous hours each day, and over as long as eight continuous months, bathing in what Cameron hypothesized would be the restorative red light. Of the fourteen patients thus treated, Cameron reported that five were discharged, one showed marked improvement, four showed slight improvement and four demonstrated no change. Although not confident that schizophrenic symptoms in some of the patients had been remediated by red light working on the endocrine system as hypothesized, he nonetheless recommended its use as a therapeutic agent. Cameron, a bit of a therapeutic gadfly, became bored with the red-light cage and dismantled it, soon after recommending it to his colleagues.

## References

Aldridge, C. (1877). Taquet on the influence of coloured light in the treatment of insanity. *London Medical Record, 5,* 117.

Cameron, D.E. (1936). Red light therapy in schizophrenia. *British Journal of Physical Medicine, 10,* 11.

Collins, A. (1988). *In the sleep room: The story of the CIA brainwashing experiments in Canada.* Toronto: Lester and Orpen Dennys.

"Colored light a cure for insanity" (1876). *United States Medical Investigator, 12,* 451.

Lisman, G.L., and Parr, A. (2005). *Bittersweet memories: A history of the Peoria State Hospital.* Victoria, BC, Canada: Trafford.

Pitres, A. (1887). *Des anesthésies hystériques.* Bourdeaux, France: G. Gounouilhou.

Reed, J.A. (1876). Annual report of the Western Pennsylvania Hospital, 1876. *Journal of Insanity, 33,* 554.

"South American Insane Hospital" (1884). *Boston Medical and Surgical Journal, 110,* 295–296.

Thompson, J.H. (1893). Hysterical disturbances of special senses *Medical Review, 28,* 87–89.

"Treatment of hysterical convulsions" (1891). *Pittsburgh Medical Review, 5,* 137–138.

"Use colors to cure insane" (1902, October 26). *New York Times,* p. 25.

# Counterirritation

*The production of irritation, tumescence, burns, lacerations or vesication of the skin in order to favorably influence the brain.*

One of the oldest asylum therapeutics, counterirritation was informed by the humoural doctrine of the ancient medical philosophers. The doctrine held that four humours, or "vital spirits," were produced by the digestive process and then circulated to the heart and brain by the heat generated by that process, thus determining and maintaining both physical and mental health. Blood, not to be confused with venous blood, was the primary of the four humours. Warm and moist, it was thought to be produced in the liver, and to determine a sanguine, that is social and expressive, temperament. Black bile, a cold and dry humour that actually was blue in color, was thought to be stored in the spleen and to determine a melancholic temperament. Phlegm could be found in any part of the body. A cold, moist and colorless humour, it resulted in the meek but trustworthy characteristics of the phlegmatic temperament The fourth humour, yellow bile or choler, was thought to be produced in the gallbladder and to determine a choleric temperament, characterized by confidence and competitiveness.

In traditional humouralism, black bile and yellow bile were most often indicted in cases of insanity. The former, when it accumulated in the spleen, contaminated the other humours and circulated peccant spirits to the brain, causing the lethargy, self-loathing and ineffable sadness that were the hallmark symptoms of melancholia. In contrast, the excessive secretion of the latter irritated the brain into frenzy and mania. Treating the melancholic and the manic, then, required counterirritation, that is, the drawing of the noxious humours away from the brain and out of the body. Such treatments were done either by derivation, that is, the application of a counterirritant close to the irritated brain, such as on the shaved skull or the nape of the neck, or by revulsion, an application distant from the irritated brain, such as on legs. Because it was believed that insanity was incompatible with another somatic ailment, if only because the body did not have the requisite power to sustain both simultaneously, the irritation, tumescence, burning or vesication caused by counterirritation would in the words of David Uwins, physician to the Peckham House Asylum in Surrey, England, "set up disorder in one part, for the purpose of knocking it down in another" (Uwins, p. 64). Balance, and mental health, in other words, would then be restored.

Although traditional humouralism had yielded slowly over time to new theories, and a new lexicon—nerves, fibers, brain congestion or inflammation, morbid action—asylum physicians remained loyal to both its logic and its therapeutics. Thus, the various techniques of counterirritation were used well into the nineteenth century, not just to treat melancholia and mania, but the growing list of their types and subtypes with which asylum patients were being diagnosed.

## References

Arika, A. (2007). *Passions and tempers: A history of the humours.* New York: HarperCollins.

Bakewell, T. (1805). *The domestic guide in cases of insanity.* Newcastle, UK: T. Allbut.

Battie, W. (1758). *A treatise on madness.* London: J. Whiston and B. White.

"Biography and psychology III: Walter Abraham Haigh" (2011). Bethlem Blog. Retrieved at http://bethlemheritge.wordpress.com/2011/08/13/biography-and-psychology-iii-walter-abraham-haigh/.

Bonhoeffer, K. (1940). *Die Geschichte der psychiatrie in der Charité im 19. jahrundert.* Berlin: Verlag Springer.

Broussals, F.J.V. (1831). *On irritation and insanity.* Trans. T. Cooper. Columbia, SC: S.J. McMorris.

Buchanan, J.R. (1879). On the centric relations of the teeth, the mouth, and the adjacent parts to the entire constitution, through the medium of the proximate portions of the brain. *Transactions of the American Dental Association,* pp. 193–212. Chicago: Knight and Leonard.

Burrows, G.M. (1828). *Commentaries on the causes, forms, symptoms, and treatment, moral and medical, of insanity.* London: Thomas and George Underwood.

Cox, J.M. (1804). *Practical observations on insanity.* London: Baldwin and Murray.

Dally, A. (1996). The lancet and the gum-lancet: 400 years of teething babies. *Lancet, 348,* 1710–1711.

Dudley, A.K. (2009). Moxa in nineteenth-century medical practice. *Journal of the History of Medicine and Allied Sciences, 65,* 187–206.

Earle, P. (1853). *Institutions for the insane in Prussia, Austria and Germany.* Utica, NY: New York State Lunatic Asylum.

Esquirol, J.E.D. (1838). *Mental maladies: A treatise on insanity.* Trans. E.K. Hunt. Philadelphia: Lea and Blanchard.

Fallowes, T. (1705). *The best method for the cure of lunaticks.* London: Author.

Ferriar, J. (1795). *Medical histories and reflections,* Vol. 2. London: Cadell and Davies.

Galt, J.M. (1846). *The treatment of insanity.* New York: Harper and Brothers.

Ghesquier, D. (1999). A Gallic affair: The case of the missing itch-mite in French medicine in the early nineteenth century. *Medical History, 43,* 26–54.

Guislain, J. (1826). *Traité sur l'aliénation mentale et sur les hospices des aliénés.* Amsterdam: J. Van Der Hay et Fils, and H. Gartman.

Hallaran, W.S. (1818). *Practical observations of the causes and cure of insanity,* 2nd ed. Cork, Ireland: Edwards and Savage.

Haller, J.S. (1980). Use of surface irritants in nineteenth-century medicine. *New York State Journal of Medicine, 80,* 1314–1323.

Haslam, J. (1809). *Observations on madness and melancholy.* London: J. Callow.

Hunter, R., and Macalpine, I. (1963). *Three hundred years of psychiatry, 1535–1860.* London: Oxford University Press.

Jenner, E. (1821). *A letter to Charles Henry Parry M.D., F.R.S. &c, &c., on the influence of artificial eruptions in certain diseases incidental to the human body.* London: Baldwin and Co.

Junod, V-T. (1875). *Traite theorique et pratique de l'hemospasie [Theory and practice of hemospasia].* Paris: A L'Imprimerie Nationale.

Kraepelin, E. (1962). *One hundred years of psychiatry.* Trans. W. Baskin. New York: Citadel.

Lutz, T. (1999). *Crying: The natural and cultural history of tears.* New York: W.W. Norton.

"M. Guislain on mental derangement, &c" (1829). *Edinburgh Medical and Surgical Journal, 32,* 97–128.

"Medico-Psychological Association notes and news" (1884). *Journal of Mental Science, 29,* 599–602.

Millingen, J.G. (1842). *Aphorisms on the treatment and management of the insane.* Philadelphia: Ed. Barrington and Geo. D. Haswell

Mills, J.H. (1999). Re-forming the Indian: Treatment regimes in the lunatic asylums of British India, 1857–1880. *Indian Economic and Social History Review, 36,* 407–429.

Monro, J. (1758). *Remarks on Dr. Battie's Treatise on Madness.* London: John Clarke.

Morris, A. (2008). William Battie's *Treatise on Madness* (1758) and John Monro's *Remarks on Dr. Battie's Treatise* (1758)—250 years ago. *British Journal of Psychiatry, 192,* 257.

Newington, S. (1865). On a new remedial agent in the treatment of insanity and other diseases. *Retrospect of Medicine, 52,* 72–74.

Pargeter, W. (1792). *Observations on maniacal disorders.* Reading, UK: Smart and Cowslade.

Perfect, W. (1800). *Annals of insanity: Comprising a section of curious and interesting cases,* 5th ed. London: Crosby and Co.

Pinel, P. (1806). *A treatise on insanity.* Trans. D.D. Davis. Sheffield, UK: W. Todd.

Porter, R. (2006). *Madmen: A social history of madhouses, mad-doctors and lunatics.* Stroud, UK: Tempus.

Prichard, J.C. (1831). On the treatment of hemiplegia. *London Medical Gazette, 7,* 425–238.

Rush, B. (1830). *Medical inquiries and observations upon the diseases of the mind,* 4th ed. Philadelphia: John Grigg.

Ryder, H. (1685). *New practical observations in surgery, containing diverse remarkable cases and cures.* London: Patridge.

Tuke, D.H. (1882). *Chapters in the history of the insane in the British Isles.* London: Kegan, Paul, Trench, and Co.

Uwins, D. (1833). *A treatise on those disorders of the brain and nervous system, which are usually considered and called mental.* London: Renshaw and Rush.

Valentin, L. (1815). *Mémoire et observations concernant les bons effets du cautère actuel [Memoir and observations concerning the good effects of the actual cautery cautery].* Nancy, France: C.-J. Hissette.

van der Kolk, J.LS. (1869). *The pathology and therapeutics of mental diseases.* Trans. J.T. Rudall. London: John Churchill and Sons.

Werber, G. (1910). Junod's blood derivations. *Journal of Advanced Therapeutics, 28,* 241–247.

## Actual Cautery

The burning or searing of the skin by an instrument such as a red hot poker or iron. The adjective "actual" was used to distinguish this therapeutic from the moxa, which sometimes also was referred to as a cautery. While the mere sight of a red hot poker often was enough to render the most obstreperous patient submissive [see **Salutary Fear**], the actual cautery also was used to create a suppurating burn, usually on the nape of the neck or the top of the head of the insane patient, and therefore was considered a counterirritant by early asylum physicians.

Perhaps the most extensive, and certainly enthusiastic, use of the actual cautery was by the early nineteenth century French physician Louis Valentin, who had published an award winning treatise on the therapeutic. Although Valentin was not an asylum physician—he was in fact a former military physician in the West Indies and specialist in diseases of the eye—he had in fact encountered a number of cases of delirium and/or mania that were the results of the malignant fevers that were epidemic in St. Domingo where he had been stationed. In those cases, he had found that the application of the actual cautery to the top of the head or the nape of neck quelled the symptoms and eventually restored reason. One of his most dramatic cures took place when he was stationed in the United States. The case was that of young girl who had been struck with mania a few years before, and would no longer speak. He applied the actual cautery and she immediately improved. Although he was unable to follow her progress, he was confident that the

**A receptacle for burning coal to heat cautery instruments. Asylum physicians debated whether it was the pain from the burn produced by the cautery or the fear of the pain that was more therapeutic (courtesy of the Wellcome Library, London).**

therapeutic had achieved its curative purpose. Upon establishing a private practice in Nancy, France, he continued the use of the actual cautery in similar cases, usually of mania, and reportedly with similar success.

Valentin downplayed, even ignored, the terror the actual cautery created in even the most insensible patient, but asylum physicians who studied his treatise did not. Jean-Étienne Dominique Esquirol, *médecin ordinaire* at the Salpêtrière Asylum in Paris, France, for example, suggested that its therapeutic efficacy was due more to its "frightful moral influence" than for the actual festering burns it produced (Esquirol, p. 411). Nonetheless, he occasionally used it, and sometimes with success. He detailed one such case:

> V.V.P., twenty-six years of age, and of a lymphatic temperament, becomes a maniac during the month of April, 1823. She is bled and bathed at home, but without success. She is admitted at the Salpêtrière on the 26th day of May following, in a state of mania, attended with a degree of agitation and fury, which nothing composes. In the month of October, I apply the actual cautery to the neck. The preparations for this operation disturb her much. Scarcely had the red hot iron been applied to her neck, when, to her cries and agitation, succeeds a moment of silence. She then sheds a torrent of tears, and afterwards makes regular progress towards recovery, which is perfected at the expiration of two weeks. She still remained for some time in the division of convalescents, and returned to her family, November 19th, of the same year [p. 411].

The actual cautery was used in some French and German asylums in the early to mid-nineteenth century. John Gideon Millingen, superintendent of the Hanwell Asylum outside of London, England, also recommended its use for monomaniacal patients who had delusions of demon possession. "The pain it excites," he wrote, "draws their attention from their melancholy apprehensions.... This sudden excitement has been known to cure patients who fancied that they heard various menacing voices denouncing perdition and celestial wrath" (Millingen, p. 60). Delimiting its use to such a specific, and probably quite rare, type of insanity made the actual cautery a seldom used therapeutic in British asylums.

## Artificial Eruptions

The raising of pustules, usually on the neck, shoulders, inside of the forearms or on the shaved head, by the vigorous frictional application of antimonial oils such as tartar emetic or croton oil, also known as *oleum tiglii*. Erupting within hours after the application, the pustules produced a burning sensation and a purulent discharge of pus before scabbing.

As with all counterirritants, the production of artificial eruptions was based on the humoural doctrine to which most early asylum physicians were devotees. As the doctrine began to wane in influence, so did the practice of producing artificial eruptions until it was revived in the early nineteenth century by the British physician Edward Jenner, who had pioneered the smallpox vaccine. In a widely cited monograph, Jenner wrote that "diseases of the skin are diversions in the animal economy for transferring diseased actions from parts vital to parts not immediately vital" (Jenner, p. 59). The artificial creation of a skin "disease" via artificial eruptions, he hypothesized, would transfer the disease of the brain of the insane patient to the skin. Although neither an asylum physician nor a specialist in insanity, Jenner nonetheless treated several cases of mania with artificial eruptions, and reported success in doing so. One of those cases was a young woman on whose shaved head he rubbed tartar emetic, producing oozing eruptions. Immediately her symptoms abated, only to return a short time later; the procedure was repeated, and once again she improved. Upon her second relapse, however, her parents, to whom her care had been entrusted, neglected to repeat the procedure, and the young woman regressed into what Jenner considered to be incurable insanity.

Jenner's treatise renewed asylum physicians'

interest in artificial eruptions, as well as in other counterirritants. After administering the therapeutic to nearly every patient at the Julius-Spital in Würzberg, Germany, quite regardless of diagnosis, Aton Müller expressed unbounded confidence in artificial eruptions. Müller had used a tartarized ointment developed by Johann Heinrich Ferdinand von Autenrieth, professor of medicine at the University of Tübingen in Germany. Autenrieth Ointment (*unguentum antimonii tartarizati*), as it was referred to, was promoted as superior to other substances, and Joseph Guislain, physician at the asylums in Ghent, Belgium, was eager to use it. His first trial was with four patients with different types of insanity, and the results were encouraging: one patient was cured, the worst symptoms of another two were ameliorated, and the reason of the remaining patient was restored although, inexplicably, she was rendered paralytic in her lower extremities.

Cautiously optimistic, Guislain then conducted a second trial on thirty additional patients, with decidedly disappointing results. No patient was cured, no symptoms were ameliorated for any appreciable length of time, and many patients suffered with deep ulcerations to the tops of the head and inflammation of the conjunctiva of their eyes. More worrisome to Guislain was that some patients who could not comprehend the reason for the therapeutic in the first place, came to see him as having "nothing but the malignity of a demon—the unrelenting author of their misery" ("M. Guislain," p. 109). Guislain was forced to conclude that whatever favorable changes might be the result of using antimonial friction to raise oozing pustules on the heads and bodies of insane patients did not in the end justify its use.

Despite this cautionary note, the use of this counterirritation therapeutic continued. And it did so with so much enthusiasm that more than a half-century after Jenner's publication George Henry Savage, physician superintendent of Bethlem (better known as Bedlam) Hospital in London, England, wondered aloud if fellow asylum physicians were, like he was, just "reverting to the old lines" by using counterirritants. After all, he reminded his colleagues, oozing pustules "did not look ornamental" ("Medico-Psychological," p. 600). To this musing, his colleague Daniel Hack Tuke replied that it would be a "great pity" to refrain from using counterirritants since so many cases of chronic insanity had improved with their use (p. 600). Tartar emetic, in fact, remained in use as a counterirritant in British asylums until the mid-twentieth century.

## *Blistering*

The creation of a localized collection of fluid on the upper layers of the skin, or under the surface of the skin. The blister usually was raised on the head, neck or extremities with an application of mustard powder or a vesicant of cantharadin in the form of powdered Spanish fly.

For early asylum physicians blistering was one of the so-called "heroic treatments" that, along with purging, vomiting and bleeding [see **Depletive Therapy**] was used routinely, even ceremonially, on patients quite regardless of their diagnosis or the duration or circumstances of their insanity. At Bethlem (better known as Bedlam) Hospital in London, England, for example, patients were blistered every spring in keeping with the humoural doctrine of seasonal repletion. It was that ritual, in fact, that drew criticism from William Battie of nearby St. Luke's Hospital, whose mid-eighteenth century treatise was one of the first monographs on the subject of insanity. Battie, a devotee of the Enlightenment movement, possessed what was in that era an unusual optimism that insanity could be cured, but only if the differences between what he called "original" and "consequential" insanity were understood, and only if treatment was individualized. "Although madness is taken for one species or disorder," he wrote, "nevertheless, when thoroughly examined, it discovers as much variety with respect to its causes and circumstances as any distemper whatever:

Madness, therefore, like most other morbid cases, rejects all general methods" (Battie, p. 94).

While Battie dismissed as unenlightened the routine and ritualized practice of blistering all patients, he did somewhat reluctantly conclude that it might be necessary and efficacious, but only if used "with great caution" and not at all with the patient who was in a "fit of fury" (p. 94). Interestingly, it was John Monro, physician to Bethlem Hospital who, without apparent irony, defended the ritual use of the heroic treatments in the asylum with which his family was so long associated, while at the same time dismissing blistering as neither a necessary nor efficacious treatment. "I never saw the least good effect of 'blisters' in madness," he wrote in his rejoinder, "unless it was at the beginning, while there was some degree of fever, or when they have been applied to particular symptoms accompanying this complaint" (Monro, p. 47).

Blistering thus became a topic of discussion, pursued with "earnestness and ingenuity" (Pargeter, p. 75) among and between asylum physicians in Great Britain and the United States. John Haslam, apothecary to Bethlem Hospital after Monro's death, found that blisters were of little use when raised on the preferred site of the shaved head, but were more effective if raised on the inside of the legs. This suggestion at first stymied Benjamin Rush who blistered many of his patients on the head at the Pennsylvania Hospital in the United States and who was resistant to relinquishing the therapeutic. Rush, however, came to realize the principle behind the change in the preferred site of administration and found in it a rationale for the continued use of the therapeutic:

> In the first stage of tonic, or violent, madness, the disease is entrenched, as it were, in the brain.—It must be loosened, or weakened, by depleting remedies, before it can dislodged or translated to another part of the body. When this has been effected, blisters easily attract it to the lower limbs, and thus often convey it at once out the body.... The blisters do the same service when applied to the wrists, and still more when applied at the same time, or alternately, to both extremities.—After the complete reduction of the pulse, they may be applied with advantage to the neck and head [Rush, p. 193].

As the humoural doctrine gave way to different theories of the causes and treatments of insanity, blistering all but disappeared from asylums. By the mid-nineteenth century it was virtually unheard of to blister a patient on any part of the body and asylum physicians were taking some pride in having relegated that therapeutic to the unenlightened past. It was a different matter in Colonial asylums, however, where blistering continued for decades longer. At the Dullunda Asylum near Calcutta, India, for example, physicians blistered patients both as a counterirritation treatment and as a punishment, as the case notes on a woman suffering from mania illustrated:

> On admission she was very violent + excited, would not wear clothes, tore everything to pieces + struck + bit every body approaching her. It was necessary to put her under restraint, a Blister was applied to the nape of her neck + sharp purgatives administered. Gradually the violence of the symptoms began to subside.... Discharged cured, October 21, 1862 [Mills, p. 420].

## Cataplasm

A poultice or plaster composed of irritating or sometimes emollient substances applied to the shaved head. It was the practice of early asylum physicians to shave the heads of most of their patients in order to cool what they assumed to be the hot and inflamed brain. The cataplasm added an additional therapeutic benefit in that when placed on the shaved head, it was thought to stimulate the circulation of blood through the brain.

Asylum physicians had their favorite substances for cataplasms. Joseph Guislain, physician to the asylums in Ghent, Belgium, favored a tincture of cantharides, or Spanish fly for the manic patient, but found the blisters it raised too stimulating for the melancholic. To treat that type of patient he experimented with Hoffman's Balsam of Life, a stimulating tincture of amber, lavender, cloves, nutmeg and cinnamon, but was disappointed in its effect. German asylum physicians tended to favor Autenrieth Ointment (*unguentum antimonii tartarizati*), but their enthusiasm for it was not shared by many others.

The fact that asylum physicians were not in consensus as to what type of substance served as the most efficacious counterirritant in a cataplasm opened the way for a considerable amount of entrepreneurship, not to overlook quackery. In regards to the latter, the case of Thomas Fallowes and his "incomparable Oleum Cephalicum," deserves mention. A private madhouse owner, Fallowes had awarded himself a medical degree before concocting his nostrum, a cure for maniacal frenzy and, he hastened to add by way of promoting the £4 a quart mix of animal, vegetable and mineral substances, any kind of insanity at all. Oleum Cephalicum, he went on to say, not only has a pleasant smell, but as a cataplasm raised small pustules on the head and stimulated the brain to release black vapors. After all, he wrote, the seat of insanity is the brain,

> which is disturbed by black vapors which clog the finer vessels thro' which the animal spirits ought freely to pass, and the whole mass of blood, being disordered, either overloads the small veins of the brain, or by too quick a motion, causes a hurry and confusion of the mind, from which ensues a giddiness and at length a fury. The abundance of bile, which is rarely found to have any tolerable secretion in such patients, both begets and carries on the disorder [Tuke, p. 93].

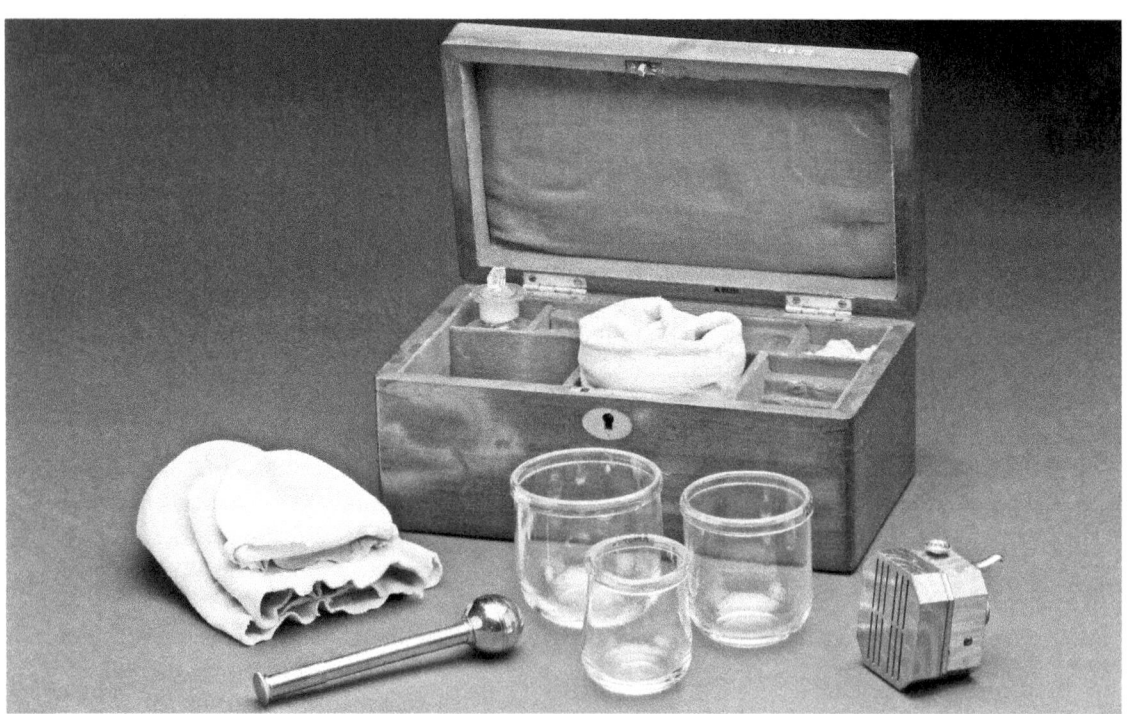

Cupping glasses and a brass scarificator. Dry cupping drew blood to the surface of the skin; the additional step of cutting the tumefied skin with a scarificator was known as wet cupping. In either case, cupping was considered an art: the placement of the cup, the duration of its application, the depth of the incision, the handling of the various cupping tools all required the skill of an asylum physician—not of a barber or self-trained empiric (courtesy of the Wellcome Library, London).

The fact that Fallowes was dismissed as a quack by his contemporaries must be reconciled with the fact that his incomparable Oleum Cephalicum was used for cataplasms by British asylum physicians well into the nineteenth century and even, on occasion, into the twentieth.

## *Dry Cupping, or Cupping, or Exhausting Cupping*

The application of a cupping instrument such as a glass, usually to the head or neck, in order to draw blood to the brain, or to the extremities to relieve the "congestion" of the brain that was thought to be a cause of insanity. The cups used in dry cupping usually were small glass orbs with thick rims that either contained a wick of burning lint or were heated on a flame before being applied for approximately ten minutes; as they cooled they drew blood to the surface of the swollen skin, bursting the capillaries. Other dry cupping instruments included animal horns, plant gourds and vulcanized rubber cups. By the nineteenth century there were numerous technological improvements on the cup heating apparatuses, from grease and alcohol lamps that afforded better heat regulation, to a cupping torch. The latter had a piece of hollow metal tubing cut at an angle on one end, through which a wick protruded. The wick was dipped in alcohol, lit and inserted into the cup to heat it; via the bulb or ring on the other end of the cupping torch, the wick was then pulled back into the tube, extinguishing the flame.

Although dry cupping was particularly recommended as an alternative to bleeding for debilitated and emaciated patients, it was a matter of debate as to how it worked. Some asylum physicians argued that it affected only the surface blood vessels, thus relieving the affected brain by inducing a distracting secondary inflammation; others posited that it affected the nervous system and through it, the secretory organs of the body. Regardless of its therapeutic function, there was startling evidence that dry cupping often was indiscriminately used. When British physician Daniel Hack Tuke visited the asylum in Toronto, Canada in the mid-nineteenth century, he found it one of the "most painful and distressing places" he had ever visited. The aggressive therapeutic regime of dry cupping had left the seventy patients with disfiguring scars on their foreheads and necks.

After conducting an autopsy on a patient who had died hours after dry cupping, the British physician George Mann Burrows, proprietor of a private madhouse in Chelsea, found that all of the blood vessels of the pericranium, cerebral membranes and the brain, itself, were richly distended with blood, thus providing evidence that dry cupping indeed had pulled blood to the surface of the head. An autopsy on a second patient who had died days after dry cupping, however, did not confirm these findings, leading Burrows to conclude that the effects of dry cupping were short-lived. To maximize those effects, he recommended that after the dry cupping the patient's head be vigorously rubbed and the feet plunged in a pediluvium in order to encourage the circulation of blood throughout the body.

## *Dry Friction*

The irritation of the skin by the hand, rough towel, horsehair glove or a brush in order to "excite the sensibility of the skin, and render perspiration more active" (Galt, p. 169). Asylum physicians often explained the use of dry friction by citing Hippocrates who had written that a physician should be skilled in many things especially in the nature of friction. Typically used after dry-cupping, douches and therapeutic baths [see **Hydrotherapy**], dry friction was considered a serviceable remedy for all types of insanity, but was particularly recommended for suicidal monomania, melancholia and hypochondriasis.

## Gum Lancing

The cutting away of the gums to expose and to hasten the emergence of new teeth. Until the twentieth century the infant mortality rate was disturbingly high. Because most deaths occurred between the ages of six months and two years, physicians theorized that teething was a common cause, thus justifying the practice of blistering, bleeding and leeching the gums, and applying cautery on the backs of the heads of infants and toddlers to hasten the emergence of their teeth. Ambroise Paré, a sixteenth century French barber-surgeon, sought a more humane alternative: he lanced or incised the gums of young children, and this procedure remained in vogue for hundreds of years.

While children that young rarely found their ways into asylums, adolescents and young adults certainly did. Often in poor physical health and inadequately nourished, these patients had an array of dental problems, among them impacted or partially erupted molars or wisdom teeth that caused persistent pain and often were prone to infections. These reactions in turn, it was argued, could excite the brain and exacerbate the symptoms of insanity or even cause insanity in the first place.

While at the Salpêtrière Asylum in Paris, France, Jean-Étienne Esquirol, observed the case of a delirious young woman who had a bloated face, salivated excessively, and complained of pain in her head and jaw. Left untreated, her delirium abated when two new teeth pierced her gums, only to return sometime later and last for several more months until two more new teeth emerged. The usually confident Esquirol was left to wonder if he should have lanced her gums to hurry the process. He speculated that the prevailing medical wisdom that teething in a young child can cause irritation of the brain very well also might be applicable to his patient, who was "rapidly approaching the period of maturity" (Esquirol, p. 197). Yet, he did not incise her gums. In his own defense, he explained that he had refrained from doing so because his young patient had been so agitated and was under the delusion that he was trying to kill her, an explanation dismissed out of hand as nothing more than evidence of "childish weakness" (p. 198) in the translator's footnote in his widely read text.

It is not evident how much gum lancing actually occurred in asylums, but that there was a robust body of medical and dental literature that posited a relationship between the molars and insanity is indisputable. After summarizing that literature, Joseph R. Buchanan concluded that the location of the molars, or wisdom teeth,

> enabled them to exert a greater power over the cerebral circulation and excitability—a depressing and deranging influence—which may be manifested in a thousand different ways, especially in melancholy gloom, disqualifying for study and the enjoyment of life, unfitting for business, and producing mental confusion and hallucinations, ill-temper, restlessness, and unpleasant dream, and in extreme cases mania and even paralysis [Buchanan, p. 198].

What lancing of the gums over the molars that did occur as a therapeutic was replaced by surgical extraction [see **Exodontia**] by the turn into the twentieth century as the theory of focal sepsis took hold and asylums in the United States and Europe added dentists and dental surgeons to their staffs.

## Inoculation of Smallpox, or Variolation

The injection of pustular fluid or dried smallpox scabs into the skin of the uninfected patient to produce a mild case of the disease that typically lasted one week. Preparations for the inoculation most often involved bleeding, purging and vomiting [see **Depletive Therapy**] to "lower" the humours. The inoculation produced a primary lesion and satellite pustules around the site of administration, and an extensive and itchy rash. The inoculation of smallpox had been a practice for centuries in India, China, many countries in Africa, and in Turkey from where it was brought to Great Britain in the early eighteenth century by Lady Wortley Montagu, wife of the British ambassador to Constantinople, and was first used there as a prophylactic against a serious acquired case of smallpox.

It is not clear how the inoculation of smallpox came into asylum therapeutics nor, for that matter, how widely it was used. In his text, Joseph Mason Cox, proprietor of the private Fishponds Asylum near Bristol, England, presented a rationale for its use as a counterirritant, but did not describe any cases he, or any of his colleagues, had actually treated:

> [E]very means employed for the removal of mental diseases, whether moral or medical, when successful, relieves by introducing some important change into the general system; but certain it is, that if any considerable commotion, any violent, new, action can be excited in maniacal complaints, by whatever means, the mental derangement is often considerably relieved if not permanently removed; thus smallpox has dissipated the most obstinate melancholia, and where affections of the intellect have resisted common remedies I should place considerable hopes on inoculation, had the party not previously had smallpox, taking care by proper medicines and management to increase the symptoms that usually attend this disease to such a degree that the whole system should be considerably affected without endangering life [Cox, p. 177].

## *Inoculation of the Itch, or Inoculation of Psora*

The rubbing on the skin, or the injection into the skin, of the pus from the scabies pustules. Scabies, a skin disease that produces intense itching, especially in the evening, and a pimple-like rash, is caused by the *Sarcoptes scabiei*, or human itch mite that burrows into the upper layer of the skin where it lays its eggs. Although the intense itching could lead to severe skin infections as the patient vigorously kept scratching, the itch was considered an effective, even curative, counterirritant, as Joseph Mason Cox, proprietor of the private Fishponds Asylum near Bristol, England, explained:

> Itch has been known to bring about the same happy effect, the cure of insanity ... by abstracting attention from the wanderings of the deluded imagination, exciting new ideas by the means of strong impressions made on both mind and body, by the irritation excited on the surface [Cox, pp. 177–178].

In the early nineteenth century when inoculation of the itch was used as a therapeutic in many European asylums, the mechanism of its transmission was a matter of some disagreement. Some asylum physicians thought that the itch was a contagious disease, spread from one person to another by direct or indirect contact. Others thought it was an infectious disease spread by the pus of the pustules. Each theory was imprecise, and had a contradictory relationship with the other, but the lack of certainty regarding the mode of transmission sometimes left asylum physicians frustrated in trying to produce this counterirritant.

That frustration was exemplified by the case Mr. deX., described in detail by Jean-Étienne Dominique Esquirol. Mr. deX., a general and inspector had "given himself up to excessive masturbation" (Esquirol, p. 187), a fact that he could not reconcile with his otherwise principled conduct. He became increasingly irritable and on occasion even threatening and in the early nineteenth century was committed to the Salpêtrière Asylum in Paris, France, where Esquirol was *médecin ordinaire*. The treatment regime focused on preventing masturbation by the use of the itch as a counterirritant.

> Hoping that I could again communicate to him the itch, I should cure him, I employed tepid baths, and friction morning and evening. He takes tonics internally and sleeps in the shirts of those affected with this disorder for fifteen nights. Professor Aibert provides me with the virus of psora. I make about the articulation of the limbs, more than eighty punctures, with no better success. I cause the patient to sleep anew in infected shirts, with no better success [p. 187].

Although Esquirol had used both the contagion and the infection approach, he much later attributed his failure to produce the itch in the patient by reference to the latter. In the years subsequent to this case, medical researchers had discovered that the pus of the scabies pustules did not contain the itch mite, and therefore was not a medium for the infection. Interestingly, it was the crowded conditions of so many asylums that was a better medium for the transmission of the itch. The superintendent of the Danvik Asylum near Stockholm, Sweden once reflected without irony that he had no need to inoculate the itch until the early nineteenth century when patients were moved from crowded dormitories into small two-person cells, thus reducing significantly the spread of scabies.

### Issue

The infliction of a lesion, wound or ulcer in order to produce a discharge of pus. An issue often was produced by the application of a cautery or with a caustic of some kind, and the wound frequently was kept open in order to maximize the duration of the discharge. As a result, the risk of infection was considerable, and both the sight and smell of the suppurating wound often was reported as distressing to the patient and physician alike. Once the wound was allowed to scab over, it was theorized that the body's effort to "throw off" the scab withdrew blood from general circulation, thus exerting a salutary influence on the brain. There was never strong support for the efficacy of the issue as a stand-alone therapeutic, however. It was used in asylums into the nineteenth century, but most often in conjunction with other therapeutics.

### Junod's Boot, or Dr. Junod's Exhausting Apparatus, or Junod's Grand Ventouse, or Junod's Hemospasic Apparatus

A metal boot, secured to the leg by a silk or rubber cap. The air was withdrawn from the boot via a flexible tube attached to a stop-cock pump; an attached manometer measured the resulting pressure. Although it remains contestable as to whether he actually invented the boot, it was so aggressively advocated in the mid-nineteenth century by French physician Victor-Théodore Junod that it bore his name.

Reflecting on the received wisdom of that era, Junod posited that insanity was caused by imbalanced blood circulation, therefore blood had to be drawn from and into other parts of the body, a process he referred to as "hemospasia." To remedy the imbalance, he advocated the boot as an alternative to the more traditional therapeutics of bloodletting and dry cupping. Its mechanism was ingenious: once attached to the leg, the air in the boot was gradually exhausted via the pump; the resulting vacuum withdrew as much as seven pints of blood from other parts of the body into the boot-encased leg even while it stimulated the absorption of serum in other parts of the body. The vacuum was maintained for as long as several hours and/or until the patient fainted, a reaction Junod interpreted as a sure sign that the remedy had been applied "to effect." Once released from the boot, the blood in the incredibly swollen leg gradually returned into circulation and into healthful balance.

Junod's theory of hemospasia appealed to competing schools of thought about the cause and treatment of insanity. Some asylum physicians, even as late as the mid-nineteenth century, were still wedded to the ancient theory of the bodily humours and cited blood as the cause of insanity and its removal as the cure. Others found the cellular theory more explanatory. They posited that the origin of insanity was in the tissues and that the flushing of toxins from them would be its cure. And then there were those more interested in the nervous system as the origin of insanity, and its restoration and revitalization as its cure. Junod's theory of hemospasia resonated with all, and his boot worked in each therapeutic modality: it withdrew and redistributed blood, drained the tissues, and deprived the brain of enough blood to reduce its power to supply nerve impulses to the rest of the body through the spinal cord.

In his 1875 text, *Traite theorique et pratique de l'hemospasie* [*Theory and practice of hemospasia*], Junod presented 293 cases in which the boot brought about either cure or remedy for patients suffering from mania, hysteria, epilepsy, apoplexy, cerebral congestion, and a variety of nervous and neuralgic afflictions. Because he also advocated the boot for the relief of medical disorders, such as laryngitis, asthma, hernias, bone dislocations, dysmenorrhea, rheumatism, gout and even cholera, the boot was widely used outside of asylums by private physicians and quacks alike. So popular had the boot become, in fact, that it was advertised in medical journals, specialty magazines and newspapers, and sold for as much as $25, a considerable sum in the mid-nineteenth century.

Junod's boot was used in asylums in France, England, Norway, the Netherlands and, to much lesser and briefer extent, in other European countries as well as in the United States. Junod's Arm, manufactured for application to the patient's arm, was less often used in asylums. And there is no evidence for the use of the Junod's Depurator, a casket-like metal case that enclosed the entire body of the patient, leaving only the head exposed, in asylums for the treatment of insane patients.

## *Lacrimation*

The inducement of the shedding of tears, or of crying. Tears were of some interest to ancient Greek physicians who believed they were "humours from the brain" and when given to excess, as so often observed in the melancholic patient, had to be purged by weeping (Lutz, p. 73).

The inducement of tears as an asylum therapeutic, however, might very well have been more for its cathartic than counterirritational effect. At the Pennsylvania Hospital in Philadelphia, the prominent physician Benjamin Rush treated grief-stricken patients not only with generous and repeated doses of opium, but by "obtruding upon the mind a sorrow of a less grade than that by which it is depressed" (Rush, p. 318) in order to produce relief through a discharge of tears.

Although he induced lacrimation only infrequently and without a great deal of confidence in its effect, Jean-Étienne Esquirol, observed a case at the Salpêtrière Asylum in Paris, France, in which crying cured insanity. Although he neither theorized as to the reasons why, nor particularly recommended lacrimation as a therapeutic, he nonetheless described the case in detail, if only to illustrate what he asserted was the puerile and proud nature of nervous disorders in women:

> A lady, thirty-four years of age, of a lymphatic temperament and nervous constitution, and of a mild and timid disposition, has always enjoyed good health, although the menstrual flux is not regular. For some months she takes care of a lady whom she tenderly loves. She labors day and night, and watches for fifteen nights in succession. Whilst greatly and constantly troubled, through fear of seeing her friend perish, she learns that her lover has fought a duel, and been wounded. After concealing her despair for some hours, she becomes delirious, and reveals her secret. They bleed her, and prescribe foot-baths and diluent drinks. After fifteen days, the violence and agitation are subdued. The patient is conscious that during her delirium, she has revealed the secrets of her heart. From this period, she believes herself despised by every one, detested by her husband, and destined to some punishment. She desires to die. Five days are spent in vain solicitations to induce her to take some aliment, and for eight days, she takes but a few swallows of broth. She is committed to my care. The countenance of the patient is pale, the lips brownish, eyes dull, the physiognomy expressive of pain, and the movements slow. At times, she heaves a profound sigh, her breath is fetid, and she suffers from constipation. On the day after her admission, I place with the patient, beside the women who serve her, a young lady of an agreeable exterior, mild and engaging, who converses at first, with an air of indifference, then with an accent of benevolence and friendship, and at length, commits to her certain confidential matters, and invites our patient to unfold her feelings. After twenty-four hours of gentle and adroit perseverance, the

patient takes the hand of her new friend, sheds a torrent of tears, and then reveals all the secrets of her heart; pointing out the cause of her delirium, the motive that induced her to resolve to eat no more, in fine, the fears that harass her. She decides also, to take some nourishment. On the day following, there is a new struggle against her notions, resolutions and fears; a new crisis, a new effusion of tears, and progress towards convalescence. After three weeks the cure is completed, on my assuring the patient that nothing that she had said was believed, but had been attributed to her delirium [Esquirol, pp. 194–195].

Although the cathartic effect of a "good cry" is still recognized, the purposeful inducement of it to relieve the irritation of the brain has long since ceased to be an asylum therapeutic.

## *Moxa, or Moxibustion*

The application of a small cylinder or cone of burning artemisia herbs to various points on the body. Used for centuries in traditional medicine, the moxa came to the attention of Dutch East India Company physicians posted in China and Japan in the mid-seventeenth century. In the traditional medicine of those countries, the balance of yin and yang was seen as crucial to physical and mental health, and for the therapeutic heat it provided the moxa most often was used as an adjunct to acupuncture. In that case, a moxa cone of rolled artemisia leaves was placed on the acupuncture point, ignited, and allowed to burn down close to the surface of the skin before being extinguished.

It is doubtful whether European physicians understood or appreciated the healing theory on which the use of the moxa was based, despite its resemblance to the humoural theory to which they were wedded. Most, therefore, used it as a counterirritant in the belief that it could draw humours from various parts of the body to a specific site, thus reducing any underlying inflammation which they presumed was the cause of insanity. British and European physicians experimented with different leaves and substances when artemisia herbs were difficult to source; these ranged from stalks of wild sunflowers to small cylinders of carded cotton wrapped in linen. They also invented specialized tools for applying the moxa. The *portemoxa,* for example, was an ebony-handled small metal ring to which three ebony ball feet were attached; the moxa could be inserted through the ring and ignited, while the ball feet kept it from direct contact with the patient's skin.

The moxa was used in general medical practice in Europe and to a lesser extent in the United States well into the nineteenth century for a variety of physical ailments, including gout, bladder inflammation, rheumatism, epilepsy and even paralysis. Its migration into asylum medicine is uncharted, however. It does appear that in France, where the use of the moxa in general medicine was being vigorously promoted, some provincial asylum physicians were experimenting with its use. It was met with less positive reactions in metropolitan asylums, however. Jean-Étienne Dominique Esquirol, *médecin ordinaire* at the Salpêtrière Asylum in Paris, France, for example, tried it without benefit in a case of dementia, and remained unconvinced of its efficacy in treating any type of insanity. The spread of the use of the moxa beyond France is evidenced by the widely read text by J. Schroeder Van Der Kolk, professor and physician to the Utrecht, Netherlands insane asylum. A somatist who believed that bodily disease was the cause of insanity and that to cure it the underlying disease first had to be treated, Van Der Kolk prescribed an astonishing array of *materia medica,* including the moxa on the crown of the head, for each and every case of insanity. The moxa, however, also held an appeal to psychists such as Karl Wilhelm Ideler. Positing that moral failure was the cause of insanity and moral discipline and re-education its cure, he used the moxa at the Berlin Charité Hospital in Germany less for its alleged ability to reduce inflammation than for its definite ability to frighten patients into moral submission [see **Salutary Fear**].

American asylum physicians made little use of the moxa. In his influential text, *Medical Inquiries and Observations Upon the Diseases of the Mind,* Benjamin Rush listed the moxa as one of several methods for the "excitement of pain" (p. 104) which he, rather like Ideler, believed was necessary for the moral discipline of the patient. He neither elaborated nor presented any cases in which it was used.

Discussion on the moxa may have been somewhat occluded in the nineteenth century asylum literature by a confusion of terms. At times moxa, which when correctly applied did not burn the skin, may have been referred to as "cautery." The term "*actual* cautery" was used to indicate the definite burning of the skin by a red hot poker or some other device.

## Mustard Pack

Only infrequently used in the treatment of the insane, the mustard pack was a cloth that had been wrapped around two handfuls of crude mustard, dipped into hot water, and then squeezed. It always was placed on the abdomen of the patient, and sometimes also on the legs, then covered with a dry towel that was secured behind the back, and further by a rubber, or mackintosh, sheet.

Samuel Newington, medical superintendent of the Ticehurst House Private Asylum in East Sussex, England, may have been the first to recommend its use as a counterirritant treatment for insanity after having experienced it himself at a spa. He wrote:

> I was induced to try the effects of being wrapped in clothes steeped in mustard-and-water, and applied to the whole legs and to the lower part of the abdomen.... I began to experience the most soothing effects, and gradually passed into a dreamy semi-conscious state, which lasted the half-hour I was under treatment. On getting up, I felt very lively and joyous, the liveliness lasted the whole day.... It occurred to me at once that this kind of application might be very serviceable in certain cases of insanity [Newington, p. 72].

Newington had experimented with the mustard pack on himself before trying it on a patient, eventually determining that two handfuls of crude mustard was the most efficacious formula. The first patient he administered it to was suffering from acute mania, and was restless, sleepless and refusing food. Before the application of the mustard pack his pulse was 180; after two hours it dropped to 60 as he drifted into what Newington described as a "semi-conscious state" (p. 73). After this single treatment, the patient took food regularly, and after a short time was released from the asylum as "perfectly recovered" (p. 73).

Theorizing that the mustard pack abstracted blood from the head, causing a state of anemia in the brain, and that it increased the circulation of blood through the capillaries, Newington increased the duration of its application from two to six or seven hours to maximize its therapeutic effect of lessening the "congestion" of the internal organs, thus bringing about calmness and sleep. At the start of the twentieth century, however, the Lunacy Commission limited the use of the mustard pack to two hours; finding that untenable, Newington ceased using the mustard pack altogether. Until this regulation, the mustard pack had been used quite frequently in British asylums.

## Nasal Discharge

The secretion of mucus as a result of the administration of any one of a number of errhines, medicated snuffs and sternutatories to the mucous membranes of the nose, causing often violent paroxysms of sneezing. Nasal discharge was favored as an adjunctive treatment by early nineteenth century asylum physicians who reasoned that the discharge was composed of "mucid lymph secreted by the glandular pituitary membrane, which lines the cavity of the nostrils and the sinuses of the brain" (Pargeter, p. 93). The relief that many insane patients reportedly felt after repeated sneezing was taken as evidence that brain congestion not only had been relieved, but that the nervous system had been healthily stimulated.

The so-called vegetative errhines, such as mustard, horseradish, white hellebore, capsicum, ginger, catharide and euphorbium, were often used to stimulate nasal discharge. So was tobacco. But some asylum physicians, such as Benjamin Rush at the Pennsylvania Hospital, found tobacco ineffective, largely due to the "insensibility of the nose to the stimulus of common snuff, from its habitual use by that class of patient" (Rush, p. 222). He preferred sulphate of mercury or muriate of ammonia, mixed with a little flour.

## Peas Therapy

The insertion of a string of peas into a four to five inch incision on the top of the head and along the sagittal suture. The string of peas kept the incision, or issue, open and suppurating, thus acting as a counterirritant to what was assumed to be the inflammation in the brain of the insane patient. Although James Cowles Prichard, an English physician and Commissioner of Lunacy is cited as the originator of peas therapy, its use as a counterirritant in cases of insanity predated by more than a century his early nineteenth century article published in the *London Medical Gazette*. A naval surgeon by the name of Hugh Ryder described his cure of a "naval lunatic" in 1685 by the application of a caustic to the crown of his head, the cutting out of the scab that had formed, and the insertion of a string of peas into the incision. The "naval lunatic," who had been bled, blistered and cupped to no avail, was immediately cured upon removal of the string of peas a month later.

There is little evidence in the nineteenth century asylum literature that peas therapy was used very often in the treatment of insanity, with the exception of an 1869 description of its use by J. Schroeder Van Der Kolk. The professor and physician to the Utrecht, Netherlands insane asylum advocated peas therapy for the treatment of visual hallucinations which, he theorized, were caused by a congestion of the optic nerves that could be alleviated by the counterirritation effect of a string of peas.

## Pediluvium

The plunging of the feet into either cold or hot water that contained an irritating substance, such as salt, ammonia, mustard powder or muriatic (hydrochloric) acid. Used during the early nineteenth century, the pediluvium was based on the premise that the irritating shock of the treatment would divert blood from the head of a manic patient, and into the extremities.

In his visit to the Stephansfeld Hospital for the Insane, near Strasbourg, France, the American physician Pliny Earle was particularly impressed not only with how often the pediluvium was used, but by the technology of its administration. He described a large room with a fixed bench along the wall, in front of which were a dozen small metallic tubs. These were fixed to the floor, and all were supplied with water from two pipes that connected them.

## Salivation or Ptyalism

The inducement of an excessive flow of saliva. Physicians had long noted that salivation increased at the onset of attacks of mania, causing furious spitting, and decreased at the onset of attacks of delusions and hallucinations, often referred to as dementia. They also observed that the suppression of excessive salivation seemed to worsen symptoms, while the stimulation of salivation appeared to ameliorate or even terminate symptoms completely. In the interest of achieving the latter, physicians experimented with a wide variety of herbs and botanicals, such as ginger and bloodroot, to spur copious salivation in their patients. But it was mercury, first used by the British physician Thomas Willis, one of the preeminent figures in seventeenth century medicine, that made its way into asylum use.

Theorizing that mercury "stimulates every part of the body, renders the vessels pervious to their natural juices, [and] coveys morbid action out of the body by the mouth" Benjamin Rush, physician to the Pennsylvania Hospital in Philadelphia, used it to "restore the mind to its native seat in the brain" (Rush, p. 103), for one of his patients, a young woman who had recently given birth:

> I once advised [salivation] in a case of [insanity] from parturition, in which the patient conceived an aversion from the infant that had been the cause of her suffering. On the day that she felt the mercury in her mouth, she asked for her infant, and pressed it to her bosom. From that time on she rapidly recovered [Rush, p. 197].

Although Rush found no use for inducing salivation as a treatment for what he referred to as "general madness" (p. 197), he did so in conjunction with other counterirritation treatments in cases of mania and dementia. Patients, however, often resisted the administration of mercury. To overcome their refusal or, perhaps, to deceive them, Rush recommended that several grains of mercury chloride, also known as calomel, be sprinkled on generously buttered slices of bread which usually overcame the reluctance of even the most stubborn of patients.

British physician George Mann Burrows also cited mercury for producing the salivation needed for cure, arguing that it equalized circulation, restored the balance between the vascular and the nervous systems, and relieved the inflammation of the brain. Unlike Rush, however, Burrows had been a somewhat reluctant convert to its use. He had never prescribed it at his private asylum in Chelsea until he witnessed the sudden recovery of an insane patient after the ingestion of a mercury-laced tonic on a cold and drafty night. He described the case of Miss C., a corpulent forty-year-old respectable businesswoman who developed delusions and fears after a friend was injured in a household accident. Gloomy and suspicious, she began planning her own death:

> Early in June she was so low-spirited and morose, that her friends were alarmed, and consulted her medical attendant, Mr. Hunter, Senior, of Mincing Lane. That gentleman prescribed a most judicious plan to be pursued; but she was refractory, and rejected his advice; and her friends, unfortunately, did not enforce it. A few days after, she contrived to squeeze herself through a small stair-window, apparently of dimensions inadequate to admit her passing, and from which there was a perpendicular descent of about thirty feet to the pavement of a court behind her dwelling. Luckily, and unknown to Miss C, some empty beer barrels had been piled up immediately under this window, and upon these she fell. By the interposition of these barrels, the height was reduced; and by the effect of gravitation, she happily came on her seat. By this means, the suicide she meditated was prevented.
>
> She was taken up, apparently not much injured, and walked into her house. Mr. Hunter came to her assistance. On examination, one of her legs was found to be considerably bruised. She complained of no other part. She was copiously bled, purged, and received such medical attention as her case required, and was very prudently placed under the supervision of a nurse accustomed to insane persons. Fever followed, without any abatement of her mental disorder ... a week after I first visited her. The countenance presented an extreme cast of despair and melancholy.... The propensity to suicide was still very active; for although, from bodily inability, she could not move from her bed, yet, by various and unequivocal little plots, she plainly indicated that was still her intention. All the features of the case at this stage were, indeed, very unpropitious.... My first object was to prescribe such means as might arrest the progress of the mortification. Sloughing to a great extent, and an immense discharge, took place, without any abatement of the mental affection. The patient's health varied much, and at length appeared to give way....
>
> She had been for some weeks taking a tonic ... calomel [mercury chloride] and squills [an herbal diuretic] were combined with it. She now mended every day and was very tractable; but all her pristine mental aberrations prevailed. After persevering in this plan a fortnight, she caught cold by falling asleep with the window open; the consequence was, saliva-

tion, but not excessive. It was suffered to take its course. Concurrent with this ptyalism was an instant amelioration of her mental symptoms. She grew more cheerful, and every aberration by degrees vanished. Three weeks from the appearance of the salivation she was so well that I took my leave [Burrows, pp. 645–646].

After that experience, Burrows experimented with mercury-induced salivation with his asylum patients, but with disappointing results. He urged his colleagues to exercise caution in its use. "The rage for prescribing this mineral, as a panacea in almost all diseases, has already tempted many to try it, and pretty indiscriminately," he wrote. "However, we may infer that the success of it has been equivocal" (p. 648). That observation notwithstanding, Burrows stated his intention to stimulate salivation with mercury when other means of cure had failed, but only as part of a general regime of counterirritation administration.

Despite Burrow's restraint, salivation remained part of the therapeutic regime in asylums throughout Great Britain, the United States and Europe well into the nineteenth century, and mercury remained the substance of choice for producing it. When used only as part of that regime, cases of mercurial poisoning were only rarely reported in the asylum literature. It should be noted, however that until the twentieth century, mercury was the primary treatment for syphilis, once known as "general paralysis of the insane." Cases of mercurial poisoning of syphilitic asylum patients, with its attendant damage to the nervous system, were much more frequently reported in the literature.

## *Seton, or Haarseil, or, Setaceum, or Pus Band*

A horsehair, silk or canvas thread, string of gauze, or a wire passed with a knife or needle through subcutaneous tissue usually at the nape of the neck or between the shoulders, and left there until it festered. The discharge of pus was believed at various times to either release the "evil humours" or relieve the underlying brain inflammation that caused insanity.

The case files of British physician William Perfect, proprietor of a private asylum in West Malling, exemplified the fact that few asylum physicians used the seton alone or, for that matter, even recommended it as a standalone treatment. In every case he detailed, the seton was used in conjunction with a variety of other medical, moral and social treatments that were part of the armamentarium of early asylum therapeutics. Case 62 illustrated that point. The patient in question was an otherwise physically healthy young boy who suffered from mania. His personal history offered no clues as to what the proximate or distal causes of his insanity might have been. Apothecaries and general physicians treated him at home for months with blisters, baths and purges, but to no avail. Coming under the care of Perfect, the child was restrained in a straitjacket when necessary, vomited repeatedly, bled often, sedated with a camphor concoction, and fed a "cooling diet" of apples, cherries and jellies. All objects that might stimulate or distract him were removed from his view, and he was encouraged to engage in mild exercise. A seton was applied to his spine and when it began to copiously discharge, the headaches and sleeplessness finally abated, and after a time, and with a host of other therapeutic interventions, he became more rational. "It is truly singular," Perfect wrote, "that since his recovery his temper and disposition have regenerated, and without the least vestige of the reserve and dullness which had always before been the prominent traits of his character" (Perfect, p. 281).

Perfect did not credit the seton with the boy's cure, but certainly stressed its importance to the therapeutic regime. Indeed, the seton was used by asylum physicians throughout Great Britain, Europe and the United States well into the nineteenth century. It was used extensively by Ernst Horn at the Berlin Charité; Pliny Earle, resident physician of the Friends' Asylum in Pennsylvania, also expressed great confidence in it as a remedy, stating that the "greater the irritation or inflammation excited by it, the greater the benefit produced" (Galt, p. 415).

Interestingly, there was a patient who would have agreed with that assessment. Walter Abraham Haigh was admitted to Bethlem Hospital in London in the late nineteenth century, diagnosed with delusional insanity. The twenty-seven-year-old Oxford University graduate was quite the favored patient at the asylum that was better known as "Bedlam." His intelligence and social class standing distinguished him from the other patients, and his active interest in his own recovery inspired confidence that he indeed would recover. But how? While editing a book manuscript written by George Savage, the asylum's superintendent, Haigh became convinced that a seton inserted in his neck would ease his delusions and hallucinations. He convinced Savage to administer it. He recovered completely and was discharged as cured. Haigh went on to become a priest and although he continued to suffer from delusions, he was never recommitted.

The use of the seton certainly outlived criticisms of it. Joseph Guislain, medical superintendent of the asylums in Ghent, Belgium, for example, found that with the exception of case studies offered by Perfect, as well as by John Ferriar, physician to the insane asylum in Manchester, England, and George Mann Burrows, proprietor and physician of a private asylum in the Chelsea area of London, England, who boasted he had cured a deranged and violent woman with a well-placed seton on the back of her shaved head, few of his colleagues gave much credit to the singular or even cumulative therapeutic effect of the seton.

## *Sweating, or Diaphoresis, or Transpiration*

The inducement of the excretion of perspiration through the pores of the skin. It long had been noted that paroxysms of mania caused profuse sweating, but it also had been observed that melancholia suppressed perspiration, thus accounting for the dry skin and brittle hair and nails of patients so afflicted. To induce healthy sweating, asylum physicians relied on a range of therapeutics, from evaporating lotions to stimulate the excretory activity of the skin, mildly acidulated drinks, warm and tepid baths [see **Hydrotherapy**], camphor, to concoctions such as Dover's Powder, a mix of ipecac and opium, all in an effort to sweat out the peccant humours that were considered the cause of insanity.

One of the nostrums given to produce sweating was Venetian Treacle or Venice Treacle, also known as theriac and mithridatium, a concoction of herbs and spices, seeds and gums, plants, and animal parts including the flesh of vipers, the original recipe of which could be traced to the second century C.E. In today's parlance "treacle" is molasses, but its use here was a corruption of the Latin *theriaca,* or antidote. During the height of its popularity in the seventeenth and early eighteenth centuries, Venetian Treacle was touted as an antidote for accidental poisoning, and as a cure for everything from common colds to the plague. And it was used with some success, but always as an adjunctive diaphoretic therapy, to treat insanity. The eminent British physician, Thomas Sydenham, was one of the strongest advocates of the distasteful elixir. He recommended its administration to cure melancholia, mania and hysteria, the latter of which occurred so frequently, in his assessment, that he diagnosed it in one out of every six of his female patients. Although it was imported to North America in the eighteenth century, there is little evidence that the use of Venetian Treacle was widespread in asylums there or in Europe, perhaps because of the increasing regulation of its production and sale.

William Hallaran, the superintendent of the County and City of Cork Lunatic Asylum in Ireland had a more innovative approach to induce sweating. He had invented a circulating swing [see **Rotation, Oscillation and Vibration**], a box that was twirled as many as 100 turns a minute by means of a windlass. He found that extended sessions in the swing tended to produce therapeutic sweating, as did the dread being placed in it.

Sweating was not just considered a cure in and of itself, but a symptom of a cure. The therapeutic success of some of the hydrotherapy techniques such as the cold wet pack and the Turkish bath [see **Hydrotherapy**], and of all of the fever induction therapeutics [see **Fever Therapy**], was gauged by how much the treated patients perspired; the greater the perspiration, it was thought, the greater the reduction of the brain inflammation that caused insanity.

# Deep Sleep Therapy (Prolonged Narcosis, Prolonged Sleep, Continuous Sleep)

*The use of drugs to keep patients deeply asleep for several continuous hours, days or as long as weeks.*

The curative value of sleep was known by the ancients and prescribed by doctors for physical ailments and mental distress for centuries. With the advent of asylums, however, restorative sleep was increasingly problematic. Overcrowded conditions, large wards filled with patients in various states of torment and misery not only left patients tired, but mentally and physically exhausted. It is little wonder, then, that asylum physicians in the nineteenth and early twentieth centuries, often devoted whole chapters in their texts to the importance of sleep. John Mortimer Granville drove home that point:

> Sleep, when the intellectual faculties are deranged or the mind is diseased, may be justly regarded as one of the most important functions to be performed by the organism.... Inability to sleep is distressing, and not unfrequently a premonitory symptom of mental disease. Slumber is anticipated as the harbinger of improvement [Granville, p. 160].

To assure the restorative and prophylactic benefits of sleep, asylum physicians relied on such drugs as opium. The "Plant of Joy" had been in use in folk medicine for millennia, and asylum physicians found its sedative effects "most effectual and salutary" (Woodward, p. 1). But opium also had deleterious side effects, most notably nausea and constipation, the latter of which often required a reliance on the anachronistic depletive treatment of purging with salts, cremor tartars, senna, calomel or jalap in order to relieve the distress [see **Depletive Therapy**]. Morphine was used as well. Administered orally when first introduced and then later subcutaneously via the newly invented hypodermic needle, it was ideal for general sedation, so ideal, in fact, that by the mid-nineteenth century morphine was the most widely used drug in asylums. Its praises were sung by one of the most prominent asylum superintendents of his generation, Samuel Woodward, of the Worcester Asylum in Massachusetts:

> The manner in which morphine has been used in this and other hospitals in this country, continuing until the symptoms have subsided, then omitting it and seeing them return, then again and again removed by the renewal of this medicine, affords unequivocal evidence of its power to subdue maniacal excitements, relieve the delusions of the insane, and restore the brain and nervous system to a sound and healthy state [Woodward, p. 62].

Hydrotherapy also was relied upon for its sedative effects [see **Hydrotherapy**]. Cold wet packs, continuous hot or warm baths, and drip sheets often calmed the most furiously insane patients and lulled them into a few hours of refreshing sleep. Even the swings, hammocks and cradles that spun, shook and swayed patients were considered soporific [see **Rotation, Oscillation and Vibration**]. Bouts of vertigo and nausea aside, patients were reported to eventually feel the "soothing, lulling effects" that were "succeeded by the most refreshing slumbers" (Cox, 139–140).

Therapeutics may have left minds vacant, but it was asylum order and routine that filled bodies enough for sleep. Large evening meals, sometimes accompanied by beer or wine [see **Diet**], exercise, and constructive activities carried out in the fresh air, if possible, were considered valuable aids to recuperative sleep.

It was in the early twentieth century that the inducement of not just restorative sleep, but deep and prolonged sleep, was made possible by the introduction of barbiturates into asylum therapeutics. Giuseppe Epifanio, a physician at the University Psychiatric Clinic in Turin, Italy, was the first to administer doses of the phenobarbital Luminal over a four day period to a young woman who had been institutionalized for manic-depressive psychosis. She fell into a deep sleep for two weeks. Upon awakening, her symptoms had been ameliorated enough that she was discharged several weeks later and remained in remission for more than two years. Published in an Italian medical journal and at the start of World War I, Epifanio's report had little international impact.

But just a few years later, Jakob Klaesi's reports did. Klaesi, a physician at Burghölzli, Zurich University's psychiatric clinic, published accounts of his successful treatment of profoundly disturbed patients with deep sleep therapy. The reports were widely read and discussed, and to this day, he is credited with the introduction of deep sleep into asylums where it remained a trendy therapeutic, especially in Europe and Great Britain, for several decades.

If Klaesi was most intimately associated with the debut of deep sleep therapy, Ewen Cameron was with its finis. The deep sleep experiments he conducted at McGill University's Allan Memorial Institute in Montreal, Canada and funded, in part, by the U.S. Central Intelligence Agency, brought opprobrium to the therapeutic. Anxious to disassociate themselves from the brewing scandal, asylum physicians turned away from deep sleep therapy and to newer and less controversial therapeutic interventions. When Cameron died in the mid–1960s deep sleep therapy, for all intents and purposes, did as well.

## References

Arieti, S. (1959). *American handbook of psychiatry.* New York: Basic Books.

Bleckwenn, W.J. (1930). Narcosis as therapy in neuropsychiatric conditions. *Journal of the American Medical Association, 95,* 1168–1171.

Bleckwenn, W.J. (1930). Production of sleep and rest in psychotic cases. *Archives of Neurology and Psychiatry, 24,* 365–375.

Bleckwenn, W.J. (1930). Sodium amytal in certain nervous and mental conditions. *Wisconsin Medical Journal, 29,* 693–696.

"Bromide Sleep" (1900). *Merck Archives,* pp. 110–111.

Cameron, D.E., Lohrenz, J.G., and Handcock, K.Z. (1962). The depatterning treatment of schizophrenia. *Comprehensive Psychiatry, 3,* 65–76.

"Catatonic cases after intravenous sodium amytal injection" (1930). Producer: W.J. Bleckwenn, University of Wisconsin at Madison. National Library of Medicine, Washington, D.C., NLM ID8501040A.

Church, A. (1900). The treatment of the opium habit by the bromide. *Illinois Medical Journal, 50,* 291–297.

Cox, J.M. (1804). *Practical observations on insanity.* London: Baldwin and Murray.

Davies, B. (2013, August 7). The zombie ward. *Daily Mail Online.* Retrieved at http://www.dailymail.co.uk/femail/article-2386477/NHS-Zombie-Ward-How-depressed-women-sleep-months-Londons-Royal-Waterloo-Hospital.html.

Dawson, W.S., and Barkus, M.R. (1926). Somnifen treatment in the psychosis. *Lancet, 208,* 1155–1156.

Epifanio, G. (1915). L'ipnosi farmacologica prolungata e sua applicazione per la cura di alcune psicopatici. *Rivista di Patologia Nervosa e Mentale, 20,* 273–308.

Fink, M., and Taylor, M.A. (2003). *Catatonia.* Cambridge: Cambridge University Press.

Gowran, C. (1944, October 17). Describes U.S. treatment of battle nerves. *Chicago Daily Tribune,* p. 3.

Granville, J.M. (1877). *The care and cure of the insane.* London: Hardwicke and Bogue.

Hock, P. (1932). Treatment of schizophrenia with prolonged narcosis. *Psychiatric Quarterly, 6,* 386–391.

Jenny, F. (1938). Treatment of schizophrenia by prolonged sleep in Psychiatric Clinic in Berne. *American Journal of Psychiatry* (supp.), 94, 184–191.

Kaplan, R.M. (2013). Deep sleep therapy in Australia. *Australasian Psychiatry, 21,* 505–506.

Kearney, J., and Courtney, P.J. (1938). Somnifaine narcosis: Results of 40 treatments in 38 cases. *British Journal of Psychiatry, 84,* 177–182.

Leys, R. (2000). *Trauma: A genealogy.* Chicago: University of Chicago Press.

Lyons, J. (1960). An interview with a mute catatonic. *Journal of Abnormal and Social Psychology, 60,* 271–277.

Macleod, N. (1900). The bromide sleep: A new departure in the treatment of acute mania. *British Medical Journal, 1,* 134–136.

MacNiven, A. (1936). Somnifaine narcosis. *British Journal of Psychiatry, 82,* 423–429.

Maw, J. (2008, April 1). Revealing the mind bender general. BBC Radio 4. London: BBC. Retrieved at http://jb_speechification.s3.amazonaws.com/Revealing-the-Mind-Bender-General.mp3.

Murray, V.F., and Burns, M.M. (1932). The use of sodium amytal in the treatment of psychoses. *Psychiatric Quarterly, 6,* 273–300.

Palmer, H.D., and Paine, A.L. (1932). Prolonged narcosis as therapy in the psychoses. *American Journal of Psychiatry, 89,* 37–57.

Ragg, P.M. (1900). The bromide sleep in a case of mania. *British Medical Journal, 2,* 1309–1310.

Shorter, E. (1997). *A history of psychiatry.* New York: John Wiley & Sons.

Walsh, J. (1947). Continuous narcosis; the advantages of oral somnifaine; a comparison. *Journal of Mental Science, 93,* 255–261.

Walton, M. (2013). Deep sleep therapy and Chelmsford Private Hospital: Have we learnt anything? *Australasian Psychiatry, 21,* 206–212.

Windholz, G., and Witherspoon, L.H. (1993). Sleep as a cure for schizophrenia: A historical episode. *History of Psychiatry, 4,* 83–93.

Woodward, S.B. (1850). Observations on the medical treatment of insanity. *American Journal of Psychiatry, 7,* 1–34.

## *Bromide Sleep*

The administration of sodium bromide to induce sleep for a continuous period of several days. In the late nineteenth century, a Scottish physician by the name of Neil Macleod who practiced in Shanghai, China, ordered a twelve ounce bottle of twelve drams of sodium bromide and directed a patient he had been treating for neuralgia to ingest a half-ounce of the mixture every four hours. The patient, a twenty-five-year-old woman, had become addicted to the morphine that had been used to treat the neuralgia, and attempts to withdraw her from it had been unsuccessful. On the first day of taking the sodium bromide the patient was drowsy; on the second day she had fallen into such a deep sleep that she could not be roused. It was evident to Macleod that she had "accidentally" exceeded the prescribed dosage and the overdose was keeping her in a deep sleep for four continuous days. During that time, she could not sit or stand, muttered answers to questions, and urinated and defecated in her bed. As she slowly awoke she became restless and confused, and mumbled incoherently. Over the next two weeks a daily improvement of her thought and speech processes was noted, and her physical strength gradually returned. Upon release from the hospital, she was astonished, as Macleod surely was as well, that she no longer had any craving for morphine.

As word of Macleod's apparent success in treating addiction spread, patients as desperate for a cure as they were to avoid the extreme discomfort of withdrawal symptoms, found their way to him. All were relieved of their various addictions to morphine and/or cocaine, with the exception of one, who died a week into the treatment from double pneumonia. That death Macleod attributed to a pneumonia epidemic in a region the patient had recently visited.

Although "bromide sleep," as Macleod christened his therapeutic, held promise for the treatment of drug addiction, it was his experiment in administering it to a woman in the throes of acute mania, without the complication of addiction, that brought the therapeutic, however briefly, into asylums. The patient, a woman, had to be brought from the interior of Japan to Shanghai, where she was to be treated for her mania. The prospect of the trip was so daunting that serious concerns were raised as to whether she would have to be restrained for its duration. Macleod suggested bromide sleep to ease her transport, and "in the hope also of benefit to the nervous condition" (p. 135). The woman not only arrived without incident, but was free of her manic symptoms upon waking from the bromide sleep.

While asylums had their share of addicted patients, Macleod's conclusion that a bromide sleep could cure, as opposed to temporarily relieve, acute mania was appealing. His reports had been republished in North American psychiatric and medical publications, most notably *Merck Archives* that stated that because "higher cerebral functions" were affected by bromide sleep, it was not only an effective cure for acute mania, but may "prove a powerful and effective means of dealing with *all* maladies of the nervous system" ("Bromide Sleep," p. 111). By attributing its efficacy to its ability to act on the nervous system, the tidy entry in the *Merck Archives* established the bona fides of bromide sleep as a somatic therapeutic. Since it was nervous maladies of all kinds that were filling asylums at the start of the twentieth century, stoking a fear that insanity was epidemic and a concomitant anxiety among asylum physicians that they were almost helpless to intervene, they were intrigued by the remedy and eager to try it.

Their experiments, however, were decidedly mixed in their outcomes. Archibald Church, a professor at the Chicago Medical College, used it with great success on a morphine addict who, upon awakening not only lost his desire for the drug, but had a renewed feeling of "strength [and] buoyancy" (Church, p. 293). His second patient, however, died during the course of the treatment, most likely from the cumulative effects of the bromide. Church's conclusion that bromide sleep was effective, albeit more risky than Macleod had acknowledged, put somewhat of a damper on its use as an asylum therapeutic. Some asylum physicians continued the treatment, much more for morphine addiction and alcoholism than for mania or the spectrum of nervous disorders, and did so with some reported success, but most considered the risk of overdose too high.

## *Deep Sleep Therapy, or Prolonged Narcosis, or* Dauernarkose

The administration of drugs to keep insane patients asleep for an extended period of time. In the early twentieth century Jakob Klaesi, a physician at the Burghölzli, Zurich University's psychiatric clinic, hypothesized that the hallucinations and delusions that were the hallmark symptoms of schizophrenia, were expression of an overactive nervous system. If so, then deep sleep for a prolonged period would reduce that activity, and thus diminish those symptoms upon waking, leaving the patient more amenable to adjunctive therapies, especially psychotherapy. On that point, Klaesi stated:

> Now that physician is needed again. The physician and the staff members now have the opportunity to present themselves as useful and necessary and gain through the treatment the patient's gratitude and confidence. The patient is forced to use meaningful words and gestures, and to consider and to adjust to the environment. If the patient establishes contact with the environment and becomes interested and concerned, then after the end of physical depression and succoring, he will not again sink into autistic habits, but become open to experiences [Windholz & Witherspoon, p. 84].

To produce that deep sleep, Klaesi first administered morphine and scopolamine, followed by the intravenous administration over a ten day period of somnifen, a compound of two barbiturates which had been developed in Switzerland a decade before and was being used in some asylums to sedate loud and boisterous patients. His first subject was a woman, successful in business until a psychotic episode brought her into the asylum where she lay naked in a padded cell that had not been used in twenty years. She was put into a deep, barbiturate-induced sleep on three separate occasions, and upon awakening from the last was free of hallucinations and delusions, and soon well enough to return home. Interestingly, although her husband was delighted in her improvement, she had confided to Klaesi before being discharged that her marriage was troubled and unhappy. Klaesi concluded that this insight was a result of deep sleep therapy, supporting his hypothesis that it would prepare patients for the work of psychotherapy.

Encouraged by the result, Klaesi went on to administer deep sleep therapy to twenty-six asylum patients, most of them women, who had been diagnosed with schizophrenia. All were kept in a state of deep sleep for ten days, with a daily dosage reduction so they could be roused to eat and use the toilet. Upon awakening, and with some adjunctive intervention, eight of the patients improved well enough to either be discharged or transferred to another, less closely supervised ward. Three patients, however, died. Klaesi attributed those deaths to pre-existing medical conditions, but the fact remained that as deep sleep therapy gained popularity as an asylum therapeutic, the mortality rate hovered between 3 and 5 percent. Other complications were noted as well: barbital rash, cardiovascular collapse, bronchopneumonia, acute renal insufficiency with anuria, respiratory depression, dehydration, fever, toxic confusional states, occasional brief delirious episodes, and withdrawal type convulsions at the termination of treatment.

Schizophrenia had already proved itself to be an frustratingly intractable disorder, so the prospect of reducing, even eliminating, its most deleterious symptoms was appealing. But what was equally, maybe even more so, appealing was that deep sleep seemed to prepare patients for intensive psychotherapy, and if it could do that, it also could be used to treat patients with other types of insanity. Not quite a panacea, deep sleep therapy nonetheless was an immensely popular asylum therapeutic, especially in Great Britain and Europe, well into the twentieth century.

It had three noticeable drawbacks, however. First, the risks associated with somnifen kept revealing themselves as considerable, thus the search for new and safer barbiturates, such as somnifaine, continued for decades. Second, deep sleep was labor intensive to administer and monitor. It required not only repeated injections of the barbiturate agent but, given its risks, close monitoring throughout the several day period of deep sleep. Not only did nurses and attendants have to rouse the patients to eat and use the toilet, but they also had to sit at their bedsides for the entire duration of the treatments to record verbatim every word the patients mumbled, as well as to describe in written detail the emergence of the patients from the sleep. Each of these was thought to reveal something about the cause of the insanity each patient was experiencing and therefore would inform the adjunctive psychotherapy that would follow.

Third, the outcomes of deep sleep therapy were mixed. Some asylum physicians reported even higher recovery rates than did Klaesi, others significantly lower, and some found no appreciable changes in their patients at all. While generally optimistic about the potential of deep sleep therapy to aid in recovery two British asylum physicians, Harold Palmer and Alfred Paine, cautioned against its panacean use. They recommended that carefully designed and controlled large scale clinical studies using various types of barbiturates, different modes of administration (injection, intravenous and oral) and doses, differently diagnosed patients, and with both short- and long-term scopes be conducted. These were not done, however. By the time that cautionary note appeared in the psychiatric literature, deep sleep therapy already was being replaced by insulin and metrazol shock therapies, and later electroconvulsive shock therapy [see **Shock Therapy**]. Although a modified version—one that kept patients in that state for a few short days to quiet their agitation—was used well into the 1970s, deep sleep therapy already had been relegated to occasional use in asylums a decade before that.

Another use for deep-sleep therapy was found during World War II. Battle-fatigued soldiers sometimes were administered barbiturates to put them into a deep sleep for several days. When the dose was reduced to bring about a state of dreamy wakefulness, the soldiers not only ate and used the toilet, but were questioned by psychiatrists about their emotional reactions to battle. What they revealed was then used as the grist of intensive psychotherapy sessions conducted over the next several days. Military physicians claimed that 75 percent of all soldiers undergoing the treatment returned to the front lines within ten days.

Despite the claim that deep sleep therapy was "the first asylum therapy that offered any hope" (Shorter, p. 205), it might be better remembered for the scandals in which it was implicated. The Ward 5 sleep room, referred to as the "Zombie Room" by its patients, at London's Royal Waterloo Hospital, for example, was the subject of considerable controversy. Overseen by William Sargant, a standard bearer for the somatic therapeutics and an expert on brainwashing, Ward 5 was reserved for intractable women diagnosed with anything from postpartum depression to anorexia. Sargant injected them with large doses of barbiturates to put them into a deep sleep and subjected them to daily electroconvulsive shocks while they slept. One of those patients, a twenty-two-year-old diagnosed with obsessional neurosis, described deep sleep therapy in Ward 5:

> It was like being buried alive. I was lying there in the dark, hour after hour, and couldn't move. I wasn't aware of my body, just my head in this darkness. You could hear people moving around and other people breathing and moaning ... I can remember the sound of the ECT [electroconvulsive shock treatment] machine being wheeled down the corridor and it being switched on and off in other rooms.... It was so frightening. First of all, they injected you and you had an awful feeling of falling backwards into yourself. After ECT, you didn't know who you were.... We were like zombies. I couldn't walk. I had to be lifted. Afterwards, they put you back to sleep again. The worst time was when I started not to be asleep. I was awake, but couldn't move or speak. It was torture, lying there for hours in the darkness [Davies, para. 3, 15, 16, 18, 19].

It was not Sargant's goal to ready his deep sleep patients for psychotherapy, which he despised, but to "re-pattern" them—wipe their brains clean of the memories that had caused their disorders. Sargant destroyed all records after he left the hospital in 1973, giving more grist to the rumor mill that Ward 5 had been an experiment in brain-washing that was funded and supported by British Intelligence and/or the U.S. Central Intelligence Agency.

While Sargant was interested in re-patterning, Ewen Cameron of McGill University's Allan Memorial Institute in Montreal, Canada was focused on *de*-patterning, that is, breaking up pre-existing memories, thoughts and patterns of behavior, and adding new ones. To that end, he isolated patients in specially built boxes in a converted horse stable on the hospital grounds, with goggles on their eyes and cardboard tubes on their arms to prevent them from touching themselves. After sensory deprivation was complete, he induced deep sleep that lasted fifteen to thirty days, with as many as three electroconvulsive shock administrations daily. Hypothesizing that patients in deep sleep were particularly suggestible, he played a continuous loop of tape over the many days the patients were asleep, with the goal of replacing their own memories with the propagandist messages on the tape. This process of "psychic driving," as he referred to it [see **Psychic Driving**], was of great interest to the Central Intelligence Agency which, it later was revealed, had generously funded these depatterning experiments on unwitting patients.

Deep sleep also was implicated in the Chelmsford Private Hospital scandal in Sydney, Australia where over fifteen years Harry Bailey put more than 1,000 patients into barbiturate-induced deep sleeps for two to three weeks, and gave them daily electroconvulsive shocks. Because the barbiturate dosage he administered was so high, the patients could not be roused, thus they had to be fed through nasogastric tubes and were left to urinate and defecate in their own beds. Although Bailey claimed an 85 percent success rate in the treatment of a range of disorders, from schizophrenia, depression, drug addiction, alcoholism, to anorexia, twenty-five of his patients died as a result of deep sleep therapy, and several hundred were left psychologically and/or physically disabled. Although there were a number of coronial inquiries into Bailey's administration of deep sleep therapy, it was not until three years after his suicide that the Chelmsford Royal Commission began an inquiry into his practice. In 1990, it filed a twelve-volume report, replete with the sordid details of Bailey's flamboyant personal as well as professional life. As a result of the report, deep sleep therapy was banned in Australia.

## Sodium Amytal Sleep, or Narcoanalysis, or Narcosynthesis

The intravenous, intramuscular, oral or rectal administration of an approximately 5 percent solution of sodium amytal, also known as amobarbital sodium and even more familiarly as "truth serum," to bring about deep sleep. The onset of sleep occurred within several minutes, and the deep sleep lasted for two to eight continuous hours, at which time patients would be awakened with painful stimuli. During their subsequent lucid intervals the patients participated in "amytal interviews" that probed their painful, repressed and delusional thoughts and desires.

The therapeutic was first used in the early twentieth century by William Jefferson Bleckwenn, a neurologist and psychiatrist who had a keen interest in Freudian psychoanalysis. In his position at the Wisconsin Psychiatric Institute in Madison, he was particularly concerned about patients diagnosed with catatonic schizophrenia. Considered incurable, many of them were unable to speak, move, feed themselves or attend to their bodily needs. Bleckwenn hypothesized that sodium amytal would relax the mind enough that upon awakening the catatonic patients not only would be able engage in daily activities but, more importantly, in insightful "amytal interviews" with asylum physicians. Such therapeutic discussions later were referred to as "narcoanalysis" or "narcosynthesis."

While Bleckwenn certainly was interested in restoring mobility and activity to catatonic patients, it was the therapeutic potential contained within the lucid interval that was more intriguing. All of the first fifty patients he treated with sodium amytal sleep experienced that interval, but none showed its narcoanalytic potential better than a twenty-year-old college student whose case Bleckwenn discussed at some length:

> J.L., aged 20, a university student, had catatonic excitement, which had had a sudden onset with confusion and mutism and refusal of food; after three weeks he went into a state of marked excitement with active hallucinations and bizarre gesticulation and grimacing. He set fire to his bed and yelled "fire." He was given 0.6 Gm amobarbitol sodium. Just before he went to sleep he said that he realized he was having a terrible time and hoped to recover to enter school in February. When he awakened, he behaved in a normal way, and discussed current topics, his illness, school, and his future plans. The lucid interval lasted for almost two hours. After a short sleep, he returned to an excited state. At the time of writing, he had made similar responses after further treatment, was less hyperactive [Fink & Taylor, p. 139].

Bleckwenn published three papers on his quite startling results, but it was a grainy black-and-white film he produced and distributed in 1930 that drew the attention of asylum physicians around the world to sodium amytal sleep. Titled *Catatonic Cases After Intravenous Sodium Amytal Injection* the silent film showed the before and after results of sodium amytal sleep: mute, posturing and unresponsive patients could be seen talking, eating and walking soon after they were awakened.

In a short time sodium amytal was being used in asylums across the country, as well as in Great Britain and Europe, and for types of insanity other than catatonic schizophrenia. It was observed to create lucid intervals for patients suffering from depression as well as from mania. The psychoneuroses also proved themselves vulnerable to the relaxing and disinhibiting effects of sodium amytal sleep, thus its use as a treatment for "combat neurosis" was widespread during World War II.

Its prevalent use as an asylum therapeutic, however, could not gloss over concerns about both the administration and efficacy of sodium amytal sleep. First, there was the problem of determining the proper dosage to induce sleep, and then the problem of assessing just how many times and over what period the therapeutic should be administered for maximum effect. Although adverse physical effects of the treatment were uncommon, it did have a mortality rate of approximately 1 percent. And then there was the concern that the lucid intervals, those windows of opportunities for catharsis and abreaction, closed all too quickly, shutting off possibilities not just for cure or remission, but for lasting improvement.

Those concerns aside, sodium amytal sleep ushered in a new era of psychopharmacology as a vast array of sedatives and hypnotics were introduced into asylums, some for producing deep sleep, but most others for calming patients and rendering them more amenable to therapeutic intervention. It might be interesting to note that sodium amytal administered at a dosage that produced hypnotic drowsiness, rather than sleep, was often used to facilitate therapeutic interviewing. Sometimes, however, using a truth serum to get to the "truth" of the problem was a daunting task. This amytal interview of a twenty-nine-year-old patient who had acute onset catatonia that had left him mute illustrated that point:

> Dr. A: You have been with us for quite a long time, and in all those days you haven't told us much. Do you think you could do it today?...
> Dr. B: We know you can talk. Suppose you tell us your name. What is your name? Huh?...
> Dr. A: Who are you? Now tell us, who are you?...Can you keep awake, huh?
> Dr. B: Supposing you tell use your name.... What is your name?
> Dr. A: Could you be good enough and tell us who you are?
> Dr. B: What is your name. Come on, tell us...
> Dr. A: Do you hear us?...Give us a sign whether you hear or not, huh?
> Dr. B. Open your eyes.... Who are you? Tell us who you are [Lyons, p. 272].

These two asylum physicians continued this line of questioning for some time before asking the unresponsive patient to write his name on a pad of paper. The patient did, and then also wrote his age when requested to do so. When asked what branch of the military he had recently served in, the patient wrote "Army" and then, speaking for the first time, said that word aloud. Then, using single words or simple phrases, he began to reply to their questions.

When the asylum physicians began to inquire about the reason for his mutism, suggesting to him that he may be hearing voices that commanded him to be silent or that he had a deep secret he was too ashamed to tell, the patient retreated once again into silence. And there he remained for many frustrating minutes. Changing tactics, the asylum physicians began inquiring about his family, and the patient, now in simple declarative sentences, replied to their questions, stating the names and occupations of his parents and siblings, and the place of his birth. Apparently encouraged by his responsiveness, the asylum physicians again turned to the reasons for his mutism:

> Dr. B: When you came in you weren't talking to us. Did you stop talking a long time before you came to the hospital?
> Patient: I never did talk too much.
> Dr. B: No, but you talked some.
> Patient: Yep, a little...
> Dr. B: Do you have any idea why you stopped talking, or did you just decide to quit?...You haven't answered my question. Why did you stop talking?...What do you say?
> Patient: I couldn't say yes and I shouldn't say unh-uh.
> Dr. B: You mean you don't know why you stopped talking?
> Patient: No [Lyons, p. 274].

Confused by his response, the asylum physicians again suggested some reasons for his mutism, and the patient again retreated into silence. This prompted the third asylum physician to ask:

> Dr. C: Can you say why you can't talk, whether it is too complicated, you don't know, or because it is so personal you just don't want to talk about it?
> Patient: One should talk when you are spoken to.
> Dr. C: Yeah—but well, that is when you are with people who aren't your friends, but you have got to feel friendly towards people.... Here we are.... You are free to say anything you want to. You will find us pretty understanding people to talk to. Did this come as a decision on your part not to—I mean, we know that there is nothing wrong with your mouth or your vocal cords, it is possible for

you to talk. Now, is this a decision on your part not to talk? Are you familiar with the old saying "You can lead a horse to..." What is the rest of that?
*Patient:* ...horse to water but you can't make him drink.
*Dr. C:* What do you think of that? Huh? Think there is any truth in it? Huh?
*Patient:* Yeah [Lyons, p 276].

The amytal interview was terminated at the point; minutes later the patient fell into a deep sleep. The asylum physicians, whose frustration was evident throughout the interview, nonetheless concluded that it revealed something about catatonic schizophrenia that was empirically investigable:

[T]he schizophrenic steps out of his own history and undertakes to refrain from any commitment to responsible action with others; that he then presents himself, not as a living person with significance to himself and to others, but in the "third person" sense of a set of statistics; and finally, that the catatonic stupor is a state of vigilance in which his declaration of lack of commitment is guarded and preserved. Stated as hypotheses, this proposal as well as all of the other issues raised, would appear to be amenable to rigorous experimental investigation [Lyons, p. 277].

When William Jefferson Bleckwenn returned to the United States after his distinguished service as an officer in the Pacific Theater during World War II his attention, just like that of most other asylum physicians, turned to the therapeutic potential of the new and dramatic shock therapies [see **Shock Therapy**] that had been introduced into asylums. Although used on occasion and well into the twentieth century, sodium amytal sleep therapy was not able to stand up against the potential of remissions and cures promised by the shock therapies.

# Depletive Therapy ("Heroic Therapy," Antiphlogistic Therapy, "Rush's System")

*Therapeutic strategies to reduce the vascular congestion, often referred to as "inflammation," of the brain that was thought to cause insanity.*

As is true with so many early asylum therapeutics, depletive therapy can be traced to antiquity. Its golden age as an asylum therapeutic, however, was between the late eighteenth and mid-nineteenth centuries, and was so intimately associated with a single physician—the inestimable Benjamin Rush of the Pennsylvania Hospital—that the term "Rush's system" soon achieved synonymity.

Rush had matriculated at the University of Edinburgh medical school and had been profoundly influenced by its most admired professor, William Cullen. A central figure in the Scottish Enlightenment, Cullen believed that the progress of medicine necessitated the development of a new nosology of disease, thus he classified all nervous diseases as "neuroses," a term he coined, and then further subdivided the neuroses into additional orders and species. One of those orders was "Vesaniae," or insanity proper, and Cullen attributed its cause to imbalanced states of "excitement" and "collapse" in the judgment faculty of the brain. The restoration of reason, then, required the use of coercive therapeutics that inspired fear and awe so intense as to diminish excitement and overwhelm collapse. Bleeding, purging, vomiting, sweating—all depletive therapies—were the recommended therapies, and it was these that Cullen's student, Benjamin Rush, relied upon in his practice at the Pennsylvania Hospital.

Departing somewhat from his mentor who had posited that too much or too little nervous energy was the cause of disease, Rush set out a unitary theory that postulated that all disease, insanity included, was due to the morbid excitement in the brain caused by convulsive actions in the blood vessels. Thus all disease, insanity included once again, urgently required depletive therapy to restore balance. And it was depletive therapy that Rush practiced with relish when, in addition to his general medical duties, he was placed in charge of the thirty to forty insane patients at the Pennsylvania Hospital in 1787. So intimidating in their administration, so dramatic in their effects and so feared by patients, depletive therapy became known as "heroic therapy," and largely because of Rush's considerable influence was used in the new private and public asylums that were being built during that era across the United States.

Rush, who was also an abolitionist, environmentalist, prison reformer, treasurer of the United States Mint, and signatory to the Declaration of Independence, eventually was castigated for his reliance on depletive therapy as a treatment of physical disease, indeed his own death from fever in 1813 most likely was hastened by his insistence that he be bled repeatedly. But depletive therapy continued for a few decades longer in the treatment of insanity, its use hidden behind the high walls of asylums. Its disappearance from asylum medicine most likely was due to a combination of reasons. New theories of the cause of insanity challenged Rush's unitary theory of disease, and new pressures on asylum physicians to bring the treatment of insanity out of the unenlightened past and in parity with enlightened medicine certainly were significant factors. Interestingly, so was the War of 1812. The conflict between the United States and Great Britain churned an animosity against the "Mother Country," and towards its medical schools. Many American medical students who aspired to be asylum physicians turned to France for their education. Although there were exceptions, of course, for the most part French asylum physicians were considerably more restrained in their use of depletive therapy in the treatment of the insane, combining it with other remedies such as hydrotherapy [see **Hydrotherapy**], or eschewing it altogether in favor of more *vis medicatrix naturae* approach that emphasized the healing power of commonsense remedies, rest, diet and fresh air. Those, in turn, were both harbingers and constituents of what became known as moral therapy [see **Moral Treatment**].

## References

Andrews, J., and Scull, A. (2001). *Undertaker of the mind: John Monro and mad-doctoring in eighteenth-century England.* Berkeley: University of California Press.
Arika, A. (2007). *Passions and tempers: A history of the humours.* New York: HarperCollins.
Author (1837). Insanity. *Boston Medical and Surgical Journal, 16,* 21.
Bakewell, T. (1805). *The domestic guide in cases of insanity.* Newcastle, UK: T. Allbut.
Battie, W. (1758). *A treatise on madness.* London: William and White.
Baumeister, A. (2011). The search for an endogenous schizogen: The strange case of taraxein. *Journal of the History of the Neurosciences, 20,* 106–122.
Bayfield, S. (1823). *A treatise on practical cupping: Comprising an historical relation of the operation through ancient and modern times.* London: Author.
Belden, L.W. (1834). *An account of Jane C. Rider, the Springfield Somnambulist.* Springfield, MA: G. and C. Merriam.
Braybooke., R.L. (ed.). (1870). *Memoirs of Samuel Pepys, Esq. F.R.S., comprising his diary from 1659 to 1669.* London: Frederick Warne and Company.
Burrows, G.M. (1828). *Commentaries on the causes, forms, symptoms, and treatment, moral and medical, of insanity.* London: Thomas and George Underwood.
Chiarugi, V. (1795). *Della pazzia in genere e in specie trattato medico analitico: Con una centuria di osservazioni.* Vol. 2. Florence, Italy: Presso Luigi Carlieri.
Coga, A. (1666-1667). An account of the experiment of transfusion, practiced upon a man in London. *Philosophical Transactions, 2,* 557–559.
Conolly, J. (1846). Melancholia—The treatment. *Lancet, 1,* 110–116.
Conolly, J. (1863). *A study of Hamlet.* London: Edward Moxon.
Doyle, D. (2005). Per rectum: A history of enemata. *Journal of the Royal College of Physicians of Edinburgh, 35,* 367–370.
Earle, P. (1854). *An examination of the practice of bloodletting in mental disorders.* New York: Samuel S. and William Wood.
Esquirol, J.E.D. (1838). *Mental maladies: A treatise on insanity.* Trans. E.K. Hunt. Philadelphia: Lea and Blanchard.
Freedman, A.M., and Ginsberg, V. (1958). Exchange transfusions in schizophrenic patients. *Journal of Nervous and Mental Disease, 126,* 294–301.
Galt, J.M. (1854). On the separation of the sexes in lunatic asylums. *New England Journal of Medicine, 51,* 492–496.
Giacometti, L. (1987). Leeching in the twentieth century. *American Journal of Cardiology, 60,* 1128–1131.

Goldstein, J.E. (1987). *Console and classify: The French psychiatric profession in the nineteenth century*. Chicago: University of Chicago Press.
Grant-Smith, R. (1922). *The experiences of an asylum patient*. London: George Allen & Unwin.
Griffin, J.P. (2004). Venetian treacle and the foundation of medicines regulation. *British Journal of Clinical Pharmacology, 58*, 317–325.
Hall, L.A. (2003). "It was affecting the medical profession": The history of masturbatory insanity revisited. *Paedagogica Historica, 39*, 685–699.
Hallaran, W.S. (1818). *Practical observations of the causes and cure of insanity*, 2nd ed. Cork, Ireland: Edwards and Savage.
Harding, T.W. (1990). "Not worth the powder and shot": A reappraisal of Montagu Lomax's contribution to mental health reform. *British Journal of Psychiatry, 156*, 180–187.
Hare, E.H. (1962). Masturbatory insanity: The history of an idea. *British Journal of Psychiatry, 108*, 1–25.
Hartnett, J.C. (1972). The care and use of medicinal leeches in 19th century pharmacy and therapeutics. *Pharmacy in History, 14*, 127–138.
Heath, R.G., Martens, S., Leach, B.E., Cohen, M., and Angel, C. (1957). Effect on behavior in humans with the administration of taraxein. *American Journal of Psychiatry, 114*, 14–24.
House of Commons (1815). *First report: Minutes of evidence taken before the Select Committee appointed to consider of provision being made for the better regulation of madhouses*. London: Author.
Hunting, P. (2010). "Old Spasm": William Cullen (1710–90). *Journal of Medical Biography, 18*, 216–217.
Kirk, R.G.W., and Pemberton, N. (2011). Re-imagining bleeders: The medical leech in the nineteenth century bloodletting encounter. *Medical History, 55*, 355–60.
Kraepelin, E. (1962). *One hundred years of psychiatry*. Trans. Wade Baskin. New York: Citadel Press.
Lawrence, G. (2002). Tools of the trade: Tobacco smoke enemas. *Lancet, 359*, 1442.
Lindsay, W.L. (1855). The histology of the blood of the insane. *Journal of Psychological Medicine and Mental Pathology, 1*, 78–93.
Lomax, M. (1921). *Experiences of an asylum doctor*. London: G. Allen & Unwin.
Macphail, S.R. (1884). Clinical observations on the blood of the insane. *British Journal of Psychiatry, 30*, 378–389.
Miller, B., and Miller, M. (1997). *Just what the doctor ordered: The history of American medicine*. Minneapolis: Lerner Publications Co.
Monro, J. (1758). *Remarks on Dr. Battie's Treatise on Madness*. London: John Clarke.
Moore, P. (2003). *Blood and justice*. New York: John Wiley and Sons.
Morris, A. (2008). William Battie's *Treatise on Madness* (1758) and John Monro's *Remarks on Dr. Battie's Treatise* (1758). *British Journal of Psychiatry, 192*, 257.
Noll, R. (2006). The blood of the insane. *History of Psychiatry, 17*, 395–418.
Pargeter, W. (1792). *Observations on maniacal disorders*. London: Smart and Cowslade.
Pfeffer, A.Z., and Pecor, M.J. (1944). Multiple transfusions for schizophrenia. *Archives of Neurology and Psychiatry, 58*, 131–134.
Pinel, P. (1806). *A treatise on insanity*. Trans. D.D. Davis. Sheffield, UK: W. Todd.
Richards, R.J. (2004). *The Romantic conception of life: Science and philosophy in the age of Goethe*. Chicago: University of Chicago Press.
Rush, B. (1830). *Medical inquiries and observations upon the diseases of the mind*. 4th ed. Philadelphia: John Grigg.
Rutkow, I. (2010). *Seeking the cure: A history of medicine in America*. New York: Scribner.
Schaffer, S. (1998). Regeneration. In C. Lawrence and S. Shapin (eds.), *Science incarnate: Historical embodiments of natural knowledge*, pp. 83–115. Chicago: University of Chicago Press.
Smith, L.D. (1993). To cure those afflicted with the disease of insanity: Thomas Bakewell and Spring Vale Asylum. *History of Psychiatry, 4*, 107–127.
Steele, W. (1892/1893). The blood in melancholia and the effect of systematic tonic treatment. *American Journal of Insanity, 49*, 604–610.
Stenger, K., and Van Neck, A. (2001). *Masturbation: The history of a great terror*. Trans. K. Hoffman. New York: Palgrave.
Tissot, S.A.D. (1832). *A treatise on the diseases produced by onanism*. New York: Collins & Hannay.
Tomes, N. (1994). *The art of asylum-keeping: Thomas Story Kirkbride and the origins of American psychiatry*. Philadelphia: University of Pennsylvania Press.
Tuke, S. (1813). *Description of the York Retreat*. York, UK: W. Alexander.
Wagemaker, H., Rogers, J.L., and Cade, R. (1984). Schizophrenia, hemodialysis, and the placebo effect. *Archives of General Psychiatry, 41*, 805–810.
Woodward, S.B. (1850). Observations on the medical treatment of insanity. *American Journal of Insanity, 7*, 1–34.

## *Bleeding, or Bloodletting, or Venesection*

The withdrawal of blood from a vein.

"Breathing the vein" to treat insanity was one of the oldest therapeutic interventions on record. Bleeding was intimately associated with the humoural doctrine of the ancient medical philosophers Hippocrates and Galen who posited that the body held a mix of four humours, or "vital spirits," that were produced by the digestive process and then circulated to the heart and the brain by the heat generated by that process. According to the doctrine, each person had a specific, although not unique, humoural constitution that had to be kept in balance to assure both physical and mental health.

Blood was one of those humours. Warm and moist, it was thought to be produced by the liver and was further associated with the spring season, during which time it was at risk for unhealthily accumulating in the body. Blood determined a sanguine temperament and when plentiful and in balance with the other humours of black bile, yellow bile or choler, and phlegm, was the reason for the sociability, pleasure-seeking, optimism and warm-heartedness that were characteristic of that temperament. When in excess, whether due to the season or to changes in the climate, diet, or life circumstances to which it, just as every other humour, was cosmologically connected, it caused the emotional and behavioral excesses of mania. The relief of this excess of blood in the brain, variously referred to as "inflammation," "plethora" or "congestion" called for the therapeutic intervention of bleeding.

As the mad-doctoring trade professionalized, asylum physicians took great interest in determining the physiological basis of insanity. Theories that focused on the pressure, flow and constitution of the blood extended the therapeutic intervention of bleeding to patients with types of insanity other than mania. Thus bleeding became *de rigueur* in asylums around the world throughout the nineteenth century and, in fact, was the preferred treatment for virtually all types of insanity. At the Bethlem Asylum in London, England, for example, bleeding not only had been part of the therapeutic regime since its establishment centuries before, but was a highly ritualized component of the asylum's culture. Patients at "Bedlam," as the asylum was better known, were bled at a particular time and on a particular day every spring. Asylum physicians moved from one patient to another, opening a vein in the arm or the foot with a sharp-pointed, double-edged blade known as a lancet. When the desired amount of blood had been removed, as measured by the line on the interior of the pewter bleeding bowl placed under the incised limb, the patient was returned to the cell.

So ritualized had this procedure become at Bethlem that it not only persisted decades after the humoural doctrine had fallen out of favor, but in the face of increasingly stinging professional criticism and even public ridicule. By the mid-eighteenth century the *zeitgeist* was changing. Insanity was being seen as more nuanced than just mania or melancholia, its cause envisioned as more complex than just congestion of the brain, and its treatment as more in need of management than bloodletting. At the vanguard of this change was William Battie whose *Treatise on Madness,* published in 1758, was the first English monograph on insanity. The entrepreneurial Battie who spearheaded the establishment of St. Luke's Asylum for Lunatics and who had a lucrative practice in the management of private madhouses in London, attacked the ritualized practice of bleeding at Bethlem, an asylum on whose Board of Governors he had once served:

> Madness, rejects all general methods, e.g. bleeding.... For bleeding, tho' apparently serviceable and necessary in inflammation of the brain, in rarefaction of the fluids, or a plethoric habit of body, is however no more the adequate and constant cure of Madness, than it is of fever. Nor is the lancet, when applied to the feeble and convulsed Lunatic, less destructive than a sword [Battie, p. 94].

The broadside, aimed squarely at Bethlem, was met by another, this one authored by John Monro, visiting physician at Bethlem and Battie's rival for esteem as the country's most authoritative mad-doctor, as asylum physicians then were known. Sarcastic in tone, Monro's rebuttal dismantled every one of Battie's assertions about the nature and treatment of insanity, including bleeding. He defended bleeding not only for its therapeutic efficacy but for the exercise of good medical judgment that prescribed its use in the first place. Although the two archrivals found common ground on more than a few points, their debate etched out the leading edge of a changing approach to the treatment of asylum patients that eventually would resign bleeding to an embarrassing footnote in the history of asylum therapeutics.

It was not just at Bethlem that bleeding was a standardized therapeutic. In France, patients in the two overcrowded insane wards at the Hôtel-Dieu were bled after the eleven o'clock meal, twice yearly, in the spring and autumn before being plunged into the river for their semi-annual bath, a standing order of physician Édouard Françoise Marie Bosquillion. So intimately was bleeding associated with this hospital, the oldest in Paris, that it often was flippantly referred to as "*traitement de l'Hôtel-Dieu.*" In Germany, Johann Christian August Heinroth, also prescribed bleeding, despite the fact that he considered insanity to be a moral, rather than a humoural, imbalance. The influential professor of physical medicine at the University of Leipzig and founder of the "psychic school' of psychiatry, rhapsodically declared that the hot blood of the insane patient should be made to gush from the veins, "as if rejoicing over its escape from the prison in which it was raging" (Kraepelin, p. 37). And in United States, there was no more staunch proponent of bleeding than Benjamin Rush, attending physician to the Pennsylvania Hospital in Philadelphia. The "Father of Psychiatry," as he posthumously came to be known, found bleeding beneficial, even curative, in its ability to relieve the plethoric condition of the brain, not to mention its ability to frighten and deceive patients [see **Pious Frauds**]. The case of a young man under his care who had become insane after killing a friend in a duel illustrated that latter point:

> In the year 1803, I visited a young man in our Hospital who became deranged from remorse of conscience.... His only cry was for a pistol, that he might put an end to his life. I told him, the firing of the pistol would disturb the patients in the neighboring cells, and that the wound made by it would probably cover his cell with blood, but that I could take away his life in a more easy and delicate way by bleeding him to death, from a vein in the arm, and retaining his blood in a large bowl. I then requested Dr. Hartshorn, the resident physician and apothecary to the hospital, to tie up his arm, and bleed him to death. The Doctor instantly feigned compliance with this request. After losing nearly twenty ounces of blood, he fainted, became calm, and slept soundly the ensuing night. The next day I visited him, he was still unhappy; not from despair and a hatred of life, but from the dread of death; for he now complained only, that several persons in the hospital had conspired to kill him. By the continuance of depleting remedies, this error was soon removed, and he was soon afterwards discharged from the hospital [Rush, pp. 127–128].

Technology kept pace with the therapeutic imperative to bleed asylum patients. The lancet, never a particularly cumbersome device but always feared for the pain it produced, underwent many improvements. The scarificator had multiple steel blades and a depth adjustor; the blades of the spring lancet, tightly fitted into a brass box, were controlled by a lever and cut to a uniform depth; the thumb lancet, protected by a cover or leaves that folded back when the blade was gripped between the thumb and index finger, was small, portable and allowed a certain degree of accuracy in the cutting. These, and other, bloodletting instruments often had bone, horn, tortoise shell, ivory or mother-of-pearl handles or covers, and were carried by asylum physicians and apothecaries in elaborately designed cases.

There were objections to the bleeding of asylum patients that was so lavishly indiscriminate by the early nineteenth century that the French reformer Philippe Pinel was given to muse aloud as to "whether the patient or his physician has the best claim to the appellation of madman" (Pinel, p. 251). Although he did not call for an end to bleeding, he recommended it only for when the exuberantly loquacious patient's complexion was flushed, pulse quickened and eyes protuberant, all diagnostic signs of an incipient paroxysm of mania. The American asylum physician Pliny Earle, however, did call for its end. The nearly half century that separated the two reformers had witnessed a sea-change of opinion about how to treat the insane, and the growing hegemony of the moral treatment approach [see **Moral Treatment**] relegated those asylum physicians who still practiced bleeding to the backwaters of asylum medicine.

"To bleed, or not bleed" was the question that opened Earle's meticulous investigation into the therapeutic (Earle, p. 9). And the answer given by the most prominent asylum physicians to the interrogative was "not bleed"—or at least, not generally and indiscriminately. Their responses indicated not just a change in therapeutic practice in mid-nineteenth century America, but a change in theory about the cause and nature of insanity. Departing from Benjamin Rush's canonical assertion that all insanity, mania in particular, was caused by an imbalance in the vascular system that inflamed the brain, the surveyed asylum physicians were more inclined to indict the nervous system, lesions on the brain, metabolic disturbances, and even moral affectations such as over-ambition, hyper-religiosity or over-indulgence as the culprits. While many recommended "local" or "topical" bleeding via leeches or wet cupping, they eschewed general bleeding for other therapeutic interventions such as moral treatment, hydrotherapy [see **Hydrotherapy**], a change in diet [see **Diet**], or simply rest and quiet. And one respondent after another cited cases in which bleeding exacerbated the insanity, rather than relieved it.

Earle's treatise tolled the demise of bleeding as an asylum therapeutic in the United States and, in many ways, the humoural doctrine that originally had influenced it. By that time bleeding almost had entirely disappeared from British and European asylums as well.

## Blood Transfusion

The replacement of withdrawn blood with blood from a donor into a vein or artery. One of the first attempts to transfuse blood from an animal to a human was performed on an insane man in the mid-seventeenth century. The anatomist Richard Lower had approached Bethlem Asylum in London, England, for a "lunatic" to be his experimental subject, less out of the belief that a blood transfusion would cure insanity than out of desperation to find a willing volunteer. The superintendent of "Bedlam," as that asylum already was known, refused his request. But a former Cambridge University divinity student who had become a "little frantic" from a brain that was "sometimes a little too warm" (Schaffer, p. 100), offered his services in exchange for one guinea. In the presence of more than forty distinguished physicians, academics and Members of Parliament, Arthur Coga was transfused with eight or nine ounces of lamb's blood.

The carotid artery of the lamb was lanced and a thin silver pipe with a quill to regulate the flow was inserted; the blood flowed into a silver porringer bowl. Coga, who was inebriated, offered his arm so that Lower could "breathe the vein" and remove several ounces of blood. A silver pipe was inserted into the wound and the lamb's blood slowly dribbled into Coga's vein. "Well and merry" during the procedure, Coga drank more wine after its completion and enjoyed a smoke (Schaffer, p. 100).

Lower had hoped that given the docile nature of the species, the lamb's blood would quiet the tempestuous disposition of Coga's insanity. And, for a time, that seemed to be true. A week after the transfusion Coga addressed the Royal Society of Medicine and proclaimed that he felt considerably better. Asked why he thought that lamb's blood, in particular, had had a salutary effect, he replied in Latin, "*Sanguis ovis symbolicam quandam facultatem habet cum sanguine Christi; quia Christus est agnus Dei*," saying, in effect that lamb's blood had symbolic power in that it was like the blood of Christ who is the lamb of God.

Whatever improvement Coga experienced

as a result of the initial blood transfusion and the second one performed a month later, was short-lived, however. When the eminent diarist Samuel Pepys was introduced to him at a local tavern, he observed that though Coga spoke "very reasonably and well," he still was "cracked a little in his head" (Braybrooke, p. 463). Coga indeed appeared quite affected by the transfusions. A letter received by the Royal Society of Medicine and signed by "Agnus Coga," who may have been his wife or mother or, for that matter, Coga himself since the name can be translated from the Latin as "Coga the Sheep," described the "forfeit of his nerves" and the "loss of his own wool" and begged for another transfusion to transform him "without as well as within" (Moore, p. 137). The Royal Society of Medicine refused his request, noting the "wildness of his mind" (Shaffer, p. 100). The discouraging outcome of the Coga experiment, coupled with the deaths of several transfusion patients in France and Italy, led the Royal Society of Medicine, as well as the French Parliament and the Catholic Church to issue prohibitions against blood transfusions. These remained in place for nearly 150 years.

Curiosity, however, persisted. It is important to note that Coga was not chosen as a subject of this transfusion experiment because he was insane, nor was the transfusion conducted to cure his insanity; rather, he was a convenient subject to test a technical procedure. Yet Coga might be seen as the embodiment of an ancient humoural question: if blood carried mental, spiritual and physical evidence of the kind of person in whose circulatory system it flowed, then was the blood of the insane different in some way from that of the sane? In the mid-nineteenth century that that specific question was investigated.

W. Lauder Lindsay, assistant physician of the Crichton Royal Institution in Dumfries in the south of Scotland, pricked the fingers of 236 insane patients and 36 staff members to examine their blood under a microscope. Pricking the fingers of the patients was no easy task and Lindsay's description of the process was a reminder of how both experimental and therapeutic interventions could be complicated by both the mental states of the patients and the total institutional context of the asylum:

> As a general rule, the insane are extremely bad subjects for such experiments.... They are extremely sensitive, restless and suspicious of operative interference, even of a slight nature. Many obstinately refused to allow their fingers to be pricked. Some did so from a firm conviction that a deep-laid conspiracy against their lives or welfare lurked under the cloak of an apparently simple experiment; others simply objected to becoming tools of experiment or amusement; some declined on the plea that in their greatly debilitated condition they could ill afford to spare even a single drop of blood; others lacked courage to submit to the operation; some demanded full explanation of the motives which led to my making a singular request of allowing their finger to be pricked by a needle; in others this formed the keynote of their delusions, delirium or vituperation.... [S]ome presented their fingers under the impression that, from the single drop of blood, the state of their constitution, the chances of cure, and the period of their removal, could infallibly be predicted [Lindsay, p. 82].

After comparing the structures of the red and white corpuscles as well as the proportion of serum, fibrin and globules in the sampled blood, Lindsay found no differences either between the blood of the insane patients and that of the staff, or between insane patients with different diagnoses. He concluded that insanity was an ordinary physical disease or, perhaps, a mental reaction to a physical disease, thus emphasizing the intimate relationship between the mind and the body.

More sophisticated laboratory methods for examining blood were made available to asylum physicians during the late nineteenth century. S Rutherford Macphail, Medical Superintendent of the Garlands Asylum in Carlisle in the north of England, for example, discovered differences in the amount of hemoglobin in the blood before, during and after episodes of insanity. This "corpuscular richness" theory was the subject of a number of subsequent published clinical observations that found that corpuscular richness was notable in asylum patients diagnosed with mania, and notably absent in those diagnosed with melancholia; that it was not distinctly different in women diagnosed with puerperal insanity as compared to other women; that it waned during an episodic attack of maniacal excitement; and that it was lower in male than in female patients who had been diagnosed with epilepsy. Clinical observations also concluded that improvement in the quality of the blood was associated with improvement in the mental condition, thus blood tonics such as iron, cod liver oil, quinine and strychnine were highly recommended. Blood transfusions, though, were not. Asylum physicians generally agreed that replacing blood lost through injury or disease was one thing, but replacing it to try to cure insanity was quite another.

That attitude was revisited in the mid-twentieth century. Experiments were conducted by a number of American physicians, most notably Arnold Pfeffer and Michael Pescor, in replacing the blood of schizophrenic patients with that of "normal" donors in order to correct the faulty metabolism of brain cells, which they hypothesized was the cause of schizophrenia. The results were not impressive. The faulty metabolism hypothesis, however, was appealing in its logic, so a decade later Robert Galbraith Heath, chair of the Department of Psychiatry and Neurology at Tulane University in New Orleans, Louisiana, and his colleagues isolated an abnormal blood protein in patients diagnosed with schizophrenia. When injected into monkeys, the protein which they called "taraxein," from the Greek *taraxis,* or confused mind, produced unusual behavior. When injected into humans, prisoners at the state penitentiary, who had never been diagnosed with schizophrenia, it produced what Heath reported was a temporary psychotic disorder that mimicked schizophrenia. He replicated this finding with sixteen other human volunteer subjects, each of whom became symptomatic—disorganized thought, depersonalization, shortened attention span, apprehension, impaired concentration—within two to ten minutes after the injection, with symptom intensity peaking at fifteen to forty minutes, and subsiding after two hours.

The Heath study immediately brought new therapeutic strategies into discussion: perhaps schizophrenia could be cured by exchange transfusions, or by hemodialysis. The press cited one asylum physician after another who was buoyed by the hope of finally curing one of the most intractable types of insanity. As is true with so many therapeutic proposals, however, the enthusiasm outpaced the sober progress of testing and evaluation. When Heath's study was replicated with better controls, the results could not be replicated.

## *Copious Bleeding*

The drawing of twenty to forty ounces of blood in a single instance. The treatment was enthusiastically advocated by Benjamin Rush, attending physician to the Pennsylvania Hospital in Philadelphia, the first colonial medical institution to treat insanity. Rush distinguished himself as the embodiment of Enlightenment ideals; he was a scientist, teacher, writer, abolitionist, signatory to the Declaration of Independence, and during his tenure at the hospital from 1783 to 1813, a psychiatric innovator. Confronted by a handful of "furious, fierce and dangerous" patients held in cells in the hospital's basement (Tomes, p. 4), Rush experimented with a variety of aggressive therapeutic interventions that came to be known as "heroic treatments," not so much for their laudable outcomes as for their daring administrations. Among those heroic treatments was copious bleeding.

Rush had matriculated at the University of Edinburgh Medical School, studying under the esteemed physician William Cullen. "Old Spasm," as Cullen was affectionately known, had set out the medical canon of that era. All disease, insanity no exception, he posited, was caused by an alteration in the excitement of the nervous system. That alteration either depressed the nervous system or, as in the case of mania, excited it, thereby producing vascular spasms that interfered with proper blood circulation. Depletive or antiphlogistic therapeutic strategies, in that case, were required to restore the balance, thus Cullen recommended bloodletting for mania. Departing from that canon, Rush posited that an alteration in the excitement of the nervous system produced "morbid excitement" of the circulation (Rush, p. 25); thus all illness, both mental and physical, stemmed from the overactivity of the vascular system. Rush, as a consequence, bled all of his patients, but copious bleeding, he argued, was the only real remedy for the "arterial disease, of great morbid excitement or inflammation in the brain" (p. 183) that was mania.

He set out the rules for copious bleeding via the jugular, occipital, or frontal vein, or the temporal artery in his text, *Medical Inquiries and Observations upon the Diseases of the Mind,* the first psychiatric text published in the United States:

> Bleeding should be copious on the first attack of the disease. From 20 to 40 ounces of blood may be taken at once, unless fainting be induced before the quantity be drawn. It will do most service if the patient be bled in a standing posture. The effects of this early and copious bleeding are wonderful in calming mad people. It often prevents the necessity of using any other remedy, and sometimes it cures in a few hours [Rush, p. 185].

With neither caveat nor criticism, Rush offered case after case in which what had appeared to be hopeless states of mania were not just relieved, but cured, by copious bleeding. And the bleeding indeed was copious. A Mr. T.H. lost 200 ounces of blood in several sessions during a two month period; Mr. D.T., who had been bled forty-seven times over nine consecutive months, lost a total of 470 ounces. Rush declared each cured.

The influence of Rush was considerable, especially in the United States where asylums were being frantically constructed and quickly filled beyond capacity. The fidelity to Rush's approach, however, would prove to be fickle, but certainly while the "Father of American Psychiatry" was alive, and then for a decade or so after his death, copious bleeding was the standing order of the day in American asylums. Yet by the mid-nineteenth century, when Pliney Earle published his comprehensive survey of asylum physicians on the therapeutic of bleeding, it was clear that Rush had steadily accumulated more detractors than supporters. Many asylum physicians simply found copious bleeding less heroic than cravenly aggressive and, in the bargain, much too risky to administer to manic patients whose resistance often was considerable. Others rejected Rush's underlying theory that insanity of all types originated in the vascular system. The strongest skepticism, however, was reserved for Rush's claims of the curative power of copious bleeding. Asylum physicians had increasingly observed that the therapeutic left patients weak, depleted, exhausted and, even more disturbingly, sometimes more floridly insane. Earle cited the case records of attending physician James Macdonald of the patients who had undergone copious bleeding at the Bloomingdale Asylum in New York City, or at other asylums before being transferred there, to illustrate these points:

> M.K. with Dementia: a striking example of the indiscriminate and excessive employment of the lancet in mental diseases. In this case, which was one of low, brooding melancholy, the most active bloodletting was employed, and repeated, day after day, until his physical energies were so far prostrated as to incapacitate the brain from performing functions common to brutes, and the heart almost circulating the blood.... [W]as discharged "by request," the expression used by that institution for unimproved.
>
> [A] woman was admitted who had been bled to the amount of eighty or ninety ounces, which had only the effect of weakening her mind without in the least allaying the violence of the paroxysms or lessening morbid strength. She remained six months and was discharged "much improved," but ...was readmitted and became a permanent resident of the institution...
>
> A/C/F/ was admitted. He had been bled

from twelve to sixteen ounces, every third or fourth day, for the space of six months. After being subjected to treatment for two years, he was discharged "by request." Two months afterwards, he was brought back and remained until his decease from typhoid fever....

J.W.J. was admitted. He had bled at different times to the amount of three or four quarts. He was discharged "cured," five weeks after his reception, but was readmitted after an absence of seven months. He was now incurable....

Admitted H.J. who had been treated by copious bleeding and other depletion. Discharged one month afterwards, "demented."

J.U....had been repeatedly bled and exceedingly reduced. Remained six months and discharged "demented."

C.R. had lost sixty-four ounces of blood in a few days before her admission. After a residence of two years, she was transferred..."demented" [Earle, pp. 19–20].

A letter to the editors of the *Boston Medical and Surgical Journal* also emphatically made all of these points. Citing cases of mania successfully treated with diet and tinctures of opium, the author implored his colleagues to question the received wisdom of the "justly celebrated Dr. Rush" that mania was the result of an inflammation and that copious bleeding was its only cure:

> Cases of [mania] are almost daily coming under my observation, and the result of the treatment [by diet and drug] has taught me an important practical lesson in insanity—*not to mistake excessive nervous action for inflammation, nor be led to consider the great muscular power of the maniac any proof of the strength and vigor which requires active depletion* [Author, p. 21, italics in original].

Some of the most eminent and respected asylum physicians around the world, who otherwise contentiously argued about therapeutics, were in agreement. Philippe Pinel, then a physician at the Salpêtrière Asylum in Paris, France, declared that "bleeding, practiced as it is without rules or bounds, is found to exasperate the complaint, and to cause periodical and curable mania to degenerate into dementia or idiotism" (Pinel, p. 252). A former advocate of copious bleeding, George Mann Burrows became its adversary. The distinguished British expert on insanity had slowly come to the realization that rates of recovery were much higher for patients who had not been copiously bled, a realization that led him to the conclusion that the therapeutic was based on an incorrect theory about the origin of mania and that, as carried out, was little more than "a practice fraught generally with mischief" (Burrows, p. 583).

The therapeutic use of copious bleeding in asylums certainly outlived its use in general medicine and, interestingly, it even outlived the concomitant blows to Rush's reputation as a physician. In 1793, more than 4,000 people died as the result of a yellow fever epidemic that struck the city of Philadelphia. Most of the patients Rush treated for the acute viral hemorrhagic disease were among those fatalities. With fidelity to his theory that all disease was vascular in origin, he had treated these patients with copious bleeding and, as a consequence, found himself being ridiculed by detractors and pilloried by the press. The English-born pamphleteer and crusading journalist William Cobbett launched a campaign against Rush, defaming him as a "potent quack" whose reliance on copious bleeding was little more than a bloody purge that killed one patient after another. Rush, his reputation sullied, sued for libel and won. Cobbett, however, fled to England and left the $8,000 judgment against him unpaid. Perhaps the ironic distance between Rush's good intentions and the bad outcomes of copious bleeding for both asylum and medical patients was captured in a letter Thomas Jefferson wrote about his good friend: "In his theory of bleeding.... I was never opposed to my friend ... whom I greatly loved; but who had done much harm, in the sincerest persuasion that he was preserving life and happiness to all around him" (Miller & Miller, p. 39).

## Leech Therapy, Leeching, or Hirudotherapy

The application of medicinal leeches, i.e., *Hirudo medicinalis,* to the skin for the localized depletion of blood. Leech therapy for the treatment of insanity dates back millennia, and was even promoted by the tenth century Persian physician, Avicenna, as a prophylactic—a regular leeching, he proposed, kept ardent lovers out of the throes of madness. During the seventeenth and eighteenth centuries, barber-surgeons sometimes eschewed the scalpels, lancets and fleams of their trade in favor of less intimidating leeches, as did military surgeons whose need for them bolstered a vigorous international trade in these segmented worms that attach with strong suckers, secrete the anticoagulant hirudin, and suck out ten times their body weight in blood before they release themselves from the skin.

Eighteenth century asylum physicians, influenced as they were by humoural doctrine, were of a mind that it was an excess, or plethora, of blood that was irritating and inflaming the brain that caused insanity, and just as the barber-surgeons and military surgeons had done, they often relied on leeches for general bloodletting. In London, England, at Bethlem Hospital, better known as Bedlam, leeches were applied in the spring to every patient, regardless of diagnosis or prognosis, since it was that season that corresponded with the vital spirit of blood, according to humoural doctrine. So ritualized had that treatment become, in fact, that it outlived the influence of the doctrine, leaving physician Thomas Monro to weakly defend leeching in front of a skeptical Select Committee that was investigating conditions at the asylum in the early nineteenth century:

> Patients are ordered to be bled about the latter part of May, according to the weather.... That has been the practice invariably for years, long before my time; it was handed down to me by my father, and I do not know any better practice [House of Commons, p. 110].

During that time most British asylum physicians had the same devotion to the time-honored treatment of leeching as had Monro, if no longer to the humoural doctrine that gave rise to it in the first place. Taking a more iatro-mechanical view, they reasoned that leeches were best suited for localized, rather than generalized, bloodletting, so their careful application to plethoric bodily sites—the forehead, behind the ears and in the nostrils for relief of melancholic congestion of the brain; the vulva and inner thighs to stimulate menses, alleviate puerperal mania, or inhibit nymphomania; the hemorrhoidal vein in the anus, thought to have an intimate sympathy with the brain, to quiet mania—became the treatment of choice.

By mid-nineteenth century, however, whatever passion there had been among British asylum physicians for bloodletting—generalized or localized—and by any means, had waned considerably in the face of high regard for moral treatment [see **Moral Treatment**]. This was evident in the response to John Conolly's recommended treatment for melancholia. Physician to the Middlesex County Lunatic Asylum at Hanwell, just outside of London, Conolly was particularly interested in melancholy, as evidenced by his highly regarded study of Shakespeare's *Hamlet,* and for its treatment he advised that leeches applied to the forehead and behind the ears would alleviate symptoms and, on occasion, cure it altogether. Only a few of his colleagues agreed. When fifty-two of them were questioned as to their treatment preferences, only thirteen were still using leech therapy for melancholia, and none for mania.

Leech therapy, in fact, always was used cautiously in cases of mania due to what often was the vigorous resistance of patients. Pundits, however, had much to say about the "leech mania" that swept across France and soon penetrated the bastilles of insane asylums. In the late eighteenth century, François-Joseph-Victor Broussais, an army physician who had once studied with Philippe Pinel at the Salpêtrière Hospital in France, advanced a new system of what became known as "physiological medicine" that attributed all illness, including insanity, to an irritation of the gastrointestinal tract that passed "sympathetically" to other organs, including the brain. The only cure, he posited, was bloodletting, but because that often weakened patients, he advocated a localized application of leeches. So popular had leeching become for illnesses ranging from colds to cancer, itches to insanity, that more than a billion leeches had to be imported into France to meet the demands that local leech farming could not. For creatures so low on the evolutionary scale, leeches became very fashionable in French culture. These fresh water invertebrate parasites, prized for their sensitivity to atmospheric conditions, also were used as barometers, and inspired the paisley-like design of brooches and of clothing, the latter of which popularly were known as "robes à la Broussais."

The influence of Broussais, who had earned both the posthumous sobriquet of "the most sanguinary physician in history," and the less flattering contemporary nickname of the "le vampire de la médicine," on the treatment of insanity in France also was considerable. The great reformer Philippe Pinel continued to use leech therapy for chronic insanity long after a new era in the humane treatment of the insane was announced by the striking of the chains of insane patients at the Salpêtrière Asylum in Paris. Another notable French asylum reformer, Jean-Étienne Esquirol, also used leeching as part of a complicated treatment regime that included tepid baths, exercise and purgings in his practice at the Charenton Asylum. His successor, Louis-Florentin Calmeil continued leech treatment well past the mid-nineteenth century, touting it as a treatment, although not a cure, of a peculiar form of insanity he labeled "monomania with paralysis."

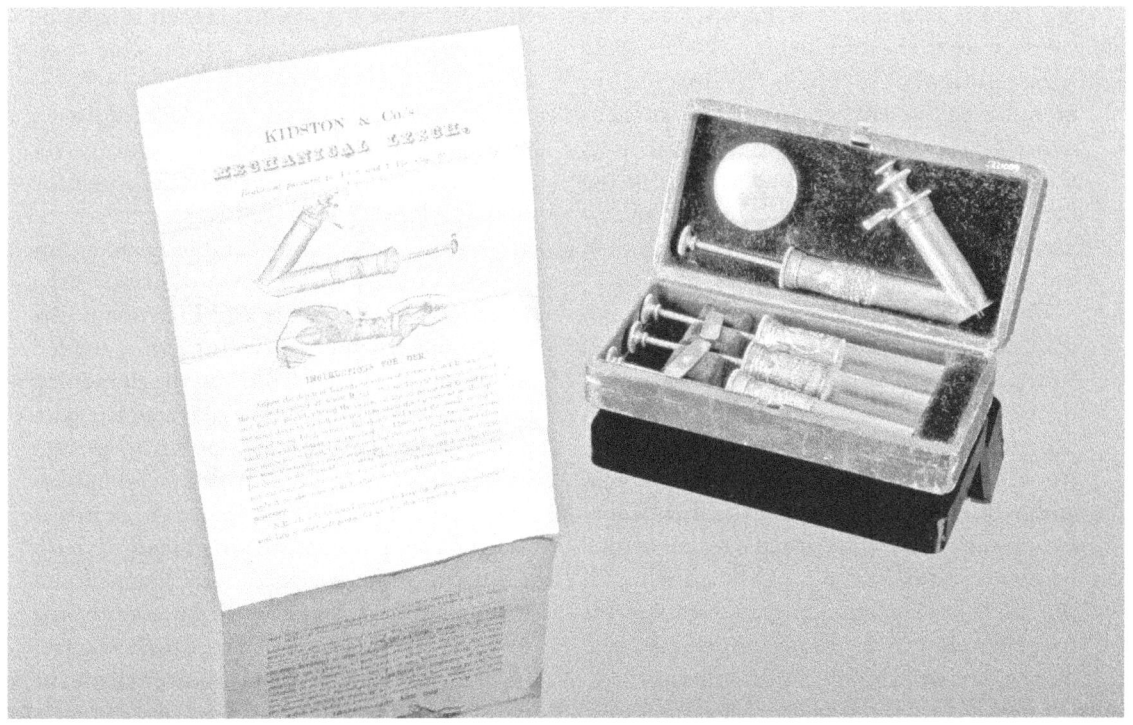

One type of many mechanical leeches that were invented in the early nineteenth century when the medical demands for *Hirudo medicinalis* was so great that it nearly led the species to extinction. Squeamish patients favored the mechanical version, as live leeches tended to drop off the skin and reattach in unexpected places (courtesy of the Wellcome Library, London).

The delusions of wealth and grandeur that were its hallmarks, he posited, inevitably would deteriorate into chronic dementia or even bring about death unless stability was gained through the repeated applications of leeches to the anus.

Leech mania also had spread to the asylums of Germany. At the small Halle-Nietleben Asylum near Leipzig, for example, physician Heinrich Damerow routinely prescribed leeches to the anus for all patients, quiet regardless of diagnosis or prognosis. That practice was so widespread that a British physician dismissed it as a peculiarly German interest in revulsion as a therapeutic; whether peculiar or not, Germany capped the exportation of leeches to the United States in the early nineteenth century for fear it would exhaust its own supply.

American asylum physician were faced with a dual dilemma in the early nineteenth century: the *Hirudo decora* leeches native to the country had less capacity for bloodletting than the *Hirudo medicinalis* of Europe, and thus were not up to the formidable task of treating "American insanity," which was imagined to be more belligerent, obstinate and autonomous—rather like the county, itself—than its European counterpart. Perhaps because of the high cost of procuring leeches, American asylum physicians used them more sparingly than did their international colleagues.

One famous American case involving leech treatment deserves mention. In 1833, Jane C. Rider, a nineteen-year-old servant of a prominent Springfield, Massachusetts, family, began experiencing episodes of sleepwalking, rising from her bed at night and wandering about, and even engaging in a parody of her housekeeping activities while asleep. Her concerned employers took her to a physician who, although believing her somnambulism was due to a paroxysm in the brain, nonetheless was quite taken by her ability to read letters with her eyes closed, recite poetry long forgotten, and mimic people while in a somnambulistic trance. His public discussions about her case brought a constant stream of fascinated laypeople and physicians to his office where, for their edification, he would subject Rider to a variety of tests that exhibited her unique abilities. Eventually unable to manage the curiosity-seekers, the physician had the "Springfield Somnabulist," as she had come to be known, admitted to the Worcester State Lunatic Asylum and placed under the care of one of the country's preeminent asylum physicians, Samuel Woodward. Already interested in phrenology, the trendy "science" of inferring character traits from the shape of the skull, Woodward concluded that Rider's persistent headaches on the left side of her head were the result of the overexcitation of the corresponding faculty of the brain, thus causing both her somnambulism and her unusual abilities. He then subjected Rider to a vigorous regime of diet, laudanum, emetics, purgatives, baths and, finally, leeches. Awaking from a somnambulistic trance to find leeches clinging to the left side of her head, Rider was "not a little surprised at her new head ornaments" (Belden, p. 91). She improved significantly although not completely, however, and was released soon after.

Leeches were stored in what often were elaborately decorated porcelain, glass or ceramic jars, and transported from the pharmacy to the asylum in pewter or silver leech carriers, all of which have considerable value as antiques in today's market. Also valuable is the so-called "mechanical leech." Invented in the early-nineteenth century, this spring loaded device simulated leech bites by the tightening and turning of springs that lacerated the skin, and the pulling back of a pump to extract blood via suction. There were several models of it and one of the first, if not the first, was designed by Jean-Baptiste Sarlandière, a French physician. Although ingeniously designed, and much preferred by squeamish patients, the use of what Sarlandière named the *bdellomètre* required considerable manual dexterity on the part of the physician and thus quite quickly fell out of what was its already rather limited use as an asylum therapeutic.

By the mid-nineteenth century leech therapy, which had been used in asylums around the world, had all but disappeared from use as humoural and inflammation theories of insanity fell out of vogue.

## *Purging*

The evacuation of the bowels produced by the administration of an aperient, enema or clyster, or smoke. The humoural doctrine had proposed that there was a link between the abdominal region, particularly the stomach and the intestines, where the humours were replenished during digestion and expelled when depleted, and some types of insanity. Thus the purging of the bowels long was thought to efficaciously expel the excessive, stale, noxious and peccant humours that could inflame the brain. Purging as a therapeutic, in fact, long outlived the humoural doctrine that first rationalized it. As more mechanistic theories of insanity achieved hegemony, asylum physicians well into the twentieth century still "cleared [the] heads, improved [the] tempers, and aborted or cut short a mental crisis," by regulating the bowels of their insane patients (Lomax, p. 99).

Asylum physicians had a veritable cornucopia of aperient herbs, flowers, roots, salts, oils and berries at their disposal to purge insane patients. Jalap, rhubarb, aloe, senna, valerian root, bryony, gamboge, Rochelle and Glauber's salts, castor oil, cream of tartar, croton oil, calomel and colocythn, among other aperients, were used alone or in combination, steeped in hot water or mixed with honey or treacle and sometimes flavored with sassafras chips or juniper berries, mixed with butter and spread on bread, or dissolved in beer, and given orally to patients as many as three or four times each day to stimulate evacuation.

The English madhouse owner Thomas Bakewell, whose flamboyant personality and widely read text on insanity still could not completely elide the fact that he had no formal medical training, was indifferent as to which purgative was best. "Most families have a predilection for some particular purge, and this may be indulged," he wrote, "for I don't

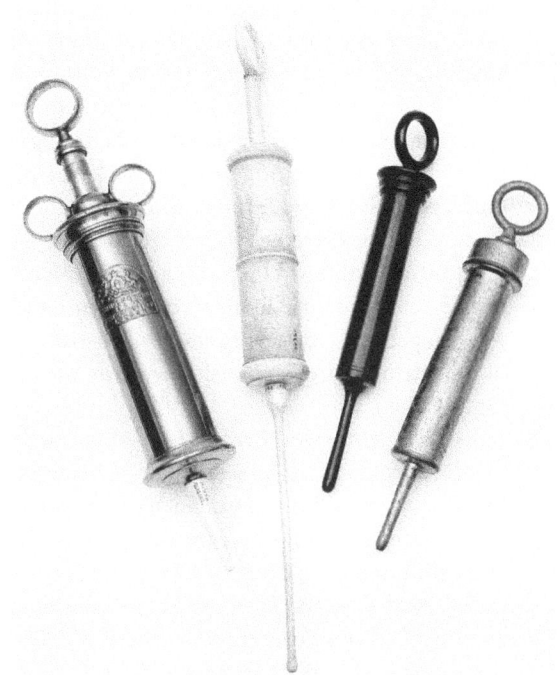

A collection of brass, ivory, ebony and pewter enema syringes. The practice of purging, or evacuating the bowels, far outlived the humoural doctrine on which it was based (courtesy of the Wellcome Library, London).

perceive it to be of any great consequence" (Bakewell, p. 64). Not everyone agreed. Jean-Étienne Dominique Esquirol, *médecin ordinaire* at the Salpêtrière Asylum in Paris, France, for example, stated emphatically that "the choice of purgatives is *not* a matter of indifference" (Esquirol, p. 86). In so declaring, Esquirol defended the steady progress of professionalizing the care of the insane—no self-taught empiric such as Bakewell, after all, was likely to appreciate that some purgatives were best suited for their special action on the hepatic system, others for their effect on the hemorrhoidal vessels, and that in all cases in which they irritated the skin, their administration had to be alternated with tepid baths. Nor was a self-taught empiric likely to know that purgatives were contraindicated for certain types of insanity: hypochondriacal insanity, for example, only worsened because of their irritating effect on the abdominal viscera where it was thought to originate; and epileptic insanity, as another example, was not at all ameliorated by the administration of purgatives. And quite contrary to Bakewell's assertion that "there is very little danger of [purgatives] being too strong, for those laboring under this disease will not at all be injured by what would be extremely hurtful to persons of sane mind" (Bakewell, p. 64), Esquirol reminded that potent purgatives can exhaust and weaken patients, rendering the administration of supplemental therapeutics, such as bleeding, particularly risky.

Esquirol eschewed only the routine use of drastic purgatives in the treatment of insanity. He, like most asylum physicians, often found it necessary to prescribe carefully concocted and calibrated purgatives to relieve the constipation that afflicted so many insane patients as a result of poor diet, sedentary conditions, the costive effects of therapeutic remedies such as opium, and even "the voluntary retention of feces so common in lunatics" (Burrows, p. 636). Because some patients resisted the therapeutic, often strenuously, asylum physicians were forced to be innovative. The eminent British expert on insanity, George Mann Burrows, recommended the use of suppositories such as a piece of soap or a twist of tobacco, the tickling of the anal sphincter with a feather, and galvanism which, when applied twice daily for one-half hour, produced a "rumbling noise in the bowel" (Burrows, p. 636) that announced evacuation. In reference to some of the emerging therapeutics of the early nineteenth century, Burrows also suggested that a stream of cold water propelled at the anus [see **Hydrotherapy**], or a session or two in a vibratory chair [see **Rotation, Oscillation and Vibration**] would work well to overcome the torpidity of the bowels.

Perhaps one of the most innovative of the purging techniques was the tobacco smoke enema. The narcotic and purgative medicinal effects of tobacco, whether smoked, chewed, inhaled, smoldered in the form of "burn cigars," swallowed as an infusion or rubbed in as a salve, had long been touted as a cure for diseases such as headaches, abdominal cramps, coughs and colds, rheumatism, toothache, and even typhoid fever and cholera. But the insufflation of tobacco smoke into the rectum of insane patients as a method of purging had an interesting history. North American indigenous groups had been using the tobacco smoke enema for as long as centuries to resuscitate those who had nearly drowned. The practice was adopted, and adapted, by European humane societies during the eighteenth century. A victim of near-drowning in London's Thames River, for example, would have been revived by the "pipe smoker medic" affiliated with the Royal Humane Society, who would blow tobacco smoke into an enema tube inserted into the victim's anus. The smoke was thought to both warm the body and stimulate the respiration, thus reviving the victim. This use of tobacco smoke also was found useful by a few asylum physicians who subjected patients to near-drowning via the bath of surprise [see **Salutary Fear**]. It may be interesting to note that the phrase "to blow smoke up one's ass" originated with this method of resuscitation, and to this day refers to getting a reaction or a rise out of someone.

Because tobacco smoke stimulated the intestinal tract as well as the respiratory system, it also acted as a purgative and for asylum physicians looking to add to their therapeutic armamentarium, the insufflation of tobacco smoke was ideal and new technological devices on the market made administration quite effortless. These "fumigators," as they were called in the United States, had metal boxes to hold the lit tobacco; a tube attached to one side of the box was inserted into the patient's rectum, and a second tube on the opposite side of the box was attached to a pair of bellows. The tobacco smoke enema was used and recommended by a few prominent asylum physicians in Great Britain, Europe and North America, but did not have widespread use.

If the use of tobacco smoke enema as a purgative was short-lived, purging was not. As a family physician who had been seconded to work during World War I in the Prestwich

Asylum in northern England, Montagu Lomax was appalled at the routine use of therapeutics which he saw as inhumane. And high on his list was the administration of croton oil as a purgative. Extracted from the seeds of Croton tiglium trees, the viscid oil raised blisters when applied to the skin [see **Counterirritation**], and caused severe diarrhea when taken internally. While Lomax agreed that the occasional administration of purgatives to relieve constipation was necessary, it was the routine and sometimes castigatory use of croton oil that he found most offensive:

> Nearly all insane persons, whether in asylums or not, are habitually constipated. And nothing tends more to clear their heads, improve their tempers, and abort or cut short a mental crisis, than the proper regulation of their bowels. This is commonplace in the treatment of all mental patients. Nevertheless, the aperients employed should be properly chosen, medically supervised, and their effects carefully noted. They should never be given indiscriminately ... and the use of stock bottles and routine treatment by the Ward Charges is to be deprecated.... When I first took office I found the use of croton oil almost universal.... [T]he drug is used much too frequently and indiscriminately, and, worse still, often as a punishment. It is in that latter light that all patients regard it.... It is probably responsible for more harm [e.g. dysentery, colitis] than all the other drugs used in asylums put together.... I once took a two minim capsule myself, for I was anxious to judge of the effects of a drug in such constant use. The experience was extremely unpleasant.... The bowels, after a strong cotton purge, may be opened ten or even twenty times. Often there is severe griping as well, and the patient may be violently sick. The pulse rate is markedly lowered, feeble cases may become blue and cyanotic, and may even faint [Lomax, p. 99].

Lomax's expose on asylum therapeutics, published in 1922, was unsettling to professionals, politicians and the public alike. A Departmental Committee was put together to examine the charges made in it and summoned Lomax to give testimony. He declined. Certain that the Committee was intent on glossing over the most serious of his allegations, Lomax took his case once again to the public whose concern about the treatment of the insane had taken on fresh urgency as asylums brimmed with shell-shocked and mind-shattered ex-soldiers. He reprinted, in book form, a series of articles that appeared in a magazine about the experiences of the pseudonymous Rachel Grant-Smith who had been held in five different British asylums. In unembellished prose, Grant-Smith described the appalling treatment she both had experienced and witnessed over the twelve years of her institutionalization. Although her complaints about maltreatment were dismissed at the time of her confinement as "delusions of persecution" by asylum officials, and the magazine articles published after her release prompted no official enquiry, the book figured significantly in what came to be known as the "Lomax Affair"—a series of investigations, enquiries, cover-ups, whitewashes and inter-professional squabbles that circuitously led to the passage of the 1930 Mental Treatment Act.

## *Spermatic Evacuation*

The ejaculation of sperm, either through masturbation or coitus. Historically, masturbation had been condemned by the Church as a sin, but it was with the 1715 publication of a pamphlet with the long-winded titled of *Onania, or the heinous sin of self-pollution, and all of its frightful consequences in both sexes considered, with spiritual and physical advice to those who have already injured themselves by this abominable practice,* that the "trinity of ideas that would come to dominate the nineteenth century—sin, vice, and self-destruction" first emerged (Stengers & Van Neck, p. 38). That trinity was reified by Samuel Auguste Daniel Tissot, an influential Swiss physician and Vatican advisor who labeled all non-procreative sexual activity as onanism and cited the ominous physical debilitations that resulted: decay of bodily strength and agility, aching in the head and joints, disorders of the intestines, and weakening of procreative power.

The earliest link between masturbation and insanity was forged by the "Father of American Psychiatry," Benjamin Rush in the early nineteenth century. Citing several cases he had treated, he conjectured that masturbatory insanity was more common than most asylum physicians realized, and that they should consider themselves well advised to be vigilant about the "train of physical and moral evils which this solitary vice fixes upon the body and mind" (Rush, p. 31). So warned, asylum physicians kept a keen eye out for signs of masturbatory insanity—and found them. After all, asylum patients often were seen masturbating, so the link between onanism and insanity was easily imagined. So easily, in fact, that in the early nineteenth century the renowned French asylum physician Jean-Étienne Dominique Esquirol declared that masturbation "is signalized in all countries, as one of the frequent causes of insanity" (Esquirol, p. 51).

While Esquirol's statement may have been hyperbolic, the fact remained that the notion of masturbatory insanity held sway throughout Western society for much of the nineteenth century and that the asylum therapeutics for treating it—wiring, circumcision, castration [see **Genital Surgery**]—were in widespread use. Therefore it is a bit ironic that spermatic evacuation by means of masturbation was ever recommended in that century for the *treatment* of insanity. That irony was compounded by the fact that it was Esquirol, himself who, however cautiously, recommended it. Esquirol cited several cases that had come to his attention in which insanity was cured by spermatic evacuation. One of those was of a twenty-four-year-old soldier who had contracted gonorrhea which, upon the advice of his comrades, he treated by drinking a tumbler of brandy in which the powder of three cartridges had been steeped. The gonorrhea disappeared, but in its place a raging insanity appeared. The soldier was wildly hallucinatory; he saw a skeleton rise from the floor of his asylum chamber, and an eagle emerge from his straw bed, ready to devour him. To protect himself, he made a circle of straw and mattress ticking on the floor, laid in the middle, and moved his head rapidly from left to right, all the time huffing and blowing to keep the skeleton and the eagle at bay. After six months in this state of fury, he began masturbating, and calmed considerably. Although both the gonorrhea and the insanity reoccurred more than once over the next several years, the calming effect of spermatic evacuation was not lost on Esquirol. Somewhat reluctant to prescribe it, he nonetheless considered the possibility that by doing so he would remove the moral condemnation from the act and that that alone would have a more salutary outcome than the act itself. "It is not easy to establish the degree of influence," he wrote, "which, in this act, belongs, respectively, to the physical and moral impression" (Esquirol, p. 197).

For Esquirol the "moral impression" of spermatic evacuation during sexual intercourse was less complicated, but he was still reticent in recommending it as a therapeutic for men or for women. Without judgment, he cited cases relayed to him by other asylum physicians of two insane patients who had engaged in the "wildest venereal transports" (Esquirol, p. 195) that cured the female and killed the male; an insane female who was cured when her long suppressed menses started again after being gang-raped; of young girls cured of hysterical melancholy by marriage. He regarded these cures as exceptions and countered that his experience showed that sexual intercourse and, for that matter, rape, marriage and/or pregnancy, risked aggravating rather than curing insanity.

A generation earlier there were asylum physicians who lauded the salutary effects of spermatic evacuation during sexual intercourse. Vincenzo Chiarugi, for example, found it to be perfectly compatible with the humanitarian reforms he was instituting at the Ospedale di Bonifazio in Florence, Italy. He had recommended it for both male and female melancholics, and actually encouraged asylum physicians to act as brokers by finding new love interests for their patients and then easing them into relationships, so as to not set off episodes of mania. Johann Christian Reil would have agreed. The physician who, although feted as the "Father of German Psychiatry" actually had little experience in treating the insane, nonetheless had strong opinions as to how they should be treated. And although the list of his prescriptions reads more like acts of medieval torture than not—hunger, thirst, red hot iron, submersion in water—he also recommended sexual intercourse, with prostitutes if necessary, to "reduce the accumulated lascivious energy that might contribute to mental disturbance" (Richards, p. 271).

That history aside, British and American asylum physicians, the latter of whom were particularly influenced by Esquirol, heeded his caution and did not recommend spermatic evacuation through sexual intercourse as an asylum therapeutic. American asylum physicians, in fact, argued whether there should be *social* intercourse between male and female insane patients within the walls of an asylum and, even more urgently, whether both sexes should be housed in the same asylum in the first place. John Minson Galt, the superintendent of Eastern State Hospital in Williamsburg, Virginia, the first asylum in the United States exclusively devoted to the care of the insane, offered an eloquent, if occasionally obtuse, argument in favor of separate asylums for the sexes. Reminding his colleagues of the "evils of this admixture" of the sexes (Galt, p. 493), and appealing to God's "unity of design" that makes it possible for birds to fly and camels to thrive in arid conditions, he argued that "it is but an extension of this idea, when we adopt the plan of providing different establishments for the two sexes, for in each case simplicity and unity are the objects sought" (Galt, p. 494).

## *Vomiting*

The inducement of the violent ejection of the contents of the stomach through the mouth. Based on the ancient humoural doctrine that insanity was both caused and worsened by an accumulation of bodily toxins, vomiting long was considered a particularly effective evacuant. It "stimulated the nerves in the abdominal region and heightened the activity of various organs; rid the stomach and upper enteron of mucus, bile, undigested foods, poisons, acids and other harmful substances; and finally, calmed or excited certain nerve centers antagonistically by inducing nausea" (Kraepelin, pp. 58–59).

A wide variety of emetic agents was used by asylum physicians to induce therapeutic vomiting. An infusion of wine with *crocus metallorum,* the yellowish or reddish oxides of some metals was favored for some time, as was black hellebore, a species of the evergreen flowering plants in the *Ranunculacea* family. "That drastic vegetable," as it came to be known, was entwined with myth, legend and superstition. In legend it was called the "Christmas Rose" because it was said to have bloomed in the snow from the tears of a young girl who had no gift to give the Christ Child in Bethlehem. Lauded by Hippocrates and Pliny for both its emetic and purgative qualities, touted in myth as having cured the insanity of the daughters of Proteus, feared for its propensity to slow and then stop the heart rate, asylum physicians administered black hellebore with both reverence and care, but not always to good effect. Philippe Pinel, physician to the Asylum de Bicêtre in Paris, France, explained why: asylum physicians were ignorant of the fact that the hellebore of legend was not black, but white and belonged to a different plant family. By the early nineteenth century the use of black hellebore as an emetic had all but ceased, and it was Pinel who eulogized its passing: "Whether we consider its empirical administration or the unfounded theories and superstitious fancies which in some instances sanctioned its employment, the disuse into which this remedy is fallen, ought to cause little regret" (Pinel, p. 254). Unwilling to give up the therapeutic with the emetic, asylum physicians then turned to ipecac syrup, powdered ipecac and especially tartrate of antimony, or tarter emetic as it was often referred to, all of which were easily administered and more efficacious in effect.

Pinel had not condemned vomiting as a therapeutic, although he, just as a number of other prominent asylum physicians of the day, had spoken out against its indiscriminate use. And for good reason. Vomiting quite recently had been the therapeutic of choice in a number of asylums and it had had its own very vocal proponents. Among them was John Monro, a member of the Monro dynasty that had been exercising its medical authority at Bethlem Hospital in London, England, since the early eighteenth century. In response to a broadside against the antiquated therapeutics of Bethlem published by William Battie, a self-proclaimed "progressive mad-doctor" at nearby St. Luke's Asylum, Monro had launched a caustic defense of the depletive therapeutics as a general method for treating insanity. On the merits of vomiting, his response to Battie dripped with sarcasm although, ironically, it actually supported his archrival's assertion that this treatment was particularly prone to misuse:

> The evacuation by vomiting is infinitely preferable to any other [depletive], if repeated experience is to be depended on; and I should be very sorry to find any one frightened from use of such an efficacious remedy by it's being called a *shocking operation, the consequence of a morbid convulsion.* I never saw or heard of the bad effect of vomits; nor can I suppose any mischief to happen, but from their being injudiciously administered; or when they are given too strong…. Why should we endeavor to give the world a shocking opinion of a remedy, that is not only safe, but greatly useful both in this and many other distempers? [Monro, pp. 50–51, italics in original].

The Monro versus Battie debate could be dismissed as nothing more that the head-butting of two physicians with sufficient ego to claim authority in all things related to insanity, but its context would argue against that dismissal. Battie's slogan "management does much more than medicine" (p. 68) anticipated the development of what came to be known as moral treatment [see **Moral Treatment**] which in its ideal, or perhaps *idealized* practice, eschewed such violent therapeutics as vomiting. But only in its idealized practice. In the daily task of caring for the insane, management perforce had to at least occasionally rely on medicine—even the violent medicine of vomiting.

Thus when the York Retreat was established in northern England in the late eighteenth century by Quaker coffee and tea merchant William Tuke, its mission of providing humane treatment of the insane was not considered compromised by the occasional therapeutic administration of vomiting. The depletive was used only when the "general health strongly indicated its necessity," and always with concomitant awareness that the "probable good would not be equal to the certain injury" (Tuke, p. 112). As moral treatment's hegemony spread, other practitioners and proponents of it also occasionally relied on what arguably was the most violent of the depletives. The forty year career of Thomas Story Kirkbride as superintendent of the Pennsylvania Hospital for the Insane in Philadelphia was co-extensive with the vogue of moral treatment in the United States. An Orthodox Quaker, Kirkbride set out a detailed plan for both the moral treatment of the insane and the moral architecture of the asylums that contained them. Yet as a physician, he was not at all opposed to using the *materia medica* of his profession, including vomiting, although more perhaps for its placebo than its medical effect. The induction of vomiting, he argued, demonstrated to insane patients that the asylum physician had mastery over their bodies as well as their minds, and that demonstration not only buoyed patients' trust in the physician but, in the process, also facilitated their recoveries. A similar philosophy underpinned the continued use of therapeutic vomiting by Vincenzo Chiarugi who introduced moral treatment to the care of insane patients at the Ospedale di Bonifazio in Florence, Italy, and by his French counterpart Philippe Pinel who, as previously noted, had spoken out against its excessive use but had incorporated it into the moral treatment regime at the Asylum de Bicêtre in Paris.

Certainly the advent of moral treatment had a great deal to do with the decline in therapeutic vomiting, as did the weakening to the point of irrelevance of both the humoural and brain inflammation doctrines that had originally justified it.

## Wet Cupping

The induction of superficial or capillary bleeding. The process of wet cupping was not only detailed in procedure but highly choreographed in execution. First, a spot free of bone and dense fat was chosen on the body of the patient and fomented with hot water. Then, a wick was dipped in alcohol, lit and swirled for mere seconds around the inside of a cupping glass [see **Counterirritation**]. The cup was placed on the chosen spot where it was to remain for only one minute, during which time the scarificator was warmed between the hands of the asylum physician. Upon removal of the cup, the tumefied skin was cut with the scarificator blades, the wick was applied once again to the cup, and the cup was placed over the incisions to collect the blood. Because each cup held approximately four ounces of blood, the juggling of multiple cups often was necessary.

"Cupping is an art," proclaimed Samuel Bayfield, a professional cupper at Guy's Hospital in London, who ran a three month course on the art in the early nineteenth century for interested students. For three guineas qualified physicians under Bayfield's stern tutelage developed the dexterity to handle glass, lamp, wick and scarificator, and the deftness to apply, reapply and remove the cups. But cupping also was a science. It was a therapeutic that was intimately linked to the theory of humouralism, and therefore made eminent sense for the treatment of insanity. It relied upon careful calibrations. Not only did the spot on the body for wet cupping have to be carefully chosen, but the blades of the scarificator had to be adjusted for the spot: one-quarter of an inch for incising the limbs, one-sixth of an inch for the scalp, one-seventh of an inch for behind the ears, and one-eighth of an inch for the temple. The amount of blood to be collected for the maximum therapeutic effect not only had to be determined before the procedure, but assessed in relationship to the physical health of the patient.

# Diet

*The treatment of insanity by the alteration of the nature, quantity and quality of the food consumed by patients.*

With changing beliefs about the nature of insanity, and about the relationship between the body, brain and mind, diet has assumed various degrees of importance to the therapeutic regimes of asylums. In the early era of asylums, and certainly before the institutionalization of the insane became *de régle,* the prevailing view of insanity was that those who suffered from it not only were deprived of reason, but of the sentience of others. What they were fed, or for that matter if they were fed at all, was of little interest. John Conolly, the medical superintendent of the Middlesex County Asylum, better known as Hanwell, reflected with disgust on his early nineteenth century predecessors' treatment of their insane patients:

> No mercy, no pity, no decent regard for affliction, for age, or for sex, existed. Old and young, men and women, the frantic and the melancholy, were treated worse, and more neglected, then the beasts of the field. The asylum resembled the dens of a squalid menagerie: the straw was raked out, and the food was thrown in through the bars; and exhibitions of madness were witnessed which are longer to be

found, because they were not the simple product of malady, but of malady aggravated by mismanagement [Conolly, 1856, p. 33].

Conolly, who had led the charge in abolishing the chains, fetters and straps of his predecessors [see **Mechanical Restraints**], took on the proper feeding of insane patients with equal fervor. Physical discomfort, he argued, impaired mental recovery, and a "scanty, ill-cooked, unwholesome diet creates a chronic uneasiness and dissatisfaction, impairs the health, and increases the mortality of an asylum" (Conolly, 1846, p. 161). To that end, he argued that diet should be regulated, at least somewhat, by the class of the patient: wealthy patients were to eat simpler and plainer food than they were accustomed to, while pauper patients were to be fed more robust and nutritious food than was their common fare. Because Hanwell Asylum was purpose-built in 1831 to care for the pauper insane, Conolly took special care with dietary arrangements. In addition to fifteen pints of fluid, the weekly quantity of solid food for female patients was slightly less than the 247.5 ounces designated for male patients. The typical menu, costing a thrifty eight-pence/day/patient, was as follows:

*Breakfast:* cocoa or milk porridge, and bread.
*Dinner:* steamed meat, yeast dumplings and vegetables on Tuesdays, Wednesdays and Fridays; baked meat on Sundays; soup and bread on Mondays; Irish stew and bread on Thursdays; and meat and potato pie on Saturdays. Each dinner meal was accompanied by a half pint of beer.
*Tea:* one pint of tea with bread and butter for female patients only.
*Supper:* cheese, bread and a half pint of beer for male patients only.

Perhaps it was inevitable that such a fare would come under criticism by those who thought it was wasted on the pauper insane who were unlikely to ever leave the asylum. The satirical magazine *Punch* certainly took a jab at it. In an article titled "The Hanwell Cookery Book," the magazine asked readers to imagine the menu that patients working in the kitchen would come up with if left to their own devices. That menu included "Apoplectic Jelly" made with 400 kangaroo eggs and steel-filings; "Methuselah Fritters" and Oltenitza Pudding"; and the perennial favorite "Croquettes a la Conolly," comprised of charred marrow bone, spring onions, oyster shells and dry glue. If left to mold, the magazine hinted, the croquettes tasted particularly good when dipped in hot treacle.

The jab aside, asylum physicians were embedded in nineteenth century society where rapid industrialization was metaphorizing the human body as a machine whose efficiency was assured by proper diet. And a properly functioning body meant a properly functioning mind—a view shared by the various regulatory bodies that oversaw public insane asylums. As a result, in their annual reports asylum physicians took great pains to discuss in detail the diets of their patients and to link them, if only inferentially, to therapeutic progress. In colonized countries such accountability was particularly problematic. Asylum physicians not only had to list the diet, but explain the nature, nutritional value, accessibility, and even the cultural and religious traditions surrounding its unfamiliar ingredients. Such was the case in Bengal, India where British physicians superintended five asylums in the late nineteenth century. Such dietary items as moong and chana dal, ghee, betel-nut, ginger and turmeric required description, as did the dietary needs of the asylums' various "Hindoo, Mahomedan, and Christian" patients (Brown, p. 5). Yet, the readers of the annual report were assured that as a result of attention to diet all patients "improve considerably in physical condition, and, with this, in most cases, there is corresponding mental improvement" (p. 64).

While a nutritious diet, in and of itself, was thought to be therapeutic, so were the social graces required for its communal consumption. In the early era of asylums, food was delivered to, sometimes even thrown into, the cells or stalls of patients. Dishes, crockery and utensils were deemed dangerous, so food had to be substantial enough to be eaten by hand. By the mid-nineteenth century, as a reflection of the growing hegemony of moral treatment [see **Moral Treatment**], communal dining was instituted in most asylums. That may seem to be nothing particularly noteworthy but, in fact, the change to communal dining was one marker of moral treatment's rejection of the age-old representation of the insane as bestial, and its acceptance of their humanity. Thus, it represented a significant reform in both procedure and philosophy. It was not instituted, however, without control and caution, as evidenced by Jean-Étienne Dominique Esquirol's description of instituting communal dining at the Salpêtrière Asylum in Paris, France:

> I chose eighty patients, and I divided them into groups of ten. In each group, I took a leader whose job it was to get the tablemates together, bring them to the table, and make sure that they all took off their hats and washed their hands when they came in. The leader was to preside over the table and make sure that at the end of the meal everyone put his spoon, fork and knife back on his plate; for I am not afraid to give them knives, on condition of course that they never take them away, and I take precautions so I will know right away who is not respecting this duty. From the very first day, everything proceeded in an orderly fashion, and from that point on letting the [patients] eat in the dining hall has been a great favor to them, a favor that works to the benefit of their cure [Leuret, pp. 170–171].

As therapeutic as good diets were, the cost of food was a hefty line item in any asylum's annual budget. In the United States, where asylums often were constructed in rural areas, many state asylums were self-sustaining, or at least, very nearly so. Traverse City State Hospital in northern Michigan, for example, purchased its first cows and a bull in the late nineteenth century and over subsequent years developed a sizeable dairy herd that included a world champion milk cow named Traverse Colantha Walker. On the asylum's grounds, the cow's gravestone commemorates the 200,114.9 gallons of milk she produced over her lifetime. The asylum also had a piggery, and an extensive system of greenhouses in which a wide assortment of vegetables were grown.

Yet, and especially in urban asylums, the temptation to scrimp sometimes was considerable. In virtually every official inquiry into the treatment of asylum patients, the quantity and quality of food was an item on the agenda. Such was the case in the investigation of the New Jersey State Asylum for the Insane in Morris Plains in the late nineteenth century. There, a legislative committee heard testimony that rotting meat, old eggs, beans filled with worms, musty tea, and bitter bread were being served to the patients. A slab of "atrocious [and] rank" butter, taken from the asylum larder, was presented in evidence, generating an "animated discussion" among repulsed committee members as to whether it was "lard, oleomargarine [or] a conglomeration of axle grease, lard and cottonseed oil" ("Bad Butter and Bread," p. 8). Its composition undetermined, sheets of paper then were placed over the slab until it was finally taken away—that way, no committee member had to look at it, or smell it. The inquiry led to the firing of the asylum's warden.

Throughout history, periods of collective trauma often resulted in food shortages and diet crises in asylums around the world. During the two World Wars, for example, food was severely rationed, resulting in the deteriorated mental and physical health of insane patients, as well as in high mortality rates. French asylums during World War II provide an interesting illustration. By 1940, the German-occupied country was verging on famine. Starving asylum patients at times were reduced to eating eggshells and grass; severe weight reduction often resulted in edema, diarrhea, chronic fatigue and, for some, coma and death. Between 1940 and the end of the war in 1945, in fact, more than 40,000 French asylum patients starved to death; if that number were to be reduced to a mortality rate, it would be more than three times higher than that of the five years both preceding and following the war.

Even in more contemporary times, the impact of civil unrests, political upheavals, economic crises, and government corruption on food security, and the consequent impact of food insecurity on the mental and physical health of asylum patients is profound. At the Accra Psychiatric Hospital, for example, asylum officials warned in 2006 that the looming food crisis in Ghana, coupled with the government's indifference towards the insane, would surely mean that patients would starve to death. That same fear was expressed in Greece in 2012. The economic crisis there left the State Infirmary of Leros without the requisite funds to feed its 350 insane patients. As late as 2013, patients in the Zanzibar Psychiatric Hospital in Tanzania were assured of a light breakfast and a light dinner, courtesy of private donors, to keep them from starving to death. The asylum no longer had funds to purchase food.

A crisis such as this was not predicted by the asylum physicians of previous eras. By the early nineteenth century virtually all agreed that a nutritious diet was therapeutic, in and of itself. But it was the distinguished German physician, Johann Gaspar Spurzheim, who warned at the time that all patients should not be nourished "out of the same kettle" (Spurzheim, p. 184). Rather, he argued, diet should be adjusted not only to the type of insanity patients suffered, but to the therapeutic strategies that were being used to treat them. This admonition, voiced by other asylum physicians as well, prompted creative attempts throughout the nineteenth century to match diet to disorder. None of these attempts proved particularly successful and most were no longer in use by the turn into the twentieth century.

## References

Atkins, P. (2010). *Liquid materialities: A history of milk, science and the law.* Farnham, UK: Ashgate.
"Bad butter and bread" (1888, April 14). *New York Times,* p. 8.
Beveridge, A. (1998). Life in the asylum: Patients' letters from Morningside, 1873–1908. *History of Psychiatry, 9,* 431–469.
Boehme, D.H. (1977). Preplanned fasting in the treatment of mental disease: Survey of current Soviet literature. *Schizophrenia Bulletin, 3,* 288–296.
Brown, J.C. (1871). *Annual reports of the insane asylums in Bengal, for the year 1870.* Calcutta, India: Bengal Secretariat Office.
Clouston, T.S. (1883). *Clinical lectures on mental diseases.* London: J. & A. Churchill.
Clouston, T.S. (1911). *Unsoundness of mind.* New York: E.P. Dutton.
Conolly, J. (1846). Diet of the insane; its influence on recovery, and on the mortality of asylums. *Lancet, 2,* 167–170.
Conolly, J. (1856). *The treatment of the insane without mechanical restraints.* London: Smith, Elder.
Cott, A. (1971). Controlled fasting treatment of schizophrenia in the U.S.S.R. *Schizophrenia, 3,* 2–10.
Cott, A. (1974), Controlled fasting treatment for schizophrenia. *Journal of Orthomolecular Psychiatry, 3,* 301–311.
Cox, J.M. (1806). *Practical observations on insanity.* 2nd ed. London: C. & R. Baldwin.
de Young, M. (2010). *Madness: An American history of mental illness and its treatment.* Jefferson, NC: McFarland.
Digby, A. (1985). Moral treatment at the Retreat, 1796–1846. In W. F. Bynum, R. Porter, and M. Shepherd (eds.), *The anatomy of madness,* Vol. 2, pp. 52–72. London: Tavistock.
Earle, P. (1841). *A visit to thirteen asylums for the insane in Europe: To which are added a brief notice of similar institutions in transatlantic countries and in the United States.* Philadelphia: J. Dobson.
Fouts, P.J., Helmer, O.M., Lepkovsky, S., and Jukes, T.H. (1937). Treatment of human pellagra with nicotinic acid. *Proceedings of the Society of Experimental Biology and Medicine, 37,* 405–407.
Gauchet, M., and Swain, G. (1999). *Madness and democracy: The modern psychiatric universe.* Trans. C. Porter. Princeton, NJ: Princeton University Press.
Hallaran, W.S. (1818). *Practical observations on the causes and cure of insanity.* Cork, Ireland: Edwards and Savage.
"Hanwell cookery book" (1853). *Punch, 25,* p. 265.
"Hanwell lunatic asylum" (1839/1840). *Eclectic Journal of Medicine, 4,* 256–259.
Haslam, J. (1809). *Observations on madness and melancholy.* London: J. Callow.
Heinroth, J.C.A. (1975/1818). *Textbook of disturbances of mental life.* Baltimore: Johns Hopkins University Press.
Hufeland, C.W. (1855). *Enchiridion medicum, or, the practice of medicine.* 4th ed. Trans. C. Bruchhausen. New York: William Radde.
Kantorovich, N.V., and Constantinovich, S.K. (1935). Effect of alcohol in catatonic syndromes: Preliminary report. *American Journal of Psychiatry, 92,* 651–654.
Karell, P. (1866). On the milk cure. *Half-Yearly Abstract of the Medical Sciences, 44,* 177–180.
Kotseli, A. (2012, June 7). "Mental institution in the

Island of Leros faces vast food shortages." Retrieved at http://Greece.greekreporter.com/2012/06/07/mental-institution-in-the-island-of-leros-faces-vast-food-shortages.
Leuret, F. (1840). *Le traitement moral de la folie.* Paris: Ballière.
Madden, R.R. (1829). *Travels in Turkey, Egypt, Nubia and Palestine.* London: Henry Colburn.
Managers of the Middletown State Homeopathic Hospital (1893). *Annual report.* Albany, NY: James B. Lyon.
Masson, M., and Azorin, J-M. (2006/2007). The French mentally ill in World War II: The Lesson of History. *International Journal of Mental Health, 35,* 26–39.
Miller, C. (2005). *Traverse City State Hospital.* Charleston, SC: Arcadia.
Mitchell, S.W. (1900). *Fat and blood.* 8th ed. Philadelphia: J.B. Lippincott.
Moran, J.E. (2000). *Committed to the state asylum; Insanity and society in nineteenth century Quebec and Ontario.* Montreal: McGill-Queen's University Press.
Pereira, J. (1843). *A treatise on food and diet.* New York: J. & H.G. Langley.
Pinel, P. (1806). *A treatise on insanity.* Trans. D.D. Davis. Sheffield, UK: W. Todd.
"Psychiatric hospital in distress" (2006, November 9). Retrieved at http://www.modernghana.com/news/119764/1/psychiatric-hospital-in-distress inmates-face-immin.html.
Rajakumar, K. (2000). Pellagra in the United States. *Southern Medical Journal, 93,* 272–277.
Rush, B. (1830). *Medical inquiries and observations upon diseases of the mind.* 4th ed. Philadelphia: John Grigg.
Simpson, F.O. (1901). Some points on the treatment of the chronic insane. *American Journal of Insanity, 57,* 601–615.
Spurzheim, J.G. (1836). *Observations on the deranged manifestations of the mind, or insanity.* 3rd ed. Boston: Marsh, Capen & Lyon.
Trustees and Superintendents of the Indiana Hospital for the Insane (1888). *Fortieth annual report.* Indianapolis, IN: Wm. Burford.
Tuke, S. (1813). *Description of the Retreat, an institution near York, for insane persons.* York, UK: W. Alexander.
Turner, B. (1982). The government of the body: Medical regimes and the rationalization of diet. *British Journal of Sociology, 33,* 254–269.
U.S. Department of Agriculture (1902). *Annual report of the Office of Experimental Stations.* Washington, D.C: Government Printing Office.
Walsh, O. (2012). Cure or custody: Therapeutic philosophy at the Connaught District Lunatic Asylum. In M. Preston and M. Ó hÓgartaigh (eds.), *Gender and medicine in Ireland, 1700–1950,* pp. 69–85. Syracuse, NY: Syracuse University Press.
Yashiro, N. (1986). Clinico-psychological and pathophysiological studies on fasting therapy. *Sapporo Medical Journal, 55,* 125–136.
Yussuf, I. (2013, October 23). "Tanzania: Psychiatric hospital short of food." Retrieved at http://allafrica.com/stories/201310230218.html.

## Gospel of Fatness

A diet composed of a large quantity of fatty foods. The gospel of fatness was preached by Thomas S. Clouston, superintendent of the Royal Edinburgh Asylum, also known as Morningside, in the late nineteenth century. It was his observation that the personal and social stresses that caused melancholia also caused poor general health, such as sleeplessness, sluggish bowels, low pulse and, most particularly, thinness. A significant gain in weight, he reasoned, would restore general health and cure melancholia. Insisting that the melancholic patient "cannot fatten too soon or too fast," he provided a steady diet of ham, eggs, cheese, fish, fowl, game, claret, burgundy, ale, porter, custard and as many as sixteen tumblers of milk every day (Clouston, 1883, p. 113). In addition, any particular food the patient especially liked was provided in as great a quantity as could be digested.

Clouston claimed great success with the gospel of fatness, although the diet was only part of a tightly regimented therapeutic regime. The case of J.R., a young melancholic, illustrated that point:

> She was ordered, and made to take, iron and aloes, with fresh air and fattening diet. She got worse at first, and hallucinations of hearing developed. She distinctly heard voices telling her she was the worst person alive. She would have refused food had she been allowed to do so. In about two months she began to improve in body and mind, especially in bodily looks and weight. For three months longer she remained depressed, and then menstruated after a series of hot baths and mustard to her feet. She brightened up from the first day of menstruation as if a cloud had been lifted off her mind, and she kept well ever after [Clouston, 1883, pp. 475–476].

Interestingly, given the fact that most of the patients in the Royal Edinburgh Asylum were paupers, many felt they benefited more from the long walks, the dances and lectures, the productive work and the sports activities that Clouston insisted upon than they did from the diet. In fact, many loathed both the quantity and the quality of the diet, as these excerpts from patients' letters indicated:

> Miss E.D.: I feel I cannot stand this place a minute longer and soon I lose the brains I had and not be able to interest myself in others and everything that goes on in the world.... I feel I shall go on degenerating in this environment into an animal that only lives to eat—as we do here!—and has not thought beyond. For really that is all the "treatment" consists of.
> Miss D.: I am suffering the most awful agonies inwardly by being forced to swallow unlimited quantities of every kind of food and liquids every few hours.
> Robert C.: I have been required to take such quantities as I could never comfortably take all my life. I assure you my life here has been one of exceptional horror, forced to eat large quantities of coarse food which I could not digest.
> George R., 26, clerk: The food here is of the very coarsest. Porridge or coffee for breakfast with dry bread, at 11 o'clock dry bread and cheese, beer or milk... Dinner at 2 o'clock broth and mutton ... then tea at 6, one cup and almost dry bread [Beveridge, pp. 431, 440].

Despite Clouston's proclamation that asylum physicians should "preach and practice the gospel of fatness in season and out of season to melancholics" (Clouston, 1911, p. 115), it was neither scientifically nor economically appealing to most of them. With the noted exception of several asylums in Australia that had used it in the early 1900s, only a few scattered and short-lived experiments with its use, all with less positive results than Clouston touted, were conducted in asylums around the world.

## *Hospital Diet*

The addition of milk, eggs and wine to supplement the standard asylum diet of tea, bread, soup, beef and potatoes. The hospital diet generally was reserved for patients whose physical health had been significantly compromised by their insanity. Such was the case at the Connaught District Lunatic Asylum in Ballinasloe, Ireland, one of the earliest of the twenty-two district asylums built in that country during the nineteenth century. There, women patients were most likely poor, often malnourished and physically exhausted from childbearing and childrearing. The health of those diagnosed with puerperal insanity was of considerable concern, and the hospital diet was found to accelerate their recovery.

## *Hunger Cure, or Famine Cure*

A diet predicated on the greatest possible abstinence from food. Over the course of several days or weeks patients' food intake was diminished by degrees until they were consuming only enough to sustain their lives. As their symptoms of insanity abated, their food intake was gradually increased. It was typical in the nineteenth century for patients undergoing the hunger cure in German asylums to also be isolated in dimly lit, closed rooms with only a light circulation of air in order to reduce any stimuli that might act adversely on them.

The hunger cure represented a depletive or antiphlogistic approach [see **Depletive Therapy**] to the treatment of aggressive and agitated types of insanity in particular. The received wisdom of this approach was that when food was withheld, the diseased and toxic humours were thrown off first, thus purifying the blood as it circulated through the body and the brain. One of the more enthusiastic devotees of this theory, and of the hunger cure as a therapeutic, was Christoph Wilhelm Hufeland the director of the medical college at the University of Berlin who also was affiliated with the Berlin Charité Hospital. He claimed to be able to cure two-thirds of all cases of insanity by irritating the abdominal nervous system which, he argued, was strongly influential on the brain. While that irritation could be produced by the administration of cream of tartar, hellebore or calomel, it was just as effectively produced, he argued, by hunger.

His colleague, Anton Müller, agreed and cited two cases of insanity cured by the hunger cure. One was of a patient who had become disorientated after a series of epileptic attacks. He had languished in an asylum for three years, his disorientation unremediated, before he was administered the hunger cure. Over several weeks his food intake was reduced to a twice daily offering of two ounces of lean meat and two ounces of bread. Within days his disorientation disappeared and he remained in remission until he returned to his normal diet. Müller somewhat reluctantly acknowledged that the remarkable cure could have been attributed to the daily administration of a sarsaparilla concoction, powdered belladonna leaves and a few grains of powdered rhubarb or, for that matter, to those substances in conjunction with the hunger cure, but the second case he cited had none of those complications. That was the case of an adolescent peasant boy whose insanity had resisted all conventional treatments. As a last resort, his food intake was reduced to a twice daily offering of two ounces of lean meat and two ounces of bread. He was discharged as cured six weeks later and suffered no remission when he resumed his normal diet.

While the hunger cure was not practiced just in German asylums, many asylum physicians outside of Germany were interested in at. At the Pennsylvania Hospital in the United States, Benjamin Rush was inclined to accept its underlying rationale, although he continued to administer a slightly more generous version of the hunger cure referred to as the "low diet." Yet, in regards to the hunger cure, he wrote: "I am disposed to think favorably of it. [It] is calculated to work in two ways....by lessening the quantity of blood by the abstraction of the ailment and by exciting the disease of hunger in the stomach to such a degree as to enable it to predominate over the disease of the brain" (Rush, p. 191).

Other early nineteenth century asylum physicians disagreed. Philippe Pinel, for one, recalled the scarcity of food during the French Revolution that reduced the diet at the Asylum de Bicêtre in Paris to one pound of bread per day per patient, leaving them wandering around the asylum in a "delirium of hunger" (Pinel, p. 32). When food supplies stabilized after the Revolution in 1792, the diet was increased to two pounds of bread per patient per day, along with one or two servings of soup. Not only did the mortality rate decrease sharply, but the overall physical and mental health of the patients increased dramatically. The experience left him with the impression that hunger fueled insanity more than it ever cured it.

Although Pliny Earle, the resident physician of the Friends Asylum for the Insane near Philadelphia, Pennsylvania, made no definitive statement on the hunger cure, it would be reasonable to assume he would have agreed with Pinel. In the first edition of his book that detailed his visits to a number of European asylums, if he mentioned food at all it was to describe its method of delivery to the patients rather than its quantity or quality. But in the second edition, to which he appended descriptions of asylums in other parts of the word penned by other physicians, the deprivation of food, whether by fate or fiat, was not glossed over. Earle appended a report from the Irish physician Richard Madden of his visit to the Cairo Lunatic Asylum in Egypt in the early nineteenth century. There he found filthy patients chained in cells who cried out for food as he passed by. He learned that they had not eaten for more than a day because the only source of food was the charitable offerings of people in the community. When two local women then came into the asylum with two cakes and a large watermelon that was broken into pieces and thrown at the patients, Madden was appalled by what he witnessed. "They devoured what they got like hungry tigers, some of them thrusting their tongues through the bars, others screaming for more," he wrote. "I have never seen nature subdued to such lowness" (Earle, p. 79).

The withdrawal of food, not for the purpose of achieving a hunger cure but for disciplining or punishing patients, was often tempting to asylum physicians. The eminent German physician Johann Christian Heinroth dismissed any concern and encouraged his colleagues to do what he himself regularly did, and that was "punish disobedience and bad manners displayed by the mentally disturbed by depriving them of food" (Heinroth, p. 297). This method of discipline certainly outlasted the hunger diet as a therapeutic. By the turn into the twentieth century, most asylums physicians agreed that a wholesome, if not generous, diet was an important adjunct to other therapeutics. And, especially in North America, where cattle and chickens often were being raised on asylum farms, and vegetables and sometimes grain were growing in surrounding fields, the diet of patients improved considerably and the deprivation of food, whether for punishment or treatment, increasingly was considered anti-therapeutic.

It may be interesting to note that the hunger cure is still practiced in some Eastern European asylums. Renamed "controlled fasting," and sometimes also referred to as "total food abstinence" or "controlled starvation," it is most often used to rest the brain and nervous system and detoxify the blood of treatment-resistant schizophrenic patients. The controlled fast, which involved twenty-five to thirty continuous days of consuming only water, was preceded by a several month long preparatory protocol that involved weekly fasting for thirty-six hours, and followed by the gradual introduction of food during a month long recovery period. Yuri Serge Nikolayev, who was in charge of the fasting unit at the Moscow Institute of Psychiatry, treated more than 6,000 such patients by controlled fasting and reported that 70 percent achieved such significant improvement that they were restored to full functioning.

One of those patients was a twenty-seven-year-old Polish student. Withdrawn, isolated, restless, he had been unable to concentrate on his studies and had traveled to Moscow to admit himself into the Institute, despite having resisted on previous occasions the suggestion that he seek psychiatric care.

> On admission he was described as being well oriented exhibiting circumstantial speech and feelings of unreality. He complained of weakness, poverty of ideation, poor memory and quick exhaustion.... His facial expression was rigid, speech was monstrous, and he found great difficulty in communicating. He felt hopeless and saw no future for himself. He was treated with insulin coma and his condition remained essentially unchanged [Cott, 1971, pp. 8–9].

After a twenty-eight day fast he was put into a recovery program, and his spirits gradually rose, his appetite returned, "his head felt clear, thinking was clear and concentration was markedly improved.... [C]olors became brighter, thinking became easier" and his feeling of emptiness was filled with the hope that he would have a bright future (Cott, 1971, p. 9).

Nikolayev's claims attracted the attention of Alan Cott, a former psychoanalyst who had an increasing interest in the trendy emerging field of orthomolecular psychiatry [see **Orthomolecular Therapy**]. After observing Nikolayev's treatment protocol, Cott selected thirty-five schizophrenic patients at the Gracie Square Hospital, a private and short-term psychiatric hospital in New York City, as subjects of his own experiment with controlled fasting. All of the subjects had been diagnosed more than five years before, and none had demonstrated any significant improvement under conventional treatments. Just as his mentor had done, Cott withheld all food from them, allowed them to drink as much water as they desired, and required that they adhere to a daily regime of outdoor walks, breathing exercises, hydrotherapy procedures [see **Hydrotherapy**], cleansing enemas and general massage. At the completion of the controlled fast, the patients remained in the hospital for a month, during which time food in the form of milk, fruit and vegetables was gradually introduced into their diet.

Cott noted significant improvement in schizophrenic symptoms for 70 percent of the patients, as long as they remained on a post-treatment low fat diet and took prophylactic fasts three to five days each month. That improvement was maintained for six years for those patients who followed the post-treatment protocol.

Controlled fasting had a short shelf life as a therapeutic. Despite having been heralded as an epochal breakthrough in the treatment of schizophrenia, the same encouraging results of the studies conducted by Nikolayev and Cott were not repeated in controlled clinical trials. The therapeutic certainly stimulated interest in the role that diet and even specific types of foods might play in both the etiology and treatment of schizophrenia, an interest that persists to the present day. And it also piqued some interest in its efficacy in treating psychoneurotic patients. In Japan, a regime of controlled fasting resulted in the significant improvement of 87 percent of the forty-nine psychoneurotic patients to whom it was administered.

## Intoxication

The creation of a state of drunkenness by the administration of large quantities of alcohol. While beer often accompanied meals in nineteenth century asylums and occasional glasses of wine were given to induce sleep, excessive imbibing by patients not only was forbidden but, for some patients, was suspected as the cause of their insanity in the first place. Thus the recommendation of Joseph Mason Cox, physician and proprietor of the private Fishponds Asylum near Bristol, England, that intoxication be used as a therapeutic, was vehemently dismissed by other asylum physicians.

Cox's argument for intoxication was based on his observation that when certain types of melancholy, particularly religious in nature, progressed as they inevitably did into paroxysms of furious mania, recovery usually quite quickly followed. Therefore, he reasoned, if paroxysms of mania could be induced by continuous intoxication, then recovery could be accelerated.

Despite the fact that early nineteenth century asylum physicians were experimenting with all types of stimuli for producing therapeutic states of excitement to counteract insanity [see **Rotation, Oscillation and Vibration**], Cox's use of continual intoxication was widely ridiculed. Among the critics was the estimable John Haslam, apothecary to Bethlem Hospital in London, who dismissed Cox's recommendation to "await the feast of Reason from the orgies of Bacchus" (Haslam, p. 307) as unworthy of detailed comment.

Unworthy of comment it may have been, but intoxication as a therapeutic maintained enough appeal that as late as the early twentieth century it was used to treat catatonic schizophrenia. Two asylum physicians, N.V. Kantorovich and S.K. Constantinovich intravenously administered a watery solution of brandy to fifteen catatonic patients at the First and Second Psychiatric Hospitals of Leningrad, Russia. Their blood alcohol concentration levels were raised to 0.2 percent, a level generally associated with slight euphoria, mild relaxation and some lightheadedness. Their results revealed that four patients showed no change in symptoms; four showed some improvement, becoming more talkative and sociable; and the remaining seven not only showed improvement but maintained it—but only as long as they were under the influence of alcohol. Continual intoxication was not strongly recommended as a therapeutic by the asylum physicians, but was used sporadically in some Eastern European asylums well into the mid-twentieth century.

## Low Diet, or Lowering Diet

A diet consisting mainly of liquids such as milk, tea and broth, with rice, gruel, or vegetables. Not to be confused with the hunger or famine cure, the low diet provided small quantities of food for antiphlogistic purposes, and under the theory that it worked as well as bloodletting in removing the excess blood that inflamed the brain causing mania and violence.

At the Pennsylvania Hospital, Benjamin Rush administered the low diet which consisted wholly of water and vegetables "of the least nutritious nature" (Rush, p. 191). He hastily noted, though, that this diet would succeed in reducing mania only if the patients had been accustomed before the onset of their insanity to a diet rich in meat and bread; for those who were not, it was unlikely to be effective. In Rush's opinion, the low diet rarely was sufficient in and of itself to deplete the cerebral vessels, thus he used it in conjunction with purging and copious bleeding [see **Depletive Therapy**].

Such allegiance to the phlogistic theory of insanity also was expressed in the therapeutics of William Rees at the Toronto Temporary Asylum in Canada. As late as the mid-nineteenth century, and much to the chagrin of his colleagues, Rees was still bleeding his patients, applying blisters and setons, and subjecting them to a low diet, all in an effort to reduce and tranquilize vascular and nervous action. Against criticism, Rees boasted a cure rate of 60 percent. Rees was, in many ways, a "transitional figure in [asylum] therapeutics" (Moran, p. 82), caught in the cross-stream of the historical humoural treatments of bleeding, purging and vomiting that assaulted the body, and the more modern suasions of moral treatment that engaged the mind [see **Moral Treatment**]. As the latter gained prominence, even hegemony, the low diet by itself or in combination with other therapeutics was increasingly disparaged.

In his description of the York Retreat in northern England, inarguably the *loco laudato* of moral treatment, Samuel Tuke described a daily menu rich in milk, bread, cheese, meat, fruit and beer and acknowledged that it would be dismissed as "more liberal than judicious" by those asylum physicians who still relied upon reducing therapeutics including the low diet (Tuke, p. 124). His own experience, however, showed that not only did the low diet fail to relieve the symptoms of insanity, but that it often exacerbated them. Feeling no inclination to alter the Retreat's menu, he cited in detail a case in which a substantial diet cured a "dangerous lunatic" after a low diet had failed to do so:

> Case 74 affords very striking evidence in favour of a liberal, nourishing diet, even when great irritation or violence exists. The patient was described as a furious, dangerous lunatic; and the reducing system had been fully tried upon him, with an aggravation of his complaint. The opposite mode was then pursued; and his appetite, from being long famished, was almost voracious for many days. It gradually lessened, till it arrived at the common standard. He took no medicine; and under the treatment he met with, his irritation of mind gradually subsided, and his recovery was very rapid and complete [Tuke, p. 125].

As phlogistic theories of insanity lost their hold by the early twentieth century, the low diet was abandoned as a therapeutic, whether stand alone or adjunctive. Diet, of course, remained a topic of considerable discussion, but that conversation between asylum physicians increasingly focused on achieving the proper restorative balance of protein, fats and carbohydrates. On the necessity of finding that balance, Arthur Van Gellhorn, medical superintendent of the Provincial Lunatic Asylum at Ueckermünde, Germany, was fond of reciting the old aphorism, "As a man eats, so he thinks," a proverb appropriate for this new interest in how the functions of the brain might be influenced by the nourishment of the body.

## *Milk Diet, or Milk Cure, or Milk Regime, or Nutritive Cure*

The substitution for, or the supplementation of, a standard asylum diet with milk consumed every few hours. Although a staple of diet today, the very idea of milk as a dietary food source, and a nutritious one at that, hid scientific, technological, legal, commercial and even moral considerations under milk's "blanket of innocent whiteness" (Atkins, p. 217). By the early nineteenth century, however, milk had become an accepted and relatively inexpensive food source in industrialized countries of the world and often was used to supplement the standard diet of insane asylum patients. Many asylums, in fact, maintained their own herds of cows and had milking barns on the grounds.

Successes in treating chronic physical diseases such as colitis, asthma and heart problems with the substitution version of the milk diet were reported in the mid-nineteenth century by the Estonian physician Philipp Karell, physician to the Emperor of Russia, and were widely reported around the world. Similar successes in treating nervousness and neurasthenia during the rest cure [see **Bed Therapy**] with the supplementation version of the milk diet were reported by the American neurologist, S. Weir Mitchell.

That said, the milk cure was not particularly portable as far as public insane asylums were concerned. It was experimented with and with disappointing results in a few asylums in Europe where, aside from Karell, it had no particularly enthusiastic proponents, In the United States, the milk cure often was used by homeopathic physicians in their outpatient practices and clinics, so when the first state homeopathic asylum was established in Middletown, New York, in the late nineteenth century, the milk cure achieved some institutional legitimacy as a therapeutic.

That homeopathic asylum proved itself loyal to its informal motto of "Meat, milk and rest." Its 875 patients had consumed nearly 75,000 gallons of milk the previous year, as a supplement to the regular asylum diet, and in service of the milk cure which, at this asylum, was a curious hybrid of Karrel's substitution and Mitchell's supplementation version. According to the annual report:

> We have come also to use more frequently than formerly a warm liquid diet. We give our patients all the milk they will drink, and use only a moderate amount of solid food. In some instances we mix raw egg with the milk; and in others we give a mixture of milk, Mellin's food [a milk modifier comprised of wheaten flour, malt and potash], and bovinine [condensed beef juice]—one pint of the former to a tablespoon of each of the latter [Managers of the Middletown State Homeopathic Hospital, p. 111].

As in all asylums, food food-refusing patients posed a difficult problem. Loathe to use the aggressive feeding techniques employed by many other asylums [see **Forced Feeding**], the physicians at Middletown came upon a unique remedy. Having read of the successful treatment of two food-refusing patients by a German asylum physician who had injected them with salt water in order to produce a burning sensation that distracted them from their delusions, the Middletown physicians mixed one teaspoon of salt with one pint of milk to produce "salted milk" that they then administered to food-refusing patients via feeding tubes. Seven of the twelve patients to whom the salted milk cure was administered began eating by the end of the day; the remaining patients were given multiple applications of salted milk and all began eating after a few days, although each reverted to food-refusal, if only on occasion, after that.

## *Pellagra Diet*

A diet that used little or no maize and that was rich in niacin, or vitamin B3. In some parts of the world, the diets of the poor were heavily reliant upon maize. This was especially true in India, Egypt, Romania, Italy and in the Southern United States. As a result, a large number acquired pellagra, a disease characterized by dermatitis and diarrhea, as well as by delirium that often brought them into asylum care. Because its cause was at first unknown, pellagra was thought to be a communicable disease and those who were diagnosed with it often were shunned in their communities as well as isolated in asylums once they were admitted.

A series of empirical and observational

studies in different parts of the world, however, eventually convinced asylum physicians that pellagra was the result of a dietary overreliance on maize and that it could be cured by a more wholesome diet. One of those studies was reported in the mid-nineteenth century by the controversial Italian physician Cesare Lombroso who posited that toxins produced by fungi that grew on maize exposed to moisture were the cause of pellagra. While this theory explained the cause of pellagra, what remained unanswered was why pellagra outbreaks also occurred *in* asylums among patients who had been admitted for other types of insanity. That had been the case at the Mount Vernon Hospital for the Colored Insane in Mount Vernon, Alabama. There, eighty-eight Black patients came down with pellagra in the early twentieth century, and more than half of them eventually died from it. Because the staff who attended them were not affected, any lingering suspicion that pellagra was an infectiously communicable disease could be dismissed. Since it was diet that differentiated the stricken patients from the staff, with the patients being fed a monotonous corn-based diet and the staff having a choice of more nutritious foods, it was theorized that corn lacked a basic nutrient for the maintenance of good health. That nutrient, niacin or vitamin B3, was isolated several years later. With public education programs, crop diversification initiatives and the fortification of processed food such as flour with niacin, pellagra was eradicated by the mid-twentieth century, thus assuring no new asylum admissions for pellagra-induced dementia. For those patients already institutionalized, the administration of niacin, then known as nicotinic acid, often reversed their delirium and restored their physical health enough to ensure their discharge.

# Electrotherapy

*The administration of electric currents to or through the body in order to treat insanity.*

The fascination with electricity as a therapeutic agent can be traced to the writings of the canonical medical authorities Hippocrates and Galen who prescribed rubbing amber, one of the so-called "electric stones,"" or applying an electric fish such as an eel or a ray, to the forehead to relieve melancholy, epilepsy and depression. From those ancient beginnings attempts to harness the therapeutic potential of electricity attracted everyone from the cleric and theologian John Wesley, to scientist-philosophers such as Benjamin Franklin, Joseph Priestley and Alexander Volta, physicians such as Luigi Galvani and Guillaume-Benjamin-Armand Duchenne, not to mention more than just a few quacks, charlatans, folk healers and stage performers. It is little wonder that the American neurologist George Miller Beard, who led the charge in the electrotherapeutic treatment of nervous disorders, once groused that it was as if "any old country Granny" could claim to be an electrotherapist (Beard & Rockwell, p. 87).

In the late nineteenth century and into the early twentieth, electrotherapy made its way from private neurology practices, nervine and health clinics, and traveling medicine shows into asylums. That transition was neither smooth nor even. Some asylum physicians were eager to try it, but budgetary constraints made the purchase of equipment and the hiring of qualified technicians onerous. Undoubtedly, a few were in equal measure in awe and frightened of its natural and even supernatural potential—this was the era of electrical machines, lighting exhibits, the electric chair and *Frankenstein*, after all. Others were skeptical about the scientific rationale for it. And for good reasons There were almost as many theories as to how electricity worked as a therapeutic as there were practitioners of electrotherapy. Promoters claimed electricity was an ethereal fluid of some kind that entered the blood vessels and then beneficially affected the brain, others claimed it was a vapor, others still, a fire; there were those who said it acted as a stimulant and those who countered that it acted as a sedative; some said it increased blood flow to the brain and others insisted it decreased blood flow to the brain; and, depending on who had the floor at the moment, electricity either bolstered healthy nervous tissue or destroyed unhealthy nervous tissue. It may have been true that during the nineteenth century the predominate metaphor of the body and the mind was that of a machine, but exactly how electricity charged that machine and kept it running was a matter of considerable disagreement.

It is interesting that the disagreement continued through what might be considered four eras of electrotherapeutics, each characterized by a distinct type of electric current: the Franklinic era of static electricity, the Galvanic era of the direct current, the Faradic era of induction coils, and the d'Arsonval era of the radiofrequency current. Each era also was characterized by a plethora of devices and gadgets, only some of which found their way into asylums. Despite the often exaggerated claims that heralded their arrival into the armamentarium of asylum therapeutics, the "golden age of electrotherapeutics" effectively ended early in the twentieth century, having fulfilled little, perhaps even none, of them.

REFERENCES

Achté, K.A., Kauko, K., and Seppälä, K. (1968). On electrosleep therapy. *Psychiatric Quarterly, 42,* 17–27.

Aldini, G. (1803). *An account of the late improvements in Galvanism.* London: Cuticle and Martin.

Beard, G.M., and Rockwell, A.D. (1892). *A practical treatise on the medical and surgical uses of electricity.* 8th ed. New York: William Wood & Co.

Beaudreau, S.A., and Finger, S. (2006). Medical electricity and madness in the 18th century: The legacies of Benjamin Franklin and Jan Ingenhousz. *Perspectives in Biology and Medicine, 49,* 330–345.

Berkwitz, N.J. (1940). Faradic shock in treatment of functional mental disorders. *Archives of Neurology and Psychiatry, 44,* 760–775.

Beveridge, A.W., and Renvoize, E.B. (1988). Electricity: A history of its use in the treatment of mental illness in Britain during the second half of the 19th century. *British Journal of Psychiatry, 153,* 157–162.

Bolwig, T.G., and Fink, M. (2009). Electrotherapy for melancholia: The pioneering contributions of Benjamin Franklin and Giovanni Aldini. *Journal of ECT, 25,* 15–18.

Céliné, L-F. (1932/1983). *Voyage au bout de la nuit (Journey to the end of night).* Trans. R. Mannheim. New York: New Directions.

Duchenne, G.B. (1872). *A treatise on localized electrization.* Trans. H. Tibbitts. London: Robert Hardwicke.

Eissler, K.R. (1986). *Freud as an expert witness.* Madison, CT: International Universities Press.

Elliott, P. (2008). "More subtle than the electric aura": Georgian medical electricity, the spirit of animation and the development of Erasmus Darwin's psychophysiology. *Medical History, 58,* 195–220.

Evans, C. (1754). A relation of a cure performed by electricity. *Medical Observations and Inquiries 1,* 83–86.

Falzeder, E., and Brabant, E. (eds.). (2000). *The correspondence of Sigmund Freud and Sándor Ferenczi, Vol. 3.* Trans. P.T. Hoffer. Cambridge: Harvard University Press.

Féré, C. (1898). Hysteria. *Twentieth Century Practice, 10,* 451–582.

Geoghegan, J.J. (1949). Electronarcosis. *Canadian Medical Association Journal, 60,* 561–566.

Gilman, S.L. (2008). Electrotherapy and mental illness: Then and now. *Journal of the History of Psychiatry, 19,* 339–357.

Jones, H.L. (1901). The use of general electrification as a means of treatment in certain forms of mental disease. *Journal of Mental Science, 47,* 245–250.

Kaufmann, F. (1916). The systematic cure of complicated psychogenic motor disorders among soldiers in one session. *Münchener Medizinische Wochenschrift Feldärztliche Beilage, 63,* 802–804.

Killen, A. (2006). *Berlin electropolis: Shock, nerves, and German modernity.* Berkeley: University of California Press.

Lerner, P. (2003). *Hysterical men: War, psychiatry, and the politics of trauma in Germany, 1890–1930.* Ithaca, NY: Cornell University Press.

Livingston, A.T. (1901). Electro-therapeutics in insanity. *Proceedings of the American Electro-Therapeutic Association,* 342–351. Philadelphia: F.A. Davis Company.

Newth, A.H. (1873). The galvanic current applied in the treatment of insanity. *Journal of Mental Science, 19,* 79–86.

Parent, A. (2004). Giovanni Aldini: From animal electricity to human brain stimulation. *Canadian Journal of Neurological Science, 31,* 576–584.

Paterson, A.S., and Milligan W.L. (1948). The technique and application of electronarcosis. *Proceedings of the Royal Society of Medicine, 41,* 575–586.

Porter, R. (2000). *Quacks: Fakers and charlatans in*

*English medicine.* Stroud, UK: Tempus Publishing.
Remak, R. (1858). On the therapeutical action of the constant galvanic current. *Retrospect of Medicine, 47,* 406–409.
Roudebush, M. (2001). A battle of nerves: Hysteria and its treatments in France during World War I. In M.S. Micale and P. Lerner (eds.), *Traumatic pasts: History, psychiatry and trauma in the modern age, 1870–1930,* pp. 53–279. Cambridge: Cambridge University Press.
Rowbottom, M., and Susskind, C. (1984). *Electricity and medicine: History of their interaction.* San Francisco: San Francisco Press.
Shelley, M. (1818). *Frankenstein, or the modern Prometheus.* London: Lackington, Hughes, Harding, Mavor & Jones.
Steinberg, H. (2011). Electrotherapeutic disputes: The "Frankfurt Council" of 1891. *Brain, 134,* 1229–1243.
Tatu, L., Bogousslavsky, J., Moulin, T., and Chopard, J-L. (2010). The "torpillage" neurologists of World War I. *Neurology, 75,* 279–283.
Weaver, B.L. (1996). Survival at the Alabama Insane Hospital. *Journal of the History of Medicine and Allied Sciences, 51,* 5–28
Wiglesworth, J. (1887). On the use of galvanism in the treatment of certain forms of insanity. *Journal of Mental Science, 33,* 385–390.

## *Electric Air Bath*

Electrification of the whole body with static electricity. The patient sat on a well-insulated glass stool to receive the therapeutic. One electrode from the static electricity machine was connected to the ground, the other fastened to the patient's clothing or held in the hand. The polarity chosen determined the effect: when connected to the positive terminal the patient experienced stimulation, when connected to the negative terminal the patient was left tired and soporific. Despite its rather disconcerting effect of raising the hair, tingling the skin, and generating a halo or corona discharge in a darkened room, most patients actually enjoyed the electric air bath. They reported that the therapeutic altered their moods, and made deep and untroubled sleep possible.

There were many variations of the electric air bath. but regardless of the design it was primarily, although not exclusively, used to treat psychoneurotic patients in British, European and North American asylums during the late nineteenth century, but only rarely after that. It had a much longer use, however, in health spas, homeopathic clinics and with private practice electrotherapists.

## *Electric Bath*

A therapeutic that combined hydrotherapy with electrotherapy. The patient reclined in an earthenware, porcelain or wood bath tub filled with warm water. A direct current was passed thought the water via plate electrodes that were fastened to the head and the foot of the tub. The plate electrode at the head of the tub was positive; this polarity was reported to be more relaxing to the patient than the reverse. The asylum physician or technician initially set the current by submerging his or hand into the water to test the sensation, but the final current was adjusted according to the patient's response.

The patient remained in the tub for fifteen to twenty minutes at a time, with treatments continuing on a daily basis. The sensations experienced while in the electric bath were not unpleasant; most patients reported feeling refreshed and often were inclined to sleep, perhaps for the first time without disturbance, after the treatment.

Robert Jones of the Claybury Asylum in Essex, England, used the electric bath to treat twenty-three adolescent patients who were suffering from what he called "anergic stupor," which he suspected was the onset of dementia praecox, or schizophrenia. The patients did nothing more than sit or stand, and were so unresponsive to their surroundings that they had to be coaxed and sometimes forced into taking nourishment. All five of the female patients who were given the electric bath treatment showed initial improvement, but the long-term results were less encouraging: two died a short time after treatment, both most likely of preexisting medical disorders; one developed epilepsy; and the remaining two were discharged as recovered. The electric bath treatment produced slightly better results for the eighteen male patients. Six recovered and were discharged; three improved notably and also were discharged; seven remained under asylum care, although their stupor had been relieved; and the remaining two, both with preexisting medical conditions, showed no improvement. Jones was cautiously optimistic about the therapeutic value of the electric bath in cases for which a steady deterioration of mental functions was otherwise expected. He theorized that the therapeutic stimulated the metabolism of patients, but he remained puzzled as to whether it was the bath or the electricity that was the more efficacious agent in doing so.

The electric bath therapeutic was popular in British, European and North American asylums for a relatively brief period. By the turn into the twentieth century, reports of its use were infrequent in the asylum literature.

## *Electronarcosis*

The alteration of the level of consciousness of the patient by electrical stimulation of the brain. The first human experiment with electronarcosis was conducted by the French biologist Stéphane Armand Nicolas Leduc, using himself as the subject. After placing electrodes behind his ear and on his forehead, his two assistants administered a gradually increasing current of electricity. Although Leduc maintained consciousness, he was unable to speak or move, a sensation he imagined was somewhat akin to sleep paralysis.

Decades later electronarcosis was tried on Soviet asylum patients who had been diagnosed with schizophrenia. Considered a humane alternative to electroconvulsive shock treatment [see **Shock Therapy**], the therapeutic was reported to have brought about considerable improvement after several applications. Since schizophrenia was the most frustratingly intractable form of insanity, the use of electronarcosis spread quite quickly through Central European asylums.

Just how electronarcosis worked to ameliorate symptoms, however, was a matter of some debate. Asylum physicians variously theorized that the electrical current changed cell oxidation, reduced brain inflammation, or restored the normal balance between the inhibitory and excitatory forces of the brain. The uncertain science behind the therapeutic and what might be considered an uneasy suspicion of Soviet psychiatry delayed the spread of electronarcosis to other European, British and North American asylums. In the mid-twentieth century, however, several asylum physicians experimented with it to treat patients with schizophrenia.

Among them was J.J. Geoghegan at the Homewood Retreat in Guelph, Ontario, Canada. In a carefully conducted trial using patients diagnosed with schizophrenia, he found that six to fifteen treatments of electronarcosis resulted in improvements for most who were in the acute stage, but that two months post-treatment almost all of those gains already had been lost. For those patients whose schizophrenia was of long-standing duration, few improvements were noted. In separate trials, British physicians A. Spencer Paterson and W. Liddell Milligan found similar results but added that they found electronarcosis to be particularly efficacious in the treatment of psychoneurotics. On that point, the cases discussed by Milligan, who was affiliated with St. James Hospital in Portsmouth, England, also hinted that the always difficult to define concept of "improvement" was assessed according to prevailing gender expectations. There was the case of "Mrs. A," aged fifty-one, who had been hypochondriacal for a decade and then sunk into a deep depression; she was suicidal and kept razor blades under her pillow. After eighteen electronarcosis treatments, she had improved enough to return home and "has been carrying out all of her household duties since then, in good health" (Paterson & Milligan, p. 578). Then there was the case of "Mr. D," a forty-two-year-old widower who had left his position as head of a large factory when he was debilitated by panic attacks and claustrophobia. After just eight electronarcotic treatments, he was able to "go anywhere without fear and within two months was back at work and feeling well, and writing a scientific monograph" (p. 579).

Although improvements were short-lived for patients with schizophrenia, there were other reasons for asylum physicians to be cautious in the administration of electronarcosis. It was found to induce cerebral convulsions and ventricular arrhythmias in many patients, some of whom also regained consciousness during the procedure. Unable to speak or to move, these patients later reported feeling as if they were being suffocated, all the while seeing bright flashing lights and hearing loud noises. The panic all of this induced compromised improvement.

The administration of electronarcosis continued in Soviet and Central European asylums well into the middle of the twentieth century, by which time it was no longer regarded an acceptable therapeutic in other countries.

## *Electrosleep Therapy*

The therapeutic induction of sleep by means of the transcranial administration of a low amplitude pulsating current. Electrosleep was developed by Vasilii Giliarovskii, a Russian physician whose holistic theory of the body-mind-environment relationship led him to eschew the use of shock therapies such as metrazol [see **Shock Therapy**] and psychosurgeries such as the lobotomy [see **Psychosurgery**] and consider those therapeutics that relied as much as possible on the body's own defenses. To that end, and after experimentation with animals, he constructed an "electrosleep machine," and in 1946 tried it for the first time on asylum patients. The machine delivered a mild and modulated electrical current for approximately fifteen to twenty minutes through electrodes pasted on the head. Most of the thirty-four patients, diagnosed with schizophrenia, upon whom it was first tried, fell asleep during the procedure and remained asleep after it ended. Although electrosleep had to be administered as many as thirty times before the patient fell into a restorative sleep, its calming and soothing effects were considered laudatory. With a bit of nationalist fervor, Giliarovskii declared that the therapeutic affirmed the Soviet principle of humaneness.

Humaneness was very much a bone of contention for British, Western European and North American asylum physicians who had embraced the various shock therapies and psychosurgeries. As a result, there were some tentative explorations of the humane alternative of electrosleep, although the current administered was higher than that used in the Soviet Union. The therapeutic tended to produce relaxation and drowsiness, generally had salutary immediate effects on those patients so treated, but also produced disturbingly high rates of neurovegetative symptoms such as tremors. The general consensus was that it was indeed humane but, in the end, not particularly effective. There was, as a result, little use of electrosleep in British, Western European and North American asylums after the mid-twentieth century.

It took a little longer for electrosleep to fall out of favor in Soviet and Nordic countries. Using the weak current favored by Giliarovskii, several physicians affiliated with the Hesperia Hospital in Helsinki, Finland, administered electrosleep to patients who had a variety of diagnoses. The patients laid on beds with their eyes closed; electrodes of one pole were placed over their eyes, those of the other on their necks, and a weak, pulsating current was delivered. Of the nineteen inpatients in the trial, twelve improved well enough to be discharged; two months later, however, almost none had maintained those improvements. The physicians were forced to consider what many of their colleagues had been considering for years: whatever positive effects of electrosleep were due more to suggestion than to the electrical current.

## Electrotherapeutic Cage, or d'Arsonval Cage, or Autoconduction Cage

A large spiral of heavy wire wound around a cylindrical frame, forming a cage in which the sitting or reclining patient experienced high frequency electrical currents with low voltage and high amperage. The patient was connected to a small solenoid by a metal electrode held in the hand; the other end of the solenoid, which contained a high-frequency oscillating magnet, was attached to a large sheet of thin metal underneath a thick cushion on the platform on which the patient sat or reclined. Although sparks flew and a lamp held in the patient's free hand became incandescent during the procedure, the patient felt no discomfort. The effect of the electrical field was general rather than localized, and most patients reported feeling energized and rejuvenated after the treatment.

The cage was invented by Jacques-Arsène de'Arsonval, a French biophysicist in the late nineteenth century, specifically as a treatment for neurasthenia and hysteria. Eager to bring their own therapeutics into the modern era, a number of British, European and North American asylum physicians invented variations of the cage. The one in use at the Steinhof Mental Hospital in Vienna, Austria, was considered the epitome of modern electrotherapeutics. Few of the cages, however, were still in routine use at the start of the twentieth century.

## Faradic Brush

An electrode embedded into a long insulated handle that ended with densely packed nickel-plated copper wire bristles that delivered currents of electricity when applied to the body in brief strokes or taps. The faradic brush was considered particularly efficacious in the treatment of hysterical anesthesia, melancholy and depression, neurasthenia, catalepsy or muscle rigidity, and as a distraction from auditory and/or visual hallucinations.

Asylum physicians acknowledged that the administration of the faradic brush was painful and distressing to patients. They also posited that it was that very pain and distress that made the brush an efficacious therapeutic. Most patients would do anything, including change and improve, in order to avoid it.

## Faradic Moxa, or Electric Moxa

The use of the faradic brush as an active electrode on dry skin. Held directly over a painful area of the body, rather than stroked over it, the faradic moxa created a burning sensation that was extremely painful. Developed by Guillaume-Benjamin-Armand Duchenne, a neurologist at the Salpêtrière Hospital in Paris, France, the moxa was intended for the treatment of localized pain, such as that which arises from neuralgia or arthritis, as well as for the treatment of tumors and enlarged glands.

One use of the therapeutic, though, found its way into a few asylums. Aphonia, that is, the inability to talk above a whisper, was not an unusual symptom of the type of hysteria most associated with young women, and with young men who were shell-shocked during World War I. If other treatments, including the faradic brush stroked on the neck over the larynx failed to restore the voice, the patients were administered the faradic moxa. In those cases, a flexible metal stem was inserted into the throat and pharyngeal cavity. The coil terminated in either small wire brushes or a metallic olive which was positioned on the larynx, delivering a faradic current. The procedure not only produced gagging, coughing and often vomiting, but was extraordinarily painful. Most asylum physicians, including Charles Féré during his tenure at the Salpêtrière and later at the Asylum de Bicêtre in Paris, France, agreed that the "mental impression" made by the device had a more curative effect than the device, itself.

## Faradization

A termed coined by Guillaume-Benjamin-Armand Duchenne, a neurologist at the Salpêtrière Hospital in Paris, France, to describe the therapeutic uses of a series of brief pulses of electricity generated by a faradic, or induction, coil. In that it both stimulated sensory receptors and produced tetanic contractions in the skeletal muscles, faradization had a much more profound physiological effect on the patient to whom it was applied than other types of electrotherapy.

There were two types of faradization administered to asylum patients. The first, general faradization or the "electric-hand treatment," involved the application of the faradic current to the body along the head-foot axis, a procedure that Duchenne had argued excited the secretions and nerve impulses. The patient was made to sit on a stool with bare feet placed on a copper electrode that was connected to one terminal of the induction coil. The other terminal was connected to a copper ball electrode covered with a moist sponge and was held by the asylum physician or electrotherapy technician with one hand, while laying the other hand on the patient's head. So positioned in series between the induction coil and the patient, the physician or therapist could assess the strength of the current as he moved his hand slowly over the head, face and neck of the patient, and down the spinal column. The optimal current was one assessed as "pleasantly painful"; by tightening or loosening his grasp on the copper ball electrode, the physician or technician could increase or decrease the strength of the faradic current. Used primarily, although not exclusively, for the treatment of hysteria, neurasthenia, insomnia and hypochondriasis, general faradization produced an immediate sensation of exhilaration and hunger, followed by drowsiness that ended in a long period of deep and uninterrupted sleep.

Duchenne practiced general medicine during the day and wandered around the wards of public hospitals and asylums, such as the Salpêtrière, in the evenings looking for patients for his faradization experi-

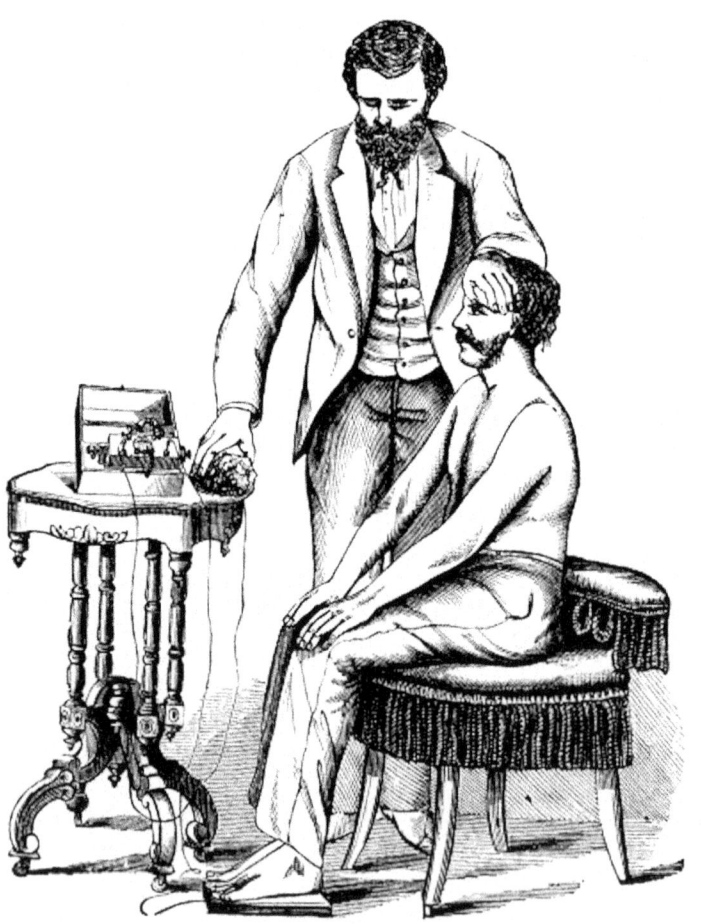

General faradization. The patient has his feet on a pedal while the asylum physician uses himself as the conductor for the electrical current passing from the machine through to the patient (G. Beard and A.D. Rockwell [1881] *A Practical treatise on the medical and surgical uses of electricity.* New York: William Wood and Company).

ments. In fact, it was there that the women diagnosed with hysteria took quite a liking to him, referring to him as "the little old man with his mischief box" (Hustvedt, p. 156), and they clamored to be his subjects.

The second type of faradization was localized, that is, the faradic current was applied to a specific region of the body. Although used mostly to treat physical disorders such as neuralgia as well as sprains and other injuries, it was occasionally used in asylums to treat hysterical paralysis and hypochondriasis.

Although faradization, just as other electrotherapeutics, had a relatively short period of popularity in asylum medicine, it made a brief reappearance in the mid-twentieth century when it was used to treat schizophrenic patients. The outcomes in these cases were similar to those noted for the convulsive shock therapies, such as electroconvulsive, insulin and metrazol [see **Shock Therapy**] that were all the rage mid-century.

## *Galvanization, or Localized Galvanism, or Galvanotherapy*

The application of a continuous current of electricity to a specific part of the body via button-shaped electrodes covered by moistened sponges that were pressed into the surface of the skin. Because the brain was implicated in most cases of insanity, the electrode often was placed on or around the head of the patient, and a current derived from a battery of anywhere from five to twenty-five cells was applied for several minutes. The effect on the patient varied with the strength of the current: a low current tended to produce warmth and sleepiness, while a higher one produced dizziness, disorientation and sometimes even convulsions.

The first recorded attempt to use galvanization therapeutically was in the early nineteenth century when Giovanni Aldini, the head of Bologna University's department of physics and the nephew of Luigi Galvani, who had discovered the electrochemical cell, convinced several Italian asylum physicians to let him try in on "hopeless lunatics." (Aldini, 113). The trials resulted in two remarkable cures. One of those patients was a twenty-seven-year-old farmer named Luigi Lanzarini, who had been institutionalized for depression for some time at the asylum at the Santo Orsola Hospital in Bologna. Before galvanizing the melancholy farmer, Aldini applied galvanism to his own head to test its effects. He described the sensation:

> First, the fluid took over a large part of my brain, which felt a strong shock, a sort of jolt against the inner surface of my skull. The effect increased further as I moved the electric arcs from one ear to another. I felt a strong head stroke and I became insomniac for several days [Parent, p. 580].

Aldini then administered galvanization to Lanzarini, using a weak voltaic pile of fifteen disks, and then gradually increasing the charge during the course of the treatment.

> I first administered the Galvanism gradually, forming the arc by means of the hands. Lanzarini, in a state of the utmost dejection, viewed the apparatus and the company present with his eyes fixed and motionless. When interrogated by the physicians and myself in regard to the origin of his malady, he gave laconic and a confused answers, which seemed to indicate a great degree of stupidity and derangement. I first moistened his hands and formed an arc with the pile at different heights to accustom him to endure the action of the apparatus. No change, however, was produced in the patient by this operation. I then repeated the experiment, placing his hands, moistened with salt water, at the bottom of the pile; and conveying an arc from the summit of the pile to different parts of his face, moistened with the same solution. A change was soon observed in the patient's countenance, and his whole demeanor seemed to indicate the degree of his melancholy was somewhat lessened [Aldini, p. 115].

Days after the series of galvanization treatments, Lanzarini had improved enough to be released. He stayed under the watchful eye of Aldini for a few days, working in his home as domestic servant, before returning to his family.

By the mid-nineteenth century galvanization had caught on. Not only was it being used with success in the treatment of a variety of neurological disorders, but for the "disorders" of daily living, such as hair loss, acne, hay fever, obesity, impotence and infertility. Those latter "cures" was being hawked by quack doctors and self-proclaimed electrotechnicians who roamed from city to city with wooden boxes containing their impressively named galvanic devices. In such a social milieu, and in the face of such exaggerated claims, many asylum physicians were more than ready to return to that early experiment by Aldini and use galvanization to treat the insane.

They had at their disposals a number of different devices, each of which came with detailed instructions that early asylum physicians seemed more interested in than they were in the effects of its administration. Such was the case of Joseph Wiglesworth, the medical superintendent of the Rainhill Asylum in northeastern England. A somewhat reluctant convert to galvanization, he had waited for the "science" of the electrotherapeutic to improve before he tried it on his patients. Once he was convinced that he could accurately measure the strength of the administered current, he galvanized eleven female patients, most of them young and suffering from melancholia. In the characteristic language of asylum physicians experimenting with a new, and in this case mysterious therapeutic force, he seemed more interested in establishing its, and thus his own, scientific, *bona fides* than in describing and analyzing the effects of galvanization of his patients. The following case study illustrates that point:

> E. P., 30, widow. Simple melancholia, without delusions. Patient was very fretful and depressed, wandering up and down the ward, moaning and groaning, and could not be got to employ herself in any way. The case had lasted two years previous to admission, and galvanization was commenced two months subsequently, no change having at that time taken place in the patient's symptoms. A large flexible plate [anode], C| in. by Z\ in., was applied to the nape of the neck, the medium-sized one [cathode] being placed on the forehead. The treatment was commenced with five milliamperes, applied for ten minutes, this strength being gradually increased to 14, which was the highest that could be employed, as patient was throughout very intolerant of the applications. The average current strength was seven milliamperes, continued for ten minutes each time. Sixteen sittings only were resorted to, and these were spread over a period of 23 days [Wiglesworth, pp. 389–390].

Wiglesworth noted that the patient "improved rapidly," becoming more "cheerful and active." She was one of three patients who had improved enough to be discharged. Three more had improved significantly, one only slightly, and the remaining five had shown no improvement whatsoever. The results shook Wiglesworth's confidence, and although he was not willing to abandon it he did caution his colleagues who were considering its use that galvanization "is certainly *not* going to revolutionize the treatment of insanity," regardless of the considerable hype that it would do so.

American asylum physicians tended to heed that admonition and were not inclined to use galvanization, but a few not only had a strong therapeutic interest in it, but a political one as well. "When legislators cease to be controlled by political considerations and become broad, philosophical statesmen," wrote Alfred T. Livingston, assistant physician at the Utica Asylum in upstate New York, "they will recognize the economy of making asylums for the insane hospitals for cure rather than places of custody, and we will then see a ratio of physicians to patients, that will allow of such work being done and such results accomplished as I have now in mind" (Livingston, p. 344). And what he had in mind was the galvanization of the acutely insane, not only to prevent their prolonged and costly institutionalization, but to demonstrate the curative power of asylum medicine.

To justify this politicized mission, which was frowned upon by many of his colleagues,

Livingston cobbled together an admittedly "crude" theory of acute insanity and its cure by galvanization. Reasoning that it was due to a congestion of the cerebral blood vessels caused by a deficiency in the strength of the vasomotor center, he argued that the electrical stimulation of that center would improve brain circulation and "relieve the exhausted and irritable brain cells" (Livingston, p. 345). Unpolished as his theory was, Livingston nonetheless claimed great successes in curing acute insanity. One of those successes was a twenty-year-old woman in the throes of acute mania:

> I found her a vigorous, violent girl, who was evidently accustomed to having her own way, and she had been running the whole establishment… She was so strong that it required three unusually large and powerful nurses to hold her upon the bed when I began to give her the electricity. Before completing the first treatment she was asleep, and this result occurred with each treatment. At the end of the month she had recovered, and has continued well since [Livingston, p. 343].

One asylum physician who shared Livingston's political agenda was Peter Bryce, superintendent of the Alabama State Hospital for the Insane in Tuscaloosa. Only twenty-six years old when appointed to the position, Bryce already had extensive interactions with some of the greatest figures in European asylum medicine, and was determined to bring "scientific treatment" to the United States. For Bryce, "scientific" meant state-of-the-art, and he found no apparent contradiction in combining a regime of moral treatment [see **Moral Treatment**] with somatic therapies such as galvanization. For both psychiatric and economic reasons he, too, was particularly interested in the treatment of the acutely insane: their cure would establish the scientific foundation of asylum medicine, attract more state funding, and keep the patient census at a manageable level during the South's dire economic times post–Civil War. Although Bryce found galvanization to be indispensible in the treatment of acute attacks of hysteria, neurasthenia and in recent onset dementia, he was unable to sustain a vigorous electrotherapy program in the face of the fact that the asylum remained underfunded and critically understaffed.

Economic realities such as this competed with a growing sense of dissatisfaction about the efficacy of electrotherapy to bring about the disappearance of galvanization as an asylum therapeutic in the early twentieth century. Its use, in one form or another, by private practice neurologists, and in health spas and clinics, however, continues to this day.

## *Leyden Jar, or Leiden Jar*

The delivery of an electrical shock via a capacitor consisting of a glass jar lined inside and out with metal foil and filled with water. A metal rod that was in contact with the inner foil lining that had been charged by an external source, protruded through the wooden cover of the jar. When the patient touched the rod, or the rod was touched on a specific part of the patient's body, a static electrical shock was delivered.

Discovered in 1745, the Leyden Jar was both small and transportable, and capable of storing electrical charges so it could deliver several successive shocks to a patient. As an early electrotherapeutic, the Leyden Jar established the precedence that others would follow: it was used by physicians, quacks and charlatans alike to cure everything from indigestion to infertility, headaches to hysteria. In regards to hysteria, in fact, the Leyden Jar enjoyed some popularity as an early asylum therapeutic. It was used to treat hysterical paralysis, a term that described a number of neurological symptoms such as paralysis, blindness, numbness, muscle weakness and convulsions that had no organic cause.

It was the American scientist-philosopher Benjamin Franklin who first suggested that static shocks could be delivered to the cranium without damaging the brain, that insight coming after he accidentally shocked himself with a Leyden jar—twice. To test the validity of his own experience, Franklin administered shocks to "C.B.," a twenty-four-year-old who suffered hysterical seizures so violent that she could not be restrained by several strong people, and that had left her on the verge of madness. The year was 1752, and "C.B's" recollection of the remedy is one of the first personal narratives of the treatment of madness published in the United States:

> At length my spirits were quite broke and subdued with so many years affliction, and indeed I was almost grown desperate, being left without hope or relief. About this time there was great talk of the wonderful power of electricity; and as a person reduced to the last extremity, is glad to catch at any thing; I happened to think it might be useful to me. Altho' I cou'd have no encouragement from any experiment in the case, I resolv'd to try, let the event be what it might; for death was more desirable than life, on the terms I enjoy'd it. Accordingly I went to Philadelphia, the beginning of September 1752, and apply'd to B. Franklin, who I thought understood it best of any person here. I received four shocks morning and evening; they were what they call 200 strokes of the wheel, which fills an eight gallon bottle, and indeed they were very severe. On receiving the first shock, I received the fit very strong, but the second effectually carried it off; and thus it was every time I went through the operation; yet the symptoms gradually decreased, till at length they intirely left me. I staid in town two weeks, and when I went home, B. Franklin was so good as to supply me with a globe and bottle, to electrify myself every day for three months. The fits were soon carried off, but the cramp continued somewhat longer, though it was scarcely troublesome, and very seldom returned. I now enjoy such a state of health as I would have given all the world for, this time two years [Evans, 1754, p. 85].

Franklin was skeptical about "C.B's" cure, reasoning that her anticipation of it may have done more to relieve her symptoms than the shocks did. Nonetheless, and because there were no asylums yet in the United States to further test therapeutic outcomes, he encouraged British and European asylum physicians to use the Leyden jar to administer static electric shocks to their melancholy patients. That was done with some frequency, but always with mixed results.

The use of this "object of fascination," as the French neurologist Guillaume-Benjamin-Armand Duchenne, once referred to it (Duchenne, p. 1102), continued several decades beyond the accumulated evidence that it cured neither mental nor physical disease. It is likely that the mysterious power of electricity and its immediate and sensational effect on the treated patient account for its relative longevity.

## *Surprise Attack Shock Treatment, or Kaufmann's Cure, or Electro-Suggestive Therapy, or Überrumpelungsmethode*

The pairing of painful currents of electricity with martial re-education to treat shell-shock. Frustrated with the failure of restorative treatments to return shell-shocked soldiers to the battlefields of World War I, neurologist Fritz Kaufmann of the Nervous Illness Station of the Reserve Infirmary in Ludwigshafen, Germany, developed the surprise attack shock treatment method to quickly and effectively coerce soldier-patients into cure after a single session.

The therapeutic consisted of four fundamental elements. First, the treating physicians engaged in "suggestive preparation" by convincing their soldier-patients that the treatment, although intensely painful, indeed would result in a cure. Second, strong alternating electrical currents of two to five minutes duration were directly applied to the body. For those shell-shocked soldier-patients who had functional impairments—paralyzed arms, for example, or feeble legs—the current was applied directly to the affected limbs; for those without such impairment, the current was applied indiscriminately to the body. The electrical current, as a matter of fact, had no salutary effect on disabled limbs or on the body in general, but its application was meant to convince soldier-patients that their distress was physical, not mental, and thus treatable by somatic means. Between sinusoidal shocks, the treating physicians ordered the soldier-patients to engage in physical exercises, assuring them as they did that they were well on the road to complete recovery. This cycle of shock and exercise continued for as long as two hours. Third, strict military discipline was maintained throughout the treatment. "Military discipline demands the most absolute, blind subordination to the orders of the superior," Kaufmann wrote, "and this creates a fertile ground for a suggestive procedure" (Kaufmann, p. 804). Fourth, no surprise attack shock treatment session was terminated before the cure was complete; to do otherwise would be tantamount to implying to the soldier-patients that their condition was incurable.

Kaufmann's rationale for the therapeutic was as pragmatic as the treatment was hardnosed. "When these patients are forced into a cure," he wrote, "...then at the very least they will be able to practice their peacetime occupations again, and the pension matter is done away with too" (Lerner, p. 102). The practicality of this logic was underscored by two indisputable facts: more than 600,000 German soldiers were treated for shell-shock during World War I, thus the urgency of getting them back to the battlefield and, after the war, to civilian life unimpaired was considerable; and the surprise attack shock treatment worked effectively to do just that. Kaufmann and his colleagues reported an astonishing cure rate of 97 percent. One of those soldier-patients, whose shell-shock had rendered him mute, described his cure in the following manner:

> The current was switched on. At first I had prickly feeling, which suddenly burst into intense pain.... The moment the doctor's suggestions began, I felt like an object with no will of its own, being fought for by two opposing powers. Gradually my own came into play as a result of both of my own reasoning and the doctor's means of domination.... I held on to the doctor's scolding as a lifeline, clung to it tightly, and pulled my nerves along with me. So the two of us pulled until I could understand and speak [Killen, p. 143].

Kaufmann's claims, demonstrated at medical meetings and published in a 1916 journal article, drew considerable attention to the surprise attack shock treatment. Many German physicians adopted it, or their own variations of it, for their treatment of shell-shocked soldier-patients. But the demonstrations and the article also drew criticisms. Condemning the treatment as unnecessarily painful and ethically suspect, other physicians adamantly refused to subject their soldier-patients to it.

Kaufmann himself responded to the quite vitriolic disagreement among his colleagues both by curbing his enthusiasm and attributing the success of the treatment more to suggestion than to the painful and humiliating electrical shocks. And as to the ethical dilemma, his response was characteristically pragmatic: the brief, however painful, treatment "serves our ultimate aim ... to help the patient quickly and make him once again a useful member of the national community" (Lerner, p. 109). His tempered interpretation of the treatment converted some of his most strident detractors, and the surprise attack shock treatment became the foundation for the treatment of shell-shocked German soldier-patients. In fact, it was estimated that by 1918, it had been administered more than a million times by more than 100 treating physicians.

Kaufmann's revised emphasis on the power of suggestion as the reason for the treatment's success, though, predicted its eventually passing from popularity into competition with other types of treatment. If it was suggestion, after all, that produced the cure, then much milder shocks could be administered for the same outcome or, perhaps, none at all. As the war dragged on, the public's sympathy tended towards the less severe treatments; after the war, its opprobrium was reserved for what was then what had come to be called the "Kaufmannization" of shell-shock treatment that replicated the traumatizing effects of war in the treatment room.

This was evident in the trial of Michael Kozlowski. A physician at the Clinic for Psychiatry and Nervous Diseases in Vienna, Austria, he treated Lieutenant Walter Kauders for shell-shock with a version of the surprise attack shock treatment. The treatment was, in Kauders' words, tantamount to medieval torture. In his complaint to the Commission for the Investigation of Derelictions of Military Duty he wrote that Kozlowski first threatened him with electrical shock, then forced him to watch it being administered to the nipples and testicles of writhing and screaming soldier-patients, before subjecting him to it. Kozlowski was sangfroid. "It is really necessary to have seen the whole procedure," he wrote in response to the charge of gross maltreatment, "...in order to realize the nonsense of these assertions by Herr Kauders" (Killen, p. 142). The Commission apparently agreed. Kozlowski was acquitted of all charges.

The larger issue of the efficacy and the ethicality of "Kaufmannized" shock treatment, however, was addressed not in the Kozlowski hearing, but in that of his supervisor, the estimable Julius Wagner-Jauregg who would go on to win the Nobel Prize for his discovery of malaria inoculation in the treatment of general paresis, or neurosyphilis. It was in this hearing that none other than Sigmund Freud testified as an expert witness, and the clash between the mentalist and the somatist was nothing more than an epic event in the respective histories of psychoanalysis and psychiatry. Freud testified that shell-shock was an unconscious desire to withdraw from the horror of war and that malingering, such as Lt. Kauders had been accused of, was rare. He went on to describe shock treatment via electricity as nothing more than a painful counterstimulus that caused soldier-patients to flee back to the front, a desire that too often was mistaken for cure. And on its ethicality, Freud was adamant: the treatment sacrificed humanity to pragmatic concerns. He had written to his close associate Sándor Ferenczi before the hearing, "I will naturally treat [Wagner-Jauregg] with the most distinct benevolence. It also isn't his fault" (p. 35). True to his word, Freud refused to accuse his colleague and friend of intentional cruelty to patients. Wagner-Jauregg was exonerated of all charges.

## Torpillage

A "persuasive" form of psychotherapy using painful faradic and galvanic electric currents to treat shell-shocked soldiers during World War I. Developed by Clovis Vincent, a French neurologist who was assigned to the military hospital in Tours, the torpillage (literally translated as "torpedoing," and so named by the soldier-patients to whom it was administered) was a revision of the shock treatment his mentor, Joseph Babinski, had used at the Salpêtrière Hospital to treat hysterical patients, mostly women, during peacetime. Convinced that shell-shocked soldiers also were psychoneurotic and that with the appropriate therapeutic intervention could return to the battlefield, Vincent replaced his mentor's use of an intermittent faradic current with a direct and continuous galvanic one aimed at the affected part of the body. Using two electrodes strapped to his hands, he applied an intensely painful galvanic current. While the soldier-patients were struggling and screaming, Vincent emphatically exhorted them to once again take up their arms in defense of their country. Most of the soldier-patients capitulated, but their treatment did not end there. They then were subjected to a physical training regime of jumping and climbing exercises, as well as an intensive re-education program, both of which were overseen by soldiers who, themselves, had been cured by torpillage.

Vincent claimed spectacular success in curing his soldier-patients of the muscle contractures, limb paralyses, and the visual, auditory and/or oral changes that were the hallmark symptoms of severe shell-shock. The torpillage therapeutic was adopted by a number of physicians in military hospitals with equal success, including André Gilles who worked at front-line psychiatric center, and who in an oft-repeated aphorism once wrote in his defense of torpillage, "These pseudo-impotents of the voice, of the arms or the legs, are really only impotents of the will; it is the doctor's job to will on their behalf" (Roudebush, p. 269). Yet, while torpillage was being heartily endorsed by the French military physicians who were being overwhelmed with shell-shocked soldiers, the therapeutic intervention and its inventor were becoming embroiled in controversy.

Early in 1916 Vincent came up against three soldier-patients who adamantly refused to undergo torpillage. Vincent responded to their obduracy by diagnosing them as malingerers, that is, as fabricating or exaggerating their physical symptoms. While it might be said in retrospect that there was little sympathy for shell-shocked soldiers in general during World War I, it also can be said with confidence that there was none for malingerers who not only were regarded as cowards and traitors, but as weak and effeminate men. Under the stigma of that label, the three soldiers were brought before a military court but were acquitted after it determined that their various physical symptoms were not only legitimate, but most likely incurable.

While these proceedings and the resulting verdict were confidential, and therefore not at all widely known, the encounter between Vincent and Jean-Baptiste Deschamps was the stuff of scandal. The soldier, with all of his equipment, had fallen from a height of nine or ten feet, landing feet-first and damaging his spine. Unable to walk upright, he was sent to several neurological centers and finally ended up at Tours where Vincent intended to cure him with torpillage. Deschamps refused, insisting that the therapeutic was tantamount to torture, and in the heated argument that ensued punched the physician several times in the face. Vincent, a former amateur boxer, reacted with several well-aimed punches of his own, but it was the soldier who was arrested and brought before a military tribunal for striking a superior officer. In a surprising finding, the tribunal gave Deschamps a six month suspended sentence, that slap on the wrist in superficial agreement with his claim that torpillage was little more than torture, but in deeper recognition of the unbridgeable chasm between the French medico-military hierarchy and the terrifying worlds of ordinary foot soldiers and war-weary civilians. The legitimacy of his therapeutic and the rationale for using it thus called into question, Vincent requested that he be reassigned to the battlefront where he served as an infantry regiment physician.

Upon the subsequent closure of the clinic at Tours, many shell-shocked soldiers were sent to Salinsles-Bains, a spa town in eastern France. It was there that neurologist Gustave Roussy had opened a clinic where he could administer a modified version of torpillage to his soldier-patients. In an attempt to reduce both the fear and the pain of torpillage, he began the treatment with a series of pain-free faradic shocks administered to the targeted areas of the body, the soles of the feet and/or the scrotum. These were followed by periods of isolation and dietary restrictions until the soldier-patients had recovered sufficiently well enough to submit to a series of military exercises under the supervision of officers who had been cured of shell-shock by the same treatment. The details of the modified torpillage treatment were described by Louis-Ferdinand Céliné in his semi-autobiographical novel, *Voyage au Bout de la Nuit* (*Journey to the End of Night*), published in 1932. Céliné had been severely concussed in battle and treated, much against his will, with torpillage. The pseudonymous Professor Bestombes who administered the treatment is skewered in this nihilistic novel that had such a profound influence on more contemporary authors such as Kurt Vonnegut and Charles Bukowski, and songwriters such as Aya Korem and Jim Morrison.

Yet the kinder and gentler version of torpillage was not without criticism either. In 1918 Roussy sent six soldier-patients before a military tribunal for refusing the treatment; each was given a suspended sentence. Privy to the findings, the local press not only invidiously compared the light sentences to that given to Baptiste Deschamps, but compared Vincent's torpillage with Roussy's modified version, and found them disturbingly similar in coerciveness. French military officials, swayed by the bad press and the public reaction to it, ceased to support the torpillage treatment of shell-shock, and by 1918 the therapeutic was no longer in use.

# Etherization

*The anesthetization of patients with ether.*

Prior to the discovery of the anesthetic properties of ether in the mid-nineteenth century surgical patients had received high dosages of narcotics such as opium, belladonna, conium, Indian hemp or hyoscyamus in what often were nothing more than futile attempts to relieve their pain. The administration of ether for the pain-free removal of a facial tumor, however, not only revolutionized surgical medicine but for a brief time enjoyed approval as an asylum therapeutic.

The first experiments with the etherization of insane patients occurred at the New York State Lunatic Asylum, later and better known simply as Utica. Sixteen patients, two of whom were female, were administered ether on anywhere from one to nine separate occasions. The ether had been dripped on a sponge inside a cup-shaped device and placed over their noses. Within minutes, each was rendered unconscious and remained so for several hours.

Originally, it was imagined that etherization would be an effective therapeutic intervention in states of mania. The unconsciousness it produced would give a respite to the patients, not to mention the asylum physicians and staff. In its first trial at Utica, however, none of the patients was manic, but each suffered from significant disturbances, including melancholia, religious despair, hallucinations or delusions, that had left distress, confusion and despair in their wake.

The patients' reaction to the etherization varied considerably. A few seemed not at all affected, a few more appeared to be intoxicated; one patient danced and another imagined he could fly. At least one, who had been in the throes of religious despair, became highly excited. He had awoken from the ether "as if from a terrible dream, and in the most violent rage seized the person who administered the ether" (Author, p. 73). After finally calming, he described his experience:

> He afterwards said that he at first dreamed he was in hell and that taking the ether had sent him there, and his rage and violence against the operator. When this excitement abated he seemed ecstatic with delight on account of the visions he had seen and the revelations that had been made to him. "I floated away," he exclaimed, "in infinity of space. I have seen a future world, what I have seen has proved the dogmas of religions, unless a man comes up to an iota, it is over with him." He said he felt "convinced of the truth of Newton's theory of the Solar System" as he saw planets "in the order and way pointed out" [p. 74].

Although none of the patients experienced any complications with etherization, neither did they experience any real remedial effects, much to the disappointment of the Utica physicians. Rather than questioning their own assumption that etherization had potential as an asylum therapeutic, the physicians resolved to "ascertain if there is not some class of the insane to whom [etherization] is especially useful" (p. 74).

The discovery of ether is a matter of considerable dispute, but credit often is given to Charles Thomas Jackson, a Massachusetts physician, chemist and brother-in-law of the poet, Ralph Waldo Emerson. Soon after its first surgical use, he was invited by Luther V. Bell, the chief physician of the McLean Asylum in Boston, Massachusetts, the very asylum, in fact, to which Jackson later would be committed and in which he was to spend the last years of his life, to etherize a "furious maniac" who had been confined naked in a padded cell to prevent him from taking his own life. Bell had had no success with the conventional asylum drugs of hashish and cannabis in calming the patient. Although the powerfully muscular patient strenuously resisted the saturated sponge, biting it and spitting on it, he eventually was subdued by the vapors and "cast into a profound snoring sleep" (Jackson, p. 105). When he awoke hours later he was calm and rational, and remained so for months, after which time he was discharged as cured.

Encouraged by the result, Jackson and Bell etherized eight suicidal female patients. They had conjectured that suicidal patients who were so ruminative and ill-at-ease as to be seriously sleep-deprived, might constitute that very "class of the insane" who would benefit most from the therapeutic, and that females would be especially "facile subjects for etherization" (p. 105). All of the patients upon awakening from the ether were cheerful and, after a day or two, some manifested considerably less suicidal ideation, although "other delusions of certainly a less dangerous character" persisted (p. 106). None of these patients was discharged as cured. Nonetheless, the outcome was promising enough for the superintendent of the asylum in his annual report to praise etherization for its "general soothing and curative influence" and to recommended it as a "valuable agent in the treatment of insanity" (Tyler, p. 28).

Many asylums in the United States, as well as in France and Great Britain, used this "valuable agent" to treat mania, agitated depression and dementia, yet years after the McLean Asylum experiments, etherization was finishing its course as a therapeutic. In a paper delivered to his colleagues, Isaac Ray, the highly influential superintendent of Butler Hospital in Providence, Rhode Island, pondered the reasons why it was not being given a "faithful trial" in the treatment of insanity (Ray, p. 165). Ray himself had used etherization with some enthusiasm, giving twenty-five patients an average of nine administrations over an unspecified period of time. All had experienced a significant alleviation of their symptoms and at least one, "the severest case" of suicidal and homicidal propensity he had ever observed, improved enough to be discharged:

> For several months [the patient's] own safety required that an attendant should be near her perpetually; and, not infrequently, this was insufficient without mechanical restraint. The night was often spent in struggles with the attendant who slept, or rather stayed, with her, with such physical and moral consequences as might have been expected. She lost flesh, her pulse rose, and countenance became wild and haggard. All other treatment failing, we thought of etherization, and it was one of the first cases in which I used it. Given at bedtime, its effect was a quiet night, several hours of sound sleep, and a well marked improvement during the day. Under its use for two or three weeks, this improvement passed into decided convalescence, and in the course of two or three months it was impossible to discern a single unhealthy manifestation. She was then discharged, and not long after was married [Ray, pp. 167–168].

Scattered reports of similar successes in other asylums, Ray conjectured, may have raised expectations above what etherization could deliver. Too many asylum physicians who, like Ray himself admitted, had found tried and true remedies to be of "utter impotence" in treating some types of insanity (p. 165), had come to anticipate that etherization would deliver a "speedy and signal benefit in the treatment of mental disease" (p. 164), and were not content with anything less. While Ray empathized with their frustration, he implored them not only to reconsider the use of etherization, but to reconsider their own *raison d'être*:

> The world ... is united in believing that its power to abolish pain under the operations of surgery renders it a signal blessing to man; and it will regard our conduct as neither humane nor judicious, if we despise its aid in suspending the still greater pains of insanity [p. 168].

Ray's plea briefly reignited interest in etherization, however the failure of the therapeutic to achieve much more than the temporary amelioration of agitation or distress predicted its falling out of favor. By the 1860s few asylums anywhere in the United States or Western Europe continued its use.

## References

Author (1848). Inhalation of the vapor of sulphuric ether in cases on insanity. *American Journal of Insanity, 4,* 73–74.

Browner, S. (1999). Ideologies of the anesthetic: Professionalism, egalitarianism and the ether controversy. *American Quarterly, 51,* 108–143.

Chipley, W.S. (1865). Memoranda on anesthetics. *American Journal of Insanity,* 22, 76–81.

Jackson, C.T. (1861). *A manual of etherization.* Boston: J.B. Mansfield.

Ray, I. (1854). Etherization in the treatment of insanity. *American Journal of Insanity, 11,* 164–169.

Tyler, J. (1859). *Annual report of the Superintendent of the McLean Asylum for the Insane, to the Trustees of the Massachusetts General Hospital.* Boston: J. H. Eastburn's Press.

# Exodontia

*The extraction of teeth to treat insanity.*

One of the most influential, albeit rather short-lived, theories in medicine was that of focal sepsis. The theory posited that localized infections spread bacterial toxins through the body via the bloodstream or lymphatic system, causing a range of chronic diseases such as nephritis, arthritis, gastritis, rheumatism and even insanity.

Although there are contenders for recognition as the most prominent and influential proponent of this early twentieth century bacteriological theory, the British physician William Hunter deserves special mention. It was he who targeted focal sepsis of the mouth, or what he referred to as oral sepsis, as the single most important cause and complication of chronic diseases. While he initially implicated oral sepsis in medical diseases, he later speculated as to it etiologic role in insanity as well. In his remarks to medical students at McGill University in Montreal, Canada in the early twentieth century, he insisted that the worst cases of "nervous disorders of all kinds, from mental depression to actual lesions on the cord" were both caused and complicated by oral sepsis (Pallasch & Wahl, p. 34).

Hunter's conclusions, although based on clinical observation rather than empirical research, prompted a vigorous public health campaign in Great Britain to extract the rotten or decayed teeth of the public, a campaign that also well-served the efforts of qualified dentists in their efforts to prohibit unregistered practitioners from plying their trade. It also prompted cautious experiments in extracting the diseased teeth of the institutionalized insane. Exodontia, in fact, often had been practiced in asylums, but for archly utilitarian purposes: it prevented biting and the tearing of clothes with the teeth, and expedited the insertions of gags, keys and tubes used in forced feeding [see **Forced Feeding**]. Hunter's theory about the role of focal sepsis in insanity, however, gave exodontia the new, and arguably, more noble purpose of ameliorating the symptoms of insanity, if not curing it altogether.

To that end, some British asylum physicians began extracting the obviously rotten teeth of their insane patients. One of those physicians was Thomas Chivers Graves, superintendent of the Rubery Hill and Hollymoor asylums in Birmingham. Determined to bring the basic principles of medicine into psychiatry and, by doing so, stave off the encroachment of a psychodynamically-orientated psychiatry that focused on the mind rather than the body, he insisted that insanity was caused by the autotoxicity of focal sepsis. Exodontia, therefore, was the preferred remedy, although certainly not the only one. Graves, just as most of the devotees of focal sepsis theory, went on to practice what amounted to a surgical detoxification by removing tonsils, appendixes, and gallbladders as well [see **Surgery**].

The urgency to do something to remedy insanity also was felt in the United States, perhaps even more dearly so due to the fact that what was referred to as "conservative dentistry" was widely practiced there. The practice of placing crowns and bridges over decayed teeth and fixing dentures on diseased teeth was, in the words of William Hunter, whose influence was considerable in that country as well, doing nothing more than creating a "veritable mausoleum over a mass of sepsis (Pallasch & Wahl, p. 34).

That admonition was heeded by Henry Swift Upson, superintendent of the Cleveland State Hospital in Ohio who, in a monograph, repeated the canonical extension of focal sepsis theory that the various types of insanity were "primarily irritative disorders of the sensory system" and that the source of that irritation was either mechanical or toxic (Upson, p. 12). If the latter, he warned, then asylum physicians would have to overcome their "disregard [and] distinct though mild dislike of the teeth as organs to be reckoned with medically" (p. 4) and attend to the dental health of their insane patients. Upson, however, recommended exodontia only when necessary, and certainly not as a routine asylum therapeutic.

One physician who found Upson's reticence to extract the teeth of the insane as overly cautious was Henry Cotton, superintendent of Trenton State Hospital, later known as the New Jersey State Hospital. Built in the mid-nineteenth century, largely as testimony to the unrelenting advocatory work of "lunacy reformer" Dorothea Dix who spent the last years of her life in an apartment on its grounds, the asylum originally had a capacity of just 200 patients. When Cotton assumed the superintendency in 1907, more than 1400 patients, most of them chronically insane and in poor physical health, were little more than warehoused there in deplorable conditions.

Cotton immediately set about improving the conditions of the asylum, but his real agenda was to introduce into what therapeutic regime it already had, a new "scientific psychiatry" based on focal sepsis theory. And, just as was the case with Thomas Chivers Graves in England, with whom he formed a fast friendship, exodontia was his initial therapeutic of preference. Using state of the art X-ray equipment to detect the focal sepsis, Cotton set about extracting the teeth of his patients. The asylum's 1919 annual report, as a matter of fact, stated that more than 800 extractions had been performed that fiscal year, in addition to the removals of the fixed bridge work, gold crowns and pivot teeth of all patients for whom X-rays showed no abscesses or infections.

The report presented the cases of several

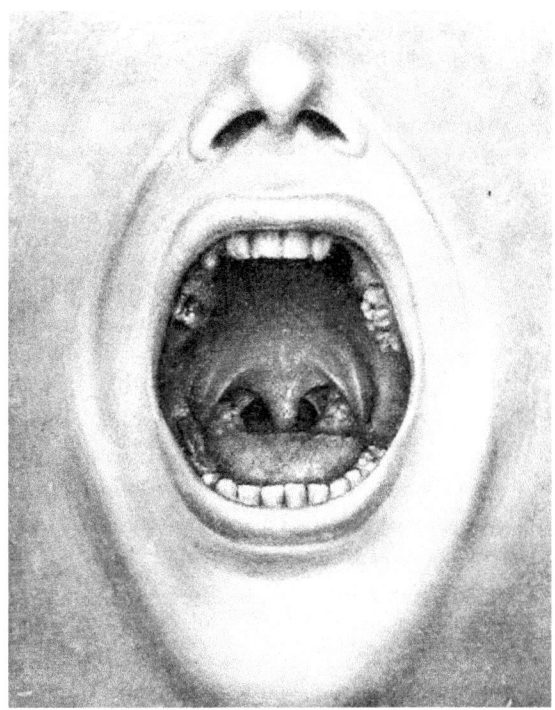

A view of the open mouth of a patient at the Trenton State Hospital in New Jersey, showing enlarged tonsils and rotten teeth. Medical superintendent Henry Cotton believed these were the result of a focal infection that spread toxins to the brain, causing insanity. The cure, as far as Cotton was concerned, was simple: the surgical removal of the tonsils and the extraction of the teeth (H.A. Cotton [1921]. *The defective delinquent and insane: The relation of focal infections to their causation, treatment and prevention.* Princeton, NJ: Princeton University Press).

patients whose conditions improved after the extraction of some or all of their teeth. One of those cases was that of M.A.S., a fifty-five-year-old woman who had been committed to the asylum several years before for agitation and depression.

> At that time it was noticed that her upper teeth were missing and her lower front teeth were in a badly decayed condition. Nothing was done for her, however, and she was transferred to the chronic wards. In September 1918, eleven bad teeth were extracted. She improved rapidly during the next weeks and on November 9, 1918, was discharged as recovered and since that time as been perfectly well. The neglect of the teeth in this patient probably is responsible for her residence of two years in the hospital for there seemed to be nothing wrong except her teeth [Board of Managers, p. 31].

Another of those cases was H.R.A., a thirty-four-year-old man who had had a previous admission to the asylum. Considered "simple-minded," he had relapsed upon release and had returned to his "untidy habits," including exposing himself to neighbors. Upon readmission he was diagnosed with dementia praecox (schizophrenia) and spent several years languishing in the asylum before two infected molars were extracted. He improved rapidly and was discharged. Monthly letters from his mother indicated that he was able to maintain employment for the first time in his life and that he no longer was a nuisance to his neighbors.

Cotton courted the attention of his asylum physician colleagues to exodontia, even while acknowledging that this therapeutic of choice most certainly must have seemed "entirely fanciful to the majority of professional men, both physicians and dentists" (Cotton, p. 269). Yet, he insisted, experience proved to him that for 25 percent of asylum patients, insanity was caused by infected teeth, and infected teeth alone. Averaging five tooth extractions per patient, Cotton was steadily transforming his asylum into a veritable "mecca of exodontia" (Board of Managers, p. 18). A visiting Swiss physician elaborated:

> I felt sad, seeing hundreds of people without teeth. Only a very few have sets of false teeth. The hospital takes care as to the pulling out of teeth, but does not provide false teeth.... The extraction of the teeth does great harm to those who cannot afford to pay for a set of false teeth, and these patients are numerous. While in the [asylum] they suffer from indigestion ... not being able to masticate their food. At home, recovered, these poor people have the same troubles, not being in a position to choose food which they would be able to eat without teeth. In addition, they are ashamed of being without teeth, since in their communities it is known to be a token of a previous sojourn in the State Hospital. They abstain from mixing with other people, refuse to go out a look for a job.... Thus, many of those recovered develop a reactive depression [Scull, p. 255].

Edentulous patients were, in many ways, the symbols of Cotton's success in not only introducing a focal sepsis based "scientific psychiatry" into asylum care, but of constructing high-tech facilities to deliver it. Just as Graves had done at the Rubery Hill and Holymoor asylums, Cotton not only had transformed Trenton State Hospital from a "holding pen for the delusional and demented" to a "center of a thorough on-going scientific assault on the root causes of psychosis" (Scull, p. 38) but, in the bargain, had reduced the staggeringly high patient census by releasing edentulous patients as cured.

And also just as it was with Graves, Cotton's interest in focal sepsis gradually moved from the teeth to other parts of the body. In fact, it was his relentless and highly controversial campaign to surgically excise insanity by removing tonsils, gallbladders, appendixes, cervixes, parts of stomachs and colons that tolled both the end of his career and the end of the hold of focal sepsis theory on asylum psychiatry [see **Surgery**].

The influence of focal sepsis theory, and on exodontia as a remedy for insanity, was particularly evident in the United States, and may be attributed, if not solely than surely largely, to the work of Henry Cotton. Asylums across the country added dentists to their staffs, purchased X-ray and other equipment, and constructed dental surgery suites, all material evidence of the influence of "scientific psychiatry." Exodontia was practiced with some enthusiasm well into the mid-twentieth century, the practice outlasting by several decades the theory that spawned it.

## REFERENCES

Board of Managers (1920). *Annual report of the Board of Managers of the New Jersey State Hospital.* Rahway, NJ: Author.
Cotton, H.A. (1919). The relation of oral infection to mental diseases. *Journal of Dental Research, 1,* 269–313.
Dussault, G., and Sheiham, A. (1982). The theory of focal sepsis and dentistry in early twentieth century Britain. *Social Science and Medicine, 16,* 1405–1412.
Hunter, W. (1900). Oral sepsis as a cause of disease. *British Journal of Dental Sciences, 43,* 741–744.
O'Reilly, P.G., and Claffey, N.M. (2000). A history of oral sepsis as a cause of disease. *Periodontology, 23,* 13–18.
Pallasch, T.J., and Wahl, M.J. (2003). Focal infection: New age or ancient history? *Endodontic Topics, 4,* 32–45.
Scull, A. (2005). *Madhouse: A tragic tale of megalomania and modern medicine.* New Haven, CT: Yale University Press.
Upsom, H.W. (1908). *Insomnia and nerve strain.* New York: G.P. Putnam's Sons.

# Expressive Therapy

*The uses of art, creative writing/poetry, dance, drama and/or music as therapeutic tools to entertain, encourage self-expression, stimulate imagination, experience the connection between mind and body, and foster activity.*

The expressive therapies emerged as asylum therapeutics in the nineteenth century, the result of the tandem influences of Romanticism and moral treatment [**see Moral Treatment**]. Partly a reaction against what the art critic John Ruskin condemned as the brutality of the artless Industrial Revolution, the Romantic movement elevated art, music and literature and valued emotional, intuitive and creative expressions over reason. Romanticism dared to imagine insanity as "an exalted state ... a privileged condition" (Beveridge, p. 595) which granted the person both access to greater truths and the genius to creatively express them. The Romantics did not have to look far for cases in point. Bedlam, as the Bethlem Asylum in London was better known, had confined artists such as Richard Dadd; the composer Robert Schumann had spent his last years in Endenich Asylum before taking his own life, and the poet Johann Christian Friedrich Hölderlin had been discharged as incurable from the university clinic at Tübingen, also in Germany; the operatic tenor and composer Pierre Gaveaux had been confined in the Charenton Asylum in France, and Bedřich Smetana, the "Father of Czech Music," who for more than a decade had been hectored by hallucinations, insomnia and depression, died in the Kateřinky Lunatic Asylum in Prague just a month after his commitment.

Romantic notions about the relationship between insanity and creativity certainly also influenced the moral treatment movement during the nineteenth century. While as a therapeutic regime, moral treatment most obviously encouraged rationality and self-regulation, it also engaged emotion, spirituality and creativity. In doing so, many nineteenth century asylums were transformed into centers of cultural activity: patients attended lectures, watched magic lantern shows, gardened, cooked, and attended religious services. They also painted and sketched, sang and danced, performed on stage and penned stories, poems and plays.

By the turn into the twentieth century, and as a result of the growing hegemony of more biological therapeutics to treat insanity, moral treatment as an ideal all but disappeared. The expressive therapies did not, though, at least not completely. Art instruction, for example, was still offered in many asylums, as was music instruction on instruments now somewhat worse for wear.

In mid-century, however, the expressive therapies enjoyed both a resurgence of popularity and a professionalization that more securely embedded them within asylum therapeutics. The popularity actually began with yet another paradigm shift in thinking about the mind. Freudian psychoanalytic theory and the psychotherapeutic "talking cure" strategies it inspired were never particularly suitable for the total institutional setting of the asylum, although both individual and group psychotherapy of one kind or another were offered in many of them. But these deeply psychological theories stimulated interest in how creative expression might represent or be used to work through the conflicts and confusions of asylum patients in either a primary or an adjunctive fashion. The mid-twentieth century timing of this renewed interest in expressive therapies was not coincidental. The patient census of almost every asylum in the United States, Europe and Great Britain was bloated by the admission of ex-soldiers. Traumatized, exhausted and dispirited, many of them were uncommunicative and immobile. And while the harsh reality was that their war-weariness was sometimes treated aggressively—with shock therapies [see **Shock Therapy**] and even with lobotomies [see **Psychosurgery**]—the prospect of engaging soldier-patients with the less intrusive expressive therapies held promise.

It was with this renewed interest in expressive therapies that its practitioners became professionalized. Credentialed in graduate training programs, registered or licensed, its practitioners often were members of newly formed national or international professional organizations that generated their own best practice and ethical standards. The expressive therapies expanded beyond art, dance, drama, music and writing, to play, cinema, sand play, journal, photo, biblio and recreational therapy, as well as integrated arts approaches. Not all of these found their ways into asylums, and some that did had only a short tenure, but the fact remains that professionalization transformed the expressive therapies. The truth be told, in the heyday of moral treatment, asylum patient involvement in expressive therapy had its odd therapeutic benefits, of course, but which expressive therapy was offered, and whether anything was offered at all, was tied more to the idiosyncrasies and access to resources of the asylum superintendent than to any larger theory of how and why it would be efficacious. The professionalization of expressive therapies a century later systematized their use, provided criteria for the evaluation of their effectiveness and eased the integration of some of them into other standard asylum-based treatment modalities.

REFERENCES

Andrews, J., Briggs, A., Porter, R., Tucker, P., and Waddington, K. (1997). *History of Bethlem*. London: Routledge.

"Answers to interrogatories" (1879, December 25). *The Meteor*, p. 3.

Beveridge, A. (2001). A disquieting feeling of strangeness? The art of the mentally ill. *Journal of the Royal Society of Medicine, 94*, 595–599.

Blumenthal, S.L. (1995). The tempest in my mind: Cultural interfaces between psychiatry and literature, 1844–1900. *Journal of the History of the Behavioral Sciences, 31*, 3–34.

Blumer, G.A. (1892). Music and its relation to the mind. *American Journal of Insanity, 48*, 350–364.

Browne, W.A.F. (1837). *What asylums were, are, and ought to be*. Edinburgh: Adam and Charles Black.

Burton, R. (1838/1621). *The anatomy of melancholy*. 16th ed. London: B. Blake.

Clark, M. (2010). *Art in madness: Dr. W.A.F. Browne's collection of patient art at Crichton Royal Institution, Dumfries*. Dumfries: Dumfries and Galloway Health Board.

Comettant, O. (1893). Hervé's mad pupils. *Musical Record and Review, 372*, 2.

Davis, W.B. (1987). Music therapy in 19th century America. *Journal of Music Therapy, 24*, 76–87.

Dickens, C. (1850). A lunatic asylum in Palermo. *Household Words, 2*, 151–155.

Dickens, C. (1852). A curious dance round a curious tree. *Household Words, 11*, 362–370.

Earle, P. (1854). *Institutions for the Insane in Prussia, Austria and Germany*. New York: Samuel S. and William Wood.

Esquirol, J.E.D. (1838). *Mental maladies: A treatise on insanity*. Trans. E.K. Hunt. Philadelphia: Lea and Blanchard.

Gamwell, L., and Tomes, N. (1995). *Madness in Amer-*

ica: Cultural and medical perceptions of mental illness before 1914. Ithaca, NY: Cornell University Press.
Gilman, S.L. (1982). *Seeing the insane*. New York: John Wiley & Sons.
Goldstein, J. (1987). *Console and classify: The French psychiatric profession in the nineteenth century*. Cambridge: Cambridge University Press.
Goodheart, L.B. (2003). *Mad Yankees: The Hartford Retreat for the Insane and nineteenth century psychiatry*. Boston: University of Massachusetts Press.
Hallaran, W.S. (1818). *Practical observations on the causes and cure of insanity*. 2nd ed. Cork, Ireland: Edwards and Savage.
Haller, B., and Larsen, R. (2005). Persuading sanity: Magic lantern images and the nineteenth century moral treatment in America. *Journal of American Culture, 28,* 259–272.
Haslam, J. (1810). *Illustrations of madness*. London: Rivingtons, Robinsons, Callow, Murray & Greenland.
Hustvedt, A. (2011). *Medical muses: Hysteria in nineteenth century Paris*. New York: W.W. Norton.
Justice-Malloy, R. (1995). Charcot and the theatre of hysteria. *Journal of Popular Culture, 28,* 133–138.
Kennedy, K. (2010). *Art in madness: Dr. W.A.F. Browne's collection of patient art at Crichton Royal Institution, Dumfries*. Edinburgh: Royal Society of Edinburgh.
Kirkbride, T.S. (1845). *Annual report of the Pennsylvania Hospital for the Insane*. Philadelphia: Pennsylvania Hospital.
"(The) Lunatics' Ball" (1874, January 24). *New York Times*, p. 5.
MacGregor, J. (1989). *The discovery of the art of the insane*. Princeton, NJ: Princeton University Press.
Mackinnon, D. (2006). Music, madness and the body: Symptom and cure. *History of Psychiatry, 17,* 9–21.
Malchiodi, C. (2005). *Expressive therapies*. New York: Guilford.
Micale, M.S. (2004). Discourses of hysteria in fin-de-siècle France. In M.S Micale (ed.), *The mind of modernism: Medicine, psychological and the cultural arts in Europe and America, 1880–1940,* pp. 71–92. Stanford, CA: Stanford University Press.
Monk, L.A. (2003). Gender, space and work: The asylum as gendered workplace in Victoria. In C. Coleborne and D. Mackinnon, *Madness in Australia: Histories, heritage and the asylum,* pp. 61–72. St. Lucia, QLD, Australia: University of Queensland Press.
Mora, G. (1957). Dramatic presentations by mental patients in the middle of the nineteenth century and A. Dumas' description. *Bulletin of the History of Medicine, 31,* 260–277.
Mora, G. (1959). Pietro Pisani and the mental hospital of Palermo in the early 19th century. *Bulletin of the History of Medicine, 33,* 230–248.
"Music as mind medicine" (1878). *Journal of Materia Medica, 17,* 82–84.
"Music cure" (1885). *Brainard's Musical World, 22,* 369.
Officers of the Retreat for the Insane (1895). *Seventy-first annual report*. Hartford, CT: Press of the Case, Lockwood & Brainard Company.
"Phrenological view of the treatment of the insane without mechanical restraint on the person" (1843). *Phrenological Journal, 16,* 209–233
Prinzhorn, H. (1972/1922). *Artistry of the mentally ill*. Trans. E. von Brocdorff. New York: Springer Verlag.
"Progress of the periodical literature of lunatic asylums" (1845). *American Journal of Insanity, 2,* 77–79.
Ray, I. (1873). *Contributions to mental pathology*. Boston: Little, Brown.
Reiss, B. (2004). Letters from Asylumia: The *Opal* and the cultural work of the lunatic asylum. *American Literary History, 16,* 1–28.
Reiss, B. (2005). Bardolatry in Bedlam: Shakespeare, psychiatry and cultural authority in 19th century America. *RLH, 72,* 769–797.
Reiss, B. (2007). *Theatres of madness: Insane asylums and nineteenth century American culture*. Chicago: University of Chicago Press.
Robertson, C.L. (1848). A report on the recent progress of psychological medicine. *Half-Yearly Abstract of the Medical Sciences, 7–8,* 314–345.
Rush, B. (1830). *Medical inquiries and observations upon the diseases of the mind,* 4th ed. Philadelphia: John Grigg.
Ruskin, J. (1870/1997). *Lectures on art*. New York: Allworth Press.
Schaeffer, N. (1999). *The Marquis de Sade: A life*. New York: Knopf.
Scull, A. (1996). *Masters of Bedlam: The transformation of the mad-doctoring trade*. Princeton, NJ: Princeton University Press.
"State of mind" (2010, February). *Dumfries & Galloway Life,* pp. 22–27.
Sueur, L., and Beer, D.M. (1997). The psychological treatment of insanity in France in the first part of the nineteenth century. *History of Psychiatry 8,* 37–53.
Weiss, P. (1964). *The persecution and assassination of Jean-Paul Marat as performed by the Inmates of the Asylum of Charenton under the direction of the Marquis de Sade*. New York: Dramatic Publishing Co.
Wright, D. (1996). *Quills*. New York: Dramatists Play Service.

## Art, or Art Therapy

Self-expression through painting, drawing, sculpting or other forms of art-making. More than any of the other expressive therapies, the therapeutic value of art was construed according to the vagaries of the era's reigning theory about the nature of insanity. Early nineteenth century Romanticism saw insanity as a source of artistic talent. When asylum patients were first encouraged to dip brushes into paint and put chalk to paper, the art they produced then was interpreted as an expression of some deeper and more profound truth about life than was accessible to those outside of the asylum who were caught up in living it in a rapidly modernizing society. Just a few decades later, the emphasis on reason and self-discipline that informed the practice of moral treatment reinterpreted artistic expression as the unsettling tension between imagination and rationality. And at the start of the twentieth century, that tension was absorbed by the theory of psychoanalysis that understood art as an expression of unconscious intrapsychic conflicts, unique to the asylum patient who produced it. Whether seen as a consequence of insanity or an expression of it, as a representation of a social truth or a manifestation of an individual struggle, art both as a material product and as an expressive process has a complex history as an asylum therapeutic.

A few of the most influential figures in the treatment of insanity stood at the starting line of that history. The French asylum physician and reformer Philippe Pinel, the American "Father of Psychiatry" Benjamin Rush, and the Bethlem Asylum apothecary John Haslam all presented cases of asylum patients whose artistic talents were awakened by their insanity. So did William Saunders Hallaran, who gave a detailed account of one of his patients at the Lunatic Asylum of Cork in Ireland, a young man whose symptoms of mania eased only to reveal a disturbing inclination to a dementia that left him resistant to any attempts at therapeutic engagement:

> This man had nearly been ranked amongst the incurable idiots, when he by accident was discovered in the act of amusing himself in drawings, with some rude colouring, on the walls of his apartment. From the specimen he had then given, he was questioned as to his knowledge of painting, and he having signified some acquaintance with the art, was immediately promised colors of better description, on the condition of his using them. This evidently gave an intelligent cheerfulness to his countenance, and he shortly evinced an impatience for the indulgence proffered to him. On being furnished with the necessary apparatus for painting, he at once commenced a systematic combination of colours, and having completed his arrangements, he requested one of the attendants to sit for him. This essay was sufficient to satisfy me that his recovery was not so remote as I had reason to suppose. The portrait was an exact representation of the person for whom it was intended.... He soon became elated by the approbation he had met with; he continued to employ himself in this manner for nearly two months after, with a progressive improvement in his mental faculties, when he was dismissed as cured [Hallaran, pp. 177–178].

While Hallaran seemed to have stumbled upon art as an expressive therapy, his Scottish contemporary, William A.F. Browne, had a keen interest in it. As the medical superintendent of the Crichton Royal Asylum in Dumfries, Browne had introduced a more continental version of moral treatment than his British Quaker colleagues who were more anxious about the unrestrained expression of emotion. He hired an art instructor and under his tutelage more than fifty of the asylum's quite well-heeled patients took to painting, drawing or sculpting as part of their therapeutic regime. Their art not only was exhibited in the asylum, but used as scenery in the elaborate theatrical productions the patients staged.

Browne saw nothing particularly revelatory in the art of his patients, that is, in his view the paintings and drawings exposed neither truth nor turmoil. Thus his interest was not so much in the material product of art-making as a diagnostic tool, but in the therapeutic process of creating it. That process, in his opinion, elevated the spirits of his patients and produced a kind of "moral contagion" of happy contentment that rippled through the asylum, affecting patients and staff alike.

It may be of interest to note that Browne also collected the art of his patients. Within his three volumes can be found the flower and bird paintings of Joanna Hutton who had spent thirty years in asylums after the unexpected death of her daughter; copies of Raphael's Renaissance paintings by John Fenn Russell, a physician by profession who was in the throes of insanity; the pen and ink drawings of other patients by William Bartholomew; and the original drawings of Joseph Askew, a Crichton patient for more a half a century, who believed that he had been adversely influenced by mesmeric powers when he lived as a young man in Peru.

Browne's collection presaged that of Hans Prinzhorn, a physician at the psychiatric hospital at the University of Heidelberg in Germany. There he was tasked with the responsibility of expanding a collection of patient art that had been started by Emil Kraepelin some years before. The result of his efforts came to be known as the Prinzhorn Collection, a compilation of more than 5,000 paintings, drawings, woodcarvings and textiles created by more than 450 patients. The Collection currently is archived at Heidelberg's University Hospital and although it continues to fascinate, it was Prinzhorn's 1922 text, *Artistry of the Mentally Ill*, that generated discussion and debate about "art brut," or "outsider art." The book contains the artistic works of ten "schizophrenic masters," all of them patients. So taken with the "autistic isolation and gruesome solipsism" of the paintings (Beveridge, p. 596), the German artist Max Ernst took the book with him to Paris where it had a significant influence on the Surrealist artists who were exploring, in their homage to Sigmund Freud and psychoanalysis, the expression of the unconscious in art.

That digression on art brut aside, art therapy, as it eventually came to be called, settled into an uncomfortable place in the moral treatment regimens of British and European asylums, in particular, during the nineteenth century. *Pace* Browne, there were some practitioners of moral treatment who feared that if imagination were given free reign, it would surely overtake reason and thus defeat the goals of restoration and cure. Others were more cautiously optimistic about the salutary effects of artistic expression and encouraged at least some of their patients to engage in it. Those physicians who did, however, were not particularly inclined to use the art for diagnostic purposes.

The familiar coda to the story of moral treatment was that for all intents and purposes it surrendered to the exigencies of the twentieth century: overcrowding, understaffing and underfunding displaced the therapeutic goal of asylums with a custodial one, and new theories about insanity replaced moral treatment with somatic therapeutics. Except for a relatively brief period of time during and after World War I when the artistic expressions of shell-shocked soldiers were read psychoanalytically as representations of unconscious conflicts, the therapeutic use of art waned and all but disappeared. It was somewhat ironic, then, that its revival occurred in that historic bastion of moral treatment, the York Retreat, in northern England. There, in the 1950s, a position was created for a staff person who, among other duties, would oversee patient engagement in the creative arts. Under his tutelage, about forty-five patients became involved in what was then called "painting therapy." True to tradition, the art produced was read neither for diagnostic nor treatment purposes, but as nothing more than an expression of the imagination.

The exhibitions, discussions and publications that came from this mid-century revival eventually led to the adoption of the term "art therapy" and by the mid–1960s the British Association of Art Therapy had been launched; the American Art Therapy Association followed a few years later. National organizations then sprung up around the world, but an imprecision in the definition of "art therapy" and the role of "art therapist," coupled with the plethora of theoretical perspectives that both informed therapeutic practice and purpose somewhat limited its use in asylums. It is typical for art therapy to have been folded into larger asylum initiatives such as occupational therapy and milieu therapy. And although its aesthetic, philosophical and structural relationship to art brut continues to be debated, the fact remains that asylum patient art is still, on occasion, exhibited and sold.

## *Dance*

The therapeutic use of rhythmic movement. Dances often were features of asylum life, especially during the nineteenth century when self-discipline and sociability were expected outcomes of a therapeutic regime of moral treatment. Patients usually were required to earn the privilege of attending a dance by good behavior and adherence to asylum rules over the weeks prior to it. Once at the event, they danced with each other and also with staff and physicians, thus the dance not only provided a distraction from the tedium of institutional life and an opportunity to rehearse the skills of reason and comportment, but personalized the patients' relationship with staff and physicians in a manner that was thought to facilitate the process of moral treatment.

One particular dance event, usually held annually, was particularly interesting. The Lunatic Ball was an extravagant event in which staff and physicians, patrons and community members joined patients for an evening of entertainment. More valuable in many ways for what it stood for than for what it was, the Lunatic Ball marked a break with the unenlightened past. Patients were no longer chained, but moved freely across the dance floor; no longer naked, they were dressed in what passed for their finery; no longer silenced, they talked and even laughed. The novelist Charles Dickens was quite taken by the way the Lunatic Ball he attended at St. Luke's Hospital in London in 1845 broke with the past, and yet just as taken by how the grip of insanity survived that rupture.

> As I was looking at the marks in the walls of the galleries, of the posts to which patients were formerly chained, sounds of music were heard from a distance. The ball had begun, and we hurried off in the direction of the music.... There were the patients usually to be found in all such asylums, among the dancers. There was the brisk, vain pippin-faced little old lady, in a fantastic cap ... there was the old-young woman, with disheveled long light hair, spare figure, and weird gentility ... there was the vacantly laughing girl, requiring now and then a warning finger to admonish her; there was the quiet young woman, almost well, and soon going out. For partners, there were the sturdy, bull-necked, thickset little fellow who had tried to get away last week; the wry-faced tailor, formerly suicidal, but much improved; the suspicious patient with a countenance of gloom ... there was the man of happy silliness, pleased with everything [Dickens, p 367].

With the keen eye of the humanitarian he was, Dickens noted the "usual loss of social habits and the usual solitude" (p. 368) among the patients, the lackluster eyes of some of them, the weariness and hopelessness of others. Yet, he felt encouraged by the experience and urged his readers to feel the same: "It may be little to have abolished from madhouses all that is abolished, and to have substituted all that is substituted. Nevertheless, reader, if you can do a little in any good direction—do it. It will be much, some day" (p. 370).

Not everyone agreed that a dance was a "little good," especially in the United States where religious revivals attended what had come to be known as the Second and Third Great Awakenings. Dance was scorned by revivalists for exciting carnal desires and passions. Although their exhortations had a considerable impact on the moral landscape of the nation, they did not completely penetrate the walls of asylums. Many asylum physicians were, in fact, religious but saw little to be worried about in the contained, supervised, controlled, medicalized and even propagandized event of the Lunatic Ball.

The Lunatic Ball has been memorialized by Katherine Drake in her 1847 painting, "Patient Ball, held in the Kitchen of the Somerset County Asylum, England." Drawings also were published in popular weekly magazines, reassuring casual readers that insanity was being tamed and domesticated within the walls of asylums.

It may be interesting to note that even in an overcrowded asylum, the therapeutic potential of dance was noted. In 1942 a dancer and choreographer was approached by the medical superintendent of St. Elizabeths Hospital in Washington, D.C., about working with traumatized soldiers, many of whom were immobile and uncommunicative. Marian Chace had always believed in the curative power of dance, so she accepted the offer and began a "communication through movement" program. Through a technique called "mirroring," in which she recreated her dancing partner's movements, she was able to establish a relationship with patients who had for all intents and purposes been unreachable. Chace also believed that mirroring allowed her to better understand the feelings and conflicts that were being expressed in the patients' movements, thus her insights informed other attempts to therapeutically engage with them. The "Mother of Dance Therapy," as she came to be called, also established a more interactive dance therapy regime, worthy of her sobriquet, with other more responsive patients. She also directed and choreographed a production titled "A Cry for Humanity: The Life of Dorothea Dix" that was performed by patients in celebration of the asylum's 1955 centennial and broadcast on television. Chace retired in 1966 after forming the American Dance Therapy Association, the first of its kind in the world.

## Drama, or Drama Therapy

The use of drama or theatrical performance, scripting or production to achieve therapeutic goals. Ironically, behind the thick walls and around the rigid rules of daily life, there always has been drama in asylums. When not gagged or medicated into silence, patients screamed, cried and chattered; when not restrained, they wandered about, most of them aimlessly, but some in search of means of escape. In their interactions with unpredictable patients, asylum physicians often had to improvise, sometimes assuming a gentle, sympathetic role, other times taking on an authoritarian air, using their penetrating gazes, booming voices and grand gestures to guide and control their unruly patients [see **Fixing**].

Therapeutic interventions also had a certain theatricality. The pious frauds, so popular in the early nineteenth century, relied upon elaborate staging and careful casting to trick or ridicule patients out of their insanity [see **Pious Frauds**]. More than a century later the shock treatments, whether delivered chemically or electrically, brought patients to what they perceived to be the brink of death by acrobatically convulsing their bodies while physicians and staff, in well-rehearsed and synchronized movements, brought them back to consciousness and, if only for a short time, some relief [see **Shock Therapy**].

Case descriptions by early asylum physicians often read more like elaborate stage directions than not. Jean-Étienne Dominique Esquirol, *médecin ordinaire* at the Salpêtrière Asylum in Paris, France, as an example, captured the theatricality of the passions in his description of mania:

> All at once he fails to recognize his surrounding objects, and losing his own identity, lives only in chaotic existence. His disordered and menacing discourses betray the disturbance of his reason. His actions are mischievous, and he desires to overthrow and destroy everything, He is at war with everybody; and hates all that he was formerly accustomed to love. He is the very genius of evil, who delights in confusion, disorder and fear which he spreads around [Esquirol, p. 48].

Decades after Esquirol's death, and still at the Salpêtrière, the "passions" of insanity and the "evil genius" of mania had given way to hysteria, the "most extroverted of the psychopathologies, its own act and audience" (Micale, p. 76). Under the Svengali-like direction of neurologist Jean-Martin Charcot, costumed and coiffed hysterical women patients performed their pathology before an appreciative audience, by going into trances, experiencing partial paralyses, acrobatically arching their bodies in an arc-de-circle, and even engaging in demonstrations of clairvoyance, telepathy and *sommeil à distance,* or telepathic communication. In the audience of these Tuesday Lectures, as the spotlighted stage for these performances of hysteria was known, were playwrights and choreographers, opera divas, and actresses such as the legendary Sarah Bernhardt, who mimicked the hysterical gestures of the patients for her role in the tragic drama "Adrienne Lecouvreur" in 1880.

It might even be said that drama played an important role in development of early nineteenth century theories of insanity in the United States. No fewer than thirteen articles of Shakespearean criticism and analysis were published in the *American Journal of Insanity,* by leading asylum physicians who clearly were taken with the mad characters who peopled the Bard's plays, and the veritable lexicon of euphemisms and clever turns of phrase he used to describe the experiences of insanity. As an homage to someone whose insights they valued as superior as their own, American asylum physicians self-consciously interpreted, analyzed and applied Shakespeare's insights, sometimes cleverly interweaving them with their own, thus boosting their own cultural authority in the new and somewhat mysterious field of asylum medicine. In the words of Isaac Ray, one of the founders of the Association of Medical Superintendents of American Institutions for the Insane: "Few men, I apprehend, are so familiar with those diversities of mental character that are, in any degree, the result of disease, as not to find the sphere of their ideas on this subject [of insanity] somewhat enlarged by the careful study of Shakespeare" (p. 524).

Art imitated life. Asylums and their patients were the subjects of quite a few early nineteenth century theatrical productions that ranged from drama to farcical comedy. These included: *The Father and Daughter* (1801), *Une Visite à Bedlam* (1818), *The Rake's Progress* (1833), and *Smiles and Tears, or the Widow's Stratagem* (1815). But the idea of performing plays *in* asylums and using *patients* in leading roles, was less a result of this genre than one of the emergence of moral treatment and its emphasis on bringing a plethora of cultural resources to the treatment of the insane.

One of the first, if not the first, asylums to stage theatrical productions with patients was Charenton, just outside of Paris, France. Under the superintendency of François Simonnet de Coulmier, a Catholic priest, elected member of the Estates-General and champion of the French Revolution, a rather unique lay version of moral treatment—one that cared for the soul, both sacred and political, as well as the mind—was instituted. Although de Coulmier emphasized "healing through art" as part of his moral treatment regime, it was not until he encountered a patient who had been transferred to the asylum from the Bastille prison that his interest in theatre was piqued. That patient was the infamous Donatien-Alphonse-François, Comte de Sade, better known to history as the Marquis de Sade.

De Sade was no stranger to the Charenton Asylum, having spent three years there until the *lettres de cachet,* such as the one that had him arrested and institutionalized for sacrilege, were abolished by the National Assembly. Free for several years, he published radical political pamphlets and actively supported the Republic. But it was his anonymously published novellas, *Justine, or The Misfortunes of Virtue*, and *Juliette* that not only caused a sensation among the French public with their graphic scenes of sexual orgies, rape, incest and torture, but that prompted Napoleon Bonaparte to order his arrest. Taken into custody in 1801, although never criminally charged, and declared insane two years later, De Sade found himself once again in the Charenton Asylum.

Ill, despondent and morbidly obese, De Sade came under the protection and tutelage of de Coulmier who encouraged him to direct plays. The plays were conventional and all-too familiar French plays, thus what drew the large public audiences to them was not the sexual license for which the "Divine Marquis" had been known for decades, but the casts of professional actors and asylum patients. While audiences heaped praise on Charenton, asylum physicians heaped scorn on de Coulmier. Bluntly stating that the plays had "no curative value," the new *médecin ordinaire* at the nearby Salpêtrière Asylum, Jean-Étienne Dominique Esquirol, went on to castigate de Coulmier for turning patients into the "object of curiosity of the frivolous, thoughtless, and sometimes wicked public" (Schaeffer, p. 486). At the heart of his remarks was a disdain not just for the priest himself, but for the pretentions of the French clergy that was clinging to its tradition of caring for the insane even while physicians, such as Esquirol, were entering asylum medicine as a specialty. Medical moral treatment, Esquirol seemed to be saying, was vastly superior to the lay moral treatment it not so much resembled as replicated.

Also critical of the theatrical productions were French government officials who were concerned that it raised the profile of a prisoner of the state who had never been charged with a crime. Arguing that even from behind the walls of the asylum De Sade constituted a threat to public morality, they suspended all theatrical performances in an 1813 decree. Although his mental and physical health had greatly improved during his years of directing and staging plays, De Sade died in his sleep a year later, wrapped in the arms of his teenaged mistress, but still confined to Charenton Asylum.

The De Sade affair at Charenton was dramatized in Peter Weiss's 1965 Tony Award-winning play, "The Persecution and Assassination of Jean-Paul Marat as Performed by the Inmates of the Asylum of Charenton Under the Direction of the Marquis de Sade," usually shortened to "Marat/Sade." A film by the same shortened title was released two years later. A later Obie-award winning play, "Quills," by Doug Wright, imaginatively recreated De Sade's last years at Charenton; it was adapted for a film released in 2000 under the same title.

The internecine politics of Charenton did not caution other asylum physicians against adding theatrical productions to their moral treatment regimes. In Palermo, Italy, in 1829 Baron Pietro Pisani, a well-to-do philanthropist and composer, converted his hillside villa into the Casa Dei Matti Asylum, later called the Royal Hospital for the Insane in Sicily, and instituted a system of gentle persuasion and productive activities that continuously engaged his 140 patients. In the garden, patients performed dramatic and musical plays in a small Greek-style theatre they, themselves, had constructed. Well regarded European and American asylum physicians visited Casa Dei Matti, eager to assess how its moral treatment was instituted and, perhaps, to compare Pisani's lay version of it with their own medical version. While Pisani did not particularly encourage lay visitors, quite aside from the fact that Sicily was not easily accessible to travelers, such luminaries as Charles Dickens, Nathaniel Parker Willis, and Alexander Dumas spent some time there, each struck by the manner in which theatrical performances soothed and quieted the otherwise restive patients in the audience.

Dumas did not write extensively about his visit to Palermo, but in a series of newspaper articles, he did describe in some detail his visit to the asylum in Aversa, near Naples, Italy. Constructed in 1813, the asylum had its own theatre that apparently was only infrequently used until Biagio Miraglia was appointed its physician in 1843. A psychiatric entrepreneur and proponent of moral treatment, Miraglia traded on what was widely believed to be the innate "agility, liveliness, intelligence, readiness in the impulses, as well as wildness and rudeness" (Mora, 1957, p. 264) of the Napoli people, and cast his patients in theatrical productions to which the general public was invited.

As a political reactionary, Miraglia chose plays with unabashed patriotic themes that would have been treated with suspicion, perhaps even censored, by government officials were it not for the fact that they were being performed by insane patients. The plays of "the Father of Italian Tragedy," Vittorio Alfieri, were popular at the asylum. Based on the theme that love of country must be greater than love of family, the plays appealed to those, such as Miraglia, who supported the populist revolutions against Austrian control.

The play Dumas attended was lesser known, but just as politically reactionary. Yet the theme of revolt against tyranny in "Le Bourgeois de Gand" by Hyppolite Romand seemed to impress Dumas less than the personal conversation he had with Miragli after the curtain had lowered. He asked Miraglia why he did the play and the physician, who later would be dismissed from the asylum and put on trial for political provocation, explained his motives in moral treatment, not political, terms:

> I wanted to show the public that the insane must not be treated as furious animals and completely rejected from the human family: a very keen observer, able to recognize which mental functions are impaired, can also recognize which ones are still intact and can improve these latter through exercise; so that insanity can be considered only as dark spot on the spirit, a dim point on the light ...Patience, perseverance, good will, and tenacity are the means to obtain the confidence of those poor patients and to lead them to the exercise of the intact functions, relaxing in the meantime the impaired functions: it is essential to put a patient in relationship with another or several other patients, in order to direct toward the same goal the intact functions of several minds partially impaired [Mora, 1957, pp. 266–267].

Miraglia's good intention, it should be noted, did not extend to his female patients. Worried that they were more inclined to improvise and deviate from the script, he used only male patients in his productions. They were cast not because of the progress they already had made at the asylum, but in the hope that they would progress as a result of their performances. The patients who appeared in the "Le Bourgeois de Gand" that Dumas saw must have found learning a script and stage cues more than a little daunting given the floridness of their insanity. That cast included a patient suffering from mania, another who had hallucinations, another who thought himself possessed by the devil; the others were described as having pathological ideas, delusions of grandeur, and senile dementia. As Dumas noted, and quite contrary to Miraglia's gendered assessment, the male patients occasionally went off script, improvised, and confused the unfamiliarity of the characters they were playing with the unreality of the insanity they were experiencing, but as Miraglia had predicted, each improved considerably after the run of the play.

Miraglia was placed on trial in 1851 and sentenced to ten years for political provocation, but an indulgence from the King released him from the sentence. He returned to the asylum at Aversa in 1853, continuing his goal of perfecting moral treatment and using theatrical productions as one means for achieving it.

The use of patient-cast theatre for the purpose of divulsion, that is, embarrassment and humiliation, in some German and Danish asylums was strongly criticized as antithetical to moral treatment by asylum physicians in other countries. Among them was William A.F. Browne. As a former student of Jean-Étienne Dominique Esquirol, who had criticized the theatrical productions at the Charenton Asylum decades before, he was loathe to engage in any activity that made laughing stocks of insane patients; as a proponent of moral treatment, on the other hand, he appreciated the therapeutic value of creative expression. When he assumed the directorship of the Crichton Royal Asylum in 1839, therefore, he struck a compromise and cautiously experimented with patient-casted and produced theatrical performances.

The Crichton Royal Asylum was ideally suited for the experiment. As part of the regime of moral treatment, the asylum offered concerts, lectures, dances and magic lantern shows to its patients who also participated in the cultural life of the southern Scottish town of Dumfries. Despite the condemnation of some Calvinist townspeople, Browne staged the asylum's first theatrical production of "Raising the Wind," a farce in two acts, in 1843, featuring both staff and patients in the

Twelfth-Night entertainment at the Hanwell Asylum in London, England, in 1848 to celebrate the end of the Christmas season. Notice the well-dressed ladies and gentlemen on the right; they most likely were prominent citizens of the community, there more to observe than to dance (courtesy of the Wellcome Library, London).

cast. It was enthusiastically reviewed in the *Dumfries Herald*:

> [Patients] constituted the main body of the audience. Many a smile escaped them, many a hearty laugh and many a bravo burst forth, and ever and anon they clapped their hands, well pleased; but all was order and regularity.... Between the two acts songs were sung...[and] at the close of the farce, an epilogue, written by a patient, was spoken; an appropriately grotesque dance wound up the whole.... Everything was, in fact, conducted as in a long-established theatre, and by a well disciplined corps of actors ["Phrenological View," pp. 226–227].

The success of the performance, and the therapeutic effects it had on both patients as performers and audience members, assuaged whatever reticence Browne had, as evidenced by his declaration that "the attempt is no longer an experiment. It is a great fact of moral science and must be accepted and acted upon" (Scull, p. 111). Theatre remained an essential mode of moral treatment at Crichton, in fact, for more than a century beyond Browne's superintendency.

In the United States where moral treatment proceeded in fits and starts, handsome state asylums designed according to the Kirkbride plan [see **Moral Treatment**] were being built across the country. Few had bespoke theatres, but most boasted large chapels or auditoriums where visiting actors troupes performed for the patients or, on fewer occasions, where patients performed plays that they wrote, or that were written for them. Quite contrary to Browne's conclusion that the therapeutic use of theatre was a "fact of moral science," however, American asylum physicians were not particularly keen on its use—with one notable exception.

Amariah Brigham was appointed medical superintendent of the New York State Lunatic Asylum in Utica when it opened in 1843. A founding member of the Association of Medical Superintendents of American Institutions for the Insane, he had a strong interest in moral therapy yet, as was the case with many of his colleagues, had no compunction about using mechanical restraints, such as the infamous Utica crib [see **Mechanical Restraints**] when more gentle interactions with patients failed. Utica, as the asylum was most often referred to, was comprised of four limestone buildings designed in the Greek Revival style. One contained a sizeable amusement hall, and it was here in 1847 that a group of patients, both male and female, and all of them white, blackened their faces with burnt cork and put on a show that was so wildly popular with patients, staff and guests, that performances, with changing casts of patients, of course, continued for almost fifty years.

The Blackbird Minstrels, as the troupe was called, mimicked a traveling black minstrel show that once had performed for the patients. Always performed by white males with blackened faces and outlandish costumes, black minstrel shows began in the country in the 1830s as a mix of savage parody of black plantation slaves and grudging respect for black cultural forms. Its performance by patients and in an asylum, though, was more than a little ironic:

> In masking themselves, the outcast actors imitated figures who were equally outcast—the slaves and urban Northern blacks who were tarred by blackness much as the actors themselves were stigmatized by the label of insanity. They enacted scenarios of slave life for the ultimate captive audience; and under the watchful eye of the asylum authorities, they turned a famously unruly form into a spectacle of their own capacity for self-control. From behind blackface masks, they spoke to each other, to their doctors (who doubled as their captors), to the curious townsfolk and even politicians who were occasionally given admittance, and to themselves—all in different codes, some still faintly decipherable, others no doubt lost

somewhere in the transmission from performer to observer [Reiss, p. 52].

Because the "Ethiopian Extravaganzas," as the productions were called, were performed by the Blackbird Minstrels before and during the Civil War, during Emancipation, Reconstruction and Jim Crow, they most likely were both performed to and received differently by their respective audiences. But the focus on hilarity, that wonderfully revulsive response that was thought to distract from delusions and buoy morose feelings, never diminished. In the words of Tilden Brown, the resident physician of the asylum, "Mirth and recreation, no longer frivolous or puerile, become dignified as instruments of cure" when embedded in a regime of moral treatment (Reiss, p. 60). In light of that rather somber framing of hilarity, the asylum went on to produce a whole variety of patient-cast theatrical productions, all comedies, farces and musicals.

At the start of the twentieth century, with the rise of the asylum patient census, the increasing patient demographic diversity and, more importantly, the supplanting of moral treatment by biological therapeutics that targeted the brain rather than the mind, the New York State Lunatic Asylum at Utica ceased staging theatrical productions. With the exception of a few annual Holiday performances, such as the one at Massachusetts's Bridgewater State Hospital for the Criminally Insane that was the subject of the controversial 1967 Frederick Wiseman documentary "Titicut Follies," the few other American asylums that used drama as a therapeutic, followed suit.

## Music Therapy, or Music Cure, or Musical Remedy

The therapeutic engagement of asylum patients in listening to music, and/or in the instrumental or vocal performance of music. The ability of music to "soothe a savage breast" was well known by the ancient physicians. Asclepiades, among others, recom-

The music therapy room at the St. Joseph State Lunatic Asylum No. 2 in Missouri. Patients were taught music and performed in a band which played for the occasional dances held for patients and staff (courtesy of the St. Joseph Museums, Inc./Glore Psychiatric Museum, St. Joseph, Missouri).

mended the use of music to calm the manic and rouse the melancholic, and Hippocrates performed music for his insane patients. Early physicians whose practice included treating the insane took counsel from their forebears. Thomas Willis, whose seventeenth century texts on insanity were canonical for generations of asylum physicians yet to come, used music to distract his melancholic patients from their woes, as did Robert Burton who declared it a "sovereign remedy against despair and melancholy, and will drive away the devil himself" (Burton, p. 372).

These proclamations were made long before the insane were separated from larger society and confined in asylums. Once congregated there, the challenge was to introduce music into large institutions teeming with differently diagnosed and situated patients. Perhaps it was not surprising that that challenge was first taken up in France where "music was the entertainment of every social class...[and] lis-

tened to in opera houses, chic parties and village fêtes" (Sueur & Beer, p. 45). At the Salpêtrière Asylum in Paris, Jean-Étienne Dominique Esquirol made cautious use of music, first to induce relaxation and eventually sleep. He had observed that insomniac patients sometimes were lulled into sleep by the percussive tapping on the wall by attendants or by the steady drip of water from a suspended pan unto the floor. Reasoning that music with such a rhythm might have the same effect, he hid musicians from the view of the restless patients and had them play tunes that would have been familiar from their childhoods. "[Music] brings peace and composure of mind," he concluded, "but it does not cure" (Esquirol, p. 80).

But could music do anything more or different than lull restive patients to sleep? An ingenious experiment was conducted in the late nineteenth century at Blackwell Island Asylum in New York City to answer that question. There, asylum physician Milo Wilson, himself a skilled musician, brought in a pianist by the name of John Nelson Pattison to perform with New York's Ninth Regiment Band under the baton of Patrick Gilmore. Then, one by one, patients were brought into the room. Their behavioral reactions to the music were observed and noted, and their pulse and respiration rates were taken and compared to their pre-concert measurements. Seven patients were tested; each of the women was chronically insane and had been unresponsive to other methods of therapeutic intervention. The "musical remedy" experiment produced impressive results. The pulse and respiration rates of the women diagnosed with melancholia increased, as did their general mood and sociability, while the pulse and respiration rates of the women diagnosed with mania decreased, as did their aggression and loquacity, as these case vignettes illustrated:

> The music aroused the interest of a thirty year old melancholic enough for her to notice her surroundings; on the second occasion of hearing it, her intelligence was further awakened; and the third time produced a "childlike affection for the genial and colossal Commissioner Thomas S. Brennan, one of the several dignitaries who observed the experiments...[Now] her days are spend counting the hours she must be away from him, and shows a babyish delight whenever she is near the Commissioner, although that is not usual unless she hears the music which first aroused her interest" ["Music as Mind Medicine," p. 83].

> A thirty year old woman with chronic mania of three year duration, and considered to have a poor prognosis, was always violent, profane, abusive and nervous. When Pattison played a "plaintive nocturne" by Chopin, her pulse was "wiry, but became fuller almost at once." She soon started talking sensibly. An adagio by Beethoven added to the tranquilizing effect, and familiar tunes such as "Home, Sweet Home" made "her nervousness pass." She was sent back to her room without the straitjacket ["Music as Mind Medicine," p. 82].

Although two additional experiments with patients diagnosed with catatonia were unsuccessful in altering pulse, respiration or behavior, the musical remedy experiment was deemed a success. Music did not cure, but it certainly had a salutary effect, either as a stimulant or a tonic, depending of course upon the diagnosis of the patient. It could be prescribed, Wilson argued, just as certainly as opium, milk, bromide, or chloral hydrate and would mimic their effects. But just as these *materia medica* could have adverse effects, so could a dose of music. The Blackwell Island Asylum experiment revealed that if patients were to listen to music unsuited for their respective condition, the results could be alarming. A melancholic patient, for example, was likely to become depressed and even suicidal while listening to a solemnly slow adagio; the manic patient, on the other hand, was likely to become excited and even violent while listening to a loud and brassy overture.

It was not just the type of music that was observed to have an effect on patients, but the instrument that played it. Antoine Chambeyron championed music as a therapeutic, observing that when one of Anton Reicha's wind quintets was performed at the Saint-Méen Asylum in Rennes, France, where he was superintendent, the fifty women patients who comprised the audience were spellbound. But it was the elegiac sound of the solo flute that seemed to enrapture the most intractably insane among them, soothing them into a contemplative silence that lasted well beyond the performance.

The "musical remedy" experiment aside, it was observations like those of Chambeyron that brought music into the therapeutic regimes of asylums. Yet, at least in one notable case, the observation was fleeting and took some time to make an impression. That was the case at the New York State Lunatic Asylum, better known as the Utica Asylum, the first publicly funded asylum in the state. In the late nineteenth century it was under the superintendency of G. Adler Blumer. A reform-minded physician, Blumer nonetheless had paid little attention to the therapeutic use of music until he observed a peculiar incident on the asylum grounds. Two pestiferous organ-grinders had wandered onto the property and had started playing beneath the window of the main building. Apparently unaware that they were on asylum grounds, they had laid their hats on the ground in the hope that coins would be tossed from the windows in appreciation. Blumer chased them away. When they returned many months later, the superintendent, ashamed of his reaction and hoping to model cordiality for his patients, invited the organ-grinders into the main building and with considerable bonhomie "conducted" their performance. Despite the fact that their music was discordant and shrill, the few patients who heard it were quite taken by it. Taking note of that, Blumer then invited the organ-grinders into the wards of the chronic patients who were similarly entranced, albeit a bit confused when the organ-grinders, who did not speak English, once again passed the hat.

Blumer realized in that moment that if unpleasant music had that salutary effect then surely pleasant music would be therapeutic. He set himself immediately to the task of creating an asylum orchestra. He advertised for musicians in the newspapers, and soon had an orchestra that played concerts for the patients and the larger community, and provided the music for the weekly patient dances. Although pleased enough with the therapeutic effects of music to recommend it to his colleagues, Blumer concluded:

> I cannot measure the precise value of music in our armamentarium. It cannot be placed on a par with drugs in this respect, and one must be content to speak of its therapeutic value in more general terms....We do know that for the moment attention is diverted from the self to the orchestra, that in so far morbid self-introspection can be checked. We know that through the nervous system the heart beats faster and the circulation is quickened, and that in so far the functions of the body are stimulated to greater activity. Similarly respiratory movement may be accelerated and the blood subjected to follow aeration. In these and other ways it may be claimed that music is helpful in the treatment of insanity, and one is inclined to bespeak for its greater consideration, as one of the readily available appurtenances of an asylum than has heretofore been vouchsafed by the craft [Blumer, pp. 361–362].

It is not known whether the Utica Asylum orchestra counted among its members musicians of exceptional talent. But it is known that asylum music sometimes did launch a few notable careers. The English composer Sir Edward Elgar began his musical career as the band conductor at the Worcester County Pauper and Lunatic Asylum, also and better known as the Powick Asylum, after the village it was near. A remarkably progressive place, the asylum confined 300 patients and made music an integral part of the therapeutic regime. Under Elgar's baton the asylum band, which was composed of both staff and patients, not only concertized for the patients, but performed the polkas and quadrilles that Elgar had composed for the Friday evening dances. The latter were collected, although never published, under the title "Powick Asylum Music" and are preserved at the Elgar Birthplace Museum. Elgar, of course went on to become a distinguished composer whose "Pomp and Circumstances" accompanies many high school and university students down the aisles during their graduation processions.

An asylum also launched the career of Ronger Florimond who at the age of fifteen was hired as the organist at the Bicêtre Asylum in Paris, France. While there, he performed for patients, composed songs, and directed them in immensely popular one-act vaudeville performances. It was an operetta he composed after leaving his position at the asylum that secured his position as musical director of the Théatre du Palais-Royal. Now known simply as Hervé, he went on to compose more than one hundred well-received operettas, and is generally credited with having established that musical genre in France.

If hearing music indeed could soothe the savage breast, then what would performing it do? That was one of the questions on the mind of nineteenth century asylum physicians who peripatetically wandered from one asylum to another to gather therapeutic ideas and practices. The American asylum physician Pliny Earle, who in the mid-nineteenth century visited asylums in Prussia, Austria and Germany, was struck by the musical instruction offered to patients but especially so by their performances. He noted that patients at the Illenau Asylum were taught to play piano by a music teacher on staff and provided weekly concerts for fellow patients and members of the Baden, Germany, community in a large saloon that recently had been constructed for that purpose. In the Kateřinky Lunatic Asylum in Prague patients transcribed quartettes and terzettes, and sang so beautifully at chapel services that "even the ear of the connoisseur would be gratified" (Earle, p. 119).

But it was at the Sonnenstein Asylum, that magnificent castle above the River Elbe near Dresden, Germany, that music therapy seemed to have reached its crescendo. Patients were not only instructed in musical performance but in musical composition, and played their original pieces in concerts to which the larger community was invited. So intimately had music been entwined within the moral treatment regime of the asylum that the mere threat of exclusion assured patient compliance and conformity.

By the late nineteenth century the principles of moral treatment that had been so welcoming to music therapy had given way to more biological strategies for the treatment of insanity, but music remained an adjunctive therapy in many asylums around the world and music therapy became an organized profession. Its widespread use in other institutions, such as general hospitals, orphanages, and residential centers for the physically or mentally disabled, attests to the continuing power of the idea that music is therapeutic.

It is worth noting, though, that a different musical form developed mid-twentieth century that could boast longevity as an asylum therapeutic. The touring asylum choir was evidence of the lingering entrancement with music as therapy, and no better example of it could be found than the Bryce Hospital Touring Choir. Established in 1950 by Virginia Dobbins, who at the time was director of patient activity at the Tuscaloosa, Alabama, asylum, the choir originally was composed of forty patients. It traveled throughout the state, singing gospels, hymns and old-time favorites, all accompanied by a patient who also was a pianist, to appreciative community audiences. By 1965 the choir had grown to eighty members ranging in age from sixteen to eighty years old, and was directed by the asylum's chaplain, B.W. Allen. Despite having no musical training, Allen was able to coax impressive performances from the immensely popular choir whose members also had the opportunity to develop their interpersonal skills in post-concert receptions with community members.

## *PhotoTherapy*

The therapeutic use of photographs. The unique spelling of the word is to differentiate this type of expressive therapy from that which involves the therapeutic application of different wavelengths of light, which is spelled "phototherapy" [see **Phototherapy**].

Asylums were the among the first institutions to use the new technology of photography. The opportunity the 1839 invention provided for cataloguing and classifying the physiognomy of insanity, as well as for "training the eye" to interpret it, was irresistible. While it must be said that cataloguing and classifying indeed were the primary purposes of asylum photography, its therapeutic potential was recognized as well. Hugh Welch Diamond, superintendent of the Women's Department of the Surrey County Lunatic Asylum for Paupers in the London, England, borough of Wandsworth, was the first to recognize the therapeutic potential of the photograph. In a paper presented to the Royal Society, he made reference to a series of four photographs he had taken of a single patient as she progressed over time from the throes of mania to eventual recovery.

The patient could scarcely believe that her last portrait representing her as clothed and in her right mind, would even have been preceded by anything so fearful; and she will never cease, with these faithful monitors in her hand, to express the most lively feelings of gratitude for a recovery so marked and unexpected [Gilman, p. 165].

While Diamond's comments could be read more as an homage to the photographer than to the patient, the idea that photographs could further therapeutic goals by increasing self-awareness and, perhaps, even fostering self-control, was intriguing to asylum physicians. Despite the cumbersome technology, quite a few experimented with its therapeutic use well into the early twentieth century although, it must be said, none was particularly impressed with its results.

Interestingly, there was a different version of photoTherapy that had been in practice a good decade before Diamond presented his paper. At the Pennsylvania Hospital for the Insane, that paragon of moral treatment, Thomas Kirkbride was using magic lantern shows to both entertain and therapeutically engage his patients. In some ways this early attempt at photoTherapy was serendipitous in its origin. Kirkbride just happened to be a friend of William and Frederick Langenheim, local photographers who were determined to make photographic images accessible to the public through the technology of a magic lantern projector that had a concave mirror in back of a light source so that a negative of a photographic image could be projected through the lens. Intrigued, Kirkbride scheduled three magic lantern shows each week, using the Langenheim brothers' slides.

The slides were carefully chosen by Kirkbride. Consistent with the demographics of his patients, they depicted topics that would have appealed to what might be called middle-class sensibilities: history, art, religion, foreign travel, famous people, advances in science. Most of the presentations ended with a humorous slide, specifically chosen by Kirkbride to lift the mood of his patients, if only to con-

A Hugh Welch Diamond portrait of an insane patient at the Surrey County Lunatic Asylum for Paupers in Wandsworth, England, circa 1840s. Diamond was a pioneer in the use of the camera to train the eye of the asylum physician to the physiognomic features of insanity, and to prompt self-awareness and self-appraisal in patients.

vince them that insane though they may be, they were not very much different from anyone else. On that point, he stated:

> Our experience here, would prove to some, that during some period of their disease, a majority of our patients are able to appreciate all the courtesies and comforts of life, and to participate in most of its employments, occupations and amusements, in a restricted way, with quite as much zest as a majority of the community of which they were recently members [Kirkbride, p. 37].

The magic lantern shows continued throughout Kirkbride's tenure as superintendent of the Pennsylvania Hospital for the Insane, a tenure that was coterminous with moral treatment in American asylums. Both it, and Diamond's subsequent attempts to use personal photographic portraits therapeutically fell out of use by the start of the twentieth century. Revived mid-century, now under the term "photoTherapy," it had, and continues to have, a somewhat limited use as an asylum therapeutic.

## *Writing and Editing*

The creation and production of an asylum newsletter, magazine or journal. During the nineteenth century there were interesting examples of using writing and editing not so much as a therapeutic, in and of itself, but as an endeavor that recognized and reinforced patient therapeutic progress. The opportunity to write and edit was granted, in some asylums, to patients who not only were literate, but who were deemed rational and sentient enough to comment in an entertaining, inspirational or educational way about their surroundings.

The first attempt to so engage patients was short-lived. The Hartford Retreat for the Insane opened its doors to just forty-four patients in 1824, only the third such asylum to do so in the United States. From its founding, its intent was to substitute kindness for cruelty, understanding for disdain—more to the point, it intended to be a model of moral treatment. Thus, in 1831 Barber Badger, the former editor of the *Christian Advocate,* among other publications, admitted himself to the Retreat for "the purpose of enjoying the benefit of the best medical advice" (Officers for the Retreat of the Insane, p. 43) and proposed that to occupy his time he publish a weekly paper. His offer was accepted. The *Retreat Gazette* originally sold for six cents per copy, or fifty cents for a dozen. More than 4,000 copies of the first edition were sold and readers, who included patients and staff at the Retreat and other asylums as well as the general public, were quite taken with it. In a letter to the editor, one local subscriber expressed his gratitude:

> I have perused [the *Retreat Gazette*] with much satisfaction, and think it much more rational than many papers I have lately seen, emanating from quarters much less suspicious, so far as the seal of public reprobation is concerned. Herewith I send you my subscription for the year, and wish you success in the enterprise. If it contributes to relieve the tedium of your sojourn, or adds to the comfort of yourself and your friends, it will be patronage better bestowed and better requited than frequently happens [Officers for the Retreat of the Insane, p. 49].

Concerns expressed by subscribers that the health of the editor may interfere with the demanding schedule of putting out a weekly newspaper were attended to. The second edition of *Retreat Gazette* came out bi-monthly at a new subscription rate of one dollar for the year. Although Badger had assumed the lion's share of the task of writing, editing and printing, he did invite patient submissions. Most of those took the form of silly observations, such as a brief essay titled "Ode to a Mosquito," and sappy doggerels such as this verse to an assistant matron:

> My dear Miss---, although it be dark,
> I cannot refrain from striking a spark
> Of grateful emotion—true heart-felt devotion
> To you for your kindness,
> In mending and starching my collars and shirts
> ["Progress of the Periodical Literature of Lunatic Asylums," p. 77].

Concerns about Badger's health aside, he recovered fully after the second edition of the *Retreat Gazette* was published, and was discharged. His duties were taken over by other patients who did not have his skill and experience. The *Retreat Gazette* was then only occasionally published over the next few years.

Its impact was considerable despite its short run. Superintendents of asylums in the United States not only were loath to fall behind their British and European colleagues who were championing moral treatment, but were keen on establishing their own *bona fides* as experts on insanity and its progressive management and treatment. Having house-organs that effectively propagandized their asylums not only went towards meeting these goals, but also in a less obvious, but still significant, way challenged prevailing notions that insanity was tantamount to a life sentence of hopelessness and despair.

Several asylums, then, started publishing newspapers, journals and magazines. The *Asylum Journal* had a several year run at the Brattleboro Retreat in Vermont. The *Opal,* arguably the best known and certainly most profitable of the patient publications, was written, edited and printed by patients at the New York State Lunatic Asylum, better known as the Utica Asylum. Over the ten years of its publication the *Opal* took on a slight edge, offering cautious insights into the daily treatment of the patients, editorials on patients' rights, and comments on asylum administration alongside poetry, open letters and religious ruminations, those so "cheery and sugar-coated" as to cause readers to forget "that the asylum was an institution with unprecedented power to rescind the liberties of the socially deviant or psychologically aberrant" (Reiss, 2004, p. 3).

A bit of subversion, though, could be found between the covers of *The Meteor,* the patient written, edited and published newspaper from the Alabama Insane Hospital in Tuscaloosa, later known as the Bryce Hospital, after Peter Bryce, its young and reform-minded superintendent. *The Meteor,* so named because like a meteor it came by surprise, and then only infrequently, yet burned brightly and intensely for its short duration, was originally published for patients and patrons, and contained the obligatory saccharine poems, pieces and platitudes. But the patients involved in its production, or perhaps Bryce himself, realized its potential to inform state officials about the ongoing needs of the asylum and to prompt them into action. The lucidly political tone of the newspaper raised questions as to who actually was writing and editing it: the anonymous patients, or Byrce. While both insisted it was the former, the patient-editor mused that perhaps his own recovery was being deliberately compromised to assure his continued involvement with the newspaper. He quite rebelliously decided that the quarterly publication would now be published "semi-occasionally," and only when he felt inclined to do so. Although none of this conflict was the subject of reportage, in the last edition of *The Meteor* the patient-editor, tongue firmly in cheek, listed several reasons why he could write such lucid commentaries and still be confined in an insane asylum: 1. some facts which

*The Opal.* **The monthly periodical was written and edited by patients at the New York State Lunatic Asylum in Utica between 1850 and 1860. The first edition was pen-printed and distributed to patients and staff; soon it was published on the asylum's printing press and by the end of its run it had 900 subscribers. The title** *Opal* **referenced the precious stone's power to prevent sickness and sorrow. It was the best known of several patient-produced periodicals in American and British asylums.**

the editor takes as facts are not facts; wrong facts are evidence of insanity; 2. latent insanity can lie beneath the surface of a lucid man and explode unexpectedly; 3. some say the editor is here for the convenience of the asylum; 4. he is fond of good eating and the Matron fears he will not get his fill if discharged; 5. he has made a pet of four deer on the asylum grounds that would miss him if were discharged; 6. if discharged, he may want to preach but because he adheres to no religious principles he would not be afforded the opportunity; 7. if discharged, he may want to edit a newspaper, but he has "too much sense to assent to any form of Communal nonsense'; and 8. "ask the superintendent" ("Answers to Interrogatories," p. 3).

House-organs also were published in Scottish asylums. The *New Moon* appeared for the first time in 1844 at the Crichton Royal Asylum in Dumfries. Edited by the superintendent, William A.F. Browne, but written entirely by patients, the newspaper whose motto was "Hail! awful madness, Hail" was a recognized effort towards moral treatment. "In resuscitating correct and healthy habits of thinking, in developing powers hitherto unknown or lost in the confusion consequent upon disease, and in giving a sphere of activity to minds which are only partially impaired," an eminent Scottish asylum physician declared, "the *New Moon* has proved most beneficial" (Lockhart, p. 326). It was also profitable. The proceeds were used to benefit the patients and to provide small allowances for those who were being discharged. In 1845 the Royal Edinburgh Lunatic Asylum followed suit and published the *Morningside Mirror.* The Murray Royal Asylum in Perth then began publishing *Excelsior* which also was written, edited and published by patients. The *Chronicles of the Cloister*, followed by *Gartnavel Gazette* were published by the patients at the Gartnavel Royal Hospital in Glasgow.

In England, too, patient publications began appearing. The *York Star,* a little octavo quarterly, was published between 1861 and 1877 by the patients at the York Asylum. And even Bethlem Asylum in London, what historically has become the quintessential asylum of collective imagination, had its own publications. The handwritten *Bethlehem Star* was circulated at irregular intervals between 1875 and 1880. Its successor, *Under the Dome,* had a longer shelf life from 1889 to 1930. Just as was the case with other asylum publications, *Under the Dome* was a collection of literary loot taken from other newspapers and periodicals, and sprinkled with light verse, religious musings, and on occasion minor complaints, most often about the food. For a brief moment a rival house publication appeared, edited by a rather mysterious patient who was simply referred to as "M." *Over the Dome* announced itself by insulting the patient-editor of *Under the Done* by calling him a "midget." The broadside thus delivered, the two editors exchanged some clever insults over the next several editions, which not only increased the sales of each publication, but demonstrated that even in an asylum as darkly unenlightened as "Bedlam" was imagined to be, something akin to moral treatment actually was taking place.

# Fever Therapy (Pyrotherapy, Pyretotherapy)

*A method of treatment in which the body temperature is raised to, and sustained at, an elevated level.*

The therapeutic value of fever was noted by ancient physicians. Hippocrates, in fact, once mused that had he the power to produce fever, he could cure all disease. As late as the nineteenth century, physicians occasionally commented on the remediating effects that typhoid fever had on the patients in their overcrowded and unsanitary asylums that were prone to epidemics.

The value of *inducing* fever to treat insanity,

rather than waiting for an outbreak or epidemic to occur, had an interesting evolution. It very well may have begun with the germ theory of disease that emerged in the late nineteenth century with the discoveries that some infectious diseases, such as malaria and typhoid that the ancient physicians would have been familiar with, were caused by microorganisms. Germ theory, as this hypothesis came to be known, replaced earlier miasma and contagion theories of disease; the former had posited that a poisonous vapor in the air carried disease, the latter that direct contact between infected people was responsible for its spread.

The scientific research of the French chemist and microbiologist, Louis Pasteur, validated the propositions of germ theory. Early in his career he had discovered that it was yeast, a living organism, that turned beet root into alcohol, but that another microbe, *Mycoderma aceti*, was responsible for souring the alcohol into vinegar. His patented process for destroying that microbe through boiling and then cooling the liquid came to be known as "pasteurization." While the discovery delighted Napoleon III who had supported his research in the hope of both saving the French wine industry and ensuring France's scientific superiority, it was the pasteurization of a much more mundane liquid—milk—that had the most potent effect on health in developing countries as well as in industrialized countries where urban growth had lengthened the supply chain between food source and consumers.

When pasteurization was patented in the mid-nineteenth century, a significant number of all admissions to asylums in industrialized countries were for what was variously termed general paresis, general paralysis of the insane, or dementia paralytica. This progressively degenerative type of insanity was first described decades before it even had a name, by John Haslam, apothecary at the Bethlem Hospital in London, England:

> Paralytic affections are a much more frequent cause of insanity than has been commonly supposed. In those affected from this cause, we are, on enquiry, enabled to trace a sudden affection, or fit, to have preceded the disease. These patients usually bear marks of such affection, independent of their insanity; the speech is impeded, and the mouth drawn aside; an arm, or leg, is more or less deprived of its capacity of being moved by the will; and in by far the greatest number of these cases the memory is particularly affected. Very few of these cases have received any benefit in the hospital; and from the enquiries I have been able to make at the private houses, where they have been afterwards confined, it has appeared, that they have either died suddenly from apoplexy, or have had repeated fits, from the effect of which they have sunk into a stupid state, and have gradually dwindled away [Haslam, p. 120].

Haslam, who did not have a formal degree in medicine, was certainly aware of the outbreaks of syphilis that had plagued Europe since the fifteenth century. The Great Pox, as it was known, had killed thousands and its venereal origin in sex and sin already had been established. Yet Haslam posited no etiologic connection between the general paresis he was seeing in Bethlem and the syphilis that was epidemic in his own country. In fact, he specifically denied it. Venereal pus, he insisted, did not infect the brain.

Antoine Laurent Jessé Bayle disagreed. The physician who practiced at the Charenton Asylum in France challenged this prevailing view that there was no organic cause of what later would be termed general paresis. On the basis of postmortem research, he proposed that the paralysis observed in these patients was but one symptom of a complex disorder that included dementia, as well as other mental symptoms. Most importantly, this disorder was caused by a chronic inflammation of the arachnoid lining of the brain. He described the progression of the disorder in detail. First, the developing inflammation caused serous fluid to press on the brain, and resulted in a mild paralysis of speech, monomania and grandiose ideas. Second, the increasing pressure on the brain produced spastic paralysis, agitation and generalized mania. Third, the now chronic inflammation, coupled with ever increasing pressure on the brain, resulted in severe paralysis, loss of sphincter control and complete dementia.

Bayle, in essence, had offered the first description of an organic brain disease; his research was to have a profound influence on asylum medicine. But it was not until 1875, several decades after the publication of his research, that Alfred-Jean Fournier, physician at the Hôpital St. Louis, a renowned hospital for diseases of the skin, would find that syphilis was the cause of this complex disorder. Fournier, who later would be appointed professor of dermatology and syphilology at the University of Paris, was once described by Oliver Wendell Holmes as the "Voltaire of pelvic literature" (Waugh, p. 232). Indeed, his catalogue of publications on the topic was impressive, as was his concern about the public, social, economic, and moral implications of the disease, a concern that definitely was shared by asylum physicians who nonetheless still remained skeptical that syphilis was the cause of general paresis. That skepticism prompted Fournier to muse, "Several times I had the experience of having to diagnose syphilitic madness in the presence of very competent and justly famous psychiatrists; and almost inevitably my opinion was received as a hypothesis that was possible, rational, perhaps tolerable, but singularly adventurous and tainted with heresy" (Quétel, p. 163).

The heretical nature of his hypothesis diminished when the spirochete bacterium *Treponema pallidum* that caused syphilis was isolated and identified by Fritz Shaudinn and Erich Hoffman in research conducted in the women's ward of the dermatology department of the Berlin Charité Hospital in 1905. The development of diagnostic tests, most particularly the Wassermann, quickly followed. To asylum physicians working on the cusp of the twentieth century, it was now apparent that general paresis, a debilitating type of neurosyphilis, was not a functional disorder after all. Its cause was neither the "competition, reckless and feverish pursuit of wealth and social position, overstudy, overwork, unhygienic modes of life, the massing of people in large cities, the indulgence in tea, coffee, tobacco, stimulants," nor even in the "sexual excesses" of rapidly modernizing societies (Kellogg, p. 657). Rather, its cause was organic—a motile spirochete that was spread by sexual contact. By the turn into the twentieth century more than 20 percent of all asylum admissions were for all types of neurosyphilis, yet physicians were just as helpless to treat it as they were before they had identified its cause.

In 1910, after 605 successive failures, the German bacteriologist Paul Ehrlich discovered "compound 606," the "magic bullet" (*magische Kugel*) that selectively targeted the *Treponema pallidum* spirochete. Salvarsan, as he referred to, was an arsphenamine, an arsenic compound that produced pain upon injection, but that offered a significant improvement over the mercury preparations used in so many asylums that too often left patients sweating and salivating, their tongues lacerated, teeth loosened by softened gum tissues, stomachs and bowels irritated, and bones so weakened that their noses collapsed and their jaws crumbled. But salvarsan was not without its toxic side effects, and certainly not without its detractors who accused Erlich of criminal negligence for aggressively marketing the drug for personal profit and for forcing prostitutes to undergo the treatment at Frankfurt Hospital. He eventually was exonerated of the charge and went on to develop neosalvarsan that was to be the treatment of choice well into the mid-twentieth century when penicillin replaced it. Yet at prescribed doses neither of these arsenical compounds crossed the blood-brain barrier, so they could do little to cure paretic neurosyphilis, although they were effective in preventing it in those asylum patients for whom early stage syphilis had been diagnosed.

Neurosyphilis continued to drain asylum resources; patients with it required intensive nursing and constant supervision. And, since the majority of those patients were middle-aged men, their commitment to asylums for care taxed their families and reduced the work force. In the face of the repercussions of this incurable type of insanity, a new and different therapeutic was needed. The Austrian physician Julius Wagner-Jauregg provided it. In the late nineteenth century he proposed that it would be possible to successfully treat paretic neurosyphilis by the induction of fever.

Wagner-Jauregg, who had only reluctantly settled on the specialty of psychiatry, developed an interest in the expanding organic approach to insanity that germ theory had generated. He had observed, while doing his obligatory residency at an asylum, that the psychosis of a female patient who had come down with erysipelas, a bacterial skin disease accompanied by high fever, remediated somewhat when the fever subsided. His interest piqued, he speculated that paretic neurosyphilis, also a bacterial disease, could be similarly and successfully treated by the induction of fever, as could other types of insanity for which bacterial causes had not been discovered. To that end, he began by injecting patients at the Clinic for Psychiatry and Nervous Diseases with the streptococcus bacterium that causes the erysipelas, or St. Anthony's Fire, that had produced the skin lesions and fever of the patient he had observed during his internship. When he received the Nobel Prize for Physiology or Medicine decades later for the fever therapy of neurosyphilis, he was to reflect upon this early trial with erysipelas as "an unfortunate experiment" that he "hardly had the authority then to carry on with" (Eghigian, p. 262).

The same reflection would have held true for his experimentation with tuberculin, a recently developed vaccine meant to be effective in cases of tuberculosis. Wagner-Jauregg injected several neurosyphilitic asylum patients with the vaccine in an effort to induce a tuberculin fever. The results were promising, despite a significant proportion of relapses, yet he was forced to abandon the treatment in the wake of alarming reports that tuberculin's toxic effects could lead to death.

In 1917, after years of experimentation, Wagner-Jauregg revived an earlier hypothesis that malaria-induced fevers would be effective in treating neurosyphilis, and they did prove to be just that. Malarial fever therapy spread quickly across the world, arresting the progression of syphilis in about 70 percent of all cases. Wagner-Jauregg's cure not only earned him the 1927 Nobel Prize for Physiology or Medicine, but "broke the therapeutic nihilism that had dominated psychiatry in previous generations" (Shorter, p. 194). After all, if the progressive dementia of the paretic type of neurosyphilis could be halted by fever, then certainly other types of insanity could be as well. For the next several decades, enterprising asylum physicians induced fevers in their patients with an array of febrile agents and raised artificial fevers with ingeniously designed machines and gadgets, all in an effort to arrest their insanity.

In the end, there was little success in treating anything other than paretic neurosyphilis with fever therapy. While many reports of its efficacy flattered to deceive, fever therapy nonetheless was considered an effective treatment available until the mid-twentieth century.

## References

Bennett, A.E., Cash, P.T., and Hoekstra, C. (1941). Artificial fever therapy in general paresis with electroencephalographic studies. *Psychiatric Quarterly*, 15, 750–771.

Braslow, J. (1997). *Mental ills and bodily cures: Psychiatric treatment in the first half of the twentieth century.* Berkeley: University of California Press.

Brown, E.M. (2000). Why Wagner-Jauregg won the Nobel Prize for discovering malaria therapy for general paresis of the insane. *History of Psychiatry, 11*, 371–382.

Carroll, R.S. (1923). Aseptic meningitis in combating the dementia praecox problem. *New York Medical Journal, 68,* 407–411.

Carroll, R.S., Barr, E.S., Barry R.G., and Matzke, O. (1925). Aseptic meningitis in the treatment of dementia praecox. *American Journal of Psychiatry, 81,* 673–703.

Dennie, C.C. (1962). *A history of syphilis.* Springfield, IL: Charles C. Thomas.

Eghigian, G. (ed.). (2010). *From madness to mental health: Psychiatric disorder and its treatment in Western civilization.* New Brunswick, NJ: Rutgers University Press.

Epstein, N.N., and Cohen, M. (1935). The effects of hyperpyrexia produced by radiant heat in early syphilis. *Journal of the American Medical Association, 104,* 883–891.

Epstein, S.H., Solomon, H.C., and Kopp, I. (1936). Dementia paralytica: Results of treatment with diathermy fever. *Journal of the American Medical Association, 106,* 1527–1533.

Freeman, W., Fong, T.C., and Rosenberg, S.J. (1933), The diathermy treatment of dementia paralytica: Microscopic changes in treated cases. *Journal of the American Medical Association, 100,* 1749–1753.

Gubser, A.W., and Ackerknecht, E.H. (eds.). (1970). *Constantin von Monakow vita mea.* Stuttgart, Germany: Huber.

Haslam, J. (1798). *Observations on insanity.* London: F. and C. Rivington.

Hershfield, A.S., Kibler, O.A., Koenig, M.T., Schmid, O.W., and Saunders, A.M. (1929). Sodoku treatment in paresis: Preliminary report on seventy-two cases. *Journal of the American Medical Association, 92,* 772–773.

Hinsie, L.E. (1927). Malarial treatment of schizophrenia. *Psychiatric Quarterly, 1,* 210–214.

Hinsie, L.E., and Blalock, J.R. (1932). Treatment of general paresis by radiothermy. *Psychiatric Quarterly, 6,* 191–212.

Kellogg, T.H. (1897). *A textbook of mental disease.* New York: William Wood and Co.

King, L.J. (2000). The best possible means of benefiting the incurable: Walter Bruetsch and the malarial treatment of paresis. *Annals of Clinical Psychiatry, 12,* 197–203.

Kragh, J.V. (2010). Malaria fever therapy for general paralysis of the insane in Denmark. *History of Psychiatry, 21,* 471–486.

Kubitschek, P.E., and Carmichael, F.A. (1928). Experimental aseptic meningitis. *American Journal of Psychiatry, 85,* 97–135.

"Medical science finds cure for paretic insane" (1928, June 2). *Chicago Defender,* p. A1.

Neymann, C.A. (1936). The effect of artificial fever on the clinical manifestations of syphilis and the *treponema palliidum. American Journal of Psychiatry, 93,* 517–532.

Neymann, C.A. (1938). Critical review: The treatment of syphilis with artificial fever. *American Journal of Syphilis, Gonorrhea, and Venereal Diseases, 22,* 92–116.

Neymann, C.A., and Koenig, M.T. (1931). Treatment of dementia paralytica: Comparative therapeutic results with malaria, rat-bite fever and diathermy. *Journal of the American Medical Association, 96,* 1858–1860.

Neymann, C.A., and Osborne, S.L. (1931). The treatment of dementia paralytica with hyperpyrexia produced by diathermy. *Journal of the American Medical Association, 96,* 7–13.

Pearce, J.M.S. (2012). Brain disease leading to mental illness: A concept initiated by the discovery of general paralysis of the insane. *European Neurology, 67,* 222–278.

Plaut, F., and Steiner, G. (1920). Recurrensinfektionen bei paralytikern. *Zeitschrift für die Gesamte Neurologie und Psychiatrie, 53,* 103–120.

Quétel, C. (1946). *History of syphilis.* Baltimore, MD: Johns Hopkins University Press.

"Rat bite fever and paresis" (1929, April 8). *Time,* p. 25.

Ross, J.R. (2005). Shakespeare's chancre: Did the Bard have syphilis? *Clinical Infectious Disease, 40,* 399–404.

Ryan, E. (1908). A visit to the psychiatric clinics and asylums of the old land. *American Journal of Insanity, 65,* 347–356.

Schamberg, J.F., and Rule, A. (1928). The effect of extremely hot baths in experimental syphilis. *Archives of Dermatology and Syphilology, 17,* 322–331.

Scull, A., MacKenzie, C., and Hervey, N. (1996). *Masters of Bedlam: The transformation of the mad-doctoring trade.* Princeton, NJ: Princeton University Press.

Shorter, E. (1997). *A history of psychiatry: From the era of the asylum to the age of Prozac.* New York: John Wiley and Sons.

Solomon, H.C. (1923). The treatment of neurosyphilis. *Journal of the American Medical Association, 8,* 1742–1748.

Solomon, H.C., Berk, A., Theiler, M., and Clay, C.L. (1926). The use of sodoku in the treatment of general paralysis: A preliminary report. *Archives of Internal Medicine, 38,* 391–404.

Solomon, H.C., Kopp, I., and Rose, A.S. (1941). Temperature swing in the treatment of general paresis: Hypohyperthermia method. *American Journal of Syphilis, Gonorrhea, and Venereal Diseases, 25,* 96–102.

Stecher, R.M., and Solomon, W.M. (1937). The complications and hazards of fever therapy: Analysis of 1000 consecutive fever treatments with the Kettering hypertherm. *Annals of Internal Medicine, 10,* 1014–1020.

Templeton, W.L. (1924). The effects of malarial fever upon dementia praecox subjects. *Journal of Mental Science, 70,* 92–95.

Thorburn, A.L. (1971). Fritz Richard Schaudinn, 1871–1906: Protozoologist of syphilis. *British Journal of Venereal Disease, 47,* 459–461.

Viner, N. (1933). A case of dementia praecox treated by intraspinal injections of horse serum. *Canadian Medical Journal, 28,* 42–422.

von Monakow, C., and Kitabayashi, S. (1919). Schizophrenie und plexus chorioidei, *Schweizer Archiv fur Neurologie und Psychiatrie, 5,* 378–392.

Wagner-Jauregg, J. (1945/1946). The history of the malaria treatment of general paralysis. *American Journal of Psychiatry, 102,* 577–582.

Warner, G.L. (1928). Malarial inoculation in cases of dementia praecox. *Psychiatric Quarterly, 2,* 494–505.

Waugh, M.A. (1974). Alfred Fournier, 1832–1914: His influence on venereology. *British Journal of Venereal Disease, 50,* 232–236.

Wisendanger, M. (2006). Constantin von Monakow (1853–1930): A pioneer in interdisciplinary brain research and a humanist. *Comptes Rendus Biologies, 329,* 406–418.

Zacon, S.J., and Neymann, C.A. (1943). Alexander

Samoilovich Rosenblium: His contribution to fever therapy. *Archives of Dermatology and Syphilology,* 48, 52–59.

## Aseptic Meningitis

The replacement of approximately twenty-five cubic centimeters of cerebrospinal fluid with an equal amount of inactivated horse serum introduced into the subarachnoid space via a lumbar puncture, in order to produce fever, headache and inflammation of the meninges surrounding the brain.

In the early twentieth century, Constantin von Monakow, director of the Brain Anatomy Institute in Zurich, Switzerland, theorized that the permeability of the choroid plexi, that is, the ventricular structures in the brain that produce cerebrospinal fluid, was compromised in patients with schizophrenia, perhaps due to a food-chemico deprivation. A resetting of the permeability by means of meningeal irritation, he reasoned, would significantly improve or even cure schizophrenia. While Monakow's contributions to the study of the brain were both far-reaching and interdisciplinary, his interest in schizophrenia was deeply personal: two of his siblings had suffered from it. In interactions with his discussion club, the "Monakow Kränzli," that included such illustrious members as Eugen Bleuler, Carl Gustav Jung and Max Cloetta, he endeavored to solve the riddle of schizophrenia which he considered one of the great mysteries of the brain. His paper, coauthored with a Japanese colleague and outlining his theory of choroid plexi permeability, prompted research interest in Great Britain, Germany and Japan.

In the United States, experiments with aseptic meningitis to actually treat schizophrenia originated with a somewhat unlikely source. Robert Carroll was director of the Highland Hospital in Asheville, North Carolina, a rather "tony" sanitarium that specialized in the treatment of nervous disorders and addictions. While the treatment regime focused on exercise, healthy diet and occupational therapy, Carroll's earlier experience as an assistant to Henry Cotton at the Trenton State Hospital in New Jersey, continued to influence him. Cotton was surgically removing the teeth [see **Exodontia**], tonsils, gallbladders and/or colons of his patients in efforts to cure the focal infections he believed caused schizophrenia [see **Surgery**]. Although he eventually would fall miserably from grace, in the early twentieth century Cotton enjoyed both professional and public adulation, although less for his therapeutic results than his grandiose claims that schizophrenia had somatic origins and its cure was in easy reach.

Carroll took a different approach to infection, positing it not as the cause of schizophrenia, but the cure. Citing a number of observations that patients with schizophrenia sometimes had lucid moments after injections of such infectious agents as typhoid fever and malaria raised their white blood cell counts, he sought to initiate a similar regenerative response that specifically would target the choroid plexi. He replaced approximately twenty-five cubic centimeters of the cerebrospinal fluid of each of five patients he had diagnosed as schizophrenic with an equal amount of inactivated horse serum in order to produce fever and brain inflammation that would not only stimulate their immune systems to attack the meningitis, but restore the permeability of the choroid plexi. "Temporary or permanent improvement" was noted for all five.

Interestingly, Carroll never wrote a case study of one of his most famous patients, Zelda Fitzgerald, for whom the horse serum injection produced a moment or two of encouraging lucidity after three days of recurring high fevers, vomiting and debilitating headaches. Diagnosed as schizophrenic, the writer, artist, dancer and wife of novelist F. Scott Fitzgerald, had been admitted into the Highland Hospital in 1936, reluctantly discharged four years later, relapsed and was readmitted several times over.

Although skeptical of the underlying theory of choroid plexi permeability, physicians at the Philadelphia Hospital for Mental Disease attempted to "submerge prejudice against it and arrive at impartial conclusions" (Carroll, Barr, Barry & Matke, p. 675) by injecting horse serum into forty-nine schizophrenic patients. The results were generally consistent with Carroll's initial findings: six of the patients went into remission, although one relapsed; twenty-eight showed continuing or marked improvement, although six relapsed after several weeks; fourteen showed either temporary improvement or none at all, and one died of a pre-existing condition. Since the evaluative terms "remission" and "improvement" remain operationally undefined, just as they did in Carroll's report, a sample of the case studies offers a glimpse into how the efficacy of this therapeutic was "impartially" assessed:

> Case 11—P.M., age 18, single, white male... with a provisional diagnosis of dementia praecox (catatonic)...On admission was superficially depressed, negativistic and mute. Cleared up and was paroled, but soon relapsed and had to be returned. Later notes state he was much overweight (gained 50 pounds in two months). Talked fairly coherently and was without judgment or insight.... Following second treatment, said "I must have been crazy or I wouldn't be here." Claims he does not remember events happening just before his commitment. Following his final treatment it was noted that he had lost a great deal of weight but was untidy and rather silly. At present ... is much brighter, relevant, cleanly and works willingly. Final result: improved physical condition, possibly due to adjustment of endocrine system. Not much improvement mentally though he seems brighter and happier. Is to be paroled soon.
> Case 26—C.N., female (colored), age 37... A case of hebephrenic dementia praecox. Symptoms, silly, foolish, untidy, evasive, hallucinated and at times excited and violent. Given five treatments, has had no attacks of excitement since last treatment (two months ago). Is quiet, tidy and works on ward, still foolish and reacts to hallucinations. Final result, better institutional adjustment.
> Case 38—R.K., white male, age 29... A case of paranoid dementia praecox of several months' duration. Symptoms: Restive, negative, seclusive, at times assaultive in reaction to tormenting hallucinations. Given five treatments. Is much brighter, talks and laughs quite normally, cheerful and helps willingly with hard work. Had formerly been regarded as a dangerous patient. His parents regard him as cured. Final result, remission.
> Case 40—F.H., white male, age 22...A case of catatonic dementia praecox of several weeks' (?) duration. Symptoms: Mute, restive, and negative. Filthy in habits and very destructive. A "runaway." Given five treatments without a particle of improvement; in fact, grew worse. Final result, nil.
> Case 42—H.Y., white male, age 34...A case of paranoid dementia praecox of several year's duration.... Symptoms: seclusive, paranoid, hallucinated and very fearful. Given four treatments. For a time appeared much better; talked coherently about his former ideas and hallucinations, laughing about them, but suddenly relapsed and became violent and homicidal in his actions. Final result, nil [Carroll, Barr, Berry, & Matzke, pp. 691, 694–695, 697].

The considerable variation in therapeutic outcome suggested to some asylum physicians that the duration of both the patients' schizophrenia and the asylum physicians' observations post-treatment should be taken into consideration. When physicians at the Osawatomie State Hospital in Kansas induced aseptic meningitis in twenty-three chronic schizophrenic patients who had been institutionalized an average of six years and had never responded adequately to any therapeutic intervention, the promising results it had immediately produced for just six of them had all but disappeared months down the road. Only two of those six patients continued to maintain "increased interests, personal, occupational and recreational, loss or great diminution of hallucinations and delusions...[and] very satisfactory institutional or social adjustment" that the treating physicians defined as "good results" (Kubitschek & Carmichael, p. 104). One of those two patients was a thirty-nine-year-old male who had been institutionalized for a decade:

> Case No. 43—H.G., a white male, 39, admitted to hospital July 24, 1915, with outstanding symptoms of muscular rigidity, attitudinizing,

alternate stupor and excitement, mute but hallucinated. Diagnosis of dementia praecox, catatonic made and confirmed by course in hospital. Patient grew careless of appearance, seclusive, restive and negativistic, took no interest or participation in occupation or recreation and was in poor physical state when treatment was started. A series of four injections was followed by slow but progressive improvement, both mental and physical, interest in his surroundings, in occupation and recreation was gradually reestablished; he became neat, cooperative and friendly; improvement continued during the following year, patient has returned home and is making a very good social readjustment. Result in this case is considered most satisfactory [Kubitschek & Carmichael, p. 134].

Persistently good results, such as was documented in H.G.'s case, however, may have had nothing to do with the horse serum or the aseptic meningitis it caused. Rather, the asylum physicians argued, the pain of repeated lumbar punctures and the fear of death evidenced by virtually all of the treated chronic patients, "made a strong appeal to the individual's instinct of self-preservation, produced a re-synthesis, to some degree, of the dissociated personality which resulted in re-establishment of contact with reality" (p. 120).

By the time Carroll's most famous patient, Zelda Fitzgerald, had died along with eight other patients in a fire at Highland Hospital in 1948, the aseptic meningitis treatment for schizophrenia had been relegated to the margins of asylum therapeutics. Long-term follow-up studies had revealed that the initial positive effects—whether from the introduction of horse serum or the fear of death—were short-lived at best, even for those asylum patients whose schizophrenia was of quite recent onset.

## Blanket Method

The prevention of the radiation of body heat by wrapping patients in blankets and adding heat from an external source. This method raised body temperature to 104° F. within two hours. For neurosyphilitic patients, five continuous hours of fever, one time per week for ten weeks was the standard protocol. Although low-tech, blanket therapy still required that patients be carefully selected; it was contraindicated for the aged as well as those who had cardiac disease or hypertension.

The blanket method was devised to treat early stage syphilis by Norman Epstein and Maurice Cohen, both affiliated with the Mount Zion Hospital in San Francisco, California. Its results, however, were disappointing. The blanket method was unable to completely eradicate the syphilitic infections of the patients to whom it was administered. It was more successful, however, in the treatment of neurosyphilis, with results largely consistent with other methods of artificial fever induction.

## Diathermy, or Electropyresis

The artificial induction of fever by high frequency electrical currents administered by electrodes which were strapped to the bodies of neurosyphilitic patients who were then insulated in rubber sheets and wrapped in heavy wool blankets. Diathermy was devised in the early twentieth century by Clarence Neymann, a faculty member of the Northwestern University Medical School and an affiliate of several asylums in Chicago, Illinois. In early experiments with diathermy, Neymann and his colleagues followed the protocol of malaria fever therapy, still the treatment of choice for neurosyphilis. On a biweekly basis, and for three months, they induced temperatures above 103.5° F. for five continuous hours. Within a short time, however, they found the protocol too conservative. They increased the number of fevers to as many as forty-nine over a three month period, their duration to as long as nine continuous hours, and their temperature to as high as 107.6° F.

The evidence for what Neymann claimed was the therapeutic success of diathermy was inconsistent. He variously reported the remission rate for treated neurosyphilitic patients as 24 and 65 percent, and provided little explanation for this significant difference. Nor did he sufficiently clarify why he reversed his opinion that fever therapies of any kind would be ineffective with "dilapidated and deteriorated patients" (Neymann & Osborne, p. 9), and began to use diathermy with "aged patients having arteriosclerosis, diabetes and advanced organic heart disease" (Neymann & Koenig, p. 1860). One other inconsistency was particularly disturbing. Neymann claimed that the "complications of diathermy treatment are absolutely nil," (Neymann & Koenig, p. 1860), yet patients often were burned, sometimes quite severely, by the diathermy electrodes. In an effort to reduce the risk of burns, a more coercive approach to diathermy was instituted. Confused or resistant patients were sedated, and their arms and legs restrained before the artificial fever was induced.

These inconsistencies and contradictions did not go unnoticed by other asylum physicians who were keen on trying therapeutics for the treatment of their neurosyphilitic patients that were more expedient, less risky and less expensive than malaria fever therapy. One of the most vociferous of them was Walter Freeman of St. Elizabeths Hospital, the federal asylum in Washington, D.C. Freeman, who would soon step into a controversy of his own making by promoting and performing lobotomies on both private practice and asylum patients [see **Psychosurgery**], acknowledged the drawbacks of malaria fever therapy but stated emphatically that the use of diathermy at St. Elizabeths "met with almost complete failure" (Freeman, Fong, & Rosenberg, p. 1750). In contrast to Neymann's various claims, only 20 percent of the neurosyphilitic patients Freeman and his colleagues had treated showed any improvement; 52 percent remained unimproved and, most alarmingly, 28 percent had died. Far from being an "innocuous treatment" (p. 1753), diathermy had disturbing results: patients sometimes were burned by the electrodes, and they invariably complained about discomfort while undergoing the treatment which more often than not left them listless, confused and dispirited—just as Freeman's lobotomy patients later, and with the same acrimony, would be described.

Freeman's criticisms were dismissed as a "clouded judgment" due to a "desire to defend the superiority of malaria [fever therapy]" by Samuel Epstein and his colleagues (Epstein, Solomon, & Kopp, p. 1527). Yet they were even more critical of Neymann's claims of therapeutic success with diathermy, characterizing them not only as another instance of "clouded judgment," but as the product of a naïve enthusiasm that was "likely to add to wishful thinking" (p. 1527). The Boston Psychopathic Hospital physicians presented their own findings on diathermy: only 27 percent of the treated neurosyphilitic patients went into remission while twice as many went into remission with malaria fever therapy. This remission rate stood in stark contrast to the claims of Neymann, and also the reports from asylums where diathermy was being met with some success. That difference between published empirical and unpublished observational findings was at the core of an exchange between Walter Bruetsch at Central State Hospital in Indianapolis, Indiana, and Neymann. Breutsch had castigated Neymann for claiming the therapeutic efficacy of diathermy in the face of such inconsistent empirical results, to which Neymann responded:

> If Dr. [Bruetsch] would have taken the trouble to scrutinize the tabulation of the results obtained in the treatment of dementia paralytica with [diathermy], he would know that these results originate from investigators all over the world, from England, Mexico, France, Italy, Belgium and even from Australia. Now everybody, all over the world, cannot be wrong. Good clinical results are, therefore, obtainable by the use of fever, produced by physical agents [Neymann, 1936, p. 531].

These acrimonious exchanges occurred several years after Neymann had developed diathermy as a treatment for neurosyphilis, and should be read as a defense of artificial fevers in general, rather than of diathermy in particular. Neymann, in fact, had all but abandoned diathermy as a therapeutic, but his enthusiasm for artificial fevers remained unabated, as did his lack of same for malaria fever therapy:

> Indeed, many physicians, and especially neuropathologists, still cling to the belief that we are dealing with something mysterious when a patient is infected with a febrile disease, or when injections of fever-producing substances are given. Many fail to recognize that fever alone is the important common factor of all such therapeutic measures. I have heard of the mythical, unproved, and much extolled action of the plasmodium of malaria in the treatment of general paresis until I have come to believe we are dealing with a fetish or taboo in the minds of its most ardent advocates [Neymann, 1938, p. 96].

Neymann may have found some vindication in the fact that the use of diathermy alone or in combination with other therapeutics, continued in asylums around the world until penicillin, the most effective cure for all stages of syphilis, was mass marketed in the mid–1940s.

## Fever Cabinet, or Electric Light Bath Cabinet, or Systemic Heating Cabinet, or Hot Box

The generic name of any one of a number of differently designed cabinets that raised body temperature to approximately 105° F. through the radiant heating devices of radiators or light bulbs. The cabinet, either box or coffin-shaped, enclosed the body and left the head of the patient free. In some designs, a small fan attached to the top of the cabinet cooled the patient's face during the treatment.

In the early years of the use of the fever cabinet, patients often experienced nausea, vomiting, cramps and precipitous drops in blood pressure due to the loss of salt during profuse sweating. These uncomfortable reactions were later ameliorated by the ingestion of salty water during the treatment. It was standard protocol to confine neurosyphilitic patients in a fever cabinet for as long as seven continuous hours and over several consecutive days.

## Hot Air Bath, or The Oven

A generic name of any one of a number of different apparatuses that circulated hot air around the patient. In the mid-nineteenth century, the preferred hot air bath method of treatment involved a fireproof wooden box, the interior of which was heated by an alcohol lamp or a gas burner and through a chimney attached to an opening at the bottom. This method was improved by manufacturer Frank Betz who developed a metal cylindrical box, lined with asbestos, into which hot air was forced and circulated. The fully clothed patient was inserted into the cylinder via a sliding frame. Usually the patient remained in the hot air bath no longer than an hour; once removed, the patient was rubbed dry, put into a change of clothes and made to rest.

The Betz Hot Air Bath, as this device was known, was extraordinarily popular in the United States where it was manufactured. In 1897 it sold for $3.50 to private practice physicians, and the price included a secret "formula" that was guaranteed to cure syphilis. The device also was used in asylums for the treatment of neurosyphilis, but generally was found ineffective in arresting this last stage of the disease. It was, however, used as an adjunct to other neurosyphilis therapeutics well into the twentieth century.

The hot air bath, usually as an adjunctive treatment, was used to treat functional, as opposed to organic, types of insanity as well. The Berlin Charité reported some success with its use in the treatment of acute schizophrenia, as did the McLean Hospital in Massachusetts. In Ireland and England, the hot air bath primarily was used to ease the coexisting physical complaints, such as arthritis and rheumatism, of insane asylum patients.

## Hot Bath Therapy, or Hyperpyrexia Bath Therapy

The elevation of body temperature by the action of hot water or steam in a closed chamber. Hot bath therapy was one of the oldest treatments of syphilis on record and was even rhapsodized in a sonnet by William Shakespeare as a "seething bath, which yet men prove/Against strange maladies a sovereign cure." So therapeutic were hot baths assumed to be that for centuries physicians sent their syphilitic patients to health resorts to "take the waters" as a cure.

The question remained, however, if hot bath therapy would have the same salutary effects on neurosyphilis, particularly of the paretic type where dementia was progressive and hopeless. In experimental conditions, Jay Shamberg and Anna Rule of the Research Institute for Cutaneous Disease in Philadelphia, Pennsylvania, determined that hot baths could raise body temperature to as high as 106° F., a temperature that attenuated the *Treponema pallidum* bacterium in recently inoculated animals.

Hot bath therapy was administered to eleven paretic neurosyphilis patients by Henry Mehrtens and Pearl Pouppirt of Stanford University Medical School in California. The temperatures of the patients were raised to 104 to 107° F. and maintained in that range for thirty continuous minutes on five consecutive days. The outcome roughly paralleled that of malaria fever therapy: two of the patients improved sufficiently enough to resume daily activities including employment; four more improved, and the remaining five were unimproved. Yet, as was the case with all of the various fever therapies, the assessment was conducted on a short-term basis, leaving unaddressed the question as to whether the positive outcomes were maintained over time.

By the early twentieth century, many asylums around the world already had built what often were palatial hydrotherapy suites and buildings [see **Hydrotherapy**], and had specially trained staff to administer and monitor the various treatments. Thus the use of the hot bath for the treatment of neurosyphilis, despite caveats as to its effectiveness, continued well into mid-century.

## Hypohyperthermia, or the Swing Method

A method of artificial fever induction developed by Harry C. Solomon at the Boston Psychopathic Hospital in Massachusetts, in which the body temperature of neurosyphilitic patients was lowered to 90° F. and then rapidly raised to 105° F. via confinement in a fever cabinet. While it had been well established by the early mid-twentieth century when this therapeutic was devised that the *Treponema pallidum* spirochete was killed by high temperatures, Solomon and his colleagues conjectured that it also may not be able to withstand low temperatures. A relatively wide swing of temperatures, then, might be particularly effective in "sterilizing the human brain of the spirochetal invaders" (Solomon, Kopp, & Rose, p. 96).

The administration of hypohyperthermia was as follows:

> The patient is prepared by a cleansing enema on the evening before and by the omission of breakfast. He is placed in a fever cabinet with the cover open, and the constantly recording rectal thermometer is inserted. After a period of ten or fifteen minutes for stabilization of temperature, the anesthetic is injected slowly to produce satisfactory anesthesia. Approximately one hundred pounds of finely-cracked or shaved ice are placed about the patient from axillae to below the knees, excluding the back. One arm is kept exposed for blood pressure readings and subsequent venipuncture. More pentothal is injected from time to time in decreasing doses to maintain the anesthesia. When the temperature falls to the desired level, the ice is removed, the body is dried, warm blankets applied, and the cabinet cover is lowered and the heat turned on. After the patient's temperature begins to rise, the inductotherm is turned on and cabinet temperature maintained at 102 to 105° F. until the patient's

rectal temperature reaches the desired level above normal. The cabinet is then opened, and the body temperature is allowed to return to normal [Solomon, Kopp, & Rose, p. 98].

The patients were described as content with the treatment, although Solomon and his colleagues hastened to note that the amnesia caused by the administration of the anesthetic during the course of the treatment most certainly had contributed to their satisfaction. At the end of several experimental trials, Solomon and his colleagues were more optimistic about hypohyperthermia's potential than its outcome. The therapeutic was never widely used in asylums.

## Inductotherm, or Electromagnetic Induction

A device that used electromagnetic induction via a current run through a large, elliptical copper strip located beneath the patient. The prone patient was sandwiched between a flat shelf and cover, and was insulated from direct contact with the inductor. The heat in the cabinet raised the patient's body temperature to 105.8° F. in approximately two hours and was kept at that level for several more hours by the hot and highly saturated air that circulated through the cabinet. The standard protocol was thirty hours of fever over eight to twelve separate treatments.

## Kettering Hypertherm

Invented in the 1930s by Charles Franklin Kettering, vice president of General Motors, in conjunction with the Fever Research Project at the Miami Valley Hospital in Dayton, Ohio, as an improvement on the radiotherm. The hypertherm had heavily insulated walls and two chambers. The larger chamber had a semi-circular portion cut out so that the patient's head and neck was exposed; the smaller chamber at the foot of the cabinet housed an air-conditioning mechanism. The hypertherm was heated by a 1550 watt resistance unit controlled by a thermostat, and humidity was secured by a pan of water heated by a 2000 watt electrical immersion heater and controlled by a humidostat. The heated and humidified air was then circulated through a blower. The therapeutic goal of the hypertherm was to raise body temperature to between 106° and 107° F., and to maintain that temperature for several consecutive hours. The typical regime for neurosyphilis was to repeat this treatment every few days.

With the assistance of the Frigidaire Division of General Motors, a supply of hypertherms was manufactured and furnished on loan to more than fifty asylums in North America and Europe. The supply, however, did not meet the demand. More than 300 asylums around the world had requested hypertherms, specifically for the treatment of neurosyphilis.

One of the more enthusiastic proponents of the hypertherm was Abram E. Bennett who had founded the Department of Fever Therapy Research at the University of Nebraska College of Medicine. At the Hastings State Hospital, with which Bennett also was associated, neurosyphilitic patients routinely were treated with a combination of hypertherm and chemotherapy (bismuth and arsphenamine), and the results were noteworthy. In one published study, Bennett and his colleagues reported that of the seventy-nine neurosyphilitic patients treated, more than half of whom were in advanced stages of the disease, 19 percent had experienced full remission and 33 percent showed improvement; the remainder showed no improvement and several patients died.

## Malarial Fever Therapy

Inoculation via intravenous injection with tertian malaria, a rarely fatal type of malaria caused by the protozoan *Plasmodium vivax*. After an incubation period of about a week, the patients experienced chills and nausea, followed by raging fevers of more than 106° F. that lasted several hours. Over the next several days, fevers alternated with chills until the patients were administered quinine sulfate to terminate the malarial infection, but not before a few milliliters of their blood were extracted to be used to infect another group of neurosyphilitic patients.

Malarial fever therapy was developed by the Austrian physician Julius Wagner-Jauregg at the Clinic for Psychiatry and Nervous Diseases. He had experimented with the production of fever in neurosyphilitic patients by inoculating them with a variety of vaccines, including typhoid fever, tuberculin, recurrent fever and erysipelas, none of which had a notably successful therapeutic outcome. Wagner-Jauregg had long suspected that malaria may be not only a more effective febrile agent, but one that produced a fever that could quite easily be arrested by quinine. He came across the opportunity to test that hypothesis during World War I when a soldier was brought from the Italian front to the clinic for treatment. Although hospitalized for shell-shock, the soldier also had a raging tertian malaria fever; left untreated with quinine, his blood was drawn and injected into a neurosyphilitic patient who was near death. "T.M.," as the 37-year-old patient has been noted in the literature, had his first paroxysm of fever a few weeks after the injection; after the sixth febrile attack his syphilitic convulsions stopped, and after the ninth, quinine was administered. Over the next few months, "T.M." steadily improved. An actor before he was hospitalized, he was now able to entertain clinic patients and staff with musical numbers and dramatic recitations.

By the time "T.M." was discharged, Wagner-Jauregg had injected an additional eight neurosyphilitic patients with malaria and had published his encouraging results. His "fever cure," a slightly misleading moniker given the fact that it actually did not cure neurosyphilis, although without question it added reasonably healthy years to patients who most certainly would have died from it, was enthusiastically received by asylum physicians around the world. In just a few short years published case studies showed that more than half of all treated patients either went into full remission or showed at least some improvement, and the popular press already had proclaimed the procedure a "therapeutic noble deed" (Brown, p. 380). Wagner-Jauregg, against whom charges of maltreating soldier-patients with painful electrical treatments had been dismissed after the War [see **Electrotherapy**], was awarded the Nobel Prize for Physiology or Medicine in 1927 for the malarial fever cure.

Quite aside from its therapeutic effectiveness, malarial fever therapy had another, more subtle, effect as its use spread throughout Europe, Great Britain and North America: it transformed the asylum physician-patient relationship. That relationship had probably reflected the larger social attitude that syphilis was the consequence of, indeed even the punishment for, moral failure. Prior to malarial fever therapy, asylum physicians had little to offer their patients except a good dose of moral condemnation; after, they began engaging their patients in a therapeutic dialogue, listening to them and soliciting their ideas and their cooperation for courses of treatment. It is possible that "shared belief and the altered relationship brought about by changes in perception created malaria fever's apparent biological success" (Braslow, p. 93).

Its effectiveness in treating neurosyphilis well established, malaria fever therapy then was tried on asylum patients who had been diagnosed with another type of frustratingly intractable insanity—schizophrenia. The results were dissatisfying. W.L. Templeton treated twenty such cases at the City of London Mental Hospital near Dartford, England. He noted that immediately post-treatment most of the patients demonstrated a "brightening of intellectual interest, a desire to converse, to read the newspapers and books" (Templeton, p. 94). Yet in the absence of supportive psychotherapy and occupational therapy at the under-financed asylum, such noted improvement could not be sustained. "At the end of two months there were few who had not materially lapsed," he observed, "and it seems only a matter of time before all or most will have resumed their former mental state" (p. 95).

Leland Hinsie also found no reason to recommend malaria fever treatment for patients diagnosed with schizophrenia. He had treated thirteen New York State Psychiatric Institute patients, all of them female, with abysmally bad results: two died during the treatment, ten remained unimproved, and one worsened. There were, he acknowledged, some improvements immediately post-treatment. One patient, for example, who had "laughed boisterously nearly all the time," ceased doing so; another who had never inquired about situations at home, asked about her family (Hinsie, p. 213). These, he hastened to add, were "fleeting and on the whole superficial" (p. 213); in the end, they were more likely attributable to nursing care during treatment, rather than to the treatment, itself.

At the Utica State Hospital in New York, George Warner treated thirty-six schizophrenic patients and found that "the results obtained have not been sufficiently encouraging to warrant a continuation of this mode of treatment" (Warner, p. 494). While his published report may be read as just another litany of ephemeral improvements, it is more revealing when read as an account of the suffering of the treated patients, the challenges they posed to asylum staff, and the havoc they must have created in their families of origin. "M.M.," for example, aged 24, had been in the asylum for thirty months:

> At the time of treatment he had been unsociable, restless, discontented and had frequently attempted to escape from the ward. He was also irritable, impulsive, and committed frequent unprovoked attacks upon other patients. He was untidy in personal habits and destructive to his clothing, requiring much supervision and resisting attention. Was also very greedy and messy at the table. He could not be induced to apply himself in any way but wandered aimlessly about the ward, usually muttering, grimacing and laughing in a silly manner and making grotesque and purposeless motions, and at times becoming for a brief period excited and noisy, screaming and banging his head against the wall, probably hallucinating. He was inaccessible and appeared very stupid, simply grinning or making some inarticulate sound in response to simple questions or directions.... He was inoculated with malaria ... and allowed to have 8 paroxysms with 62 hours of fever above 102 degrees.... During treatment he continued restless and noisy, particularly at night, but he was cleanly in his personal habits, and immediately following treatment a change in his attitude and conduct was observed. Although still unsociable, he had become relatively quiet, composed and compliant.... He was able to understand directions given and when interviewed appeared more intelligent.... The improvement lasted two months.... He has slumped to his previous low regression and has since shown no amelioration of symptoms [Warner pp. 501–502].

While the weight of evidence accumulated that malaria fever was ineffective in treating schizophrenia and other psychoses, "the malarial treatment of the paretics was a standard procedure in nearly all of the institutions for the insane" (Dennie, p. 18). But it was not without its own complications. It was tricky to dispense, requiring the careful matching of blood type between donor and recipient, and the laboratory confirmation that it was tertian malaria, and not some other strain, that was being administered. The question of how many paroxysms of fever should occur before quinine was administered, and at what temperature, or perhaps temperatures in the plural, the series should reach for each treated patient was never satisfactorily resolved. Relapses were noted in some cases, fatalities in others. And there were ethical concerns, most notably raised by William Alanson White, superintendent of St. Elizabeths Hospital, the government asylum in Washington, D.C. White had not particularly shared the optimism of his colleagues regarding malaria fever therapy, but had felt an obligation to do something about neurosyphilis which was, to all extent and purposes, a death sentence. To that end, he ordered a supply of a dozen mosquitoes contaminated with tertian malaria. Only one survived the transit from Puerto Rico. That single mosquito was placed in a small wire mesh cage that was then attached to the arm of a neurosyphilitic patient. After being infected by the bite, the blood of that patient was drawn and used to treat an additional group of neurosyphilitic patients, and so on. While the treatment was largely effective the risks were high, in White's opinion, that a misdiagnosis would mean that a patient without syphilis would be infected with malaria. The risk exceeded the benefit in his calculation, and he refused to authorize the continued use of syphilitic donors.

Few other asylum physicians, however, came to the same calculation; neither did the American Psychiatric Association which generally endorsed the therapeutic innovations that were sweeping across the country in the early twentieth century. In Denmark, however, the ethical questions raised by malaria fever therapy brought about the first regulations regarding patient consent to treatment in that country's history. Malaria fever therapy had been introduced in Danish asylums in the early twentieth century after an asylum physician witnessed the administration of the therapeutic during a study tour in Austria and convinced Axel Bisgaard, the director of the Sankt Hans Hospital in Copenhagen, to use it. Accompanied by an asylum physician and a nurse, Bisgaard took two neurosyphilitic patients to Wagner-Jauregg's clinic in Vienna where they were inoculated with malaria. The blood of these patients then was passed on to other patients. Of the twenty-one infected, ten improved enough to be discharged and the remainder, although still institutionalized, had improved significantly. Bisgaard, however, was reticent to declare a therapeutic victory over neurosyphilis. "Time," he declared, "must decide here and as elsewhere, how long these improvements will last" (Kragh, p. 447).

Time, in fact, was not on the side of cure. Although one of the patients who had been infected in Vienna was discharged and remained in remission for years, the other was recommitted a year later and died during a convulsive seizure. Yet the administration of malaria fever therapy spread quickly through Danish asylums, where the mortality rates were carefully calculated. Noting those rates, the Directorate of the State Mental Hospitals issued a an informed consent directive in 1924, the first regulation of its kind in Denmark. The directive required that all asylum patients who were being considered for malaria fever therapy had to give their consent to the treatment; if unable to do so, such consent had to be obtained from a spouse, parent or other relative.

A second complication of malaria fever therapy was that it was expensive to administer. Treated patients required close medical supervision and vigilant nursing care, a staffing expense that taxed underfunded and overcrowded asylums. Vials of infected blood had to be stored in optimum conditions and were for some asylums, quite difficult to obtain. There was, in a fact, an interesting trade in malaria infected blood. Thermoses of it had to be shipped between asylums. In those asylums in which infected mosquitoes, rather than the blood of syphilitic patient donors were used to infect, special rooms had to be constructed to assure the safety of other patients as well as the staff. That was necessary at Sankt Hans Hospital, for example, where the windows of the purpose-built treatment room had to be covered with a fine mesh net that the mosquitoes could not pass through, and an extra entrance door had to be put in place to make it possible to look for mosquitoes before entering the room.

It was not effectiveness, ethics or expenses that brought an end to malaria fever therapy, however. Its therapeutic hegemony was first challenged by the introduction of machines and gadgets that produced artificial fevers to the same effect, and then quashed by the introduction of penicillin, which quickly proved itself many times more effective for the treatment of neurosyphilis.

## Radiothermy, or Ultra-High Frequency Oscillation

An alternative to diathermy, radiothermy eliminated the need for electrodes. The neurosyphilitic patient was suspended on interlaced cotton tapes stretched across a wooden frame; an eight inch high celotex cover was placed over the body, allowing the head to protrude from the cabinet. At each end of the cabinet there was an aluminum condenser plate covered with hard rubber. Between them a short-wave radio field was concentrated via a vacuum tube oscillator. The heat produced circulated around the recumbent patient, raising the body temperature to 103.5° F. Ordinarily, the patient was not kept in the radiothermy cabinet after the desired temperature was achieved; rather, the body temperature was maintained by wrapping the patient tightly in heavy wool blankets and surrounding him or her with hot water bottles. This treatment typically was repeated bi-weekly for ten to twenty weeks.

Just as the diathermy it was designed to replace, radiothermy carried risks of burns by arcs produced by the radio waves that tended to concentrate in the perspiration on the patient's skin. Radiothermy also raised the risks of dehydration and collapse, and was considered too risky to use with patients whose neurosyphilis was in an advanced stage.

At the New York Psychiatric Institute and Hospital, Leland Hinsie and Joseph Blalock used a radiotherm apparatus provided by the General Electric Company to treat sixty-eight neurosyphilitic male and female patients. The clinical remission rate was 18 percent, a rate comparable to a comparison group of patients who had been treated with malaria fever therapy, but much lower than expected for each group. Hinsie and Blalock attributed that finding to the fact that females were included in both the radiothermy and the comparative group of malaria fever patients. They took pains to point out that in the "thousands of reports in the literature on results with malarial treatment there is an outstanding silence on the results among women," except for the passing observation that they have a "relatively lower remission rate" (Hinsie & Blalock, p. 205).

Gender aside, Hinsie and Blalock also were concerned about the fact that six of the sixty-eight patients treated with radiothermy died, two of them during the treatment, itself, and the rest months after the treatment. While they considered it safe to say that in the latter case the radiothermy was not the proximate cause of death, it certainly was for the other two. One died as a result of having "lost the temperature regulating mechanism within the body" (p. 206), and the other from convulsive seizures.

Hinsie and Blalock concluded that radiothermy, despite its risks, was a less hazardous febrifacient agent than malaria fever therapy.

## Rat-Bite Fever Therapy, or Sodoku

The injection of *Spirochaeta morsus-muris* (later renamed *Spirillum minor*) to produce paroxysms of fever with temperatures of 104° to 105° F, along with swelling of the lymph glands, eruptions of the skin, thirst, nausea and vomiting, and anxiety sometimes accompanied by hallucinations. The spirochete is found in the saliva of infected rats and produced the same reaction—commonly known in the West as rat-bite fever and in the East as sodoku—in injected asylum patients as it did in those outside of asylums who had been bitten or scratched by infected rats. The course of rat-bite fever was quite easily arrested by salvarsan (arsphenamine).

The treatment of choice for neurosyphilitic asylum patients in the early twentieth century was malarial fever therapy, but it was not without its drawbacks. Looking for an alternative, Harry C. Solomon of the Boston Psychopathic Hospital began injecting neurosyphilitic patients with *Spirochaeta morsus-muris* to produce rat-bite fever. The hospital had been established just a decade or so before to treat acute cases of insanity and to serve as a teaching hospital for Harvard University Medical School. Experimental therapeutics would be its métier for decades to come. As its chief of therapeutic research, Solomon was able to address his own interest in neurosyphilis through a variety of what he referred to as "non-specific" interventions with either "greater power of permeation into the nervous tissue," or more capability of "inducing greater immunity on the part of the patient" (Solomon, p. 1728). Among those interventions was rat-bite fever.

It may be interesting to note that the strain of spirochetes used by Solomon was obtained from a baby hospitalized at the time with rat-bite fever; the strain was then passed through two mice, two rabbits and four guinea pigs. From the hearts of these lab animals, blood was extracted and injected into the thighs of eight neurosyphilitic patients, one of whom died of the disease before the treatment could be concluded. After a couple of days, the temperatures of the remaining seven patients rose and remained at elevated levels for a few hours to a few days before subsiding, only to rise again. This cycle continued for two weeks until it was terminated by salvarsan. Although detailed in their description of the treatment, Solomon and his colleagues were conjectural in their appraisal of its outcome, stating that it was "too early to attempt to evaluate the therapeutic results" (Solomon, Berk, Theiler, & Clay, p. 404), but that the observation of improvements in some of the patients was "at least suggestive of the therapeutic value of the method" (p. 404).

Despite this cautious appraisal, other asylum physicians were ready to use rat-bite fever as a therapeutic. Alex Hershfield and his colleagues set out a regime for its use in three Illinois asylums. They injected a total of seventy-two neurosyphilitic patients with the rat-bite fever spirochete. All patients were then confined to bed, their temperatures recorded every four hours. The inoculation period varied from eight to fifteen days, and started with an inflammation at the site of the injection and was followed by swelling of the lymph glands, and fever that ranged from 102° to 105° F., lasting four or five days. The fever reoccurred over the next several weeks. Some complications were noted: more than half of the patients suffered from severe neuralgia post-treatment; two developed delirium and had convulsions, and another two suffered from disorders of the heart and shortness of breath. All of the complications were satisfactorily resolved with one or two administrations of arsphenamine. In addition, ten patients died during the treatment, although Hershfield and his colleagues stated that only two of those deaths could be attributed to the treatment.

Hershfield and his colleagues observed patients for a year post rat-bite treatment and concluded that 50 percent of them "were more or less physically improved," 20 percent showed "from slight to marked mental improvement," 20 percent did not show any difference mentally," and 10 percent showed initial mental improvement and "then became worse" (Hershfield et al., p. 773). The outcome of "physical improvement" was not defined, except for a brief statement that many patients had gained weight; "mental improvement" remained undefined as well. Curiously, the description of the treatment ended with neither the authors' endorsement nor their dismissal of rat-bite fever as a therapeutic for the treatment of neurosyphilis. The press, nonetheless, reported the findings with some enthusiasm. *Time* magazine, for example, lauded it as a valuable alternative to malaria fever treatment; the *Chicago Defender*, somewhat ironically given the headline "Medical Science Finds Cure for Paretic Insane," merely repeated Hershfield's conclusion that some of the treated patients showed some mental improvement.

## *Relapsing Fever*

The induction of fever by injections of the human louse spirochete, *Borrelia recurrentis* (previously named *Spirochaeta duttoni*). Relapsing fever therapy dates to the late nineteenth century when Alexander Samoilovich Rosenblum (sometimes spelled "Rosenblium") infected thirty-two patients at the Odessa Psychopathic Hospital in Russia with relapsing fever, typhoid, or malaria. The patients had been diagnosed with either schizophrenia or manic-depression and none had neurosyphilis. He claimed to have cured sixteen of the patients, all of whom had been treated with malaria; the effects of both relapsing fever and typhoid were negligible. Published in an obscure medical journal, his findings were largely ignored although Julius Wagner-Jauregg, who would later be lauded as the founder of fever therapy, cited them in his early papers on malaria fever therapy.

The use of relapsing fever for the treatment of neurosyphilis was tried with some success by German physicians Felix Plaut and G. Steiner at the German Research Institute for Psychiatry in Munich, decades after Rosenblum had published his study. Hypothesizing that because there was a close relationship between the relapsing fever and the syphilis spirochete, the former would produce antibodies that affected the latter, they injected neurosyphilitic patients with a domestic relapsing fever virus. The course of the resulting recurrent fever was easily arrested by salvarsan. Although the results were encouraging, they did not meet expectations. Plaut and Steiner then injected an African strain of the virus into six patients with paretic neurosyphilis and two with schizophrenia. The paroxysms of fever lasted several days and were accompanied by chills, profuse sweating, headaches and nausea. Unexpectedly, the fever of this African strain could not be arrested by salvarsan, so it was left to run its course for each patient. Once again, the results were encouraging, but only just that: one of the neurosyphilitic patients went into remission, two improved, and the remainder showed no improvement. Both of the schizophrenic patients remained unimproved by the treatment.

Plaut and Steiner remained uncertain as to whether the results obtained were caused by the recurring fever treatment, or coincident with it. As a result, they did not enthusiastically endorse it. In the wake of what often were overinflated success stories about the effects of malaria fever therapy on paretic neurosyphilis, relapsing fever therapy was never widely used.

## Fixing (The Eye, Catching the Eye, the Gaze, the Clinical Gaze)

*The intense stare used by an asylum physician to subjugate, and later to diagnose, an insane patient.*

Fixing may have been influenced by the spellbinding command to "gaze into my eyes" delivered by mesmerists, professional and quack alike, who were plying their trade across Europe in the late eighteenth century. It most certainly was influenced, however, by the power dynamics of the asylums that were being built during that same period. It was there that physicians were ardently establishing, and jealously protecting, a kind of godlike supremacy over their hapless patients.

A clash between god-like supremacy and royal supremacy was famously played out in Francis Willis's treatment of George III, King of Great Britain and of Ireland, and fixing was a contentious issue in it. Willis, a clergyman as well as a physician, hence the sobriquet "the Duplicate Doctor," owned a private madhouse in the Lincolnshire countryside where, it was said of him, he controlled his patients with his gaze. Of that inimitable skill, one of his contemporaries wrote:

> Of the celebrated Willis it has been said, that the utmost sweetness and affability is the usual expression of his countenance. But, when

looks a maniac in the face for the first time, he appears instantly to change character. His features present a new aspect, such as commands the respect and attention, even of lunatics. His looks appear to penetrate into their hearts, and to read their thoughts as soon as they are formed. Thus does he obtain an authority over his patients, which afterwards cooperating with other means, contribute to restore them to themselves and their friends [Pinel, 1806, pp. 49–50].

Authority over the insane King, however, already had proved difficult to establish. Other treating physicians had used everything from a straitjacket [see **Mechanical Restraints**], to purging and vomiting [see **Depletive Therapy**] to blistering [see **Counterirritation**] in the treatment of the mad King, but it was through fixing him with the eye that Willis finally established supremacy over him and secured his submission.

So piercing was Willis's gaze, in fact, that the estimable Edmund Burke, House of Commons Opposition leader, shied away from it during a 1789 meeting with him to discuss his treatment of the King. A particular point of that discussion had been to ascertain why Willis had allowed the imperiously defiant King to have a razor. Burke had demanded to know,

"If the Royal patient had become outrageous at the moment, what power the Doctor possessed of instantaneously terrifying him into obedience?"

"Place the candles between us, Mr. Burke," replied the Doctor, in an equally authoritative tone—"and I'll give you an answer. There, Sir! by the EYE! I should have looked at him *thus*, Sir—*thus!*"

Burke instantaneously averted his head, and, making no reply, evidently acknowledged this *basiliskan* authority [Macalpine & Hunter, p. 272].

The desire, and the need, to exercise a "basiliskan authority" over asylum patients who were more riffraff than royalty, led many physicians to emulate Willis and use fixing both as an expression of their authority and an exertion of power not only over their corporeal patients, but over their corporeal patients' incorporeal hallucinations, delusions, and fantasies. To that end, fixing was a necessary requisite for producing the salutary fear that controlled, manipulated and sometimes humiliated and ridiculed patients into what physicians believed would be rational thought and behavior [see **Salutary Fear**].

Willis's influence even reached over the ocean and the just as wide political divides between the "Mother country" and a former colony. From the Philadelphia Hospital in Pennsylvania, Benjamin Rush had kept up a lively correspondence with Willis, trading ideas about the most efficacious strategies for treating asylum patients. He was obviously impressed by Willis's use of fixing, since it appealed to that odd combination of supremacy and suggestion that characterized the treatment regime put into place by the "Father of American Psychiatry." On fixing, Rush wrote:

[T]he first object of a physician, when he enters the cell or chamber of the deranged patient, should be, to catch his EYE, and look him out of countenance. The dread of the eye was clearly imposed upon every beast of the field. The tiger, the mad bull, and the enraged dog, all fly from it; now a man deprived of his reason partakes so much of the nature of those animals, that he is for the most part easily terrified, or composed, by the eye of a man who possess his reason. [A stern or ferocious look] may sometimes be necessary; but a much greater effect is produced, by looking the patient out of countenance with a mild and steady eye, and varying its aspect from the highest degree of sternness, down to the mildest degree of benignity; for there are keys in the eye, if I may be allowed the expression, which should be suited to the state of the patient's mind, with the same exactness that musical tones should be suited to the depression of spirits in hypochondriasis [Rush pp. 173–174].

Rush went on to suggest that what the physician sees when fixing on the patient should determine his comportment with the patient. Fixing, therefore, was transformed from a coercive strategy to a diagnostic assessment and a therapeutic tool:

VOICE: In governing mad people it should be harsh, gentle, plaintive, according to circumstances...

COUNTENANCE: It should assist his eye and voice in governing his deranged patients. It should be accommodated to the state of the patient's mind and conduct. A grave countenance in a physician has often checked the frothy levity of a deranged patient in an instant, and a placid one has suddenly chased away his gloom. A stern countenance in like manner has often put a stop to garrulity, and a cheerful one as extorted smiles even from the face of melancholy itself...

CONDUCT: It should be uniformly dignified.... He should never descend to levity in conversing with them. He should hear with silence their rude or witty answers to his questions, and upon no account ever laugh at them or with them...

ACTS OF KINDNESS: [A]ll his directions for discontinuing painful or disagreeable remedies, and all his pleasant prescriptions, should be delivered in the presence of his patients; while such as are of an unpleasant nature, should be delivered only to their keepers. Small presents of fruit or sweetcake will have a happy effect in attaching maniacal patients to their physicians for it is a fact, that in proportion to the intensity of misery, the subjects of it feel most sensibly the smallest diminution of it [Rush, pp. 175–178].

It has been argued that as the result of the Enlightenment, and Rush indeed was the embodiment of the American Enlightenment, sight was valued as the most rational of the senses. The visual arts of that era gave testimony to that. In paintings, sketches and drawings asylum physicians were always depicted as having a steady and evaluative gaze that was meant to represent the epitome of rationality, and that stood in stark contrast to the distracted, wild or plaintive gazes of the depicted insane patients. Thus, the role of sight, if not fixing in the manner that Willis and Rush had so successfully used it, became central to the asylum physician-patient interaction.

John Haslam, apothecary to Bethlem, better known as "Bedlam," Hospital in London agreed that an informed gaze was necessary for the evaluation of patients, but was critical of the blunt use of fixing. In his well-regarded text, *Observations on Madness and Melancholy*, he suggested that the "fascinating power" of fixing "ought now be lamented among the *artes deperditae*" (p. 277). Could the

A Carl Josef print of an asylum physician with eyes so bulging as to "fix" a patient with an intense stare. This "awful imposition of the eye" was condemned by John Haslam, apothecary to Bethlem Hospital in London, but valued by most of his early nineteenth century contemporaries (courtesy of the Wellcome Library, London).

attention of the insane be fixed, and could they be reduced to obedience by nothing more than the eye, Haslam asked? The fact, he replied to his own interrogatory, was "notoriously otherwise" (p. 275). And he seriously questioned both the claims and the integrity of those asylum physicians who thought differently:

> It has, on some occasions, occurred to me to meet with gentlemen who have imagined themselves eminently gifted with this awful imposition of the eye, but the result has never been satisfactory; for, although I have entertained the fullest confidence of any relation, which such gentlemen might afterwards communicate concerning the success of the experiment, I have never been able to persuade them to practice this rare talent *tetè a tetè* with a furious lunatic [Haslam, p. 278].

Yet Haslam acknowledged that gaining some ascendancy over insane patients was necessary for their management. Self-deprecatingly, he admitted that had no "rare qualities" that other asylum physicians were boasting—"no thunder in my voice, nor lightening in my eye" (p. 295)—therefore it was necessary for him to have recourse to other expedients:

> A mildness of manner and expression, an attention to their narrative, and seeming acquiescence in its truth, succeed much better [than staring them out of countenance]. By such conduct they acquire confidence in the practitioner; and if he will have patience, and not too frequently interrupt them, they will soon satisfy his mind as the derangement of their intellects [Haslam, p. 296].

Haslam's comments presaged a different understanding and use of fixing. As coercive mechanical restraints increasingly were being replaced in the early nineteenth century with the persuasive techniques of moral treatment [see **Mechanical Restraints; Moral Treatment**], fixing symbolized a new relationship between physician and patient—one that involved the physician's comportment as well as his authority.

Fixing might very well have been reduced to a footnote in the historiography of asylum therapeutics were it not for the critique of medical power by the twentieth century French philosopher Michel Foucault who was no fan of moral treatment. The "gaze" or "observing gaze," as he variously referred to it, led patients to believe that physicians could penetrate artifice and deceit, ignorance and naïveté, to see through to the truth, he argued. That vested asylum physicians with an unchallengeable wisdom that assured both their authority and their status in a modernizing and secularizing society that was finding it increasingly necessary to confine the diseased, disordered and the discontents in purpose-built institutions.

In Foucault's argument, the gaze served to benefit nineteenth century asylum physicians. It did nothing of the kind, however, for asylum patients. The gaze stripped them of their individuality and their agency, reduced them to their diagnoses, and granted asylum physicians supremacy over their minds.

## References

Foucault, M. (1989). *The birth of the clinic: An archaeology of medical perception.* Trans. A.M. Sheridan. London: Routledge.
Gillman, S.L. (1995). *Health and illness: Images of difference.* London: Reaktion Books.
Haslam, J. (1809). *Observations on madness and melancholy.* London: J. Callow.
Hunter, R., and Macalpine, I. (1963). *Three hundred years of psychiatry, 1535–1860.* London: Oxford University Press.
Macalpine, I., and Hunter, R. (1991). *George III and the mad-business.* London: Pimlico.
Pinel, P. (1806). *A treatise on insanity.* Trans. D.D. Davis. Sheffield, UK: W. Todd.
Rush, B. (1830). *Medical inquiries and observations upon the diseases of the mind.* 4th ed. Philadelphia: John Grigg.

## Forced Feeding (Forced Alimentation, Gavage)

*A method of putting food into the body of patients who were incapable of feeding themselves, or who refused to do so.*

In a statement that captured the seventeenth century take on insanity, William Salmon declared that "those taken with this disease seem to be mad as wild beasts, nor do they differ much from them...[They have] a prodigious Herculean strength ... endure the greatest hunger, cold, and stripes without any sensible harm" (Salmon, 56). Although he concocted physics, cast horoscopes, practiced alchemy and defended his quite dubious medical credentials, Salmon's characterization of the insane as insensible, in every sense of that term, was shared by his contemporaries who bona fides were not in question. Among them was Thomas Willis. Physician, founding member of the Royal Society, and Sedleian Professor of Natural Philosophy at Oxford University, Willis affirmed that "madmen, what ever they bear or suffer, are not hurt; but they bear cold, heat, watching, fasting, strokes, and wounds, without any sensible hurt" (Willis, p. 205).

This image of the insane as "wild beasts" persisted well into the eighteenth century, and certainly influenced what was passing at that time for asylum therapeutics. Whippings and beatings [see **Salutary Fear**], seclusion in cold and dark cells [see **Isolation**], mockery and harassment by physicians, attendants and gawking visitors alike were endured by insane patients who were imagined to have neither the sense nor the sentience to be very much inconvenienced by any of it. In the confines of asylums, this confrontation between "man and beast" made food irrelevant [see **Diet**], and what patients ate, or for that matter, if they ate at all, was a matter of little concern.

Revolutions—political, social, industrial, intellectual—encouraged a new, more humanitarian, view of insanity and an imperative to treat, rather than control, it. Food now was considered not only essential for fueling the bodily machine, but for healing the ravages of the mind. When patients refused to eat the food offered to them, then, asylum physicians were faced with a new and disturbing dilemma. Loathe to carry on the coercive practices of their predecessors, they nonetheless were faced with the prospect of having to force feed their food-refusing patients.

The influential reformer Philippe Pinel, so intimately associated with the moral treatment movement [see **Moral Treatment**], found nothing contradictory between his humanitarian approach and the forceful methods sometimes needed to feed patients. While at the Salpêtrière Asylum in Paris, France, he both used and recommended the use of feeding bottles and the nasal feeding tubes used with success by his former pupil Jean-Étienne Dominique Esquirol to nourish food-refusing patients until they gained the requisite strength and insight to eat on their own. On his advice, feeding tubes were so regularly used in French asylums that there was little discussion among and between asylum physicians about the method or, for that matter, the ethics of their use.

An article published in a widely read medical journal in 1845, however, initiated a lively debate about the practice among French asylum physicians who soon were joined by their German and British contemporaries. The instigator of this debate was François Leuret, chief physician at the Bicêtre Asylum in Paris. Leuret had departed from the prevailing ideas of that era by insisting that the origin of insanity was, in fact, unknown, therefore it was necessary to supplement the suasions of moral treatment directed at the mind with rough handling directed at the body. In the article, though, Leuret focused his discussion on the technical problems with the use of the standard nasal feeding tube on food-refusing patients. In its place, he recommended a more flexible tube of his own design. The article prompted other French asylum physicians to discuss their own preferred methods of forced feeding, thus revealing for the first time not only the wide range of technical devices actually in use behind asylum walls, but the sheer extent of food-refusal among insane patients.

German asylum physicians followed the technical debate with some interest. The preferred method of forced feeding there was the manual forcing open of the mouth, a low-tech method, certainly, but a low-risk one as well. Nasal and gastric tubes were rejected for the most part, and rectal feeding was promoted in their place, an alternative that British asylum physicians, who had entered the debate when Leuret's article was re-published in the *Lancet,* rejected emphatically in favor of the stomach pump. In response to both the German and British reactions, Jules Baillarger, a long-time physician at the Salpêtrière in Paris, promoted a technological innovation: electricity. Well-placed charges to the neck, he argued, both opened the mouth and forced swallowing. His recommendation made strange bedfellows not only of British and German asylum physicians, but his French colleagues as well who declared the method dangerous and unnecessary.

The international debate continued for some time, focusing more on the best technology for forced-feeding rather than the underlying, and in many ways more unsettling questions, about how to calculate the degree of force needed against the degree of resistance demonstrated; how to determine when acceptable force crossed the threshold into unacceptable violence; and whether patients had some inherent right to refuse food, and if their insanity diminished that right. Typologies of food-refusing patients, also known as sitophobic patients, also were constructed. The clinical nuances of food-refusal were discussed, albeit briefly during the mid-nineteenth century. Physical illness certainly could cause it, asylum physicians agreed, as could anorexia nervosa and bulimia, delusions about poisoning and filth, shame, defiance and obstinacy, and suicidal intention. Whether the dynamics of each of these required a different technological approach, however, was not often a matter of discussion among asylum physicians whose attention turned once again to the improvement of the technology of forced-feeding and stayed on that topic into the early twentieth century.

That technological debate had not just to do with the type of device to administer the food, but where the food should be delivered. Whether food was to be placed in the mouth alone, or into the esophagus via the mouth, or through the nose with or without entering the esophagus, or into the stomach, or via the rectum, not only determined the type of device that was used, but the nutriment that was administered. Beef-tea and brandy were considered best for feeding by mouth; eggs, milk and pearl barley for feeding by nose; butter, port wine and beef tea for feeding by rectum. Some devices worked best if the patients were physically or mechanically restrained; others if they were sedated, perhaps by a whiff or two of chloroform.

When the technological debate over forced-feeding finally waned, however, the ethical issues waxed. From the imprisoned British suffragettes who were violently force-fed in reaction to their hunger strikes, to the Irish Republican prisoners at the start of the twentieth century and the Guantanamo Bay prisoners at the century's end, to the terminally ill, the elderly, the intellectually handicapped, and the insane, forced-feeding has become a complex human rights issue. In regards to the latter, it is entwined with mental health legislation and with considerations of "best interests," "medical justification," and "informed consent."

REFERENCES

Baillarger, J. (1845). Du cathétérisme de l'oesophage chez les aliénés. *Gazette Médicale de Paris, 9,* 568–570.
Dickens, C. (1852). A curious dance round a curious tree. *Household Words, 11,* 362–370.
Digby, A. (1985). *Madness, morality and medicine: A study of the York Retreat, 1796–1914.* Cambridge: Cambridge University Press.

Doyle, D. (2005). Per rectum: A history of enemata. *Royal College of Physicians Edinburgh, 35,* 367–370.
Friedenwald, J., and Rühräh, J. (1906). *Diet in health and disease.* Philadelphia: W.B. Saunders.
Gostin, L.O. (2000). Human rights of persons with mental disabilities: The European Convention on Human Rights. *International Journal of Law and Psychiatry, 23,* 125–129.
Haslam, J. (1809). *Observations of madness and melancholy.* 2nd ed. London: G. Hayden.
Herbert, W.W. (1894). The forcible feeding of the insane. *British Medical Journal, 1,* 462.
Howe, E., Kosaraju, A., Laraby, P.R., and Casscells, S.W. (2009). Guantanamo: Ethics interrogation, and forced feeding. *Military Medicine, 174,* iv–xiii.
"The Kalamazoo Asylum: In a general way its affairs are found all right" (1878, April 15). *Daily Gazette,* p. 1.
Leuret, F. (1845). Note sur une nouvelle sonde destinée à l'alimentation des aliénés. *Gazette Médicale de Paris, 1,* 540–541.
Mickle, W.J. (1884). Rectal feeding and medication. *New York Medical Abstract, 4,* 152–156.
Moxey, D.A. (1869). On the administration of food and medicine by the nose when they cannot be given by the mouth. *Lancet, 93,* 394–395, 425–426.
Neumann, H. (1859). *Lehrbuch der psychiatrie.* Erlangen, Germany: Verlag ver Ferdinand Enke.
"On the feeding of the insane" (1850). *Journal of Psychological Medicine, 3,* 219–221.
Pritchard, T. (1855). To the editor of the *Asylum Journal. Asylum Journal of Mental Science, 1,* 189–190.
Reeve, J.F. (1851). An apparatus for administering nourishment to insane persons who refuse food. *Lancet, 2,* 90–91.
Salmon, W. (1686). *Systema medicinale, a compleat system of physic, theoretical and practical.* London: T. Passinger, T. Sawbridge and T. Flesher.
Sammet, K. (2006). Avoiding violence by technologies? Rectal feeding in German psychiatry, c. 1860–1885. *History of Psychiatry, 17,* 269–277.
Smith, L.A. (1878). *Behind the scenes, or, life in an insane asylum.* Chicago: Culver, Page, Hoyne, & Co.
Stiff, W.P. (1858). On simple sanguineous cyst of the ear in lunatics. *British and Foreign Medic-Chirurgical Review, 21,* 222–227.
Sutherland, H. (1875). On the artificial feeding of the insane. *Journal of Psychological Medicine and Mental Pathology, 1,* 98–115.
Tuke, D.H. (1892). *A dictionary of psychological medicine.* London: J. & A. Churchill.
Tuke, H. (1858). Forced alimentation. *Journal of Mental Science, 4,* 204–222.
Williams, E.A. (2008). Gags, funnels and tubes: Forced feeding of the insane of suffragettes. *Endeavor, 32,* 134–140.
Williams, E.A. (2010). Stomach and psyche: Eating, digestion and mental illness in the medicine of Philippe Pinel. *Bulletin of the History of Medicine, 84,* 358–386.
Williams, S.W.D. (1864). Remarks on the refusal of food in the insane. *Journal of Mental Science, 10,* 366–380.
Willis, T. (1684). *Practice of physick.* London: Dring, Harper, and Leigh.

## Balmanno's Feeding Apparatus, or Balmanno's Syringe

Intended to supersede the use of the stomach pump for the forced feeding of the food-refusing patient, the feeding apparatus was comprised of a narrow tube that was inserted into the nose, rather than the mouth, passed into the pharynx, and then into the stomach via the action of the constrictor muscles. The insertion required little force, and except for a slight choking sensation it was not particularly uncomfortable to the asylum patient. The nutriment liquid was then dispensed via a syringe through the several inches of tube that remained outside the nose.

Thomas Prichard, physician at Abbington Abbey, a private lunatic asylum in Northampton, England, stated that he had kept food-refusing patients alive for several weeks with the feeding apparatus. He cited the case of a patient who had refused all nourishment for some time, having made a vow to starve himself to death. In a weakened state, he was forced-fed with the feeding apparatus and after several administrations he was able to sit up in bed, and soon developed a hearty appetite.

The feeding apparatus was invented by John Balmanno, visiting physician to the Glasgow Royal Asylum. It used throughout Scotland and in some asylums in England during the mid- to late nineteenth century.

## Eguisier's Irrigateur

A metal-encased pump that ejected nourishing liquids through an attached tube that was snaked down the patient's throat and into the stomach. The irrigateur worked rather like a cafetiere in which hot water is poured into a receptacle and then forced, by pressure, through the coffee beans.

In the mid-nineteenth century the irrigateur, which had been patented in France by its inventor, Maurice Eguisier, an obstetrician, was used with some enthusiasm in European and in provincial British asylums. Phillip Stiff, resident physician at the County Asylum in Nottingham, England, reported on his success in improving the physical health of a fifty-year-old patient who was under the delusion that he had been sold to the devil. He had refused all food. His breath became fetid, his tongued furred, and his bones were evident under his skin. At times, Stiff recounted, "he appeared to be sinking" (Stiff, p. 225). The patient was forcibly fed with the irrigateur twice daily for three weeks. Although he gained weight and looked healthy as a result of the forced-feeding, his state of mind remained unimproved.

The eminent British asylum physician Harrington Tuke was unimpressed with the device, stating that he did not much admire the "clock-work plan of squirting sustenance into the stomach" (Tuke, p. 216), adding almost parenthetically that he did not care for its bulky appearance either. He rather reluctantly conceded that it might be of more use in provincial asylums where physicians and attendants were in short supply, than in the more modern and better staffed city asylums where the skills of physicians were put to better use than do nothing more than attaching a tube and priming a pump.

It may be interesting to note that the alternative placement of the tube of the irrigateur also made the device handy for performing enemas and vaginal douches.

## *Feeding Spoon, or Forcing Spoon*

A metal spoon with a long point bent at a right angle that was inserted into the pried open mouth of the patient; a funnel at its other end dripped liquid nutriment into the mouth. The feeding spoon was used in asylums around the world throughout the nineteenth century. Some asylum physicians were opposed to it; the often protracted struggle to insert the spoon exhausted both the patient and the physician. Other asylum physicians, however, reported satisfaction with its use. Among them was S.W.D. Williams of the Northampton General Lunatic Asylum in England, who set out a detailed and choreographed plan for the successful use of this very low-tech device for forced-feeding:

> With the aid of three attendants the patient is placed on his back on a mattress on the floor, and covered by bedclothes, being, as *sine qua non,* in his night dress, as far as the armpits, the arm being free. The head rests on a well-filled bolster, an attendant kneels on each side of the bedclothes covering the patient, and thus easily but effectually secures his body. One hand is placed on the patient's wrist, and the other presses of his shoulder. By these means he is perfectly restrained in the least irksome way to both patient and attendant, and, which is of primary importance, but few if any bruises need be inflicted.... The operator kneels at the patient's head, and, if the patient is very restive, may steady his head with his knees, but that is seldom necessary. A third attendant takes his place at the operator's left elbow.... The next operation is to get the spoon into the patient's mouth: this, if the patient be a woman, is generally easily done by getting her to talk, and slipping it in when the mouth is opened to speak; this device failing, however, persistent but moderate pressure with the spoon against the teeth, aided, if necessary, by inserting a finger between the upper and lower gums behind the last molar, will soon effect our object. Of course, in putting a finger into the mouth, one must look out for being bitten; but if the spoon is firmly pressed against the teeth so as to slide between them immediately the masseters are relaxed, such an accident cannot readily occur. [The spoon] should be placed far enough into the mouth to command the tongue.... It should then be restrained by the thumb and index finger of the left hand, the palm and remaining fingers firmly grasping the chin and preventing any to-and-fro or lateral motion of the head. The third attendant now passes his right hand under the operator's engaged arm and firmly closes the nostrils....

The operator can now with his right hand pour the food into the patient's mouth [Williams, pp. 374–375].

A variation of this method was the simultaneous use of two feeding spoons. For this administration the patient could sit or lie down, the mouth was pried open and kept open with one of the feeding spoons, and liquid was poured from the second spoon into the first. The asylum physician or attendant then gently touched the back of the pharynx with the first spoon while the nose was being pinched, thus forcing the patient to swallow the liquid.

The feeding spoon, in its single and double use, was used in asylums around the world throughout the nineteenth century, including the York Retreat, an asylum in northern England that not only was dedicated to non-restraint, but that could claim credit for having initiated the moral treatment movement [see **Moral Treatment**]. In a letter dated 1829, superintendent George Jepson described the necessarily forceful use of the spoon to feed a food-refusing patient:

> The way we have found effectual is to fasten the patient in a chair a little leaning backward with a person to hold the head and another the hands. If the patient refuses to open her mouth it becomes necessary to force it open by inserting the handle ... of a key between the teeth in the mouth and then turning it by hold of the web so as to force the mouth open to make room for the introduction of the spoon. Then with another spoon nearly fill that between the teeth and push it forward till the point passes the ridge of the tongue, then lean the patient backwards till the liquid is passed down the throat and if she should refuse to swallow, by closing the nostrils a short time and gently stroking the throat she may be inclined to do so. A teacup of milk and the yolk of an egg beat up [in] it and a little sugar and, if she be very reduced, a little brandy may be added [Digby, p. 132].

One of the most persistent problems with forced-feeding by mouth was that patients sometimes spat out the food or liquid. Henry Sutherland, physician to a number of private asylums in England and a well-regarded lecturer on insanity at the Westminster Hospital, had no hesitance in recommending that force be used to preclude this disgusting response. He suggested that an attendant wrap an arm around the resistant patient's neck and then use his hand to clamp the mouth closed until the food is swallowed. That force, coupled with well-timed "threats and shaming" by the asylum physician (Sutherland, p. 100), usually secured the cooperation of even the most recalcitrant patient.

## *Gag*

A straight or curved piece of wood with a hole in it that was inserted into the mouth that had been opened by a screw or by some other means. The gag had a hole through which a tube was threaded so that liquids could be slowly decanted down the esophagus via a funnel at the other end of the tube.

The gag posed several problems in administration: patient resistance made it difficult to insert, even if the mouth was being kept open by a screw; the hole could be covered by the tongue; the threading of the tube through the open hole required considerable skill and because it bent against the posterior wall of the pharynx before entering the esophagus, it often caused severe retching and contraction of the pharynx.

## *Galvanic Method*

The insertion of two needles connected to a voltaic pile, an early form of an electrical battery, into the digastric muscles. The resulting shock opened the mouth widely so that the patient could be fed. Although there is some dispute as to its originator, Angelo Filipi of Milan, Italy claimed he was the first to use it in the mid-nineteenth century to feed a particularly intractable case of food-refusal. Upon the second and third administration the patient, who had come to believe that he was dealing with a supernatural, rather than electrical, force, capitulated and agreed to feed himself. He was quite quickly cured and discharged from the asylum.

Although the galvanic method forced open the mouth so food could be placed in it, it could not ensure that the patient would swallow the food. Addressing that issue, Jules Baillarger, physician at the Salpêtrière Asylum in Paris, France, applied electrical plates to each side of the neck of a food-refusing patient to force him to swallow. The patient, a twenty-seven-year-old who had continued to lose weight while being fed via a nasal tube, the preferred practice at that time in French asylums, improved significantly over six weeks of such treatment.

Despite criticisms that the use of electricity was dangerous and unnecessary, the galvanic method was used with some success in Italy, France as well as in Austria in the mid-nineteenth century.

## Haslam's Key

A large iron key that pressed down on the tongue on the food-refusing patient while keeping the jaws apart; once inserted via a long wooden handle, the nose of the patient was pinched to keep the mouth open so that fortifying liquids could be slowly poured through a hole in the center of the key. The key was invented by John Haslam, apothecary at Bethlem Hospital, better known as Bedlam, in London, England, in 1798 after having come across a "number of interesting females who, after having suffered a temporary disarrangement of mind, and undergone the brutal operation *of spouting,* in private receptacles for the insane, have been restored to their friends without a front tooth in either jaw" (Haslam, p. 317, italics in original).

Although intended to be a humane alternative to the spouting boat, the use of the key required some initial deception. The patient was blindfolded, "which never fails to alarm him, and urges him to enquire what the persons around him are about," according to Haslam (p. 320). The administration of a pinch of snuff or pepper, or the use of a feather to tickle the nose, caused the patient to sneeze, which opened the mouth sufficiently for the insertion of the key.

Haslam boasted that the key had never deprived a patient of a tooth, yet its administration required a considerable degree of force, as he described:

The manner in which this compulsory operation is performed, consists in placing the head of the patient between the knees of the person who is to use the instrument: a second assistant secures the hands, (if the straight-

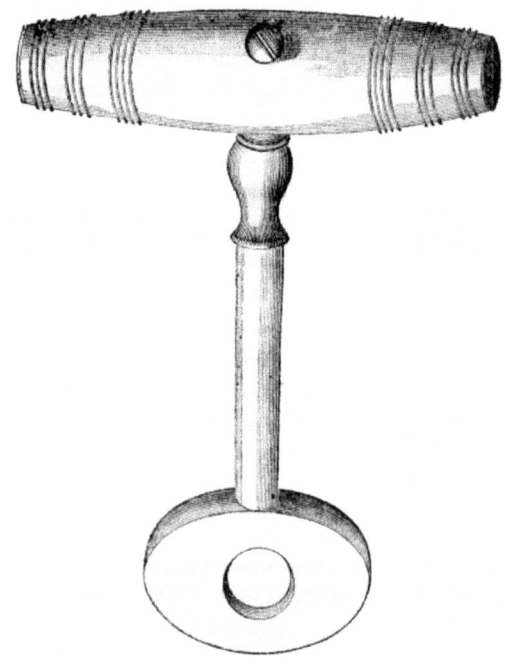

One of many devices, screws and gags that were used to force-feed patients. Haslam, apothecary to London's Bethlem Hospital, intended the key to be a kinder and gentler alternative to other devices that broke teeth, but realized soon that patients were none too keen on his invention. Thus it was often necessary for them to be blindfolded, then a little pinch of snuff or a tickle on the nose with a feather forced them to open their mouths just enough for the key to be inserted (P.S. Knight [1827]. *Observations of the causes, symptoms and treatment of derangement of the mind.* London: Longman, Rees, Orme, Brown and Green).

waistcoat be not employed) and a third keeps down the legs. The nose of the patient is held by the person who uses the instrument [Haslam, p. 319].

Replaced by nasal tubes in the early nineteenth century, Haslam's key became a symbol of what the author Charles Dickens referred to as the "unconscious cruelty" in the treatment of asylum patients in previous generations. Its abandonment as a technology of forced-feeding was, to him, a marker of the "substitution of humanity for brutality, kindness for maltreatment, peace for raging fury; in the acquisition of love instead of hatred; and in the knowledge that, from such treatment, improvement, and hope of final restoration will come, if such hope be possible" (Dickens, p. 370).

## *Manual Force*

The use of the hands to open the mouth of the food-refusing patient. Although this undoubtedly was the fallback technique used by frustrated asylum physicians around the world, it was the preferred technique of German asylum physicians in the nineteenth century. Karl Hergt, physician at the Illenau Asylum near the Black Forest in Baden, Germany, described how manual force was to be used:

> The patient is laid down in the horizontal position ... pelvis, shoulders, hands and head are to be held by a sufficient number of attendants. The physician standing by the side of the patient presses the lower jaw with the hand which is positioned under it against the upper jaw meanwhile fixing the middle finger of the same hand between the opened lips at the line where both rows of teeth meet. The forefinger of the other hand, crooked like a hook, is introduced into the free corner of the mouth into the outer mouth cavity and with the help of the ... thumb, by pulling, ... a pocket is made in which ... liquid is gradually poured [Sammet, p. 262].

Hergt, who practiced in an asylum at the vanguard of moral treatment, not only found such a technique necessary, but actually advantageous. Unlike many of the devices, such as the gag and the key, it did not break teeth, and unlike the various nasal and gastric tubes, it posed no danger of perforation or laceration.

It was not the use of manual force that was of concern to one of the leading German asylum physicians of that era, but the reliance on it that was disturbing. Heinrich Philipp August Damerow argued that its quite easy use undermined the dogma of individualization, that is, the calibration of therapeutic intervention to the special needs of the individual patient. Damerow, who loathed the positioning of any technology, including the hands, between the patient and the asylum physician, encouraged his colleagues to be innovative, even spontaneous, in their treatment of the sitophobic patient. Although inspiring, his idealism stood at odds with the daily management of large and complex asylums and had little impact on the use of manual force as a method of forced-feeding food-refusing patients.

## *Mouth-Opener*

A face mask composed of an elliptic piece of wood or a metal plate with an aperture over the area of the mouth. When opened, a shutter over the aperture allowed food to be introduced in the mouth; when closed, the shutter prevented the patient from spitting or otherwise ejecting the food. The mouth-opener was used well into the nineteenth century in asylums in France and Germany.

## *Nasal Tube*

An oiled flexible tube that was passed through one nostril and as far as the cavity of the pharynx so that it did not enter the esophagus. A nutriment liquid then was poured into the tube, via a funnel, and the patient's nose and mouth were pinched shut. This method of forced-feeding was attributed to French asylum physician Alexandre Brierre deBoismont who presented it as a "vigorous, striking, and energetic measure" to overcome what he assessed was the obdurate stubbornness and sly deceptiveness of the sitophobic patient (Tuke, 1858, p. 210).

While the nasal tube assured that the patient's teeth would not be broken as they so often were with the feeding spoon and the spouting boat, it had its own drawbacks. The tube often was difficult to insert due to the accumulation of mucus within the nose, and when inserted at times became plugged with mucus, requiring that it be withdrawn, cleaned and reinserted, sometimes repeatedly and almost always to the great distress of the patient. In addition, it pitted the asylum physician against the resistant patient, thus reducing the former's moral authority. Another complication that initially had not been anticipated by asylum physicians is that some patients were able to contract the muscles at the back of the pharynx, thus forcing the tube into the larynx, causing choking. Others were able to twist the tongue backwards behind the tube, force it forward between the teeth, and bite it in two.

French asylum physicians, such as Jules Baillarger and Guillaume Ferrus, the latter affiliated with the Bicêtre Hospital in Paris, improved the design of the nasal tube by adding stylets of iron and whalebone, to carry the tube into the nose. A significant design improvement was the articulated stylet, or articulated catheter. Invented by Emile Blanche of the Salpêtrière Asylum in Paris, France, it was composed of thirty-one rings controlled by a watch-spring; the stylet moved the gum elastic tube quite freely when flexed, but made it rigid when extended. In its flexed state the tube was inserted in the nostril and on to the pharynx, and then was straightened by a pull on the watch-spring of the stylet so as to avoid the larynx. When it reached the esophagus, liquid nutriment was introduced through the tube. The stem connected to the stylet's watch-spring then was released making the tube flexible, thus allowing for its easy withdrawal. Although recognized for its ingenuity, the articulated stylet was not often used by asylum physicians who found it unnecessarily technologically complex. In his survey of forced feeding techniques, the eminent British asylum physician Harrington Tuke revealed that Blanche himself rarely ever used his own invention, preferring instead the simple gum-elastic feeding tube that it was designed to improve. In fact, none of the improvements did much to expedite the insertion of the nasal tube and, in the end, were deemed largely unnecessary.

## *Nasogastric Intubation*

The insertion of a nasal tube that delivers nutriments directly to the stomach. In use today, it allows for the continuous feeding of food-refusing patients through the use of a gravity-based system in which the bag containing the liquid is situated above the patient's head. The end of the tube, which is plastic, is lubricated and an anesthetic spray often is applied before insertion through the nose. Its position in the stomach can be affirmed, if necessary with a chest/abdomen X-ray.

## *Nose Feeding*

The insertion of a funnel or syringe, or the emptying of a spoon or feeding cup of nutriment liquid into the nostril of the recumbent patient. D. Anderson Moxey, medical officer at the Hants County Lunatic Asylum in Hampshire, England, in the mid-nineteenth century, was one of the first physicians to call attention to this method of forced-feeding. The patient's arms and legs were restrained by three to five attendants, and a funnel was placed in one of the nostrils. Liquids, such as milk, beef tea, broth, coffee, wine or spirits diluted with water, or semi-solid foods such as soup, or eggs mixed with milk, were then poured from a sauceboat into the small Wedgewood funnel and into the nostril of the patient.

Moxey had experimented with the method,

administering diluted brandy and eggs mixed with milk to himself without adverse results. Neither painful not irritating, the experience nonetheless was "sufficiently unpleasant" to cause him to appreciate "why many patients, after a very short trial, prefer to take their food in the usual way." (Moxey, 1869, p. 425).

The wholly unanticipated lack of resistance of patients during that "very short trial," however, was explained by Moxey as a consequence of three factors. First, he argued, even the insane "have a tolerably shrewd appreciation of the power of numbers" (p. 426), so when confronted by several attendants "a feeling of alarm often prompts them to give in, even before they are laid down on the couch" (p. 426). Second, restraint by the attendants degraded and produced a feeling of utter powerlessness that was "not agreeable to the natural vanity of anyone, sane or insane" (p. 426), thus bringing about unconditional surrender. Third, the administration of nutriments via the funnel was sufficiently disagreeable, as Moxey himself testified, to "bring most patients to terms, particularly when the luxury of a stout resistance is so completely precluded" (p. 426).

Nose feeding was used during the late nineteenth century, despite the concern of many asylum physicians about the degree of restraint it required for its administration. In most asylums it eventually was replaced by the nasal tube.

## *Nose Holding*

The low tech method of pinching the nose to force the mouth open to receive food. It was commonly used in asylums prior to the mid-nineteenth century.

## *Paley's Feeder*

A glass-covered funnel with a spout shaped like a goose's bill. The spout was forced between the teeth of the patient, a spring lever was then compressed to release liquid down the throat. The glass cover on the funnel allowed the asylum physician to measure each release of liquid. Paley's Feeder was not recommended for the resistant patient, since it was likely to break teeth or injure the tongue.

## *Rectal Feeding, or Clyster, or Nutrient Enema*

The delivery of nutriments in concentrated form by injection or insertion into the rectum of the food-refusing patient. Although Egyptian papyri dating back to 1500 B.C.E. list more than 700 different medications that could be administered through the rectum, it may have been the Mongols who were the first to administer nutrients via an animal bladder filled with nourishing fluid and attached to one end of a cow's horn.

Although the origin of rectal feeding as an asylum therapeutic is unclear, the role of Bernhard Oebeke and Franz Richarz, both of whom were affiliated with a private asylum near Bonn, Germany, is notable. In the mid-nineteenth century they initiated a lively debate among their peers about sitophobic patients, their humane treatment, and the ethical responsibilities of attending physicians that went on, unresolved, for several decades. The debate was hardly parochial: asylum physicians around the world were expressing discomfort with the standard technologies, such as the stomach tube and the screw, that required such force to administer that they terrified and injured patients. Some were declaring forced-feeding unethical; others were insisting that the reliance on technology in any form to deal with food refusal breached the very physician-patient relationship that was necessary for recuperation and cure in the long-term. All also were agreeing that forced feeding, at times, was absolutely necessary. Oebeke and Richarz proposed rectal feeding as a compromise: it was non-violent in its administration and, as a result, did not disrupt the therapeutic alliance, and it saved lives. But it also posed a significant problem: its occasional use in asylums in the past led to the conclusion that it was a "poor and insufficient substitute for natural feeding" (Neumann, p. 207).

Oebeke and Richarz, armed with more recent physiological findings that the rectum absorbs more nutrients than previously thought, then set out to increase the nutritional value of the nutriment to be rectally injected. They conferred with chemist Hans Heinrich Landolt who recommended cold Liebig's meat extract, a viscous black spread comprised of reduced meat stock and salt that, he asserted, had all the nutritional value of lean meat. Oebeke and Richarz rectally administered this meat extract peptone to ten of their food-refusing asylum patients. Although they reported encouraging results, the death of a patient who had refused repeated injections was a stark reminder of the obduracy of the problem of sitophobia.

The reluctance of asylum physicians to adopt this technology of forced feeding could be accounted for, in part, by the ream of research that was being conducted on Leibig's meat extract. Nearly 500 tons of it was being produced yearly in a manufacturing plant in Uruguay in anticipation of its proposed use to supplement the diets of the under-nourished and feed the famished people around the world. The research quite consistently found that it was absorbable by the rectum, but that it had little nutritive value and could not, by itself, sustain life.

Oebeke resisted this conclusion of the scientific community and argued that in the case of the food-refusing asylum patient, the rectal injection of Liebig's meat extract could act as a "prophylactic measure before the voluntary taking of food," thus buying time for the patient to develop the requisite insight that food acceptance was necessary to continue living (Oebeke, p. 469). Despite this objection, the weight of scientific findings decreased the enthusiasm of even Oebeke and Richarz for its use in the rectal feeding of the food-refusing patient. Physicians at other asylums experimented with other nutritive substances, such as Mickel's formula of milk, hot water, bicarbonate soda, and Benger's liquor pancreaticus; or Dujardin-Beaumont's formula of milk, egg yolk, bicarbonate and laudanum; or Riga's formula of milk, eggs, salt and red wine. The outcomes, however, were not encouraging. Without a nutritive substance that could be well absorbed and that could sustain life for some time, rectal feeding as a forced-feeding technology all but disappeared by the start of the twentieth century from those asylums that had ever used it.

As an interesting aside, the popularity of Liebig's meat extract did not suffer from the scientific findings. The extract was further refined into a granular powder and remarketed as the Oxo bouillon cube. This handy trick to assure "flavorsome home cooking" can be purchased in any supermarket today.

## *Screw, or Screw-Gag, or Screw Key, or Fish Tail Gag*

Two plates of iron that when inserted in the mouth were slowly separated by means of a screw, thus forcing the mouth open. Fortifying liquids then were poured either directly down the throat, or through a tube that was inserted into the esophagus. The screw was used in many asylums around the world well into the twentieth century and was notorious for breaking teeth, lacerating the tongue, and even fracturing the jaw of the food-refusing patient.

Daniel Hack Tuke refined the screw in the late nineteenth century to expedite the threading of a tube into the esophagus. Using iron prongs, as opposed to iron plates, his fish tail screw, as he referred to it, was easier to insert between the teeth and left more space in the opened mouth for the insertion of a tube.

## *Spouting Boat*

A teapot-shaped vessel constructed of soft metal with a long tin pouring spout that was forced between the teeth. Its use in the early nineteenth century required such force that it inevitably broke the teeth of the resisting patient. This "most destructive and devilish instrument," as Bethlem Hospital apothecary John Haslam once called it (Haslam, p. 316) was marginally easier to use if the patient had no teeth to clench, thus many asylum physicians as a matter of expediency pulled the teeth of their patients.

In the mid-nineteenth century John Foster Reed, resident medical officer at Kensington House, a private asylum in London, redesigned the notorious spouting boat which was so feared by asylum patients and physicians alike. He constructed a teapot-shaped vessel with a pewter mouthpiece to fit around the chin, and strong flattened mouth tube, perforated at the sides, slightly curved, and with a blunt, wedge-shaped apex. He described how it was to be used:

> First, fill the vessel with the required liquid.... The patient is then to be placed on a bed, in the recumbent position; the head, supported on a pillow, must be firmly held by the assistants, as well as the trunk and extremities.... The instrument is then to be taken in the right hand, and while the spout is applied to the lips, a small quantity of the contained fluid may be allowed to flow over them; at the same time the nostrils should be compressed with the thumb and forefinger of the left hand. By this means it will be found the patient is soon compelled to open his mouth, and gasp for breath, when the spout of the instrument should be quickly insinuated between the teeth. The vessel can be maintained in its situation, with the pewter mouthpiece applied firmly to the face. The flow of the liquid can be regulated at pleasure by the application of the thumb to the valve at the top of the handle [Reeve, pp. 90–91].

## Stomach Pump, or Stomach Tube

A narrow twenty-eight inch long tube, inserted through the mouth and into the stomach, into which a nutriment liquid could be passed via a funnel, syringe, or valve and piston driven pump. The tube often had a rounded wooden end with openings on each side so that if it rested against the walls of the stomach liquid could still flow through it.

The use of the stomach pump required considerable expertise, and could not be left to staff or attendants. The asylum physician began the procedure by dipping the end of the stomach tube in warm liquid, then passing it through the mouth of the patient to the back of the pharynx, over the epiglottis, down the esophagus and into the stomach. Once in place, the nutriment liquid was administered, and the tube was withdrawn. Although a few patients were sedated with chloroform before the procedure, most were not, and the effect of the procedure on them was considerable. Daniel Hack Tuke warned his colleagues of this:

> The patient should be kept lying down when the feeding is over, as the operation generally causes no little shock to the nervous and circulatory systems. This is partly due to the struggle which almost always ensues, and to the anxiety which is frequently produced in the patient's mind by the process, and also partly due to some obscure nervous connection between the stomach and the heart through the medium of the pneumogastric and sympathetic nerves [Tuke, 1892, p. 500].

The infamous spouting boat that was used to force feed food-refusing asylum patients. This one was constructed of pewter and when forced into the mouth, the long spout often broke teeth and lacerated the tongue and cheeks (courtesy of the Wellcome Library, London).

The term "stomach pump" is somewhat misleading today, since it refers to the process of pulling out the contents of the stomach through a long tube, rather than putting in liquid nutriments. As an indication of a method of forced-feeding, however, the term "stomach pump" was used throughout the nineteenth and into the early twentieth centuries.

## Wedge

A block of wood, five to six inches in length, approximately one inch thick at one end and tapering down to a lesser thickness on the other end, that was inserted into the mouth of the patient to keep it open so that nutriments could be poured down the throat. The insertion of the wedge invariably broke teeth and lacerated the tongue and palate.

Lydia Smith, a patient at the Michigan Asylum for the Insane in Kalamazoo, Michigan, in the mid-nineteenth century, described in her asylum memoir her experience with the wedge:

> I soon felt the weight of the attendant on me, with one knee pressing directly on my stomach, and one hand, like the grip of a tiger, on my head. The wedge was then forced into one side of my mouth, crowding out a tooth in the progress—a tooth which had been filled not long before—causing the most excruciating pain. I cannot tell why, unless it was convulsions, caused by the great pressure on my stomach, but my teeth were set, my lips seemed glued together, and I could not have opened my mouth, even had I known what they wanted me to do. Crash! Crash! went another of my teeth, and another, until five were either knocked out or broken off. I laid in a pool of blood that night [Smith, p. 4].

In state hearings about the treatment of patients at the Michigan Asylum for the Insane, Smith, who had escaped from the asylum and was subsequently declared sane by a court of law, testified as to the use of the wedge. In the face of contradictory testimony by asylum physicians and staff, and by the submission into evidence of her case file in which the wedge was not noted, her testimony was treated with skepticism by hearing officers, and mocked as "merest moonshine" by the press. She was not accused of perjury, however, because, as the press noted, "It is a curious fact connected with the restoration of the person to sanity that some of the delusions which possess the mind while unsound are still believed in implicitly" ("Kalamazoo Asylum," 1879, p. 1).

The use of the wedge for the forced feeding of the food-refusing patient continued into the early twentieth century in many asylums. It was gradually replaced with the stomach pump and the nasal tube.

## Genital Surgery

*Surgical procedures performed on the otherwise healthy sex organs of male and female asylum patients.*

There may be no asylum therapeutic that was so inextricably entwined with the ideologies of the era than genital surgery. To separate the strands of the skein would be challenge enough; to retangle them to make sense of the surgical obsession with the sex organs of asylum patients in the late nineteenth and early twentieth centuries would be no less a challenge.

Any attempt, though, had best begin with a discussion of gender ideology or, perhaps better stated, "ideologies" in the plural. While it would be a facile overstatement to maintain that social attitudes and ideas about the appropriate roles, rights and responsibilities of men have been historically and culturally invariant, it would not be to insist that in Western culture, at least, men always have enjoyed a position of power and privilege. Women, in contrast, have not. More often defined by their biology and the destiny that was imagined to follow it—wife, mother, helpmate, caretaker, empathizer, moral standard bearer, epitome of fragile innocence—they have been in a state of relative dependency. So deeply was this ideology engrained, repeated and represented, that it passed as "natural," as truth with a capital "T." Thus women's challenges, whether incidental or determined, to male hegemony in that era were often pathologized. New diagnostic categories—ovariomania, nymphomania, masturbatory insanity, neurasthenia, uterine epilepsy—were added to the quintessential women's insanity of hysteria, bringing more women into asylums and under the clinical gaze of male asylum physicians. And because all of these disorders were thought to be the reflexive consequences of their sex organs, genital surgery was considered a logical therapeutic intervention.

Men, too, were subjected to genital surgeries, although the therapeutic rationale for performing them was never as convincing as it was in the case of women. The social control rationale, however, was overt. In an era of rapidly changing morals and mores, sexual psychopath statutes were hastily passed, criminalizing a long list of male-perpetrated sexual offenses, from rape and child molestation, exhibitionism and voyeurism, to consensual same-sex acts. Convictions resulted not in prison sentences, but in asylum commitments. Discharge from the asylum, then, was contingent on the reduction of the threat the sexual psychopath posed to society, and because that threat was considered to be the result of what were imagined to be uncontrollable sexual urges and desires, genital surgeries once again were logical therapeutic interventions.

Fears about the sexual psychopath arose from another ideology of that era, and that was eugenics. Eugenics, literally translated as "good in birth" or "well born," was both a scientific ideology and a vigorous social movement to better society. It was predicated on the notion that the undesirable traits of those deemed unfit were inheritable and passed on to the next generation. Just as was the case with the diagnostic categories of hysteria and sexual psychopath, "unfit" was a pliable category that could be used to label criminals, alcoholics and drug abusers, chronic paupers and ne'er-do-wells, the feeble-minded and the insane—in other words, those who were filling asylums. The solution to the problem they posed was obviously surgical: involuntary sterilization.

Class ideology entwined around eugenics ideology. Those most likely to be seen as unfit and committed to asylums were the urban and rural poor who lacked the resources and opportunities to change their station and life, and the social capital to resist their labeling and commitment. Racial ideology also was influential. In the United States, foreign-born asylum patients were far more likely to be involuntarily sterilized than native born patients; black and Latino patients far more than whites. Mixed-race asylum patients in Sweden, Denmark, Finland and Norway, all of which had vigorous eugenics initiatives, also underwent the "surgical solution" at higher rates than native-born patients. That racial ideology was made brutally obvious during World War II. In Nazi Germany more than 450,000 unfit people, many of them asylum patients, were involuntarily sterilized in the name of preserving the "Master Race."

Ideologies do change. Even those as deeply entrenched as gender, class and race ideologies yield to one degree or another, and in one way or another, to politicized resistance, organized social movements, new knowledge, and the changing conditions of society. Its ideological underpinnings challenged by changing gender roles, new theories about the causes of insanity, resistance to the surgical solution by some asylum physicians and their patients, and social adaptation to emerging moral and social orders, genital surgeries all but disappeared as an asylum therapeutic in the mid-twentieth century.

## REFERENCES

Barrus, C. (1894/1895). Gynecological disorders and their relation to insanity. *American Journal of Insanity, 51,* 475–491.
Battey, R. (1880). Summary of the results of fifteen cases of Battey's operation. *British Medical Journal, 1,* 510–512.

Braslow, J.T. (1997). *Mental ills and bodily cures*. Berkeley: University of California Press.

Broun, L. (1906). Preliminary report of the gynecological surgery in the Manhattan State Hospital West. *American Journal of Insanity, 62,* 407–447.

Brown, I.B. (1866). *On the curability of certain forms of insanity, epilepsy, catalepsy and hysteria in females*. London: Robert Hardwicke.

Brown-Séquard, C-E. (1889). *The elixir of life*. Boston: J.G. Cupples Company.

de Young, M. (2010). *Madness: An American history of mental illness and its treatment*. Jefferson, NC: McFarland.

Ellis, W.C. (1839). *Treatise on insanity*. London: Samuel Holdsworth.

Esquirol, J.E.D. (1838). *Mental maladies: A Treatise on insanity*. Trans. E.K. Hunt. Philadelphia: Lea and Blanchard. 1845.

"Excision of the clitoris as a cure for masturbation" (1862). *Boston Medical and Surgical Journal, 66,* p. 164.

Friedman, E.B. (1987). Uncontrolled desires: The response to the sexual psychopath, 1920–1960. *Journal of American History, 74,* 83–106.

Griesinger, W. (1861). *Mental pathology and therapeutics*. Trans. C.L. Robertson and J. Rutherford. London: New Sydenham Society.

Groneman, C. (1994). Nymphomania: The historical construction of female sexuality. *Signs, 19,* 337–367.

Hare, E.H. (1962). Masturbatory insanity: The history of an idea. *British Journal of Psychiatry, 108,* 1–25.

Have, P. (2007). Sterilization under the swastika: The case of Norway. *International Journal of Mental Healthy, 36,* 45–57.

Human Betterment Foundation (1939). *Human sterilization today*. Pasadena, CA: Author.

Inmate, Ward 8 [Woodson, M.M.] (1932). *Behind the door of delusion*. New York: Macmillan.

Kline, W. (2001). *Building a better race: Gender, sexuality and eugenics from the turn of the century to the Baby Boom*. Berkeley, CA: University of California Press.

Kopp, M.E. (1938). Surgical treatment as sex crime prevention measure. *Journal of Criminal Law and Criminology, 28,* 692–706.

Lancaster, R.N. (2011). *Sex panic and the punitive state*. Berkeley: University of California Press.

LeMaire, L. (1956). Danish experiences regarding the castration of sexual offenders. *Journal of Criminal Law and Criminology, 47,* 294–310.

Longo, L.D. (1979). The rise and fall of Battey's operation: A fashion in surgery. *Bulletin of the History of Medicine, 53,* 244–259.

Mitchinson, W. (1982). Gynecological operations on insane women: London, Ontario, 1895–1901. *Journal of Social History, 15,* 467–484.

"Notes and news" (1877). *Journal of Mental Science, 22,* 336–337.

Obendorf, C. (1912). The sterilization of defectives. *State Hospital Bulletin,* 106–112.

"Removal of the ovaries as a therapeutic measure in public institutions for the insane" (1893). *Journal of the American Medical Association, 20,* 135–137.

Rodriguez, S.W. (2008). Rethinking the history of female circumcision and clitoridectomy: American medicine and female sexuality in the late nineteenth century. *Journal of the History of Medicine and Allied Sciences, 63,* 323–347.

Schoen, J. (2005). *Choice and coercion: Birth control, sterilization and abortion in public health and welfare*. Chapel Hill: University of North Carolina Press.

"Sex organ changes in insanity" (1915). *Journal of the American Medical Association, 65,* 254–255.

Shortt, S.E.D. (1986). *Victorian lunacy: Richard M. Bucke and the practice of late nineteenth century psychiatry*. Cambridge: Cambridge University Press.

Skae, D. (1863). A rational and practical classification of insanity. *Journal of Mental Science, 14,* 309–319.

Smith-Rosenberg, C., and Rosenberg, C. (1973). The female animal: Medical and biological views of woman and her role in nineteenth century America. *Journal of American History, 60,* 332–356.

Stern, M., Folsom, R.P, and Ritter, I.S. (1924–1925). Vasectomy and its influence upon 100 cases of dementia praecox studied at the Manhattan State Hospital. *State Hospital Quarterly, 10,* 404–412.

Studd, J. (2006). Ovariotomy for menstrual madness and premenstrual syndrome: 19th century history and lessons for current practice. *Gynecological Endocrinology, 22,* 411–415.

Tissot, S-A. (1776). *Onanism, or a treatise upon the disorders produced by masturbation*. Trans. A. Hume. London: J. Pridden.

van der Meer, T. (2008). Eugenic and sexual folklores and the castration of sex offenders in the Netherlands (1938–1968). *Studies in the History and Philosophy of Science, 39,* 195–204.

Warren, C.A.B. (2004). Genital surgeries and stimulation in nineteenth century psychiatry. In *Gender perspectives on reproduction and sexuality, vol. 8,* M.T. Segal and V. Demos (eds.), pp. 165–198. Amsterdam: Elsevier.

Warsh, C.L.K. (1989). *Moments of unreason: The practice of Canadian psychiatry and the Homewood Retreat, 1883–1923*. Montreal, Quebec, Canada: McGill-Queens University Press.

Wiglesworth, J. (1885). On uterine disease and insanity. *British Journal of Psychiatry, 30,* 509–531.

Witte, M.E. (1906). Surgery for the relief of insane conditions. *American Journal of Insanity, 62,* 449–465.

Wright, S. (1871). Dr. Strethill Wright's case of ovariomania. *Edinburgh Medical Journal, 11,* 245–249.

## Castration

The surgical removal of the testicles. The first castrations of asylum patients were carried out in the late nineteenth century at the

Burghölzli, the psychiatric hospital of the University of Zurich in Switzerland. Founded as a modern clinic for the humane treatment of insanity, the Burghölzli had achieved international recognition for its unique combination of moral treatment [see **Moral Treatment**] and somatic therapeutics. The physician Emil Oberholzer, who later would emigrate to New York City and establish a private psychoanalytic practice, described the first three cases of surgical castration at the Burghölzli:

> *Case 1.* A man, who on account of uncontrollable sexual longings and perversions, eagerly desired operation, submitted to castration, which resulted not only in enabling him to refrain from perverse practices (especially homosexuality) but from other breaches of the law of which he had previously been guilty. Shortly after castration, however, an inexplicable, though transient anxiety state, with vague ideas of reference, developed in the patient.
> *Case 2.* An alcoholic delinquent, with very strong sexual abnormalities, was castrated at his own request, but the operation was ineffectual in diminishing his sexual phantasies. He was permitted to leave the hospital on the ground that he was no longer a social menace, but his psychosexual desires continued unabated. Failure to have erections in response to psychosexual stimulation and also his impotency were a great and constant source of irritation to him.
> *Case 3.* A worthless, criminal imbecile permitted the operation for testicular neuralgia. Notwithstanding his comparatively advanced age of 34 at the time of the castration, physical changes soon occurred so that at the age of 41, he had the appearance of a youth of 20, with a feminine distribution of adipose deposits, which persisted in spite of a generalized emaciation, and with a general diminution of the hairy growth. The operation in no way affected his mental state, for although physically impotent, his psychic cravings were not lessened. He indulged in copulation with his mistress, but, curiously enough, is said not to have regretted the operation. Some years after the operation he developed hemorrhages from the urethra every six weeks, with general physical and mental disturbances such as women experience at the menstrual periods [Obendorf, pp. 110–111].

The case studies made no compelling argument that castration was therapeutically efficacious. Its continued use could only be legitimated by linking the best interest of the embodied patient with the best interest of the body politic. The passage of sexual psychopath laws in many countries during the early twentieth century formalized that link. By treating the individual's best interest as synonymous with society's best interest, castration could be used for the dual purpose of treatment and protection. Under those laws if an individual were convicted of molestation, rape, sodomy, corrupting the morals of a child or indecent exposure, as examples, and was also diagnosed as a sexual psychopath, he was civilly committed to an asylum, rather than criminally sentenced to a prison. Castration then could be used therapeutically to ease the symptoms of sexual psychopathy and/or to protect society from further offenses upon his discharge.

In Denmark, for example, an asylum patient so committed could be castrated if the Medico-Legal Council had convinced the Minister of Justice that the therapeutic would resolve the mental suffering and social opprobrium caused by his sexual psychopathy, and also reduce his risk for re-offending after his release. The Netherlands had enacted a similar legal procedure in the late 1930s; over the subsequent three decades, 400 asylum patients who had been diagnosed with sexual psychopathy had been castrated. The majority of them were homosexual child molesters. In twenty U.S. states sexual psychopathy was broadly enough defined that homosexuals could be committed to asylums for sex acts with consenting adults. In seven of those states they could be castrated in order to suppress their "unnatural desires" and, somewhat ironically if only because it anticipated the failure of castration as therapeutic, to protect society from them.

By the mid-twentieth century much of the panic over sex and its threats to innocence and morality had dissipated, as panics inevitably do, and the legal, psychiatric and social implications of the sexual psychopath laws were more heatedly debated. In the United States, Michigan was the first state to repeal its psychopath law and to abolish the legal category of "criminal sexual psychopath." Most states followed suit.

The repeals had essentially disarticulated psychopathy and sexual threat. By doing so, sexual offenders were criminally sentenced to prison. No longer therapeutically necessary, castration now was legitimated largely in terms of the protection of society. That was evident when the state of Florida passed the Chemical Castration Statute in 1997. It mandated that anyone convicted of sexual battery undergo chemical, as opposed to surgical, castration by means of weekly injections of Depo–Provera (medroxyprogesterone acetate, or MPA). The drug reduces the production of testosterone in the testes and adrenal glands, thus reducing the sex drive. No therapeutic counseling was mandated in conjunction with castration. Eight additional states passed similar chemical castration statutes, all predicated on the best interest of society, although few chemical castrations actually have been carried out. International interest in chemical castration has waxed and waned, but in quite recent years forcible chemical castration laws have been passed in Poland, Moldova, and Estonia, and proposed in Macedonia and India.

## Clitoridectomy, or Female Circumcision

The surgical excision of the clitoris.

In late nineteenth century there were four types of clitoral surgery: removal of smegma from the glans of the foreskin and the labia minor; separation of adhesions to the hood of clitoris; circumcision, in which the hood of the clitoris was excised; and clitoridectomy. In deference to the fact that clitoral stimulation was considered essential to women's healthy sexual desire and drive, physicians turned to the clitoridectomy only as a surgery of last resort.

The "last resort" was turned to most often in cases of chronic masturbation, considered in that era to be both a cause and a consequence of insanity. The medical logic was as such: female sex organs sympathetically influenced the brain, and their periodic irritation by menstruation, pregnancy and menopause, coupled with chronic masturbation, increased the risk for insanity; insanity, in turn, reduced social appropriateness and self-control, thus increasing masturbation and exacerbating the insanity. In this endlessly recursive logic, women indeed were both the "product[s] and prisoner[s] of [their] reproductive systems" (Smith-Rosenberg & Rosenberg, p. 334).

As a specialty gynecology had achieved considerable status by the mid-nineteenth century, and in Great Britain there was no more esteemed practitioner than Isaac Baker Brown who was senior surgeon at the London Home for Surgical Diseases of Women, which he had founded. Baker Brown had been frustrated by patients whose gynecological problems were complicated by that quintessential women's insanity—hysteria—and had found in the reflex irritability dogma an avenue for resolving that frustration. Hysterical women, he concluded, must be chronic masturbators and that unspeakable vice must be damaging and depleting the central nervous system. It did so, he hypothesized, in stages: first chronic masturbation caused the restless, excited, ailing and complaining symptoms of hysteria, then it irritated the spinal nerves causing hysterical epilepsy, then cataleptic fits and then epileptic fits which collectively led to idiocy, then mania, and then death. The surgical extirpation of the cause of the irritation, then, not only seemed a logical conclusion but a medical imperative. "The treatment must be the same," he insisted, "whether we wish to cure functional disturbance, arrest organic disease, or, finally, if we have only a chance of averting death itself" (Baker Brown, pp. 8–9).

Thus Baker Brown performed a clitoridectomy on his first patient, a twenty-six-year-old dressmaker who was a patient at his proprietary hospital and had all of the symptoms of hysteria, obviously caused by the "peripheral irritation of the pudic nerve" (Baker Brown, p. 33), a medically polite term for masturbation. He anesthetized her, seized her clitoris with a forceps, ran the thin edge of a red hot iron around its base until it was loosened, and then cut it away. He then severed the adjacent nymphae with a sawing motion of the hot iron which he then used to saw the surfaces of the labia. After the surgery, he waited for her to regain her health after two days of heavy post-operative hemorrhaging. She recovered completely and remained in cheerfully grateful contact with him after her discharge.

Baker Brown discussed her case as well as those other patients on whom he had performed the surgery in his 1866 book, *On the Curability of Certain Forms of Insanity, Epilepsy, Catalepsy and Hysteria in Females*. The slim red volume created quite a sensation. In the parlance of the day, it traversed social taboos with its discussion of female sexual anatomy and sexual desires, and suggested a certain patriarchal zealousness in controlling both. Many of his colleagues were outraged, not so much at the genital surgery as Baker Brown's relentless pursuit of public attention for performing it. After a series of vitriolic exchanges with and between contributors to several prestigious medical journals, Baker Brown was ignominiously expelled from the Obstetrical Society. He died some time later, impecunious and defamed, but not before his book had come to the attention of asylum physicians in the United States.

The fact was that clitoridectomies already were being performed in the United States, mostly on the patients of gynecologists in private practice. A few years before Baker Brown's book was published, for example, a report was published in a local medical paper about the successful clitoridectomies performed on two girls who were "addicted to the habit of masturbation," as a prophylactic against insanity ("Excision of the Clitoris as a Cure for Masturbation" p. 164). One was cured of the habit, the other not.

Baker Brown's thesis that clitoridectomy could not only prevent insanity, but remedy it, was intriguing to some asylum physicians, although most were reticent, if not completely resistant, to leaving their carefully cultivated art of treating the insane to scalpel-wielding gynecological surgeons. The waning of the reflex irritability theory of insanity certainly rendered the decision to use clitoridectomy sparingly as an asylum therapeutic easier to make. There was little discussion of its use in the asylum literature, although quite recent archival research of patient records show that clitoridectomies were occasionally performed as late as the mid-twentieth century.

## *Oophorectomy, or Ovariectomy, or "Normal Ovariotomy," or Battey's Operation, or Female Castration*

The surgical removal of the ovaries. One of the first published reports of the castration of female asylum patients was authored by Emil Oberholzer, physician at the University of Zurich's psychiatric hospital, the Burghölzli. There, four patients were surgically castrated in the late nineteenth century. All were released after the surgery but the therapeutic outcome for each failed to meet even low expectations: one improved temporarily before mania recurred; one had a recurrence of psychosis and had to be readmitted to the asylum, although she was later discharged; another experienced no change in her mental symptoms; and the remaining woman died of post-surgical peritonitis.

Oberholzer's may have been one of the first published observations on female castration, but some of his predecessors already had experimented with the surgical removal of the healthy ovaries of women. One of those physicians was a Rome, Georgia, surgeon by the name of Robert Battey who in 1872 performed his first "normal" ovariotomy on a thirty-year-old woman. Death, she had averred to him, would have been a relief from the epileptiform convulsions that accompanied her occasional menstrual periods, the gastric and rectal bleeding that left her depleted and exhausted. Battey surgically removed both of her ovaries, which from all appearances were normal. Although she developed post-surgical peritonitis, she recovered fully.

Battey's discussion of his first case, published in a regional medical journal, set out the single criterion for the surgery: "any grave disease which is either dangerous to life or destructive to health and happiness, which is incurable by other and less radical means" (Longo, p. 249). Only a few years later, and having performed the procedure on many more patients, Battey added "in cases of insanity or epilepsy caused by uterine or ovarian disease; and in cases of protracted physical and mental suffering associated with monthly nervous and vascular perturbations" (Longo, p. 249) to his growing list of surgical indicators. These additional criteria expanded the pool of potential patients from the nervous and anxious women who often requested their private physicians to "Batteyize," them, as the surgical procedure was colloquially known, to the insane women who were confined in asylums.

It was the underlying rationale for Battey's operation that erased any distinctions between private and public patients. The surgery was based on the rather simple, and even by the late nineteenth century rather antiquated, theory of reflex irritation, that is, that every organ of the body affected every other organ, including the brain. The periodic irritation of the ovaries by menstruation, pregnancy and menopause, it was argued, was transmitted to the brain via the sympathetic nerves, thus accounting for the disproportionate number of women confined in asylums.

The sociological rejoinder to this conclusion eluded Battey and his nineteenth century colleagues, and that was that the diagnostic criteria for what was considered at the time types of insanity unique to females, including menstrual, pregnancy, puerperal, lactation and climacteric insanity, as well as nymphomania, neurasthenia and hysteria, were broadly and vaguely defined. In addition, new and accommodating gender-specific diagnoses were being proposed with something tantamount to wild abandon, thus widening further the diagnostic net. One of those new diagnoses was ovariomania, sometimes also called uteromania or "Old Maid's Insanity." David Skae and Thomas Clouston, both physicians to the Royal Edinburgh Asylum for the Insane, also known as Morningside, took credit for the new diagnosis. One of their colleagues provided a case description of a thirty-five-year-old ovariomanic woman who had been admitted on two separate occasions to the asylum. On the first, she was depressed and complained that spirits were "tearing her entrails, to which they gained admission by the vagina" (Wright, p. 247). This state of excitement abated, however, and she was released several months later. Upon second admission she insisted that her neighbors were accusing her of having given birth to a child, whom she had murdered. She also complained that the spirits were torturing her again, this time by thrusting sharp objects into her womb. She died of exhaustion and malnourishment before an oophorectomy could be performed.

It was not just new diagnostic language that brought more women into asylums in the late nineteenth century and decades beyond, but the considerable influence of eugenics ideology. Quite regardless of the diagnosis, insanity was thought to be largely inherited and thus inheritable. And while that assumption, along with Battey's expanded indicators for the oophorectomy should have eased the entry of the surgical procedure into asylums, that was not always the case. Many asylum physicians resisted the challenge to their status as experts on insanity, and were loath to vest gynecological surgeons with authority over their patients. Some asylums did add gynecological surgeons to their staff, others such as the Norristown State Hospital for the Insane in Pennsylvania, hired them as visiting physicians. Norristown, however, provided an interesting example of the turf wars and professional jealousies that tolled the demise of the oophorectomy as a therapeutic procedure. Visiting gynecological surgeon Joseph Price had performed four oophorectomies on patients there and had fifty more on his waiting list when the Committee on Lunacy of the Pennsylvania State Board of Charities visited in 1893. They were far from impressed with the procedure nor the fervor with which it was being pursued. Their report, published in part in an editorial in the *Journal of the American Medical Association,* was unusually acerbic:

> The zeal of the gynecologist is being carried to an unusual extent when it proposes to use a State Hospital for the Insane as an experimental station, where lunatic women are be to subjected to doubtful operations for supposed cures. If it is to be permitted in some forty or fifty cases, as proposed, it might be well to practice the experiment on the entire female lunatic population, so that the gynecologist may have the large opportunity he doubtless craves to see just what would happen. At the expense of some lives, the continued and aggravated insanity of most of his subjects, with a few supposed cures and improvements, he could read his conclusions learnedly to his gynecological brethren, with the resultant added forward movement up his ladder of fame ["Removal of the Ovaries," p. 136].

The editorial agreed with the Committee's findings, if not with the sarcasm with which they were offered. It appropriately pointed out that oophorectomies had not been shown to ameliorate insanity, quite regardless of diagnosis, and that they had a disturbingly high mortality rate of 20 percent. It also questioned the reflex irritation theory that had legitimated the procedure in the first place, conceding at the same time that if the theory were viable "the brain and spinal cord have doubtless become permanently altered, or impelled to disordered action," so removal of the irritating organs would offer no relief ("Removal of the Ovaries," p. 135). In addition, the editorial appealed to the personal rights of asylum patients and the legal ramifications of violating them. Arguing that because of their insanity patients could not give consent to the surgery which, it hastened to add, extirpated otherwise healthy organs, it came down adamantly against the surgery.

There are no reliable data on how many asylums patients underwent oophorectomies. There is information, however, that the surgical procedure was practiced in Great Britain, where it was called "Tait's surgery" after the "Father of Gynecology," Lawson Tait, and in many European countries, as well as in the United States. Few of these surgeries specifically for the treatment of insanity were reported in the literature after the turn into the twentieth century.

## *Tubal Ligation, or Female Sterilization*

A surgical procedure for female sterilization that involves the cutting of the fallopian tubes. The sterilization of asylum patients during the late nineteenth and early twentieth centuries was justified on two fronts: as an intervention in the mother and wife role, and as the prevention of future reproduction.

While many more asylum patients were sterilized for the latter eugenical justification, the former deserves mention. In an era where the causes of women's insanity were still largely attributed to essential difference in biology, sex and sexuality, there was recognition that the stresses and strains of women's lives, especially in regards to their roles as mothers and wives, at times caused and more often exacerbated their mental instability. Asylum physicians for the most part were heeding the plea of Clara Barrus, assistant physician to the Middletown State Hospital in New York and, in the late nineteenth century one of the few women asylum physicians in the United States, to see women patients as something different and more than just their biology:

> The causes of insanity in women may be, nay, they probably are, as varied, and many of them identical with, the causes of insanity in men; for we have always to remember that both before and after one is a wife and mother, one is a human being, and the elements that enter into the causation of mental aberration in women will develop along the line of the experiences

and inheritances that come to her as a human being, *with the addition* of those which to her as human being of the female sex [Barrus, p. 477, italics in original].

Those "additions" included the demands of the still strictly prescribed roles of mother and wife. So when twenty-six-year-old Alma H., diagnosed with schizophrenia, told physicians at the Dorothea Dix Hospital in Raleigh, North Carolina, that she was overwhelmed by her household duties, frightened that she would become pregnant for the fourth time, and feared that she would kill her young children when their crying exhausted her, she was sterilized. And when Nelly S., a twenty-three-year-old who had tried to poison her seven children who ranged in age from four months to eight years, was committed to the same asylum, she was sterilized as well.

Like Alma H. and Nelly S., many young women confined to asylums could anticipate being discharged to return to their children and husbands. Their symptoms often ameliorated with little more than rest, and although not recovered, and certainly not cured, they would have been considered well enough to return to their roles as mothers and wives. Asylum physicians reasoned that if some of the stress, distress and fear that attended either one or both of those roles could be relieved by the assurance of no additional pregnancies and childcare burdens, sterilization served a therapeutic end. In addition, it was a relatively low-cost and low-risk procedure that, according to the received medical wisdom of the era, had no deleterious effects on the nervous system or brain.

Determining if these "additions," as Barrus referred to them, indeed factored in as cause or consequence of any woman asylum patient's insanity was more daunting than the surgery, itself. Most asylum physicians were men and in possession of cultural capital—education, style of speech, intellect, clothing and authoritative comportment—that women patients especially in state or public asylums did not have. So discussions about these "additions," and coming to agreements that ster-ilization was a viable therapeutic option, were sometimes awkward, as this transcribed interview revealed:

*Doctor:* How are you?
*Patient:* I don't feel very good.
*Doctor:* You have been tired out a long time?
*Patient:* Yes.
*Doctor:* How many children have you at home?
*Patient:* Five at home and one died and I am six months pregnant...
*Doctor:* How many babies do you want, about a dozen?
*Patient:* Oh lord, I got enough [Braslow, p. 66].

Regardless of whether that Stockton State Hospital physician in that case was engaging in good natured jesting or a stern reminding of the patient's "proper" role as mother and wife, he decided that the patient should be sterilized after giving birth to her sixth child. She became one of the 9,000 female asylum patients who underwent tubal ligations between 1900 and 1940 in the United States.

The number, though, is misleading. Some asylums also confined women who were not insane, but "unfit to breed" because of feeble-mindedness, low intelligence and/or moral deviance. Hastily passed laws in most states in the United States and in many other countries mandated their *involuntary* sterilization. The purpose here was clearly and unabashedly eugenic: the best interest of society trumped the therapeutic best interests of the patients.

## *Vasectomy*

The surgical cutting and sealing of part of each vas deferens, typically as a means of male sterilization. An editorial published in the prestigious *Journal of the American Medical Association* in 1915 drew attention to research conducted in Italy by Carlo Todde who had compared the testicles of 200 asylum patients with thirty subjects who had no history of insanity. Todde found that the testicles of the asylum patients were smaller than those of the comparison patients. The differences, however, were particularly noted for those twenty-five patients of the group who had been diagnosed with dementia praecox. Their testicles not only were smaller in size and weight, but had "altered structure and function" including an "alteration in the filial cells ... a degeneration of the cells which have to do with the production of spermatozoa, or an atrophy of the seminiferous tubules" ("Sex Organ Changes in Insanity" p. 254). This observation was confirmed by a number of asylum physicians and researchers, most notable among them Frederic Mott, then the director of the laboratory of the Claybury Asylum, a London county council asylum. Mott, who would go on to become president of the Royal Medico-Psychological Association, described the testicles of patients with dementia praecox as looking like those of elderly men, suggesting to him that dementia praecox may be a "precocious senility" caused by the premature atrophy of the gonads.

The prospect that changes in the testicles were pathogenic was intriguing to asylum physicians who were frustrated with the intractability of dementia praecox. They considered the possibility that there was an intimate relationship between spermatozoa and the cells of the cerebral cortex of the brain. Undischarged spermatozoa, they hypothesized, were reabsorbed into the bloodstream and carried to the brain, bathing it in the very lecithin, cholesterin and phosphorus that were the chief constituents of brain tissue. If the testicles of asylum patients were pathological, then such secretions were compromised, adversely affecting the brain and causing dementia praecox. Following that logic, a reasonable therapeutic response by asylum physicians was to inject their dementia praecox patients with testicular extracts, or to administer any one of the many popular nostrums, such as Brown-Séquard Elixir [see **Organotherapy**]. The results, however, were far from satisfactory.

The hypothesis, though, remained intriguing and asylum physicians had another therapeutic strategy consistent with it: vasectomy. The organotherapist Charles-Édouard Brown-Séquard, whose elixir had failed to ameliorate the symptoms of dementia praecox, had also insisted that vasectomy restored the "senile testicles" of the elderly, thus it may very well do the same for the precociously senile testicles of the patients with dementia praecox. Thus in the early to mid-twentieth century, even as the diagnosis of dementia praecox evolved into that of schizophrenia, vasectomies were performed in any number of asylums in the United States, Great Britain and Europe.

At the Manhattan State Hospital, for example, 100 patients underwent the surgical procedure in the early 1920s. All of them were under thirty years old at the time of admission and had been diagnosed with dementia praecox. The results failed to live up to expectations: seventy-one of the patients showed no mental or physical improvement; seventeen has some physical improvement in that their weight increased and their physical appearance improved; six demonstrated a slight mental improvement characterized by a diminution of combative and impulsive behavior; the remaining six showed a slight degree of both mental and physical improvement. As a result of the study, the asylum physicians were unable to substantiate the claim that vasectomy was of any value in the treatment of dementia praecox.

Early findings such as this did not necessarily dampen the interest that many asylum physicians had in treating dementia praecox with vasectomy. The fact that the therapeutic intervention not just continued but actually revved up in some places as opposed to others suggested that larger and more local eugenical interests may have intersected or even merged. The state of California provided an interesting case study. There was no more vigorous eugenics program, no more vociferous and prominent eugenics promoters, no more thorough cultural saturation of eugenics propaganda, than in the "Golden State." So effective was its initiative that in the 1930s representatives of the nascent Nazi party sought the advice of the state's eugenics promoters as to implementing a similar program in Germany.

All of that, in part, may account for why

vasectomies were performed on patients with dementia praecox in so many California asylums, without apparent regard for the emerging conclusion that they were therapeutically ineffective. One of those asylums was Stockton State Hospital where a state-wide survey conducted by the Human Betterment Society revealed that its physicians endorsed the procedure. The transcript of a conversation between one of those physicians and a patient who had just been admitted for the second time for nervousness and depression, showed just how smoothly vasectomy had emerged as a therapeutic alternative, for physician as well as patient:

> *Doctor:* You are back again?
> *Patient:* Yes, sir.
> *Doctor:* What was the trouble this time?
> *Patient:* Oh, about the same thing...
> *Doctor:* Have you ever been sterilized?
> *Patient:* No.
> *Doctor:* You had better let us operate on you while you are here.
> *Patient:* That will certainly be all right with me and my wife also.
> *Doctor:* We will do that then.
> *Patient:* Doctor, will that bring better composure to the nervous system?
> *Doctor:* It is supposed to, it has in a number of cases, we do not guarantee it, but in a number of cases it has had marked beneficial effects. It cannot hurt you and does not interfere with your sexual life in any way...
> *Patient:* I will be very much obliged to you, sir [Braslow, 64–65].

It is estimated that between 1910 and 1950, Stockton State Hospital physicians performed vasectomies on more than 1,500 patients, but with few therapeutic benefits. At the Sonoma State Hospital, in contrast, the therapeutic value of the procedure was never really considered. It was here that vasectomy was used in its most eugenical form—as a measure of social control. Founded as a state hospital in the late nineteenth century, the Sonoma State Hospital originally confined mentally disabled children and adolescents. With the passage of the state's eugenics law, however, with its generous definition of "mental defective," the asylum was transformed into a "revolving operating room" (Kline, p. 53). People were committed for social and moral violations, such as alcoholism or petty vice crimes, sterilized within days, and discharged days later. Sonoma State Hospital, according to best estimates, sterilized more "mental defectives" than any institution in the world.

In states that had passed eugenic sterilization laws, but that had less vigorous promotion of them, asylum patients were more fearful of the procedure. One of them, Marion Marle Woodson, who under the pseudonym "Inmate, Ward 8" published a memoir of his years as a patient in the Eastern State Hospital in Vinita, Oklahoma, described the impact of state's sterilization law on his fellow patients:

> The patients on the receiving ward are in seething unrest. The two thousand men and women in the institution are in a foment. I suspect that this is true in every asylum in the state.... The spectre of sex sterilization has been thrust over us. The legislature has passed and the governor has signed a measure permitting the desexualization under certain circumstances, of any male of female inmate who is too aged to procreate. And the patients are frightened, wrought up, angry and muttering. They know little about the law, therefore they are the more frightened.... They gather in knots and discuss the fate which may be hanging over them. But they do not do it where the attendants can hear. They are afraid to do that.... And so the fears, the loneliness, and the near hopelessness of the Locked-ins have an added terror [Inmate, Ward 8, p. 112].

Whether vasectomy was intended to be used to relieve the suffering of insane patients or to protect society from social and moral degenerates was not always evident. That said, it is estimated that in the United States alone more than 9,000 vasectomies were performed between 1900 and 1940 on patients confined to state asylums.

## *Wiring*

A procedure if not developed by, certainly popularized by, David Yellowlees, superintendent of the Glasgow Royal Asylum in Scotland, which involved the surgical insertion of a silver wire ring into the foreskin of the penis, making it impossible to masturbate without pain or injury. Like many asylum physicians in the late nineteenth century, Yellowlees was influenced by the work of the Swiss physician Samuel Tissot who had posited that by increasing the peripheral circulation, the act of masturbation dangerously rushed blood to the brain and that ejaculation had a more debilitating effect on the nervous, circulatory and digestive systems than losing forty ounces of blood. And like most asylum physicians of that era, Yellowlees witnessed his male patients masturbating, leading him to the conclusion that the act was not only a cause of insanity, but also one of its effects. Curing insanity, then, required preventing masturbation.

Yellowlees's conclusion certainly had the backing of some distinguished asylum physicians. Jean-Étienne Esquirol of the Salpêtrière Asylum in Paris, France, earlier had argued that masturbation caused insanity, not via a sudden rush of blood to the brain but by the depletion of blood from the brain, and that unless it could be prevented it would be "an insurmountable obstacle to cure" (Esquirol, p. 388). On that latter point William Ellis, the superintendent of the Hanwell Asylum near London, England, agreed, as did the revered German reformer Wilhelm Griesinger, albeit with some hesitation. He suggested that the secrecy and shame surrounding the act of masturbation contributed more to insanity than the act, itself. David Skae, resident physician at the Royal Edinburgh Asylum, agreed as well, and was the first to propose a new category of insanity—masturbatory insanity—to be added to the categories of mania and melancholia.

Whether they considered it a cause and/or an effect of insanity, or a distinct clinical category, asylum physicians were frustrated in both preventing and treating masturbation. They tried blistering the penis or smearing it with croton oil, shocking the spine or restraining the hands, increasing the exercise of the patient in question or altering his diet, but all to no avail. Surgical procedures such as castration were discussed, and almost always rejected. So in the late nineteenth century when Yellowlees suggested the minimally evasive procedure of wiring, there was considerable interest in the procedure.

Yellowlees surgically inserted wires into the penises of twelve of his patients with what he declared were good results. Not only did the wiring prevent masturbation, but the surgical process itself, in his opinion, seemed to have a strong moral effect on the consciences of his patients, one of whom wept when he learned that the wire eventually would be removed once he had learned the proper habit of self-restraint.

Richard Maurice Bucke, superintendent of the Provincial Asylum for the Insane in Hamilton and later the London Asylum, both in Ontario, Canada, tried the procedure on twenty-one patients specifically selected "as belonging to a class in which the habit seemed to some extent a cause of the insanity" (Shortt, p. 126). Case records show that the patients, most of whom were laborers or farm workers, were all in their early twenties and, with one exception, were single. Their diagnoses upon admission varied: twelve had been diagnosed as manic, four as melancholic, three as imbecilic, one as demented; the remaining patient, for reasons not explained, was undiagnosed.

While Yellowlees had reported no pre- or post-surgical complications for his patients, Bucke could not claim the same. Many of his patients resisted the procedure, several developed serious infections; for one reason or another, eight of the patients had to be wired twice, and three underwent three separate procedures. And while Yellowlees described a "good" outcome, Bucke did not. The casebooks show that of the twenty-one patients, only two showed "marked improvement" and three "slight improvement." The rest remained unchanged. On the basis of this trial, Bucke, who had taken on the task with enthusiasm, asserting that "a good many cases could be relieved and cured which are now hopeless"

(Warsh, p. 59), was forced to reconsider his position. Not only did he think wiring was insufficient to the task of preventing masturbation, but he questioned whether masturbation could be considered the sole cause of insanity in the first place.

Experiments in wiring were conducted in a number of British, European and American asylums in the late nineteenth century, but with disappointing results. A concomitant sea-change in opinion about the cause-and-effect relationship between masturbation and insanity caused many asylum physicians to reject their own theories and the therapeutics they had recommended, or used.

# Hydrotherapy (Hydropathy)

*The internal or external application of water in any of its forms—liquid, ice or vapor—as a therapeutic treatment.*

The use of water to treat insanity dates to antiquity. Celsus, Galen and Hippocrates, among other physicians, prescribed its use not just for the relief of physical ailments but for the mental disorders they were presumed to have caused. When asylums were but few and far between, physicians often treated insane patients with what usually was a staggering array of therapeutics that included some type of application of water.

Daniel Oxenbridge was a case in point. The Puritan physician plied his trade in London in the early seventeenth century and treated a number of insane patients in their homes. His journals, anonymously published many decades later, detailed his treatment of one Mrs. Miller, aged twenty-four, the wife of a well-to-do cloth merchant, who had been insane for a couple of years. Hardly parsimonious in his treatment, he bled, purged and vomited her, as was *de rigueur* in that era, made her swallow copious quantities of apple cider and a concoction of borage, endive, succory (chicory), fumitory and even more apples. He shaved her head and applied to it the warm lungs of lambs, sheep and pigeons, and then, in what she must have reveled in as relief, he bathed her head in warm water infused with rosemary, sage, lavender and betony (mint). He plunged her feet nightly into warm water to dispose her to sleep, and as time passed and the weather warmed, he placed her in a bath of lukewarm water where she remained for hours at a time. Although his cure of her hardly could be attributed to water alone, the case demonstrated the same kind of therapeutic use of it as is found in the case notes and texts of such eminent physicians as Robert Burton and Richard Napier, contemporaries of Oxenbridge.

Despite the weight of history and the imprimaturs of such distinguished physicians, hydrotherapy or hydropathy was generally not incorporated into the therapeutic regimens of early asylums, at least not in the form that easily would have been recognized by its bygone proponents. Water was used in them not so much to achieve some therapeutic end in and of itself, but more as a means to terrify, subjugate and punish [see **Salutary Fear**]. Thus, asylum patients were ducked, drenched and nearly drowned during much of the eighteenth and early nineteenth centuries—hydrotherapeutic methods, if indeed they could be so termed, that left little question as to their intent.

Over the years, however, sometimes elaborate and always expensive hydrotherapy suites and buildings were being constructed in asylums around the world, signaling a change in attitude in favor of the therapeutic, as opposed to coercive, potential of water. While there may be many reasons for this, three are especially noteworthy. The first springs from an unlikely source—the significant influence of a Silesian peasant by the name of Vincent Priessnitz. As a boy he had witnessed a deer drag itself to a stream and submerge its injured limb in the cold water; it did so day after day until its strength returned. Deeply moved by what he believed was both the healing and the spiritual property of water, Priessnitz assumed the role of folk healer, treating villagers' aches and pains with cold water immersions and compresses. He healed himself, as well. In 1816 he was run over by a wagon loaded with oats. The physician who examined him declared that if he lived, he most surely would be an invalid for the remainder of his life. Priessnitz set out to heal himself when the physician's poultice of herbs stewed in wine failed to relieve his pain. He leaned over a chair and held his breath in what he mistakenly believed was a successful effort to realign his fractured ribs, and then applied cold water compresses, changing them every few hours. After ten days he declared himself cured although, as a matter of interest, he wore wet compresses around his chest to relieve the pain for the remainder of his life.

His remarkable recovery secured his reputation among laypeople as a "water-doctor" and among qualified physicians as a quack. The hydrotherapeutic clinic he built in his home, however, was lauded by the Imperial Commission sent to investigate it, and Priessnitz was given a license to practice "hygienic remedies," an honor that had never before been bestowed on a layperson. Among the many patients who took the "water cure" by subjecting themselves to cold baths, showers and wet packs, and drinking copious amounts of cold water, were physicians who were curious about its curative claims. Most left impressed; some were evangelical in their zeal about the cure, thus it was not long before hydrotherapeutic clinics, often known simply as "hydros," were being built across Europe. The patients who flocked to them, most of them quite well-to-do, were suffering not only from the aches and pains of work and life in a rapidly industrializing society, but from the mental strains and stresses that were produced by modernization. It would not have been unusual in the mid-nineteenth century to find a "nervous" patient following an arthritic one into a hydro's cold shower room.

Second, the putative success of the water cure in ameliorating mental distress garnered the attention of asylum physicians. Faced with stinging criticism that their tried and true "heroic" methods of treatment—bleeding, blistering, purging, vomiting [see **Counterirritation; Depletive Therapy**]—were not only feeble but dated, they were interested in modernizing their approach. And by using water in less threatening ways than their predecessors, they were able to claim some therapeutic success. Hydrotherapeutic applications soothed and calmed the manic, stimulated and invigorated the melancholic, and improved the general physical health of patients while checking the spread of communicable diseases and freshening the odor of overcrowded asylums in the bargain. Although certainly well suited for coercion and, to be frank, sometimes still boldly used for that purpose alone, by the mid-nineteenth century hydrotherapy more often was being used as a therapeutic substitute for the mechanical restraints, "heroic" interventions and befuddling drugs of old.

In his travels, Frederick Peterson of the Hudson River State Hospital for the Insane in New York was quite taken with how widespread the use of hydrotherapeutics had become in asylums around the world. He commented,

> [F]or the insane in Germany, Holland, France, Belgium, Italy, and Austria in the winter of 1886–1887, I was surprised to find how universally hydrotherapy was employed in the treatment of certain conditions of insanity, and with what excellent results; and in a visit to the new insane asylum in Athens, Greece, in 1892, I was astonished to note how well equipped a hydrotherapeutic establishment it possesses, although in a country we are disposed to consider somewhat out of the track of modern progress [Peterson, p. 371].

Had he traveled to Mexico, Peterson would have been just as surprised. San Hipólito Asylum for the Insane was established in 1566, the first asylum of its kind built in the Americas. Almost from the start, however, its compassionate mission was undermined by ideological conflicts between the Catholic Church which had founded it, the wealthy benefactors who funded it, and the often poorly trained physicians who ran it. The overcrowded asylum fell into horrible disrepair, its patients neglected, underfed and often abused by coercive applications of water—the bath of surprise and forced immersions in tubs of cold water. By the 1880s, just about the time that Peterson was visiting European asylums, San Hipólito had placed itself on the "track of modern progress" by transforming its custodial function into a therapeutic one with the installation of a rather elaborate hydrotherapy suite with showers, douches and tubs used to treat anything from melancholy and mania to hysteria and hypochondriasis.

Modern asylum medicine, after all, required modernized facilities and, it might be added, modernized facilities made the practice of modern asylum medicine possible. When patients were being nothing more than bled and shackled, purged and leg-locked, there were few reasons for improving asylums, save for the construction of wings and outbuildings to accommodate the ever-increasing patient census. The therapeutic, as opposed to coercive, use of water required specialized facilities and trained staff, the building and hiring of which provided the opportunity to transform asylums from hopeless and antiquated institutions into hopeful and modern ones.

The costs of adding hydrotherapeutic facilities were considerable. A 1902 report from the Government Hospital for the Insane, later known as St. Elizabeths, in Washington, D.C., where 1,199 patients in the previous year had been treated with 22,210 baths, estimated an outlay of $3,000 to build a hydrotherapeutic facility in a single ward, and $36,000 to $40,000 to build one in a new and separate building. It also advised that each facility be staffed with skilled operators or specially trained attendants, adding significantly to personnel costs.

Such costs, it was argued, would be offset by the benefits of the therapeutic use of water. The 1907 Biennial Report of the Illinois Public Board of Charities provided an interesting glimpse into the rather peculiarly unbalanced structure of this argument that was being presented in many asylums around the world: costs were being calculated in cold financial terms; benefits in impressions, observations and hopes.

To begin, the report framed the argument by visually linking the modern asylum with modernized therapeutics. The report's frontispiece has two series of photographs, one titled "The Old Way," the other "The New Way." The former is of chains, straitjackets, restraining chairs, and a bottle ominously labeled "stupefying drug"; the latter is of bathtubs, showers and footbaths. Determined to bring the "New Way" into its state asylums, the Public Board of Charities estimated the costs of constructing hydrotherapeutic facilities as $290,000, a cost that would be offset, it argued, by the significantly increased cure rates that would "relieve the state of the care of such patients" (p. 251). To bolster its benefit analysis, the report offered testimonials by American asylum physicians already experienced in the therapeutic applications of water. The tributes illustrated what was being touted as a modern remedy whose benefits far exceeded its costs:

> From our experience here I am inclined to the belief that no other therapeutic agent is so valuable in such an institution. We expect by the aid of hydrotherapeutic measures to practically do away with all forms of restraint whatever, either mechanical or chemical [p. 13].
>
> The various methods in which water must be applied makes necessary a certain amount of apparatus.... All this involves, in its installation, a certain outlay, yet it seems to me the state has no right to deny this proved means of greatest utility and curative power to its wards, especially when its economic value in restoring health and sanity is considered [p. 254].
>
> Your legislature must permit this step of progress to be made or be left behind and see your insane hospitals discreditably trailing along in the rear [p. 255].
>
> I have observed with great interest that hydrotherapy has won a prominent place in the therapy of the insane and that in the most

progressive hospitals it is substituted for injurious hypnotics and narcotics ... no matter how expensive the hydrotherapeutic apparatus may be, its use is always profitable [pp. 256–257].

Physicians always had relied upon declarations and anecdotes like these to justify the coercive uses of water in the early years of asylums. It was, in fact, the oft-repeated story originally told by the Flemish physician and chemist, Jean Baptiste van Helmont in the mid-seventeenth century, of a carpenter who was cured of his insanity when he escaped his captors by leaping into a deep pond and nearly drowning, that gave reason for the uses of the bath of surprise and ducking—those greatly fearsome and feared coercive uses of water. Modern asylum medicine, however, had to be based on sounder stuff, and it was the science that built up around the therapeutic uses of water that is the third reason for the widespread and enthusiastic use of hydrotherapeutics in asylums.

Neither a researcher nor a scientist, Priessnitz had kept no records of the thousands of patients who took his water cure; he had published nothing, and he had never addressed his contemporaries in a professional meeting. But he had a devotee who did. Wilhelm Winternitz, an Austrian medical student, conducted extensive research for his dissertation on the patients who took Priessnitz's water cure. He measured their pulses and took their temperatures before and after treatments; he took plethysmographic readings to measure the accumulation of blood in the parts of the body exposed to particular treatments. He theorized that the temperature stimulant of water not only acted on the organs proximate to its administration, but on nerve points that affected other organs, as well as glands and muscles, through the neural pathways of reflex arcs. An ice pack on the foot, he hypothesized, indeed would affect the brain.

Graduating as a neurologist, Winternitz founded his own hydrotherapy establishment in the popular resort town of Kaltenleutgeben in the southern Vienna Woods where he treated nearly 13,000 patients over a quarter of a century. While doing so, he carried on his research and published extensively on the therapeutic uses of water, and was admitted to the medical faculty of the University of Vienna as a private docent for hydrotherapy. It could be convincingly argued that hydrotherapy was the first asylum therapeutic whose rationale was derived from rigorous adherence to the scientific method, albeit that little of that research used insane patients as subjects, and indeed it was this modern approach to therapeutics that asylum physicians were eager to embrace. For his research and work, Winternitz is referred to as the "father of scientific hydrotherapy," a sobriquet that reveals that this therapeutic not only was empirically and theoretically grounded, but that it constituted a discipline, of sorts, that asylum physicians could be taught, as well as a technique in which they could be trained.

Winternitz had his own devotees who furthered scientific hydrotherapy. Among them was Simon Baruch. It was through his tireless advocacy that American asylum physicians, many of whom were skeptical at first, were eventually convinced of the efficacy of hydrotherapy. A general practitioner with no experience in treating insanity, Baruch nonetheless meticulously documented the experiences and the research of asylum physicians around the world who were skilled in its use. Among them, was the American asylum physician Frederick Peterson whose appeal to "modern progress" was a clarion call for a new and different approach to asylum therapeutics. Like Winternitz, Baruch was given an academic position. As professor of hydrotherapy at Columbia University's College of Physicians and Surgeons, he assured that the future generation of asylum physicians were schooled in the theory and research of hydrotherapy in the treatment of insanity.

With credentials such as this, it would be reasonable to expect that hydrotherapy would have had a long and vital tenure as an asylum therapeutic. By the 1920s and certainly for several decades after, however, the expensive hydrotherapy facilities were being re-purposed for the new shock therapies [see **Shock Therapy**] that were making even stronger claims of scientific legitimacy and bolder promises for cures. And even after those therapies had all but run their ultimately disappointing course, hydrotherapy did not return as a therapeutic. Thorazine and other neuroleptic drugs that came into asylum use in the mid-twentieth century provided an easily administered, low cost alternative to the showers, baths and douches that were once hailed as markers of modern asylum medicine.

REFERENCES

Amaral, D., and Rogers, S.J. (2011). Against *le packing*: A consensus statement. *Journal of the American Academy of Child and Adolescent Psychiatry, 50,* 191–192.
Baruch, S. (1903). *The principles and practice of hydrotherapy.* New York: William Wood.
Beam, A. (2003). *Gracefully insane: The rise and fall of America's premier mental hospital.* New York: PublicAffairs.
Bell, J. (1859). *Treatise on baths.* Philadelphia: Lindsay & Blakiston.
Bradley, I. (2012). Keep taking the liquids. *History Today, 62,* 44–46.
Bucknill, J.C., and Tuke, D.H. (1879). *A manual of psychological medicine.* London: J. & A. Churchill.
Burrows, G.M. (1828). *Commentaries on the causes, forms, symptoms, and treatment, moral and medical, of insanity.* London: Thomas and George Underwood.
Burton, R. (1621). *The anatomy of melancholy.* Oxford: Cripps.
California Commission in Lunacy (1872). *Insanity and insane asylums.* Sacramento, CA: T.A. Springer.
Cox, J.M. (1806). *Practical observations on insanity.* London: C. and R. Baldwin.
Cumming, W.F. (1899). *Notes on lunatic asylums in Germany, and other parts of Europe.* Edinburgh: Neill and Co.
Delion, P. (2005). *Le packing avec les enfants autistes et psychotiques.* Ramonville-Saint-Agne, France: Erés.
deViesca, M.B.R. (2000). Hydrotherapy as a treatment for mental illnesses during the XIX century in Mexico. *Salud Mental, 23,* 41–46.
"Dr. Jacobi on the nature and treatment of insanity" (1846). *British and Foreign Medical Review, 22,* 1–18.
"Dr. K.G. Neumann and the springs of Germany" (1846). *London Medical Gazette, 38,* 71–73.
"The drip sheet" (1893). *Canada Lancet, 25,* 395.
Earle, P. (1853). *Institutions for the insane in Prussia, Austria and Germany.* Utica, NY: New York State Lunatic Asylum.
Farmer, F. (1972). *Will there really be a morning?* New York: G.P. Putnam's Sons.
Finnane, M. (1981). *Insanity and the insane in post-famine Ireland.* Totowa, NJ: Barnes & Noble.
Fordyce, O.O. (1913). Hydrotherapy in the treatment of the insane. *Annual Report of the Ohio Board of Administration,* 15–23.
Gerhard, W.P. (1895). The rain-bath—A novel form of bath and new method of bathing insane patients. *American Journal of Insanity, 52,* 23–36.
Hinsdale, G. (1910). *Hydrotherapy.* Philadelphia: W.B. Saunders.
Howells, J.G. (1975). *World history of psychiatry.* New York: Brunner/Mazel.
Illinois Board of Public Charities (1907). *Biennial report.* Springfield, IL: Phillips Bros.
Jacobi, M.P., and White, V.A. (1880). *On the use of the cold pack followed by massage in the treatment of anemia.* New York: G.P. Putnam's Sons.
Jones, M. (2008). The most cruel and revolting crimes: The treatment of the mentally ill in mid-nineteenth century Jamaica. *Journal of Caribbean History, 42,* 290–309.
Kennedy, M., Helms, P., and Dykstra, M. (1936). The sedative wet sheet pack. *American Journal of Nursing, 36,* 53–60.
Kraepelin, E. (1962). *One hundred years of psychiatry.* Trans. Wade Baskin. New York: Citadel.
Lathrop, Clarissa Caldwell (1890). *A secret institution.* New York: Bryant Publishing.
Letchworth, W. P. (1889). *The insane in foreign countries.* New York: G.P. Putnam's Sons.
Leuret, F. (1840). *Du traitement moral de la folie.* Paris: Chez J.-B. Baillierè.
"The lunatic asylums of Denmark" (1861). *Medical Times and Gazette, 2,* 389.
MacDonald, M. (1981). *Mystical Bedlam: Madness, anxiety and healing in seventeenth century England.* Cambridge: Cambridge University Press.
Madsen, J. (1966). Some pages from the history of Sct. Hans Hospital. *Acta Psychiatrica Scandinavica, 41,* 13–56.
McDowall, T.W. (1883). Danish retrospect. *British Journal of Psychiatry, 29,* 305–311.
Metcalfe, R. (1898). *Life of Vincent Priessnitz, founder of hydrotherapy.* London: Simpkin, Marshall, Hamilton, Kent, & Co.
Micale, M.S. (1990). Charcot and the idea of hysteria in the male: Gender, mental science, and medical diagnosis in ate nineteenth-century France. *Medical History, 34,* 363–411.
Newington, S. (1865). On a new remedial agent in the treatment of insanity and other diseases. *Retrospect of Medicine, 52,* 72–74.
Officers of the Hospital (1902). *Report of the Government Hospital for the Insane.* Washington, D.C.: Government Printing Office.
Oxenbridge, D. (1715). *General observations and prescriptions in the practice of physick.* London: W. Mears, J. Brown, and T. Woodward.

Peterson, F. (1893). Hydrotherapy in the treatment of nervous and mental disease. *Gaillard's Medical Journal, 65,* 370–379.

Power, T. (1865). *Report on the effects of the Turkish bath in the treatment of insanity, for the Board of Governors.* Cork, Ireland: Author.

Quinton, R. (1904). *L'eau de mer milieu organique.* Paris: Ed. Masson.

Robertson, C.L. (1861). On the sedative action of the cold sheet in the treatment of recent mania. *British Journal of Psychiatry, 7,* 265–277.

Rowland, H. (1938). Interaction processes in the state mental hospital. *Psychiatry, 1,* 323–337.

Rush, B. (1830). *Medical inquiries and observations upon the diseases of the mind.* Philadelphia: John Grigg.

Sanborn, F.B. (1898). *Memoirs of Pliny Earle, M.D.* Boston: Damrell & Upham.

Seabrook, W. (1935). *Asylum.* New York: Harcourt, Brace.

Shepard, C.H. (1900). Insanity and the Turkish bath. *Journal of the American Medical Association, 34,* 604–606.

Sheppard, E. (1866). Cases treated by Turkish bath. *British Journal of Psychiatry, 12,* 74–83.

Stevenson, S. (1988). Madness and the picturesque in the Kingdom of Denmark. In W.F. Bynum, R. Porter, and M. Shepherd (eds.), *The anatomy of madness, Vol. III: The asylum and its psychiatry,* pp. 13–47. London: Routledge.

Svedberg, G. (2000). Narratives on prolonged baths from psychiatric care in Sweden during the first half of the twentieth century. *International History of Nursing Journal, 5,* 28–35.

Swartz, S. (2010). The regulation of British Colonial lunatic asylums and the origins of colonial psychiatry, 1860–1864. *History of Psychology, 13,* 160–177.

Tuke, D.H. (1885). *The insane in the United States and Canada.* London: H. K. Lewis.

Tuke, D.H. (1892). *A dictionary of psychological medicine.* London: J. & A. Churchill.

Tuke, H. (1858). On warm and cold baths in the treatment of insanity. *Journal of Mental Science, 4,* 532–552.

Turner, T.H. (1992). A diagnostic analysis of the casebooks of Ticehurst House Asylum, 1845 to 1890. *Psychological Medicine (Monograph), 21,* 1–70.

"The virtues of sea water" (1905). *American Monthly Review of Reviews, 32,* 495–496.

White, W.A. (1909). *Bulletin: St. Elizabeth's Hospital.* Washington, D.C.: Government Printing Office.

White, W.A. (1916). Dangers of the continuous bath. *American Journal of Insanity, 72,* 481–484.

Widroe, H.J. (2010). *Diary of a medical student: Hospital of horrors.* Charleston, SC: CreateSpace.

Winslow, F.B. (1857). Prolonged shower bath in the treatment of the insane. *Journal of Psychological Medicine and Mental Pathology, 10,* 1–28.

## Beach Bathing, or Strand Bathing

The practice, especially popular in the Scandinavian countries and France, of bathing patients in the sea. Sea bathing was said to have considerable advantages over other types of cold water bathing:

> Sea bathing is usually preceded by some exercise, a walk or ride to the beach; it is accompanied by some muscular exertion—struggling against the waves, or, in the more robust, by attempts to swim: with others, again, the whole affair is attended by a dread of danger which powerfully affects the nervous system, and causes hurried breathing, palpitation, and increased rapidity of circulation. The immersion also is in a dense fluid largely impregnated with salts, by which the skin is sensibly stimulated and even irritated. This surface is, besides, actively impressed by the movement of the waves impinging on it, and causing a kind of massage. Add to these, exposure at one time to often a cool and keen wind from the sea, and at another to the full blaze of the meridian sun, and we can readily conceive that sea bathing presents a more complex problem for solution than the mere use of a cold bath [Bell, p. 399].

In Denmark, sea bathing was used with great enthusiasm. At Stk. Hans Asylum, most of the 700 patients were bathed daily between late May and early October. In the opinion of the superintendent, "the beginning of convalescence, or at least essential improvement in both body and mind [could be dated] from the day when the patient began strand bathing" (Lechworth, p. 211). It was also reported that the daily promenade of patients from the asylums to the fjords had additional beneficial therapeutic effects.

Beach or strand bathing was part of a therapeutic regime that idealized rural life. The move of Stk. Hans Asylum from the city of Copenhagen to the Bistrupsgaard Manor overlooking the Roskilde Fjord, for example, was predicated on the assertion that the patients soon would "emulate the pure and innocent customs of the locals, and fall into the natural rhythms of sound sleeping and healthy eating" (Stevenson, p. 29). Fresh air, long walks and bathing in the cold water of the fjord were considered antidotes to the stresses of city life that either caused or contributed to insanity.

The rural idyll also was reflected in Harald Selmer's prize-winning essay on the topic of "On the General Principles to Be Adopted in the Treatment of the Insane," submitted in a contest sponsored by Philiatria, an association of young physicians. Selmer, a physician at Stk. Hans, set out a plan for a model asylum that would treat the insane with dignity by providing refuge, employment and recreation in a pleasant and healthy rural setting. The essay prompted the Danish government to establish the Jütland Asylum in Aarhuis in the mid-nineteenth century and to name Selmer its first superintendent. The asylum was purposely built close to the sea so that its patients would benefit from beach or strand bathing.

Although the Wards Island Asylum was in close proximity to the Atlantic Ocean, patients were not taken to the sea, rather, the sea was brought to them. Under the superintendency of Alexander MacDonald, a 220 by 30 foot open air bath was cut out of the rocks at the southern tip of the island; a sluice allowed the water of Hell Gate, a narrow tidal strait in New York City's East River, to flow into it. On his mid-nineteenth century tour of the asylum, British physician Daniel Hack Tuke saw as many as 200 patients bathing in the two-and-a-half feet deep sea water "to their heart's content" while "evidently enjoy[ing] their immersion immensely" (Tuke, 1885 p. 63).

## Cold Water Ingestion

The drinking of an hourly pint of cold water for several continuous days or weeks. Cold water ingestion was promoted by Austrian physician Leopold Avenbrugger for the cure of suicidal propensity. If, during the course of the treatment, the patient remained pensive and taciturn, Avenbrugger also recommended the sprinkling of cold water on the eyes, forehead and temples until the patient "becomes more gay and communicative" (Burrows, pp. 449–450).

In the early nineteenth century the prevailing theory, elaborated by Jean-Étienne Esquirol, the prominent *medécin ordinaire* at the Salpêtrière Asylum in Paris, France, was that suicidal propensity was the result of either a "delirium of the passions," set off by personal crises that extinguished free will, or a chronic pathological obsession in an otherwise healthy mind. It was that latter explanation, referred to as suicidal monomania, to which Avenbrugger subscribed. The received wisdom at the time was that monomania was an organic disorder, originating in the stomach, thus he reasoned that the copious consumption of cold water would stimulate the functions of the stomach and the liver, dilute stomach acids, lessen appetite, distend the blood vessels, and remove toxins from the body.

A proto-sociological challenge to this theory was thrown down by Jean-Pierre Falret, *chef de l'hospice* at the Salpêtrière Asylum who posited that suicidal propensity was neither the result of the delirium of the passions nor of monomania. Rather, he argued that it was a an act of free will that had been influenced by both the predisposing causes of heredity, age, gender, education and temperament, and the indirect causes of romantic, financial and/or domestic problems. Interestingly, he also recommended cold water ingestion as a treatment, but expressed some skepticism that it would be effective for any patient who already had not made significant progress towards full recovery.

## Cold Water Pour

The streaming of cold water down the coat sleeves of the patient so that it descended into the armpits and down the trunk of the body. Recommended by Benjamin Rush, "the Father of American Psychiatry," and physician to the Pennsylvania Hospital, the cold water pour was used as one method of last resort to "establish a governance over deranged patients ... in order to prevent their destroying their clothes and the furniture of their cells, as well as to punish outrages upon their keepers and upon each other" (Rush, p. 182).

## Cold Wet Pack, or Packing

The tight wrapping of a patient in a cold wet sheet or blanket. The cold wet pack is said to have been invented by Vincent Priessnitz, the innovator of hydrotherapy and was brought into asylum use in the mid-nineteenth century by C. Lockhart Robertson of the Sussex Lunatic Asylum in Hayward's Heath, England. Controversially, it remains in use in some asylums to this day. Robertson described the method of its use as follows:

> A piece of mackintosh cloth is laid over a mattress, and a folded blanket laid over that. An ordinary sheet is then wrung out of cold water and laid on the blanket. On this the patient is laid on his back, and the sheet is rapidly wound round him so as to include the arms in it folds. The blanket is then tucked over the body, and three or four other blankets laid over these. There is often a little shivering at first, but this passes off as the sheet gradually warms and the blood so determined to the surface [Robertson, p. 267].

Particularly suited for the treatment of what were referred to as the "feverish symptoms" of mania—hot head, rapid pulse, increased respiration, hot and dry skin—Robertson left the patient in the cold wet pack for an hour or more, at which time the patient was removed, rubbed with a dripping wet sheet, drenched with several pails of cold water, and then rewrapped in another cold wet pack. This process, Robertson pointed out, had to be repeated either several times over a long period, or even during the course of a single day before its soothing and sedative effect was noted. He described a case of a young blacksmith whose mania was cured by the administration of the cold wet pack after other treatments had failed:

> Arrived under strong personal restraint.... The symptoms of mania are well marked; there was general perturbation of all the mental powers, with noise and violence; the expression of countenance wild ... face flushed.... [O]rdered to be packed every two hours, with dripping sheet after. This was continued all day, and at night he was placed in the padded room. This treatment was continued during the 12th March; that night he slept five or six hours. On the 13th March he could, for a few seconds, collect his thoughts, and the violent symptoms were subsiding. This packing was continued once a day, with two cold pails after, for a week, by which time he was calm and quiet in mind, though still much confusion of intellect.... The packing was then discontinued.... On the 26th November he was discharged cured [p. 270].

Beyond conjecturing that the cold wet pack reduced the "feverish symptoms" of mania, Robertson did not elaborate upon its physiological action. Physicians with specialties other than asylum medicine however did. Max Schüller, a Berlin surgeon, used the cold wet pack in experiments on trephined rabbits and found that within two hours of its application, it contracted the cerebral blood vessels, lessening the blood supply to the brain, slowed the pulse and respiration rate, and increased the quantity of lymph in the brain, thus hastening sleep. Mary Putnam Jacobi, an American obstetrician, went on to describe how the respiratory, circulatory and heat regulatory centers then were excited, resulting in a dilation of the cutaneous vessels and an increase in body temperature. The skin, as a result of two hours in a cold wet back, became so filled with blood that steam arose when the blankets were removed from the patient. These combined long-term physiological effects, she argued, increased perspiration, urination and defecation, thus relieving the body of impurities and toxins.

The use of the cold wet pack was rationalized on the basis of empirical studies and controlled observations. As a result, its recommended use was extended beyond mania to cases of hysteria, alcoholism, general paresis (syphilis), melancholy and neurasthenia, as well as to general restlessness, agitation and insomnia. Its potential for abuse, most particularly for use as a mechanical restraint [see **Mechanical Restraint**] rather than as a hydrotherapeutic, however, was noted. After investigating allegations of abuse of the cold wet pack, the Lunacy Commission in 1873 placed restrictions on its use and recategorized it as a mechanical restraint. In the face of the still powerful non-restraint movement, British asylum physicians grew increasingly reticent to use it. By the early twentieth century, it had all but disappeared from the armamentarium of British asylums.

At the same time and in the United States, however, the conclusion that the cold wet pack was a mechanical restraint was vigorously rejected. Rather, it was accepted and so enthusiastically used as a hydrotherapeutic that one physician commented that "the [asylum] packroom is the true bedlam of modern psychiatry" (Rowland, p. 333). The method and mode of its application, however, varied considerably. A 1936 survey of seventeen asylums found that the recommended duration of the cold wet pack varied from twenty minutes to six hours, and the temperature from 48° to 80° F. Other variations also were evident more than a half century later in a retrospective audit of the files of forty-six patients who had been treated with the cold wet pack over a three year period of time at a single asylum. The patients received anywhere from one to more than fifty applications; the majority experienced "calming effects" that were not further described and a few found the treatment so soothing that "they became addicted and required a behavioral modification plan to be weaned" from it (Ross, et al., p. 244).

In regards to that last finding, the cold wet pack was not always feared by patients. Some, such as William Seabrook, actually found it pleasant. The journalist, who had admitted himself into the Bloomingdale Asylum in New York City for alcoholism and depression, wrote this about his cold wet pack experience:

They [the attendants] fixed the bed so it wouldn't soak through to the mattress, then laid me straight and naked on the bed with my arms pressed along my sides like a soldier lying at attention and began swathing me, rolling me one side and then the other, in tight wet sheets, so that the weight of my body rolling back would pull them smoother and tighter, over and over again.... I was flat on my back. Except that my head stuck out and lay comfortably on a pillow. I was the mummy of Rameses. I couldn't bend my elbows or knees. I couldn't even double my fists. My hands were pressed flat. I couldn't move a muscle.... This was the famous "pack." ... After a while my mind began to work and I discovered that I liked it.... I remembered theories that we all have a subconscious longing to be back in the womb—that we remember subconsciously how nice and safe and warm it was.... I went lax presently and was beginning to sweat. I sweated, time passed, and the tension was gone and the jangling nervousness disappeared too, faded slowly as it does under a strong soporific. I was soon as peaceful as a four month fetus [Seabrook, p. 43].

The "longing to be back in the womb" underlies the controversial contemporary use of the cold wet pack on institutionalized autistic children in France. The therapeutic was brought to France in the 1970s by American psychiatrist Michael Woodbury who had been affiliated with the Chestnut Lodge Asylum in Rockville, Maryland, where packing was routinely used. It was embraced by French psychiatrists whose understanding of autism was strongly influenced by Freudian theory. Most notable among them was Pierre Delion, head of Child Psychiatry at the University Hospital in Lille, who suggested that while wrapped in the cold wet pack the child, whose autism was the result of either cold or cloying mothering, undergoes a regression and re-experiences the safe and secure fetal environment. Used widely throughout France to integrate the senses and reduce self-harming behaviors, the use of the cold wet pack was featured in a 2011 documentary film titled *The Wall (Le Mur)*, which critically interrogated this psychoanalytic approach to autism. The film, which was posted on the internet, caused an international uproar.

The treatment of autistic children in France, 75 percent of whom are institutionalized and few of whom ever attend school, had been the subject of criticism from international advocacy and human rights groups for a number of years, but it was the treatment of the cold wet pack that both accelerated and politicized the controversy. While acknowledging that there is scant empirical evidence for the efficacy of packing, French psychiatrists argued that it often produced spectacular results; they, and a number of psychiatric organizations such as the World Association of Psychoanalysis, called for its continued use. Parents' groups and international human and disability rights organizations, such as Autism Rights Watch, declared it barbaric and called for its elimination. A consensus statement published by eighteen internationally recognized experts on autism declared the treatment unethical, adversative to the "evidence-based practice parameters and treatment guidelines" of other countries, and oppositional to children's "basic human rights to health and education" (Amaral & Rogers, p. 191). In early 2012 Prime Minister François Fillon called for a new national plan on autism that will bring France in line with the standards of practice and care of other Western countries; a month later, the French government specifically came out against packing.

## *Continuous Hot Bath, or Refractory Bath, or Waterbed Treatment*

The lowering on a hammock of a restrained patient into a tub where a series of valves and temperature gauges assured there was a continuous flow of 95° to 110° F. water. The tub was then covered with a canvas sheet or wooden cover with a hole for the head of the patient. The patient usually remained in the tub for eight to twenty-four hours before the sedative effect on the nervous system was experienced.

Various theories were proposed for the efficacy of the treatment. Some physicians argued that the continuous hot bath eliminated toxic impurities from the body by stimulating the excretory function of the kidneys and the skin; others that it lowered the pulse and blood pressure and raised respirations; and others still that it relieved the "congested brain" by warming the blood and soothing the nervous system. Regardless of the theory, physicians around the world used the continuous hot bath with zeal, and cited case after case where it ameliorated, even cured, the restlessness, agitation and confusion associated with mania.

One of those cases was Daniel D., a thirty-year-old who was committed in the early twentieth century to the Pennsylvania Hospital for the Insane. Described in admission notes as "garrulous, vituperative, restless, noisy, and hostile in manner" (Hinsdale, p. 173), he was placed in the continuous hot bath where he remained for five days, at which time his mania completely receded. He was released as cured.

In Sweden, the continuous hot bath was an often relied upon treatment. One nurse described the treatment as it was carried out at Västra Marks Hospital:

> A canvas sheet was placed over the tub.... It happened on one occasion that patients could live in there for three weeks at a time in the bath. They slept in the bathtubs, too. We fed them in the bath and held the drinking glass up to their mouths.... They peed and defecated in the water, of course.... Some patients became calmer from it, they really did! It exhausted them. That was the reason why they had to lie there like that. They were so very restless. They spat on us. The names they called us! [Svedberg, p. 29].

The death of a patient while in the continuous hot bath in a Swedish asylum in 1922 brought both criticism and defense of the treatment, just as deaths, usually from scalding, had brought in other countries around the world. In the United States, William Alanson White, the distinguished superintendent of the Government Hospital for the Insane, later named St. Elizabeths, in Washington, D.C., excoriated his colleagues for their reliance on the continuous hot bath as a therapeutic. He argued that the risks to the patient were considerable, not just from the temperature of the water, but from the length of exposure to it, and the restraints that kept the agitated patient from splashing, pulling the plug, or tearing the canvas cover. He concluded that if asylums would do away with this "crude and useless device that is nothing more than a makeshift and an excuse for lack of exertion," then more effort would have to be placed on interacting with disruptive patients with patience and intelligence (White, 1916, p. 482).

The continuous hot bath was known as the refractory bath in France, and the waterbed treatment in Denmark. In most asylums around the world, it was used until the mid-twentieth century.

## Continuous Warm Bath with Application of Cold to the Head

The placing of a patient in a tub of tepid water, often for several hours, while a cold affusion was applied to the head. The method of application varied, from cold wet towels wrapped around the head, jugs of cold water poured on the head, ice bags placed on the head, to a cold spray from a douche pipe directed at the head. The continuous warm bath with application of cold to the head was deemed to be more efficient in reducing the plethora of blood in the brain than the tepid or warm bath alone.

The sedative and soothing effect of this treatment was so pronounced that asylum patients often requested it. The risk that the continuous warm bath with application of cold to the head would either agitate or debilitate the patient, however, required that its application be carefully monitored.

## Douche

A steady stream of cold water falling from a hose or pipe held or fixed in place above the head of the restrained patient. The douche became a popular feature of the hydrotherapeutic regime in asylums during the nineteenth century and well into the twentieth. The diameter of the douche hose or pipe, and its distance to the head of the patient had significant implications: a small hose held a few inches from the head was deemed to have a decidedly tonic effect and was usually reserved for the melancholic or otherwise morose patient; a large hose, perhaps one to two inches in diameter, held a few feet above the patient's head tended to produce shock, faintness, vomiting and physical exhaustion and was recommended for the raving maniacal patient.

The douche also acted morally, as a means of repression, since most patients greatly feared it. Most asylum physicians, in fact, conceded that whatever efficacy it had was due more to the shock and fear it produced than the percussion of cold water on the head, and therefore greatly circumscribed its use so as to avoid any impression of punitiveness. A notable exception to that rule was François Leuret, principal physician at the Bicêtre Asylum in Paris, France, who had a dubious reputation for substituting "the continuous but more painful blow of a torrent of water ... for a shower of blows from the stick" (Bucknill & Tuke, p. 661).

American asylum physician Pliny Earle visited the Bicêtre in 1838, and described in detail the repressive use of the douche by Leuret:

> Dr. Leuret showed the bathing room, and explained his use of douche for mental and moral disciplines, which appears to me injurious. The scene of this treatment contained about a dozen bath-tubs, over each was a douche-pipe with a capacity for a three-quarter-inch stream. In two tubs we saw patients, each kept from leaving the tub by a board fitted to his neck where he sat, as a man stands in the pillory. One was a robust man, subject to varying hallucinations, who now thought himself the husband of the widowed

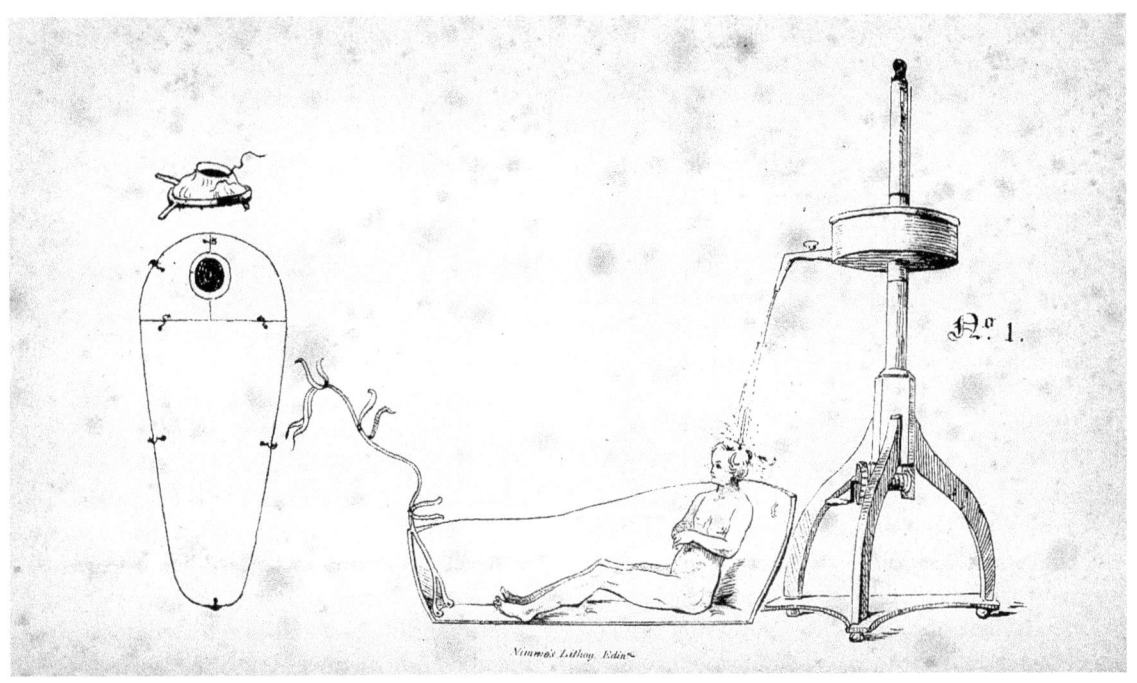

The douche. This rather low-tech contraption poured a steady stream of cold water on the patient's head through a pipe approximately one inch in diameter, while the patient reclines in a bath, the cover of which can be seen on the left. The device was portable and was devised by Domenico Gualandi of the Hospital for the Insane at Bologna, Italy, probably in the early nineteenth century (A. Morison [1828]. *Cases of mental disease*. London: Longman and Highly).

Duchess of Berri, and had been permitted the day before to have writing materials on condition that he would not write such vagaries as that he was a favorite of the exiled Bourbons and of Louise Philippe. He had written, however, his usual absurdities about the Duke of Bordeaux, Charles X., etc. Dr. Leuret, with this letter in his hand, reminded the patient of his promise, read him the nonsense he had written, and asked him if he still believed that. "Oui, Monsieur." "Give him the douche," said Dr. Leuret to the attendant, who at once turned the cock and discharged the stream on the madman's head. He screamed and writhed, and begged to have it stopped. It was checked; and he was asked, "Do you still believe you are the intimate friend of Charles X.?" "I think I do." "Let him have the douche." He again floundered, shouted and begged for mercy. "Well, are you the chum of Charles X. and the Duke of Bordeaux?" "I—I presume so." "Give him the douche once more." In this way, sometimes with argument and sometimes with the cold stream, the doctor labored for half an hour to break up his fantastic notions. At last the patient gave in, and his tormenttor gave him a lesson to be learned for the next day.

Turning to the other man in his tub, Dr. Leuret said he had yesterday refused to do a task assigned to him, leaving the work untouched. He then asked the man why he had neglected to work. "To tell the truth, Monsieur, I did not feel any special desire to work." This was said with a jocose leer which almost made us laugh. "Well, will you work hereafter when you are told?" Reflecting an instant, with the same comic air he said, "*Parole d'honneur*, I will *not* work." "Give him the douche," said Dr. L. The effect of the stream was now instantaneous. Like a child who is whipped, he cried, "I will, I will!" The douche was then stopped, and orders given that he should do the task before night [Sanborn, pp. 95–96].

Leuret believed that the cause of insanity was not yet, and perhaps never would be, known, therefore its treatment demanded the "reasonable use of all means which influence directly the mind and the passions of the insane" (Leuret, p. 156). Many of his contemporaries argued that the cause of insanity was an as yet unidentified lesion on or in the brain and that treatment, therefore, had to be directed at the body. The vituperative debate these two opposing views created waged during much of the later nineteenth century, not only in France, but around the world. The douche, arguably the one hydrotherapeutic most easily adaptable to either therapeutic or coercive purposes, was central to that debate.

## Drenching

The pouring of as many as forty to fifty buckets of ice cold water from a distance of ten to fifteen feet above, unto the patient's head. The pouring was done either by hand or by what became increasingly complicated series of pulleys and winches that raised and tipped the buckets. Drenching was strongly advocated by Ernst Horn of the Berlin Charité Hospital and was used there and in some other German asylums into the mid-nineteenth century. Horn argued that drenching

> calms and soothes the insane; it cools the head made feverish by congestion of the blood; it makes unruly patients docile and orderly; it enables the dumb to speak; it changes the outlook of those bent on self-destruction; it awakens self-consciousness in the motionless melancholic obsessed by his brooding; it has a salubrious effect on imbecile patients; and in many instances it contributes to the maintenance of calm and order in its role as an instrument for shocking and punishing patients [Kraepelin, p. 65].

Some of Horn's German colleagues agreed that drenching was an effective punishment of the intransigent patient. Even the reformer Ernst Pienitz, superintendent of the Sonnenstein Asylum in Pirna, used it occasionally, but only when accompanied by "a certain ritual exhortation and admonition" (Kraepelin, p. 65). Most of his colleagues, however, disagreed that drenching was an effective therapeutic. The superintendent of the Siegburg Asylum, Maximilian Jacobi, related that in one German asylum he had visited, 300 buckets of ice cold water had been poured over the head of one patient over several successive weeks, without ameliorating a single one of his symptoms.

## Drip Sheet

A variant of the cold wet pack, it was administered to a patient who stood in a tub of approximately twelve inches of 100° F. water. The sheet, which had been dipped in 75° F. water was then wrapped around the patient and tucked in at the neck and the legs. Two or three basins of 60° F. water were then poured over the head and shoulders of the patient; each was followed by several minutes of vigorous rubbing and slapping of the patient's sheeted body by the physician or nurse. Upon leaving the tub, the sheet was removed and the patient was dried with a warm towel.

The sedative effect of the drip sheet, which American neurologist S. Weir Mitchell proclaimed was a "remedy past praise," was found to be efficacious as a treatment of hysteria, neurasthenia, psychoneurosis and melancholia ("Drip Sheet," p. 25). It was used in North American asylums well into the twentieth century.

## Dripping Machine

A bucket positioned above the restrained and often blindfolded patient that slowly and steadily dripped cold water on a single spot on the forehead. Used extensively in French and German asylums in the mid-nineteenth century by devotees of the "somatic school" that posited organic causes of insanity, the dripping machine was used most often to treat persistent nervous headaches and insomnia, secondary symptoms of the congestion of blood in the head that was thought to have caused the insanity.

In the mid-nineteenth century Russia was divided into states, each with its own "Yellow

House," or asylum. The dripping machine may have been used in many of them, but certainly was at Poltava, a small asylum with just twenty patients who slept on straw covered floors and were daily subjected to the dripping machine, more as punishment than for therapy.

Interestingly, the dripping machine was better known throughout history for causing insanity than for treating it. As early as the fifteenth century, the Italian jurist Hippolytus de Marsiliis observed how a steady drip of water could hollow out a stone, and concluded that the same process, if directed to the forehead of a person, would cause insanity. In the eighteenth century the term "Spanish water torture," referencing a method of torture used during the Spanish Inquisition, was used to describe the device, but by the early twentieth century, the term "Chinese water torture" came into parlance, perhaps as a result of one of escapologist Harry Houdini's tricks in which he was suspended by his feet in what he called a "Chinese water torture cell," actually a steel cabinet, while it was being quickly filled with water. Regardless of its moniker, the dripping machine long has been more intimately associated with torture than with treatment.

## Fan Douche

A modification of the douche, it was administered by placing the thumb over the nozzle of the hose or pipe, breaking the jet of usually cold or cool water into a fan-shaped stream. On its own, the fan douche had few beneficial effects, and therefore was used as an adjunct to other types of hydrotherapies.

## Fomentation

The application of moist heat via a large square piece of woolen flannel or a sponge that had been dipped in boiling water and wrung out. The action of fomentation was similar to that of a poultice, in that it relieved tension by increasing the circulation in the part of the body, usually the abdomen or spine, to which it had been applied. Because fomentation lost its heat quite rapidly, the flannel or sponge had to be changed every fifteen to twenty minutes.

At times, counterirritants [see **Counterirritation**] such as turpentine were added in an effort to draw out impurities, or narcotics such as laudanum or poppies to produce sedation. The poppy fomentation, as the latter was referred to, was prepared by boiling a half a pound of deseeded poppy heads in four pints of water, and then dipping the flannel or the sponge into the strained liquid.

On occasion, dry fomentation was used as an asylum treatment. This involved the application of a hot brick wrapped in flannel, or of a heated bag of salt or bran, to the abdomen or spine of the patient. In addition to its sedative effect, the dry fomentation was thought to relieve indigestion, thus increasing the appetite of the patient.

## Liver Spray

A needle spray administered through a perforation in the sitz bath tub. The liver spray was directed at the upper right section of the abdomen, in the general direction of the liver. By drawing blood to the surface of the body and stimulating the flow of bile secretions, the liver spray relieved the liver and the intestines of the stasis that caused constipation.

Whether due to poor diet, poor general health, or large doses of opiates, chronic constipation was a problem peculiar to many asylum patients. Since the amount of putrefaction in the organs was thought to influence both temper and temperament, the liver spray was deemed a necessary adjunct to other hydrotherapeutic methods.

## Mustard Bath

A tepid bath into which five or six handfuls of crude mustard were dissolved. The mustard

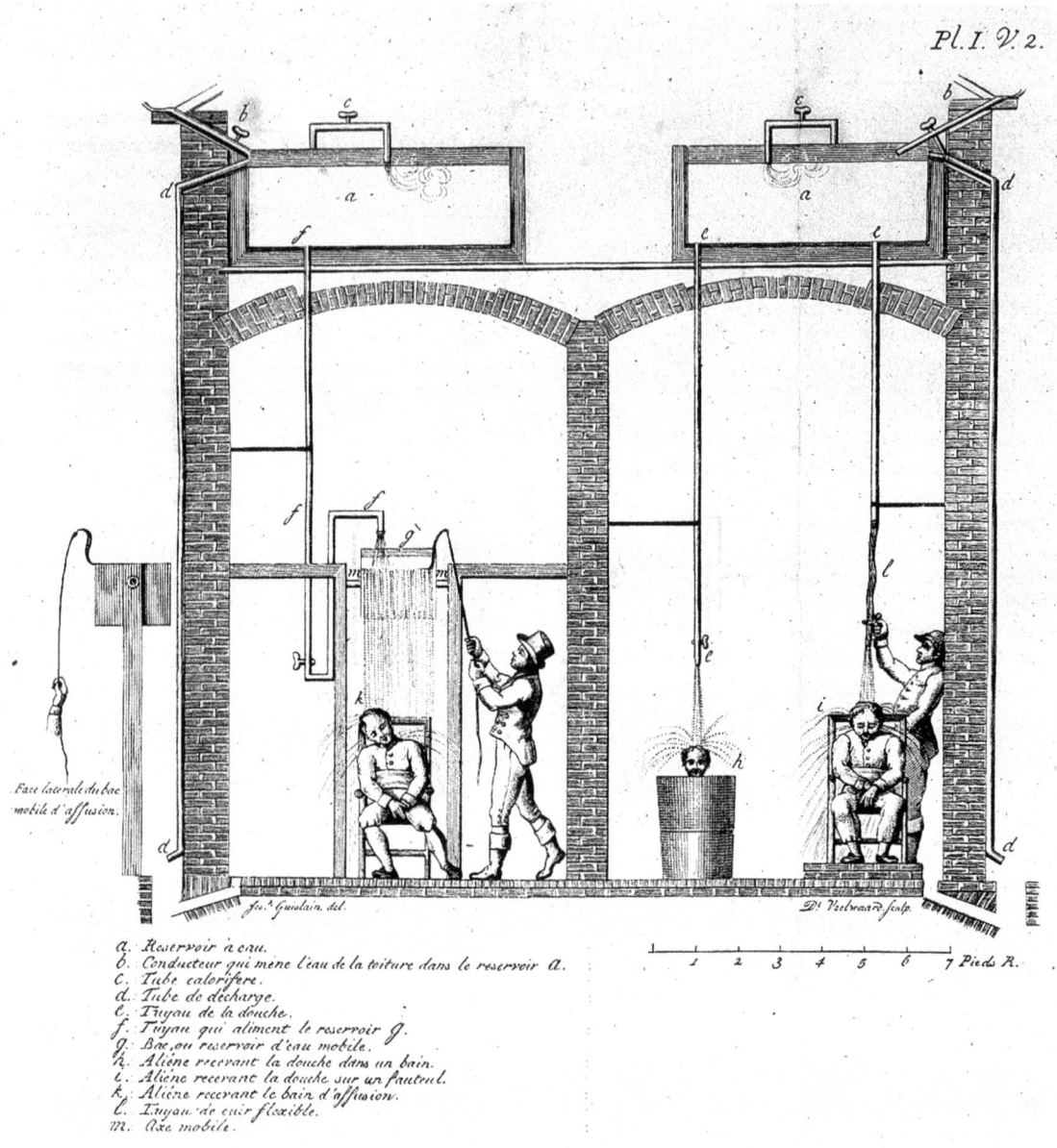

More high-tech versions of the douche, depicting from left to right: the rain bath or shower, the steady pour on the head, and the fan douche on the head and neck (courtesy of the Wellcome Library, London).

bath was enthusiastically endorsed by Samuel Newington of Ticehurst House Private Asylum in East Sussex, England, who had found it effective in the treatment of severe cases of mania. He described a patient, Mr. W., who had been brought to Ticehurst in a straitjacket while being further restrained by attendants. Despite repeated doses of opium, Mr. W. did not sleep for nearly a week; he was restless, excited and talkative. He was placed in a mustard bath where he remained for thirty minutes, and was "perfectly red upon being taken out" (Newington, 1865, p. 73). Over the next eight days he had six of these baths, and at the end of two weeks was released to his family.

The mustard bath was believed to lower body temperature and decrease blood circulation, however the risk of skin irritation and even superficial burns to the body was considerable. Although infrequently used as an asylum therapeutic, those physicians who did use it significantly decreased the duration of the mustard bath, from the thirty minutes recommended by Newington, to ten minutes with cloths protecting the patient's genitals.

## Needle Spray

Multiple horizontal sprays of water, under twenty to thirty pounds of pressure, from nozzles that surrounded the body. The needle spray was administered while the patient stood in a iron box or in an otherwise enclosed shower. Valves allowed for the regulation of water temperature. The needle spray most often was used as an adjunct to other forms of hydrotherapy, most notably the spinal douche.

It did have its own independent therapeutic effect, however. Although the needle spray did not lower body temperature, it did dilate the superficial blood vessels and had both a tonic and a sedative effect on the patient. At St. Elizabeths Hospital in Washington, D.C., the needle spray was a favorite hydrotherapeutic for staff and patients alike. Staff found it easy to administer and patients enjoyed it.

What might have been the prototype of the needle spray used at Hôpital Sainte-Anne in Paris, France, decades earlier, did not elicit such a positive response. American physicians touring the asylum observed patients standing in the middle of hoops of metal pipes, approximately one inch in diameter, that had been perforated with small holes through which jets of water sprayed out. "It seemed to us a frightful ordeal through which to pass," one of them wrote, "and from the contortions and grimaces of the patients we infer it was regarded in the same unfavorable light by them" (California Commission in Lunacy, p. 179).

## Neptune's Girdle, or Neptune's Belt

A variant of the cold wet pack, the girdle was a linen compress, soaked in 60° F. water, folded several times over and placed on the patient's abdomen. It was secured there by a flannel that was wrapped around the patient's trunk and fastened behind the back.

Some version of the girdle had been used in German folk medicine for a century before it found its way into German asylums where it was considered an effective treatment of any number of symptoms, including mania and melancholy. One of its proponents was Karl Neumann whose mid-nineteenth century treatise on hydrotherapy enthusiastically described its use, both in insane asylums and in the hydro spas that were popular in his native Germany. An anonymous English physician who reviewed his book, however, was not nearly so impressed. He dismissed the alleged beneficial effects of the girdle on nothing more than the "principles of hocus pocus" ("Dr. K.G. Neumann," p. 73). Regardless, the girdle was used in asylums throughout Europe.

At the McLean Asylum in Boston, Massachusetts, the girdle was a particularly favored treatment for the female patient suffering from hysteria, neurasthenia or psychoneurosis, all of which were considered related to the female reproductive system. Theorizing that the abdominal skin had the most immediate reflex reaction with the abdominal viscera, the cold and the mild pressure of the girdle on the abdominal region was thought to ease cramping and "uterine restlessness," as well as regulate and relax the genital organ's function. The girdle was used there and in many other American asylums as late as the mid-twentieth century.

## Nightcap, or Wet Cap, or Ice Cap

A double linen cap either dipped in cold water or with shards of ice placed between its folds, or a bladder or clay cap filled with ice. The nightcap was placed on the shaved head of the patient to reduce irritation and fury, and to induce sleep. Its use was predicated on the theory that what generally was referred to as "mania," was caused by a plethora of blood in the brain. In the words of Joseph Mason Cox, medical superintendent of Fishponds, a large private asylum near Bristol, England, that excess produced "grotesque and incongruous catenations of thought, while the sense of sight, hearing, and feeling are morbidly affected" (Cox, p. 27). It also caused the patient "to retain heat with great tenacity" (p. 120), a symptom that could be easily relieved through the application of the nightcap.

To equalize the circulation of blood through the body, many physicians took the advice of Achille-Louis-François Foville, medical superintendent of the Saint-Yon Asylum in Rouen, France, and immersed the patient's feet or entire body in warm water while wearing the nightcap. Foville recommended the patient be kept in the warm bath for as long as two to three hours, and for many as two to three times a day, observing that anything less would increase, rather than decrease, agitation. He claimed so much success with this treatment that he boldly declared, *"la folie est curable."*

The nightcap was used in asylums throughout the world during the nineteenth century. Its use far outlasted the "plethora" theory of madness that had given rise to it in the first place.

## *Pail Douche, or Pail Pour, or Bain d'Affusion*

The pouring of pails of water of any temperature, or of alternating temperatures, over the head and shoulders of a patient who was kneeling, crouched over or restrained in a bath tub. The height from which the water fell was thought to moderate the intended effect, thus water poured from a short distance was considered more stimulating than water poured from a longer distance. The pail douche often was given just before bedtime, and its nightly administration over a period of two to three weeks was found particularly effective in easing the symptoms of melancholia and advanced dementia.

It had a decidedly punitive use, as well. At the Bicêtre in Paris, France, principal physician François Leuret used the pail douche to punish refusal to participate in the therapeutic regime he had set out. He described one such case, that of a patient named Mr. Dupré, a former army officer, who had adamantly refused his order to write the history of his own life:

> I now determined to employ my last and strongest arguments. I had the patient carried into the bath-room, undressed, and placed in a *baignoire;* two pails of water thrown over his body. On his promise to write, he was allowed to dress, but when dressed, he refused to keep his word. He was again placed in the bath, and *four* buckets of water poured over him. He again persisted he would write, again dressed, and again broke his promise; *eight* pails were then ordered to be brought, and when he saw them ranged before him, and had become convinced that I was likely to carry out my threat, he gave up further resistance, and devoted the rest of the day to writing his life in all its details [Tuke, 1858, pp. 551–552].

The pail douche was used in many European, British and American asylums well into the early twentieth century.

## *Pelvic Douche, or Perineal Douche, or Ascending Douche*

The direction of a forceful jet of 60° to 80° F. water for as long as ten continuous minutes at the genital area of the patient who was seated on a box or stool with an opening at the center. The pelvic douche was used primarily to relieve the plethora of blood and the hyperesthesia believed to be contributing causes of hysteria in women. The therapeutic was used in many asylums around the world.

By the time hydrotherapy had become the peerless remedy for almost all types of insanity in the mid-nineteenth century, the canonical assumption that hysteria was a uniquely women's affliction, a consequence of the wandering womb, had been successfully challenged by prominent French asylum physicians, such as Pierre Briquet of the Hôpital de la Charité and Jean Martin-Charcot at the Salpêtrière Asylum. Hysteria in men was assumed to have the same origin in the nervous system as that of women, and their symptoms—paralyses, limb contractures, seizures and hemianesthesias—were identical to women's, although more likely to be set off by physical, rather than emotional, traumas. The latter point is an important differentiation, and one that helps account for the fact that the pelvic or perineal douche was much more often administered to women than men: physical traumas were transient events that left their traces in the bodies of otherwise strong and reasonable men; emotional traumas were enduring events that left their traces in the bodies of otherwise weak and irrational women. Men, therefore, were thought to be able to "get over" hysteria, while women had to be treated for it.

While the pelvic douche was not often administered to hysterical men, it was to men whose insanity was thought to be either the cause or the effect of excessive masturbation. Maximilian Jacobi, director of the Seigburg asylum near Bonn, Germany, described in detail the case of J.R., who had been committed to the asylum in the early nineteenth century for restlessness, aggression and "vehement expressions of the will and propensities" ("Dr. Jacobi," p. 4). After dismissing an irregular excitement of the nervous system as the cause of his insanity, Jacobi determined that J.R. had been "excessively addicted to masturbation" (p. 4) since he was a boy. The plan of treatment was complicated, and involved a spare diet, active employment in the open air, sleeping in a straitjacket or camisole [see **Mechanical Restraints**] while being watched over by an attendant and, especially, cold douches on the perineum. The treatment regime was successful; J.R. refrained from masturbation for several months, and was released from the asylum.

## Prolonged Cold Bath, or The Soak

The placing of a restrained patient into a tub of continuously flowing 50° to 70° F. water; the patient typically remained in the tub for several continuous hours. The prolonged cold bath was said to have a sedative effect on the nervous system by contracting the capillaries and drawing the blood into the body and to the heart. Upon removal from it, the patient often was wrapped in a warm blanket until color had returned to the face and the lips were no longer blue. It was during this warming phase that the patient experienced the tonic effect of blood rushing back to the surface of the skin. This "perceptive shock to the nervous system" (Tuke, 1892, p. 118), however, had to be used repeatedly to produce lasting sedative benefits to the manic or agitated patient.

Michael Viszanik, medical director of continental Europe's oldest asylum for the insane, the Narrenturm, colloquially called the "Fools' Tower," in Vienna, Austria, claimed remarkable success with what he referred to as the cold water cure, stating that fully one-third of his patients were cured by it, and it alone. American physician Pliny Earle, who not only visited the Narrenturm, or the "Babel-Tower," as he dismissed it, but methodically reviewed its annual reports, argued that this remarkable cure rate could be attributed to the fact that all cases of delirium tremens and many of febrile delirium that had been admitted into the general hospital were immediately transferred to the Narrenturm and then conveniently rediagnosed as insanity. These disorders, which Earle argued were not insane at all, would have been quickly cured by Visznik's cold water cure.

The risks to patients of the prolonged cold bath were considerable. And patients feared it. Clarissa Caldwell Lathrop, who had been institutionalized at the Utica Asylum in New York, described the deaths of two women who had been subjected to it:

> Two women met their death from a "soak," as it was called, of five hours in cold water. One

of these, a Mrs. S., had never evinced the slightest indication of insanity beyond a depression natural to her imprisonment. She was a bright, refined little woman, and was pronounced sane and was to go home if she would sign a certain paper, which she protested frequently she would not sign as it disposed of her property in a way she did not approve. Finally, she did sign the paper, and directly after signing it a "soak" was prescribed for her. She died within a day or two. The other lady, a Mrs. J., was placed in the "soak" in a "camisole," a garment which rendered her perfectly helpless, and she died shortly afterwards [Lathrop, p. 207].

The prolonged cold bath was used well into the twentieth century. Frances Farmer, a well-known actress who had been involuntarily committed to the Western Washington State Hospital for the Insane in the mid-twentieth century was subjected to repeated prolonged baths which she loathed but that had their desired therapeutic effect. She vividly described the experience in her memoir:

> The trustee ...steered me... into a small room with three bathtubs. Before I could organize myself, the trustee had taken down three canvas straps from the hook on the wall and looped one around my chest, pinning my arms against my sides until my breath was cut short. The second was buckled around my thighs, the third around my ankles.... They picked me up, one by the ankles, the other by the shoulders and dropped me into the empty tub, bruising my spine...
> The first crash of icy water hit my ankles and slipped rapidly up my legs. I began to shake from the shock of it, screaming and thrashing my body under the sheet, but the more I struggled, the more I realized that I was helplessly restricted in a frozen hell...
> For the next twenty-four days I was depersonalized in hydro. The physical pain, the spiritual injury, the mental torture mashed one day into another, until all thoughts hinged on either being in or out the tub. Nothing else existed.... Hydro was prescribed for a three hour duration, but seldom did the treatments terminate on time, and the endless hours in cold water attacked my bowels and bladder. Lying in the water, with my nerves and system violated, knowing that my [menstrual] blood and waste were mingling with it, offended and grieved my spirit beyond description. My femininity was mauled, my power to reason or struggle vanished. I simply existed in chilling confusion.
> I was unnaturally calm at the end of three weeks, for I had been systematically de-energized. All personality was washed away and all that was left was a water-logged robot.
> I had been tamed [Farmer, p. 173].

## Salt Glow Bath

The placement of a patient in a tub of 104° to 115° F. water to which salt had been added. The patient was then vigorously rubbed for eight to ten minutes with salt crystals that had been dampened in the tub water until the body glowed, and then was rinsed with warm water. The salt glow bath had a tonic effect and was most often prescribed for cases of melancholia.

## Scotch Douche, or Douche Écossaise

The rapidly alternating sprays of cold and hot water shot through a pressured hose and directed at the back and the trunk of the patient. The Scotch douche was valued for its tonic and thermal effects on the body.

In his annual report to the Ohio legislature, O.O. Fordyee, medical superintendent of Athens State Hospital, described the use and the benefits of the Scotch douche in some detail:

> One of our favorite treatments is the modified Scotch douche, which is given as follows: Beginning at about 98 F., and gradually rising to 110–120° F., and covering a period of three or four minutes, then suddenly drop to about 70° and apply momentarily.... It is best to begin with ten or fifteen pounds of pressure and gradually increase with the tolerance of the patient to thirty of forty pounds, or even more.... I regard its use, given in connection with a preparatory treatment, such as a salt glow, wet sheet pack, tub bath, or cabinet bath, the most

active hydriatic tonic we have, and recommend its extensive employment in the convalescent, dementia praecox, functional neurosis, depressed states of manic depressive insanity after the patient has reached the state of subjective sufficiency, and, in fact, whenever a tonic agent is indicated. It is tonic, alternative, revulsive and calmative, and it good for anyone [Fordyee, p. 22].

By the mid-twentieth century, the use of hydrotherapy had gone out of vogue in asylums around the world and few asylum physicians shared Fordyee's enthusiastic declaration that the Scotch douche was "good for anyone." In his memoir of his psychiatric rotation at Manteno State Hospital near Chicago, Illinois, in the mid-twentieth century, Harvey Widroe's reaction reflected the new attitude that the Scotch douche was less therapeutic than it was punitive:

> [T]he door to the [Scotch douche] room burst open, admitting two burly attendants dragging a large man, thrashing and screaming, struggling against the straight jacket that bound his arms to his body.... Within almost no time at all, he was tightly secured to the metal post at the end of the room opposite the fire hoses. Aimed directly at him, the hoses were turned open full blast, and high pressure streams of water hit him from different angles. Assaulted by forceful torrents, he cursed and threatened for a minute or two and then began screaming and moaning. After a very long five minutes he slumped to the floor, now a silent and limp rag doll.... After a five minute interval the hoses were turned on again even though the patient appeared to have become docile.
>
> It may have made difficult patients more manageable, but I realized that this inhuman procedure was not treatment. This was torture! [Widroe, pp. 14–15].

## *Sea Water Injection, or Marine Plasma Injection, or Ocean Plasma Injection, or Quinton Plasma Injection*

The subcutaneous injection once every five to eight days, of an approximately 700 gram dose of diluted and cold-sterilized sea water that had been collected at least thirty-five miles from the shore. Lauded as a cure for everything from melancholia, to dementia, to epilepsy, sea water injection typically produced chills, thirst, loss of appetite, insomnia, weakness and slight nausea that lasted one to two days, followed by a gradual increase in improvement that culminated several days later in restoration, if not recovery.

French biologists, most notably Réne Quinton, promoted the therapeutic in the early twentieth century, based on two premises: that insanity was the result of some peculiar, but unidentified, toxin that infected the brain, and that sea water was 98 percent identical to blood. They hypothesized that by bathing cells in the plasma of sea water, in which all minerals on earth were concentrated, they would be purified and, if they had not already been irreparably damaged, restored to proper functioning. Quinton elaborated on the theory:

> Man is a marine animal by descent (like all animals). Now, in order to render to the human organism its primitive environment, which a long line of descent has modified, it is feasible to place it (the organism) in sea water, or its original environment. It is easy enough to admit that if infection is really the point of departure of mental maladies, it (infection) may be combated by marine serum, because using that means makes it possible to wash out the toxins which clog and destroy the central brain cells as rust, if allowed to rest upon the steel, clogs and ruins machinery, and that it may be possible to renew the strength of the brain cells by placing them in sea water ["Virtues of Sea Water," p. 496].

Quinton was an unabashed evolutionist and, in fact, often was referred to as the "French Darwin." It actually was his argument that sea water was the "original environment" of cells that provoked the strongest reaction, even from physicians who were willing to entertain his toxin theory of insanity. One of them, an anonymous American reviewer of Quinton's book titled, *L'eau de Mer Milieu Organique*, struck an uneasy compromise between belief and science by reminding readers that "the action of sea water is not divine.... Sea water is not the creator of human life, and therefore diseased brains... may be recuperated by the water of the sea, but not re-created if dead" ("Virtues of Sea Water," p. 496).

While Quinton and his colleagues demonstrated considerable success both in France and in Egypt in treating diarrhea, athrepsia and cholera in infants, and psoriasis and eczema in adults with sea water injections, the extent to which the insane recuperated at all was a matter of some contention among those French and Belgian asylum physicians who were experimenting in the early twentieth century with its use. Interest in sea water injection to treat insanity waned considerably over the years as a result. Despite a post–World War II revival of interest in the use of a vast range of products derived from Quinton's Plasma, such as isotonics, hypertonics, nasal and dermo-sprays in health spas and alternative medicine clinics in Europe and North America, there was no concomitant revival of interest in treating insanity with sea water injection or any of the derivative products.

## *Shower Bath, or Rain Bath, or Spray Douche*

A modification of the douche, that delivered water through a rose-shaped nozzle in the form of a spray rather than a stream. The advantages of the shower bath over the prolonged bath were considerable, and guaranteed its steady implementation in asylums around the world. Because the water did not remain in contact with the body, the shower bath produced an initial shock to the patient, the recovery from which required a greater, and more restorative, expenditure of physiological energy than that required by the prolonged bath. The descending water also assured that the patient did not have prolonged contact with his or her own dirt and disease. Cheaper to construct than a bath tub and, because it used less water, cheaper to use, the shower bath was considered an efficient and effective asylum therapeutic for both mania and melancholia.

It was not always a safe therapeutic, however. When first used in European asylums, the shower bath subjected the patient, who was unaccustomed to such an ablution, to twenty to thirty continuous minutes of rapidly descending water. The risk of death from shock was unexpectedly high.

The 1856 death of a pauper patient by the name of Daniel Dolley, confined in the Surrey County Lunatic Asylum in south London, and the vigorous defense of the shower bath as a therapeutic by Charles Snape, the physician who had ordered it, illustrates how risk was imagined and negotiated in an asylum. Dolley had been subjected to a twenty-eight minute shower bath that had put him a "state of vital depression"; upon his removal, he was administered a two grain dose of tartaremetic (Winslow, p. 1). He died shortly after. Snape was indicted for willful negligence, unskillful and unscientific treatment that caused Dolley's death. The grand jury, however, threw out the indictment and Snape was reinstated to his position in the asylum. The reinstatement left unresolved the larger question as whether the shower bath could be considered "a safe, efficient, judicious, and curative process of treatment" (p. 2). The nature of the shower bath, in this case, was a matter of dispute. A civil engineer, hired by the Commissioners in Lunacy who were involved in the case, had estimated that an average of twenty gallons of water per minute fell on Dolley; a civil engineer hired by Snape had estimated that it was no more than four-and-a-half gallons per minute. While the exact nature of the shower bath remained unresolved, the larger issue of the risk asylum physicians should take in treating the insane prompted considerable debate. Snape argued that:

> The science of medicine in all its branches will ever be a science of unusual difficulty and doubt, from the necessity of treatment being based upon "surmise"; and, after all, he is the ablest practitioner who guesses most correctly, and assumes most justly the real seat and na-

ture of the disease to be grappled with. But it is still "surmise"; and if in the treatment of bodily ailments there be so much doubt, how much greater is the doubt in references to mental disease? [Winslow, pp. 4–5].

The reaction to this statement was swift. "The profession of medicine would indeed be reduced to a very low ebb, and the practitioner of this exalted art would be in a humiliating position," Forbes Winslow argued, "if the noble science which he cultivates and practices were based upon *'guesses,' 'assumptions,'* and *'surmises'*" (Winslow, p. 5). Yet even Winslow, an expert on insanity and a vocal critic of the inhumane treatment of the insane, acknowledged that the specialization of asylum medicine was being practiced in the absence of a complete understanding of insanity, and with the hope that "fresh resources" eventually will cure it. Snape had defended the shower bath as one of those "fresh resources," and had castigated his fellow asylum physicians for not taking the risk in using it.

In the end, the Lunacy Commission ruled that the duration of the shower bath should not exceed three minutes, that it should not be used punitively, and that tartar emetic should not be administered after it. The larger, and more pressing, scientific and philosophical controversy over the state of asylum medicine, however, was left unresolved.

In the United States, the shower bath was an integral feature of the public health and hygiene movement. Simon Baruch, a physician who went on to become a professor of hydrotherapy at Columbia University's College of Physicians and Surgeons, was the driving force behind the building of public bath houses in New York City, and the first institutional shower bath in that city's Juvenile Asylum. His passionate promotion of the therapeutic drew the attention of Amariah Brigham, medical superintendent of the Utica State Hospital in upstate New York who set up a shower bath facility in the former bakery on the asylum grounds in the late nineteenth century. The facility had four rows of eight feet high showers with nickel-plated brass nozzles that sprayed seven-and-a-half gallons of water per minute at twenty-five pounds of pressure.

With its growing use in asylums around the world, the shower bath was subjected to recommendations beyond that concerning its duration. It was proposed that it be administered only in the morning at least an hour after breakfast, in that its tonic effect was likely to interfere with sleep if administered later in the day or in the evening. To prevent fainting, it was advised that the patient sit on a stool or lean forward from a standing position so that the water descended on the neck, rather than the head. A vigorous rubbing of the patient with a coarse towel or flesh brush was recommended after the shower, and was to be followed by gentle exercise. The shower baths of various duration, pressure and temperature were used in asylums around the world until the mid-twentieth century.

## *Sitz Bath, or Hip Bath, or Half Bath*

A small tub of approximately 98° F. water in which the patient sat so that only the pelvic portion of the body was submerged, while the legs were bent over the rim of the tub. Originally, the sitz bath was prescribed for the female patient whose insanity was thought to be caused by, or resulted in, dysmenorrhea or amenorrhea. By congesting the blood vessels in the pelvic viscera, the sitz bath stimulated the flow of menstrual blood. The treatment usually commenced two to three days before the expected menstrual period and continued for a week; it often was repeated the following month.

## *Spinal Douche, or Charcot Douche*

Invented by Karl Wilhelm Ideler of the Berlin Charité Hospital in the early nineteenth century. The spinal douche directed a jet of cold water against the patient's spine for several continuous minutes. Ideler, a proponent of what was then called the "psychic school" of thought that took a philosophical approach to insanity, viewing it as a result of moral failings, argued that the spinal douche was effective in disciplining the patient to the norm of reason, thus it was effective both as punishment and a therapeutic.

Upon his visit to the Berlin Charité, British physician William F. Cumming was quite taken aback by the use of this "cruel remedy" which he described in detail:

> This cruel remedy is resorted to on alternate days in every case, male and female, when its use is not contraindicated by complications of epilepsy, phthisis, or paralysis; and it is administered in the following manner:—
>
> Between 10 and 11 A.M. the patients are placed singly in an empty bath, furnished with a formidable array of straps and buckles, to secure them during the torture. A small jet of cold water is forced out of a pump by the combined strength of four men, against the spinal column, along which it is made to play for the space of two minutes. The victim is then released, and his place occupied by another. My [host] acknowledged to me that the pain of this discipline was excessive. He had himself made trial of it, and with all his resolution could hardly support it for thirty seconds. On my remarking on the cruelty of the practice, he said, that many of the patients, notwithstanding their great dislike to the douche, derived much benefit from its use, and confessed that they felt better and more comfortable on the days of its application than on the intervening days [Cumming, p. 18].

During his tour, Cumming came across no other German asylum in which the spinal douche was, or had been, used. In fact, most asylums physicians dismissed it out of hand, relegating it to the imaginings of a "clever and enthusiastic man, whose better judgment was in this instance warped by a favourite theory" (Cumming, p. 19). The comment could be read both as a condemnation of the spinal douche as a therapeutic, and of the German psychic school of medicine that by the time of Cumming's visit had been usurped by a biological approach to insanity.

Although Cumming was quick to conclude that the spinal douche only was used at the Berlin Charité, it was in fact used in asylums throughout Europe as well as the United States. In fact, it was used with such therapeutic enthusiasm at the Salpêtrière Asylum in Paris, France, for the treatment of hysteria, that it was known there as the Charcot Douche, after the legendary neurologist and chief physician, Jean-Martin Charcot. It was at the Salpêtrière that Charcot aimed a jet of 45° to 60° F. water, at twenty to thirty pounds pressure, at a small section of the hysterical patient's spine for less than thirty seconds. While far from the only therapeutic used in the treatment of hysteria at the Salpêtrière, the spinal douche was touted as a method of stimulating the nervous system and redistributing nervous energy through the body. The Charcot Douche now is used in spas, especially in Eastern Europe, rather than in asylums, although for the same purpose.

The spinal douche also was used in American asylums, but with some variation: the jet was of warm water or of pulsating cold water, the duration was only a few seconds, and it typically was used in combination with other hydrotherapy therapeutics.

## *Tepid Bath, or Warm Bath*

A contested treatment in which the restrained patient was lowered in a hammock into a tub where there was a continuous flow of 85° to 95° F. water. The tepid bath, usually several hours in duration, was recommended by a number of physicians for the treatment of recent onset mania or melancholia. Joseph Mason Cox, medical superintendent of the Fishpond Asylum near Bristol, England, claimed much success in treating mania by enticing the patient into a tepid bath that had been infused with rosemary or other aromatic plants; John Thurnam, resident physician at the York Retreat in northern England, claimed the same success in treating melancholia when mild stimulants such as soap or salt were added. At the Salpêtrière Asylum in Paris, France, the weekly, and sometimes daily, tepid bath was the preferred treatment for hysteria. It was there that Etienne-Jean Georget found the tepid bath particularly useful for diminishing the excitement, dissipating the tension, and calming the nervous organs of the hysterical patient.

In the United States the most prominent proponent of the tepid bath was Simon Baruch. As a visiting physician to St. Elizabeths Hospital in Washington, D.C., he made sure it became a significant feature of the asylum's hydrotherapy program. Between 1923 and 1924 alone, nearly 109,000 tepid baths were given to 4000 patients at this federal asylum.

Some detractors, however, found it difficult to comprehend the rationale for using a tepid bath at all, reasoning that since water temperature was below body temperature, the bath "does not raise the temperature of the body, and can give rise to no reaction, and cannot affect the circulation in the central nervous ganglia" (Tuke, 1892, p. 118). Taking an even more dismissive attitude, Philippe Pinel, physician of the infirmaries at the Hospice of Bicêtre near Paris, France, argued that the tepid bath produced such debilitation that it risked rendering the patient incurable.

## Turkish Bath, or Hot Air Bath

A continuous flow of 160° to 190° F. steamy air that circulated through a tiled room in which the patient sat. The purpose of the Turkish or hot air bath was to cause intense perspiration that softened the skin, increased circulation, and encouraged deep and refreshing sleep. The Turkish bath, or Haman, long a tradition in Middle Eastern culture as well as a therapeutic in that region's asylums, was introduced in Great Britain by David Urquhart. A diplomat who had traveled extensively through the Middle East, Urquhart not only wanted to popularize that region's culture, but address both the personal hygiene and health concerns of the British people. To that end, he built a Turkish bath at the St. Anne's Hill Hydropathic Establishment near Blarney, Ireland, in the mid-nineteenth century. An immensely popular component of what became known as "the water cure," the Turkish bath was thought to cure everything from cancer to baldness.

Thomas Power, resident physician of the nearby Cork District Lunatic Asylum, speculated that the Turkish bath might also cure insanity. He had one constructed and reported with great enthusiasm the results of the first 124 patients who had been treated by it: ten had been cured and released; two had been cured, released, but relapsed; fifty-two had improved significantly; sixty, most of whom had been long-term patients of the asylum, remained unchanged. On the basis of these data, Power ventured that cure rates would double if all asylums administered Turkish baths to patients.

In addition to its curative effect, Power found that the Turkish bath had one other decided advantage: it all but eradicated the noxious odor of the insane. He, along with many of his colleagues, theorized that the peculiar and disgusting stench of the insane was "exhaled from the skin and its minute glands and follicles" and that it must have arisen from "an unhealthy state of the blood, which must exercise a deleterious influence on the system generally, and on the organs connected with operations of the mind in particular." The Turkish bath, he reasoned, removed the "vitiated humours and other secretions and probably cures the diseased and tainted system where other means have failed" (Power, p. 3).

In the wake of this report, Turkish baths were installed in asylums across Great Britain. Urquhart designed a magnificent panopticon style bath for the Colney Hatch Asylum, the largest in the country, but financial constraints significantly altered its scale. Nonetheless, medical director Edgar Sheppard, reported that eight of the ten patients to whom it was first administered were cured and released. The case of one of those patients who was released as cured after two months of institutionalization and several Turkish baths, was presented as follows:

> W.S.N., 30 admitted 1865, with delusions, aural hallucinations, great depression of spirits, and impaired memory. Received a great shock two months ago by the death of his only child. He thinks the child has been taken away by women, and will be restored to him. Complains of constant pain in his head and of sleepless nights, when he fancies the child is under the bed. At times is quite confused and stupid; bowels costive, tongue furred, skin harsh and dry.... Was taken to the Turkish bath, temperature 180°. In about twenty-five minutes the patient was bathed in profuse perspiration; expressed satisfaction and enjoyment, pain in the head being the only drawback.... Dropped asleep in the cooling room, where animated conversation was going on, fifteen minutes after reclining on the couch, and woke up decidedly relieved. Said his skin felt as it never felt before—soft, supple, and clean. Went to bed at 8 p.m. *without an opiate,* and slept soundly to 5 a.m. on the following morning [Sheppard, pp. 75–76].

Although Sheppard saw no drawbacks to the Turkish bath, some of his British colleagues did. John Bucknill was not particularly impressed with its therapeutic outcomes at the Devon County Asylum where he was medical superintendent. He wrote that the Turkish bath was "more calculated to improve the health of chronic and incurable patients than to act remedially on those whose malady is recent and curable, or at most that its role will be to supplement methods of treatment which are capable of being applied more constantly" (p. 744). He, just as other skeptics, was inclined to worry that if the Turkish bath was used too often it would become "a luxurious and wholesome habit rather than a remedy" (Buknill & Tuke, p. 744).

With the construction of municipal water systems, the Turkish bath became part of the hydrotherapeutics of a number of asylums around the world. Charles Shepard, a public health physician, was its most prominent promoter in the United States, arguing that this simple and inexpensive therapeutic purified the blood and relieved its congestion in the brain. He was instrumental in the building of a facility in the New York City Asylum for the Insane where 2280 Turkish baths were administered in 1873 alone.

Over the decades since its introduction in the Cork District Lunatic Asylum, enthusiasm over the Turkish bath waned as the claims of its curative power were challenged. By the mid-twentieth century, and with the advent of Thorazine and other neuroleptic drugs, the administration of the Turkish bath all but disappeared as an asylum therapeutic.

## *Vapor Bath, or Russian Bath, or Steam Bath, or Cabinet Bath*

The subjection of the body of the patient to the action of steam in a closed chamber. The vapor bath was used in some asylums less as a specific therapeutic for insanity than for the relief of physical complications, such as rheumatism or dropsy (edema), experienced by many asylum patients. The 120° F. temperature did not produce the sedative effect of the Turkish bath and therefore was considered less exhausting to the patient.

# Hypothermia (Cold Narcosis, Refrigeration Therapy, Frozen Sleep)

*The therapeutic lowering of body temperature for a prolonged period.*

Influenced by the writings of the ancient medical authority Hippocrates, eighteenth and early nineteenth century asylum physicians applied ice packs to the shaved heads of their patients. Hippocrates had posited that if patients were covered with mud, the parts of their bodies that dried first were the warmest, and where there was excessive heat, there was disease. For early asylum physicians insanity was a disease of the brain, therefore a perfectly sensible therapeutic intervention was to cool the heads of their insane patients.

Cooling techniques proliferated during the nineteenth century. The British physician George Mann Burrows, for example, suggested that in addition to ice packs, drops of ether, diluted alcohol, or a mixture of spirits, vinegar and water would produce a "calming and even soporific effect in violent mania" (Burrows, p. 595). Asylum physicians also sprayed their patients with cold water douches, forced them to swallow pints of cold water, wrapped them in cold wet sheets, and restrained them in cold baths in order to relieve the "feverish" symptoms of their insanity [see **Hydrotherapy**]. They also swung them to and fro on hammocks while pouring cold water on their heads [see **Rotation, Oscillation and Vibration**], and plunged them into vats of cold water to gather up their senses [see **Salutary Fear**].

It was, in fact, the plunging of insane patients into cold water that was cited by McLean Asylum physicians John Talbot and Kenneth Tillotson as a precedent for inducing hypothermia in patients with schizophrenia. At that time, the early 1940s, hypothermia was being used to treat some forms of cancer as well as drug addiction, and although it was much too early to determine its effectiveness in either case, the two physicians were determined to use it to treat the asylum's most intractable patients. They began with ten patients. Each was sedated with a barbiturate and a muscle relaxer, and wrapped in a Therm-O-Rite blanket, also known as a "mummy bag," through which the physicians circulated a refrigerant. A stomach tube pumped glucose into each patient and a rectal thermometer transmitted body temperature readings every other minute. So wrapped, the patients, whose body temperatures dropped an average of 15° F, stayed in a hypothermia-induced stupor for as long as sixty-eight continuous hours.

The patients had been chosen for their failure to respond to other therapeutics, such as insulin and metrazol, yet several reacted to the induced hypothermia with either a "persistent and reassuring modification of the mental picture," or with a "temporary or quasi-permanent" modification (Talbot & Tillotson, p. 123). The physicians presented the case of S.R., a sixteen-year-old who had been diagnosed with catatonic schizophrenia, as an example of one of the four patients for whom the treatment's effects were positive and enduring. After the hypothermia treatment, during which his body temperature dropped to 92° F, he became quiet, polite and friendly. His hallucinations and "queer ideas" disappeared, and after several months he was discharged as cured (p. 122). One of the three additional patients for whom the effects were temporary was H.M., a thirty-nine-year-old woman who had been diagnosed with paranoid schizophrenia a decade before. She was wrapped in the Therm-O-Rite blanket until her body temperature dropped to 74.6° F. The treatment left her "less aggressive for a few days," but she regressed to her pretreatment condition before the end of the week (p. 119).

Two more of the patients in this trial run of therapeutic hypothermia were not at all affected by the treatment. Talbot and Tillotson hypothesized they may have experienced an "irreparable morphological damage to the central nervous system" as a result of having had schizophrenia for some time (p. 126) and that that had rendered them resistant to the treatment. The remaining patient, a forty-eight-year-old man who was kept in a hypothermic stupor for fifty continuous hours, died of circulatory collapse as his body temperature rose from 80° F to 92° F towards the end of the treatment.

On the basis of this initial trial with ten patients, Talbot and Tillotson believed therapeutic hypothermia held out a "modicum of hope" in the treatment of schizophrenia (p. 126), particularly that of relatively short duration. That "modicum of hope," however may have been too tiny to make hypothermia a really promising intervention for most asylum physicians. Its risks were considerable. A temperature of 95° F is required for normal metabolism and bodily functions and the reduction required by the therapeutic literally brought patients to a state of near-death. The consequences such a state could have for patients were considerable. Two Longview State Hospital physicians found that out when they initiated their own version of what they called "refrigeration therapy." Douglas Goldman and Maynard Murray chose sixteen patients whose schizophrenia was intractable from the Cincinnati, Ohio asylum. They placed them, already packed in ice, into cooled cabinets, kept them refrigerated for as long as forty-eight continuous hours, and dropped their body temperatures to 84° F. Three of the patients died of pneumonia, and most of the others suffered a variety of physical complaints, including serious lung infections. None demonstrated any lasting change in schizophrenic symptoms. The physicians conceded "with a sense of keen disappointment" that refrigeration therapy did not meet expectations (Goldman & Murray, p. 165).

Nor did it meet the expectations of Thomas Hoen and his colleagues at the Central Islip State Hospital in New York. They administered therapeutic hypothermia to thirteen patients diagnosed with schizophrenia, rapidly reducing their body temperature to 85° F at which time the refrigerating machine was turned off. In most cases the temperature dropped another three degrees over the following hour before slowly rising. Although the use of the therapeutic gave Hoen and his colleagues some insight into the physiological consequences of induced hypothermia, the clinical results were not significant.

Hoen and his colleagues hypothesized that it was not the therapeutic but the patients that were the problem in attaining good outcomes. They conjectured that hypothermia might very well be more effective with patients who had a better prognosis than the intractable schizophrenics for whom the therapeutic originally was designed. In fact, James Spradley and M. Marin-Foucher had already given that a try. The Trenton State Hospital physicians had treated thirty patients variously diagnosed with schizophrenia, manic-depression, involutional psychosis, and psychosis with mental deficiency, wrapping them in Therm-O-Rite blankets to maintain steady body temperatures of 90° F for anywhere from forty-eight to seventy-two continuous hours.

One patient, a twenty-eight-year-old woman who had been diagnosed with manic-depression, not only improved remarkably but rapidly; she was discharged a month after her hypothermia treatment, her anxiety, anorexia, and flights of ideas gone completely. Fourteen more patients improved enough to be released as well; the remaining patients all showed improvement, although the term "improvement" remained undefined and unmeasured.

Spradley and Marin-Foucher were optimistic about the outcomes and predicted that the curative power of induced hypothermia would be boosted if patients could only be kept longer than seventy-two hours in frozen sleep without the significant risk of vascular damage. Although they acknowledged that there were "a multitude of other details to be solved" (Spradley & Marin-Foucher, p. 238), they concluded that the possibilities offered by hypothermia "appear to be unlimited" (p. 238).

None of that possibility was realized. The few asylum physicians who induced hypothermia in their patients were faced with lackluster outcomes, and were never able to develop a scientific rationale as to why the therapeutic was not working or, for that matter, why it should have worked in the first place. With the exception of a few sporadic attempts to test its efficacy, induced hypothermia all but disappeared as an asylum therapeutic by the mid-twentieth century.

In the end, though, it may have been something else that hastened its disappearance. Writing just four years after the end of World War II, and three years after the Nuremberg trials of Nazi physicians, Spradley and Marin-Foucher had cited the Dachau experiments in which concentration camp prisoners were subjected to freezing conditions as precedent for the therapeutic use of hypothermia with asylum patients. Although quick to condemn the experiments as "iniquitous attempts ...inspired by the perverted mind of Heinrich Himmler" (p. 235), they just as quickly lauded them as "the most complete investigations in the biophysiological field" (p. 235). This curious acknowledgment left Spradley, Marin-Foucher and other asylum physicians practicing hypothermia, or interested in doing so, vulnerable to invidious comparisons, and that most surely hastened the disappearance of the therapeutic from asylum practice.

### References

Beam, A. (2001). *Gracefully insane: The rise and fall of America's premier mental hospital.* New York: PublicAffairs.

Burrows, G.M. (1828). *Commentaries on the causes, forms, symptoms, and treatment, moral and medical, of insanity.* London: Thomas and George Underwood.

Goldman, D., and Murray, M. (1943). Studies on the use of refrigeration therapy in mental disease with report of 16 cases. *Journal of Nervous and Mental Disease, 97,* 152–165.

Hoen, T.I., Morello, A., and O'Neill, F.J. (1957). Hypothermia (cold narcosis) in the treatment of schizophrenia. *Psychiatric Quarterly, 1,* 696–702.

Spradley, J.B., and Marin-Foucher, M. (1949). Hypothermia: A new treatment of psychiatric disorders. *Diseases of the Nervous System, 10,* 235–238.

Talbott, J.H., and Tillotson, K.J. (1941). The effects of cold on mental disorders. A study of ten patients suffering from schizophrenia and treated with hypothermia. *Diseases of the Nervous System, 2,* 116–126.

# Isolation

*The physical and social separation of a patient from the rest of the asylum population.*

Isolation was, and arguably still is, the leitmotif of insanity. In the pre-asylum era the insane often were confined in the attics and cellars of their own homes, present in a physical sense, yet absent from the daily interactions of their family members. Such was the case in Ireland, as an example, in the decades before the building of the first asylum:

> There is nothing so shocking as madness in the cabin of the Irish peasant, where the man is out laboring in the fields for his bread and the care of the woman of the house is scarcely sufficient for attendance on the children. When a strong man or woman gets the complaint, the only way they have to manage is by making a hole in the floor of the cabin, not high enough for the person to stand up in, with a crib over it to prevent his getting up. The hole is about five feet deep, and they give this wretched being his food there, and there he generally dies [Letchworth, p. 172].

Those without families often were left to wander the countryside alone, begging for food and shelter. Some were even licensed to do so. In England, insane patients who had gained a modicum of their senses while in the care of London's Bethlem Asylum were released to fend for their own. Their left arms adorned with an armlet of tin that was the official "license" that distinguished them from the "sturdy beggars" who were otherwise fit and able to work, they drifted around the country, begging for food and for drink that would be poured into the hollowed out ox horn they had strung around their necks.

Even in the almshouses, poor houses, workhouses and hospices that sprung up to separate the destitute, disabled and disorderly from rapidly modernizing society, the insane were often separated from other residents. Then, if they were particularly difficult to manage, they were further separated from each other by confinement in solitary pens, stalls and purpose-built "lunatic boxes."

The nineteenth century boom in asylum construction might be understood as having resolved that leitmotif of isolation. After all, it was in these institutions that the insane were congregated. Yet, by reading history against the grain, asylums as brick-and-mortar institutions also could be understood as perpetuating isolation. Consider their locations. It is a fact that there were plenty of urban asylums; centrally situated, only walls, fences and gates isolated their patients from the sociability of daily interactions and the hustle and bustle of daily commerce. Yet, the majority of asylums were built as far from urban centers as possible. Essential to the Kirkbride Plan that guided the construction of public asylums in the United States, for example, rural locations were essential to the regime of moral treatment [see **Moral Treatment**]. As Thomas Kirkbride himself declared:

> It should never be forgotten, that every object of interest that is placed in or about a hospital for the insane, that even every tree that buds, or every flower that blooms, may contribute in its small measure to excite a new train of thought, and perhaps be the first step towards bringing to reason, the morbid wanderings of a disordered mind [Kirkbride, p. 47].

Kirkbride, no stranger to insanity as he was the superintendent of the Pennsylvania Hospital for the Insane, was not just waxing rhapsodic on the rural idyll, but also suggesting that isolation of insane patients from the stresses and strains of their familiar lives was therapeutic. So therapeutic was this isolation from "precipitating influences"—families, work, social interactions—thought to be that asylum physicians with perhaps a soupçon more imagination than Kirkbride whimsically proposed that asylums should isolate the insane from *everything* familiar by becoming, themselves, completely unfamiliar. Such was the desire of François Emmanuel Fodéré, then physician to the Marseille Lunatic Asylum in France:

> I would like these [asylums] to be built in sacred forests, in steep and solitary places, amid great upheavals, like the Grande-Chartreuse.... It will often be useful for the latest arrival to be brought down by machines, for him to traverse ever new and astonishing places before he reaches his destination; the ministers of these places should wear special costumes!...Phantasmagoria and the other resources of physics, music, water, lightning, thunder, etc., would be used by turns...[Asylums must] offer to the senses of the insane objects entirely different from those to which they were accustomed, new faces, other furnishings, other sites, other manners, a total change, finally, in all the objects that surround them [Fodéré, p. 215].

That was nothing more than ripe imagining, but the fact remained that the geographic and social isolation of asylums also made possible the therapeutic control of insane patients, impressing upon them what the French asylum physician Philippe Pinel termed "the deep and durable conviction of [their] dependence" (Pinel, p. 105). To that end, isolation also was used behind the walls of brick-and-mortar asylums as a therapeutic intervention. The dingy cells, dark pits and padded rooms became the sites of uncontested medical power: social contact, food, light, space, temperature, activity were controlled within their walls to achieve therapeutic ends.

As is true with many therapeutics, reputation tarnished with age. In the twentieth century and beyond isolation was used less frequently and the conditions of it were improved considerably. Patients were confined in what was being referred to as "limited containment suites," and their health, both mental and physical, was carefully monitored on a daily basis. But a new phrase had been introduced in many countries in contemporary times, one that would have been foreign to asylum physicians of the past but that would have captured the concerns that occasionally were being voiced about isolating patients in cells and strong rooms. That new phrase is "human rights." It signifies a different understanding about insanity and more particularly about those who experience it. Patients in many countries no longer suffer a civil death with their confinement, but have rights that are both protected and enforced by law. In the United States, for example, both federal and state legislation mandate that isolation only be used in emergencies to protect asylum staff and other patients; while laws do not cap the consecutive days patients can be so detained, or at least allow for exceptions if they do, they do require that physicians approve each twenty-four hour segment.

During the latter part of the twentieth century, the deinstitutionalization initiative in the United States, Great Britain and much of Europe decanted most asylum patients into communities and created a new model of community-based care. In many poor and developing countries, however, the asylum-based model persists to this day, and it is in those countries that isolation as a therapeutic strategy *cum* social control mechanism *cum* torture device *cum* expression of indifference is also being recast as a human rights issue. The advocacy efforts of Disability Rights International has brought to light the plight of asylum patients in Paraguay, for example, by exposing the isolation of two adolescent males in cells containing only wooden benches and holes in the floor as latrines. Although each had been allowed four hours every other day in an outdoor pen littered with garbage and human excrement, they had remained in isolation cells for more than four years. Other Paraguayan asylum patients shared their plight. The organization's exposure of the continued use of isolation led to a 2005 agreement with the Paraguayan government to release patients confined in the country's asylums and to integrate them into newly developed community-based service networks.

### References

Arens, K. (1996). Wilhelm Griesinger: Psychiatry between philosophy and praxis. *Philosophy, Psychiatry, & Psychology, 3,* 146–163.

Arnold, C. (2008). *Bedlam: London and its mad.* London: Simon & Schuster.

Bartlett, P. (1998). The asylum, the workhouse, and the voice of the insane poor in nineteenth century England. *International Journal of Law and Psychiatry, 21,* 421–432.

Beers, C.W. (1908). *A mind that found itself.* New York: Longmans, Green, and Co.

Coleborne, C. (2009). Challenging institutional hegemony: Family visitors to hospitals for the insane in Australia and New Zealand, 1880s–1910s. In G. Mooney and J. Reinarz (eds.), *Permeable walls: Historical perspectives on hospital and asylum visiting,* pp. 289–307. Amsterdam: Rodopi.

Coleborne, C., and MacKinnon, D. (eds.). (2003). *Madness in Australia: Histories, heritage and the asylum.* Queensland, Australia: University of Queensland Press.

Committee of the General Assembly (1883). *Report of the Committee of the General Assembly appointed to investigate the charges against Dixmont Insane Asylum and the affairs of the Western Penitentiary.* Harrisburg, PA: Lane S. Hart.

Committee of Visitors (1875). *Annual report of the Newcastle-Upon-Borough Lunatic asylum.* Newcastle-Upon-Tyne, UK: Daily Journal Office.

Conolly, J. (1856). *The treatment of the insane without mechanical restraints.* London: Smith, Elder & Co.

de Young, M. (2010). *Madness: An American history of mental illness and its treatment.* Jefferson, NC: McFarland.

Earle, P. (1853). *Institutions for the insane in Prussia, Austria, and Germany.* Utica, NY: New York State Lunatic Asylum.

Engstrom, E. (2003). *Clinical psychiatry in imperial Germany.* Ithaca, NY: Cornell University Press.

Esquirol, J.E.D. (1838). *Mental maladies: A treatise on insanity.* Trans. E.K. Hunt. Philadelphia: Lea and Blanchard.

Fodéré, F.E. (1817). *Traité du délire.* Paris: Croullebois.

Gauchet, M., and Swain, G. (1999). *Madness and democracy: The modern psychiatric universe.* Trans. C. Porter. Princeton, NJ: Princeton University Press.

Goldberg, A. (2002). The Mellage trial and the politics of insane asylums in Wilhelmine Germany. *Journal of Modern History, 74,* 1–32.

Haviland, C.F. (1915). *The treatment and care of the insane in Pennsylvania.* Philadelphia: Public Charities Association of Pennsylvania.

Haw, C.M. (1989). John Conolly and the treatment of the mentally ill in Victorian England. *Psychiatric Bulletin, 13,* 440–444.

Hippius, H., Möller, J., Müller, N., and Neundörfer-Kohl, G. (2008). *The University Department of Psychiatry in Munich.* Munich: Springer Medizin Verlag Heidelberg.

Kaufman, D. (1999). Science as cultural practice: Psychiatry in the First World War and Weimar Germany. *Journal of Contemporary History, 34,* 125–144.

Kelm, M.L. (1994). Women, families and the Provincial Hospital for the Insane, British Columbia, 1905–1915. *Journal of Family History, 19,* 177–193.

Kirkbride, T.S. (1842). *Annual report of the Pennsylvania Hospital for the Insane.* Philadelphia: John C. Clark.

Lerner, P. (2003). *Hysterical men: War, psychiatry, and the politics of trauma in Germany, 1890–1930.* Ithaca, NY: Cornell University Press.

Letchworth, W.P. (1889). *The insane in foreign countries.* New York: G.P. Putnam's Sons.

Lisman, G.L., and Parr, A. (2005). *Bittersweet memories: A history of the Peoria State Hospital.* Victoria, BC, Canada: Trafford.

Mental Disability Rights International (2007). *Ruined lives: Segregation from society in Argentina's psychiatric asylums.* Washington, D.C.: Author.

Micale, M.S. (1985). The Salpêtrière in the age of Charcot: An institutional perspective on medical history in the late nineteenth century. *Journal of Contemporary History, 20,* 703–731.

Michigan State Board of Corrections and Charities (1895/1896). *Thirteenth biennial report.* Lansing, MI: Robert Smith Printing Co.

Mitchell, S.W. (1908). The treatment by rest, seclusion, etc. in relation to psychotherapy. *Journal of the American Medical Association, 25,* 2033–2037.

Morison, A. (1848). *Outlines of lectures on the nature, causes and treatment of insanity.* London: Longman, Green, and Longman's.

Museum of Dr. Guislain (2012). *Neither rhyme nor reason: History of psychiatry.* Tielt, Belgium: Lannoo Publishing.

Noll, R. (2007). *The encyclopedia of schizophrenia and other psychotic disorders.* New York: Facts on File.

Perfect, W. (1800). *Annals of insanity.* London: Chalmers.

Philo, C. (2004). *A geographical history of institution provision for the insane from Medieval times to the 1860s in England and Wales.* Lewiston, NY: Edwin Mellen Press.

Pinel, P. (1806). *A treatise on insanity.* Trans. D.D. Davis. Sheffield, UK: W. Todd.

Ptok, U., and Dilling, H. (1999). The psychiatrists Oscar Wattenberg and Johannes Enge and the history of psychiatry in the Hanseatic city of Lübeck between 1900 and 1945. *History of Psychiatry, 10,* 319–328.

"The restraint system in French public asylums for the insane" (1865). *British Journal of Psychiatry, 11,* 442–443.

Robertson, G.M. (1901). Note on the use of padded room and the practice of locking up patients by day in single rooms. *Philadelphia Medical Journal, 57,* 195–199.

Rush, B. (1830). *Medical inquiries and observations upon the diseases of the mind,* 4th ed. Philadelphia: John Grigg.

Sandwith, F.M. (1889). The Cairo Lunatic Asylum. *Journal of Mental Science, 34,* 473–490.

Savill, T. (1889). *Clinical lectures on diseases of the nervous system delivered at the infirmary of la Salpêtrière by Professor J.-M. Charcot.* London: The New Sydenham Society.

Silverman, J.A. (1997). Charcot's comments on the therapeutic role of isolation in the treatment of anorexia nervosa. *International Journal of Eating Disorders, 21,* 295–298.

Tuke, S. (1813). *Description of the Retreat, an institution near York, for insane persons of the Society of Friends.* York, UK: W. Alexander.

"Use Colors to Cure Insane" (1902, October 26). *New York Times,* p. 25.

Zilborg, G. (1948). Russian psychiatry—Its historical and ideological background. *Bulletin of the New York Academy of Medicine, 19,* 713–728.

## Basses-Loges, *or* La Chapelle

The subterranean cells of the Salpêtrière and the Bicêtre Asylums, respectively. The cells of the Paris, France, asylums were notorious. Tiny and dank, with straw-covered planks for sleeping and sitting attached to the wall, they were lit by small holes over the doors through which food was passed to the patients who were likely also to be chained, fettered or restrained in an iron collar [see **Mechanical Restraints**]. The *basses-loges* were particularly loathsome in that they were on the same level as the sewer system; when the Seine River swelled with rain, sewer rats made their way into the cells and bit the restrained patients.

An early eighteenth century visitor to Paris described the "cry of the hospital" that sometimes emanated from the patients held in the *basses-loges* of the Salpêtrière:

> Sometimes, in the middle of the night, the residents ... would hear a clamor rise up, a sort of savage groaning at regular intervals. It was the cry of the hospital. Held in, suppressed for months, the energy and fury that filled the souls of the poor creatures would slowly increase and then burst forward.... This cry of alarm coming from the place produced in us a terrifying feeling [Micale, p. 708].

The cells at both asylums were demolished in the early nineteenth century under the superintendency of Philippe Pinel.

## *Dark Chamber, or Dark Room, or Dark Cell*

A windowless asylum room, with or without furniture, in which intractable patients were confined. The dark was a subject of some controversy among early asylum physicians. Some insisted that insanity could be caused not by the dark, *per se,* but by the fear of it. William Perfect, a physician who owned a private madhouse in the English market town of West Malling, for example, presented the case of a respectable and genteel young seminarian who was so terrified of the dark and the prospect that his mischievous classmates would confine him in it, that he "lost his reason, and has never since emerged from a state of the most deplorable idiot" (p. 357). Other asylum physicians worried that the dark exacerbated the confusion and aggression of maniacal patients in particular; yet others, still, believed it calmed, perhaps cured, even the most unmanageable patients by reducing distractions and encouraging silence. Among the latter was the American physician Benjamin Rush who in the early nineteenth century used four dark chambers, approximately ten feet square in size and fronted by heavy doors with small bolted hatches through which food could be passed. He explained the effect of the dark on maniacal patients at the Pennsylvania Hospital:

> Solitude is indispensably necessary in [mania]. The passions become weak by the abstraction of company, and by refraining from conversation. For this reason, visitors should be excluded from the cells and apartments of highly deranged people, and there are times in which the visits of a physician, and of the cellkeeper or nurse, should be as seldom and short as are consistent with the proper treatment and care of the patient.... Darkness should accompany solitude in the first stage of [mania]. It invites to silence, and it induces a reduction of the pulse, by the abstraction of the stimulus of light, and by the influence of fear, which is naturally connected with darkness [Rush, pp. 189–190].

Confinement in a dark chamber was not at all considered inconsistent with the principles and practices of moral treatment [see **Moral Treatment**], as long as patients were not further restrained by straitjackets or chains. At the York Retreat, so intimately associated with moral treatment that its name was synonymous with it, patients in the throes of mania were confined in chambers that the residing physician preferred to describe as "gloomy," rather than dark, so that they "may not be affected by the stimulus of light or sound; such abstraction more readily disposing to sleep" (Tuke, p. 164). And at the asylum in Ghent where Joseph Guislain introduced moral treatment to Belgium, maniacal patients were confined in dark chambers often for weeks at a time until they calmed and became more amenable to the therapeutic regime.

The "color cure" [see **Color Cure**] offered a serviceable alternative to dedicated dark chambers in overcrowded asylums around the world. At the Juliusspital in Würzburg, Germany, physician Aton Müller painted the walls of a room black; while the room could be used for any patients, when the window also was shuttered, the most furious of them became tranquil. Black rooms, promoted as particularly suitable for female patients with hysterical insanity, also were found in a number of asylums across the United States, including the Wards Island Asylum in New York City, and at the Peoria Asylum for the Insane in Illinois where its superintendent, George Zeller, distinguished himself as a proponent of the color cure as an adjunct to moral treatment.

Yet no matter how vigorously the dark chamber was rationalized as a more humane alternative to the straitjacket or chains it could never distance itself from the pits and cells in which the insane were confined before moral treatment became *de rigueur*. The investigation into the Dixmont Asylum near Pittsburgh, Pennsylvania, in the late nineteenth century illustrated what was the often considerable difference between the rhetoric of moral treatment and the reality of managing the insane. Katie Fondelier, an "acutely insane" young patient with a talent for escape, had been found dead in a dark chamber. It was less the cause of her death than the reason for her confinement—therapeutic or punitive—that led to the grilling of asylum physicians and staff by state representatives as the transcript of the inquiry revealed:

> *Q.* Doctor, you have testified here this morning in regard to Katie Fondelier, that Katie was not put in a dark room for punishment.
> *A.* No, sir.
> *Q.* What was she put there for?
> *A.* She was put in for—more when she came back—when she was brought back to the hospital, she was brought back in a

paroxysm. She was acutely insane, had an acute attack, and was very much excited, noisy, boisterous in manner, and also tearing her clothing, destructive of furniture and clothing, and all window glass. About the window glass, I don't know whether she ever broke any, but she was destructive of furniture. She broke two chairs, and, taking all these things into account, we knew she would escape if she could, and for these reasons we put her in a dark room.
Q. She had escaped?
A. Yes, sir.
Q. Isn't it true she had escaped and been recaptured, and that the purpose of placing her in such confinement was that she could not escape again, and for that reason you placed her in a dark room?
A. No, sir; because we could not keep her in the hall. She was too excitable to be kept in the hall. She had excited all the patients around her.
Q. Why not put her in her own room?
A. Her own room had just an ordinary window, and I was afraid to.
Q. So that you were afraid she would break out the glass and commit suicide?
A. I thought it was best to put her in a dark room where she would be more quiet. I know by putting patients in a dark room that way it has done a good deal of good [Committee of the General Assembly, pp. 404–405].

Just a couple of years later, an exchange of letters between the Michigan State Board of Corrections and Charities and the superintendent and board members of the Upper Peninsula Hospital for the Insane in Newberry illustrated not only how quickly the very term "dark chamber" conjured images of patient abuse and punishment, but just how much it unsettled the goal of enlightened asylum medicine:

*Letter from the Board of Corrections and Charities:* The Board was surprised to find that dark rooms in which no windows were provided (regular dungeons), had been planned for inmates. No such means for the easy though cruel, restraint of troublesome patients, by attendants could meet the approval of this Board, and it would therefore urgently recommend to your honorable board that such dark rooms near the dining rooms in each story be thrown into and made a part of the dormitory adjoining them.

*Reply from the chairman of the asylum building committee:* In regard to the dark rooms will say that this board never intended them for places of punishment. These rooms were placed in the hospital department of the institution as a means of treatment for certain classes of patients, a means the most humane and beneficial known to science for these cases. We have no places or modes of punishment. These rooms are designed for new lines of medical treatment, and when your honorable board fully understand their use and the benefits that will follow I do not think they will object to them.... This is an era of progress and if we cannot advance in the treatment of the insane by all known methods, we should cease to try to employ medical men.

*Reply from the Board of Corrections and Charities:* I am instructed to say in reply that this Board did not say in its communication, and regrets that it was so understood, that your board intended the dark rooms for places of punishment....That the temptation to use them would be great, and that such temptation would be yielded to at times, is beyond question with this Board in the light of past experience. We would respectfully suggest that the '"new lines of medical treatment"' which the eminent alienists of your board propose to adopt, be so planned as to prevent, as far as possible, the old and still existing attempts of attendants to make their official actions as easy as may be, when not under the eye of the medical superintendent or one of his assistants [Michigan State Board of Corrections and Charities, pp. 67–69].

The use of the dark chamber in American, British and European asylums certainly ended in the twentieth century with the introduction of Thorazine and other major anti-psychotic drugs, and in response to patients' rights initiatives. But in other countries, the use continues into contemporary times. Argentina provides an example. Its first asylum was established in 1876 and founded on the principles of moral treatment that slowly eroded under the familiar pressures of overcrowding and underfunding. By 2004, there were more than 25,000 patients in teeming public asylums that were in considerable disrepair. Investigations conducted by Disability Rights International and the Center for Legal and Social Studies documented egregious human rights violations behind the closed doors, and focused most critically on the use of dark chamber isolation. Patients in one of the country's psychiatric penal units, for example, were confined in filthy, hot chambers that measured four by six feet and had no toilets, ventilation or light. Some had been so confined for months, either to protect themselves or others from harm, or to observe them before placing them in the wards. At the Colonia Montes de Oca, the national asylum, physicians strenuously defended the use of the dark chamber as a means to make easier the work of the few attendants on staff by isolating the most distracting and disruptive patients from the larger patient population. That dark chamber isolation often has been found to exacerbate symptoms and arrest any progress towards rehabilitation or cure, was ignored in the name of bureaucratic efficiency until a scathing report was filed by the investigating organizations. That report, coupled with the advocacy work of a number of human rights activists and organizations, led to significant and continuing asylum reform. In 2007 Argentina became the first country to ratify the United Nations Convention on the Rights of Persons with Disabilities, and passed Mental Health Law #26.657 that, in part, protects the rights of asylum patients from abusive treatment, including confinement in the dark chamber.

## *Isolation Therapy*

The suppression of visits from family and/or friends. Although a few asylums, such as the original Bethlem (or "Bedlam") in London, England, and the Salpêtrière in Paris, France, were exceptions, historical encounters between asylum and place more often meant that asylums were built at some geographic distance from centers of population. This was especially true in the United States. Between the mid- to late nineteenth century scores of public asylums were being built across the country not only according to the "moral architecture" blueprint of Thomas Kirkbride, chief physician at the Pennsylvania Hospital for the Insane in Philadelphia, but in deference to his moral treatment plan as well. Built in secluded and tranquil places, the asylums were far from the social and moral influences that Kirkbride believed caused insanity [see **Moral Treatment**], not to mention the hereditary one. For most asylum physicians of that age, the prospect that insanity indeed was hereditary in nature, placed them in a tense relationship with the "dangerously contaminated pool(s) of lunacy and dementia" that were their patients' families (Kelm, p. 181).

Away from public and even political scrutiny, the geographic isolation of asylums allowed their superintendents and physicians to exercise a patriarchal power over their patients. But that power was far from hegemonic. Even from a distance, sometimes in fact a great distance, families and friends attempted to mediate and negotiate the treatment of their loved ones, as these letters to asylum superintendents illustrate:

> Please sir, is my wife any better since she last wrote me. Please ask her if she would like to see me or her sisters. Please give me her answers in her own words....
> 
> Doctor, I have this day sent a letter containing a picture to Mrs. L. As I was her most intimate girlfriend please let me know how she receives it and if she recognizes the face. I take much interest in her and sincerely hope you can benefit and help her [de Young, p. 134].

When families and/or friends did visit, they did so according to asylum rules; they came at designated times and days, congregated in designated places within the asylum walls or on the grounds and under the watchful eye of staff, and conversed about designated topics so as to not further excite or disturb their loved ones. The potential for visitors to upset institutional order and its therapeutic agenda was a pressing concern for asylum superintendents and physicians. And for good reason.

Occasionally visitors uncovered ugly realities, and in doing so made the private troubles of asylum life into public issues. Such was the case for the sisters of a Helen H. who had been committed to the scandal-plagued Provincial Hospital in British Columbia, Canada in 1913. There, they found her restrained in a straitjacket and severely bruised from a beating by a female attendant. They demanded to see the superintendent, Charles Edward Doherty, who acquiesced to their insistence that she be discharged, although he made it clear that he did so against medical advice. The sisters then contacted the Provincial Secretary and demanded an investigation into the treatment of patients at the asylum; their adamancy was dismissed by Doherty as evidence of the insanity that Helen apparently also had inherited. In the end, no investigation ensued, if only because Helen had been returned to the asylum by her family who found themselves once again unable to care for her. Upon her recommitment, Doherty received a letter signed by the Provincial Secretary insisting that the family's complaints were to not adversely affect Helen's future treatment at the asylum.

Asylum superintendents and physicians debated for some time about whether to restrict or refuse visiting. But it was Jean-Martin Charcot at the Salpêtrière Asylum in Paris, France, who triangulated the issue: at the apex was the powerful asylum physician with superior expertise and knowledge; at the base, the inferior patient at one angle, the family at another, and a wide distance between them. The asylum physician's influence on the family, then, was necessarily as strong as it was on the patient, but because the family also influenced the patient, it was his obligation to restrict or refuse their visits. All of this, of course, was therapeutically rationalized as being in the best interest of the patient, and was given the label "isolation therapy."

Isolation therapy was part of the treatment regime at the Salpêtrière where the "Napoleon of Neurosis," as Charcot enjoyed being called, treated a large number of women patients who had been diagnosed with hysteria. Upon admission, he refused to allow their families to visit. It was not until the patients' often astonishing array of hysterical symptoms slowly abated over the ensuing weeks, months or years, that he allowed only occasional visits.

In one of the twenty-five clinical lectures he delivered on the nervous system, Charcot defended isolation therapy by relating a detailed story of its success. The case was that of a fourteen-year-old anorexic girl, "bordering on hysteria," who was starving herself to death. The girl's distraught father had begged Charcot to come to their home in Angoulême in southwestern France to treat her. Charcot demurred, and told the father to bring his daughter to Paris, "place her in one of our hydrotherapeutic establishments. Leave her there, or at least when you go away make her believe that you quitted the capital, inform me of it, and I will do the rest" (Silverman, p. 279). Weeks later, an Angoulême physician, familiar with the family, informed Charcot that the girl indeed had been admitted to such an establishment, but that she was still refusing food and was close to death. The father had not contacted Charcot, he revealed, because he and his wife refused to leave their dying daughter.

Charcot visited the establishment only to come across the tall, emaciated girl with her drooping head, weak voice and cold extremities. "There was indeed every reasons to be uneasy," he told his colleagues, "very uneasy." He continued:

> I took the parents aside, and after having addressed to them a blunt remonstrance, I told them that there remained, in my judgment, but one chance of success. It was that they should go away, or pretend to go away, which amounted to the same thing, as quickly as possible.... They went immediately. Their acquiescence was difficult to obtain in spite of all my remonstrances. The father especially failed to understand how the doctor could require a father to leave his child in the moment of danger. The mother said as much, but I was animated by my conviction. Perhaps I was eloquent, for the mother yielded first, and the father followed, uttering maledictions, and having I be-

lieve but little confidence in the prospect of success.

Isolation was established; its results were rapid and marvelous. The child, left alone with the nun who acted as nurse, and the doctor of the house, wept a little at first, though an hour later she became much less desolate than one would have expected. The very same evening, in spite of her repugnance, she consented to take half a little biscuit, dipped in wine. On the following days she took a little milk, some wine, soup, and then a little meat. The nutrition became improved, progressively but slowly.

At the end of 15 days she was relatively well. Energy returned and a general improvement in nutrition, so far that at the end of the month I saw the child seated on a sofa, and capable of lifting her head from the pillow. Then she was able to walk a little... and 2 months from the date of the commencement of the treatment she could be considered as almost completely cured [Silverman, p. 298].

Eulogized by his former student Sigmund Freud as a *"visuel"* who had little interest in talking to his hysterical patients and even less in listening to them, Charcot nonetheless conversed with the girl he had successfully treated, who reaffirmed the hierarchical underpinnings of isolation therapy:

As long as papa and mamma had not gone—in other words, as long as you had not triumphed (for I saw that you wished to shut me up), I was afraid that my illness was not serious, and as I had a horror of eating, I did not eat. But when I saw that you were determined to be master, I was afraid, and in spite of repugnance I tried to eat, and I was able to, little by little [Silverman, p. 298].

Charcot's influence, in the matter of isolation therapy as in all, was considerable, and the therapeutic was widely used in France into the twentieth century. In fact, it became so associated with him that the American neurologist S. Weir Mitchell took umbrage. In 1875 Mitchell had developed the rest cure [see **Bed Therapy**], a treatment for neurasthenics, most of them women, that entailed several weeks of isolation. To correct the widespread impression that isolation therapy was Charcot's brainchild, he challenged the famous asylum physician and, in doing so, staked a claim for the inventiveness of American medicine:

Charcot is quoted as claiming for its use ... precedence of invention [but I cannot] find proof of this in his books. He was given to such claims, and I have twice before suffered in like manner at his, Charcot's, hands. I think it just, less on my account than to American medicine, that I a little protest [Mitchell, p. 2034].

## *Oubliette, or Fool's Pit*

A cylindrical pit, large enough to accommodate a single patient, dug into the basement floor of an asylum and covered with a heavy metal grate, or a makeshift wooden stall constructed in the basement and fronted by a metal grate. As the French word *"oubliette"* suggests, the strong room was a "forgotten place" used in the nineteenth through early twentieth centuries in asylums around the world to confine violent and otherwise unmanageable patients, and most likely for centuries before asylums were established. One such oubliette, then called a fool's pit, was observed in a Munich general hospital decades before an asylum was constructed in that German city:

In the hope of seeing wide, light rooms, I entered the cellar; instead of fresh, healthy air a repugnant vapour hit me and instead of dry cleanliness I met damp dirtiness. No separate and free-standing beds, but human stalls made of wooden slats were to be seen. These areas were the pits. The overseers of the fool's pits were called the strikers [Hippius, Möller, Müller & Neundörfer-Kohl, p. 3].

## *Padded Cell, or Padded Room, or Rubber Room*

An asylum room with cushioned walls and floors into which refractory or suicidal patients were placed. The origin of the padded room has been attributed to Johann Heinrich Ferdinand von Autenrieth, professor of medicine at the University of Tübingen in Germany in the early nineteenth century. Although he had little contact with insane patients, Autenrieth's writings greatly influenced the therapeutic regimes of German asylums where padded rooms, their walls and floors covered with rubber stretched over cork chips, first appeared.

In the emerging era of moral treatment [see **Moral Treatment**], many British asylum physicians found padded rooms to be viable alternatives to coercive methods of mechanical restraint [see **Mechanical Restraints**]. Padded rooms were introduced into the basement wards of London's Bethlem Asylum, better known as Bedlam, in 1844. Visiting physician Sir Alexander Morison described their design and purpose and offered a few caveats about their use:

> In almost every case of excitement, seclusion in a padded room, as it is called, will be found to be sufficient. This consists of a small room padded with cushions, stretched on a framework of wood, and stuffed with horse-hair or cocoa-nut fibre, and having the floor covered in the same way. In [Bethlem] the padded rooms are lined with a composition consisting of India-rubber and cork; but although possessing the advantage of being more easily cleaned, I prefer the first mentioned, as I consider them to be too hard, so that a resolute maniac, if so determined, might easily inflict injuries upon himself, by throwing himself against the walls. As light is often a source of great irritation, so darkness is a powerful auxiliary in obtaining quiet, and preventing the renewal of raving. But we should as speedily as possible ascertain that darkness does not beget real terror.
>
> Many, besides the ignorant and superstitious, have an unaccountable dread of being left in the dark; and the worst consequences might follow, by their being so treated. Although we cannot enforce too much the employment of soothing means to calm and restrain the violent and mischievous insane,—still, if these entirely fail (and especially when the patient is in a condition to be sensible that his conduct has called for marks of disapprobation), these become necessary [Morison, pp. 397–398].

If Morison seemed somewhat hesitant about using padded rooms to soothe the "resolute maniac" and the "violent and mischievous insane," his rival John Conolly was far from it. At the forefront of the non-restraint movement, Conolly was determined to render "both mechanical restraints and muscular force unnecessary" for the control of even the most refractory patients at the nearby Middlesex County Asylum, better known as the Hanwell Asylum (Conolly, p. 44). It was there that Conolly not only unhesitatingly used the bare rooms that were padded from floor to ceiling with cocoa-nut fiber enclosed in ticking and illuminated by whatever light came through wire blinds across the windows, but set out strict guidelines to prevent their misuse:

> The seclusion and the reasons for it, are always immediately reported to the superintendent or physician, and, in the case of female patients, to the matron also. The ward is visited from time to time by these officers, and an accurate knowledge of the state of the secluded patients is obtained by means of an inspection plate or covered opening in the door of the room. The patient is not left to suffer from thirst or hunger, nor are his personal state and cleanliness unattended to; nor is he allowed to remain in seclusion longer than his excited state requires. A written report of each instance of seclusion, and of its duration, is sent to the physician at the close of each day, and copied by him into a book which is inspected at every meeting of the Committee. Thus are obtained all the advantages of seclusion, without any abuse of it [Conolly, p. 460].

The padded rooms, in Conolly's opinion, soothed and quieted distressed patients, but their "cure commenced" before they were even coaxed or carried into them. Because they were subjected neither to mechanical restraints nor muscular force the patients, he argued, were more inclined to trust their best interests were being served; the timely introduction of "good tempered" attendants (p. 47), offering food and drink after they had calmed, drew patients to the inevitable conclusion that they were under good and kind care. He offered the case of a twenty-four-year-old woman in support of his contentions. In a state of "violent excitement" (p. 111), she was convinced she would be burned alive for some real or imagined sin and had to be carried into a padded room. Then,

> the tranquility and the solitude at first appeared to surprise her. She got up, and walked around the room as if to examine it; then lay down again, and became quiet and composed. It was some hours before she became quite calm enough to take a little food, and by this time the appearance of the attendants scarcely seemed to alarm her. After three days careful nursing and management she had quite gained enough confidence in them, and it was practicable to remove her to a bed in the infirmary. She recovered and was released weeks later" [Conolly, p. 113].

As a therapeutic innovator of some repute, Conolly's promotion of padded rooms had considerable influence on asylum medicine in Great Britain. Heralded as an "all important aid to the Modern System of humane treatment" (Arnold, p. 184), they could be found here and there along the six miles of corridors that wound through Colney Hatch, the newly built asylum in north London that, with 3500 patients, was the largest in Europe. Conolly's influence was felt in the Commonwealth of Australia where the addition of padded rooms at the Adelaide Lunatic Asylum in the mid-nineteenth century was praised as the first enlightened step towards moral treatment. And it was felt as far away as Egypt, then under British rule. At the Cairo Lunatic Asylum, the only asylum in that country, five padded rooms were constructed and filled with leather cushions stuffed with vegetable horse hair and palmetto from Algiers. Although so effective in calming maniacal patients that the heavy neck chains that once had held them to the walls were no longer needed, straitjackets or camisoles were still on hand. Despite the assessment of the British asylum superintendent that "healthy-minded Egyptians are very like grown-up children, and when insane are almost invariably quite easy to manage" (Sandwitch, pp. 485–486), occasional mechanical restraint still was required.

Colonial condescension aside, the Cairo Lunatic Asylum illustrated one of the incongruities of padded rooms: they could not always replace mechanical restraints entirely. Sometimes, in fact, they were used in conjunction with them. In the United States where their use was relatively infrequent, Clifford Beers, a university student who would go on to be the founder of the American mental health hygiene movement, described in his bestselling memoir his confinement in a padded room while also restrained in a straitjacket:

> The [padded room] I was forced to occupy was practically without heat., and as winter was coming on, I suffered intensely from the cold. Frequently it was so cold I could see my breath. Though my canvas jacket served to protect part of that body which it is at the same time racking, I was seldom comfortably warm; for, once uncovered, my arms being pinioned, I had no way of rearranging the blankets [Beers, pp. 133–134].

Beers's experience revealed another incongruity of padded rooms. Conolly's rigid regulations for their therapeutic as opposed to punitive use aside, they invited abuse. Conolly's influence most likely did not extend to Russia where asylums, also known as "dollhouses," a perversion of the German *"Tollhaus,"* and later as "yellow houses," had not been used to confine the insane until the late eighteenth century. Small, poorly run, and cruel, the use of padded rooms also known as "isolators," to torture as much as treat, was common.

Some British asylum physicians pointed out the definitive incongruity of padded rooms and that was that they were, in fact, little more than capacious versions of the straitjackets and camisoles they were designed to replace. That position was taken by George M. Robertson, physician-superintendent of the Royal Edinburgh Asylum, also known as Morningside:

> I place [padded rooms] ... in the same category as mechanical restraint, which is only resorted to most exceptionally and in the direct neces-

sity. Of course, it is possible to say that if mechanical restraint be necessary and does good in one case for one day in 100,000, that to that extent the practice is desirable. A similar limited desirability may be claimed for the padded room...[I]t is a form of treatment handed down to us from the past, and had its origin in, and was adopted from, the jails. It became naturalized in the madhouses one hundred years ago because these institutions were not mental hospitals, but prisons for the insane.

I venture to say that no medical student from the hospitals or graduate, seeing the practice adopted for the first time, but feels more keenly its prison-like characteristics with compassion for the individual subjected to it, than a realization of its medical and therapeutic blessings...[T]he sight of a patient locked up in a room will never fail to create an impression, often indelible, on a layman visiting an asylum for the first time. The impression is never favourable, and its always accompanied by sympathy for the unfortunate sufferer [Robertson, pp. 195–196].

In a concluding statement that was more disturbing for its prescience than its condemnation, Robertson went on to warn that padded rooms very well could become "magnified in importance and in frequency of employment out all semblance of the truth" (p. 196) in the eyes of the public for whom asylums were unsettling and insanity unnerving. Indeed, padded rooms, just like the straitjackets they were meant to replace, are to this day associated in the public imagination with the brutal and unenlightened treatment of the insane.

## *Psychic Abstinence Treatment, or Deprivation Therapy*

The isolation of patients from all human contact and in total silence for a period ranging from several days to several weeks. Developed by the Swiss born psychiatrist, Otto Binswanger, who at the start of World War I was a professor at the University of Jenna in Germany, psychic abstinence treatment was administered to soldiers suffering from the most severe manifestations of shell-shock. Often disparagingly referred to as "war hysterics," "tremblers," or "war neurotics," these soldiers were a source of considerable shame not only to the German body politic, but to psychiatrists such as Binswanger who lionized war as an antidote to the degenerating forces of modernity. War also was glorified as a test of manhood. According to Binswanger:

> In the course of the last year and on the outbreak of the war, I have been treating a whole series of young men with weak nerves: anxious, timid, vacillating, weak-willed individuals whose consciousness and feelings were determined only by their own ego and who exhausted themselves in complaints about their physical and mental pain. Then the war came. Their morbid sickliness fell away from them at a stroke, they reported for service—and all have so far proved their worth [Kaufman, p. 128].

By the end of the first year of the war, however, nearly 112,000 German soldiers had been diagnosed with what eventually came to be known as shell-shock, and treating them was a daunting challenge to physicians. Binswanger, taking inspiration from the at-home rest cure for middle class neurasthenic women developed in the United States by S. Weir Mitchell, isolated his soldier-patients in single rooms [see **Bed Therapy**], demanded complete silence and forbade any human contact. Patients who violated the strictures of psychic abstinence treatment were deprived food. Only the most severe cases of shell-shock were subjected to this disciplinary therapy, and Binswanger claimed a 66 percent success rate.

An even higher rate of success was claimed by his colleague Ernst Kretschmer who, after the war, would serve as a founding member of the General Medical Society for Psychotherapy. Kretschmer isolated his shell-shocked soldier-patients in darkened rooms at the Württemberg Hospital and visited them once daily; no other staff were allowed to enter the rooms. The patients were confined to their beds and activity, indeed movement in general, was forbidden. Positing that such "boring to death" treatment, as it came to be called, would calm the patients' frayed nerves, Kretschmer found that the symptoms of shell-shock—the trembling, tics, stutters, stumblings, as well as the disturbing impairments of the senses—improved in one to two weeks, and disappeared in four to six weeks.

## *Solitary Cell or Isolation Cell*

A room that isolated uncontrollable or self-injuring patients from the larger asylum population. The solitary cell usually was quite well lit and ventilated, and often was furnished with a bed or pallet for sleeping; patients placed in it typically were not further restrained. That was the case at the Het Dolhuys (The Madhouse) in Haarlem in the Netherlands, where fourteen solitary cells, known as "*dolcellen*," were built for the insane patients who in the sixteenth century joined the lepers already isolated there. Each of the cells was approximately four feet wide by four feet long, and nearly six feet in height, had a stone floor and walls, a barred inner door and a heavy wood outer door. Hot stones were placed between the doors in the winter to provide some heat for the patient who slept in a small wooden crib and had a bucket for bodily wastes. An iron hatch, approximately one foot square, was built into the wall above the cell and could be opened to provide light and air.

Solitary cells were used in asylums around the world, but not without a great deal of discussion and debate about the exigencies of their use. For reformers determined to introduce moral treatment into asylums that had relied on chains, cuffs and straitjackets to control and subjugate patients, solitary cells offered in equal measure a caring intervention and an opportunity for cruel abuse. The prominent French asylum physician Jean-Étienne Esquirol, pondered that dilemma. While acknowledging that solitude "exercises a mysterious power which reestablishes the moral forces that have been exhausted by the passions," (Esquirol, p. 78), he nonetheless warned that "it is not easy to determine the period at which isolation should cease. To prevent abuse, extreme caution and tact are requisite. Here, experience is slow to decide" (p. 78).

Indeed, the duration of solitary cell confinement in French asylums was the subject of a broadside by the British physician C. Lockhart Robertson, whose career included the superintendency of the Sussex County Asylum, the presidency of the Medico-Psychological Association, and Visitor to the Chancery lunatics. Lockhart, who was known for his unbridled criticism of patient abuse, discovered in his tour of French provincial asylums that in one of them two patients, diagnosed with nymphomania, had been confined in solitary cells for two years. He attributed that "barbarous" practice to the bureaucratic interference of lay governors and, above all, of "stupid old *réligieuses*" ("The Restraint System," p. 443), and called on more enlightened French colleagues to "insist such scandals shall cease to disgrace France" (p. 443).

The use of the solitary cell was the subject of scandal and not just in France. In the late nineteenth century a tavern keeper named Heinrich Mellage in Iserlohn, Germany, published a pamphlet that detailed how he rescued Alexander Forbes, a Scottish priest, from Mariaberg Asylum where he had been involuntarily confined for more than three years. Written in hyperbolic prose, the pamphlet detailed the abuses of patients at the private Catholic asylum, including long periods of confinement, after having been stripped naked, in unheated solitary cells. The pamphlet, *39 Monate bei gesundem Geiste als irrsinnig eingekerkert* ["39 months of a sane man's imprisonment as insane"] was widely read by a public ghoulishly fascinated not only with insanity and its commitment, but by the vindictively applied label of insanity by incompetent physicians and the prospect of false commitment. The pamphlet did not go unnoticed by the asylum or the state that, in a joint action, brought a libel suit against Mellage. His nine day trial, covered by both the international press and by psychiatric journals and communiqués, ended in his acquittal, prompted asylum reforms, and mounted a vituperative public backlash against asylums and their physicians. Forbes, the alcoholic, explosively violent and unrepentantly "un-priestly" priest who was the subject of the pamphlet, was released from Mariaberg after having been certified as sane by a consulting physician.

The abuse at Mariaberg was considerable, and certainly not limited to the solitary cell. But the fact that such a cell, so reminiscent of the unenlightened past, was still being used stood in stark contrast to the wide-sweeping German asylum reforms that had been put into place by such notable theorists as Wilhelm Griesinger, and into practice by such asylum physicians as Oscar Wattenberg at the State Hospital in Lübeck. It was there that Wattenberg had abolished completely the use of the solitary cell, and did so "on principle":

> One can sense, that it [i.e. the isolation of patients] is not as it should be, it is an open sore that one does not like to put a finger on. That must change! We have to use the sharp knife of humanity for this putrid wound and cut it from the core. We have discontinued the use of strait-jackets, we have invented the agricultural colony, the family care and the open door system, we have reduced the use of isolation cells—why don't we totally abolish them? [Ptok & Dilling, p. 321].

For asylum physicians in other countries, as eager as their German colleagues to jettison "the ballast of [their] sinking public image" (Engstrom, p. 69) while at the same time controlling their asylums, misunderstandings about the continued use of the solitary cell had to be adamantly confronted. Such was the case at the Newcastle-Upon-Borough Lunatic Asylum in northeast England in the late nineteenth century, when visiting members of the Lunacy Commission criticized the use of the solitary cell by stating, "we cannot but express a hope that by care and perseverance some other and less objectionable means may be adopted in the management and treatment of cases of the descriptions now under consideration" (Committee of Visitors, p. 12).

Medical superintendent R.H.B. Wickham offered a strong rejoinder by reminding the Commission that the patients confined in solitary cells were "objects of terror to the well-disposed patients, and the feelings of the quiet and orderly" (p. 15). He further emphasized that while the Commission had counted more than 3,000 hours of seclusion cell use, the majority of that total actually reflected the repeated use of the cell over time for a small number of particularly difficult patients. One of those, a homicidal male, was secluded sixty-nine separate times for a total of 700 hours; another an acutely manic female, thirty-eight times for a total of 353 hours. That said, Wickham somewhat reluctantly agreed to "almost entirely" relinquish the use of the seclusion cell despite disagreeing with the Commission that its use was "wrong, inhumane, or retrograde" (Committee of Visitors, p. 16).

## *Strong Room*

A room, usually with a reinforced or a double door and grates on the window, to confine violent or self-injuring patients. Often disparagingly referred to as an oubliette, the strong room in fact was considerably less oppressive; patients usually were allowed to remain clothed and seldom were further restrained. A strong room typically was well lit, aired and heated in the winter months, but additional features were matters of both planning and pride. At the Sonnenstein Asylum, housed in a castle overlooking the river Elbe near the German city of Dresden, the floor of the strong room was brick and heavily varnished so bodily excretions and odors would not be absorbed, an innovation that was consistent with its status as Germany's first moral treatment asylum. At the West Riding Pauper Lunatic Asylum in Wakefield, England, the thirty strong rooms had silicate-covered walls and flush-paneled doors that opened outward to they could not be blocked by patients. Similar design novelties could be found in asylums across the United States although some, such as a county asylum in Pennsylvania that replaced the easily damaged plaster walls with sheets of tin, were put into place more out of necessity than any pretense of promoting moral treatment.

## Masks, Gags and Toggles

*Coverings strapped or otherwise secured over the face, or placed around or in the mouth, to prevent speaking, screaming, spitting and biting.*

Upon a visit to Bethlem, England's first insane asylum, a visitor observed:

> It seems strange that anyone should recover here: the cryings, screechings, roarings, brawlings, shaking of chains, swearing, frettings, chafings, are so many, so hideous, so great, that they are more able to drive a man that hath his wits, rather out of them, than to help one that never had them, or hath lost them, to find them again [Ackroyd, p. 619].

That observations was made in the early seventeenth century when Bethlem held thirty-one insane patients in a dark and dingy building designed to hold just twenty-four. Over the years the asylum, originally located on a patch of ground between two open sewers, would become better known as "Bedlam," the Cockney contraction of "Bethlem," and a word synonymous with noise.

In that sense, "Bedlam" was typical of early insane asylums. But it was not just the often impenetrable noise that was considered both the consequence of insanity and the cause of it that was problematic. It was also the fact that patients sometimes ingested inappropriate things—the straw or mattress ticking of their beds, the dirt on the floor and the grounds, even their own feces—ripped their clothes with their teeth, spit, and bit themselves, each other, as well as attendants and asylum physicians. Case notes such as this one from the files of the Hampshire County Lunatic Asylum in southern England could be found in any mid-nineteenth century asylum anywhere in the world: "Attacked ... the Charge Attendant of his ward whilst on the seat of the W.C. Tried to bite off his nose & ear & to gouge out his eyes, and did bite him about 11 places but only superficially" (Carpenter, p. 126).

Hampshire was a provincial pauper lunatic asylum, holding patients who had spent months, perhaps years, in workhouses under often execrable conditions; they were and most likely always had been, poor, and many were uneducated, even illiterate. But insanity was a great leveler. Once in the throes of it, class distinctions blurred and pauper and private asylums alike were plagued by the same problems of discipline and danger. This was evident from the case files at the Bloomingdale Asylum in New York City. The private asylum catered to the well-to-do and was a model of moral treatment [see **Moral Treatment**]. Rules were posted on the walls of the elegant Federal style brownstone building, encouraging patients to engage in civilized comportment: no screaming, spitting or biting was allowed. But in the throes of insanity, such rules were meaningless and their violation posed as much of a problem of management as it did in any pauper or public asylum, as this case illustrated:

> Miss--- was admitted to Bloomingdale Asylum, December 7, 1888, in her third attack of insanity. Her age was 23 years.... Her case pursued a course of increasing violence and excitement, at the height of which her actions were most violent, destructive, filthy, abusive and insulting to those around her.... The first entry in her case records state that she was admitted in an excited state, singing, striking, and biting.... [S]he acknowledges that she is very bad, but again glories in being so, and says the best thing she has done since she came here was to bite a patient. She never loses an opportunity to bite or strike [Lyon, p. 109].

While mechanical restraints [see **Mechanical Restraints**] could deter patients from biting, they could not silence screaming; and while isolation [see **Isolation**] could mute the screaming, it could not deter the biting and self-injury. Sedatives such as opium, morphine, chloral and bromide were used to calm boisterous and aggressive patients, but in some nineteenth century asylums, particularly in Europe, masks, toggles and gags were valuable additions to the therapeutic armamentarium. In significantly modified versions, masks of some kind or another were in use well into the twentieth century.

REFERENCES

Ackroyd, P. (2000). *London: A biography*. London: Vantage.
Arnold, C. (2008). *Bedlam: London and its mad*. London: Simon & Schuster.
Brown, A.R. (2010). Reform and curability in American insane asylums in the 1840s. *Constructing the Past, 11*, 12–29.
Carpenter, D.T. (2010). Above all a patient should never be terrified: An examination of mental health care and treatment in Hampshire 1845–194. Doctoral Dissertation, University of Portsmouth. Portsmouth, UK.
Farrell, L. (1995). Some things never change. *British Medical Journal, 311*, 634.
Giles, H.H. (1888). *The insane, and the Wisconsin system for their care*. Madison, WI: Democrat Printing Co.
Heinroth, J.C.A. (1975/1818). *Textbook of disturbances of mental life*. Baltimore: Johns Hopkins University Press.
Lyon, S.H. (1895). Dual action of the brain. *New York Medical Journal, 62*, 107–110.
Meranze, M. (1996). *Laboratories of virtue: Punishment, revolution, and authority in Philadelphia, 1760–1835*. Chapel Hill: University of North Carolina Press.
Millingen, J.G. (1842). *Aphorisms on the treatment and management of the insane*. Philadelphia: Ed. Barrington & Geo. D. Haswell.
Szasz, T. (2010). *Coercion as cure: A critical history of psychiatry*. New Brunswick, NJ: Transaction Publishers.
Tuke, D.H. (1882). *Chapters on the history of the insane in the British Isles*. London: Kegan Paul, Trench & Co.
Webster, J. (1852). Additional notes on provincial asylums for the insane in France. *Journal of Psychological Medicine, 5*, 124–139. 229–255.

## *Autenrieth's Mask, or* Autenrietische Maske

A well cushioned leather mask with openings for the eyes and nostrils, and with a tight leather strap that was slipped under the chin. The mask was designed by Johann Heinrich Ferdinand von Autenrieth, professor of medicine and founder of the inpatient clinic at the University of Tübingen in Germany in the early nineteenth century. Although he had little direct contact with insane patients, his writings had a significant, albeit brief, influence on their treatment, particularly in Germany. Autenrieth identified with what was known as German Romantic Psychiatry, a movement that emphasized the quasi-mystical nexuses between psychiatry and philosophy, and that posited psychic, rather than somatic, origins of insanity. In the manner of his colleagues in that movement, Autenrieth posited that insanity was tantamount to passion unrestrained by free will, thus therapeutics should restore the will of insane patients through the benevolent tyranny of iron-clad discipline. He wrote:

> The doctor can never sufficiently impress upon himself and others the fact the insane are identical in more respects to stubborn, ill-mannered children and, like them, require stern (not cruel) treatment…. Is not the treatment of mental patients frequently comparable to the education of children? Every finding indicates that comparison is apt [Szasz, p. 77].

How apt that comparison was in practice was evident in the case of Autenrieth's most famous patient, the lyric poet Friedrich Hölderlin whose metaphysical influence on the development of the philosophical movement known as German Idealism was considerable. Physically and mentally exhausted, the poet was taken in the early nineteenth century by friends to Autenrieth's clinic where he was administered the standard course of stimulants and sedatives, immersed in baths of cold water [see **Hydrotherapy**], wrapped in a straitjacket [see **Mechanical Restraints**] and, when his outbursts were intolerable, fitted with Autenrieth's mask. Silenced, but not improved, he was later discharged as incurable and taken in by a local cabinet-maker with whom he lived quite peacefully until his death, thirty-six years later.

Although one of the leaders of the German Romantic movement in psychiatry, Johann Christian August Heinroth, went out of his way to disabuse asylum physicians of their concern that the Autenrieth mask was cruel, since its aim, he argued, was "to produce one of the most healing restrictions" (Heinroth, p. 294), the mask was never well accepted nor widely used. That said, modifications of the mask found their way into asylums in Europe. At the Ospedal San Lazzaro in northern Italy, for example, what was variously referred to as the "cap of silence" or the "helmet of silence," a leather cap with a heavy chin strap held in place by a strap buckled behind the head, was used well into the nineteenth century to silence loud patients. In its tour of provincial English asylums around that same time, the Lunacy Commission came across similar leather caps with mouth-closing chin straps. Most of these were in storage, and the Commission was assured that they had not been used for many years. And although John Minson Galt, the superintendent of Eastern State Hospital in Williamsburg, Virginia, dismissed the mask in all of its versions as "merit[ing] but little confidence" (Galt, p. 181), it occasionally was used until the mid-nineteenth century in some American asylums as well.

## Brank

A locked metal frame that fit over the head with an iron bit approximately two inches long and one inch wide to press down on the tongue. The brank was used in the Middle Ages to punish and humiliate women who were "common scolds," that is, who talked shrewishly, gossiped and nagged, hence the early term for the device was the "scold's bridle" or "gossip's bridle," or "witch's bridle."

In a mid-nineteenth century series of lively lectures, replete with quotes from early English poets and dramatists and illustrated with hand drawn pictures, T.N. Brushfield told his audiences that branks had been used as late as decades before in Scottish and some provincial English asylums to silence loud patients. His claims on that point were considered questionable at the time, although he insisted he had found a brank in storage at the Cheshire Lunatic Asylum, where he was medical superintendent, and had been told by an elderly patient that years before she had been forced to wear one to silence her loud screams.

## Gag

A horseshoe-shaped iron pallet that was inserted into the mouth and that pressed down the tongue. The gag had chains on each end that were drawn tightly towards the jaws and then fastened behind the head with a lock. The gag had wide use in a variety of disciplinary institutions, including jails, prisons and even in the military, and was the subject of occasional investigations and official inquiries, especially when its use resulted in death. It also was used in asylums around the world as late as the early twentieth century.

## Muffle

A simple cotton cloth tied over the mouth of the patient to prevent talking and screaming. The muffle was used in eighteenth century asylums.

## Toggle, Pear, or Bulb

A piece of pear-shaped hardwood placed in the mouth of the patient and secured at the back of the neck by leather straps attached to a crossbar. Johann Christian August Heinroth, professor of medicine at Leipzig University in Germany, urged asylum physicians to use the device, which many had considered cruel, for its ability to bring refractory patients into submission, if not silence:

> Since the oral cavity of the patient is more or less filled by this instrument, the patient can obviously utter no articulate sounds, but can still utter stifled screams, which is the more undesirable as the patient has to make a greater effort to do so; except that he might grow tired of this effort and become quiet.... Just as badly brought up children, or rather spoiled children, given vent to their malice through screaming, and thus enjoy themselves, so unruly patients give vent to their rage and obstreperousness by screaming and roaring if they cannot do so in any other manner, and tend to scream more the more they are forbidden to do so. If they are prevented from screaming, they lose their only remaining weapon and must finally acknowledge their total impotence [Heinroth, p. 294].

It was Heinroth who suggested that because Autenrieth's mask did not prevent the patient from opening his or her mouth, that the pear be used in conjunction with it to assure silence.

## *Wire Mask, or Net Mask, or Grating Mask, or Net Cap*

A bowl-shaped devise made of quite tightly woven wire or fabric mesh, fitted over the head of the patient and secured around the neck with a leather strap that was locked behind the head. The mask did not prevent the patient from talking, but did prevent biting, tearing clothes with the teeth, spitting, or eating objectionable substances. Although an American physician who was touring provincial French asylums in the mid-nineteenth century was quite taken aback by the site of patients, both male and female, wearing wire masks, such masks were in occasional use in asylums throughout Great Britain, Europe as well as in the United States into the twentieth century.

# Mechanical Restraints

*Devices of various kinds that restrict, inhibit or prevent movement of all or part of the body.*

Above the fourteen foot high portal of Bethlem Asylum, the "Bedlam" of both history and imagination, were two Portland stone sculptures carved in the late seventeenth century by Cajus Gabriel Cibber. Each depicted a figure reclining on a mat of straw. One, known as "Melancholy," was free of mechanical restraint, perhaps because he required none; his pose, on his side, one leg crossed back over the other, his thick neck barely holding up his head, signified defeat; his facial expression was sad and distant. The other, known variously as "Raving Mania" or "Raving Madness" or just as "Raving," was more intimidating. On his back, he seemed to have been caught in the act of rising, his muscled legs arching and his fists clenched. His head was thrown back, his facial expression tormented, his mouth open as if he were about to bellow. Around his wrists were thick manacles connected by a short and heavy iron chain.

The "Brainless Brothers," as they were ungraciously referred to, became icons of that most iconic London asylum, Bedlam. But "Raving," in particular, also became the representation of a contentious debate that had as much to do with the treatment of the insane as it did with the claims to expertise of the asylum physicians who were treating them. That debate centered on the manacles around "Raving's" wrists, that is, on mechanical restraints.

There is no question that in the early years of asylums mechanical restraints were necessary to control and contain those insane patients whose behavior was injurious to themselves and posed a threat to others. Some drugs were relied upon to calm them—calomel and opium, as examples—but neither worked well nor for long. Asylums provided the hothouses, as it were, for the growing of the new profes-

The "Brainless Brothers," Melancholy and Mania. The statues were carved out of Portland stone and graced the portals to the entrance of Bethlem Hospital, better known as Bedlam, in London, England (courtesy of the Wellcome Library, London).

sion of asylum physician and for the cultivation of specialized skills for treating insane patients. The mere sight of chained and manacled patients spoke little of the profession and even less of its expertise. In the not too distant past, the insane had been restrained in their own homes, in the private madhouses that were run by untrained do-gooders and entrepreneurs, and in monasteries and convents by clerics and nuns. How, the question was being asked both in Great Britain and in parts of Europe, had asylums and their physicians improved upon the unenlightened past?

There were notable contenders for the recognition of having started the non-restraint movement—Philippe Pinel in France, Vincenzo Chiarugi in Italy, William Tuke in York, England—all deserve mention. But there was perhaps no one more idealistically devoted to the movement than Robert Gardiner Hill, a physician at a Lincoln, England, asylum. "Restraint," he declared in 1838, "is never necessary, never justified, and always injurious, and its application consequently unjustified" (Hill, p. 12). Those were bold words for a twenty-four year physician in a provincial asylum, and if Hill's later jeremiad was truthful, he was stigmatized by his colleagues who remained bound to tradition as "one bereft of reason ... a speculator, peculator, and a practical breaker of the sixth commandment by exposing the lives of attendants to the fury of the patients." And, if that were not enough, his system of non-restraint was called a "piece of contemptible quackery, a mere bait for the public ear" (p. 12).

But not by everyone. An asylum physician of no less stature than John Conolly, was so impressed with the tranquility of the asylum upon his visit that he abolished restraints in the massive Middlesex County Asylum, better known as Hanwell, where he was resident physician. Conolly, older, distinguished, well established in his specialty, took credit from

**Mechanical Restraints**        210        Encyclopedia of Asylum Therapeutics

the brash upstart for the idea and for years the two engaged in a shrill debate over who should be lionized as the originator of the non-restraint movement. Of that debate, a patient at Hanwell versified:

> We have in the asylum, Sir,
> Some doctors of renown
> With a plan of non-restraint
> Which they seem to think their own.
> All well-meaning men, Sir,
> But troubled with a complaint
> Called the monomania
> Of total non-restraint
> [Scull, MacKenzie & Hervey p. 48].

While they debated, the movement gained momentum. It reached the United States before the mid-nineteenth century. New to asylum-keeping and the treatment of the insane, and geographically distant from their more experienced British and European colleagues, U.S. asylum physicians read journals, exchanged letters, hosted distinguished international visitors and were hosted in return, in order to mainstream themselves into the profession. Well aware of the spreading non-restraint movement, they nonetheless were reluctant to join it. The American insane, they argued, were different from the British or European insane. They were ruggedly individualistic, daring and aggressive—much like the country, itself—and thus unusually difficult to control without mechanical restraints. So deeply entrenched was that view that the Association of Medical Superintendents of American Institutions for the Insane (AMSAII) declared that any "attempt to abandon entirely the use of all means of personal restraint is not sanctioned by the true interests of the insane" (Curwen, p. 7). Arguing that mechanical restraint was a "moral instrument," the members agreed with one of its own who urged pride in the belief that "we have an American practice in the use of restraint, which is at once benevolent, enlightened and practicable" (Shrady, p. 61).

That conclusion was the subject of scorn by British asylum physicians, such as the prominent asylum reformer and head of the Lancet Commission that had investigated the conditions of British asylums, J. Mortimer Granville. He reminded that the treatment of the insane could be divided into three distinct

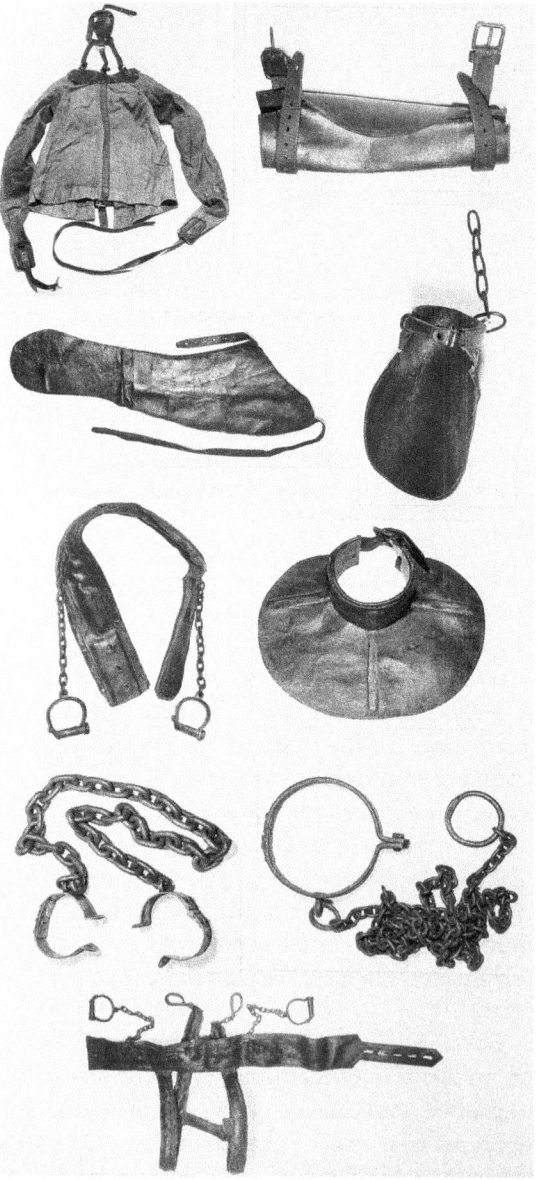

A variety of nineteenth-century mechanical restraints used at the Hanwell Asylum. Established in 1831, Hanwell was the first purpose-built asylum in England. Under the superintendency of John Conolly all mechanical restraints were abolished (courtesy of the Wellcome Library, London).

periods: the barbaric in which they were regarded as wild beasts and were "chained, tamed, or destroyed, as convenience should dictate" (Granville, p. 705); the humane in which some compassion was expressed; and the remedial in which insanity was finally recognized as a malady that had to be treated and cured. In the United States, he retorted, "the treatment of lunatics can hardly be said to have made progress even in the stage of development which we have reluctantly described as the humane" (p. 706). It was scarcely believable, he added, "but we are almost forced to the conclusion, that our friends across the Atlantic have not yet mastered the fundamental principles of the remedial system. They adhere to the old terrorism tempered by petty tyranny" (Granville, p 707).

If that were not criticism enough, another British physician, John C. Bucknill who had spent several months in the United States visiting asylums, also ridiculed the assumption that the American insane were somehow different, and therefore more deserving of mechanical restraint.

> Our American brethren tell us, indeed, that there is some wonderful peculiarity in the American character which distinguishes it from that of the parent race in the old country in preferring the restraint of instrumental bonds to that of moral influence.... It can, however, scarcely be doubted by those who know even a little of America ... and the "inherent quality" attributed to the "universal Yankee" of peculiar resistance to moral influences and rebellion against kindly and sympathising treatment is an unjust and unfounded libel upon him.... The essence of the non-restraint system is to lead the lunatic by such remains of mental power and coherence as the physician can lay hold upon, and where there has been least mind there will be the slightest means of moral guidance; but to make the men of the United States an exception because they, more than others, have learned how to rule themselves, is a blundering censure upon their culture and their virtues [Bucknill, pp. 84, 85, 86].

These and other broadsides only hardened the resolve of the country's first generation of asylum physicians to continue the practice of mechanical restraint, but it embarrassed the new generation that was poised to take over the leadership of the AMSAII and to establish themselves as experts on insanity. For them, joining their international colleagues in promoting non-restraint was "the mark of a new, more scientific approach" to the care of asylum patients (Tomes, p. 214).

The truth be known, that "more scientific approach" did not, in fact, could not, preclude the use of mechanical restraints all together. In virtually every asylum they were easily at hand when needed. Many asylum physicians scrabbled for high ground by designing new restraints that were less "mechanical" than "moral." Thus a pair of leather hand-muffs could be dismissed as remnants of a barbarous past, while a pair of leather hand-muffs with ventilation holes could be heralded as the harbingers of an enlightened future.

Yet even an enlightened future was not free of mechanical restraints. In post–World War II exposes on public asylums by such notable investigative journalists as Alfred Q. Maisel and Albert Deutsch, stark black and white photographs of straitjacketed or leg-locked patients raised the question once again as to whether asylums and their physicians had indeed improved upon the unenlightened past. While it may be tempting to conjecture that the introduction of Thorazine (Chlorpromazine) and other powerful psychotropic drugs into asylums in the mid-twentieth century precluded any need of mechanical restraints, that was not so. And while it may be even more tempting to further conjecture that more recent patient rights legislation precluded the use of mechanical restraints, that, too, was not so.

While the use of mechanical restraints is rare in Great Britain, for example, it is not in the United States. One to three patients in asylums or other psychiatric facilities die each week from aspirating vomit, strangulation, heart attack or stroke while confined in straitjackets, wrist or leg straps, or other devices. In 2011 a dozen distinguished scholars debated the therapeutic, legal and ethical implications of the continued use of mechanical restraints. Among them was Elyn Saks who spoke out against the forced treatment of patients and argued for preserving their dignity by putting them at the center of restraint decisions. Saks knows of what she speaks. Diagnosed as schizophrenic when she was a university student, she was institutionalized on several occasions and spent as long as twenty continuous hours in mechanical restraints. Saks is now the Orrin B. Evans Professor of Law, Psychology and Psychiatry and the Behavioral Sciences at the University of Southern California. The forum was the first in a series on the contemporary treatment of the mentally ill sponsored by the Saks Institute for Mental Health, Law, Policy and Ethics that she founded and directs.

## References

"Asylum Workers Association" (1916). *British Journal of Psychiatry, 62,* 639–645.
Atkins, G. (2003). *Gay Seattle.* Seattle: University of Washington Press.
Author (1826). Characteristics of French medicine. *American Medical Review and Journal, 3,* 5–25.
Author (1869). The Charlesworth and Gardiner Hill controversy. *Medical Times and Gazette, 2,* 287–289.
Beers, C. (1908). *A mind that found itself.* New York: Longman, Greens.
"Bethlem's Court of Governors Minutes" (1814, June 28).
Blumer, G.A. (1898–1899). The insane in the Antilles. *American Journal of Insanity, 55,* 713–723.
Bucknill, J.C. (1876). *Notes on asylums for the insane in America.* London: J & A Churchill.
Chiarugi, V. (1793). *Della pazzia in genere e in specie trattato medico analitico: Con una centuria di osservazioni.* Florence, Italy: Presso Luigi Carlieri.
Committee on Madhouses in England (1815). *Report of the Committee on Madhouses in England.* London: J. McCreery.
Cruden, A. (1739). *The London-citizen exceedingly injured, or a British inquisition display'd.* London: Cooper & Dodd.
Cumming, W.F. (1852). *Notes on lunatic asylums in Germany, and other part of Europe.* London: John Churchill.
Curwen, J. (ed.). (1875). *History of the Association of Medical Superintendents of American Asylums for the Insane.* Warren, PA: E. Cowen.
Deas, M.P. (1896). The uses and limitations of mechanical restraint as a means of treatment of the insane. *British Journal of Psychiatry, 42,* 102–113.
deHalsalle, H. (1916). *Degenerate Germany.* London: T.W. Laurie.

Deutsch, A. (1948). *The shame of the states.* New York: Harcourt, Brace.
Dickens, C. (1852). A curious dance round a curious tree. *Household Words, 11,* 362–370.
Dix, D. (1845). *Memorial soliciting a state asylum for the insane, submitted to the legislature of Pennsylvania.* Philadelphia: Isaac Ashmead.
Doerner, K. (1981). *Madmen and the bourgeoisie: A social history of insanity and psychiatry.* Oxford: Basil Blackwell.
"Dry and wet packs" (1895). *Journal of Mental Science, 41,* 94–98.
Earle, P. (1848). *History, description and statistics of the Bloomingdale Asylum for the Insane.* New York: Egbert, Hovey & King.
Earle, P. (1853). *Institutions for the insane in Prussia, Austria and Germany.* Utica, NY: New York State Lunatic Asylum.
Ellis, W.C. (1838). *A treatise on the nature, symptoms, causes, and treatment of insanity.* London: Samuel Holdsworth.
ENUSP (2012, February 22). Czech Republic must stop caging human beings. Retrieved at http://www.enusp.org.
"Forty-two years in a crib" (1907, March 10). *Chicago Daily Tribune,* p. F6.
Foucault, M. (1965). *Madness and civilization.* New York: Pantheon.
Galt, J.M. (1846). *The treatment of insanity.* New York: Harper & Brothers.
Gerard, D.L. (1997). Chiarugi and Pinel considered. *Journal of the History of the Behavioral Sciences, 33,* 381–403.
Granville, J.M. (1877). *The care and cure of the insane, Vol. 1.* London: Hardwick and Bogue.
Greenfield, L. (2013). *Mind, modernity, madness: The impact of culture on human experience.* Cambridge: Harvard University Press.
Hallaran, W.S. (1819). *Practical observations of the causes and cure of insanity.* Cork, Ireland: Edwards and Savage.
Haslam, J. (1798). *Observations on insanity.* London: F. and C. Rivington.
Heinroth, J.C.A. (1975/1818). *Textbook of disturbances of mental life.* Baltimore: Johns Hopkins University Press.
Hill, R.G. (1857). *A concise history of the entire abolition of mechanical restraints in the treatment of the insane.* London: Longman.
"The Holloway Pack Pill" (1895, January 24). *The Truth,* pp. 210–212.
Holt, E. (2004). Rest and restraint. *Lancet, 365,* 829–830.
House of Commons (1815). *First report: Minutes of evidence taken before the Select Committee appointed to consider of provision being made for the better regulation of madhouses.* London: Author.
House Special Committee (1907). *Report of the special committee on investigation of Government Hospital for the Insane.* Washington, D.C.: Government Printing Office.
Hunter, R., and Macalpine, I. (1963). *Three hundred*

*years of psychiatry, 1535–1860.* London: Oxford University Press.

"Insane asylum methods" (1880, December 2). *New York Times,* p. 8.

"Investigating asylums" (1880, December 7). *New York Times,* p. 12.

Knight, P.S. (1827). *Observations on the causes, symptoms and treatment of derangement of the mind.* London: Longman, Rees, Orme, Brown, and Green.

Kraepelin, E. (1962). *One hundred years of psychiatry.* Trans. W. Baskin. New York: Citadel.

Lathrop, C.C. (1890). *A secret institution.* New York: Bryant Publishing.

Letchworth, W.P. (1889). *The insane in foreign countries.* New York: G.B. Putnam.

Lindsay, W.L. (1878). The protection bed and its uses. *Edinburgh Medical Journal, 23,* 716–724.

MacBride, David (1772). *A methodical introduction to the theory and practice of physick, 1772.* London: Strahan.

"Mad-Houses: Bethlem" (1815, August 31). *The Times,* p. 2.

Maisel, A.Q. (1946, May 6). Bedlam 1946. *Life,* pp. 102–110, 112, 115–116, 118.

"Medical institutions of Naples" (1831). *North American Medical and Surgical Journal, 11,* 17–61.

Meier, M. (2009). Creating order: A quantitative analysis of psychiatric practice at the institutions of Burghölzi and Rheinau between 1870 and 1970. *History of Psychiatry, 20,* 139–162.

Mills, J.H. (1999). Re-forming the Indian: Treatment regimes in the lunatic asylums of British India, 1857–1880. *Indian Economic and Social History Review, 36,* 407–429.

Moddler, M. (1879, November 23). "A crying disgrace." *New York Herald,* p. 7.

Nichols, C.H. (1855). Proceedings of the tenth annual meeting of the Association of Medical Superintendents of American Institutions for the Insane. *American Journal of Insanity, 1–2,* 39–101.

Pinel, P. (1806). *A treatise on insanity.* Trans. D.D. Davis. Sheffield, UK: W. Todd.

Porter, R. (1990). *Mind-forg'd manacles: A history of madness in England from the Restoration to the Regency.* London: Penguin.

Redjinski, J. (1971). The Utica crib. *Bulletin of the Menninger Clinic, 35,* 202–206.

Rush, B. (1830). *Medical inquiries and observations upon the diseases of the mind,* 4th ed. Philadelphia: John Grigg.

Saks, E.R. (1986). The use of mechanical restraints in psychiatric hospitals. *Yale Law Journal, 95,* 1836–1856.

Saks, E.R. (2008). *The center cannot hold: My journey through madness.* New York: Hyperion.

Scull, A., MacKenzie, C., and Hervey, N. (1996). *Masters of Bedlam: The transformation of the mad-doctoring trade.* Princeton, NJ: Princeton University Press.

Shrady, G.F. (1959). Proceedings of the fourteenth annual meeting of the Association of Medical Superintendents of American Institutions for the Insane. *American Journal of Insanity, 16,* 42–96.

Smith, L. (1879). *Behind the scenes; or, Life in an insane asylum.* Chicago: Culver, Page, Hoyne.

Smith, S. (1916). *Who is insane?* New York: Macmillan.

"(A) Social Blot" (1870). *British Medical Journal, 2,* 441–443.

Stevenson, S. (1988). Madness and the picturesque in the Kingdom of Denmark. In W.F. Bynum, R. Porter, & M. Shepherd (eds.), *The anatomy of madness,* Vol. III, pp. 13–47. London: Routledge.

Tomes, N. (1994). *The art of asylum-keeping: Thomas Kirkbride and the origins of American psychiatry.* Philadelphia: University of Pennsylvania Press.

Tuke, D.H. (1885). *The insane in the United States and Canada.* London: H. K. Lewis.

U.S. Patient Office (1907). Ellen E. Perkins, of Beaver Bay, Minnesota: Sexual Armor. Specification of letters patent, Serial No. 380,468.

"The Week: Topic of the Day" (1869). *Medical Times and Gazette, 2,* 549.

Weiner, D.B. (2008). Philippe Pinel in the twenty-first century. In E.R. Wallace & J. Gach (eds.), *History of psychiatry and medical sociology,* pp. 305–312. New York: Springer.

White, W.A. (1938). *William Alanson White: An autobiography of purpose.* Garden City, NY: Doubleday.

Willis, T. (1684). *The practice of physick: Two discourses concerning the soul of brutes.* London: Dring, Harper, and Leigh.

Windholz, G. (1995). Psychiatric treatment and the condition of the mentally disturbed at Berlin's Charité in the early decades of the nineteenth century. *History of Psychiatry, 6,* 157–176.

Wood, W.M. (1852). Description of a new bed and bedstead for the use of insane and other patients. *Journal of Psychological Medicine, 5,* 395–398.

Yamanaka, H. (2003). Scandal and psychiatry in early nineteenth century Prussia. *History of Psychiatry, 14,* 139–160.

## *Arm-Chair*

A wooden chair with padded boxes on the arms. It was designed in the early nineteenth century by Sir William C. Ellis, the first medical superintendent of the Middlesex County Asylum near the village of Hanwell, west of London. Better known as the Hanwell Asylum, it was the first purpose-built asylum in England and one which, under Ellis's superintendency, experimented with non-restraint. Finding it occasionally necessary to restrain refractory patients, however, Ellis constructed the arm-chair as a more humane alternative to the tranquilizing and coercion chairs which were in wide use across Europe and the United States at the time.

He described the arm-chair as a convenient and easy mode of confinement, and laid out the details of its construction in his published treatise on the causes and cures of insanity:

> Each of the arms of the chair forms a padded box, which *incloses the arm of the patient, from a little below the elbow to the wrist*. The box ought to be sufficiently large to contain the arm quite loosely and without any pressure, and the hand will remain at liberty. A board, which forms a very convenient rest, is attached by hinges to the inner side of one of the arms of the chair, and is fastened to the other arm. When the confinement of the arm is unnecessary the box may be opened, and the patient may still remain fastened in the chair, by means of a loose strap passing in front of the body, through two holes at the back of the chair, and there buckled. The chair may be fitted with a foot-board, a little elevated above the floor, and perforated with holes. Under this board a vessel constantly filled with hot water ought to be kept in cold weather [Ellis, pp. 165–166].

Ellis resigned just a few years after he assumed the superintendency of Hanwell in protest against the bureaucratic interference of the asylum's magistrates, but content that he had instituted a benevolent therapeutic regime. As necessary as he found the arm-chair to be, and as humane he felt was its design, just a few decades later it was caustically dismissed by the Lancet Commission on Lunatic Asylums as nothing more than an instrument of "tender-hearted torture" (Granville, p. 94).

## *Aubanel's Restraining Bed, or Utica Crib, or, Protection Bed, or Enclosed Bed, or Safety Bed, or Preservation Bed, or DeKalb Crib*

A bed with a hinged convex latticework lid that locked at the front. The bed was wide enough for the patient to change positions, but not high enough for the patient to sit. Invented by Honoré Aubanel, medical superintendent of the Marseilles Lunatic Asylum in France in the mid-nineteenth century, the bed was offered as a humane alternative to the straitjackets used to restrain violent, suicidal or demented patients.

In 1846 Amariah Brigham introduced the bed into the New York State Lunatic Asylum in Utica, New York, where he was medical superintendent. It was in use there for several years before he directed his resident officer, Tilden Brown, to make some structural modifications on the original design. The reconstructed bed, completed in 1854, resembled a child's crib with spindled sides that allowed more circulation of air. The Utica crib, as it came to be known, was built of pine and ash and was six-and-a-half feet in length, three feet in width, and just fifteen inches from top to bottom. The latticed cover was composed of one-by-two inch strips of pine, spaced two inches apart, as were the side spindles. With only various slight modifications, such as using chains to suspend it in the air so that it could be rocked, the prototype was reproduced in asylums across the United States and Canada. In some American asylums it was also known as the DeKalb crib.

In a discussion with other asylum physicians, Tilden Brown stated that the first patient placed in the crib at Utica had become so enamored with it that when he was deprived of it for a few nights he begged to go back in it, saying "You know Doctor, we are all creatures of habit, and I can't sleep without it" (Nichols, p. 60). Although some of Brown's colleagues favored any form of restraint that a patient did not resist, others expressed concern that the lack of resistance indicated the restraint was not "obnoxious" enough to have a therapeutic effect (Nichols, p. 61).

The Utica crib, in fact, had been in use for some years before it became the subject of that spirited debate at the tenth annual meeting of the Association of Medical Superintendents of American Institution for the Insane (AMSAII) in 1855. Thomas Kirkbride, medical superintendent of the Pennsylvania Hospital for the Insane and one of the most vocal proponents of moral treatment [see **Moral Treatment**], conceded that the recumbent position of the patient in the crib might soothe delirium, but found it so repulsive as to never allow one in his asylum. Similar objections as to the appearance of the crib and the impression it left on medical and lay visitors were voiced by C.H. Nichols of the Government Hospital for the Insane (later renamed St. Elizabeths Hospital), who described it as an "ungracious looking machine" (Nichols, p. 59), but also reluctantly endorsed its use in certain cases. After discussion, the superintendents authorized the use of the crib, and the specifications for its construction were read into the record.

The crib certainly did leave an indelible impression on medical and lay visitors to American asylums. One of them was William Hammond, the Civil War Surgeon General and founder of the American Neurological Association, who referred to the crib as a "barbarous contrivance" and called on the New York state legislature to investigate its use (Moddler, p. 7). In the late nineteenth century, a three-person committee took testimony from superintendents, physicians, attendants and trustees about the use of the crib and other mechanical restraints at New York state asylums. The hearings exposed the growing rift between the specialties of asylum psychiatry and neurology, with the use of the crib vigorously defended by most asylum superintendents and physicians, and just as vigorously denounced by neurologists. T.M. Franklin, medical superintendent of the women's ward at the Blackwell Island Asylum, for example, lamented that he had only four cribs available, and expressed the desire to have an open dormitory filled with cribs to restrain violent patients. Neurologist Edward Spitzka, on the other hand, testified that the cribs were overused with little consideration of their effects. He had performed autopsies on two Wards Island Asylum patients who had been confined in cribs; the lower extremities of both had been paralyzed by the confinement. The final report of the investigating committee conceded that some patients had been mistreated by the use of the crib as well as other types of

The crib best known in the United States as the Utica Crib. Brought over from France in the 1840s, it was introduced at the New York State Lunatic Asylum in Utica and used there as in most asylum across the country for decades. The "ungracious looking" device became so controversial during the era of moral treatment that some asylum physicians made quite a show of throwing it onto a bonfire by way of announcing a new era of kinder and gentler treatment (courtesy of the St. Joseph Museums, Inc./Glore Psychiatric Museum, St. Joseph, Missouri).

mechanical restraints, but found insufficient evidence to conclude that mistreatment was widespread throughout New York asylums.

During his visit to American and Canadian asylums, British physician Daniel Hack Tuke dismissed the crib as an "unpleasant object [that] invariably suggests, when occupied, that you are looking at an animal in a cage" (Tuke, p. 55). He hoped that it would never find its way into British asylums, apparently not realizing that a similar crib, known as the enclosed bed, had been constructed as early as 1852 by William Wood, medical officer of Bethlem Hospital (better known as Bedlam) in London, or that a modified version of the crib, known as the protection bed, and sometimes referred to as the safety or preservation bed, had been designed by W. Lauder Lindsay, physician at the Murray Royal Institution in Perth, Scotland, in the mid–1870s, and was in use in a few Scottish asylums. Tuke apparently also was not aware that Lindsay's protection bed had been shipped to Australia at the request and with the enthusiastic endorsement of F. Norton Manning, the Inspector General of the Insane, and to Canada where eleven were in use at the Provincial Hospital for the Insane in Halifax, Nova Scotia, alone.

Lindsay, in fact, was the most outspoken advocate of the bed or crib in all of its variations. He argued that it was the only restraint that could prevent serious self-injury, accidents, as well as injury, sometimes fatal, by attendants in acts either of necessary physical restraint or unnecessary physical violence. He reminded critics of the English Lunacy Commissioners' 1870 findings that rib fractures, for example, were very common among asylum patients. In one of the cases the Commissioners detailed, a patient had repeatedly "slammed his chest with his open hand," breaking two ribs and his sternum; in another, an attendant twice lifted a patient and dropped him to the floor, breaking his rib ("Social Blot," p. 441). He further argued that the scandalous death of a patient at the Hanwell Asylum could have been avoided by the use of the bed or crib. That case involved Santa Nistri, an Italian immigrant, who was admitted to the asylum in 1869. An unmanageable patient, he was placed in a padded room and kicked, punched and bit the attendants when they came to feed and dress him. He also was reported to have slipped against a stair rail while he was being moved by attendants from one part of the asylum to another. Nistri died approximately one week after admission; the postmortem examination revealed a fractured sternum and eight fractured ribs. A jury exonerated the asylum and its attendants of any criminal responsibility for his death, a decision that created a heated debate about whether the use of mechanical restraints, including the bed or crib, would have prevented his death ("The Week," p. 549).

Tuke did not reflect on this controversy, but took the side of those who opposed the use of the bed or crib by asserting that it was a "so temptingly facile mode of restraint," that it easily could be abused and that patients would experience it as abusive (Tuke, p. 55). Indeed, patient accounts spoke strongly to that observation. Clarissa Caldwell Lathrop, who had spent two years as a patient at Utica, was not herself restrained in the crib, which she referred to as "an instrument of torture" (Lathrop, p. 201), but witnessed its effect on other patients:

> How the poor patients would labor to get out. Night and day they would work away at some loose slat when unobserved, and, perhaps, after many long, persevering efforts, they would crawl out and up to freedom through the narrow aperture below the mattress, only to be again imprisoned by the careless attendant. When one realizes what a comfort it is when suffering to be able to change one's position occasionally, it may be easy to imagine what it is to be shut up in one of these wooden cages, and forced to lie flat on your back [Lathrop, p. 202].

While confined at the Michigan Asylum for the Insane in Kalamazoo, Lydia Smith was placed in the crib soon after admission. She described the experience in the following way:

> A crib is a square box, on which is a cover, made to close and lock, and has huge round

posts, separated so as to leave a small space between for ventilation. The strap attached to the muff [confining the hands] was fastened to the crib in such a manner as to tighten around my waist, and across the pit of my stomach, with such pressure that it actually seemed to me that I could not breathe. My feet were fastened to the foot of the crib so tight, and remained there so long, that when they did unfasten them they were swollen so that it was impossible for me to stand upon them [Smith, p. 3].

Tuke's concern that the crib was available for abuse also was confirmed by growing news coverage of both crib-related deaths and long periods of confinement, in one case as long as forty-two years ("Forty-two Years," p. F6), in asylums across the United States. Bowing to growing peer and public pressure to abolish this type of restraint, G. Alder Blumer, the new superintendent of Utica, collected the forty or more cribs in his asylum and publicly burned them in 1887. Other superintendents followed suit, and by the turn into the twentieth century, the crib was infrequently used.

## Autenrieth's Chamber, or Chamber of Palisades

A tall wooden or metal palisade or cage that held otherwise unrestrained patients. The chamber was used not only for confining and isolating patients but, because it was wheeled, also for transporting them from one part of the asylum to another. The chamber was designed by Johann Autenrieth, a professor of medicine at the University of Tübingen in Germany in the early nineteenth century as an alternative to chains and fetters. Convenient, portable and, allegedly, humane, it was used in many European asylums where large rooms that were often referred to as "cage rooms" were filled with individual chambers and where on any given day patients so confined could be seen being wheeled across the asylums' grounds.

The chamber was not without its critics, however. Johann Christian August Heinroth, who had served as "physician for mental illness" at the St. George Home in Leipzig, Germany, before his tenure as Dean of the medical faculty at the University of Leipzig, was particularly critical of it. His rather lengthy harangue not only revealed the deep philosophical schism in German psychiatry during that era between the psychic and somatic schools of thought, but about the proper role of the asylum physician and the mundane practicalities of asylum administration. As to the chamber, Heinroth wrote:

> We find ourselves unable to recommend it in any way, for the following reasons. Firstly, use of the contrivance precludes any curative achievement; for if the patient is allowed to rage as much as he likes and move about within the space allotted to him, he remains master of himself and acts according to his own will. Now it is precisely this will which is bad and which must be restrained, since the whole power, the whole form of the disease is concentrated in it. Autenrieth's chamber thus prevents all medical influence on the patient. Secondly, even if our purpose is the safety of the patient, who must be prevented from inflicting injury on himself, it must be remembered that the patient can ram his head against the bars of the wooden cage just as effectively as against a stone wall.... Finally, since in any hospital or asylum... there are almost always a few candidates for Autenrieth's chamber, or since it may happen that several such patients qualify for the chamber on the same day, are we to lock them all together in the chamber, since all are to receive the same care and treatment? And if we do not wish to do this, how many such chambers must we build for each institution, and at what cost? [Heinroth, p. 295].

## Ball and Chain

Heavy iron ball at the end of a chain attached to the patient's lower leg, thus allowing slow walking but no running. The ball and chain was more often used on jail and prison inmates than asylum patients, but in his analysis of "certain unpublished returns of restraint made in 1800" (Tuke, p. 54), the British physician Daniel Hack Tuke found twenty-one cited instances of the use of the ball and chain to restrain patients. He thought the use was most likely confined to the "Southern or far Western institutions" (p. 55) he had not personally visited, but in fact the ball and chain was in use in many American asylums, especially those at which patients were outside performing agricultural work, until the twentieth century.

### *Belgian Cage, or Lunatic's Cage, or Idiot's Cage*

A wooden cage on short posts. The cage had been used for centuries before asylums were established, often for the display of the insane to the public. Within asylums, the cage was used to restrain the violent or demented patient. Although the cage was used throughout Europe, it became known as the Belgian cage when it was displayed at the National Fair in Brussels in 1880. At the time of the fair, it already had been banned from use in Belgium for more than thirty years.

### *Boot Hobbles, or Quarter Boots*

Constructed of bed-ticking and leather, the boots were locked by their soles to the foot of the bedstead, thus keeping the patient in a prone position on the bed. The boots were de-

**Belgian Cage, also known as the Lunatic's Cage or Idiot's cage. Asylums in countries around the world had their own versions of the cage that were used both to restrain and display insane patients to curious asylum visitors (W.P. Lechworth [1889].** *The insane in foreign countries.* **New York: G.P. Putnam's Sons).**

signed in the 1830s by Edward Parker Charlesworth, physician at the Lincoln Lunatic Asylum, also known as the Lawn Asylum, in Lincoln, England, to reduce the chafing produced by iron leg-chains. Because the boots allowed restricted movement of the legs, however, their use often resulted in deep skin abrasions and abscesses. Nonetheless, they were still in use more than twenty years after their invention. In a vituperative debate over who should be lauded as the originator of the British non-restraint movement, Charlesworth's protégé, Robert Gardiner Hill, cited the invention of the boots to discredit his former mentor's claim that he deserved recognition for being the first physician to abolish chains and manacles at an asylum.

## Cage Bed, or Net Bed, or Veil Bed

A bed with a cage of metal bars, or alternatively heavy netting, affixed to an approximately three feet high tubular metal structure; one side of the bed could be lowered for access to the restrained patient, and when raised, could be locked into position. The bed was first used, primarily in Eastern and Central European countries, in the early twentieth century as an enlightened alternative to the straitjacket or camisole.

Its use continued for more than a century until the United Nations, Amnesty International, Disabilities Rights International, and the European Council charged that it violated Article Five of the Universal Declaration of Human Rights, which all countries joining the European Union ratified. Article Five, which prohibits the subjection of any person to "torture or to cruel, inhuman or degrading treatment or punishment" made the continued use of the bed in asylums in the new European accession countries of Slovenia, Slovakia, the Czech Republic and Hungary, the target of a vigorous campaign by disability and human rights activists. Hungary was quick to ban the bed in 2003; Slovenia phased out its use by 2004. Slovakia also banned the bed in 2004, but with some resistance. Asylum physicians there protested that without the availability of the bed, more coercive restraints of violent or demented patients would be necessary.

It was in the Czech Republic that the deeply ethical, social and political underpinnings of the ban were exposed. For many years, psychiatrist Jan Pfeiffer had been campaigning for the ban on cage beds in the outdated and underfunded Czech asylum system. His campaign drew the attention of J.K. Rowling, author of the internationally acclaimed *Harry Potter* series, who wrote an open letter to the Czech government, protesting their use. Reprinted in newspapers around the world, the letter specifically targeted the use of the bed for disabled children in state homes, but initiated an international media investigation on the use of the bed in asylums as well. The most thorough media inquiry was conducted by the British Broadcasting Corporation (BBC) in 2004. In it, Michel Celetka described the week he had been locked in a cage bed while a patient at the asylum in Brno. Desperate for help, he had admitted himself to the asylum where he was immediately tranquilized and locked in the bed. He spoke of feeling "confused and trapped," and because he was not allowed to leave the bed to eat or to use the toilet, he even considered drinking his own urine to quench his thirst (Holt, p. 829).

Soon after the Rowling letter and the BBC exposé, the Czech Minister of Health issued a statement that he had instructed all institutions to cease the use of the cage bed by the end of the year. Czech President Vaclav Klaus, however, criticized that decision, declaring that it was a premature reaction to populist attacks against the standards of care in the country. Many asylum physicians criticized it as well, asserting that the bed was more humane than other restraint techniques, but others rejoined that no type of mechanical restraint, including the bed, would be necessary if Czech asylums were better regulated and funded, and their physicians better trained. In the wake of the exposé, there also were calls in the country for more enlightened views and research on insanity in this post-communist country, and on more liberating strategies, such as deinstitutionalization and community care, for dealing with it.

Cage beds were removed in asylums by order of the Czech Health Ministry in 2004, but because they were not officially banned, they remained in use for extreme cases. One of those cases was that of thirty-year-old Vera Musilova, a patient at the Bohnice Psychiatric Hospital in Prague, who died after choking on her own feces while restrained in a cage bed in 2006. Her parents' lawsuit against the hospital was dismissed in 2012, the same year that a patient at the Dobřany Psychiatric Hospital hung herself just a few hours after being placed in a cage bed. Her death has renewed the international campaign against the use of the cage bed in Czech asylums.

## *La Ceinture à Bracelets Mobiles*

A broad leather belt for encircling the body to which softly padded leather wristlets were attached by small chains; the belt was further secured by straps that went over the shoulders, in suspender fashion. The belt bracelets allowed some movement of the hands, and the entire restraint could be worn under the clothes, so as to give the patient a dignified appearance. They were designed by J.A. Peeters of the Gheel Lunatic Colony in Belgium in the mid-nineteenth century and were used primarily for patients who tore their clothes.

## *Chains, or Shackles, or Fetters*

A series of thick interlinked metal rings that were secured at one end to a bed, wall or some other stable object, and at the other end to the patient's legs, wrists, waist and/or neck. Chains were the original method of mechanical restraint used in asylums around the world; inexpensive to forge and quite easy to apply, chains were used to maintain some control in asylums that throughout history have been overcrowded and understaffed.

The use of chains in early asylums was not just a matter of cost and expediency. The insane patient was thought to be akin to a brute or a wild beast, bereft of reason and incurable in the bargain. "Madmen are still strong and robust to a prodigy," the English physician Thomas Willis warned, "so that they can break cords and chains, break down doors or walls, one easily overthrows many endeavoring to hold him" (Willis, p. 205). Such a patient, therefore, had to be tamed, domesticated, and chained for the well-being of self and others during that tedious and treacherous process.

By the nineteenth century, this bestial view of the insane was being challenged by proponents of moral treatment [see **Moral Treatment**] who were arguing not only that the insane retained the vestiges of humanity, but that they could be restored to reason. This *"rupture épistemologique,"* as it sometimes is so referred, rendered the obdurate use of chains in Western asylums barbaric, archaic and damnable, as the case of James Norris illustrated.

James Norris, sometimes referred to as William Norris, was an American seaman who was admitted to Bethlem Hospital in London in 1800 and transferred to its incurable wing a year later. Exceptionally strong and very cunning, Norris quickly established a reputation as the most violent and devious patient at Bethlem. Because he had small wrists and hands, he could easily slip off the manacles that were used to restrain him and use them as weapons against attendants and other patients. In 1804, the apothecary of Bethlem, John Haslam, frustrated that there was not room enough in the overcrowded asylum to confine Norris in two rooms where his restless energy could be better contained, worked with a number of others to design a complex system of chains to secure Norris to the wall of his cell. The restraint was described by asylum reformer Edward Wakefield as follows:

> He was fastened by a long chain, which passing through a partition, enabled the keeper, by

going into the next cell, to draw him close to the wall at pleasure; that to prevent this Norris muffled the chain with straw, so as to hinder its passing through the wall; that he afterwards was confined in the manner we saw him, namely, a stout ring was riveted round his neck, from which a short chain passed to a ring made to slide upwards or downwards on an upright massive iron bar, more than six feet high, inserted into the wall. Round his body a strong iron bar about two inches wide was riveted; on each side the bar was a circular projection, which being fashioned to and inclosing each of his arms, pinioned them close to his sides. This waist bar was secured by two similar bars which, passing over his shoulders, were riveted to the waist bar both before and behind. The iron ring round his neck was connected to the bars on his shoulders, by a double link. From each of these bars another short chain passed to the ring on the upright iron bar.... His right leg was chained to trough [bed]; in which he had remained thus encaged and chained more than twelve years [House of Commons, pp. 11–12].

On his second visit to Bethlem, Wakefield brought an artist who sketched Norris chained to the wall of his cell. Engraved by George Cruikshank, the sketch appeared in newspapers across Great Britain, and prompted a Parliamentary Select Committee inquiry. Although both Haslam and the Governors of Bethlem defended the chaining of Norris, averring that "however unsightly [the chains were] on the whole rather a merciful and humane, than a rigorous and severe imposition" ("Bethlem's Court of Governors Minutes" p. 1), the Parliamentary Select Committee and much of the public were more critical. In 1816, Haslam was relieved of his position.

Norris died from tuberculosis just three weeks after being released from his chains. For decades to come, however, the sketch of this "ferocious madman," as Haslam had characterized him, served as an icon for the British non-restraint movement which ultimately removed chains and shackles from asylums across the country, even while it prompted other countries to do so as well.

In colonized countries, however, the use of chains continued, rationalized by a racialized psychiatry that relegated indigenous people to brutes and wild beasts, quite regardless of their mental condition. Thus in the French colonies of Morocco and Syria, for example, insane patients in the "martisans" or asylums were found in heavily chained leg locks as late as the early twentieth century, long after the chains had been struck at the Asylum de Bicêtre in Paris; and in India, then under the sovereignty of the British Empire, insane

**Drawing of James Norris, also known as William Norris, an American seaman who was confined at Bethlem Hospital in London. Agile and very crafty, Norris was able to slip out of manacles and use them as weapons. The Bethlem apothecary John Haslam designed this complicated restraint system that involved chains and iron bars. The "ferocious madman," as Haslam referred to him, was so restrained for twelve years (courtesy of the Wellcome Library, London).**

patients were chained long after chains had been abolished at the Hanwell Asylum outside of London.

As another symbolic gesture in the mid-twentieth century, asylum chains were melted and cast into a 300 pound "Mental Health Bell" in the United States. The bell, which can be found in Baltimore, Maryland, has the following inscription: "Cast from shackles which bound them, this bell shall ring out hope for the mentally ill and victory over mental illness."

In some countries, however, chains are still the preferred method of restraint of insane asylum patients. In 2010, the World Health Organization piloted the "Chain-Free Initiative" in Afghanistan, and in Somalia where it is estimated that 90 percent of asylum patients are chained by their wrists and/or legs to beds, trees in the asylum yard, or to large stones in a common area. The organization also noted that asylum patients are still being chained in a number of countries, including Ghana, Eritrea, Kenya, Malaysia, Indonesia, Pakistan and India.

## *Coercion Chair, or English Chair, or* Zwangstuhl

A significantly modified version of the tranquilizing chair invented by Maximilian Jacobi, superintendent of the Siegburg Asylum in Germany, a former monastery situated on a steep rock overlooking the town, and used extensively throughout that country and Austria well into the twentieth century. The coercion chair was tall, constructed of wood, had long, wide arms, and was supported by a wooden base, rather than legs. When the patient was seated, a hinged door at the base was closed and locked in front of the feet, a lid was closed over the thighs, and a board fitted into grooves was maneuvered down in front of the trunk, so that only the head of the patient was visible. In at least a few asylums, for example, the Imperial Provincial Lunatic Asylum in Hall, Austria, and the Gieseing Asylum near Munich, Germany, another block of wood with a small door that could be opened to feed the patient was fitted over the head.

In his tour of European asylums, the American physician Pliny Earle was appalled by the coercion chair. After describing it in detail, he concluded, "We advance no pretensions to inventive genius, but, really, it appears as if there were one thing wanting to make this chair just what it ought to be; and that is—to heat it a few hours in the midst of a large and brisk fire" (Earle, p. 148).

## *Cruciform Stance*

Vertical form of the bed saddle in which the patient was secured in a standing position for eight to twelve continuous hours via a ring in a belt to a heavy cord that ran from ceiling to floor. The patient's arms were encased in the

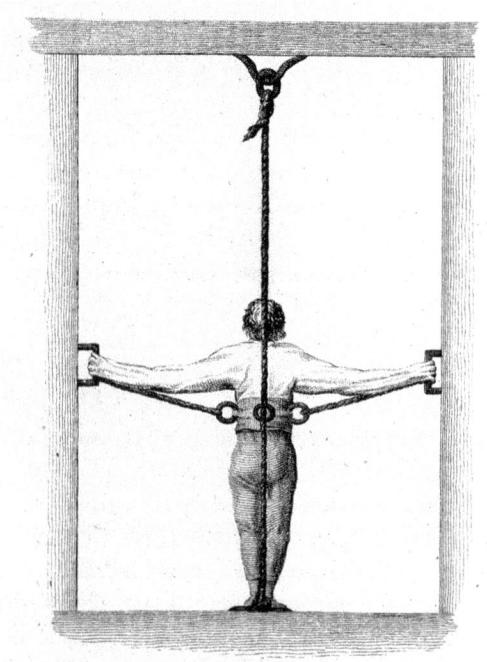

The cruciform stance. The origin of this method of mechanical restraint is unknown but it is most often associated with Ernst Horn of the Berlin Charité Hospital (courtesy of the Wellcome Library, London).

long sleeves of a straitjacket, and fastened to rings in opposite walls. The origin of the cruciform stance as a restraint is unclear. There is evidence that some German neurologists used it to calm nervous patients in their private practices before Ernst Horn, with whom it is most often associated, began using it at the Berlin Charité Hospital as a method to reduce the delirious outbursts of the belligerent and uncooperative patient who was at risk of injuring self or others. The cruciform stance, Horn argued, rendered the patient harmless, submissive and more respectful of the physician. He further boasted that any patient who had been subjected to this type of mechanical restraint one or more times would become orderly and obedient at the mere mention of it.

The cruciform stance was not widely used in asylums outside of the Berlin Charité and a few other German asylums, although the psychiatric reformer, Emil Kraepelin, favorably described it as "one of the most innocuous, comfortable and safest devices for calming patients" (Kraepelin, p. 86).

## Cuirass

A heavy leather breastplate composed of stout oxhide attached by iron rings to a leather back-plate, thus resembling the piece of armor after which it was named. The cuirass also had long leather sleeves ending in enclosed gloves, and straps on each side and at the back that were used to secure the patient to a chair, or to an iron ring in the wall. It was used in many European and British asylums, but is most associated with German asylums where its use continued until the late nineteenth century.

The cuirass was the special target of a furious broadside against German asylum therapeutics delivered by prominent British physician Sir James Crichton-Brown at the annual meeting of the Asylum Workers Association in London in 1915. In the throes of World War I, many asylum attendants either were being retrained to work with the wounded or were themselves conscripted into service. Crichton-Brown cautioned that it was too early to speculate about the effects the war would have on the body of knowledge informing the care of asylum patients in England, but that it was certain that "it will explode and utterly demolish the spurious deference and respect hitherto bestowed on German teachings and methods" ("Asylum Workers Association, p. 641).

To great applause, and with more than a little nationalist fervor, Crichton-Brown went on to declare that the British had nothing to learn from the Germans who lagged shamefully behind in the humane treatment of the insane. He offered the continued use of the cuirass restraint decades after it had been abandoned in British asylums as evidence of a "coldness, a severity. and indifference to human suffering that is revolting... [and] that contrast(s) with the urbanity and sympathy we are accustomed to here" (p. 642).

## Dry Pack

A warmed sheet or blanket and several broad leather straps that were connected at intervals by loops with two long strips of webbing. The blanket was wrapped tightly around the patient from head to toe, and secured by long and heavy safety pins. Once packed, the patient was laid on one strip of webbing; the other strip was brought down over the body and secured to the one underneath. The leather straps then were pulled tightly to restrain movements of the arms and legs, and the upper part of the blanket was folded and then sewn back to prevent interference with breathing. The patient usually was briefly released from the dry pack two to three times during a twenty-four hour period. The dry pack was used most often in cases of homicidal or suicidal mania.

The dry pack so exhausted the patient by reducing the pulse and body temperature, and by greatly increasing perspiration, that the risk of death was considerable. Indeed, several cases of patients dying as the result of having been restrained in it attracted a great deal of public attention and made asylums physicians wary of its use. One of those case was Thomas Weir, a twenty-five-year-old patient at Holloway Asylum in London, who had become extremely agitated and had violently attacked two other patients. He was dry packed for several hours. Upon release from the restraint, he refused food and attacked three attendants when they tried to force feed him. He was again dry packed, this time for five hours. He once again became violent after that period of restraint, and asylum physicians found it necessary to keep him under continuous, and unsupervised, dry pack restraint. Four days later, he died. The coroner's inquest determined that "Weir died from exhaustion, following mania. The jury are of opinion that not sufficient medical supervision was exercised, and that the mechanical restraint was excessive and too long continued" ("Dry and Wet Packs," pp. 97–98).

A subsequent investigation of Weir's death by Lunacy Commissioners led to a finding that condemned the use of the dry pack in any asylum and under any circumstance. The press also called for elimination of this form of mechanical restraint, stating that Weir's death "is a story of the slow torturing to death of a helpless maniac by methods of barbarity which must be apparent to the most callous observer" ("Holloway Pack," p. 212). Shamed by the resulting public outcry, British asylums gradually stopped using the dry pack, although European and American asylums continued to use it well into the twentieth century.

In some American asylums, the term "dry pack" actually was a euphemism for a straitjacket or camisole. A few asylum superintendents were able to cleverly reduce the incidence of straitjacket use in their annual reports by increasing the incidents of dry pack use, apparently reasoning that the latter would be mistakenly understood as a therapeutic intervention rather than a mechanical restraint.

## *English Clock Case, or English Coffin, or Pen, or Lunatic Box, or Box, or Press, or Isolation Cell*

An upright wooden case resembling a grandfather clock into which a patient was placed. A hinged panel was then locked, securing the standing patient inside. Only the

The English Clock Case. Upright wooden cases like this were used in many asylums during the nineteenth and early twentieth centuries. It was thought to be particularly effective in calming manic patients, some of whom would stand upright in the box for days, even weeks, at a time (courtesy of the St. Joseph Museums, Inc./Glore Psychiatric Museum, St. Joseph, Missouri).

face of the patient was visible through an opening at the top of the case which could be closed with a sliding or swinging door. The case was thought to be particularly effective in treating the manic patient because it "reduce[d] excitement by the expenditure of excitability, from the constant exertion of the muscles which support the body. The debility thus induced in those muscles would attract morbid excitement from the brain and therefore relieve the mania" (Rush, p. 191). The patient remained in the case for several continuous hours or even days, was fed through the open door at the top; bodily wastes were not usually removed from the case until the treatment was terminated.

Although the case had been in use in some provincial English asylums for years, for example at St. Peters in Bristol where it was called a pen, Johann Christian August Heinroth of Leipzig University in Germany was sometimes mistakenly cited as its inventor. Heinroth was the leader of the "psychic school" of thought in Germany, also known as "Romantic psychiatry," that linked psychiatry with philosophy and poetry, and saw insanity as the result of a moral failing that required that the patient be re-educated to the norm of reason. By both restricting movement and causing humiliation, the case forced the patient to relinquish earthly passions and bodily needs, and recommit to a moral life. The case was reserved for the restraint of the incorrigible patient whose stubbornness and bravado posed more problems to re-education than did the diagnosed mental condition.

An English visitor to the Siegburg Asylum, housed in an old monastery near Bonn, Germany, commented on its use:

> I saw several patients of both sexes under restraint, and notably two who were enclosed in a wooden sentry box, with only their necks and heads exposed. I was not a little struck with this apparatus, which looked more like a Chinese punishment than a means of medical treatment; but on asking Dr. Föcke the history of so strange a practice, I had the mortification of learning that the model of the apparatus had been brought ... from England many years ago. I trust that no such instrument of durance is to be found in England in the present day [Cumming, p. 59].

A similar case, known as an isolation cell, was used in Australian asylums in the late nineteenth century. The cell was constructed of strong tongue and groove timber, with straight wings on each side of the front that allowed it to be wedged into a corner. The door was curved, had a metal handle and mortise locks, and an oval window just below head height. The patient either stood or sat on a small ledge inside in the box and was further restrained by leather straps.

## *Enveloping Bag, or Envelope Bag*

A long canvas or woolen bag that enveloped the patient; a collar fixed to the open end of the bag was secured loosely around the patient's neck. So confined, the enveloped patient was further restrained by straps that ran through handles on the side of the bag that then were secured to the bed. The enveloping bag was used with some frequency in British colonial asylums, long after moral treatment [see **Moral Treatment**] had made such restraints unfashionable. Arguing for the continued use of the enveloping bag at the asylum in Bengal, India where he was medical superintendent during the mid-nineteenth century, Arthur Payne reminded his colleagues that although non-restraint was in vogue in the British Isles and had become the epitome of enlightened and compassionate asylum medicine, it was necessary, if only occasionally, to use it in the management of the insane in the far reaches of the Colonies.

## *Five-Point Restraint*

The addition of a thick cotton cord or sheet tied around the waist of a patient who already was secured to the bed in a four-point restraint. A former patient, Jackie Cachero, who had been involuntarily committed by her mother in the mid-twentieth century to the Western State Hospital in Washington because she was a lesbian, described being placed in the five-point restraint where she had remained for two to three continuous weeks:

> They strapped me down in a little tiny room with nothing in it but a hospital bed, and they put these leather straps around my wrists, strung a belt through them, and they had me spread-eagled, my legs tied to the other end of the bed. They had a strap around my waist, too [Atkins, p. 52].

## Four-Point Restraint

One of the few forms of mechanical restraints still in use for subduing the violent patient who is placed face-up and spread-eagle on a bed, with hands and feet tied to the bedstead with thick cotton cords.

## Gyve, or Leg-Lock

An iron bar, approximately two feet long, with a shackle at each end to secure the feet; a chain fastened it to an iron belt to which handcuffs dangled from chains. During the Parliamentary Select Committee inquiry into asylums and mad-houses in England in 1815, Godfrey Higgens, a Governor of York Asylum, discovered a rusted gyve in a locked closet. No one was able to tell him how the twenty-four pound restraint, apparently first called a gyve by Shakespeare in *Othello* ("I will gyve thee in thine own courtship," II, I, 170), came into the asylum and whether it had been recently used.

In asylums in the colonies of the British Empire, gyves were in use well into the twentieth century. Whether they were cast of iron or made of heavy wood, they usually were referred to as leg-locks.

## Hallaran's Belt

A broad leather strap that encircled the body and had leather loops which encircled the patient's arms just above the elbows, thus allowing limited movement of the forearms and hands. The belt was closed at the patient's back with loop holes and rings secured by a small iron pin and padlock. To assure that it did not slip up or down on the body, a suspender of leather bands was placed over the patient's shoulders and locked onto the belt behind the back. Designed in the early nineteenth century by William Saunders Hallaran, physician to the Cork Lunatic Asylum in Ireland, the belt was intended to free the patient from prolonged confinement in a straitjacket which, in Hallaran's opinion, only instilled a "vicious disposition ...as if from consciousness on the part of the patient, of injurious treatment, and the justice of resenting it" (Hallaran, p. 134).

## Hand-Muffs, Locked Gloves, or Soft Gloves

Heavy leather or canvas mittens, with air holes punched in them for ventilation, and secured at the wrists with specially designed screw bolts that were unlocked with a key. The muffs were invented by Paul Slade Knight, medical superintendent of the Lancaster County Lunatic Asylum in Lancaster, England, who described their efficacy in managing a violent patient:

> An intriguing, unruly, vicious male lunatic was detected by myself with a piece of iron, which he had contrived to shape like a dagger, with a handle firmly fitted to it. Of course I had it removed. He immediately became excessively abusive, and I directed some restraint to be placed on him; and he was secured with the hand-muffs which I had invented.... On this he lost all command of temper, and uttering the most revolting imprecations, explained—*"I'll murder you yet: I am a madman, and they cannot hang me for it."* I took no particular notice of his threat. I deemed it prudent, however, to

have my eye more particularly upon him, and kept the hand muffs on about three weeks, when all restraint was removed, and he was placed under a somewhat strict superintendence for a short period; but as he *abstained* from any absolute violence he was free from coercion of any kind" [Knight, pp. 72–73, italics in original].

A century after its invention, the hand-muff was still in use in American asylums. The mental hygiene reformer and former asylum patient, Clifford Beers, described his restraint in it in the following manner:

> I was subjected to a detestable form of restraint that amounted to torture. To guard me at night while the remaining attendant slept, my hands were imprisoned in what is known as a "muff." A muff, innocent enough to the eyes of those who have never worn one, is in reality a relic of the Inquisition. It is an instrument of restraint which has been in use for centuries and even in many of our public and private institutions is still in use. The muff I wore was made of canvas, and differed from a muff designed for the hands of fashion only in the inner partition, also of canvas, which separated my hands, but allowed them to overlap. At either end was a strap which buckled tightly around the wrist and was locked [Beers, p. 122].

The hand-muff also was used in asylums to prevent masturbation. As late as the mid-twentieth century it was theorized that masturbation was both the cause and the effect of insanity. Because the vigilant supervision of asylum patients in the evening was often compromised by understaffing, the hand-muff was an essential preventive device.

## Haslam's Belt, or Haslam's Girdle

A leather belt, eight to ten inches wide, that was passed around the lower part of the body and fastened to the back with buckles; the patient's hands were placed in leather bags on each side of the belt and secured in that position with cloth bandages. The belt was invented by John Haslam, apothecary to Bethlem Hospital in London, in the early nineteenth century as a "salutary restraint" (Haslam, p. 126) and humane alternative to the straitjacket. Upon its 1814 visit to Bethlem, however, a committee of reformers, headed by Edward Wakefield, found little use of Haslam's Belt; rather, most patients were leg-locked and chained to the walls. Asylums throughout Europe did use some version of the belt, though, and any number of asylum physicians took credit for its invention.

## High Collar

A thick leather or iron collar, sometimes lined with linen or cotton, placed over the head of the patient and fastened behind the neck with a lock. The collar not only was used to prevent biting, tearing clothes with the teeth, and excessive head movements of the manic or delirious patient, but to focus the distracted patient's attention in one direction or on one thing. The collar was in use in England and Ireland until the mid-nineteenth century, and in Germany for decades after that.

## Horn's Sack, or Horn's Bag

Invented by Ernst Horn at the Berlin Charité Hospital in the early nineteenth century, the sack was approximately seven feet long and two feet wide and composed of rough burlap. The inner layer was covered with waxed linen at the head of the bag to prevent the entry of any light; the outer layer was fitted with straps at one end so that it could be drawn closed over the recumbent patient who usually also was confined in a straitjacket or camisole. Horn had observed that highly agitated patients often quieted and calmed in the dark, so he had experimented with placing these patients in potato or sugar sacks. Upon finding that with this simple method he could cure 25 percent of them, he designed the double layered sack.

The sack was the subject of what might have been the first psychiatric malpractice charge ever filed, and certainly of the subsequent bitterly divisive scandal that ensued. In August 1811, a young woman named Luise Thiel was brought to the Charité; she was depressed, emaciated due to anorexia, and screamed uncontrollably at any attempt to feed her. Over the following eleven days, she was subjected to the standard treatments of the lunatic ward which included hydrotherapy, the administration of emetics, and sessions in the rotary device known as Cox's Swing [see **Rotation, Oscillation and Vibration**]. Her condition, however, did not improve. Horn then ordered her to be placed in the sack where she remained for one hour. Somewhat calmed by the restraint, she was removed for a short time, and then placed again in the sack where she was found dead three hours later.

The cause of her death was a matter of some dispute. The town physician concluded she had asphyxiated. Experts brought in disagreed, saying the sack was too porous to cause asphyxiation. Their conclusion was supported by an experiment conducted by a physicist in which the flame of an oil lamp, enclosed in the sack, continued to burn for some time, giving evidence that there was sufficient air in the sack to sustain life. Rumors that Thiele actually had been enclosed in two sacks, one doubled over the other, precluded any closure to the dispute.

Although with just thirty-nine rooms the psychiatric section was a relatively small component of the very much larger Charité Hospital, it was rife with petty bickering and much more consequential philosophical and scientific arguments over the causes and treatments of insanity. The day after Thiel's death, the Charité's Second Surgeon, Henrich Kohlraush, wrote a letter to the Chief Medical Councillor, Johann Langermann, describing Horn's treatment of her as "cruel" and "barbaric." The letter was forwarded to the police, as was a petition received the following day from a relative of Thiele's, demanding a criminal investigation. The Chamber Court immediately began an informal investigation which concluded a month later with the finding that there was insufficient evidence to pursue criminal charges against Horn. Refuting the finding, the police commissioner pressed the Ministry of Justice to launch its own formal investigation.

The investigation not only exacerbated the rift between Horn and Kohlraush, but revealed the ideological differences within German medicine. Horn was a proponent of philosophical medicine, that is, medicine tied to theory and science and learned in the academy; Kohlraush advocated a more pragmatic and skill-based approach. The experts called in the investigation to give their opinions were champions of philosophical medicine; as a result, they not only concluded that the sack was an appropriate method of treatment and not the cause of Thiele's death, but took the opportunity to excoriate Kohlraush and his approach to medicine.

A series of newspaper and magazine articles on the case continued that theme, thus elevating the status of both Horn and the philosophical medicine he practiced. In 1814, Kohlrausch resigned from the Charité in disgrace. Two years later, however, an anonymous article published in a major newspaper stated that the sack that the experts had examined before giving their opinions was not the double layered sack in which Thiele had died, but a single layered sack without the waxed linen that blocked both air and light. That article, and several that followed, called for a new investigation. Although Horn then quickly published a book in an effort to vindicate himself, he could not stop the medical community's growing criticism not about his philosophical approach to asylum medicine, but about his specific use of the sack, which by then increasingly was referred to with the term Kohlrausch had first used: "*der Sterbesack*," or "death-sack." In 1818 Horn resigned under duress from the Charité His career, however, was not adversely affected. He was appointed a professor of therapeutics at Berlin University and published quite extensively on asylum therapeutics.

## Lacing

A simple restraint in which the patient first is confined in a straitjacket, then laid on a bed and covered with a blanket; ropes were then laced over the blanket and secured to the sides of the bed, much in the manner of lacing a corset. The German physician Johann Christian August Heinroth enthusiastically recommended lacing for female patients who needed restraint "not so much on account of their wild behavior but because they display morbid stubbornness and refractoriness, and because of their perverted actions, and who would only laugh at mere confinement in a straitjacket" (Heinroth, p. 296). Lacing, he argued, served the dual purpose of restraint and punishment.

## Leather Hobbles

A narrow strap of leather wrapped around the ankles and secured with a lock, allowing the patient to walk in very small steps. Considered a humane alternative to chains and gyves, hobbles could be found in asylums around the world, and were in use well into the mid-twentieth century.

## Locked Jumpsuit

A contemporary version of the strong dress/suit. The jumpsuit was a one-piece garment closed and locked at the back with large safety-pin-like devices through steel grommets, or a heavy zipper. The arms of the patient were not enclosed, so the hands could be secured in wristlets attached to a waist belt or chain. The locked jumpsuit is still in use in asylums around the world.

## Mad Box, *or* Daarekiste, *or* Dollkasten

A wooden box, constructed of heavy planks, typically about nine feet square with a small hole to let in air and some light. The *daarekiste* contained a latrine and a plank bed, and was used in Denmark into the nineteenth century for restraining violent asylum patients. Because there were few asylums in Denmark, the insane often were restrained in *daarekiste* that had been built on the grounds of general hospitals, jails, town halls and even in private homes.

The physician Ole Jørgen Rawert visited seventeen general hospitals in Denmark in the early nineteenth century and commented that the arrangement of *daarekiste* at Odense Hospital were reminiscent of pigsties. About the nine *daarekiste* on the grounds of Elsinore Hospital, he wrote:

> Lunatics are supposed to be able to stand greater cold than healthy people but in Denmark, generally speaking, we go a little too far in testing just how much cold they can stand: here they get just as little warmth in the winter as at most places [Stevenson, p. 34].

In Germany, the mad box was referred to as the *dollkasten*. It was of identical construction to the Danish *daarekiste* with the exception that it was movable.

## Manacles, *or* Handcuffs, *or* Wrist Shackles

A pair of lockable linked iron rings, often weighing as much as ten pounds, for securing the wrists, which sometimes were further secured by a chain to an iron waistband. Like chains, handcuffs were inexpensive to forge and relatively easy to apply, thus they were one of the first methods of mechanical restraint to be used in asylums, and one of the last to be abolished.

In his testimony before the 1815 Parliamentary Select Committee investigating the conditions of asylums in England, John Haslam, the apothecary of Bethlem Hospital in London, defended the use of handcuffs in a this exchange with a skeptical committee member:

> *Member*: Might not violence be effected with both hands?

*Haslam*: You cannot be afraid of any man so secured.
*Member*: You think that the hands so secured with irons, is less objectionable than when secured by the strait waistcoat?
*Haslam*: A thousand times.
*Member*: Can the patient move his hands to his face?
*Haslam*: Certainly; it is merely a security around each wrist.
*Member*: Is he not capable of doing an injury with his hands secured in that way?
*Haslam*: No; he is not able to strangle himself, or to fix the apparatus to hang himself, or do any injury to himself or any body else...
*Member*: Is he not capable of striking another person with his hands secured with irons?
*Haslam*: The hand put up even of a timid person would prevent it.
*Member*: Is he not capable of striking another person that may come in his way?
*Haslam*: Not to hurt him; he can strike him, but not to hurt him ["Mad-Houses," p. 2].

## *Maniac's Bed*

A bed frame on four very short legs to which the patient was secured via an iron bar passed through loops at the back of a shoulder harness, cotton wristlets hooked to each side of the bed and cotton anklets hooked to the foot of the bed. The bed itself was padded for the comfort of the patient who typically was propped up against large pillows. A hole at the bottom of the mattress allowed the passage of bodily wastes into a bucket. The bed was designed by Vincenzo Chiarugi, physician in chief at the at the Ospedale di Bonifazio in Florence, Italy, in the late eighteenth century. Some version of the bed could be found in most asylums around the world.

## *Monkey Jacket*

A heavy canvas sack-like dress in which the feet and arms of the patient were enclosed. Straps attached to the sack were locked on the sides and the foot of the bed. In his tour of American asylums in the late 1800s, the English physician Daniel Hack Tuke did not come across a patient in the monkey jacket, but was surprised to find that many asylums had the jackets stored in closets.

## *Osier Basket, or Osier Cage, or Wicker Basket, or Basket of Force*

A coffin-shaped wicker basket, approximately six feet long and one-and-a-half feet wide, in which a recumbent patient was secured by a heavy wicker lid that left the head exposed. The basket was invented at the Charenton Asylum near Paris, France, in the early nineteenth century by physician Charles François Simon Giraudy. With some variation in design and construction materials, it was used in many asylums throughout Europe.

## *Perkins Sexual Armor*

Designed and patented in 1908 by Ellen Perkins, a registered nurse. Perkins sexual armor was a complicated unisex chastity belt that prevented the insane patient from masturbating. Expounding on both the received wisdom of the early twentieth century that masturbation was the most common cause of insanity in the young, and the harsh reality that asylums were understaffed, Perkins designed the sexual armor to "accomplish the redemption of [the insane] from such habits" without constant vigilance by staff (U.S. Patent Office, p. 1).

A cloth garment much like an armless and short-legged bathing suit, Perkins sexual armor had an inverted arch-shaped thin metal crotch plate with a perforated central opening for the passage of urine when unlocked by a key. The rear plate was secured by hinged extensions that were stitched into the garment. The inner portions of the legs of the garment were covered with heavy leather reinforcements that were attached to the sides of the crotch plate; the shirt portion was reinforced with leather shoulder and neck straps, the ends of which were secured by a small padlock. Perkins asserted that the sexual armor could be both comfortably and discretely worn. In her patent application, Perkins stated that the sexual armor had been used and found "highly efficient" (p. 2).

The Perkins sexual armor was given patent number 875,845 in 1908. It is not known how widely or extensively it was used in asylums. A plaque commemorating her invention can be found at the Green Door, a liquor store and bar in Beaver Bay, Minnesota, her home town.

### Pillory Wicker

Invented by Charles François Simon Giraudy in the early nineteenth century. The pillory was a body-sized basket composed of strong woven wicker that was placed over the patient and secured by suspenders over the shoulders. The pillory allowed some movement of the arms and legs, but because of its wide circumference, movement was slow and awkward. There is no evidence the pillory was used anywhere other than for a brief time at Charenton Asylum near Paris, France, where Giraudy was a physician.

### Pocket Muffs

A variation of the hand-muffs comprised of two long leather sleeves, fastened around the shoul-

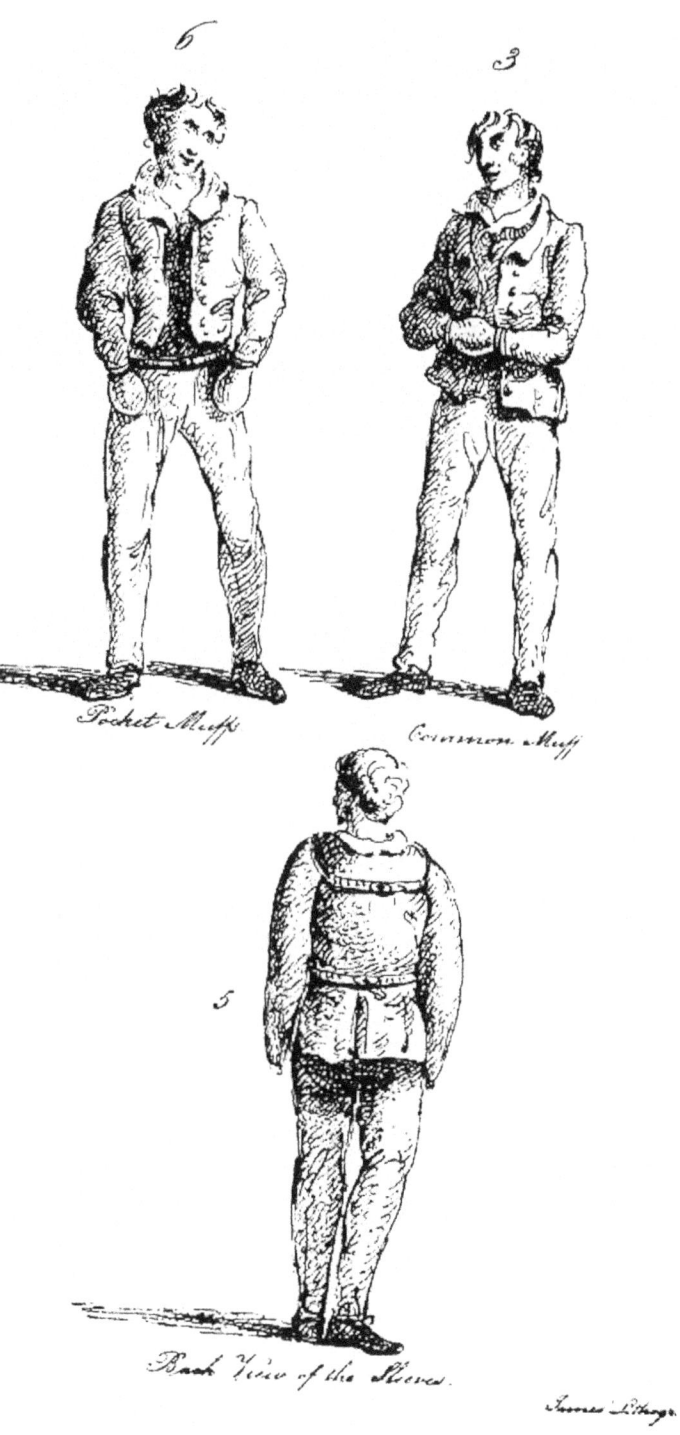

Paul Slade Knight's versions of pocket muffs, common muffs and sleeves. Asylum physicians were incredibly inventive in finding ways to restrain patients. These, Knight boasted, were so lightweight and comfortable that most patients said that wearing them brought back memories of strolling around with their hands in their pockets (P.S. Knight [1827]. *Observations of the causes, symptoms and treatment of derangement of the mind.* London: Longman, Rees, Orme, Brown and Green).

ders with a strap and lock, terminating in separate heavy leather mittens with small holes punched in them for ventilation, and further secured to leg locks on the thighs and a chain to each ankle. The pocket muff was invented by Paul Slade Knight, medical superintendent of the Lancaster County Lunatic Asylum in Lancaster, England, in the early nineteenth century. Knight noted that many patients were pleased to be restrained in the pocket muffs since they were comfortable and brought pleasant memories of strolling around with hands in pants or jacket pockets.

## *Posey Vest, or Criss-Cross Vest*

A strong, lightweight vest with a mesh strap that can be secured to the sides of a bed or the back of a chair laced through the middle. The vest, which is currently in use in asylums, allows the patient to sit up and move arms and legs, but prevents leaving the bed or chair. Laws in many states in the United States require that the vest be applied with the opening at the patient's chest in order to prevent choking or strangulation.

## *Restraining Girdle*

A broad leather girdle with straps holding the hands at the side. The girdle was used on the patient who had difficulty tolerating the pressure that the straitjacket or camisole exerted on the chest.

## *Side-arm Dress, or Maillot de bain*

A heavy, swaddling garment with long closed-end sleeves sewn to its sides or terminating in pockets, thus preventing arm movement but not inhibiting walking. The dress was used extensively on both female and male patients during the late nineteenth and early twentieth centuries at asylums throughout Europe. It was vigorously defended as a type of restraint by respected physicians such as Valentin Mangan of the Hôpital Sainte-Anne in Paris, France, who argued that it was a compassionate and more effective method of soothing agitated patients and preventing self-injury than the straitjacket or camisole, which he asserted only exacerbated excitement. Although asylum physicians were not inclined to publicly defend it on this point, they also found the dress useful in preventing masturbation.

Another convert, however reluctant, to the use of the side-arm dress was P. Maury Deas, superintendent of the Cheshire County Asylum in northwest England, who was quick to describe himself as "strong an opponent of mechanical restraint as could be found anywhere" (Deas, p. 103). His asylum experience, however, had moderated his conviction. He was forced to conclude that there was a certain "class" of patients for whom mechanical restraint not only was necessary, but therapeutically beneficial. He described in detail one of those cases:

> Case VI., that of a lady with no hereditary predisposition, suffering from melancholia. Intensely depressed and suicidal, refusing food; hears voices; anemic; amenorrhea. Was bent on suicide, and tried it in so many ways, that for three days of the week after admission she was restrained by side-arm dress for thirteen to eighteen hours. In the next two months improved a good deal, and suicidal tendency less acute. Then worse again; jumped over rail on top of steps. Improved a little again, but seven months after admission became more acutely suicidal; tried to smother herself, and to put herself on fire. Was restrained 27 nights by side-arm dress. After this slowly improved, and had no return to acute symptoms, but remained depressed. Twelve months after admission had improved considerably, and was soon after removed to another asylum [p. 106].

Deas argued that in cases such as this, the advantages of the mechanical restraint of the side-arm dress outweighed the disadvantages.

> First, there is greater security for your patient. You feel that you are doing your best and your

mind is at rest; you are able to check injurious habits, which is extremely difficult, if not impossible to do.... And then it is first of all constant; it does not relax in vigilance; it does not lose its temper [pp. 109–110].

## Six-Point Restraint

The addition of a thick cotton cord or sheet tied around the knees of a patient who already was secured to the bed in a five-point restraint.

## Sleeves

Two wide leather sleeves, closed at the bottoms, fastened across the shoulders and the elbows by a locked strap, and attached in front by a broad belt around the waist. If the patient strenuously tried to break the strap across the shoulders, another strap was be passed around the thighs and through loops sewn into the bottom of each of the sleeves. Designed by Paul Slade Knight, medical superintendent of the Lancaster County Lunatic Asylum in Lancaster, England, and made by a local saddlemaker, the sleeves were touted as the best method for securing a violent lunatic. Knight often kept a patient in the sleeves for months, with no injury to the patient or to others.

To many asylum physicians, the sleeves offered significant advantages: they were not as hot as restraint in as a straitjacket or camisole, put less pressure on the chest so that breathing was not impeded, and usually required no additional types of restraint, save a strap around the ankles, if necessary.

## Spring Straps

Broad, soft bands placed around the calves of the patient. The straps prevented the patient from kicking or running, but did allow slow and clumsy walking. The straps were used in many European asylums in the late nineteenth century.

## Stock

A heavy wooden base with half circles through which the patient's legs were placed, topped with another heavy wooden slab with aligned half circles that secured the legs in place, thus completely immobilizing the patient. More familiar as a publicly humiliating type of punishment for the medieval or colonial criminal or rule violator, the stock also was used in asylums throughout the world. Commissioner of Lunacy, Stephen Smith, was startled to find the stock still in use in state asylums in New York as late as the 1880s.

## Straitjacket, or Camisole de force, or Strait-waistcoat, or, Madd-Shirt, or Polka

A vest of strong materials with long sleeves that either were tied or locked behind the back. The first reference in print to the straitjacket is in a 1739 pamphlet by Alexander Cruden who was confined on three occasions in a private madhouse in London. Cruden, who often referred to himself as the "Corrector of the Morals of the Nation," was the author *A Complete Concordance to the Holy Scriptures,* which is still in print today. Writing in the third person, he described how he was put into a straitjacket "made of strong Tick, with long Sleeves which came a great way below the ends of his Fingers; and so the Keeper clasped the Arms of the Prisoner upon his Breast, and his Hands round his Sides toward his Back, where his Hands were tied very firmly by large strong strings of Tape" (Cruden, p. 7).

Cruden's account shows that the straitjacket was in use decades before it was first described in the medical literature by British physician David MacBride (1772), who often is mistakenly credited as its inventor:

> These waistcoats are made of ticken, or some strong stuff; are open at the back, and laced on like a pair of stays; the sleeves are made tight, and so long as to cover the ends of the fingers, and are there drawn close with a string, like a

purse, by which contrivance the patient has no power of using his fingers; and when he is laid on his back in bed, and the arms brought across the chest, and fastened in that position, by tying the sleeve-strings fast round the waist, he has no power of his hands. A broad strap of girth-web is then carried across the breast, and fastened to the bedstead, by which means the patient is confined on his back; and if he should be so outrageous as to require further restraint, the legs are secured by ligatures to the foot of the bed [Hunter & Macalpine, pp. 591–592].

Cruden's account also questions the received wisdom that the straitjacket was invented in 1770 by an upholsterer named Guilleret for use on unmanageable patients at the Hospice of Bicêtre near Paris, France. Although that asylum's physician of the infirmaries, Philippe Pinel, is given credit for striking the chains and shackles of the patients soon after his arrival in 1793 in an act that ushered in the age of moral treatment [see **Moral Treatment**], he continued to use and to recommend the straitjacket, both for restraint and punishment. His widely read 1801 text, translated five years later as *A Treatise on Insanity,* argued that the judicious use of the straitjacket was not incompatible with moral treatment, thus encouraging its occasional use by all but the most strident opponents of mechanical restraint around the world for decades to come.

Still widely used in asylums around the world, the straitjacket cannot shed its association with both insanity and unenlightened responses to it.

## *Strong Dress/Suit, or Locked Dress/Suit*

A swaddling garment made of strong linen or wool, lined throughout with flannel, that completely enclosed the arms and hands. The dress/suit routinely was worn by both female and male patients in asylums across Europe in the late nineteenth century, and in the face of the vigorous non-restraint movement, was defended as absolutely necessary for the management and care of the most violent and destructive patients, by esteemed physicians such as George Savage, physician superintendent of Bethlem Hospital (better known as Bedlam) in London.

## *Suspended Sack*

A course linen sack, approximately ten by fifteen feet that was kept expanded at the top and the bottom by a strong wood or metal rim and was hoisted with a suicidal or dangerous

**An early nineteenth century drawing of a patient in a French asylum restrained in a straitjacket. One version or another of this mechanical restraint is still used in asylums around the world (courtesy of the Wellcome Library, London).**

patient in it to the ceiling by ropes. The sack was designed in the early nineteenth century by Johann Tschallener, the medical superintendent of the Imperial Provincial Lunatic Asylum in Hall, near Innsbruck, Austria. Although visiting physicians such as Pliny Earle, who would later become the resident physician at the Friends Asylum in Pennsylvania and then the Bloomingdale Asylum in New York, were fascinated by the sack, there is no evidence of its widespread use.

## *Swaddling Bed, or Swaddling Basket*

A bed with a deep wooden trough running down the middle, filled with fresh straw or oats and covered with a sheet folded four times. The sheet was swaddled around the reclining patient who was further secured in the bed by cuffs around the feet and long arm sleeves crossed over the chest and secured to the opposite sides of the bed. The bed was designed in the mid-nineteenth century by Louis Florentine Calmeil, head physician at the Charenton Asylum near Paris, France, specifically for delirious and agitated patients in the tertiary stage of syphilis, which he was the first to identify as a distinct neuropsychiatric disease.

## *Ties and Cuffs*

Developed as an alternative to the straitjacket or camisole by Vincenzo Chiarugi, physician in chief at the Ospedale di Bonifazio in Florence, Italy, in the early nineteenth century. Two cloth and leather bands were wrapped around the body and knotted behind the patient to tie the arms to the sides; cuffs of cloth and leather, reinforced with iron, shackled the hands and feet. Chiarugi preferred the ties and cuffs not only for the ways they could be altered in their application according to the patient's condition, for example, the use of the ties alone for a less disturbed patient in need of restraint, but for the fear they induced in all patients. He considered the passion of fear to have a sedative effect on the disturbed patient.

## *Tranquilizing Chair, or Restraint Chair*

Invented by Benjamin Rush, physician at the Pennsylvania Hospital and the "Father of American Psychiatry" in the early nineteenth century. The chair had a board fitted to the back that could be raised or lowered according to the height of the patient. Affixed to the board was a wooden frame, lined with linen, which was placed over the patient's head; a small keyhole in the frame, covered with black linen, let in some light. Leather chest, belly, upper arm and wrist bands secured the patient to the chair, as did wooden cuffs at the bottom of the chair that held the feet. A close-stool pan, half filled with water was on wooden tracks under the seat, and could be slid out for emptying.

Rush designed the chair for manic patients, theorizing that four to twenty-four continuous hours in it "opposes the impetus of the blood towards the brain, lessens muscular action everywhere, reduces the force and frequency of the pulse, [and] favours the application of cold water and ice to the head, and warm water to the feet," which he also recommended in the treatment of mania (Rush, p. 179). Rush claimed great success with the chair, and its use spread quickly in asylums across the United States. It did have its detractors, though. Asylum physicians complained that it often caused edema in the legs, and the risk of gangrene was considerable from the chafing caused by the leather bands. The asylum reformer, Dorothea Dix, voiced another complaint that the chair was as much an "instrument of inquisitorial torment" (p. 43) as the chains, manacles and straitjackets it was designed to replace. During her tour of asylums and almshouses where the insane sometimes also were kept, she came across a patient strapped in the chair:

I found in the men's ward, a poor man in a "tranquilizing chair," whose countenance wore an expression of agonized suffering I can never forget. His limbs were tightly bound, his legs, body, arms, shoulders, all were closely confined, *and his head also*. Feeble efforts to move were broken down by this inexorable machine. Upon the head, sustained by the apparatus which confined the movements of the neck, was a quantity of broken ice. This, as it gradually melted, flowed over his person, which, however, was in some degree protected from the wet by a stiff capo, either of canvass or leather. It was a very hot day, but he was deadly cold, and oh, how suffering! To suffer would have been his lot, perhaps, under any circumstance; but this treatment, "employed to *keep him still*" was a fearful aggravation of inconceivable misery. I asked how long he had been under this restraint. "Four days!" "What, day and night?" "No, at night we take him *off*, and strap him upon the bed." "How long will you keep him so?" "Till he is quiet." "How long have you ever kept the patients in this condition?" "Nine days, I believe, is the longest." It does not require much knowledge of the human frame, and of its capabilities to endure suffering, and resist destructive and injurious influences, to know whether such a mode of treating insane persons is remedial and restoring in its effects, or whether it does not seriously endanger life, and lay the foundation of various fatal ailments, in addition to the malady under which they are suffering [Dix, p. 43, italics in original].

Calls by Dix and others to abandon all methods of restraint, including the chair, in favor of moral treatment [see **Moral Treatment**] were rejected by members in the 1844 meeting of the Association of Medical Superintendents of American Institutions for the Insane (AMSAII). Arguing that mechanical restraint is itself a "moral instrument," the members agreed that the American practice of mechanical restraint, including the chair, was compassionate, enlightened, and practical.

The tranquilizing chair was the first American asylum therapeutic that was exported to Europe, where it was enthusiastically received, especially in Germany. Friedrich Groos, medical superintendent of the University of Hei-

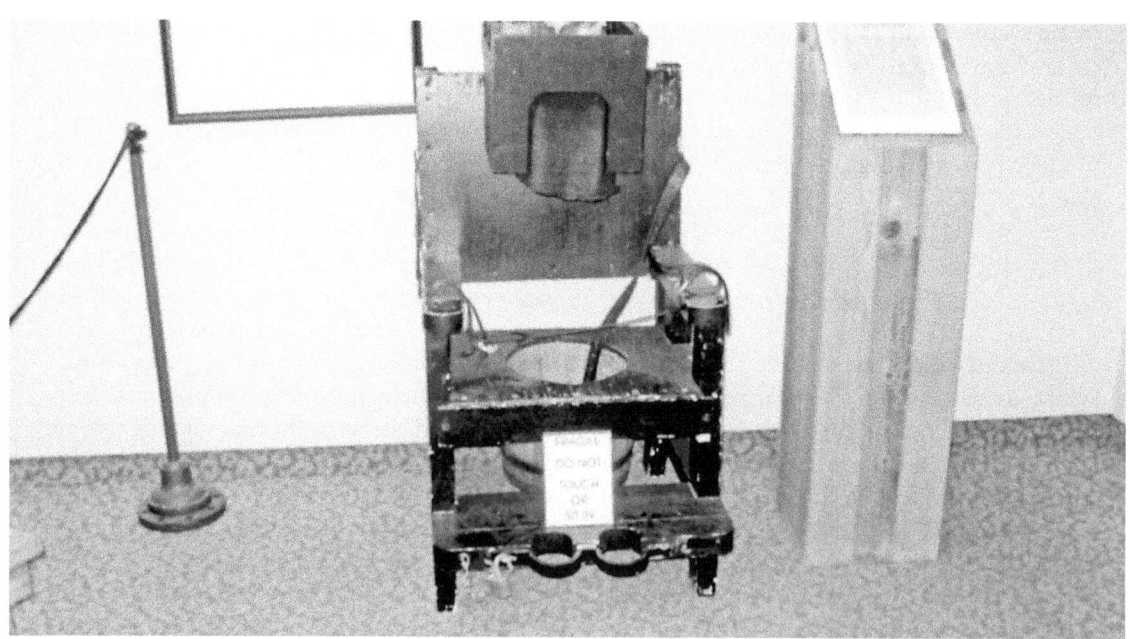

Benjamin Rush's famous tranquilizing chair, the only American asylum therapeutic that was exported abroad. The dark hood attached to the top of the chair slid over the patient's face; the bucket beneath the chair collected bodily waste (courtesy of the St. Joseph Museums, Inc./Glore Psychiatric Museum, St. Joseph, Missouri).

delberg Hospital for the Insane, for example, confided that he had used the chair so often that he would not care to continue to practice asylum medicine without it. Ernst Horn of the Berlin Charité Hospital remarked that it had an extraordinary effect on the psychology of the patient by forcing the patient to calmly and thoughtfully cope with the discomfort of being confined in it. Johann Christian August Heinroth, physician to St. George's Asylum in Leipzig, kept patients in it for as long as several weeks with no deleterious effects. In the Ghent Lunatic Colony in Belgium, where the chair also was well received, the physician Joseph Guislain observed that many patients had been so long confined in it that they walked with their knees bent.

A number of modifications in the original design of the tranquilizing chair occurred with its use. At the Gartnavel Royal Asylum in Glasgow, Scotland, for example, the chair was placed on springs so that the least movement of the patient's body caused a motion not unlike that of a soothing carriage-ride. At the Maison Coloniale de Sante in Martinique, an iron rod was driven through the arms of the chair, wedging the patient in, but leaving the arms and legs free. In Saint Luke's Hospital in London the wooden head frame of the chair was removed, but wooden boxes were added to enclose the patient's legs, as was a heavy cross board that was fastened across the thighs to both further restrain the patient and serve as a table. In his visit to St. Luke's, the author Charles Dickens referred to tranquilizing chairs like this as "hideous curiosities" (Dickens, p 366.). In France, the restraining chair was known as the *la chaise de force,* or *fauteuil de force,* or force chair. Simply a padded chair to which the patient was secured by leather straps, the force chair did not have a wooden head frame so that the forced feeding of the patient would be expedited.

A contemporary version of the chair is known as the restraining chair. Once made of wood, but now of heavy vinyl, the chair has belts and cuffs to prevent any movement of the legs, arms or torso. There is a large cup beneath the chair to hold bodily wastes, however, unlike the original tranquilizing chair, there is no enclosure for the patient's head. The chair, advertised as "like a padded cell on wheels," is used in jails, prisons and detention centers, as well as asylums. Reports of deaths and injuries resulting from its use prompted Amnesty International in 1999 to call for a federal investigation; to date, however, none has been conducted. The chair is still in use in asylums around the world.

## *Wall Camisole*

A straitjacket placed on a standing patient and secured to the wall by bolts through metal plates at the shoulders. The sleeves of the camisole were crossed at the waist and also bolted to the wall. The patient was left standing, often for days at a time, in a wooden bucket that collected bodily wastes.

A modified version of the wall camisole was invented by Giovanni-Maria Linguiti, a cleric who was superintendent of the Ospedale Psichiatrico S. Maria Maddalena, also referred to as the Aversa, after the town it was located in near Naples, Italy. A visitor described the device which, he was assured by the physician who was acting as his guide, was more for show than use:

> Another means of repression proposed [by Linguiti], consisted in placing and securing the patient vertically against a wall. This was to be effected in the following manner: the patient's arms being secured by a straitjacket, and the flexion of the fingers prevented by hard leather gloves, he was fastened to the wall by means of a semicircular piece of iron, covered with soft leather, and passing over the chest; the legs being at the same time secured in a board provided with holes for that purpose. The patient was made to remain several hours in this position ["Medical Institutions of Naples," pp. 25–26].

The wall camisole was used in Germany and some Eastern European asylums well into the twentieth century.

## Wyman Bed-Strap, or Bed-Saddle

Invented by Rufus Wyman, the first superintendent of McLean Asylum for the Insane in Boston, Massachusetts, in the early nineteenth century. The strap or saddle consisted of an eighteen by twenty-two inch strap of leather, with two side straps at the top, two at the bottom, and one in the middle. The central strap was centered and secured on a cross of thin strips of metal attached to the bed. The patient was placed on a saddle-shaped cushion in the middle of the strap; the side strap was passed over the waist and secured on the other side of the bed and the top straps were crossed over the chest and buckled to the waist strap, thus confining the patient's body to the cushion. The feet were secured in rings attached to the lower side straps that were then locked on the foot of the bed. Although the strap or saddle held the patient securely to the bed, it did allow some movement back and forth.

Even the most ardent proponents of non-restraint encountered patients in their asylums whose aggressive confusion exhausted them and sapped the energy and the patience of physicians and attendants alike. The use of the bed strap or saddle on those patients was rationalized as a humane alternative to other mechanical restraints, as well as to physical restraint that often resulted in injuries. Pliny Earle, physician to the Bloomingdale Asylum in New York City and advocate for non-restraint, praised the strap or saddle as "invaluable" and promoted it as "method of restraint with which every institution should be supplied" (Earle, p. 37).

Indeed, the strap or saddle was widely used in American public asylums even after most other types of mechanical restraint had long been abolished. It was also used in the federal asylum, St. Elizabeths Hospital in Washington, D.C. But in 1904, when the new superintendent, William Alanson White, came across a patient strapped to it, he immediately issued an order discontinuing its use. In his autobiography White wrote that he had never seen "such a cruel apparatus as this" (White, p. 95).

Testimony before a 1907 House Committee investigating the conditions of St. Elizabeths, revealed that the saddle, as it was more commonly referred to there, was still in occasional use a couple of years after White's order, and on at least two occasions with his personal permission. Under questioning by two Committee members, a former attendant described one of those times:

*Smyser*: What about you three [attendants] putting a saddle on a patient?
*Lloyd*: I helped perform that duty.
*Smyser*: What was the condition of affairs? Did the patient's condition require this treatment?
*Lloyd*: He was very much disturbed and was molesting other patients by disturbing them, you know, causing others to fight this patient, and we thought it best to restrain this patient to keep him from injuring the patients.
*Smyser*: As well as himself?
*Lloyd*: As well as himself.
*Smyser*: And in doing it how was it done? Was it done humanely or cruelly?
*Lloyd*: You have to use as much force as is necessary in order to use the appliance known as the bed saddle, which has wristlets, and which has anklets, and a strap that fastens over the chest, and similarly it is fastened to the bedstead. That requires, if the patient resists, to take him bodily by force and hold him down there in the bed, by his arms and by his legs, until you get the straps fastened. It requires sometimes, all the strength of an attendant to hold one limb of those furious patients.
*Smyser*: But in using force that you did use were you cruel and rough?
*Lloyd*: We could not be otherwise—that is, if I understand the word cruelty. If I understand the meaning of the word cruelty—to force a patient down against his will, and to do that using all the strength that you can maintain, in order to carry into execution the order of the physician who gave the orders for this patient to be restrained— if I understand the world cruel, it must be cruel.
*Smyser*: But it was not done for the purpose of hurting the patient?
*Lloyd*: It was not. It was to preserve the patient

against attacking others and prevent himself from injuring himself.

*Barchfeld*: That is not cruelty. That is merely force [House Special Committee, pp. 1504–1505].

The unclear distinction between cruelty and force called into question the continued use of the strap or saddle in asylums across the country. Although some relied upon it well into the early-twentieth century, most others discontinued it use.

## Metallotherapy (Metalloscopy, Burquism)

*The therapeutic external application or internal ingestion of metals.*

In the mid-nineteenth century French physician Victor Jean-Marie Burq serendipitously discovered that metals such as gold, silver, platinum and zinc had an unexpected effect on patients who had been diagnosed with hysteria. In fact, he had accumulated evidence that he actually could cure some of the most mysterious symptoms of hysteria, such as limb paralysis or even hemianesthesia, by the simple application of an appropriate metal disc to the affected part of the body, or by having the patient ingest a metal compound solution.

In an effort to convince his skeptical colleagues, Burq filed dozens of reports on this new therapeutic which he coined "metallotherapy," with the Academies of Science and Medicine and demonstrated it on the patients of various French hospitals and asylums. One of those asylums was the Salpêtrière. He visited well before the "Golden Age of Hysteria" so intimately associated with that Parisian asylum, and well before Jean-Martin Charcot had achieved his fame as the impresario of that golden age, but Burq's description of the patients he encountered there presaged both:

> There, in a single vast hall, the sad refuge of the incurables, unfortunate women by the hundreds, some still young, are confined. The most dreadful disorders as well as destitution have relegated them to public charity. All these wretches beyond the reach of ordinary medicine live apart in this last asylum where they are visited on the run by a physician.... It's pitiful to see sometimes 10 or 20 of these women, immobilized by very solid restraints ... scream, roar, foam at the mouth, twist, and struggle.... The disorders are so heart rending that the hospital administration believes it cannot permit anyone other than those working on the service to enter this hall Although accustomed to these kinds of patents, I myself needed several days to get used to such sights [Goetz, Bonduelle, & Gelfand, pp. 177–178].

Charcot, who was an intern at the time of Burq's visit, may very well have witnessed the metallotherapy demonstration, but whatever impression it made on him took decades to leave its mark. In fact, it was only after Burq contacted the president of the Société de Biologie in 1876, asking him to form a committee to investigate his claims that Charcot's interest was piqued in metallotherapy. Charcot, who had been appointed the chair of the investigating committee, was joined by Jules Bernard Luys of the Charité Hospital and Amédée Dumontpallier of the Hôpital de la Pitié. Each set out to replicate Burq's claims.

The *dramatis personae* of hysterical women patients at the Salpêtrière was long, but none would become as famous as Blanche Wittmann. The "Queen of the Hysterics," as she soon would come to be called, was then an eighteen-year-old, newly committed to the asylum for convulsions, transient paralysis and fainting spells, and diagnosed with hysteria. She was among the first of the patients to undergo metallotherapy. Because she was found to have a particular sensitivity to gold and copper, two copper plates were applied to her numb leg; within several minutes sensation returned in a zone several centimeters above and below the site of application. Charcot produced the same results with other hysterical women patients, thus confirming Burq's claims.

The effects of metallotherapy were short-lived—hardly the cure that Burq had boasted. That, however, did not pique Charcot's interest as much as the observation that for some patients the hysterical symptom moved from one part of the body to the other. If a gold disc, for example, was placed on the numb right hand of a patient, feeling was restored but at the same time it was lost in the otherwise sensate left hand. It was Dumontpallier, his colleague on the commission, who had come across the same thing in his work at the Hôpital de la Pitié, who called this phenomenon "transference." Charcot found that he could direct the transfer of symptoms from one part of the body to another not just by the application of metals, but by the use of magnets, turning forks and electrical currents. Because all of these restored sensation, Charcot labeled them "aesthesiogens."

Blanche Wittmann took a starring role in these aesthesiogen demonstrations. Paralysis moved from one of her legs to the other under the influence of metal discs; under the influence of a magnet her right leg swung over her left and, though naturally right-handed, she began writing with her left hand. The aesthesiogens also erased memories and created new ones, and transferred emotions in a process that came to be known as "psychic polarization." It also transferred hallucinations. When Blanche was told that she had a pigeon perched on her hand and that she would only be able to see with her left eye, she could no longer see it when that eye was closed. While she was stroking and talking to the imaginary bird a magnet was then discretely placed on the table. Standing up suddenly, Blanche seemed confused and walked away; when asked, she could no longer see the bird. When she returned to the table, however, Blanche saw the imaginary bird once again, and resumed petting and talking to it.

At the Charité Hospital in Paris, incredible observations also were being made by Luys. He, too, had confirmed Burq's metallotherapy claims and, like Charcot, was experimenting with the therapeutic potential of other aesthesiogens. To that end, Luys used a magnet to transfer the limb paralysis of a hysterical patient to a hypnotized patient. Upon being awakened, not only did the limb paralysis disappear from the hypnotized patient, but from the hysterical patient as well. Not content with a single metal disc or a simple magnet to produce these results, Luys invented a magnetic crown. Shaped like a horseshoe, it was placed on the head of an hysterical patient whose symptoms included contractures and hemiplegia, removed after five minutes, and then placed on the head of hypnotized patient who, when awakened, had assumed not only the hysterical symptoms but the very personality of the hysterical patient.

Burq also had claimed that the internal ingestion of metals would have the same salutary effects as the external application. Charcot investigated that claim using his favorite hysterical patient, Blanche Wittmann. He found that the external application of gold, her preferred metal, "very quickly produced cutaneous sensation in the neighborhood of the metallic plaques, but as quickly relapsing anesthesia was produced in the same points." When gold was taken internally in the form of a solution, Blanche "recovered peripheral sensation and muscular power, and, for a month she had no hysterical attacks" (Goetz, Bonduelle, & Gelfand, p. 33). His star patient's reaction was sufficient reason for Charcot to substantiate Burq's claim.

The investigating committee, then, not only confirmed Burq's metallotherapy findings, but went far beyond them in their fascination with the alleged therapeutic power of magnets, tuning forks, and electrical currents. It put into circulation a lexicon of newly coined terms—"aesthesiogen," "transference," "magnetic amnesia," "consecutive oscillations," "psychic polarization"—and an untidy list of scientific rationales for their observed outcomes. Charcot, like Burq, theorized that the metals and other aesthesiogens worked by producing a slight electrical current that affected the nervous system; others explained effects with reference to electro-capillary currents, or to a chemical reaction produced by the contact of metal with the moist surface of the skin, or to molecular vibrations.

The committee published its report in 1877. The esteemed president of the Société de Biologie was bewildered by the findings, but in true spirit with the "Golden Age of Hysteria" finally conceded that perhaps science was still running to catch up with the mysteries of the nervous system. Others were more critical. The committee's nod to Burq as the discoverer of metallotherapy was criticized for its ahistoricity. Not only had metals in the forms of rings, amulets and bracelets been used to cure disease in ancient times, but both metals and magnets had been used on occasion, and almost always with controversy, during the eighteenth and early nineteenth centuries by some physicians, mesmerists and, more notoriously, charlatans and quacks.

More serious criticisms were leveled at the committee's findings. Skeptical asylum physicians in Germany, Italy, Great Britain and the United States were able to demonstrate similar, if not identical, results for hysterical patients with the administration of mustard plasters, wooden cylinders, tortoise shells, rubber, minerals and shards of ice, thus simultaneously calling into question the therapeutic power of the aesthesiogens and raising the question of "expectant attention," that is, suggestion.

Charcot vehemently disagreed that the therapeutic effects he had produced were due to suggestion, declaring it impossible that women of such low status and poor education would ever know how to invent or simulate what had been scientifically discovered by chance. Without a doubt a brilliant neurologist, Charcot was nonetheless a poor social psychologist, overlooking the ways in which expectations were shaped and reinforced by his own interactions with his hysterical patients, and how the patients, crammed into crowded wards, trained each other to perform. That was evident to George Robinson. The Royal Edinburgh asylum physician brought along a healthy dose of Scottish skepticism when he visited Paris to learn more about metals, magnets and hypnotism. At the Charité Hospital where Luys was using metallotherapy, Robinson noted that hysterical patients had been used by medical students to write clean copies of their hastily scribbled notes and observations, and that former patients had been recruited to be hypnotized for transference sessions with hysterical patients. Former and present hysterical patients mingled freely with each other, he discovered, and even read articles in the periodical *Revue des Sciences Hypnotiques* together. In Robinson's opinion, "expectant attention" was being primed at the Charité and, in the end, had more to do with the successes of metallotherapy than the applied or ingested metals ever did.

There was no compromise to be had in the debate over metallotherapy: the therapeutic results were due either to the metals and magnets, or to the suggestibility of hysterical patients. For every case that was discussed or published that showed the efficacy of one aesthesiogen or another, there was a case that showed the power of suggestion; for every asylum physician who tried it for the first time, there was another who refused to continue its use. Yet, by the turn into the twentieth century, metallotherapy was a thing of the past. Its denouement certainly coincided with the waning of the "Golden Age of Hysteria," especially in France, but there were other factors at work as well. For one thing, metallotherapy had served as a bridge into the more intriguing subject of hypnosis and its therapeutic potential and, to a lesser extent, into psychoanalysis and the therapeutic potential of exploring the unconscious. And for another, metallotherapy had become entwined with the spread of Spiritualism with its clairvoyants, mediums, spinning tables, spirit healings, conversations with the dead and other paranormal trappings. While Spiritualism as a belief system survived criticism and condemnation, the esotericism of metallotherapy only marginalized it further as an asylum therapeutic.

## References

Caplan, E. (2001). *Mind games: American culture and the birth of psychotherapy*. Berkeley: University of California Press.
Charcot, J.M. (1878). Lecture on metalloscopy and metallotherapy applied to the treatment of grave hysteria. *Scientific American, 5,* 1959–1961.
Dumontpallier, M. (1878). Metallotherapy and metalloscopy of Dr. Burq. *British Medical Journal, 12,* 548–552.
Dumontpallier, M., Charcot, J-M., and Luys, J.B. (1878). Report on the metallotherapy and metalloscopy of Dr. Burq. *British Medical Journal, 2,* 548–552.
Goetz, C.G., Bonduelle, M., and Gelfand, T. (1995). *Charcot: Constructing neurology*. New York: Oxford University Press.
Harrington, A. (1987). *Medicine, mind and the double brain*. Princeton, NJ: Princeton University Press.
Harrington, A. (1988). Metals and magnets in medicine: Hysteria, hypnosis and medical culture in fin-de-siècle Paris. *Psychological Medicine, 18,* 21–38.
Hustvedt, A. (2011). *Medical muses: Hysteria in nineteenth-century Paris*. New York: W.W. Norton.
Muller, F., and Tuke, W.S. (1880). Cases of hysteria, with paralysis, treated by metallotherapy. *British Journal of Psychiatry, 26,* 56–66.
Robertson, G.M. (1892). Hypnotism at Paris and Nancy. *Journal of Mental Science, 38,* 494–531.
Tuke, D.H. (1879). Metalloscopy and expectant attention. *British Journal of Psychiatry, 24,* 598–609.

# Moral Treatment
# (Moral Management, Moral Therapy)

*Curative discipline by means of a range of non-medical strategies.*

The very term "moral treatment" has become synonymous with the reforms in the treatment of the insane that began in the late eighteenth century in response to changing ideas about the insane, insanity and its curability. Its philosophy has become intimately associated with larger-than-life asylum reformers in France, Italy, England and the United States, and with specific asylums that ranged from large public institutions to small private facilities. Moral treatment, on occasion, has been rhapsodized as the greatest single reform in the history of asylum therapeutics, and panned as the most duplicitous exercise of social control in that history.

If not ambiguous, then "moral" was, and remains, a somewhat confusing term, better understood for what it connoted than denoted. It referred to the passions, the emotions, the sentiments, the affections of insane patients, in other words, their psychology. Enlightenment thinking had replaced the historic view of the insane as insensate, no more than wild beasts, with one that favored their subjectivity that could be engaged, interrogated and directed in order to bring about cure. And although "treatment," "management" and "therapy" implied subtly different types of interactions between asylum physicians and patients, the terms often were used interchangeably. Whatever the interaction, asylum physicians were to carry out moral treatment with kindness and firm authoritativeness. That said, though, it was not at odds with the philosophy of moral treatment to use persuasion, rousing, calming, manipulating, disabusing, distracting, deceiving, frightening and humiliating if any one or combination of these strategies most effectively engaged and directed the patients. It is also important to note that moral treatment, which sometimes is conflated with the non-restraint movement [see **Mechanical Restraints**], did not at all preclude the use of restraints, although its practitioners had relegated the more brutal devices to the dark and unenlightened past. Thus, while moral treatment signified a rupture in attitudes about the insane, it maintained ties to much, although certainly not all, of their historic treatments.

On that point Philippe Pinel offered an interesting example. The French physician, immortalized in paintings by Charles Müller and Tony Robert-Fleury that depict him heroically striking the chains of patients, was widely regarded as the originator of moral treatment. While his status as such was more mythic than real, the fact remains that insane patients at the Bicêtre Hospice and the Salpêtrière Hospital were indeed freed from their chains. On Pinel's orders, however, they were then confined in straitjackets. Pinel saw no irony in that. In his view, *traitement moral* involved "the art of subjugating and taming the alienated ... by placing him in a strict dependency upon a man who, by his physical and moral qualities, is apt to exercise on him an irresistible empire and to change the vicious chain of his ideas" (Pinel, p. 58). And straitjackets did just that. Pinel related that in the first days after their liberation from chains, it took seven or eight attendants to get the patients into straitjackets; later it took four, and then only two. In the end the patients put themselves into the straitjackets. The "irresistible empire" that Pinel had exerted in the name of moral treatment, not only had disciplined the insane patients but had engaged their own subjectivity sufficiently enough to cause them to discipline themselves.

Pinel never developed a comprehensive theory of the cause of insanity, but he proposed that its cure was to be found within the environs of the asylum as an institution. To facilitate moral treatment, he argued, the asylum had to be a well-ordered place, staffed by competent, trained and closely supervised personnel. It required for its smooth running the skills of "thoughtful, philanthropic, courageous, physically imposing and inventive leaders ... devoted to order without violence" (Pinel, p. 52). In this paternalistic view, the asylum was a family made up of "turbulent and skittish and volatile" children who had to be controlled, socialized and disciplined by a firm and kind father-figure (p. 213).

Moral treatment, however, was more than surveillance and discipline. It also was custodial care. In that regard, Pinel's asylum reforms indeed were significant. He increased the quantity and quality of the dietary allotment, thus relieving many patients not just from hunger, which he believed was the "most powerful motive of action of both savage and civilized man," but from the weakness and disorders, both physical and mental, that resulted from it (pp. xxii–xxiii). He engaged them in work in the asylum and on its grounds, and provided educational and recreational opportunities. And within the asylum walls, he listened to them as well as to the staff who interacted with them, as is evident in his widely read and translated text *Traité Médico-Philosophique sur L'aliénation Mentale, ou la Manie*. The book was rife with clinical vignettes and case studies that demonstrated Pinel's shrewd appraisals of the causes and the dynamics of particular cases of insanity. From arguing a patient out his delusion that he was the king, to consoling another who was grief-stricken, to staging an elaborate ruse [see **Pious Frauds**] to threaten a food-refusing patient into eating, the book laid out his strategies for tailoring moral treatment to the unique cause and symptoms of each patient's insanity.

Pinel was familiar with the work of Vincenzo Chiarugi, although he apparently thought it too formulaic to be of interest. "Always follow the beaten path, speak of madness in general in a dogmatic tone, then consider madness in particular and resort once again to the old scholastic order of causes, diagnosis, prognosis, and indications to follow," he wrote, "that is the task that Chiarugi has accomplished" (p. xxv). In truth, Chiarugi had accomplished more than that, and some contemporary historical revisionists credit the Italian physician, and not Pinel, as the originator of moral treatment. His seminal text on the treatment of the insane had been published years before Pinel's, but had remained untranslated, and therefore not widely known. It is certainly true that Chiarugi struck the chains of the insane patients at the Ospedale di Bonifazio in Florence a good four or five years before Pinel had achieved notoriety for doing so at the Bicêtre and the Salpêtrière. It is also, and incidentally, true that neither physician had done so on his own initiative: Chiarugi had acted in respect of the wishes of the asylum's founder, the Grand Duke of Tuscany, and Pinel at the request of his lay superintendent Jean-Baptiste

Pussin, who also was a former asylum patient. In regards to insanity their etiological perspectives differed: Pinel focused on the passions, Chiarugi on the neural activity of the common sensorium of the brain. Although Pinel's *traitement moral* was different enough from Chiarugi's *la cura morale* to be a point of contention, they found common ground on the necessity of the humane treatment of the insane.

Like Pinel, Chiarugi believed the asylum as a brick-and-mortar institution played an essential role in moral treatment. Upon assuming the medical director title in 1788, Chiarugi transformed the Bonifazio into a model asylum, admired for its orderliness, cleanliness, tranquility and even beauty. Patients worked in the asylum and on its grounds, engaged in recreational activities, educational programs and religious services, if so inclined. Diversionary and entertaining activities, especially listening to and performing music, which Chiarugi thought to be particularly therapeutic, were part of the daily activity within the asylum.

Chiarugi also codified a set of regulations for asylum commitment. No one could be committed without a medical certificate signed by the magistrate and chief judge; that certificate had to describe in some detail what behavior, thoughts, feelings or desires of the person were considered evidence of insanity. The person then would be evaluated at the Bonifazio and classified as maniacal, melancholic or demented. Each type of insanity had the same three general treatment strategies—sedative, stimulating and secondary— but the specifics of each allowed for a more individualized treatment plan. For example, all patients were given sedative treatment, but whether the sedative administered was a cold bath, a purge, blistering or bleeding, depended on the symptoms and needs of the individual patient.

Mechanical restraints were used, but only if necessary. Chiarugi disliked the straitjacket but was not at all opposed to using a modified version of restraint which he referred to as the "ties and cuffs" or, for that matter, the "maniac's bed," to which the disruptive or dangerous patient was secured via a shoulder harness, wristlets and anklets [see **Mechanical Restraints**]. And, just as was true of Pinel, the use of persuasion, manipulation, deception and fear were not inconsistent with Chiarugi's approach to moral treatment [see **Pious Frauds; Salutary Fear**].

Pinel's prominence eclipsed Chiarugi's, and his posthumous canonization relegated Chiarugi to little more than a historical footnote. Yet, as a matter of fact, there was another and quite unlikely contender for recognition as the originator of moral treatment, and that was a coffee and tea merchant in northern England. William Tuke was a Quaker and when his co-religionists attempted to visit a young Quaker widow who had been committed to the York Asylum for melancholy, they had been told she was not in a suitable state to be seen. The young woman subsequently died, and although the circumstances of her death were never explained by asylum officials, the Quaker community suspected she had died from abuse or neglect, a not unreasonable suspicion given the fact that the asylum had been investigated for mistreatment on a number of previous occasions. At the urging of Tuke, the Society of Friends agreed to fund a private asylum for Quaker patients that was based on religious and humanitarian principles.

The York Retreat was established in 1792, the term "Retreat" deliberately chosen to distinguish it from the scandal-wracked asylums and madhouses of England, and to connote a quiet, restful and safe institution. Situated on eleven acres of wooded countryside just a half mile from the eastern gate of the city of York, the original building accommodated just thirty patients who paid anywhere from eight to fifteen shillings a week for their care. As the facility expanded over time, tree-lined walks led to a small working farm, a large vegetable garden and courtyards in which caged animals such as rabbits, or tethered birds such as hawks, could be found.

Although from its start the Retreat always had a physician on staff, little faith was ever placed in the power of traditional medicine. Bleeding, blisters, setons and other therapeutics were given trials but were judged inadequate to the task of relieving or curing insanity. More confidence was placed in warm and cold baths [see **Hydrotherapy**] and in a generous and healthy diet [see **Diet**], along with exercise and fresh air. But it was moral treatment in which the most faith was invested.

Writing some years after the establishment of the Retreat, Samuel Tuke, grandson of the founder, set out the tenets of moral treatment: assisting patients in controlling their own disorders; restraining patients when absolutely necessary; and promoting the general comfort of patients. Each tenet, of course, required different therapeutic strategies. Thus the induction of fear, for example, was considered a perfectly appropriate strategy to prompt insane patients, all of whom were considered capable of rationality, into self-control; the straitjacket or isolation in a dark and quiet room was used to promote self-restraint; and kindness in all interactions, diversionary amusements, and an aesthetically pleasing institutional environment all lessened "the irritation of the mind" (Tuke, p. 177). Thus from its architecture to its daily interactions to its therapeutic regime, the Retreat "was designed to encourage the individual's own efforts to reassert ... powers of self-control" (Scull, 1993, p. 99). The following case exemplified that therapeutic mission:

> Some years ago a man, about 34 years of age, of almost Herculean size and figure was brought into the [Retreat]. He had been afflicted several times before, and so constantly, during the present attack, had been kept chained, that his clothes were contrived to be taken off and put on by means of strings, without removing his manacles. They were however taken off. When he entered the Retreat, he was ushered into the apartment where the superintendent was supping. He was calm; his attention appeared to be arrested by his new situation. He desired to join in the repast, during which he behaved with tolerable priority. After it was concluded, the superintendent conducted him to his apartment, and told him the circumstances on which the treatment would depend; that it was his anxious wish to make every inhabitant in the house as comfortable as possible, and that he sincerely hoped the patient's conduct would render unnecessary for him to have recourse to coercion. The maniac was sensible of the kindness of his treatment. He promised to restrain himself, and he so completely succeeded that, during his stay, no coercive means were ever employed towards him [Tuke, pp. 146–147].

The innovative approach of moral treatment drew the attention not only of asylum physicians in Great Britain and Europe but in the United States where in the early nineteenth century the confinement of the insane was a new and growing enterprise. At the Pennsylvania Hospital the putative "Father of American Psychiatry," Benjamin Rush, took up the practice of moral treatment although it could be argued convincingly that his was a rather uniquely American version of it. While very much influenced by the Enlightenment's emphasis on humanity and reason, Rush was skeptical about the assertions of Pinel and Tuke that the efficacy of psychological therapeutics was superior to medical therapeutics in the treatment of the insane. To him, and most of his yet still small cadre of American asylum physicians, that radical assertion seemed to hark back to pre–Enlightenment notions that insanity was a spiritual conundrum, better dealt with by ministers and empathetic lay persons than qualified physicians. Having none of that, Rush asserted that insanity was a disease of the brain, not a disorder of the mind, and that the occasional use of gentle suasion, distracting amusements and pious frauds aside, it was best cured by medical interventions such as copious bleeding [see **Depletive Therapy**], and by cleverly designed restraints such as the tranquilizing chair [see **Mechanical Restraints**]. This Americanized version, then, medicalized moral treatment in a way that would have been unsettling to Pinel and most certainly to Tuke, although it likely would have been more appealing to Chiarugi whose interactions with American asylum physicians, if there were any at all, were certainly few and far between.

This Americanized version of moral treatment was practiced in the small corporate asylums that dotted the northeast. Whether established by Quakers, such as the Friends Asylum in Frankford, just outside of Philadelphia, or by Congregationalists, such as the McLean Asylum in Boston, Massachusetts, these new asylums claimed as much success with the Americanized version of moral treatment as did their European and British counterparts. In them, the classical medical therapeutics of bleeding, purging, vomiting and blistering directed to the body and hence to the diseased brain often were used alongside the psychological therapeutics of rest, relaxation, education, recreation, and resocialization.

It was at the Pennsylvania Hospital for the Insane that moral treatment reached its apogee in the United States. The hospital was purpose-built in 1841 to accommodate the new admissions for insanity at the Pennsylvania Hospital which, as a general hospital, had limited facilities for their care and custody. Thomas Story Kirkbride, an Orthodox Quaker, was appointed its first superintendent, and his forty year career was co-extensive with the vogue of moral treatment in the United States. Insisting that "the insane are really 'the wards of the State,' and ...every State is bound by all the dictates of humanity, expediency, and economy, to make proper provision for those not able to provide for themselves" (Kirkbride, 1880, p. 80), he set about creating a comprehensive program of moral treatment that in the United States became synonymous with his name:

> Early hours are always desirable in a hospital for the insane,—early hours for retiring at night, and early hours for rising in the morning. To many this is a radical change in their habits, and this change itself is often of very marked advantage.... By six, it is intended the patients should be getting ready for breakfast, which meal, during the whole year, is taken at half past six o'clock, and previous to which, medicine is given to those for whom it may be deemed desirable in the different wards.... Immediately after breakfast, the rooms and wards are put in order.... [A]rrangements are made for driving, walking, visiting interesting places, and for the special occupations and amusements of the patients during the day.... After the outdoor exercise, the usual indoor resources are at command—reading, writing, conversation, games of nearly every kind, and whatever work is likely to be interesting to individual patients.... At noon, medicine is again administered to those who are taking it regularly, and preparations are made for dinner, which is on the table at half past twelve. Early in the afternoon, the hour depending somewhat on the season, all are expected to be again in the open air, and securing, as much as possible, the advantages which result from it, sunshine, exercise, and whatever else can be combined with these valuable agents for preserving as well as restoring health.... Tea is ready at six o'clock in winter, and at half past six in summer; after which, except in very warm weather, few go outside of the yards connected with the wards. Then begin the special arrangements for making the evenings pass pleasantly. Preparations are made for the lectures and other entertainments in the lecture room, or gymnastic halls, or for the officers' tea parties.... After leaving the lecture rooms, the patients frequently assemble in the parlors, and have music, games, and other diversions, filling up the time to half past nine, between which and ten o'clock, all persons are expected to retire for the night [Kirkbride, 1880, pp. 276–280].

This highly structured routine of moral treatment, in Kirkbride's opinion, was necessary for breaking the careless habits that were both the cause and the effect of insanity. Those patients who responded favorably to the regime were rewarded with improved ward assignments, with the upper wards reserved for those whose behavior was consistent with the rules and norms of the institution. This strategy also had been found effective by Pinel and Tuke. In an asylum setting, whether a massive public asylum like the Salpêtrière or a small private one like the York Retreat, diagnosis usurped identity and individuality was absorbed by uniformity. The ward hierarchy system was an effective moral treatment strategy

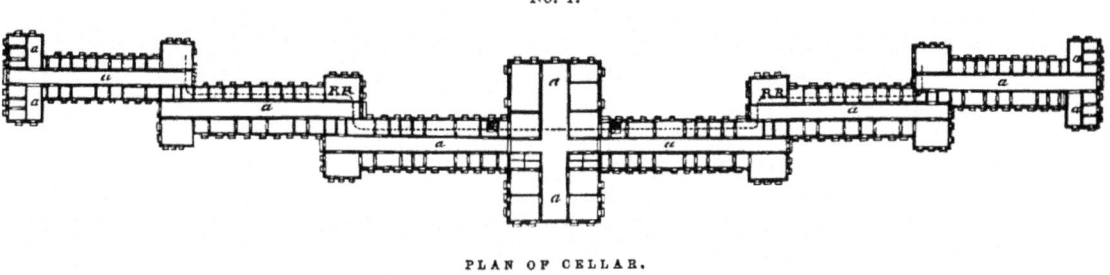

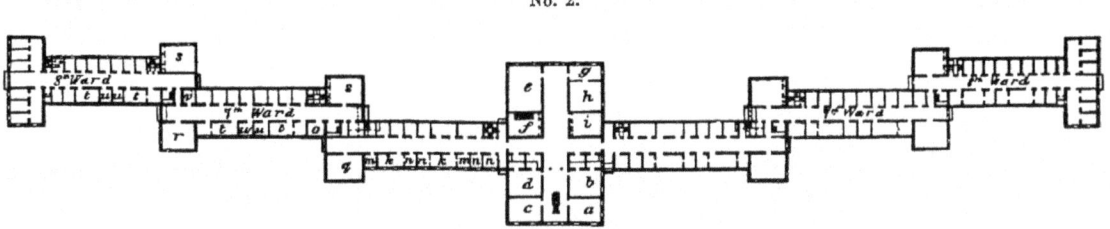

The Kirkbride Plan for moral architecture. Developed in the mid-nineteenth century by Thomas Kirkbride, superintendent of the Pennsylvania Hospital, the plan maximized the comfort and privacy of patients, and assured their exposure to fresh air and sunlight. Most state asylums in the United States were built according to the Kirkbride Plan (T.S. Kirkbride [1880]. *On the construction, organization, and general arrangements of hospitals for the insane.* Philadelphia: J.P. Lippincott).

to assist insane patients in achieving and maintaining status.

In keeping with the Americanized version of moral treatment, Kirkbride also used the *materia medica* of his profession. Opium, morphine, conium, a mixture of iron and quinine, black henbane, and chloral hydrate were routinely administered to patients who also were bled, blistered, purged to counteract the constipating effect of morphine, wrapped in wet blankets, doused with buckets of cold water, given mustard foot baths and camphor rubs. Those who refused food were force fed. And, although mechanical restraints were used only as a last resort, Kirkbride did not hesitate to wrap a violent or self-injuring patient in a partial straitjacket known as "the sleeves."

Moral treatment for Kirkbride was not only built into the daily regime of the asylum, but into the asylum, itself. Kirkbride was an impassioned advocate of "moral architecture," a term used first by Samuel Tuke in describing the design of the York Retreat. Kirkbride proposed that handsome buildings on beautiful grounds not only made moral treatment within their walls possible but created in their very brick and mortar a sober moral order that facilitated treatment. Although he had not designed the Pennsylvania Hospital for the Insane, he saw in its simple plan of a central hall with two wings, the template for moral architecture.

Over the years of his tenure as superintendent, Kirkbride developed an asylum plan that also came to be synonymous with his name. The Kirkbride Plan was a congregate plan, with all of the patients living under the roof of a single linear building that was comprised of small, connected pavilions, and arranged in the shape of a shallow "V." While Kirkbride discouraged the building of expensive and ornate asylums, he insisted that they should have a cheerful and comfortable appearance, every thing repulsive and prison-like should be carefully avoided, and even the means of effecting the proper degree of security should be masked, as far as possible, by arrangements of a pleasant and attractive description. For the same reason, the grounds about the building should be highly improved and tastefully ornamented; a variety of interest should be collected around it, and trees and shrubs, flowering plants, summer-houses, and other pleasing objects, should add to its attractiveness. No one can tell how important all these may prove in the treatment of patients, nor what good effects may result from first impressions thus made upon an invalid on reaching a hospital [Kirkbride, 1880, pp. 52–53].

The American Romanticism movement of that era definitely had left its imprint on the Kirkbride Plan. The movement's emphasis on the salutary effects of beauty and order on the mind, and on the restorative qualities of nature were echoed in the Plan's specifications for the sizes of rooms and the dimensions of windows, the curve of the staircases, the lighting and style of furniture, and the design of the landscape in which native flora and fauna took pride of place. In the words of Kirkbride:

It should never be forgotten, that every object of interest that is placed in or about a hospital for the insane, that even every tree that buds, or every flower that blooms, may contribute in its small measure to excite a new train of thought, and perhaps be the first step towards bringing to reason, the morbid wanderings of a disordered mind [Kirkbride, 1842, p. 47].

Kirkbride was instrumental in the founding of the Association of Medical Superintendents of American Institutions for the Insane (AMSAII), the nation's first medical organization. Although there was some disagreement among his twelve co-founders as to the model architectural design for asylums, the Kirkbride Plan prevailed. In the mid-nineteenth century the AMSAII published the architectural guidelines for the Plan and Kirkbride himself published a weighty guide to its most minute details. In the flurry of construction that followed, the linear arrangement that was moral architecture could be found in virtually every newly built state asylum across the country.

Whether moral treatment could be practiced within the moral architecture of state asylums was another matter altogether. Certainly it was the intention of the AMSAII that it would be. That was also the intention of an unyielding advocate, a former school teacher by the name of Dorothea Lynde Dix, who was waging a relentless international campaign for asylum reform. While in England, preparing for a hectic schedule of visits and meetings, Dix spent some time at the York Retreat and with the descendants of its founder, William Tuke. The experience left her convinced that asylum reform meant more than just improving hygienic conditions and striking chains; rather, it meant instituting moral treatment. Upon return to the United States she sought out Kirkbride and over the following years the two worked through that era's conundrums about gender and status—a woman in equal partnership with a man; a layperson in alliance with a professional—to form a strong coalition that brought moral treatment into the moral architecture of the new state asylums.

By the time the second edition of Kirkbride's influential book was published in 1880, however, both moral architecture and moral treatment had fallen out of vogue not only in the United States but in Great Britain and Europe as well. Some of the reasons why were provincial, but others crossed national boundaries. Certainly one of the primary reasons for its disappearance had to do with the fact that a consensus definition of moral treatment had never been settled on; the notion of "kindness," in the end, might have been the only thing that really linked the *traitment moral of* Pinel with the *la cura morale* of Chiarugi, and those with moral treatment at the York Retreat and the Pennsylvania Hospital for the Insane.

As moral treatment spread geographically, its underlying rationale and set of constitutive practices spread as well, rendering a consensus definition even more difficult to achieve. As an example, the "Belgian Pinel," as Joseph Guislain sometimes was referred to, posited

A postcard depicting Traverse City State Hospital in northern Michigan, circa 1930. The asylum, whose motto was "Beauty Is Therapy," was the quintessential example of moral architecture. Closed in 1989, it is in the process of being transformed into apartments, condominiums, shops and restaurants under the name the Village at Grand Traverse Commons.

that because the mind resides in the brain then insanity *ipso facto* was a disorder of the brain. Therefore his approach to moral treatment at the asylums in Ghent was highly somatic. He bled, purged, blistered, douched and spun his patients in Cox's chair [see **Rotation, Oscillation and Vibration**] in order to stimulate their sensory nerves and, as an outcome, focus their attention, prod their imagination, sharpen their memory and judgment, and hone their reasoning. In contrast, the "Dutch Pinel," as J. Schroeder van der Kolk was referred to, might more appropriately have been referred to as the "Dutch Tuke," such was his allegiance to the familial model of moral treatment as was practiced at the York Retreat. In the antiquated asylum in Utrecht that he reformed and in the handful of asylums that were built upon that model throughout the Netherlands, van der Kolk instituted a regime of moral treatment that reflected the ideal of the middle-class Christian family, replete with gentle but firm pedagogical discipline and paternalistic supervision. Johann Gottfried Langermann, as another example, struck a compromise between Pinelean reform and German Romanticism. Insanity was, to Langermann, an idiopathic disorder of the soul in which the soul suffers from the conscious and deliberate pursuit of the passions at the expense of reason. The insane, then, were considered morally responsible for their irrationality while at the same time still reasoned enough to also be morally responsible for their own cure. Moral treatment, then, as he had instituted it at the asylum in Bayreuth, Germany, was an uncompromising regime of re-education, re-socialization, repetitive physical activity, religious exercises and self-discipline, all under the threat of flogging, isolation and other punishments.

The ambiguity of the very term moral treatment, the differences in rationales and practices such ambiguity engendered, also meant that the assessment of its success in remediating or even curing, insanity was highly subjective. And it is true that its practitioners boasted success. The York Retreat claimed that in its first fifteen years, 67 percent of patients with recent onset mania and 62 percent of those with melancholia had recovered well enough to be discharged. Although the statistics were less impressive for those whose insanity had been of a longer duration, they still were respectable: 16 percent of patients with chronic mania and 28 percent of those with chronic melancholia had been discharged as recovered. Pinel, whose meticulous statistical tables and calculations were in the service of embedding moral treatment within a scientific paradigm, claimed 51 percent of all patients with mania, and 62 percent of those with melancholia, were cured by moral treatment over four years. The findings, however, were biased by his choice of subjects: his results were limited only to patients who had never been previously admitted or treated at the Salpêtrière Hospital or any other asylum. Pliny Earle, the medical superintendent of the Bloomingdale Asylum in New York City, declared that 62 percent of that asylum's patients were cured by moral treatment, a claim he came to regret decades later when his analysis of the yearly reports of twenty American asylums that practiced moral treatment revealed that the cure rate had been inflated by counting as separate cures each discharge of any patient whose recurring insanity had brought him or her back to the asylum multiple times in a given year. Earle, once a vigorous proponent of moral treatment, went on to assert that its cure rate was unduly influenced by the "temperament of the reporter; each man having his own standards, or criterion" (Earle, 1887, p. 56). And it was influenced by the invisible hand of politics. On that point, Earle suggested that some asylum physicians "cooked statistics" to garner political and public support for their asylums, their work in them and their practice of moral treatment (p. 226).

The second major reason for the disappearance of moral treatment had more to do with sociological than ideological or statistical factors. Moral treatment was best suited for small asylums with a high physician-to-patient ratio and, diagnosis aside, a relatively homogeneous patient population. As reform movements, especially in Great Britain and the United States, successfully advocated for the building of new public asylums those desirable factors were compromised. These new asylums were larger, often much larger, than those that had been highly regarded as bastions of moral treatment; more expensive to run, they had much lower physician-to-patient ratios, and their patient populations were considerably more diverse.

Worcester Asylum offered an example. Built in the 1830s as the first public asylum in the state of Massachusetts, it revealed from its start the consequences of the compromises that had made its very establishment possible. Quickly and cheaply built, it originally accommodated just 120 patients, most of them working class Yankee farmers, craftspeople and fishermen whose families already had lived in that area for generations. Perhaps because of its successful use of moral treatment—its medical superintendent Samuel B. Woodward boasted a recovery rate between 82 and 91 percent for patients who had been insane a year or less—the asylum was soon filled far beyond its capacity. As a result of the advocatory activities of Dorothea Lynde Dix, funds were procured for its expansion and the "quiet and happy family" of patients, physicians and staff, as Woodward had once described it, was soon disrupted by the admission of the chronically insane who had been languishing in poor houses and jails, the deeply impoverished, as well as by much-maligned Irish immigrants. State funding lagged behind the changes and, as a result, the ratio of asylum physicians to patients decreased more than three times. With neither the time to interact with each patient on a daily basis, or the resources to design, implement and oversee individualized treatment plans, Woodward was forced to compromise the asylum's mission of moral treatment, and then abandon it altogether in favor of custody. Even given the fact that Woodward's original claim of an 82 to 91 percent recovery rate would soon be proved as egregiously over-inflated by Pliny Earle, the fact remained that as moral treatment was replaced by custody and control, the recovery rate at the Worcester Insane Asylum precipitously plummeted to a mere 23 percent.

By the mid- to late nineteenth century, therapeutic pessimism encroached on the optimism that had always attended moral treatment. Although moral treatment was an umbrella term for a set of diverse practices, places and practitioners, its *raison d'être* was that humane, kind and respectful treatment cured insanity. The "cult of curability" had its critics within the emerging profession of asylum medicine, but it was the criticism of the treatment, itself, especially by former patients that constitutes the third major reason for its disappearance.

In England, for example, John Thomas Perceval, son of the assassinated Prime Minister Spencer Perceval, was committed for "religious excitement" to Brislington House, a private asylum in Bristol. Run by Edward Long Fox, the asylum was highly regarded as a paragon of moral treatment, but in a two volume memoir published after his release Perceval revealed that moral treatment was more rhetoric than reality.

> Nothing did I require but wholesome diet, moderate and healthy exercise, and pure air; instead of which I was drenched with the most nauseous medicines against my will and against my conscience: I was fastened in a strait-waistcoat, or huge, hot leathern armcases, and compelled to lie day and night in the same bed, and in the same room, and fed on slops of bread in broth [Perceval, p. 14].

Perceval joined other former patients and their allies and advocates to form the Alleged Lunatics' Friend Society, an incredibly active group that papered Parliament with proposals for asylum reform and requests for official inquiries into asylum management and the treatment of patients. It lambasted moral treatment as nothing more than social repression achieved by treating patients as if they were children. So formidable was the Society that the estimable Thomas Harrington Tuke, proprietor of the Manor House, a small moral treatment asylum in Chiswick, once declared "I assure you I would rather see the devil in my asylum than you" (Hervey, p 272).

Isaac Ray might have said the same of one of his patients. Ray, an eminent asylum physician, brought moral treatment to the Maine Insane Hospital in Augusta when he was appointed superintendent in 1841. There, he encountered a patient by the name of Isaac Hunt who, for the three years of his confinement, would prove himself difficult and obstreperous, and for the years after his release, an embittered foe. Hunt not only brought suit against Ray for "mal, barbarous and inhuman, and cruel treatment" (Weiss, p. 385), but revealed in a widely read memoir the iron fist in the velvet glove of Ray's version of moral treatment. Published in 1851, *Astounding Disclosures! Three Years in a Mad House* detailed the "confinement, treatment, torture of body and mind, and ... malpractice" that not only prolonged Hunt's recovery, but that worsened the "wild mania" that caused his friends to commit him in the first place (Hunt, p. 10). From the forced ingestion of stupefying drugs, the drudgery of demeaning labor, the cruelty of staff who jeered at his delusions and threatened him with beatings and restraint, to the alleged machinations of Ray himself to keep him in the asylum once he had recovered to prevent him from going public with his complaints, Hunt revealed that moral treatment was little more than a chimera. Published just months after the Maine Insane Hospital had burned to the ground in 1850, the memoir concluded with a plea so reminiscent of those who had first brought moral treatment into asylum practice:

> As I have said, I suppose the institution will be rebuilt, and if it must be, I hope that for their strong cells, they will take as a model the new jail at Boston, and as an act of humanity let

them be for the wild, noisy patients, at a distance from the peaceable and quiet ones sufficient not to disturb them, and under no circumstances should the shower bath or cold bath be permitted to be used, as it has been used, as an instrument of torture, under penalties which would consign those who thus abuse their power to the State prison. Let the people see to it that none are abused, for the insane, of all human beings, are the most to be pitied, and they should be protected from abuse, as much as the public should be protected from their violence. If the people knew that institution as I know it, they would abandon it forever, for all the good that it could accomplish in a thousand years of the very best treatment, could never repay the horrid atrocities that have been practiced there in the ten years that it has been in operation; and it should be abandoned forever, and its ground enclosed and planted with weeping willows, and its walls allowed to crumble with time, and remain as a monument to designate it as the field of blood, and the curse of an avenging God [Hunt, p. 355].

Kindness, the *sine qua non* of moral treatment, was also exposed as more rhetoric than reality in none other than the Pennsylvania Hospital for the Insane. A prominent carriage-maker named Ebeneezer Haskell had been committed for "breach of the peace." Asserting that he had been falsely committed by family members who owed him money, Haskell escaped from the asylum four times, the last time fracturing his leg while scaling over the wall. While recovering in a hospital he learned that his attorney had filed a writ of *habeas corpus,* securing his release from the asylum and paving the way for an inquest of lunacy before the Court of Common Pleas. A parade of witnesses, from family members, servants and neighbors, to asylum physicians, to the asylum superintendent, Thomas Story Kirkbride, testified over the eleven day hearing. In his charge to the jury, the judge instructed them to decide whether Haskell's excitability, irritability, quick temper and talkativeness had changed in quality and quantity from "peculiarities" to insanity, as a result of a failed business venture several years before, as had been alleged in court, and whether he was, as a result, deprived of reason and understanding and therefore unable to manage his own affairs. After an hour's deliberation, the jury returned a verdict that declared Haskell was, and always had been, sane.

Haskell, too, published a memoir. In it he alleged that patients in the Pennsylvania Hospital for the Insane, the quintessence of moral treatment, were choked, douched with buckets of cold water, strapped to their beds, confined in bare dungeons, berated, humiliated, beaten by attendants and physicians, and lied to and about by Kirkbride, himself. Not content to allow readers to come to their own conclusions, Haskell spent the next several years in a vigorous and public anti-asylum campaign where he repeated his charge that little resembling the ideal of moral treatment could be found behind the locked doors and high walls of asylums.

In its absence, there has been a tendency to idealize moral treatment as if it was, and always had been, a set of discrete therapeutic practices that operationalized a set of agreed upon theoretical principles. A century after its disappearance, the French philosopher and historian Michel Foucault revisited the occasionally heard criticism that moral treatment really was moral oppression, and that asylums that were dedicated to it were really a "juridical space in which [the patients] were accused, judged, and condemned, and from which [they were] never released except by the version of this trial in psychological depth, that is, remorse. Madness will be punished in the asylum, even if it is innocent outside of it" (Foucault, 1988, p. 269). Although Foucault balanced his argument by crediting Pinel and Tuke, in particular, for insisting on more humane treatment of the insane, he concluded that within the walls of the asylum, and as practiced by the paternalistic and judgmental asylum physicians, moral treatment "results in nothing more than the conversion of medicine into justice, of therapeutics into repression" (p. 266).

Foucault's assessment has both its supporters and detractors, but the fact remains that the lingering influence of moral treatment's "law of kindness" and its highly individualized approach can be found to this day in therapeutic communities, recovery initiatives and occupational therapy programs.

REFERENCES

Charland, L.C. (2007). Benevolent theory: Moral treatment at the York Retreat. *History of Psychiatry, 18,* 61–80.
Chiarugi, V. (1793). *Della pazzia in genere e in specie trattato medico analitico: Con una centuria di osservazioni.* Florence, Italy: Presso Luigi Carlieri.
Deutsch, A. (1937). *The mentally ill in America: A history of their care and treatment from Colonial times.* Garden City, NY: Doubleday.
de Young, M. (2010). *Madness: An American history of mental illness and its treatment.* Jefferson, NC: McFarland.
Digby, A. (1985). *Madness, morality, and medicine.* Cambridge: Cambridge University Press.
Earle, P. (1848). *History, description and statistics of the Bloomingdale Asylum for the Insane.* New York: Egbert, Hovey & King.
Earle, P. (1887). *The curability of insanity: A series of studies.* Philadelphia: J.B. Lippincott Co.
Edginton, B. (1997). Moral architecture: The influence of the York Retreat on asylum design. *Health & Place, 3,* 91–99.
Foucault, M. (1973). *The order of things: An archaeology of the human sciences.* New York: Vintage.
Foucault, M. (1988). *Madness and civilization: A history of insanity in the Age of Reason.* New York: Vintage.
Gerard, D.L. (1997). Chiarugi and Pinel considered: Soul's brain/person's mind. *Journal of the History of the Behavioral Sciences, 33,* 381–403.
Goldstein, J. (1987). *Console and classify: The French psychiatric profession in the nineteenth century.* Cambridge: University of Cambridge Press.
Goodheart, L.B. (2003). *Mad Yankees: The Hartford Retreat for the Insane and nineteenth-century psychiatry.* Amherst: University of Massachusetts Press.
Grange, K.M. (1963). Pinel or Chiarugi? *Medical History, 7,* 371–380.
Greenfeld, L. (2013). *Mind, modernity, madness: The impact of culture on human experience.* Cambridge, MA: Harvard University Press.
Grob, G.N. (1962). Samuel B. Woodward and the practice of psychiatry in early nineteenth century America. *Bulletin of the History of Medicine, 36,* 420–443.
Guislain, J. (1826). *Traité sur l'aliénation mentale et sur les hospices des aliénés.* Amsterdam: J. Van Der Hay et Fils, & H. Gartman.
Haskell, E. (1869). *The trial of Ebenezer Haskell.* Philadelphia: Author.
Hervey, N. (1986). Advocacy or folly: The Alleged Lunatics' Friend Society, 1845–1863. *Medical History, 30,* 245–275.
Hunt, I. (1851). *Astounding disclosure! Three years in a mad house.* Boston: Author.
Johnson, H. (2001). *Angels in the architecture.* Detroit, MI: Wayne State University Press.
Kirkbride, T.S. (1842). *Annual report of the Pennsylvania Hospital for the Insane.* Philadelphia: John C. Clark.
Kirkbride, T.S. (1880). *On the construction, organization, and general arrangements of hospitals for the insane.* 2nd ed. Philadelphia: J.B. Lippincott.
Laffey, P. (2003). Psychiatric therapy in Georgian Britain. *Psychological Medicine, 33,* 1285–1297.
Livi, C. (1882). Life of Chiarugi. *Alienist and Neurologist, 3,* 93–118.
Luchins, A.S. (1989). Moral treatment in asylums and general hospitals in 19th-century America. *Journal of Psychology, 123,* 585–607.
"M. Guislain on Mental Derangement, &c." (1829). *Edinburgh Medical and Surgical Journal, 32,* 97–113.
Michel, S. (1994). Dorothea Dix: Or, the voice of the maniac. *Discourse, 17,* 48–66.
Perceval, J.T. (1840). *A narrative of the treatment experienced by a gentleman during a state of mental derangement.* London: Effingham Wilson.
Piddock, S. (2007). *A space of their own: The archeology of nineteenth century lunatic asylums in Britain, South Australia and Tasmania.* New York: Springer.
Pinel, P. (1801). *Traité médico-philosophique sur l'aliénation mentale, ou la manie.* Paris: Caille et Ravière.
Porter, R. (1990). Foucault's great confinement. *History of the Human Sciences, 3,* 47–54.
Scull, A. (1979). Moral treatment reconsidered: Some sociological comments on an episode in the history of British psychiatry. *Psychological Medicine, 9,* 421–428.
Scull, A. (1993). *The most solitary of afflictions: Madness and society in Britain 1700–1900.* New Haven, CT: Yale University Press.
Smith, L. (2008). A gentleman's mad-doctor in Georgian England: Edward Long Fox and Brislington House. *History of Psychiatry, 19,* 163–184.
Sueur, L., and Beer, D.M. (1997). The psychological treatment of insanity in France in the first part of the nineteenth century. *History of Psychiatry, 8,* 37–53.
Szasz, T.S. (2007). *Coercion as cure: A critical history of psychiatry.* New Brunswick, NJ: Transaction Publishers.
Tomes, N. (1984). *The art of asylum-keeping: Thomas Story Kirkbride and the origin of American psychiatry.* Philadelphia: University of Pennsylvania Press.
Tuke, S. (1813). *Description of the Retreat, an institution near York, for insane persons of the Society for Friends.* York, UK: W. Alexander.
Weiner, D.B. (1979). The apprenticeship of Philippe

Pinel. *American Journal of Psychiatry, 136,* 1128–1134.

Weiss, K.J. (2013). Isaac Ray, malpractice defendant. *Journal of the American Academy of Psychiatry and Law, 41,* 382–390.

Whitaker, R. (2002). *Mad in America: Bad science, bad medicine, and the enduring mistreatment of the mentally ill.* New York: Perseus Publishing.

Yanni, C. (2007). The *architecture of madness.* Minneapolis: University of Minnesota Press.

Ziolkowski, T. (1990). *German Romanticism and its institutions.* Princeton, NJ: Princeton University Press.

## Organotherapy (Opotherapy, Séquardotherapy, Histotherapy, Zootherapy, *Materia Medica Animalis*)

*The treatment of insanity with preparations derived from animal endocrine organs or glandular extracts.*

The use of animal organs to treat disease dates to antiquity. Hippocrates and Celsus, for example, recommended the liver of a pigeon or a wolf to treat hepatic disease, and the brain of a hare to remedy tremors. Pliny the Elder prescribed the testicles of a bear to ameliorate the seizures of epilepsy, and the castor sacs of a beaver to relieve menstrual disorders.

Perhaps the most recited recipe of animal offal, albeit for more nefarious purposes than the treatment of disease, is found in Shakespeare's *Macbeth* (Act IV, Sc. 1):

> Double, double toil and trouble;
> Fire burn and cauldron bubble.
> Fillet of a fenny snake,
> In the cauldron boil and bake:
> Eye of newt and toe of frog,
> Wool of bat and tongue of dog,
> Adder's fork and blind-worm's sting,
> Lizard's leg and howlet's wing,
> For a charm of powerful trouble,
> Like a hell-broth boil and bubble.

The medicinal, as opposed to necromantic, use of animal organs was re-discovered in the late nineteenth century during the laboratory revolution in medicine that spawned the specialties of bacteriology, serology, immunology, and endocrinology. Here, the role of Mauritian-born physiologist and neurologist, Charles-Édouard Brown-Séquard, deserves brief mention. Towards the end of a peripatetic career that brought him to France, England and the United States in the various roles of physician, researcher and educator, Brown-Séquard shocked the Société de Biologie in Paris in 1889 with the claim that the testicles of animals could invigorate men and prolong their lives. He, at the age of seventy-two and having experienced what he referred to as "spermatic anemia" (Brown-Séquard, p. 22), enjoyed the physically, mentally and sexually rejuvenating effects of ten subcutaneous injections of a filtered solution of testicular blood, seminal fluid and testicular extract from healthy dogs and guinea pigs. In an era as prudish in its comportments as it was extravagant in its claims that sexual excess and impropriety caused ill health, not to mention insanity, Brown-Séquard concluded by appealing to his female colleagues to concoct an equally potent elixir of crushed animal ovaries for women.

Testicular extract, better known and aggressively marketed as Brown-Séquard Elixir, became all the rage in the United States and Europe in the early twentieth century. Variously feted in song, satirized in poems and cartoons, and sensationalized in the press, it eventually was dismissed by most physicians as nothing more than a nostrum that worked only if the user believed it would. Yet the hypothesis underlying it—that disorder and disease could be caused by a deficit or a surplus of internal secretions—continued to intrigue.

The interest in what was to become known as organotherapy can be traced in the medical and psychiatric literature. In 1893 the *New York Therapeutic Review* published a series of articles that urged the use of organ extracts for the treatment of a variety of not just physical, but mental illnesses. Just two decades later, more than 8,000 articles and reports on their uses had been published in the literature worldwide. And as the medical specialty of endocrinology developed, journals devoted to the field conveyed the optimism that the cause of insanity, at last, could be found in the interstitial or metabolic auto-intoxication caused by the internal secretions of the duct and ductless glands. The restoration and balancing of these hormones, as they were now being termed, through vigorous regimes of organotherapy would not only treat, but perhaps even prevent and cure, insanity.

Asylum physicians tried an astonishing array of organotherapy preparations to treat their patients, as well combinations of pure glandular extracts and of patented products such as Hormotone, a mix of thyroid, pituitary, ovary, testis, pancreas and spleen hormones that was touted as a cure for neurasthenia, premature senility and sexual neurosis. A 1923 case from the records of Maudsley Hospital in London, England, illustrates not only the enthusiastic approach to organotherapy, but the canonical link during that era between endocrinology and psychiatry. The patient was a twenty-one-year-old woman who gave her illness the moniker, "the slow." It had begun during her adolescence with pains in her head and neck, and over the years had developed into peculiar habits such as touching things repeatedly and getting in and out of bed before finally settling down to sleep. When admitted to the Maudsley she was diagnosed with compulsion neurosis that, it was theorized, was caused by her sex organs or, more to the point, by her "infantile uterus" (Evans & Jones, p. 261) that had resulted in late onset menstruation, underdeveloped breasts and a pathological desire to "remain a child, cared for and dependent upon her mother" (p. 261). She was treated with a combination of pure thyroid extract, a thyro-ovarian extract mix and Hormotone, and was released as significantly improved, although not cured, eight months later.

Organotherapy of some type or another was used as an asylum therapeutic well into the twentieth century in Europe and North America. Having been hyped so enthusiastically, it was somewhat destined to disillusion, but it was not just the disappointing therapeutic outcomes that brought its end. Asylum physicians and psychiatric researchers, eager to establish the specialty of their discipline and increase the status of their practice, turned away from somatic explanations of insanity and towards the brain. A new discourse emerged, and with it a new practice: autointoxication theory was replaced by brain metabolism theory, the focus on hormones by neurohormones, as neurotransmitters originally were termed, and the use of glandular extracts to treat asylum patients by a plethora of psychotropic drugs.

REFERENCES

Borell, M. (1976). Brown-Séquard's organotherapy and its appearance in America at the end of the nineteenth century. *Bulletin of the History of Medicine, 50,* 309–320.

Brown-Séquard, C-E. (1889). *The elixir of life.* Boston: J.G. Cupples Company.

Clouston, T.S. (1904). *Clinical lectures on mental diseases,* 6th ed. Philadelphia: Lea Brothers & Co.

Cobb, I.G. (1922). *Aids to organotherapy.* New York: William Wood and Company.

Evans, B., and Jones, E. (2012). Organ extracts and the development of psychiatry: Hormonal treatments at the Maudsley Hospital 1923–1938. *Journal of the History of the Behavioral Sciences, 48,* 251–276.

Goodall, E., and Craig, M. (1894). The insanity of the climacteric period. *British Journal of Psychiatry, 40,* 235–242.

Hoskins, R.G. (1946). *The biology of schizophrenia.* Philadelphia: W.W. Norton.

Kraepelin, E. (1917). *Lectures on clinical psychiatry,* 3rd ed. New York: William Wood and Company.

Marland, H. (2003). Disappointment and desolation: Women, doctors and interpretations of puerperal insanity in the nineteenth century. *History of Psychiatry, 14,* 303–320.

Noll, R. (2007). Kraepelin's "lost biological psychiatry"? Autointoxication, organotherapy and surgery for dementia praecox. *History of Psychiatry, 18,* 301–320.

Noll, R. (2011). *American madness: The rise and fall of dementia praecox.* Cambridge: Harvard University Press.

Robertson, A. (1893). Observations on the action of the brain of the sheep in disease of the central nervous system and mind. *British Medical Journal, 16,* 1319–1320.

Robertson, A. (1896). A discussion on the treatment of mental and nervous diseases by animal abstracts. *British Medical Journal, 2,* 800–802.

Rohé, G.H. (1893). Lactational insanity. *Journal of the American Medical Association, 21,* 235.

Smith, W.M. (1912). On the use of brain extract in the treatment of various forms of insanity. *British Medical Journal, 2,* 1451–1454.

Trede, K., Baldessarini, R.J., Viguera, A.C., and Bottero, A. (2009). Treatise on insanity in pregnant, postpartum, and lactating women (1858) by Louis-Victor Marcé: A commentary. *Harvard Review of Psychiatry, 17,* 157–165.

Watson, W.S. (1898). Melancholia and its treatment. *Journal of the American Medical Association, 30,* 831–834.

Wilson, E.A., and Christie, T. (1925). Puerperal insanity. *British Medical Journal, 31,* 797–798.

## *Brain Extract, or Myelin, or Cerebrinin*

An extract of the cortex of a sheep's brain administered by teaspoon three times daily before meals. The extract, concocted by Alexander Robertson, physician to the Royal Infirmary and City Parochial Asylum in Glasgow, Scotland, was flavored with cinnamon, dyed red with cochineal and referred to as myelin in fear that the patients would revolt if they realized it was sheep brain extract.

Myelin was first given to seventeen patients whose diagnosis varied from melancholia, mania, dementia to organic disease of the spinal cord. The extract had no appreciable effect on most of the patients, with the exception of three: a melancholic woman who became "more or less maniacal" post-treatment (Robertson, 1896, p. 800); another melancholic woman who continued the improvement she had made before the treatments began; and a forty-year-old man diagnosed with dementia. It was in the latter case that results were the most remarkable:

> His memory and intelligence were both greatly impaired, and there was some thickness in speech. He also had palsy of both legs and weakness of both arms. After five weeks of ordinary treatment he was not better but rather worse. Three days after the myelin was begun there was marked improvement both in mind and body. In five days he could not only stand, but also walk a few steps; in nine days he walked up and down the ward; and in less than six weeks after the myelin was begun he left the hospital to resume his employment. Though nearly well, his recovery could not be said to be perfect [Robertson, 1896, p. 800].

The more concentrated form of brain extract, which Robertson called cerebrinin, was administered to an additional five patients, two diagnosed with mania and the remaining three with melancholia. The results were mixed: both of the manic patients became more so, although one also experienced "greater lucidity" (Robertson, 1896, p. 800); one of the melancholic patients remained unchanged, while the remaining two "distinctly improved" (p. 800), although how and for how long was not discussed. On the basis of these observations, Robertson concluded:

> These, then, are the results of my experience with this preparation. They cannot be said to be either definite or striking. And yet the impression remains on my mind that there is a constituent in the brain of the sheep, and doubtless also of other animals, which acts as a stimulus to nerve tissue, cell and fibre, in the human subject in certain morbid states of these structures [Robertson, 1893, p. 1320].

In the late nineteenth and early twentieth centuries "impressions," such as this, were important to asylum physicians who were eager to expand their armamentarium of therapeutic resources. One of those physicians was W. Maule Smith at the Barnsley Hall Asylum in Worcestershire, England. Following the lead of Robertson, he boiled finely divided sheep brain tissue in a mixture of alcohol and ether and strained it though muslin; when cooled, he decanted the fluid from the thick deposit that was then poured into a boiling saline solution with glycerine. The resulting emulsion, rich in cerebrinin, was then administered to a range of patients with a concomitant range of results: eight of the twelve females with dementia "showed improvement" as observed in their manageability, increased appetites and better sleeping habits; six of the eight cases of delusional insanity reported fewer hallucinations; none of the five cases of manic-depression showed any improvement; six of the thirteen cases of epileptic insanity improved, although none experienced a decrease in the number and severity of seizures; eight of the fourteen cases of dementia praecox showed less restlessness and calmer mental states; and seven of the nine cases of melancholia improved. One of the cases in that latter category was a woman who

> showed unsurpassed distress both day and night at the idea of her being condemned and in the power of Satan, whose medium for evil she was. It would be difficult to find a case in whom the agony, hopelessness, and despair were more marked than in this patient. Prior to admission she made a desperate attempt to end her life by exposure and sheer starvation. No improvement was recorded for four months after admission; she was then given the extract during the height of a paroxysm of acute distress at Easter. Since then the whole complexion of the case has altered; she now occupies herself usefully and takes an interest in others, she has also slept well without the aid of any sedative, and morbid brooding and concern for her spiritual welfare are reduced to practically nothing [Smith, p. 1454].

Smith was left with the impression that brain extract worked most effectively in cases with recent onsets of insanity, quite regardless of the specific type. Hardly a cure, it instead quieted, calmed and relieved the more distressing symptoms, thus Smith hardly endorsed it over the more expensive hypnotic and sedative drugs that often had unpleasant side effects.

## *Ovarian Extract, or Oöphorin*

An abstract of cow or sow ovaries, typically administered in dry powder or tablet form in a dose of three to five grains, two to three times daily. The belief that women's insanity was intimately related to their reproductive organs, specifically the ovaries, can be traced to Hippocrates who conjectured that the periodic irritation of these organs in monthly menstruation, occasional pregnancy, birth and lactation, and in menopause, reflexively and adversely affected the brain. It was in the nineteenth century, however, with the rise of the medical specialty of obstetrics and its subsequent influence on psychiatry, that conjectures such as these became canonical in medical literature and practice. Very specific types of reproductive insanity—pregnancy, puerperal, lactation and climacteric—which had been surveyed by French psychiatrist Louis-Victor Marcé in an influential 1858 monograph, now were being diagnosed by influential asylum physicians. By the mid-nineteenth century, as a matter of fact, these types of reproductive insanities accounted for anywhere from seven to as much as 25 percent of all female asylum admissions.

That era's prevailing theory of reproductive insanity improved on Hippocratic conjecture by positing that periodic irritation temporarily depleted ovarian secretion which was needed for proper brain metabolism. The introduction of ovarian extract, then, would reestablish brain metabolism in each type of reproductive insanity. This appealing logic made differential diagnosis necessary, and led to keen observations of the symptomatic expressions of the various types of reproductive insanity. Pregnancy insanity, asylum physicians observed, was rare and occurred most often in first pregnancies. Its melancholic symptoms typically lasted a few weeks to a few months. Puerperal insanity, sometime also referred to as parturition insanity, was much more common. Its manic symptoms of excessive talking, excitement, insomnia, refusal of food, obscenity in language and behavior, indifference to personal appearance and hygiene and, most disturbingly, aversion to the newly born child and/or the husband, usually began two to six weeks after the birth of the child. Like pregnancy insanity, although more common, lactation insanity was characterized by melancholic symptoms and occurred most often in women who had had several previous children. Some of these cases, asylum physicians observed, resulted in dementia, that is, in hallucinations, delusions and disordered thinking. Finally, climacteric insanity typically occurred during the prodromal stage of menopause and manifested itself in periods of melancholic confusion and stupor, increased alcohol or drug consumption, occasional acts of sexual perversion, and olfactory hallucinations, that vacillated with longer periods of animation and socially appropriate activity.

It was both the disturbing symptoms of the various types of reproductive insanity, and the equally disturbing prospect of keeping women who were wives and mothers in asylums and away from their families and homes, that prompted asylum physicians to experiment with ovarian extract. And the results were encouraging. Physicians at the Dundee Mental Hospital in Scotland described five cases in which hypodermic injections of ovarian extract re-established menstruation and terminated cases of puerperal insanity. One of those cases was "Mrs. A.," a twenty-five-year-old who had given birth to her first child six months earlier:

> [Her insanity] continued until she was admitted to the [asylum]... in an emaciated state. She remained in a condition of acute mania for the next twelvemonth, during which time she had calmer periods and gained weight, but only to lose ground again. There was no menstruation. At the end of the nineteenth month a hypodermic inject of extract of ovary corresponding to 30 grains of fresh gland was given, and at intervals of from four to nine days successive injections, amounting to eight in all. From the first injection improvement was seen, and within six weeks she was up and going about, rational, interested in her surroundings, sleeping well and eating well. Menstruation began again, and in the twenty-third month since her breakdown she was discharged home as cured. She has since undertaken her regular household duties with success, and has undergone another pregnancy with no trouble [Wilson & Christie, p. 797].

The asylum physicians reported a similar success in a case of climacteric insanity. The patient in this case was "Mrs. F.," fifty-six years old, who had started menopause a couple of years before her admission into the asylum.

> She was stated to be light-headed, extremely talkative, asking senseless questions, and being sometimes delirious, at others stuporous. On admission she was depressed, stuporous and incoherent, and was treated on general principles. It was noticed after a time that she had spells of confusion at regular intervals. She would be acutely confused for about a week, then apparently recover, and act in every way as a rational woman, taking an interest in everything and working well. Her spells of mental confusion occurred regularly every three weeks, and inquiry elicited the fact that her menstrual periods had been at intervals of twenty-one days. One week before the next attack was due I gave her an injection every second day. She never had another attack, as I anticipated when each spell was due. And so for three spells. Then I omitted injection for two spells and she was discharged. No further attacks have been recorded [Wilson & Christie, p. 798].

The keen clinical observations that began the therapeutic use of ovarian extract also brought about its end. Despite the heartening results, asylum physicians could not dismiss the fact that most cases of reproductive insanity resolved themselves with no more complicated therapeutic intervention than bed rest, quiet and a good diet. Pregnancy insanity, they noted, almost always terminated with childbirth, puerperal insanity and lactation insanity usually were resolved within six months after childbirth, and climacteric insanity within a year of onset. What many asylum physicians also noted were the social, sometimes referred to as "moral," contributors to reproductive insanity: the anxieties associated with childbirth, the demands of motherhood, the loneliness of middle age and, especially for poor women who disproportionately found their ways into asylums, the stresses of single motherhood and the shame of illegitimacy. These keen observations—that reproductive insanity tended to resolve itself, and that its causes may be more social than biological—eventually weakened the assumed link between women's reproductive organs and insanity, thus obviating the need for ovarian extract treatment.

## Thyroid Extract

An abstract of sheep thyroid, specifically for the cure of myxedema, or hypothyroidism. The British physician George Redmayne Murray had discovered this successful cure for a disease that in its most severe manifestation produced changes in mental status, including lethargy, stupor and delirium. In the late nineteenth and early twentieth centuries, patients with myxedema could be found in virtually every asylum in Europe and North America.

At one of those asylums, the Royal Edinburgh in Scotland, medical superintendent Thomas Clouston had eight cases under his care. Their symptoms varied significantly, but their decline into insanity was marked by the hallmark signs of myxedema: slowness in mental activity, depression, irritability, suspiciousness and loss of self-control. Although Clouston boasted that the discipline of asylum life was sufficient to assure the "recovery" of some of these patients, he did concede that the "cure" of the rest was due to thyroid extract treatment. "The contrast between the disturbed, stupid, inert subject of myxdematous insanity, and the active, intelligent, bright and alert person who is seen after two or three months' treatment," he wrote, "is most dramatic" (Clouston, p. 668).

The "dramatic" cures Clouston wrote about, however, were not always noted. Some asylum physicians, in fact, found reason to conclude that only the most degenerated cases of myxedema should be treated with it. W.S. Watson, physician at the Riverview Sanitarium in New York, for example, discussed the cases of four female patients with mild myxedema who had deteriorated dangerously during treatment. One of them was " Miss P.," a thirty-three-year-old whose

> whole disposition had changed from an active worker and unassuming maiden to the belief that she belonged to some man or ought to, showing marked eroticism in various ways, whole mind seemed to be upon men, how this or that one could save her, etc. Thyroid was given in increasing doses, beginning with .32 grams t.i.d. [three times per day], believing the extract might be indicated from the degenerate tendency of the mind; after the dose had been increased to 1 gram t.i.d. [three times per day], the eroticism had so increased as to make it necessary to watch the patient every moment, lest she, in her uncontrollable condition, would make a show of herself; every expression and movement as well as her words showed intense sexual excitement. The thyroid was discontinued [Watson, p. 833].

While many asylum physicians were debating just what symptoms of myxedema merited thyroid extract treatment, some were experimenting with its use on the related diagnosis of cretinism. In these cases the congenital or endemic deficiency of thyroid hormones produced what often were very large goiters, as well as physical deformity and intellectual disability. While special asylums and training schools had been built in Europe and North America for cretin children, inspired by the philanthropic work of Swiss physician Louis Guggenbühl, adults with cretinism could be found in many public asylums in the late nineteenth century and beyond. The eminent German psychiatrist Emil Kraepelin described one of these asylum patients, a thirty-two-year-old "grotesque being," who was short, flabby and had a broad face with protuberant eyes, a flat nose and a huge double chin. She insisted her name was "Nobody":

> It is quite impossible at present to form an idea as to whether she is clear about her surroundings.... Her mood is cheerful and exalted. She often breaks out into a short, jerky laugh, without any cause, or begins to sing a ballad or street song in a shrill voice. She obeys orders with reluctance; she puts away her hand when she is asked to give it, but then strikes hands with a loud clap. She sometimes repeats words she hears or questions that are asked her several times over, and she has a decided tendency to make rhymes.... She writes her name correctly on the blackboard, and does a simple sums. All further attempts to test her knowl-

edge are defeated by her resistance, accompanied by vacant laughter and clucking movements of the tongue. It is easily seen from the patient's behavior that she suffers from a considerable degree of imbecility [Kraepelin, pp. 337–338].

Kraepelin held out little hope for a cure of adult cretinism with thyroid extract, although he did find that treatments improved the overall health of afflicted patients. He was fascinated, however, by the observation that the "imbecility" of Nobody and patients like her resembled the last stages of dementia praecox. Kraepelin, in fact, was the first to describe dementia praecox as an incurable psychotic disorder that had its onset in late adolescence or early adulthood and resulted in confusion, delusions, hallucinations and often incoherent speech and bizarre behaviors. He also was one of the first to theorize that its cause was autointoxication, that is, a disorder of metabolism that morbidly affected the brain. Because dementia praecox resembled the imbecility of cretinism and, to a lesser extent, paralleled the development of myxedema, he targeted the thyroid gland as the source and experimented with the administration of thyroid extract on dementia praecox patients.

Kraepelin's autointoxication theory was met with more than a little skepticism by his colleagues, many of whom were convinced that more psychodynamic factors were at play in this mysterious and pernicious type of insanity. And although he never really relinquished his autointoxication theory, his experiments with the thyroid extract treatment of dementia praecox were disappointing and by the start of the twentieth century he had abandoned them completely.

The thyroid gland indeed may have "served as a paradigmatic organ for early human ... experimentation on the function of glands and their role in disease processes" (Evans & Jones, p. 254), but thyroid extract treatment for various forms of insanity waned over time. By the mid-twentieth century, in fact, thyroid extract treatment had been administered to literally thousands of asylum patients in North America and Great Britain, but with disillusioning results. Despite some evidence of positive short-term therapeutic success in some types of insanity, virtually no long-term therapeutic success was noted, even for the most chronic and debilitating types of insanity such as dementia praecox, schizophrenia and manic-depressive psychosis.

## *Thyroid Shock Therapy, or Hyperthyroid Treatment*

The administration of large doses of thyroid extract over a short time period to produce an acute reaction that beneficially stimulated the nervous system. By the early twentieth century, much of the therapeutic optimism that small doses of thyroid extract would be as efficacious in treating chronic insanity, such as dementia praecox, as it was for treating the relatively uncommon cases of myxedema psychosis, had been deflated by disappointing outcomes. In 1924, William S. Dawson of the Maudsley Hospital in London, England, observed that the debilitating melancholia of patients with another type of severe insanity—manic depressive psychosis—would benefit from doses of thyroid extract that were large enough to produce significant weight loss and fatigue, but that were followed by "remarkable improvement[s] in the mental condition" (Dawson, p. 126).

The case of a twenty-six-year-old who was admitted to the Maudsley Hospital for melancholia two months after giving birth gave reason for this new therapeutic optimism. Doubting her ability and her worthiness as a mother, and plagued by thoughts about smothering her newborn, the woman deteriorated significantly after admission. She was semi-stuporous, and sometimes begged the staff to poison her for her wickedness. She was then administered a ten day intensive course of thyroid shock therapy over which the dose of thyroid extract was incrementally increased from ten grains to thirty, and then gradually reduced before being ceased completely. One week after the treatment, the staff noted that she was more aware of and responsive to her surroundings; a month after that she was described as "active [and] cheerful" (Evans & Jones, p. 266). She was released on a pass and showed a great interest in her baby. Soon after, she was discharged, "free from doubts" and "completely well" (p. 266).

Thyroid shock treatment," a precursor of insulin shock therapy [see **Shock Therapy**], also was promoted by Henry Devine, medical superintendent of the Holloway Sanatorium in southwest London. Purpose-built for the "middle class insane," the magnificent Franco-Gothic design facility housed approximately 300 patients who wandered its elegant corridors, played cricket and croquet on its expansive lawn, and listened to concerts and dramatic readings in the evenings. Holloway also was a site of therapeutic innovation, and Devine had a particular interest in using glandular agents not only for their physiological effects in supplying what the organism lacks, but also as "shock" agents with a view to the modification of the humoral-neurovegetative tonus.

This hypothesis not only stirred some interest in thyroid shock therapy, but also helped explain the rather puzzling observation that males suffering from insanity sometimes improved with doses of ovarian extract, while their female counterparts occasionally improved with doses of testicular extract. The glandular extract in these cases did not act specifically, but generally in shocking the system.

# Orthomolecular Therapy

*The treatment of insanity with large doses of vitamins and minerals in order to restore biochemical balance.*

The successful use of vitamin B3 (niacin) to treat pellagra in the early twentieth century suggested that vitamins and minerals could be used with efficacy to treat a variety of physical and mental disorders. At that time, outbreaks of pellagra already had been widespread throughout Southern Europe and the Mediterranean countries for centuries, and now was endemic in the American South. The dermatitis, diarrhea and inflamed mucus membranes that were symptomatic of the early stages of the disease often gave way to the dementia and delusions that were the hallmark symptoms of pellagra psychosis, and that necessitated admission into asylums. Because its cause was unknown pellagra was at first thought to be a communicable disease, thus pellagra patients usually were isolated from other asylum patients. So confined, they were treated with a range of therapeutics from the administration of arsenic, to prophylactic doses of quinine, to blood transfusions.

A series of observational studies by Joseph Goldberger, who had been appointed by the U.S. Surgeon General to examine the virulent epidemic of pellagra in the South, seemed to confirm the findings of earlier Italian studies that germs were not the source of the disease. Instead, Goldberger reasoned, diet was the culprit. The rural poor Southern diet of corn and molasses, he posited, deprived its consumers of an essential ingredient. From an epidemiological perspective, this explained why a disproportionate number of patients diagnosed with it could be found in Southern asylums; why pellagra outbreaks occurred *in* asylums among patients who had been admitted for other types of insanity; why asylum staff, who enjoyed a more nutritious diet, remained free of the disease; as well as why pellagra was cured by a diet rich in vegetables, meat and milk.

Although Goldberger did not live long enough to identify the essential missing ingredient, subsequent research isolated vitamin B3 (niacin). With nutrition programs, crop diversification initiatives and the fortification of processed food, such as flour, with niacin, pellagra was eradicated by the mid-twentieth century, thus assuring no new asylum admissions for pellagra-induced dementia. For those patients already institutionalized, the administration of niacin, then known as nicotinic acid, often reversed their dementia and restored their physical health enough to ensure their discharge.

In the early decades of the twentieth century, vitamins were expensive—far out of the reach of most cash-strapped asylums. As some research money gradually became available, however, the use of vitamin B3 for the treatment of schizophrenia, the dementia and delusions of which most resembled those caused by pellagra, underwent cautious experimentation. The findings were mixed. When other vitamins were substituted for, or added to vitamin B3, the findings remained mixed. John Notkin and his colleagues at the Hudson River State Hospital in Poughkeepsie, New York, for example, administered massive doses of vitamins A and D over several months to fifteen female and seventeen male schizophrenics and compared their reactions to that of an equal number of controls. Only two of the experimental group patients showed any significant improvement, but doubts remained as to whether that could be attributed to the vitamin therapy alone. At the Worcester State Hospital in Massachusetts, L.H. Chase gave large doses of vitamin B1 to ten schizophrenic male patients for two months and noted neither clinical improvement nor deleterious effects. Eva R. Balken and her colleagues, however, found significant improvements as measured by the Grace Arthur Point Performance Scale for forty-six chronic schizophrenic male patients in Elgin State Hospital in Elgin, Illinois, after they were administered vitamins A, D, B1 and B2, as well as iron.

These scattered and inconsistent findings would have had little influence on everyday asylum medicine were it not for a rather serendipitous set of circumstances. Abram Hoffer, a Canadian physician with no specialized training in psychiatry, had been appointed by the Saskatchewan provincial government in the mid–1950s to bring its two asylums into the mainstream of twentieth century psychiatry. Joining him were Humphry Osmond and John Smythies who had collaborated in the development of what was known as the M-hypothesis that postulated that schizophrenia was caused by an unknown toxin related to adrenalin and with the psychological properties of the powerful hallucinogenic drug mescaline. Reasoning that an efficacious treatment for schizophrenia would relieve the congested backwards of the asylums they were appointed to reform, the three physicians set out first to discover its cause. Reconsidering the M-hypothesis, they proposed that the unknown toxin that caused schizophrenia was adrenochrome, a product of the excessive oxidation of adrenaline, and that the most effective treatment would be to block this toxic metabolite with large doses of niacin (vitamin B-3) and ascorbic acid (vitamin C).

The adrenochrome hypothesis, as it was now called, was then tested on a male patient whose catatonic schizophrenia had been unrelieved by the conventional treatments of insulin and electroconvulsive shock therapies [see **Shock Therapy**]. Large doses of niacin and ascorbic acid were administered through a stomach tube. His recovery was so remarkable that he was discharged as cured a month later. With funding from the Rockefeller Foundation, Hoffer and his colleagues went on to conduct several double-blind, placebo-controlled studies with the same encouraging results. In them, they administered up to six grams per day of vitamin B3 as well as large doses of vitamin C to schizophrenic patients as additives to the regular treatment regime. Not only was the recovery rate of the experimental group of patients twice that of controls, but the re-admission rate was half and the positive results still were noted in follow-up studies conducted more than a decade later.

Noting these findings, Linus Pauling in a 1968 article published in the prestigious journal *Science,* coined the term "orthomolecular therapy" for the treatment of insanity with vitamins and proper diet. Long interested in mental illness (his mother had succumbed to pellagra and had suffered bouts of pellagra psychosis), Pauling had concluded that abnormalities in enzyme function had adverse effects on the brain and produced the hallmark symptoms of schizophrenia and other types of debilitating insanity. These effects, he proposed, could be effectively treated with mega doses of vitamins in combination with a proper diet.

The imprimatur of Pauling, a Nobel laureate in chemistry and later of peace, raised the profile of the orthomolecular treatment of insanity—and the controversy. The American Psychiatric Association put together a task force to study the claims for its success and found them wanting. It scathingly criticized the studies of Hoffer and his colleagues, and declared orthomolecular therapy of no therapeutic value. In conclusion, it stated:

> This review and critique has carefully examined the literature produced by megavitamin proponents and by those who have attempted to replicate their basic and clinical work. It concludes in this regard that the credibility of the megavitamin proponents is low. Their credibility is further diminished by a consistent refusal to perform controlled experiments and to report their new results in a scientifically acceptable fashion. Under these circumstances this Task Force considers the massive publicity which they promulgate via radio, the lay press and popular books, using catch phrases which are really misnomers like "megavitamin therapy" and "orthomolecular treatment," to be deplorable [Lipton, p. 48].

Hoffer fought back with a comparably scathing book-length *ad hominen* attack on task force members whom he characterized as biased, inept and insensitive, and on the task force itself whose actions, he declared, only could be understood "if one took into account the spirit of Watergate then rampant in Washington, among some of the government agencies and the American Psychiatric Association, headquartered in Washington" (Hoffer, p. 122).

The battle waged for some time. Orthomolecular therapy not only had its vehement proponents, dismissed as a "cult following" by a nutrition committee of the American Pediatric Association, but its popularization in the larger culture guaranteed its use for treating other vexing disorders, such as autism, learning disorders, hyperactivity and developmental disabilities, that only infrequently were found among asylum patients. It was lauded in popular self-help literature with intriguing titles such as *The Way Up from Down,* and *Down Syndrome and Vitamin Therapy*; praised in popularized psychiatric books, many of them written by Hoffer himself, such as *How to Live with Schizophrenia,* and *Healing Schizophrenia: Complementary Vitamin and Drug Treatment;* and commended in the autobiographies and testimonials of former patients such as Sister Theresa Feist, the actress Margot Kidder, and Mark Vonnegut. In a newly revised edition of his bestseller, *The Eden Express,* however, Vonnegut who is now a physician himself, retreated from his enthusiastic endorsement of the orthomolecular treatment of the schizophrenia that led to his institutionalization.

> At the time I wrote my book I felt that the large doses of vitamins with which I was treated, along with more conventional approaches, had a great deal to do with my recovery. It was my hope that many people diagnosed as schizophrenic would get better if only their doctors would become more open-minded and treat them with vitamins. Since that time I've seen people with breakdowns like mine recover every bit as completely as I did without vitamin therapy. I've seen many cases where vitamin therapy didn't make any difference and a lot of cases like mine where it's hard to say exactly what did what.... I continue to feel that the debate over whether or not vitamins might have a role in the treatment of some forms of mental illness has been miserably handled by both sides. What I can no longer do is to maintain that the vitamins played a major role in my recovery.... I remain very proud of the [first edition] of the book but if I could have one line back I'd delete "The more the vitamins took hold..." [Vonnegut, p. 298].

Some studies heralding the success of orthomolecular treatment continued to appear in the scientific literature, many of them published in the *Journal of Schizophrenia*, now titled the *Journal of Orthomolecular Medicine*, founded by Hoffer. Most were either contradicted by larger and better controlled studies, or summarily dismissed as unscientific by the specially constituted task forces of professional organizations such as the National Institute of Mental Health. It is in the court of public opinion that orthomolecular therapy has been holding its longest sway.

Hoffer claimed to have successfully treated thousands of asylum patients throughout Canada with orthomolecular therapy, but the controversy that always attended it impeded its use in other countries. Yet its influence still was felt. The usually bland and monotonous diets of asylum patients were supplemented whenever and wherever possible with vitamin and mineral rich foods. Although few asylum physicians were willing to ascribe to the premise that vitamin deficiency caused insanity, many were willing to settle for the proposition that insanity and nutritional states were to some extent interdependent. By improving the general physical health of patients, they reasoned, they also would improve their overall mental health.

### REFERENCES

Balken, E.R., Maurer, S., and Falstein, E.I. (1936). Variations in psychological measurements associated with increased feeding of vitamins A, D, B1 and B2 and iron in dementia praecox. *Journal of Comparative Psychology, 21*, 387–403.

Chase, L.H. (1939). Vitamin B1: Effects in schizophrenia. *American Journal of Psychiatry, 95*, 1035–1038.

Cole, H.P. (1909). The transfusion of blood as a therapeutic agent with report of transfusion in a case of pellagra. *Southern Medical Journal, 2*, 631–638.

Committee on Nutrition of the American Academy of Pediatrics (1976). Megavitamin therapy for childhood psychosis and learning disabilities. *Pediatrics, 58*, 910–912.

Feist, T. (1979). *Schizophrenia cured*. Regina, Saskatchewan, Canada: Canadian Schizophrenic Association.

Fouts, P.J., Helmer, O.M., Lepkovsky, S., and Jukes, T.H. (1937). Treatment of human pellagra with nicotinic acid. *Proceedings of the Society of Experimental Biology and Medicine, 37*, 405–407.

Hampson, S. (2007, May 14). Lois Lane Returns. *Globe and Mail*, p. L-1.

Hoffer, A. (1974). History of orthomolecular psychiatry. *Orthomolecular Psychiatry, 3*, 223–230.

Hoffer, A. (1976). *Megavitamin therapy: In reply to the American Psychiatric Association task force report on megavitamin and orthomolecular therapy in psychiatry*. Regina, Saskatchewan, Canada: Canadian Schizophrenic Association.

Hoffer, A. (1992). *How to live with schizophrenia*. New York: Citadel.

Hoffer, A. (2004). *Healing schizophrenia: Complementary vitamin and drug treatment*. Toronto, Ontario, Canada: CCNM Press.

Hoffer, A., and Prousky, J.E. (2008). The proper treatment of schizophrenia requires optimal daily doses of vitamin B3. *Journal of Orthomolecular Medicine, 23*, 191–195.

Lipton, N. (1973). *Task force report on megavitamin and orthomolecular therapy in psychiatry*. Washington, D.C.: American Psychiatric Association.

McCafferty, E.L. (1909). Pellagra among the colored insane at the Mt. Vernon Hospital. *Gulf States Journal of Medicine and Surgery and Mobile Medical and Surgical Journal, 14*, 228–236.

McLeod, K. (2003). *Down syndrome and vitamin therapy*. Ottawa, Ontario, Canada: Kemanso Publishing.

Noll, R. (2007). *The encyclopedia of schizophrenia and other psychotic disorders*. New York: Facts on File.

Notkin, J., Krasnow, F., Huddart, V., Thompson, W.J., and Watts, L.E. (1936). Effects of vitamins A and D in dementia praecox. *American Journal of Psychiatry, 92*, 925–935.

Pauling, L. (1968). Orthomolecular psychiatry. *Science, 160*, 265–271.

Rajakumar, K. (2000). Pellagra in the United States. *Southern Medical Journal, 93*, 272–277.

Slagle, P. (1994). *The way up from down*. New York: Random House.

Vonnegut, M. (2002). *The Eden express: A memoir of insanity*, 2nd ed. New York: Praeger.

# Ovarian Compression

*Forcible pressure on the ovaries by the hands, fists, body or with a specially designed compression belt, in order to prevent, terminate or initiate an attack of hysteria.*

There are few mental disorders that have a longer history than hysteria, and fewer still, if any at all, that have such a wide range of culturally idiomatic symptoms, from suffocation, choking, mutism, paralysis, seizures, anesthesia, hallucinations, dissociation, anorexia, somnambulism, florid emotionality, drama, seductiveness and deception. What is constant, however, is that hysteria always has been considered the quintessential women's malady. That gender specificity was set in the very origin of the word "hysteria," derived from the Greek *hystera,* or womb. The ancients posited that when its generative function is unfulfilled, the womb "is distressed and sorely disturbed, and straying about in the body and cutting off passages of the breath, it impedes respiration and brings the sufferer into extremist anguish and provokes all manner of diseases besides" (Plato p. 87).

Over subsequent millennia hysteria was appropriated by the Church and interpreted as an embodiment of sin or possession, and then by nineteenth century neurology that translated it as a nervous disorder, and finally by twentieth century Freudian psychoanalysis that described it as somatic symptoms arising from repressed emotions and memories. Yet, through all of its iterations, the female reproductive organs were never far from consideration.

That was no more evident than in the practice of Jean-Martin Charcot. The renowned neurologist was the director of the Salpêtrière Hospital in Paris, France, and it was in that "museum of living pathology," as he once referred to it (Shorter, p. 169), that hysteria became a spectacle. Charcot paraded his hysterics into the hospital amphitheater and coaxed, coerced and coddled the women into not just demonstrating, but *performing,* their hysterical symptoms before appreciative audiences. On command they had seizures that arched their backs, or went into hypnotic trances that left them rocking top hats to and fro as if they were babies; their otherwise paralyzed limbs were made to gesture and dance, and their apparently unfeeling bodies were pierced with needles.

Such performances, though, were scripted by Charcot's theory of hysteria. He insisted that hysteria was an inherited disorder of the nervous system, set off by an *agent provocateur,* such as a shock or a trauma. Although it left no lesions in the spinal cord or brain that could be seen in a postmortem examination, he remained adamant that hysteria had an organic origin. Evidence for that, he proposed, could be found in the "hysterogenic zones" on the body. Located above and below the breasts, under the rib cage, on the hips and over the ovaries, these were "the more or less circumscribed regions of the body where pressure or simple rubbing brings about the more or less occurrences of the phenomenon of the *aura,*" he wrote, "that may be followed on occasion, if one persists, by an hysterical attack" (Charcot, p. 88).

Since hysteria's organic cause remained elusive, so did its remedy. Thus, Charcot was much less interested in curing it, than in demonstrating it to an audience and in managing it in the crowded environs of the asylum. Demonstrations were carried out in the controlled context of the Tuesday Lectures held in the asylum amphitheater, a long room lit by gas lamps with frosted globes the light from which was further diffused by the red painted walls. There, Charcot would touch the hysterogenic zone of the patient, setting off the hysterical symptoms or sometimes even changing them dramatically mid-course, all the while lecturing to his audience. But the daily management of hysteria posed a more formidable problem. The patients who filled the wards were often on the brink of hysterical attacks or in the throes of them, and because of the wide range of their spectacular symptoms their control was required. Asylum staff were directed to touch their respective hysterogenic zone in order to arrest an attack, an intervention that usually was effective, unless the zone was over the ovaries.

Not all hysterics, however, were "ovarian subjects," as Charcot referred to them (Eghigian, p. 198), but those who were had a particular tenderness and sensitivity associated with that hysterogenic zone. Intervention required more than a touch. Charcot advised his staff to use a more forceful approach:

> The best position... is for the patient to be stretched out horizontally on the floor, or if possible, on a mattress....Then the doctor, with one knee on the ground, plunges his closed fist into [her ovarian region]. Most important, he must call on all his forces in order to vanquish the rigidity of the abdominal muscles [Hustvedt, p. 52].

With uncharacteristic modesty, Charcot admitted that this ovarian compression technique was used as early as the sixteenth century when placing heavy stones on the belly, hitting it with iron bars, or jumping on it were used to interfere with hysterical attacks. Indeed, Charcot's somewhat less brutish method had been used for many decades in asylums. So overly confident were asylum physicians in the reflexive relationship between the ovaries, the nervous system and hysteria, that ovary compression was rarely discussed in the literature. One notable exception was the observation by John Gideon Millingen, then medical superintendent of the Hanwell Asylum outside of London, England, that hysterical attacks often were remedied either by a nurse's "clenched hand," or by her heavy body sitting on the abdomen of the patient (Milligen, p. 129).

It is not clear if Charcot's staff objected to the plunging of their closed fists into the stomachs of hysterical patients or, for that matter, if the patients did, but in the late nineteenth century he directed one of his interns, Dr. Poirier, to design an ovary compressor, an ingenious modification of an abdominal tourniquet. Applied to the patient's abdomen, the descending knob of the heavy leather and metal belt applied continuous pressure on just one of the sensitive ovaries; the pressure could be easily adjusted by the patient, herself, with a twist of the handle of the knob. One famous performing Salpêtrière hysteric, Blanche Wittmann, was particularly fond of the compressor. The "Queen of the Hysterics," as she was widely known as a result of her dramatic Tuesday Lecture demonstrations, wore the contraption for as long as forty-eight continuous hours. As soon as it was removed, she went into a paroxysm of hysteria.

The Poirier compressor was bulky and uncomfortable to wear, and had the added disadvantage of compressing only one ovary at a time. A few years after its invention, another of Charcot's interns, Gilbert Ballet, who would go on to become the chair of clinical psychiatry and brain disorders at the Hôpital Sainte Anne in Paris, designed a more comfortable version that pressed on both ovaries simultaneously. Other modifications soon followed. One, designed by Charles Féré, another of Charcot's interns, was in the form of stiff truss. The point of support was on the spine; on the front, rubber pads attached to metal clasps pressed into the ovarian region.

There is not much evidence that ovarian compression, whether by hands, fists or belts, was used in the treatment and management of hysteria in asylums outside of the Salpêtrière Hospital. It was there, after all, that Charcot himself had ushered in the "Golden Age of Hysteria" that was unparalleled anywhere else in the world. Upon his death in 1893, that golden age ended and hysteria was quickly appropriated by his most renowned pupil, Sigmund Freud, who reinterpreted it as psychological disorder, more suitable for treatment by the talking cure of psychoanalysis than ovary compression.

Parenthetically, it should be noted that Charcot always, and somewhat controversially, asserted that men could suffer from hysteria, too. *Sans* ovaries, their hysterogenic zones included the top of the head, below the clavicle, below the nipples, at the bottom of the rib cage, between the shoulder blades, on the lower back and, for some, on the spermatic cord, the skin of the scrotum, or in the testes. One of his patients, Gui, a twenty-seven-year-old locksmith, whose athletic contortions during the *grand hystérie* attack were photographed and published in several of Charcot's treatises on male hysteria, always experienced a "testicular aura" before the attack. The feeling rose to his esophagus, making it difficult to breathe and creating a loud ringing in his ears. When he lost consciousness, his body would convulse and his back would arch high into an *arc-en-cercle*. Hysterical attacks such as this terminated only when his right testicle was squeezed, and were prevented if it were squeezed during the prodromal phase. Charcot noted, however, that even in those male hysterics for whom the testes were hysterogenic zones, squeezing was not always an effective intervention. In some males, it only prolonged the hysterical attack.

REFERENCES

Charcot, J-M. (1890). *Leçons sur les maladies du système nerveux*. Paris: Lecrosnier & Babè.
Eghigian, G. (2010). *From madness to mental health: Psychiatric disorder and its treatment in Western civilization*. New Brunswick, NJ: Rutgers University Press.
Evans, M.N. (1991). *Fits and starts: A genealogy of hysteria in modern France*. Ithaca, NY: Cornell University Press.
Goetz, C.G., Bondulle, M., and Gelfand, T. (1995). *Charcot: Constructing neurology*. New York: Oxford University Press.
Gorbach, F., and Train, M. (2005). From the uterus to the brain: Images of hysteria in nineteenth century Mexico. *Feminist Review, 79*, 83–99.
Hustvedt, A. (2011). *Medical muses: Hysteria in nineteenth century Paris*. New York: W.W. Norton.
Meek, H. (2013). Medical men, women of letters, and treatments for eighteenth century hysteria. *Journal of Medical Humanities, 34*, 1–14.
Micale, M.S. (1985). The Salpêtrière in the age of Charcot: An institutional perspective on medical history in the late nineteenth century. *Journal of Contemporary History, 20*, 703–731.
Micale, M.S. (1990). Charcot and the idea of hysteria in the male: Gender, mental science, and medical diagnosis in late nineteenth-century France. *Medical History, 34*, 363–411.
Micale, M.S. (1990). Hysteria and its historiography: The future perspective. *History of Psychiatry, 1*, 33–124.
Micale, M.S. (1995). *Approaching hysteria: Disease and its interpretation*. Princeton, NJ: Princeton University Press.
Millingen, J.G. (1841). *Aphorisms on the treatment and management of the insane*. London: John Churchill.
Møllerhøj, J. (2009). Encountering hysteria: Doctors' and patients' perspectives on hysteria in Denmark, 1875–1918. *History of Psychiatry, 20*, 163–183.
Plato (2000). *Timaeus*. Trans. D.J. Zeyl. Indianapolis, IN: Hackett Publishing Co.
Scull, A. (2009). *Hysteria: The biography*. Oxford: Oxford University Press.
Shorter, E. (1992). *From paralysis to fatigue: A history of psychosomatic illness in the modern era*. New York: Free Press.
Wenegrat, B. (2001). *Theatre of disorder: Patients, doctors and the construction of illness*. New York: Oxford University Press.

# Phototherapy (Light Therapy)

*The therapeutic exposure to natural sunlight or to specific wavelengths of light via various specially designed devices.*

During the nineteenth century, nearly 300 asylums were constructed in the United States alone, most of them according to what was known as the "Kirkbride Plan." This unique plan was based on the idea that moral treatment [see **Moral Treatment**] was best accomplished within moral architecture, that is, within asylums that were not just constructed to provide security, order and comfort, but aesthetic appeal. The Kirkbride Plan called for windows—tall, elegant windows in the common areas; higher, smaller and unbarred windows in the patients' rooms—porches and pavilions where patients could congregate out of doors and enjoy the beautifully landscaped grounds. Sunlight was essential to moral treatment, not as a therapeutic in and of itself, but as a refreshing tonic.

In the early twentieth century, after moral treatment had had its heyday, the therapeutic value of sunlight or, more particularly of ultraviolet light, was discovered. It was found to cure rickets, a softening of the bones caused by the deficiency or the impaired metabolism of vitamin D, calcium or phosphorus. The discovery immediately led to the prospect that ultraviolet light would cure other diseases and improve general health in the bargain and that, in turn, had a fascinating effect on lifestyle and fashion. People took to the beaches to bask in the sun; two-piece bathing suits for women, short-bathing suits for men, and sun suits for children became all the rage; sun tans were fashionable and make-up that simulated them was marketed; ultraviolet lamps became a booming industry; and glass that let in, rather than screened, ultraviolet light was often used in the construction of sunrooms and conservatories.

The claims made about sunlight eclipsed its curative power, but they did raise the interesting prospect that exposure to ultraviolet light might have more than just the tonic effect that practitioners of moral treatment had touted. And, they suggested that exposure to other wavelengths of light, most particularly infrared and X-ray, also may have a curative effect on insanity.

Thus began a series of experiments *cum* treatments conducted by a number of asylum physicians in the United States, Great Britain and Europe during the early to mid-twentieth century. None left much trace in the asylum practice literature, and if it can be said at all that a consensus was reached about phototherapy, it was that it was ineffective in ameliorating the symptoms of insanity, let alone curing it, but that it many cases it did indeed have a general tonic effect.

### REFERENCES

Albert, M.R., and Ostheimer, K.G. (2002). The evolution of current medical and popular attitudes toward ultraviolet light exposure: Part 1. *Journal of the American Academy of Dermatology, 47,* 930–937.
Albert, M.R., and Ostheimer, K.G. (2003). The evolution of current medical and popular attitudes toward ultraviolet light exposure: Part 2. *Journal of the American Academy of Dermatology, 48,* 909–918.
Albert, M.R., and Ostheimer, K.G. (2003). The evolution of current medical and popular attitudes toward ultraviolet light exposure: Part 3. *Journal of the American Academy of Dermatology, 49,* 1096–1106.
Andrews, J. (1997). *The history of Bethlem.* London: Routledge.
Barfoot, M. (2009). David Skae: Resident asylum physician; scientific general practitioner of insanity. *Medical History, 53,* 469–488.
Beam, A. (2001). *Gracefully insane: The rise and fall of America's premier mental hospital.* New York: PublicAffairs.
"Beauty and sunburn" (1931, August 15). *New York Times,* p. 12.
Bynum, W.F. (2001). Nature's helping hand. *Nature, 414,* 2.
Corcoran, D. (1933). Light therapy. *Psychiatric Quarterly, 7,* 234–244.
Humphris, F.H. (1992). *Artificial sunlight and its therapeutic uses.* 5th ed. London: Oxford University Press.
Jackson, J.A., and Chamberlain, L.R. (1927). Heliotherapy in the treatment of mental patients. *Medical Journal and Record, 126,* 731–734.
Licht, S.H. (1967). *Therapeutic electricity and ultraviolet radiation.* Baltimore, MD: Waverly Press.
Mould, R. (1993). *A century of X-rays.* London: Institute of Physics Publishing.
Myerson, A., and Neustadt, R. (1939). Influence of ultraviolet irradiation upon excretion of sex hormones in the male. *Endocrinology, 25,* 7–12.
Scull, A. (2005). *Madhouse: A tragic tale of megalomania and modern medicine.* New Haven, CT: Yale University Press.
Trustees of the Danvers State Hospital (1932). *Annual report of the trustees of the Danvers State Hospital.* Gardner, MA: Gardner State Colony.
Yanni, C. (2007). *The architecture of asylums: Insane asylums in the United States.* Minneapolis: University of Minnesota Press.

## Heliotherapy, or Ultraviolet Therapy

The therapeutic exposure to the sun or to an ultraviolet lamp. The warmth produced by the sun was thought to be a general tonic for asylum patients, thus they were encouraged to spend time out of doors, either walking and recreating on the grounds, or congregating on sun porches. Heliotherapy, as it was called, was so crucial to the management of mood, that physicians in urban asylums went out of their ways to assure patients were exposed to it. At the St. Elizabeths Asylum in Washington, D.C., for example, a fifth floor heliotherapy deck used by consumptive or phthisical patients, that is those with the highly contagious bacterial infection of tuberculosis, was opened for other patients to benefit from the sun.

The invention of the ultraviolet lamp solved the problem for urban asylum physicians and for those who practiced in asylums located in colder and darker climes. Ultraviolet therapy was used, but only for a short time, at the Bethlem Hospital in London in the early twentieth century. Patients did not care for it. Accustomed to the dreariness of London, just a minute of the treatment tended to uncomfortably irritate their skin.

The ultraviolet lamps was put to a different therapeutic use by Abraham Myerson and Rudolph Neustadt, at that time affiliated with the Boston State Hospital. Influenced by research that found that hens exposed to additional light at night laid eggs earlier than those that were not, they set out to examine whether ultraviolet light exerted an influence on the formation and excretion of the sex hormone testosterone in males. Because they used asylum patients as subjects, they also were interested in the effect of ultraviolet radiation on their mental states. Three of the patients, all of them fifty-four years old, were in the depressive phase of manic-depression; the two remaining patients, one who was twenty-eight years old and the other forty-five, had been diagnosed with psychopathy with depressive features.

Using a small ultraviolet lamp, they radiated different parts of the body for eight continuous minutes; subsequent sessions gradually increased the time of exposure to twenty minutes. Testosterone excretion was measured by a colorimetric method. Although they were not at all certain, Myerson and Neustadt assumed that the greater excretion would be the result of a greater production of the sex hormone. The findings revealed that testosterone excretion increased 120 percent when the patients were irradiated on the head, chest, genitals and thighs, and 200 percent when they were irradiated on the genitals alone. Although these findings were significant, the effect of the increased sex hormone production and excretion on the depressive mental states of the patients remained unclear. Although they noted that the ultraviolet radiation on the two patients who had been diagnosed with psychopathy with depressive features had a "good influence" it apparently had none worthy of mentioning on the remaining three patients. Myerson and Neustadt were forced to conclude that "Any relation of the depressive mental states of our patients to the formation and excretion of male hormones is not discernible" (Myerson & Neustadt, p. 11).

Myerson, for one, was unwilling to abandon ultraviolet light as a therapeutic tool. A few years after the publication of his study, he joined Boston's McLean hospital where a unique therapeutic strategy was being implemented. Total push, as it was called [see **Total Push**] was the application of all available therapeutics in the asylum's armamentarium to treat the chronically insane who languished in the backwards. This "everything but the kitchen sink" approach included, at Myerson's insistence, ultraviolet irradiation of the male patients' genitals, although he admitted that this treatment was "not related insofar as we know at present to the general well-being of the individual" (Beam, p. 82).

## Infrared Therapy, or Photothermal Therapy

The use of infrared radiation to increase circulation to a particular part of the body. When administered by a lamp, the long infrared rays are absorbed by the skin and slightly penetrate deep tissues, thereby generating heat and perspiration, lowering blood pressure, stimulating the nervous system and reducing overall nervous tension and anxiety. Infrared therapy typically produced a feeling of relaxation and mental well-being. Long before infrared lamps were invented, asylum physicians had relied upon such low-tech devices as hot water bottles and, later, heating pads to produce the same results.

Many of the early to mid-twentieth century asylum annual reports list infrared therapy as one of the treatment strategies administered to patients, but details as to how and why it was used, and with what particular types of patients, were not offered. Neither are outcomes. Clarence Bonner, medical superintendent of the Danvers State Hospital in Massachusetts, however, was slightly more forthcoming on these issues than his contemporaries. Under his superintendency more than 4000 infrared treatments were administered yearly to patients via a zoalite infrared lamp. Bonner declared the treatments produced "gratifying results" (Trustees of the Danvers State Hospital, p. 65), although he did not elaborate.

Although Bonner never mentioned it, his use of infrared therapy most likely was influenced by focal sepsis theory. The prospect that a localized infection, in the colon as an example, spread toxins through the blood system and into the central nervous system causing insanity, had been cautiously proposed decades earlier. It had a significant effect on the practice of medicine but had taken its time in garnering the attention of asylum physicians. When it finally did, it generated a veritable passion of tooth-pulling [see **Exodontia**] and surgery [see **Surgery**] in some asylums, leaving patients not just struggling with insanity, but with poor physical health. Infrared therapy was tried in a number of asylums as an alternative to these more invasive methods.

## X-Ray Therapy

Treatment with high energy and short wavelength electromagnetic radiation capable of penetrating the body. Discovered in 1895 by Wilhelm Conrad Röntgen in his laboratory at the Physical Institute of the Julius-Maximilians University in Bavaria, the therapeutic, as opposed to the diagnostic, potential of X-rays was almost immediately recognized. Just as was true with the other phototherapies, though, that potential remained unrealized in the case of insanity.

One of the most ambitious efforts to use X-rays therapeutically was led by Mihran Krikor Kassabian, a radiologist by specialty, who treated twelve epileptic patients confined in the Insanity Department of the Philadelphia Hospital in Pennsylvania in the early twentieth century. Hypothesizing that he could cure their epilepsy by X-rays directed at the anterior and occipital areas of the brain, he administered five minute exposures, three times a week for a total of three months to the patients, all of them male, who ranged in age from six to sixty. The type, severity and frequency of epileptic seizures varied considerably among them.

The two youngest patients died subsequent to the course of treatment, one two months after its completion, the other five months. Autopsies showed "congestion of the brain" in each patient but it was unclear as to whether that was the cause of death. The remaining ten patients, all of whom had suffered hair loss but no other adverse effects, had fewer seizures over the year following the treatment. One patient had 433 epileptic seizures that year, a stunningly high number but, in fact, about one-half of the number he had had over the year prior to X-ray therapy. Although Kassabian cautiously concluded that the trial was a success, the therapeutic effects did not persist. Other asylum physicians who replicated the treatment had similar disappointing results.

# Pious Frauds
# (Salutary Demonstrations, Innocent Ruses, Curative Ruses, Suggestive Therapies)

*Ruses, deceits and trickeries to humor, distract, challenge and sometimes ridicule the content of delusions, hallucinations and fixed thoughts and ideas.*

The therapeutic was informed by, although not derived from, the philosopher John Locke's doctrine of associations that posited that thinking was the process of organizing incoming sense-data as opposed to engaging with a stock of built-in-ideas. Insanity, therefore, was the result of the "wrong connexion of ideas [that is] mistaken for truth" (p. 13). Pious frauds were relied upon to tear the mind loose from its erroneous trains of thought and perception.

The term "pious frauds" was coined in the early nineteenth century by Joseph Mason Cox, proprietor of the private Fishponds Asylum near Bristol, England. Although a trained physician, Cox eschewed a medical in favor of a management approach designed, in part, to outwit the insane patient with "certain deceptions contrived to make strong impressions on the senses by means of unexpected, unusual, striking, or apparently supernatural agents" (Cox, p. 47). While Cox conceded that pious frauds deviated from what he acknowledged was the "accustomed routine of practice," he justified their use on the "smallest hope of success" they offered in "some cases that have resisted the usual methods" (p. 46). He offered a detailed description of one of those cases:

> Mr. ___, aged 36, of full habit, melancholic temperament, extremely attached to literary pursuits, and subject to depression of spirits without any obvious cause. His lucubrations were sometimes extended through whole days and nights in succession, and at these periods he was very abstemious, drank only water, and avoided animal food; his friends remonstrated with him on the hazard of such proceedings; and his housekeeper being urgent for his adopting some plan that had his health for the immediate object, the idea struck him of her having some sinister design, and that she intended to destroy him by means of a succession of poisoned shirts, under the baneful influence of which he believed himself then suffering. No arguments availed, and all reasoning was ineffectual, the hallucination therefore was humoured, a suspected shirt was exposed to some simple chemical experiments, continued, repeated, and varied with much ceremony, and the result so contrived as to prove the truth of the patient's suspicions; the housekeeper, notwithstanding all her protestations of innocence, was served with a pretended warrant, and in the presence of the patient, hurried out of the house by the proper officers, and secluded from his observation for a time, while he supposed she was in gaol expecting an ignominious death. After this preface, a formal consultation was held, certain antidotes prescribed, and after a few weeks he perfectly recovered; a new plan of life and regimen were adopted, and he has ever since continued to enjoy *mens sana in corpore sano* [p. 68].

The patient, now of a "sound mind in a healthy body" was never apprised of the deceit to which he had been subjected, and Cox insisted that be the case in all pious frauds. To reveal the deceit, he argued, would not only jeopardize any renewal of confidence in the physician, but any use of yet another pious fraud should the patient relapse. What Cox did not consider, however, was that being apprised of a pious fraud actually may cause a relapse. Jean-Étienne Dominique Esquirol, *médecin ordinaire* at the Salpêtrière Asylum in Paris, France, presented the case of a patient who had imagined that the persistent pain in her head was being caused by a worm devouring her brain. Esquirol humored her delusion and made a small incision in her head, removing a tiny piece of fibrin and presenting it to her as the irksome worm. The pain in her head was relieved, and the suicidal thoughts that had brought her into the asylum disappeared. When she showed other patients the worm, however, they laughed and told her that Esquirol had "made a game of her credulity" (Esquirol, p. 9). Apprised of the pious fraud, her head pain returned as did her delusion that a worm was the cause of it.

The power of the "wrong connexion of ideas" was evident in reports by other asylum physicians that some patients who had been relieved of their delusions or hallucinations by pious frauds had developed new ones in their place, and often had done so quite quickly. Aton Müller, physician at the Julius-Spital in Würzberg, Germany, related the case of a patient who suffered from the delusion that a demon inside his abdomen was constantly hectoring him. An elaborate pious fraud was perpetrated to eradicate the delusion. A thick vesicant was smeared on his stomach and left there long enough for a large blister to form. Müller then incised the blister and showed the patient a small obstetrical mannequin that had been secreted into the room, telling him this was the source of the voice in his stomach, and then dashing it to the floor. The patient was greatly relieved, but a few minutes later became convinced by the sight of his own navel that another demon, this one silent, must have been overlooked by the physician.

Sham surgeries and other medical procedures were the epitome of pious frauds, and asylum physicians eagerly shared their case examples in the psychiatric literature. Vincenzo Chiarugi, physician to the Ospedale di Bonifazio in Florence, Italy, for example, advised that if a patient imagined that frogs inhabited his or her stomach, the physician should administer an emetic and then "artfully place frogs in the basin into which the patient vomits" (Chiarugi, pp. 68–69). Benjamin Rush, of the Philadelphia Hospital in Pennsylvania, used purgatives for the same effect, showing the patient the corpse of the imagined animal that had been cleverly placed in his stools. And Joseph Guislain, superintendent of the Ghent asylums in Belgium, reported the case of an asylum physician who treated a patient who believed that every vessel of her body was full of light and ready to burst into flame, by rubbing a solution of phosphorous oil on her skin that made her believe her body's luminescence was caused by the light he had expelled from her blood vessels.

These and other pious frauds directed at the body of the patient, as theatrical as they were, paled in comparison to those directed at the mind. Those pious frauds not only required masterful deceit, but a cooperative cast of actors, and sometimes even costumes and elaborate sets. William Pargeter, a private madhouse owner and physician in England, reported the cure of a patient who believed himself already dead, and thus refused to eat, by costuming his friends in shrouds and sending them with plates of food into his darkened bed-chamber where they began to eat heartily.

The disordered man, seeing this, asked who they were, and what they were about. They replied, they were dead persons. *What then,* says the patient, *do the dead eat? Yes, yes,* say they, *and if you will sit down with us, you may eat likewise.* Upon this, he jumps out of bed, and falls to with the rest; and having made a hearty meal, and drank a composing draught which they provided for him, he went to bed again, fell into a fine sleep, and in a short time recovered his health and senses [Pargeter, pp. 45–46].

One of the most elaborately staged and scripted pious frauds in the literature involved a tailor who had publicly mused upon the fate of Louis XVI during the French Revolution and became so convinced that he would be executed at the guillotine as a traitor that he was committed to the Asylum de Bicêtre in Paris, France. There, the noted physician of infirmaries Philippe Pinel set about to disabuse the patient of his delusion. He secured the assistance of three young physicians, had them costumed in the black suits of magistrates and then brought the patient into a room where they were sitting at a table. They proceeded to relentlessly interrogate him about his daily activities, and his political and ideological leanings. Leaving the patient to worry about his fate, they loudly and contentiously argued amongst themselves before they delivered the carefully scripted verdict, saying, "In virtue of the power that has been delegated to us by the national assembly, we have entered proceedings in due form of law, against Citizen --- and having duly examined him, touching the matter whereof he stands accused, we make our declaration accordingly. It is, therefore, by us declared, that we have found the said Citizen --- a truly loyal patriot; and pronouncing his acquittal we forbid all further proceedings against him" (Pinel, p. 227). The tailor's delusions of persecution disappeared upon pronouncement of his acquittal but, just as in so many cases of even the most elaborate pious frauds, returned at a later date. Pinel then declared him incurable.

For Pinel, the enactment of pious frauds was not inconsistent with a program of moral treatment [see **Moral Treatment**]; in fact, many of the most crafty authors of pious frauds in the early nineteenth century were also the most outspoken advocates of kind and gentle interactions with the insane. Among those was the lay director of the Casa Dei Matti Asylum, later called the Royal Hospital for the Insane, in Palermo, Italy. Baron Pietro Pisani was a wealthy philanthropist who had converted his villa into a small, thoroughly regulated asylum and put into practice a gentle, kind, albeit very paternalistic, form of moral treatment that was both lauded and envied by international visitors.

Pisani, however, was not above tarnishing his "halo of moral sublimity" ("Palermo," p. 163) by engaging in pious frauds. He was fond of recounting the details of his encounter with a woman patient who, for reasons unstated, had resolved to never stand up straight; rather, she stooped as low as she could while still resting on the soles of her feet. This awkward position required that her knees were painfully bent, but no tender ministrations convinced her to change her posture. Thus, Pisani engaged in a rather elaborate pious fraud: he came to her one morning and confided that he no longer could bear being celibate and asked for her hand in marriage. After some persuasion, she agreed. The nuptials were held the next day. The patient, dressed in a hastily procured bridal gown, was carried to an elaborately decorated arbor where a feast had been prepared for the guests of the ceremony, all of them patients at the asylum. One of the attendants, dressed as a padre, conducted the counterfeit ceremony and not only declared her the wife of Pisani, but bestowed upon her the title of baroness. Still unable to walk, she was carried back to the asylum and, eager to be worthy of the marriage and the title, engaged in an active regime of exercise and moral treatment that restored her ability to walk and her sanity. She was released from the asylum and had a life-long friendship with Pisani, often enjoying a laugh with him at the elaborate pious fraud that had restored her sanity.

During the early to mid–1800s asylum physicians published detailed descriptions of their pious frauds in the psychiatric literature, and told and retold their own and others' ruses so often that sometimes the retelling took on the nature of well-worn jokes. "Everyone knows the anecdote of the patient who feared to pass water lest he should deluge the world," wrote John Minson Galt, the superintendent of Eastern State Hospital in Williamsburg, Virginia, "and was made to do so by being told the city was on fire, and that he could quench the flames" (Galt, p. 141). What did not become part of the psychiatric literature or, for that matter the psychiatric lore of pious frauds, were detailed observations of the therapeutic value of these ruses, deceits and trickeries. Some patients were declared "cured" on the basis of having surrendered their delusions, others altered the content of their delusions or developed new ones, and still others relapsed, but discussions of how the pious frauds worked, or more likely did not, to break the "wrong connexion of ideas" were largely absent.

In the end, it was the very tenacity of delusions, hallucinations and fixed ideas that caused asylum physicians to speculate how deeply they must be marked in the brain. Pious frauds, with all of their deceitful theatrics, increasingly were seen as inadequate to the task of restoring patients to sanity. By the mid–1800s, most asylum physicians were "adapting the technological inventiveness of the age to the task" (Scull, p. 73) by turning away from pious frauds and to a variety of ingenious therapeutics such as circulating swings [see **Rotation, Oscillation and Vibration**], and douches [see **Hydrotherapy**].

A widely read manual by two of the most highly respected asylum physicians, John Bucknill and Daniel Hack Tuke tolled the demise of pious frauds as a therapeutic:

> Systematic works on insanity generally contain examples of the cure of delusions by artifice... [W]e should not think it worth while even to try the effect of legerdemain upon mental disease. We have seen so many painful instances

of objective reality failing to influence delusion in the smallest degree, that we have not the slightest faith in the effect of trick.... We are sorry to be able to yield but very imperfect belief to the accounts of the cure of delusions by legerdemain. The modern examples are so uncommonly like the old ones, that it is impossible to resist the suspicion that they have been copied from them [Bucknill & Tuke, p. 680].

War, however, often necessitates the modernization of antiquated ideas. The ravages and horrors of World War I did just that as tens of thousands of shell-shocked soldiers filled military hospitals and public asylums. Their symptoms of anxiety, sensory and gait disturbances, and disorientation were not easily resolved by conventional treatments. With no physical wounds or injuries as their cause, these symptoms were seen as hysterical in nature and therefore particularly susceptible to the sway of suggestion.

The suggestive therapies, as they were referred to, that were used to treat shell-shocked German soldiers during World War I modernized the clever yet naïve pious frauds of the previous generations of asylum physicians. Max Rothman, for example, used the "wonder drug fraud" in which he persuaded his soldier-patients that a new drug recently had been developed that was certain to cure their symptoms. Because it was painful to ingest, he went on to explain, it would have to be administered with a short-acting general anesthetic. When the patients awoke from the anesthetic, having had no such wonder drug administered, of course, they were invited to demonstrate that their symptoms had been successfully treated. And, according to Rothman, and a number of German physicians who had followed suit with this ruse, most of them did just that.

Two of the most intractable symptoms of shell-shock were deafness and deaf-muteness. Unable to hear commands or give them, soldiers who suffered from these symptoms not only could not return to the front lines, but could not be duped by these modernized pious frauds that relied only on verbal suggestion and manipulation. Arthur Hurst, a physician at the Seale Hayne, a military hospital in Devon, England, shrewdly overcame that hurdle. He claimed to have cured three deaf soldiers by convincing them, via written communications, that a simple operation would restore their hearing. A local anesthetic was applied and a small incision was made behind their ears and dabbed with gauze. Just as the bloody gauze passed before the eyes of the soldier-patients, a loud bell was rung behind them. All of them were startled, not to mention convinced that the sham surgery had restored their hearing.

Robert Sommer, a professor at the University of Giessen in Germany and head of its psychiatric clinic, also cured deaf and deaf-mute soldier-patients with an elaborate technological device that tricked them into responding to an audible signal. Resembling a polygraph machine, the device recorded on graphs the movements of the middle and index fingers of the seated and strapped patients. When the attention of the patients had focused on how subtle movements of their fingers were being charted, a loud bell was rung behind them; the jerk of their hands upon hearing the bell, often accompanied by startled cries, were simultaneously charted on the graphs. Sommer described the therapeutic effect of this technological ruse:

> Immediately there occurred a twitching of the forearm, which brought forth the evidence that the patient must have heard the tone. Then through calm encouragement vis-à-vis the curve in front of him, the patient's attention was directed to the fact that there could no longer be the slightest doubt that he could hear. From this moment on in point of fact he could hear clearly and reacted correctly to every acoustic-verbal situation [Lerner, p. 117].

Even the most innocuous of interactions between asylum physician and patient—"You'll be fine," "This will make you feel better"—has the hint of suggestion. Pious frauds, though, no matter how elaborately staged or technologically sophisticated, were based in trickery and deceit. As such, they problematized the difference between curing patients and persuading them they were never ill in the first place.

REFERENCES

Bucknill, J.C., and Tuke, D.H. (1874). *A manual of psychological medicine.* Philadelphia: Lindsay and Blakiston.
Chiarugi, V. (1793). *Della pazzia in genere e in specie trattato medico analitico: Con una centuria di osservazioni.* Vol. 2. Florence, Italy: Presso Luigi Carlieri.
Cox, J.M. (1806). *Practical observations on insanity: To which are subjoined remarks on medical jurisprudence as connected with diseased intellect.* London: C. and R. Baldwin, and J. Murray.
Esquirol, R. (1833). *Observations on the illusions of the insane, and on the medico-legal question of their confinement.* London: Renshaw and Rush.
Galt, J.M. (1846). *The treatment of insanity.* New York: Harper & Brothers.
Guislain, J. (1826). *Traité sur l'aliénation mentale et sur les hospices des aliénés.* Amsterdam: J. Van Der Hay et Fils, & H. Gartman.
Jones, E. (2011). *War Neurosis* and Arthur Hurst: A pioneering medical film about the treatment of psychiatric battle casualties. *Journal of the History of Medicine and Allied Sciences, 67,* 345–373.
Kraepelin, E. (1962). *One hundred years of psychiatry.* Trans. W. Baskin. New York: Citadel.
Lerner, P. (2003). *Hysterical men: War, psychiatry, and the politics of trauma in Germany, 1890–1930.* Ithaca, NY: Cornell University Press.
Locke (1690). *Essay concerning human understanding.* London: Edward Mory.
Mora, G. (1959). Pietro Pisani and the mental hospital of Palermo in the early 19th century. *Bulletin of the History of Medicine, 33,* 230–248.
"Palermo" (1835). *The Friend, 7,* 161–163.
Pargeter, W. (1792). *Observations on maniacal disorders.* Reading, UK: Smart and Cowslade.
Pinel, P. (1806). *A treatise on insanity.* Trans. D.D. Davis. Sheffield, UK: W. Todd.
Rush, B. (1830). *Medical inquiries and observations upon the diseases of the mind,* 4th ed. Philadelphia: John Grigg.
Scull, A. (1993). *The most solitary of afflictions: Madness and society in Britain, 1700–1900.* New Haven, CT: Yale University Press.

# Psychic Driving, Accelerated Psychotherapy, or Automated Psychotherapy

*Exposure to a continuously repeated audio message via a looped tape, in order to alter cognitions and/or behavior. The content of the cue communication was derived from what had been determined during a previous psychotherapeutic session to be the source of the patient's current mental problems.*

Psychic driving was developed by D. Ewen Cameron, a Scottish psychiatrist who in the mid-twentieth century was affiliated with the Allan Memorial Institute of Psychiatry in Montreal, Quebec, Canada. An Italian Renaissance mansion. the Allan Memorial had been donated to McGill University and its affiliated Royal Victoria Hospital by the Allan family in honor of their three children who were casualties of World War I. Cameron's inspiration for psychic driving had come from an unusual source: having come across an advertisement for a Cerebrophone, a bedside phonograph with pillow speakers that taught its purchasers a foreign language while they slept, he considered a similar approach to treating asylum patients. He originally thought that psychic driving would be most efficacious for the psychoneurotic patients at Allan Memorial, and it is with them in mind that he designed the therapeutic.

First, Cameron audiotaped psychotherapy sessions with a selected patient; then with the assistance of technician Leonard Rubenstein, he edited a twenty to thirty second extract of the sessions into a looped tape that was given to the patient to "work on," that is, listen to and write about. The patient was to listen to the tape two hours in the morning, again for two hours in the afternoon, and once more for two hours in the evening—hearing the same single extract each time—and all the time writing everything that crossed his or her mind while listening. The written responses were collected and given to Cameron, and if in the next psychotherapy session the patient showed some insight or disclosed a revelation based on the extract, he or she would be given a new tape and the process would continue.

In its original iteration, the taped extract, also known as a "cue communication" or a "dynamic implant," was reflective of what Cameron had assessed was the origin of the patient's psychoneurosis. Despite his disdain for all things psychoanalytic, Cameron had a rather deterministic approach to mental problems, believing that they originated in childhood conflicts, rejections and disappointments. Thus, the tape might feature a brief exchange between Cameron and the patient as to whether the latter felt loved by his mother, or ignored by her father. At times, Cameron also played the tape during the next psychotherapy session to personally gauge the patient's reaction to it. And reactions often were intense. Patients reported they ruminated on the taped extracts, were overrun by memories, lost sleep. Some had to be sedated until their "fire blizzard," as he referred to it, had passed (Collins, p. 125).

Other patients seemed unmoved by the taped extract, or resistant to really hearing it. This realization prompted Cameron to do the first of many revisions of the psychic driving therapeutic. To intensify the impact of the taped extracts, he had patients hear them through headphones, so that they became tantamount to voices in the head. In fact, he designed head gear, rather like football helmets, through which the taped extracts directly entered the ears of the patients. Then, operating on the hypothesis that a distorted extract may prompt more attentiveness, he filtered the cue communications by varying pitch, volume and tone.

These technological changes did work to increase attentiveness, in Cameron's impression, but further changes were needed. To that end, Cameron began administering adjuvant drugs. Patients were injected with a combination of the amphetamine desoxyn and sodium amytal, the so-called "truth drug." And they were administered lysergic acid diethylamide, better known as LSD. Cameron, however, was not keen on the psychedelic drug's effects, and soon stopped using it altogether. He had no similar misgivings, however, about also using hypnotism and sensory isolation to render his patients more receptive to the taped extracts.

And he used deep sleep therapy [see **Deep Sleep Therapy**]. With a potent combination of drugs such as seconal, nembutal, sodium amytal, and chlorpromazine (Thorazine), he put some of his patients into a deep sleep and bombarded them with the taped extracts for as long as sixteen hours each day. As a matter of interest, the combination of powerful drugs and prolonged sleep, to which repeated electroconvulsive shock treatments were added, constituted another of Cameron's therapeutic innovations known as "depatterning" [see **Shock Therapy**], and was thought to render patients particularly receptive to psychic driving.

Along with improving technological methods, and rendering his patients more vulnerable to the taped extract, Cameron expanded his psychic driving pool of patients by including schizophrenics. At the time, the predominate theory of the cause of schizophrenia was psychoanalytic in nature and focused on bad mothering—a subject that produced a veritable treasure trove of cue communications.

Diagnosis aside, Cameron initially claimed therapeutic success with psychic driving, although he neither defined nor measured that outcome. Oblivious to the skepticism and the scorn of many of his professional colleagues, he courted the press before he published his findings in psychiatric journals or gave papers in professional meetings. It very well may have been the press that first used the word "brainwashing" to describe psychic driving. Although Cameron publicly eschewed the term, he acknowledged that the "reorganization of the personality may be brought about without the necessity of solving of conflicts or abreaction or the reliving of past experiences" (Cameron, Levy, & Rubenstein, p. 742) was the therapeutic goal of psychic driving, making it a first cousin in relatedness to brainwashing.

Just saying the word "brainwashing" in the Cold War era was bound to draw more than a little attention. In the end, who said it first was immaterial. The fact remains that in the mid-1950s Cameron was contacted by Colonel James Monroe of the Society for the Investigation of Human Ecology (SIHE), a front for the United States Central Intelligence Agency (CIA). The CIA's Scientific Intelligence Division was more than a little interested in mind control and in the potential that psychic driving had, both on its own and in combination with depatterning, to accomplish it. It funded Cameron's work, known as MKULTRA subproject 68, for three-and-a-half years, and to the tune of $64,243. The Canadian government added another $200,000.

Since the CIA was neither in the position to monitor the use of psychic driving at Allan Memorial nor criticize the ethics of it, Cameron continued to act as a free agent. In 1963, after administering psychic driving to more than 300 patients, Cameron finally conceded defeat. In a 1963 Presidential address to the American Psychopathological Association, an organization devoted to the scientific investigation of disordered human behavior, he offered a *mea culpa*, saying that he had taken a "wrong turn" in pursuing psychic driving (and depatterning) as a cure for psychoneurosis and especially for schizophrenia.

A decade after Cameron's death, a *New York Times* expose revealed the CIA link to his work, prompting several former psychic driving (and depatterning) patients to file suit. In 1988, nine former patients received a $750,000 out-of-court settlement with the CIA. The Canadian government also compensated each of Cameron's patients $100,000.

Although there was scattered and infrequent use of psychic driving in some Canadian and British asylums during the 1950s, and both proposals and attempts to use it in on inmates in maximum security prisons, the therapeutic had limited appeal on scientific, ethical and practical grounds.

### References

"Brainwash suit settled: CIA to pay $750,000" (1988, October 15). *The Gazette*, p. A1.
Cameron, D.E. (1956). Psychic driving. *American Journal of Psychiatry, 112*, 502–509.
Cameron, D.E. (1957). Psychic driving: dynamic implant. *Psychiatric Quarterly, 31*, 701–712.
Cameron, D.E., Levy, L., and Rubenstein, L. (1960). Effects of repetition of verbal signals upon the behavior of chronic psychoneurotic patients. *British Journal of Psychiatry, 106*, 742–754.
Collins, A. (1988). *In the sleep room*. Toronto, Ontario, Canada: Lester & Orpen Dennys.
Farnsworth, C. (1992, November 19). Canada will pay 50s test victims. *New York Times*, p. A-2.
Gilman, D. (1988, October 22). Inside the strange mind of Ewen Cameron. *Ottawa Citizen*, p. B3.
Horrock, M.N. (1977, August 2). Private institutions used in CIA effort to control behavior. *New York Times*, pp. 1, 16.
Klein, N. (2008). *Shock doctrine: The rise of disaster capitalism*. London: Picador.
Marks, J. (1979). *The search for the Manchurian candidate: The CIA and mind control*. New York: Norton.
Rauh, J., and Turner, J.C. (1990). Anatomy of a public interest case against the CIA. *Hamline Journal of Public Law and Policy, 11*, 307–363.

## Psychosurgery

*The treatment of insanity by a surgical procedure on an anatomically normal brain.*

The early twentieth century witnessed a crisis in psychiatry: academic psychiatrists, thoroughly committed to lofty theorizing and lab research, were at odds with clinicians who were just as committed to hands-on practice; both were at odds with the marginalized asylum physicians, still referred to as "alienists," who plied the specialty in overcrowded and understaffed state asylums; and all were at odds with neurologists and the newly emerging neuropsychiatrists who were vying for authority in treating the insane. The crisis enveloped asylums as well: were they to function only as warehouses that kept the insane out of social circulation, or could they aspire to be the kind of centers of healing, perhaps even cure, that returned them to social circulation? Might asylums even become laboratories in which the theories of academic psychiatry, the insights of clinical psychiatry and the findings of neurology were put to the test?

By the end of World War I, and in the wake of its traumatizing effects on soldiers and civilians alike, the need for answers to these questions took on urgency. They were addressed by any number of psychiatrists but none so prominent, perhaps, as Adolf Meyer, the Swiss-born physician whose tenure as a neuropathologist in American asylums led to professorships in psychiatry at Cornell and then later at Johns Hopkins University in Baltimore, Maryland. The "Dean of American Psychiatry," as he was known in his own lifetime, envisioned a specialty that not only was united by theory and practice, but by a monistic concept of mind and body, a psychobiological approach that made insanity the subject of both psychic and somatic interventions.

To unite academics, practitioners and alienists under the single heading of "psychiatrist" also required a more liberal conceptualization of insanity, itself. After the war, the restorative project of restoring social cohesion and cooperation was vital, thus extending the definition of insanity to misfits, miscreants, ne'er-do-wells and perverts fit well with the larger social agenda, and allied psychiatrists with social reformers, policy-makers and politicians. Psychiatry had finally found its place, Albert Barrett proclaimed in his presidential inaugural address to the American Psychiatric Association, as the "liaison between medicine and social problems" (Barrett, p. 13).

Philanthropists were interested in this liaison, as well. The Rockefeller Foundation provided ample funds for research that investigated everything from the endocrine system to low intelligence as possible causes of insanity, and everything from shock therapies to brain surgery as its cure. In regards to the latter, the Foundation backed the research of John Fulton of Yale University. Reflecting on battlefront observations that soldiers who sustained wounds to the frontal lobes, the dominant control centers of the brain, often were rendered euphoric, giddy and childlike, Fulton severed the frontal lobes of a lab chimpanzee named Becky in a procedure called a lobectomy. Becky, who had never given in to the rigors of problem-solving training and had a propensity for temper tantrums when she did not receive a reward for an incorrect response to a training exercise, was left complacent and easy to manage, although still unable to problem-solve. Curiously, a second lab chimpanzee named Lucy demonstrated the opposite reaction to the lobectomy. She had been a well-trained problem-solver who had exhibited little emotion when incorrect responses were unrewarded. After the lobectomy, however, she not only made more incorrect responses but had loud and violent temper tantrums when shown the food withheld from her because she had.

In a paper delivered at the Second Annual Neurological Conference in London, England, in 1935, Fulton described the lobectomy in detail. There are a few apocryphal stories in the history of asylum therapeutics. One is that Egas Moniz, the Portuguese neurologist who would go on to transform Fulton's laboratory experiment into a therapeutic procedure, and would be awarded the Nobel Prize in the bargain, was in the audience and had asked Fulton if the lobectomy would have the same outcome on insane patients. Fulton, as he told the story many years after the incident, was nonplussed and replied that that procedure was "too formidable" to ever justify its use on humans. In fact, Fulton's memory may have been self-serving. It was not until Moniz had achieved a certain infamy for his surgical destruction of parts of the frontal lobes of his insane patients that Fulton recollected this encounter, and his ethical, if not noble, response to it. But the fact remains that shortly after the conference, Moniz began his experiments with the leucotomy, the predecessor of the slightly modified but much better known psychosurgical technique of the prefrontal lobotomy.

Psychosurgery actually has a meandering history that predated Moniz and postdated the American physician Walter Freeman whose name is synonymous with the lobotomy. Its history features larger than life physicians whose altruistic motives often were overshadowed by their blazing desire to be the first to discover a cure for intractable insanity. It reveals the role of the press in both the pace of psychosurgery and the expansion of the potential patient pool from the insane, to the depressed, anxious or bored; from asylum patients, to outpatients, to the imprisoned; from adults to adolescents and children; from those who had not lived in larger society for decades, to the dissidents, nonconformists and political radicals who were trying to change society. Its history also reveals the silence of the medical profession and its unwillingness to police itself, even as psychosurgery fell from grace. And that fall, itself, was a fall through decades of changing ideas about the relationship between the mind and the body, between insanity and sanity, between physician and patient; it was a fall through evolving notions of civil and human rights, and it was a fall through different perspectives on how much "spontaneity, sparkle and flavor" (Freeman & Watts, 1937, p. 30) a person, even an insane person, could lose and still be a person.

The quintessential example of psychosurgery—the lobotomy—all but disappeared in the 1970s, but psychosurgery is still being performed on carefully chosen patients. Gone are the leucotomes, curved spoons and ice picks of the halcyon days of the lobotomy. Modern psychosurgery relies instead on radiosurgical gamma knives, ultrasound, proton beams and stereotactic techniques.

## References

Barrett, A.M. (1922). The broadened interests of psychiatry. *American Journal of Psychiatry, 79,* 1–13.

Berrios, G. (1997). The origins of psychosurgery: Shaw, Burckhardt and Moniz. *History of Psychiatry, 8,* 61–81.

Bigelow, N. (1949). Topectomy—New light on a stab in the dark. *Psychiatric Quarterly, 23,* 156–163.

Burroughs, W.S. (1959). *The naked lunch.* Paris: Olympia Press.

D'Astous, M., Cottin, S., Roy, M., Picard, C., and Cantin, L. (2013). Bilateral stereotactic anterior capsulotomy for obsessive-compulsive disorder: Long-term follow-up. *Journal of Neurology, Neurosurgery and Psychiatry, 84,* 1208–1213.

de Young, M. (2010). *Madness: An American history of mental illness and its treatment.* Jefferson, NC: McFarland.

Diefenbach, G.J., Diefenbach, D., Baumesiter, A., and West, M. (1999). Portrayal of lobotomy in the popular press: 1935–1960. *Journal of the History of the Neurosciences, 8,* 60–69.

Dully, H. (2007). *My lobotomy.* New York: Crown.

El-Hai, J. (2005). *The lobotomist: A maverick medical genius and his tragic quest to rid the world of mental illness.* Hoboken, NJ: John Wiley & Sons.

Ellison, R.W. (1952). *The invisible man.* New York: Random House.

Freeman, W. (1962). West Virginia Lobotomy Project: A sequel. *Journal of the American Medical Association, 181,* 1134–1135.

Freeman, W., Davis, H.W., East, I.C., Tait, H.D., Johnson, S.O., and Rogers, W.B. (1954). West Virginia Lobotomy Project. *Journal of the American Medical Association, 156,* 939–943.

Freeman, W., and Watts, J. (1936). Prefrontal lobotomy in agitated depression: Report of a case. *Medical Annals of the District of Columbia, 5,* 326–328.

Freeman, W., and Watts, J. (1937). Prefrontal lobotomy in the treatment of mental disorders. *Southern Medical Journal, 30,* 23–31.

Freeman, W., and Watts, J.W. (1950/1942). *Psychosurgery in the treatment of mental disorders and intractable pain.* Springfield, IL: Charles C. Thomas.

Hirose, S. (1966). Present trends in psychosurgery. *Psychiatry and Clinical Neurosciences, 20,* 361–379.

Hohne, H.H., and Walsh, K.W. (1970). *Surgical modification of personality.* Melbourne, Australia: Victorian Mental Health Authority.

"Ice-pick surgery is tried en masse" (1952, August 24). *New York Times,* p. 61.

Kesey, K. (1962). *One flew over the cuckoo's nest.* New York: Viking.

LeBeau, J.L. (1951). The surgical uncertainties of prefrontal topectomy and leucotomy (Observations on 100 cases). *British Journal of Psychiatry, 97,* 480–504.

Lewis, N.D.C., Landis, C., and King, H.E. (1956). *Studies in topectomy.* New York: Grune and Stratton.

Livingston, K.E. (1969). The frontal lobes revisited: The case for a second look. *Archives of Neurology, 20,* 90–95.

Macpherson, J., and Wallace, D. (1891/1892). Remarks on the surgical treatment of general paralysis of the insane. *Transactions of the Medico-Chirurgical Society of Edinburgh 11,* 167–183.

Mark, V.H., Sweet, W.H., and Erwin, F.R. (1967). The role of brain disease in riots and urban violence. *Journal of the American Medical Association, 201,* 895.

Mashour, G.A., Walker, E.E., and Martuza, R.L. (2005). Psychosurgery: Past, present and future. *Brain Research Review, 48,* 409–419.

McKissock, W. (1951). Rostral leucotomy. *Lancet, 258,* 91–94.

"Medicine: Losing nerves" (1947, June 30). *Time,* p. 45.

Menninger, W.C. (1948). Facts and statistics of significance for psychiatry. *Bulletin of the Menninger Clinic, 12,* 1–25.

Moniz, E. (1937). Prefrontal leucotomy in the treatment of mental disorders. *American Journal of Psychiatry, 93,* 1379–1385.

Mueller, C. (1960). Gottlieb Burckhardt, the father of topectomy. *American Journal of Psychiatry, 117,* 461–463.

Ögren, K., and Sandlund, M. (2005). Psychosurgery in Sweden, 1944–1964. *Journal of the History of the Neurosciences, 14,* 353–367.

Oral histories (2005). Sound portraits. Retrieved at http://soundportraits.org/on-air/my_lobotomy/oralhistory.php.

Pool, J.L., Heath, R.G., and Weber, J.J. (1949). Topectomy: Surgical indication and results. *Bulletin of the New York Academy of Medicine, 25,* 335–344.

Pressman, J.D. (1998). *Last resort: Psychosurgery and the limits of medicine.* Cambridge: Cambridge University Press.

Raz, M. (2013). *The lobotomy letters: The making of American psychosurgery.* Rochester, NY: University of Rochester Press.

Rück, C., Karisson, A., Steele, J.D., Edman, G., Meyerson, B.A., Ericson, K., Nyman, H., Asberg, M., and Svanborg, P. (2008). Capsulotomy for obsessive-compulsive disorder: Long-term follow-up. *Archives of General Psychiatry, 65,* 914–921.

Sargant, W.W. (1967). *The unquiet mind.* Boston: Little, Brown.

Shaw, T.C., and Cripps, H. (1890). On the surgical treatment of general paralysis. *British Medical Journal, 1,* 1364.

"Southern doctors" (1936, November 30). *Time,* pp. 66–67.

Starr, M.A. (1893). *Brain surgery.* New York: William Wood.

Stone, J.L. (2001). Dr. Gottlieb Burckhardt—The pioneer of psychosurgery. *Journal of the History of the Neurosciences, 10,* 79–92.

Strecker, E.A., Palmer, H.D., and Grant, F.C. (1942). A study of prefrontal lobotomy: Neurosurgical and psychiatric features and results in 22 cases, with a detailed report on 5 chronic schizophrenics. *American Journal of Psychiatry, 98,* 524–530.

"Surgery for insanity" (1952, April 14). *Newsweek,* pp. 100–101.

Tranøy, J., and Blomberg, W. (2005). Lobotomy in Norwegian psychiatry. *History of Psychiatry, 16,* 107–110.

Valenstein, E.S. (1986). *Great and desperate cures: The rise and decline of psychosurgery and other radical treatments for mental illness.* New York: Basic Books.

Wagner, C.G. (1890). A case of trephining for general paralysis. *American Journal of Insanity, 47,* 59–66.

Warren, R.P. (1946). *All the king's men.* New York: Harcourt, Brace.

Whitty, C.W.M. (1955). Effects of anterior cingulectomy in man. *Proceedings of the Royal Society of Medicine, 48,* 463–469.

Whitty, C.W.M., Duffield, J.E., Tow, P.M., and Cairns, H. (1952). Anterior cingulectomy in the treatment of mental disease. *Lancet, 259,* 475–481.

Wolfe, B. (1952). *Limbo.* New York: Ace.

Worthing, H.J., Brill, H., and Wigderson, H. (1949). 350 cases of prefrontal lobotomy. *Psychiatric Quarterly, 23,* 617–656.

## Capsulotomy

The drilling of very small holes in the skull through which tiny electrodes are inserted and then heated, thus destroying the adjacent cellular structures. The lesions created interrupt the cortico-striato-thalamo-cortical circuitry in the brain and simultaneously cause metabolic decreases in other regions of the brain. The capsulotomy, developed in Sweden in the late 1940s by Lars Leksell and Jean Talairach, initially was performed on chronic schizophrenic patients, but with disappointing results. In more recent years, and with the added advantage of more advanced technology such as the gamma knife and proton beam, it has been found to be more effective as a treatment of last resort for obsessive-compulsive disorder, producing immediate improvements in most patients.

The findings of studies focusing on long-term results, however, are mixed. In a follow-up study of twenty-five Swedish patients, nine remained in remission a decade after surgery, but only three of them were free of adverse effects. Ten additional patients were found to have impairments in reasoning and judgment, and were apathetic and/or disinhibited. No significant changes in obsessive-compulsive symptoms were reported for the remaining six patients. A long-term study of nineteen Canadian patients, however, had somewhat more optimistic findings: seven remained significantly improved seven years after the surgery, and two more were considered improved, although none had gained full relief of obsessive-compulsive symptoms.

## Cingulectomy

The surgical excision of a portion of the cingulate gyrus in the frontal lobe of the brain and the immediate surrounding tissue. A thin ribbon of gray matter that is a conduit between the more primitive limbic system and the frontal lobes, the cingulate gyrus regulates emotions and pain, and is thought to drive the body's unconscious responses to unpleasant experiences. It was surgically targeted as a result of the common ground that two antagonists briefly scrabbled for in the late 1940s: both John Fulton and Walter Freeman agreed that selective surgical destruction of the cingulate gyrus would improve short- and long-term outcomes for patients, the former on the basis of empirical studies with animals, the latter on his observation that patients seemed to be less psychologically tense when fibers near the cingulate gyrus were severed during the prefrontal lobotomy.

The first to try this refined method was Sir Hugh William Bell Cairns, a prominent British neurosurgeon who, among many other recognitions, had been called upon to treat T.E. Lawrence, the soldier-author better known as "Lawrence of Arabia" after the motorcycle accident from which he never recovered. In the late 1940s Cairns and his colleagues performed cingulectomies on eighteen chronic and deteriorated asylum patients. The results were less than satisfactory: three died post-surgery and for the remainder "no permanent clinical benefit resulted," although aggressive outbursts and obsessional thoughts seemed to decline (Whitty, p. 465).

Taking particular note of that decrease in obsessional thoughts, Cairns and his colleagues then selected seventeen additional anxious or obsessional patients as candidates for the cingulectomy, and produced more satisfying results. Two of the patients improved to such an extent that they could be considered cured, although Cairns and his colleagues were reticent to use such a "bold" word (Whitty, p. 466); four more improved significantly enough to return to their families and/or work obligations, although their full functioning was somewhat limited by the persistence of their symptoms; and with the exception of one patient, all of the others improved. What was unsettling, however, was that improvement was not lasting for two of the otherwise significantly improved patients; both relapsed within two years of the surgery and were readmitted to the asylum.

By the 1970s there had been a sea-change in opinion about the psychosurgical treatment of insanity. In fact, that year only 300 psychosurgeries were performed in the United States, a startling low figure given that an average of 5,000 had been performed each of the previous five years. The cingulectomy, however, did not fall from grace as precipitously as had the lobotomy that it was designed to improve. With improved stereotactic techniques and on carefully chosen patients—those with anxiety, moderate depression, obsessions and/or compulsions—significant success is still being claimed.

## Prefrontal Lobotomy, or Leucotomy, or Freeman-Watts Procedure

The surgical severing of the neural connections to and from the prefrontal cortex, the anterior part of the brain's frontal lobes. The Portuguese neurologist Egas Moniz is credited as the first to have performed a leucotomy (from the Greek term *leukos,* or white), a surgical procedure that came to be better known as the prefrontal lobotomy. A colorful character whose birth name was António Caetano Abreu Freire, he had assumed the *nom de guerre* of Egas Moniz during his university years when he penned left-leaning political tracts. Indeed, Moniz remained politically active throughout his early career, variously serving as a minister to Spain and minister of foreign affairs before serving as Portugal's signatory to the Treaty of Versailles, which ended World War I. He was equally accomplished in his medical specialty. In 1927 he developed angiography, a medical imaging technique that allowed the visualization of intracranial lesions, earning him his first Nobel Prize nomination the following year.

Moniz also was ambitious. Insanity was, even then, the last frontier for neurology and for Nobel Prize aspirants as well. As his interest grew he developed a working hypothesis that persistent insanity must be the result of "fixed ideas" that were supported by neural pathways in the prefrontal area, that highly developed part of the brain associated with reason and judgment. If those neural pathways were surgically interrupted, he conjectured, then the fixed ideas would disappear, and so would the insanity. Whether Moniz ever really queried John Fulton about performing chimpanzee lobectomies on human patients, the fact remains that after that Second Annual Neurological Conference in London, England, in 1935, he was eager to give it a try.

Unable to perform the surgery himself due to the disabling effects of gout, Moniz enlisted the assistance of neurosurgeon Almeida Lima. In 1935, just months after the conference, the two had engaged in a practice surgery on a cadaver, another month later they performed the first leucotomy. Their patient, a sixty-three-year-old woman who had been institutionalized at the Bombarda Asylum, had been diagnosed with agitated depression and paranoia; her anxiety, restlessness, continual crying and insomnia had rendered her a particularly unlikeable and annoying patient, and it may have been more for that reason than the nature of her insanity that she was chosen to undergo the first leucotomy. Her hair was shaved, Novocaine was administered for local anesthesia, and then two holes were drilled in her skull. A syringe was inserted into each burr hole and 0.2 cubic centimeters of alcohol were injected into her frontal lobes, dehydrating and killing the nerve fibers. The pioneering leucotomy took just a half-an-hour to perform.

Five hours later the patient was questioned by Moniz. She was able to state her address and her preference for milk over bouillon, but she could not recall the name of the hospital nor her age. She was returned to the asylum and Moniz had little if any additional interaction with her, relying instead on the reports of nurses and a visiting psychiatrist who wrote that two months after the leucotomy:

> The patient behaved normally. She is very calm, anxiety is not apparent. Mimicry still a little exaggerated. Good orientation. Conscience, intelligence and behavior intact. Mood slightly sad, but somewhat justified because of her concern about her future.... There are no new pathological ideas or other symptoms and for the most part previous paranoid ideas are primarily gone [Valenstein, p. 104].

Moniz, who had anticipated success, declared her cured. He immediately repeated the procedure on seven additional asylum patients, some of whom, in fact, underwent the procedure more than once. Those who showed the best results, Moniz observed, were not the psychotic back-warders, but those who were anxious, depressed or agitated, such as the seventh patient, a forty-six-year-old woman who had anxiety attacks and hypochondriacal preoccupations. In and out of asylum for years, she was leucotomized and cured of her anxiety, but not of her hypochondriasis.

Whatever impressions that the alleged successes and the obvious failures of this first cohort of patients made on Moniz was never clear, but for whatever reasons he decided that the leucotomy procedure had to be modified. So, beginning with his next patient he used a leucotome, rather than alcohol injections, to destroy the nerve fibers in the frontal lobe. The leucotome was a knife-like instrument with a retractable wire loop that cored the nerve fibers from the frontal lobes. Two corings were done on the first patient who underwent this modified procedure; as many as four were done on some of the subsequent patients. All twenty of the leucotomies were performed in just a few days.

Four months later Moniz reported his results at the Academy of Medicine conference in Paris, France. There, he asserted that although six of the patients remained unimproved, seven had improved and the remaining seven had been cured. The boldness of this assertion was undermined by several facts that the otherwise impressed conferees may or may not have been privy to. First, since it was just four months after the leucotomies had been performed, there had been hardly enough time for a careful follow-up on the patients by any of Moniz's colleagues, let alone Moniz himself had he even been inclined to do so. Second, Moniz had varied the leucotomy procedure, itself, quite considerably as he operated on one patient after another. The first patient, of course, had a single alcohol injection on each side of her brain, but for some of the subsequent patients, the injections were raised to six. Of those who had been operated on with the leucotome, one received a single coring on each side of the brain, three received two, and six patients received four corings on each side of the brain, and some of them also had later alcohol injections. Some of the patients also had more than one version of the leucotomy after the first failed to produce immediate positive results. Third, Moniz's evidence of the leucotomy's success was impressionistic. Using words like "calmer" and "more alert," he suggested that manageability was a desired outcome, but failed to explain if that predicted successful adaptation to life outside of the asylum.

Moniz published his findings in a French medical journal just weeks after the conference; the monograph, in which he coined the term "psychosurgery," was subsequently translated into several languages, reaching a wide audience that turned out to be considerably less credulous than the conferees. Moniz was roundly criticized for his naïve theory of insanity, the crudeness of the leucotomy procedure, and the rhetorical sleight of hand of using anecdotal data to claim therapeutic success.

He also had his admirers and imitators. After an invitation to discuss and demonstrate the leucotomy in Italy, the psychosurgery was instituted at the Racconigi Asylum near Turin, where Emilio Rizatti went on to perform as many as 200 leucotomies between 1937 and 1939 alone. Leucotomies also were performed in asylums as far away as Romania, Hungary, Japan, Cuba and Brazil. In fact, it was in Brazil that Aloysio de Mattos Pimenta, a neurologist at the Hospital Psiquiátrico do Juqueri in São Paulo, leucotomized four patients in 1936, thus performing the first psychosurgeries in the Americas.

The most ardent admirer of Moniz and the leucotomy was the chair of the Department of Neurology at George Washington University in Washington, D.C. Walter Freeman had begun his career at St. Elizabeths Hospital in that capital. Once known as the Government Hospital for the Insane, the sprawling facility housed more than 5,000 patients whose vacant expressions, shabby clothes and unsociability had disgusted and shamed him. He stayed in the laboratory as much as possible, learning all he could about the brains of psychotic patients who had been brought for autopsy. His occasional forays into the wards revealed his penchant for unconventional therapeutics: he subjected catatonic patients to carbon dioxide and variations in air pressure [see **Cerebral Stimulation**], and performed "jiffy spinal taps" (El-Hai, p. 70) by inserting needles into the bases of patients' skulls as they leaned over chairs.

Now a professor with a thriving private practice, Freeman was redoubling his efforts to find the cause of insanity in the brain. To that end, he communicated with Moniz. His rather fawning fan letter included a promise to bring the leucotomy to the United States and to arrange to have both Moniz's book and his paper on his first cases published in English. Freeman made good on all of his promises, none more pressing than bringing the leucotomy into practice. After extensive research and rehearsal with the leucotome knives that they had ordered from France, Freeman and his neurosurgeon partner James Watts performed their first leucotomy in 1936 on Alice Hood Hammatt, a sixty-three-year-old private patient. Diagnosed with agitated depression, she had been restless, anxious and garrulous; in Freeman's words, she was "a master at bitching and really led her husband a dog's life.... She was a typical insecure, rigid, emotional, claustrophobic individual throughout her mature existence" (Freeman & Watts, 1950, p. xviii).

In preparation for the prefrontal lobotomy, her scalp was cleaned and daubed with gentian violet. Three incisions were made into the violet markings and an auger was used to make holes in her skull over the left and the right frontal lobes of her brain. The leucotome was inserted four centimeters into the exposed surface of her brain. The wire loop was rotated full circle to cut a round core of neural fibers, withdrawn one centimeter to cut another core, and another centimeter to cut a third core. The instrument was withdrawn and then reinserted at a different angle and three additional cores of neural fiber were removed in a surgical procedure that took approximately one hour. Four hours after the surgery Hammatt was calm, almost too calm for Freeman's liking, but over the next few days became more responsive and alert. On the following day she answered questions correctly, first in simple monosyllables and then with more detail:

> Q: Are you content to stay here?
> A: Yes
> Q: Do you have any of your old fears?
> A: No
> Q: What were you afraid of?
> A: I don't know. I seem to forget.
> Q: Do you remember being upset when you came here?
> A: Yes, I was quite upset, wasn't I?
> Q: What was it all about?
> A: I don't know. I seem to have forgotten. It doesn't seem important now... [Freeman & Watts, 1950 p. xix].

Freeman and Watts declared Alice Hood Hammatt cured. Eager to share their success, the partners presented her case to the District of Columbia Medical Society where they were met with incredulity. Undeterred, they wrote up the case for publication in the *Medical Annals of the District of Columbia,* referring to the procedure as a "lobotomy," rather than a leucotomy in order to stamp it with their own imprimatur.

After Hammatt's apparently successful surgery, the physicians quickly lobotomized five more psychiatric outpatients, with mixed immediate results: two were able to return to work, two others relapsed within a couple of months, and the remaining patient, a forty-seven-year-old woman who had lost a great deal of blood when a couple of blood vessels accidentally were severed during the lobotomy, suffered seizures and incontinence and remained anxious and forgetful. Freeman and Watts, however, were confident in the prefrontal lobotomy. They presented a paper on their first six patients to the Southern Medical Association, after having first contacted the press for advanced publicity. While colleagues attending that meeting were hardly unanimous in their support of the surgery, the press coverage was more than favorable. *Time* magazine, for example, declared the prefrontal lobotomy a "noted example of therapeutic courage" and generally dismissed those who challenged the procedure on scientific or ethical grounds as "lesser experts" ("Southern Doctors," p. 67).

It was at this meeting that Freeman and Watts defined their evaluation of what a prefrontal lobotomy would have on patients whom they would consider cured. "Every patient probably loses something by this operation," they stated, "some spontaneity, some sparkle, some flavor of the personality, if it may be so described" (Freeman & Watts, 1937, p. 30). Over the subsequent decade, it had become increasingly apparent what the loss of "sparkle" meant for lobotomized patients: disorientation to time, place and self; inertia that transformed some of them into "wax dummies" who had to be tickled and prodded into activity; euphoria; restlessness that was remediated for some with electroconvulsive shock treatments; food cravings and sloppy eating habits; affective incontinence, that is, a tendency to react with unrestrained joy, sorrow or anger to rather trivial events; childish stubbornness; loss of dignity, shame, reserve and self-consciousness; incontinence and sloppy bathroom habits; reduction of creative talent; and reliance on concrete rather than abstract or strategic thinking.

None of Freeman and Watts's first cohort of prefrontal lobotomy patients was institutionalized at the time of surgery. Indeed, they had initially reasoned that the prefrontal lobotomy would be of no benefit to the "chronic deteriorated patients" who inhabited the wards of asylums across the country, and who already were the subjects of insulin and metrazol shock therapies [see **Shock Therapy**]. But as they continued to perform prefrontal lobotomies on outpatients, report to their colleagues, and as the press that they actively courted continued to laud the procedure as a potential cure of all manner of distress, disease and disorder, some asylum physicians were eager to try it on their insane patients.

Prefrontal lobotomies were expensive to perform. They required a surgical suite, an anesthesiologist, nursing assistance and the skill of a neurosurgeon. Few public asylums in the United States had the facilities, staff or money to invest in the procedure. It is estimated that between 1940 and 1945, fewer than a thousand prefrontal lobotomies were performed, and only a fraction of those were done in state asylums. In Minnesota, for example, ninety-two patients were lobotomized at the Willmar and the Rochester state hospitals; two hundred were lobotomized at the Missouri State Hospital #4 in Farmington and sixty-seven of them improved enough to be discharged. With a grant from the Rockefeller Foundation, the Institute of Pennsylvania Hospital clinical director Edward Strecker, broke with protocol and performed prefrontal lobotomies on twenty-two severely deteriorated back-warders. His results were mixed. Two patients with chronic schizophrenia improved remarkably; three more improved, although not enough to be discharged; the remaining patients showed only some improvement. While the press hyperbolized the outcomes, and while Strecker encouraged his colleagues to use the prefrontal lobotomy for chronic schizophrenics, in a published article he was more circumspect about the therapeutic potential of the procedure. In regards to the prefrontal lobotomy, a "potentially dangerous and definitely brutal method to use in the treatment of mental dysfunction," he and his colleagues wrote, "recovery must not be expected" (Strecker, Palmer & Grant, p. 530).

Henry Worthing and his colleagues at Pilgrim State Hospital in Brentwood, New York, both followed Strecker's example of lobotomizing refractory asylum patients and confirmed his low expectations, as selected case studies illustrated:

*Case No. 4.* This woman, born in 1898, was admitted to Brooklyn State Hospital, where she was diagnosed as dementia praecox, catatonic type. She was transferred to Pilgrim State Hospital in 1936. Since 1940, she was assaultive and noisy; she wet and soiled and was a feeding problem. Prefrontal lobotomy was done on June 10, 1947. She is now obese, quiet, smiling, friendly, does a small amount of work. There is massive regression and chronic hallucinations, but she is clean [Worthing, Brill & Wigderson p. 647].

*Case No. 38:* Born in 1923, this man was admitted to Pilgrim State Hospital on February 18, 1942. The diagnosis was dementia praecox, catatonic. There was no reaction to adequate therapy; he was subsequently regressive, disturbed, and hallucinated. Lobotomy was performed on January 16, 1948, followed by a gradual improvement in behavior. The patient was released on convalescent care.... At home, he was somewhat childish but in the main well behaved. He is idle, requires some slight supervision and is dependent.... His parents are grateful, since they had never been able to adjust to the idea of leaving him in the hospital, and yet could not manage him at home before the lobotomy [p. 649].

*Case No. 49:* This man, born in 1922, had had a previous attack at Pilgrim State Hospital when he was treated by one of the authors. He was readmitted June 22, 1945, after which there was failure with both insulin and electric shock. Lobotomy was done on February 19, 1948, after the patient had been in a withdrawn state, actively hallucinating for more than a year. There was striking improvement. The patient described his previous hallucinations with insight—as happens after insulin. Released on convalescent care April 18, 1948, he was discharged one year later. He was well-adjusted, working, without apparent residual defect; but he began drinking and is said to have indulged in marijuana. There was a full relapse and he was recertified [pp. 649–650].

*Case No. 231:* Aged 57, this man was diagnosed with dementia praecox, paranoid, onset more than ten years ago. There were delusions of persecution, economic incapacity, withdrawal from family, letters to authorities. He was admitted to Pilgrim State Hospital in 1947. In the hospital, he was furiously resistive, actively hallucinated, resentful, grandiose, unapproachable.... Lobotomy was done on February 8, 1949.... The patient admitted that he had been "imagining things." He became friendly and approachable. On close examination, residual psychotic content was noted.... The man was released June 4, 1949. On first report, he was comfortable, but economically dependent. He was well-behaved. No loss of intelligence in conversation was observed, but no will to work [p. 654].

Just ten prefrontal lobotomies were performed at the Delaware State Hospital. Its superintendent, Mesrop Tarumianz, had estimated that successfully lobotomizing just ninety-nine patients would save the state more than $300,000 over a decade, but the fact remained that at a minimum of $250 per lobotomy, the asylum could ill afford to continue the procedure.

The economic constraint was less burdensome, or perhaps less worrisome, in other countries. Sweden was an example. By the mid-twentieth century, prefrontal lobotomies were being performed in more than half of the country's twenty-eight asylums. One of them, the State Mental Hospital of Umedalen, chose the most obstreperous and unruly patients, most of them women diagnosed with schizophrenia, as candidates for the procedure. The results were not particularly remarkable. Only a small percentage of the patients were discharged as cured; if there were any significant changes in the remaining patients it was that they had become more tractable, and therefore better suited for asylum life.

In Finland, where there were just 2500 asylum beds for the more than 12,000 insane patients, the prefrontal lobotomy was only a reticently used therapeutic. During the mid–1940s approximately fifty patients, most diagnosed with schizophrenia, were lobotomized using the standard Freeman-Watts technique. Although that number increased over subsequent years, Finnish physicians were more inclined than some of their international colleagues to use the prefrontal lobotomy as a last resort after all other therapeutic interventions had failed. From a more practical standpoint, the small number of qualified neurosurgeons in Finland may have had as much, if not more, to do with the reluctance to perform the procedure than any rigid adherence to the "last resort" protocol.

After the ravages of World War II, in fact, the number of prefrontal lobotomies increased in all European countries that had sufficient numbers of neurosurgeons. In England, for example, Sir Wylie McKissock posed a formidable post-war challenge to Freeman and Watts, who were still somewhat scrounging for patients, with the sheer number of procedures he performed, not to mention the speed with which they were performed. By his own estimation the neurosurgeon lobotomized nearly 3,000 patients, some in thirty minute procedures using a standard brain needle rather than a leucotome, which he had disdainfully dismissed as nothing more than a "mechanical egg-whisk." His patients ranged from adolescents to the elderly; some were casualties of the war and a few were what were called "mental defectives," in the parlance of the day, but the majority had been diagnosed with schizophrenia. His results, too, suggested that the standard prefrontal lobotomy, as well as the rostral variation he had devised of accessing the frontal lobes through burr holes at the top, rather than the temporal region, of the skull, had limited therapeutic success with asylum patients: one-third improved enough to be discharged to home care; one-third improved slightly and the remaining one-third showed no improvement.

Despite these forays into the psychosurgical cure of insanity, it had become increasingly clear by the mid–1940s that the prefrontal lobotomy was neither an efficient nor an expedient asylum therapeutic. The desire to find a surgical solution that would empty asylums was only intensifying, however, in the face of what was becoming an international crisis. In the United States alone, there were more than 250,000 admissions in 1946 to state asylums where there was, on average, only one physician for every 250 patients. Meeting just the minimum standards for asylum patient care, inpatient treatment in that same year would have cost approximately $600,000,000; in truth, only one-sixth of that amount actually had been spent. Asylums in every country were in similarly dire straits. With no control over the number of admissions, and little over budget appropriations, the only control asylum physicians did have was in regards to discharges. To that end, and with the confidence that psychosurgery would be the means to empty asylums, a cheaper and quicker version of the prefrontal lobotomy was desperately needed.

It may be interesting to note that in the late 1990s a Swedish investigative report revealed that prefrontal lobotomies had been performed on thousands of patients in Swedish asylums, many without their or their relatives' permission. In addition, nearly 500 children, many of them developmentally delayed and institutionalized in national training schools, had undergone the procedure as well. Pleas for compensation by surviving lobotomy patients were denied by Parliament. Just a couple of years earlier, however, the Norwegian government had agreed to pay approximately $18,500 to each of the country's 500 surviving lobotomy patients. It was estimated that 2500 lobotomies had been performed there.

## Topectomy, Cortical Ablation, or Frontal Gyrectomy

The surgical excision of part of the cerebral cortex in order to relieve the symptoms of insanity. The first topectomy, as the psychosurgery later was to be termed, was performed by the Swiss physician Gottleib Burckhardt in 1888 at the Prefargier Psychiatry Clinic on the shore of Lake Neuchatel at the foot of the Jura Mountains. That such an idyllic setting was the site of the first attempt to alleviate, even cure, insanity, by surgical intrusion into the brain is worthy of mention, as is the fact that Burckhardt often is historically overlooked as the founder of psychosurgery. Little of the fame or the infamy that sobriquet carries with it today is associated with his name.

Influenced by late nineteenth century animal and human experiments and autopsy studies that focused on the functional specialization of the brain, Burckhardt theorized that psychotic symptoms such as aggression, delusions and especially hallucinations could be relieved in insane patients by the surgical removal of part of the cortex of the brain. According to Burckhardt,

> If excitation and impulsive behavior are due to the fact that from the sensory surfaces excitations abnormal in quality, quantity and intensity do arise, and do act on the motor surfaces, then an improvement could be obtained by creating an obstacle between the two surfaces. The extirpation of the motor or sensory zone would expose it to the risk of grave functional disturbances and to technical difficulties. It would be more advantageous to practice the excision of a strip of cortex behind and on both sides of the motor zone creating thus a kind of ditch in the temporal lobe [Berrios, p. 69].

Burckhardt, who had little surgical experience, performed topectomies on two women and four men. Five of the six had been diagnosed with *"primäre Verrücktheit,"* a diagnosis equivalent to schizophrenia. All of the patients were aggressive, restless, experiencing auditory hallucinations and delusions, and had not responded to conventional treatments. The site of the procedure varied with the target symptom of the patient: for the three who were violent and experiencing auditory hallucinations, the excision was made in the temporal lobe; for one who was aggressive, the parietal-temporal area; for another with paranoid delusions, the temporo-frontal area; and for the remaining patient, Friedrich August N., the frontal lobe was the site of excision.

It was the targeting of the frontal lobe that decades later would come to define the psychosurgical procedure known as the lobotomy, and Friedrich August N., a lithographer by trade, was the first patient to undergo it. It was his excitability, complicated in the eighth year of his asylum stay by hallucinations, unpredictable body movements, delusions of grandeur and increasingly explosive behavior that drew Burckhardt's attention to his frontal lobes. So in a two-and-a-half hour surgical procedure, he opened the skull of the thirty-one-year-old patient with a trephine, opened the dura, and removed some of the frontal cortex with a sharp spoon. The dura and then the skull were closed with cat-gut sutures. Improvement was noted almost immediately post-surgery. Friedrich August N. was calmer and more conversational, but he also suffered several seizures that had to be treated with bromide. Disappointed with the outcome, Burckhardt determined he needed a second procedure.

Friederich August N. was one of the three patients who had shown improvement after the topectomy, although one of them drowned, whether by suicide or accident, a short time after her discharge from the Clinic. Two others in the initial group had not improved, and one had died five days post-surgery from a subdural hematoma and pneumonia. Burckhardt, however, was confident that the psychosurgery held promise for the relief of psychotic symptoms and presented his findings at the Berlin Medical Congress in 1899. His confidence was not at all shared by the members of his audience. His presentation, in fact, "caused a chill in the room" (Stone, p. 89), and while the comments and questions from his audience were polite enough, the reports they later published in leading journals about the presentation often were scathingly critical of both the psychosurgical procedure and its theoretical rationale. The distinguished German physician Emil Kraepelin dismissed the procedure as nothing more than trying to pacify restless patients by "scratching away the cerebral cortex," and the Italian physician Giuseppi Seppili declared that Burckhardt's theory of localization ignored the more influential theory that psychosis was the result of a diffuse pathology of the cerebral cortex (Berrios, pp. 69–70).

Burckhardt retreated to Switzerland where he wrote a lengthy and decidedly defensive paper that reviewed the relevant clinical and experimental literature, laid out in detail his theory of psychosis and the rationale for its psychosurgical treatment. The paper was quoted quite widely, but more often in the service of criticism than praise. The American neurologist Moses Allan Starr, for example, concluded that despite Burckhardt's assertions to the contrary, "there is no reason to conclude that insanity not traumatic in origin is amenable to surgical treatment, and Burckhardt's proposal ... to trephine in chronic cases and make incisions at random into the brain, deserved the severe censure with which it is met" (Starr, p. 271). The most devastating criticism, however, was levied a few years after his death in a paper published by neurosurgeons Vladimir Bechterev and Ludvig Puusepp. "We have quoted this data to show not only how groundless but also how dangerous these operations were," they concluded after reviewing Burckhardt's findings. "We are unable to explain how their author, a holder of a degree in medicine, could bring himself to carry them out" (Berrios, p. 71). This rhetoric of rectitude was somewhat undermined by the fact the Puusepp, who had an appointment at the University of Tartu in Estonia as professor of neurosurgery, the first such academic appointment in the world, had already performed three psychosurgeries. In them, he had severed the nerve fibers between the frontal and parietal lobes of the patients in order to relieve their manic-depressive psychoses. The outcomes were thoroughly discouraging so he had never published the cases.

That aside, the criticism had essentially marginalized Burckhardt who never performed another procedure, but it had not marginalized the intriguing idea that severe psychosis might just possibly be cured by a much more refined version of his procedure. In the mid–1940s J. Lawrence Pool, then affiliated with Columbia University Medical Center in New York City, developed just that procedure which he christened the topectomy (from the Greek "*topos*" or place, and "*ektome*" for excision). The topectomy was a limited bilateral ablation of cortex in the frontal lobes, with cortical removals begun at 2.5 centimeters from the coronal suture when it crosses the midline, and 1.9 to 2.0 centimeters in depth, thus each excision was carried to the depth of the brain's gray matter but did not extend into the underlying white matter. Although ill-suited for the violently insane, this more conservative approach was predicted to bring relief to those who still manifested "some evidence of 'drive' and some indication of emotional reaction or affect" (Pool, Heath, & Weber, p. 336).

For a time, topectomy posed a formidable challenge to prefrontal lobotomy, and to the newly designed procedure of the transorbital lobotomy. The claims made about each essentially were put to the test in a series of comparative studies known as the Columbia-Greystone Project, and later called the New York State Brain Research Project, hailed as "one of the most extraordinary research projects in the history of medical science" (Bigelow p. 156). The first study began in 1947 and was designed to determine which part of the frontal lobe could be excised to the greatest benefit and the least harm to the patient. To that end, Pool performed topectomies on forty-eight patients at the New Jersey State Hospital in Greystone Park, while Walter Freeman performed transorbital lobotomies on eighteen patients. The results indicated that the topectomy had a slight advantage in relieving symptoms, an advantage that Freeman who, incidentally, left the tip of his leucotome in the brain of one his patients, attributed to post-operative care, rather than to the procedure itself. In the second study, Freeman performed transorbital lobotomies on an additional nine patients and, although more impressed with the outcomes, Pool continued to claim a slight advantage.

Yet there was little evidence of topectomy's "slight advantage" in Pool's assessment of his psychosurgical patients. About twenty-four hours after surgery, the patients' psychotic symptoms accelerated, and some became hostile and resentful. Four or five days post-surgery improvements began to be noted and these continued for some of the patients, despite the fatigability and the dulling of their mental activity. Approximately one-third of the patients temporarily became incontinent, and some had postoperative convulsive seizures. Pool concluded that "good results" were obtained for approximately 20 percent of the patients, although he did not define the term; and that "significant improvement" was noted for another 20 percent. The latter were patients who were discharged "so that they are at home and capable of housework, etc. but are not capable of earning their living" (Pool, Heath & Weber, p. 343). The remaining patients showed no improvement, although Pool hastened to add that with the exception of two of them, "we do not think any of our patients have been rendered the worse for their operations" (p. 343).

Whatever advantages might have accrued to the topectomy as a psychosurgical procedure were surely undercut by the fact that it was poorly suited to the noble cause of emptying out asylums. It was a complicated procedure, lasting anywhere from four to eight hours, that required the careful selection of patients and the skill of a neurosurgeon. Few state asylums had the surgical facilities in which the procedure could be performed, nor did they have the staff necessary for appropriate aftercare. If there was a contest between

Pool and Freeman, the latter might have been declared the winner. The transorbital lobotomy, after all, was cheap, easy and although ugly in its crudeness, better suited for asylum practice.

Pool eventually conceded that he could not claim the topectomy was superior to the transorbital lobotomy. Indeed, others such as Jacques LeBeau in Paris, France, who was reporting good results, had by the mid-twentieth century lost interest in the topectomy as a psychosurgical technique as well.

## *Transorbital Lobotomy, or Ice Pick Lobotomy*

The surgical severing of the neural connections to and from the prefrontal cortex via the insertion of an ice pick or an orbitoclast above the eyeball and through the boney orbital ridge. The transorbital lobotomy was devised by the American neurologist Walter Freeman as a quicker and cheaper procedure than the prefrontal lobotomy, and therefore more suitable for use as an asylum therapeutic.

Freeman's innovation was influenced by the work of Amarro Fiamberti, an Italian physician who had been experimenting with streamlining the lobotomy by using a transorbital method that accessed the frontal lobes of the brain through the bony eye socket. After anesthetizing the patient, Fiamberti had entered the brain by inserting a sharply pointed hollow instrument, known as a trocar, into the eye socket and forcing it through the thin orbit of bone. He then had inserted a hypodermic needle filled with alcohol or formalin through the hollow tube of the trocar and plunged it about two centimeters into the frontal lobes of the brain.

Keen to take advantage of, or perhaps to improve upon, the innovation of Fiamberti, Freeman began experimenting on cadavers, using an ice pick from his home to crack through the bone and then moving it back and forth, rather like a windshield wiper, to sever the nerve fibers. Confident that he had mastered the technique, he tried the procedure for the first time on a patient from his private practice. Her name was Sally "Ellen" Ionesco, a twenty-nine-year-old wife and mother who had been in the throes of rapid mood swings, alternating between periods of depression that left her bedridden and periods of mania that made her violent. In 1946, Freeman anesthetized her with three short bursts of electroconvulsive shock, pinched her upper eyelid between his thumb and forefinger, easing it well away from the eyeball, and inserted the ice pick into the conjuctival sac. He bent down on one knee while aligning the ice pick parallel to the bony ridge of her nose and then pulled its handle as far laterally as the rim of the eye socket allowed in order to sever the nerve fibers at the base of the frontal lobe. Returning the instrument half way to its initial position, he then pushed it into the frontal lobe to a depth of seven centimeters from the margin of the upper eyelid. He then moved the ice pick fifteen to twenty degrees medially and

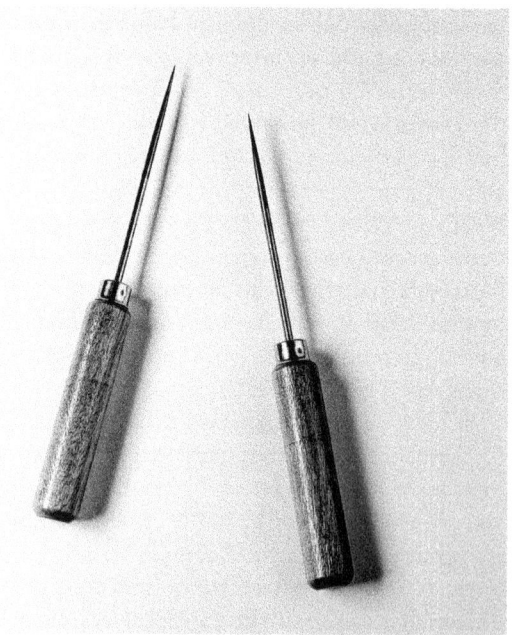

A pair of "orbitoclasts" used to perform transorbital lobotomies. The devices were designed by the American lobotomist Walter Freeman to replace the kitchen ice pick he had been using (courtesy of the Wellcome Library, London).

thirty degrees laterally, returned it to the mid-position, and withdrew it with a twisting motion, all the while exerting pressure on the eyelid to prevent hemorrhaging. While in subsequent transorbital lobotomies the procedure would be immediately repeated through the other eye socket, he asked Ionesco to return several weeks later for that part of the procedure.

Left with swollen black eyes, Ionesco returned home for a long recovery that required full-time care. Her mood swings disappeared, and after some time she was able to work as a nurse, and later as a nanny. Freeman declared her surgery a success, but like so many lobotomy patients, whether prefrontal or transorbital, her good health was impermanent, although not short-lived. As she aged, her mental state declined; she hallucinated and had delusions of persecution.

Freeman performed several more transorbital lobotomies in rapid succession in his office, all with similar results as the Ionesco surgery, with the exception of the fourth patient who hemorrhaged when he sliced a blood vessel. Although the patient survived, he suffered epileptic seizures and was left so lethargic by the psychosurgery that he had to be cared for by his family. After nine successive transorbital lobotomies, Freeman finally apprised his neurosurgeon partner, James Watts, of his activities. Watts was appalled, and immediately ended their partnership. He explained why:

> It is Freeman's opinion that transorbital lobotomy is a minor operation.... If he is correct in his view [it] should take precedence over more time consuming psychiatric techniques. On the other hand, if [it] is a major operation, as I believe it is, it should be performed only rarely in mental cases that are not disabled. In both mental and physical disease, surgical intervention should be reserved for cases in which conservative therapy has been tried and failed or in cases where such treatment is known to be ineffective. It is my opinion that any procedure involving cutting of brain tissue is a major surgical operation, no matter how quickly or atraumatically one enters the intracranial cavity. Therefore, it follows logically, that only those who have been schooled in neurosurgical techniques and can handle complications which may arise should perform the operation [Freeman & Watts, 1950, pp. 59–60].

Undeterred, Freeman began seeking out patients at state asylums. Arriving first at the Yankton State Hospital in South Dakota in 1946, he was invited to perform transorbital lobotomies on a dozen chronic schizophrenics, patients whom a decade before he would have thought inappropriate for the surgery. The following year he revisited Yankton and then went on to perform thirteen transorbital lobotomies on schizophrenic patients in Western State Hospital in Steilacoom, Washington, where the success of the surgeries was trumpeted by the press. But it was in 1948 that Freeman started in earnest his nearly decade-long "head-hunting trip" (El-Hai, p. 243), criss-crossing the country, visiting nearly 200 state asylums, many of them more than once, teaching asylum physicians how to perform the transorbital lobotomy, and performing more than a few himself. While the prefrontal lobotomy had been considered the surgery of last resort for agitated and depressed outpatients, Freeman promoted the transorbital lobotomy as the surgery of first choice for the psychotic and institutionalized insane.

Not content with the assembly-line lobotomies he was performing at large state asylums on patients selected for him by asylum physicians, Freeman proposed a "mass lobotomy" project that would bring the benefits of the surgery to smaller and more isolated asylums. This was not the first time such a proposal had been offered. Just a few years earlier the British psychiatrist William Sargant, who had been awarded a Rockefeller Scholarship to study at Harvard Medical School, and who had once derisively laughed at the very idea of psychosurgery and now was its enthusiastic proponent, had suggested that a mass lobotomy project be carried out at the Tuskegee State Hospital in Alabama. Patients were selected, permissions from relatives were obtained and the services of Walter Freeman were procured before this bold attempt to "rescue the Negro patient" was banned by the Veterans Administration (Sargant, p. 130).

Now, Freeman was determined to carry out a version of this plan. In 1952 he convinced the West Virginia Board of Control to fund what he was calling the "West Virginia Lobotomy Project." Over a twelve-day period, he lobotomized 228 patients from four small asylums in the nation's poorest state. Julius McLeod, then an eighteen-year-old attendant at Lakin State Hospital, the state's segregated asylum for Blacks, remembered how the lobotomies were performed and his reaction to them:

> [Freeman] took a surgical looking nail and a surgical looking hammer, and he drove the nail between the bridge of the nose and the eyes, one on each side. He pushed in one or two times, up through the frontal lobe, crossed it a couple of times, moved it back and forth.... After all this time, I still can't put into words what I felt other than anger and disgust. These people were human, not cattle [de Young, p. 358].

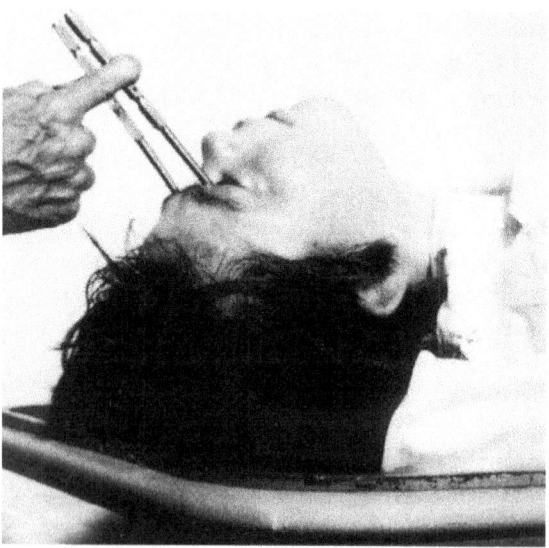

The trajectory of the transorbital lobotomy: above the eyeball, through the boney orbital ridge, and into the prefrontal cortex. The procedure was designed by Walter Freeman as a quick and inexpensive alternative to the prefrontal lobotomy, and therefore ideally suited for the assembly-line treatment of asylum patients.

Helen Culmer arrived as a nurse at Lakin State Hospital just as the West Virginia Lobotomy Project began, and assisted Freeman in the procedure. She recalled the press of people, not just physicians and nurses, but laypeople from the town, who came to witness the procedure:

> [Freeman] came, and I held the patient's head and he did the lobotomy. He had an instrument—to me it looked like a nail, a great big nail. It had a sharp point, and he inserted this in the corner of the individual's eye and banged it with a mallet, I guess it was. And then he pulled from one side and pulled to other side. It wasn't easy.... It wasn't easy to watch ... and I know that we lost one patient because they couldn't stop the bleeding and I can't remember if any others died.... It wasn't—it wasn't what I thought it might be. To me it was cruel. But that was my opinion. Remember, I've seen all kinds of things in my line of work, so if I stopped and dwelled on each little thing, I'd be hurting ["Oral Histories"].

Freeman published the results of the West Virginia Lobotomy Project in the prestigious *Journal of the American Medical Association,* and reported that four of the 228 patients died as the result of their transorbital lobotomies, and of the remaining 224 patients, 85 (38 percent) were released from the asylums within one year post-surgery, a rate more than forty times higher than of the comparison group of 202 patients whose relatives had refused permission for the surgery. That difference certainly gave face validity to Freeman's claims that "the lobotomy gets them home."

The patients' before and after photographs that were published in the report provided another kind of "face validity" for the success of the transorbital lobotomy, in that the "distorted expressions of fear, hate and torment give way to relaxed and sometimes smiling friendliness" (Freeman, Davis, East, Tait, Johnson, & Rogers, p. 941). The report also provided glimpses into the loss of "sparkle" that resulted from the procedure. Upon discharge, Freeman and his colleagues explained, the lobotomized patients have a couple of weeks of "relaxed friendliness, indolence, some confusion, and forgetfulness," but this "rather easy period" was followed by a more protracted "echo" period of "irritability, defiance and perhaps resurgence of complaints" (p. 941). Indeed, visits to the homes of the eighty-five lobotomized patients who had been discharged revealed that their adjustment varied greatly. Some were working or attending school, others were keeping house "in a more or less effective fashion," others still were in "less satisfactory condition" and had to be closely supervised by family members (p. 942).

The published report touched only lightly on the fact that in addition to the eighty-five lobotomized patients who had adjusted upon discharge, there were an additional fifty who had not. They had proven themselves too difficult for relatives to handle and had to be readmitted. The report also only briefly mentioned that seventeen of the total group of lobotomized patients had to have a second transorbital lobotomy the following year because they either had shown insufficient improvement or had relapsed.

The cost of the West Virginia Lobotomy Project was $2,300. In this poverty-stricken state, the per diem cost of housing an insane patient was $2.04. Freeman calculated a $48,000 savings to the state in the year following the project, thus showing the financial bottom line for "getting them home." The project was refunded. The next year Freeman and his associates lobotomized an additional 285 West Virginia patients, 115 more the following year, and 159 more the next year, claiming an overall success rate, as measured by discharge alone, of 38 percent for the grand total of 787 patients.

A 38 percent discharge rate for patients, most of whom had been diagnosed with schizophrenia, was, in fact, more than any other therapeutic could boast. But the question about the quality of life for discharged transorbital lobotomy patients lingered. To address it, Freeman conducted a brief statistical follow-up as patients reached their fifth through eighth year post-transorbital lobotomy. Of the 703 still alive, 309 (44 percent) were now living outside of the asylums. As to the quality of their lives, Freeman quite shrewdly concluded that "the losses in intelligence, memory and other measureable abilities are due to the [pre-existing] psychosis, not to lobotomy" (p. 1134).

Freeman's cleverly worded findings in published articles, his addresses to his peers and the generally favorable press coverage he continued to receive drew the attention of his international colleagues. He was invited to demonstrate the transorbital lobotomy in England where prefrontal lobotomies were still being performed; although riveted and repulsed in equal measure, in the end British asylum physicians showed little interest in using the procedure. In Germany, just recently shamed by the Nuremberg Trials that had made public the medical atrocities committed by Nazi physicians during World War II, Freeman's invited demonstration was met with reproach by Karl Kleist, the country's foremost biological psychiatrist. Kleist declared the transorbital lobotomy a "mutilating surgery," and warned that "Germans should avoid further world criticism for experimental procedures" (Valenstein, p. 218). Indeed, even in those countries sill performing the prefrontal lobotomy, the transorbital innovation held little appeal. While not uniquely American, its use was significantly more widespread across the United States than it ever was in Great Britain, Europe or anywhere else in the world.

By the 1960s, though, the transorbital lobotomy had lost much of its appeal, and Freeman much of his reputation. The ethical questions about the procedure that he had overlooked now loomed large. Longer term studies of patients post-transorbital lobotomy found that the best results produced little more than inertia, inattentiveness, lack of initiative, blunted affect, docility, all of which were leading to the conclusion "that the treatment was worse than the disease" (Mashour, Walker, & Martuz, p. 412). In that tumultuous decade, rumors floated around that lobotomies were being considered to change political attitudes, quell student protests, and quiet racial conflicts. Novels such as *All the King's Men* and *The Naked Lunch* further tarnished the surgical procedure, as did the play *Suddenly, Last Summer* later made into a popular film and, of course, the novel *One Flew Over the Cuckoo's Nest,* later made into a blockbuster film. The public also was getting a glimpse at the role of lobotomy-like procedures in a future technologically totalitarian society in novels such as *The Invisible Man* (Ellison, 1952) and *Limbo* (Wolfe, 1952), and in films such as "A Clockwork Orange." Press coverage took a negative turn, and critics who had been graciously silent now were impolitely vocal.

Freeman's reputation declined precipitously. He was dismissed from one hospital in California where he had moved when he recommended that a schizophrenic child be lobotomized; his surgical privileges were severely restricted at two other hospitals. He performed his last transorbital lobotomy in 1967 on a woman he had lobotomized on two previous occasions. This time he ripped open a blood vessel. The patient died a few hours later.

Although hers was the last lobotomy he ever performed, Freeman remained enthusiastic until the day he died in 1972 about the surgery's ability to "bring them home." His enthusiasm, however, was long past being shared by his peers, the public or the press. The procedure was restricted in many states, requiring the approval of a specially constituted review board before it was carried out; it was similarly restricted, or even banned, in countries such as Japan, Australia and Germany, and the former Soviet Union. Medical and psychiatric organizations, both national and international, published strict guidelines for its acceptable use; lawsuits by lobotomized former patients were settled, almost always in their favor.

The tides of psychiatric and public opinion had turned during the decades of the sixties and seventies. In Freeman's own lifetime, the lobotomy had been lauded as "an example of therapeutic courage" ("Southern Doctors," p. 67) to being finally damned as "the most uniquely infamous" asylum therapeutic in history (El-Hai, p. 1).

## *Trephining, or Trephinization, or Trepanning, or Trepanization*

Although the procedure of drilling or scraping a burr hole in the skull in order to expose the dura mater of the brain can be traced to the Neolithic era, the term "trephining" also was used in the late nineteenth century to label surgeries that involved the sectioning of the dura mater in order to drain cerebrospinal fluid that was hypothesized to have created intolerable intracranial pressure. Although there is some debate as to the originator of the procedure, Claye Shaw laid claim to the title. As medical superintendent of the Middlesex County Asylum in Banstead, England, he had directed surgeon Harrison Cripps to drill holes in the skull of a paretic patient, section the dura over the motor cortex of the frontal lobes and drain cerebrospinal fluid. The patient recovered and was discharged. Shaw's report of the trephination was widely criticized by some of his colleagues who voiced the same concerns about the procedure, its ethics and its scientific rationale that would be posed decades later about the lobotomy. But it also inspired imitators and contenders for glory. The following year, J. Batty Tuke, medical superintendent of the Asylum for Fife and Kinross in Scotland, performed the same procedure on a paretic patient with a good outcome. Shaw quickly countered by trephinating another patient who also improved enough to be discharged, that success somewhat tempered by Shaw's admission that the good results for the first trephined patient had not persisted. He had developed epilepsy several months after his discharge, and had died a short time later.

While Shaw and Tuke vied for recognition, and while the British Medical Association debated trephination, other asylum physicians experimented with it on their patients who had been diagnosed with general paresis, also known as general paralysis of the insane, a form of neurosyphilis. The results were mixed. Charles Gray Wagner, physician at the Utica Asylum in New York, used a chisel and hammer to trephine the skull of a paretic patient; the thirty-two-year-old Black man showed some initial improvement but died two months later. George Zeller, medical superintendent of the Peoria Asylum in Illinois reported even more distressing results: he had operated on nine paretic patients, but only one survived. The survival rate of trephined paretic patients was much higher at the Stirling District Asylum in Scotland where John Macpherson and David Wallace treated five paretic patients. The results, however, were more than disappointing. The asylum physicians found "no permanent or marked benefit conferred upon our patients" and were forced to conclude that the present state of knowledge about general paresis was "so imperfect that as yet surgical treatment ... can be of no material benefit whatsoever" (Macpherson & Wallace, pp. 178–179).

Although Shaw remained an advocate of the trephining procedure to relieve intracranial pressure in general paresis cases, the therapeutic did not outlive his enthusiasm for it. By the turn into the twentieth century the procedure was no longer being reported in the literature.

# Rotation, Oscillation and Vibration

*The use of various devices to spin, swing and shake insane patients in order to increase pressure on the brain, thereby inducing calm and sleep.*

The idea of therapeutically spinning, swinging and shaking asylum patients had its origins in a conversation between the British physician Erasmus Darwin and James Brindley, an engineer and fellow member of the Lunar Society, an informal learned society whose membership boasted some of the leading figures of the nineteenth century Midlands Enlightenment movement. Sleep was the topic of that particular conversation. Brindley told the story of how he had once seen a millwright stretch out on the large stone of a corn mill and contentedly fall asleep as the stone began to whirl. The story piqued Darwin's interest. Long interested in the potential of sleep to cure physical diseases, the physician conjectured that if a patient were stretched out on a couch that was fixed to a perpendicular shaft that ran from the ceiling to the floor and then whirled around that shaft with increasing velocity, "sleep might be produced, and probably the violence of the actions of the heart and arteries might be diminished in inflammatory fevers" (Darwin, pp. 436–437).

Since the use of such a "rotative couch" was somewhat impractical in the setting of Darwin's private medical practice, he never had one constructed. But in his widely read text, *Zoonomia,* in which he set out his theories of anatomy, disease, psychology and evolution, the latter theory expanded upon by his grandson Charles Darwin, the famous naturalist, he recommended that hospital physicians try this unique approach to treating disease and disorder. Not many took up that call, but *asylum* physicians certainly did. Within a decade of the 1801 publication of *Zoonomia,* asylums across Europe were spinning, swinging and shaking their patients in a wide variety of cleverly designed couches, chairs, mats, swings, beds and hammocks, not just for the purpose of sedating but stimulating them.

Before observations were made as to therapeutic efficacy there were those asylum physicians who found the devices barbarous and even ludicrous. One of them was John Haslam, former apothecary to the Bethlem ("Bedlam") Asylum in London. In an oft-repeated phrase, he described such devices as doing nothing more than "spinning a mad-man round on a pivot" (Haslam, p. 340), and dismissed them as nothing more than whimsical.

Whimsical or not, it was not just the novelty of such devices that appealed to asylum physicians, nor was it just the way they resembled the tools and machines that were both cause and consequence of that era's Industrial Revolution. These "mechanical anodynes," as they were sometimes called, produced the same effects as the old-fashioned humoural therapeutics of bleeding, purging and vomiting that asylum physicians were eager to move beyond. They had an additional advantage, best summed up by William Hallaran, medical superintendent of the County and City of Cork Lunatic Asylum in Ireland and inventor of a circulating swing: "Since the commencement of the use of [mechanical anodynes], I have never been at a loss for a direct mode of establishing a supreme authority over the most turbulent and unruly" (Hallaran, 1810, p. 60).

That "supreme authority" predicted the punitive potential of the mechanical anodynes. That potential was recognized by Joseph Mason Cox who was the first of the asylum physicians to take on Darwin's challenge to bring these devices into hospital practice. His eponymously named chair was, in fact, the prototype for virtually every other such device that was invented and used during the first half of the nineteenth century. But the potential of their misuse in the service of "supreme authority" was never far from his consideration. "The employment of such Herculean remedies," he warned, "requires the greatest caution and judgment." Not every asylum physician heeded that warning.

By the mid-nineteenth century rotating, oscillating and vibrating devices had outlived their novelty. There was increasing skepticism being expressed about their efficacy and, as moral treatment became *de rigueur*, increasing criticism about their ethicality. Fatalities resulting from its use had been reported in a number of asylums. In Italy, for example, the medical commission of Milan barred its use at the Senavra Asylum after several deaths were reported. By that time, most of the rotation, oscillation and vibration devices had either been relegated to the cellars and basements of asylums, or appropriated by scientific laboratories for experiments on the functioning of the vestibular system. Their legacy, however, can be found today in funfair and amusement park whirligigs and rollercoasters.

REFERENCES

Baillon, H. (1893). Mechanical treatment "fads." *American Medico-Surgical Bulletin, 6,* 211–215.
Burrows, G.M. (1828). *Commentaries on the causes, forms, symptoms and treatment, moral and medical, of insanity.* London: Thomas and George Underwood.
Charcot, J.M. (2011/1892). Vibratory therapeutics. *Journal of Nervous and Mental Disease, 199,* 821–827.
Conolly, J. (1847). *The construction and government of lunatic asylums and hospitals for the insane.* London: Churchill.
Cox, J.M. (1804). *Practical observations on insanity.* London: Baldwin and Murray.
Darwin, E. (1801). *Zoonomia, or, the laws of organic life.* Vol. 4. 3rd ed. London: Johnson.
Dodge, R. (1923). Habituation to rotation. *Journal of Experimental Psychology, 6,* 1–35.
Galt, J.M. (1846). *The treatment of insanity.* New York: Harper & Brothers.
Goetz, C. (2009). Jean-Martin Charcot and his vibratory chair for Parkinson disease. *Neurology, 73,* 475–478.
Gordon, A.G. (2007). Erasmus Darwin (1731–1802): Neurologist. *Neurology, 68,* 1239–1240.
Granville, J.M. (1883). *Nerve vibration and excitation.* London: J. & A. Churchill.
Guarnieri, P. (1988). Between soma and psyche: Morselli and psychiatry in late-nineteenth century Italy. In W.F. Bynum, R. Porter, and M. Shepherd (eds.), *The anatomy of madness, Vol. III: The asylum and its psychiatry,* pp. 102–124. London: Routledge.
Hallaran, W.S. (1810). *An enquiry into the causes producing the extraordinary addition to the number of insane.* Cork, Ireland: Edwards and Savage.
Hallaran, W.S. (1818). *Practical observations of the causes and cure of insanity.* Cork, Ireland: Edwards and Savage.
Harsch, V. (2006). Centrifuge "therapy" for psychiatric patients in Germany in the early 1800s. *Aviation, Space, Environmental Medicine, 77,* 157–160.
Haslam, J. (1809). *Observations on madness and melancholy.* London: G. Hayden.
Hoolihan, C. (2008). *An annotated catalog of the Edward C. Atwater collection,* Vol. 3. Rochester, NY: University of Rochester Press.
Knight, P.S. (1827). *Observations on the causes, symptoms and treatment of derangement of the mind.* London: Longman, Rees, Orme, Brown, and Green.

Kraepelin, E. (1962). *One hundred years of psychiatry.* Trans. W. Baskin. New York: Citadel.
"Lunatic asylums" (1857). *London Quarterly Review, 101,* 199–215.
"M. Guislain on mental derangement, &c." (1829). *Edinburgh Medical and Surgical Journal, 32,* 97–113.
Maj, M., and Ferro, F.M. (eds.). (2002). *Anthology of Italian psychiatric texts.* New York: Wiley InterScience.
Patrick, H.T. (1894). Vibratory medicine. *Chicago Medical Recorder, 7,* 236–240.
Rush, B. (1830). *Medical inquiries and observations upon the diseases of the mind.* 4th ed. Philadelphia: John Grigg.
"The vibrating electric helmet for nervous disease" (1892). *The Electrical Engineer,* 251–252.
Wade, N.J. (2005). The original spin doctors—the meeting of perception and insanity. *Perception, 34,* 253–260.
Wade, N.J., Norrsell, U., and Presly, A. (2005). Cox's chair: "A moral and a medical mean in the treatment of maniacs." *History of Psychiatry, 15,* 73–88.
Windholz, G. (1995). Psychiatric treatment and the condition of the mentally disturbed at Berlin's Charité in the early decades of the nineteenth century. *History of Psychiatry, 6,* 157–176.

## *Chiarugi's Cradle, or Chiarugi's Swing, or Restraining Cradle*

A suspended cloth cradle into which the patient's body was enclosed, with only the head exposed. The cradle was rocked gently back and forth to calm the furiously maniacal patient, and to eventually bring about sleep. Designed by Vincenzo Chiarugi, physician in chief at the Ospedale di Bonifazio in Florence, Italy, in the late eighteenth century, the cradle was an alternative to the mechanical restraints [see **Mechanical Restraints**] that Chiarugi, an ardent reformer, had campaigned against. In a letter to a colleague, Chiarugi described the cradle and its use in detail:

> To prevent a furious insane subject from coming to harm and getting into danger at night following his strange movements, I put him in a cradle in the air like a child as follows: one can hang this suspended cradle made of double, very resistant cloth onto the walls of every room; the two extremities are equipped with leather in which holes have been bored; a little mattress is placed in the cradle together with one cushion to put under the head. The furious insane subject is comfortably placed therein with his head out and his arms inside, so that he is free to turn on both sides. Then, starting from the neck one passes the thick rope through to the two holes at the extremities of the cradle down to his feet, where it remains attached, so that it prevents the insane subject, who is thus sewn therein, to throw himself out of the cradle, even if he were Hercules. A quiet insane subject remains the whole night in the same room with him to keep him company; if the furious subject is a woman, the quiet insane subject will be another female. The quiet subject will have the duty to rock the cradle, whenever the furious one begins to scream and the rocking must continue until the former falls asleep. The work of the quiet one is generously rewarded the next day [Maj & Farrow, p. 61].

It is interesting to note that Chiarugi's cradle preceded by several years the publication of Darwin's *Zoonomia* which is usually credited for the development of rotation, oscillation and vibration therapeutics. Chiarugi apparently had found the inspiration for the cradle in the works of the first century Roman medical writer Aulus Cornelius Celsus and the seventh century Greek physician Paulus Aegineta, both of whom had mentioned in passing that a rocking motion often soothed even the most furious maniac.

## *Cox's Chair, or Cox's Swing*

A common Windsor chair, suspended by a hook in the ceiling by two parallel ropes attached to the rear legs; two additional ropes, joined by a sliding knot, attached to the front legs regulated the elevation of the chair. The patient, restrained in a straitjacket, was strapped in the chair by a broad leather belt across the waist as well as straps that secured the legs to the front legs of the chair. The chair was then either swung back and forth, or rotated by an attendant.

The chair was designed by Joseph Mason Cox, proprietor of the private Fishponds Asylums near Bristol, England, in the early nineteenth century, and was the first attempt to put Erasmus Darwin's ideas into therapeutic practice. Its first use was for swinging, and although Cox often used it in that manner, he found the oscillatory movement considerably less therapeutic than the rotary movement, especially in producing restorative sleep. "After a very few circumvolutions, I have witnessed the soothing, lulling effects, when the mind has become tranquilized, and the body quiescent," he wrote. "A degree of vertigo has often followed, which has been succeeded by the most refreshing slumbers" (Cox, 139–140).

In Cox's opinion, the valuable property of the chair was that it worked on both the body and the mind of the patient. It produced vertigo, nausea, copious evacuations, and often vomiting, which Cox just as many asylum physicians did, valued as "among the most successful remedies" in the treatment of insanity (p. 144). And its use left a lasting impression on the patient who was quite inclined to docilely accept any therapeutic regime offered in its place, as the following case illustrated:

> Mr. ——, aged 34, naturally of a gloomy, morose, reserved disposition, had been indulged in every wish of his heart from his infancy, became suspicious, revengeful, and impatient of control.... All the more common means [of treatment] had failed, and he obstinately resisted medicine.... (H)e made some resistance to being placed in the chair, but when properly seated and secured, he was at first turned round very gently, and after a few revolutions, he appeared to experience some unpleasant sensations, his attention was roused, and he made some violent but unavailing struggles; the motion being increased he became pale, and begged the operation might be discontinued, promising compliance with my wishes as to food, medicine, &c. I therefore directed his immediate liberation; he complained of giddiness, nausea, seemed exhausted, and had nearly fainted; being laid on the bed, I found his pulse 60, the inspirations fifteen, the expressions of features changed, the extremities and superficies cold, he soon fell into a profound sleep, which continued three hours; but on waking I found him in mind and body just as before the [chair] was employed, all his promises were forgotten, and he refused food and physic; next day the [chair] was repeated as before, when similar effects were soon excited.... [H]e entreated to be relieved, and repeated his former promise, I again complied, and he was taken out the swing in the most helpless state imaginable, was put to bed, where he soon feel asleep, and did not wake for six hours.... [H]is former mental peculiarities soon after returning, the [chair] was prepared, and the necessary steps taken for its employment, but rather than repeat the ride in the whirligig, as he termed it, he submitted entirely to my wishes.... I had the pleasure to see him gradually improve till he advanced to perfect reason [Cox, pp. 145–148].

It was the effects of this mechanical anodyne on body and mind that led Cox to speculate that the chair also could be used to provide some relief in hopeless cases of insanity. In those cases, however, he imagined that the fear caused by the chair had to be enhanced, by using it in the dark, "where, from unusual noises, smells, or other powerful agents acting on the senses, its efficacy might be amazingly increased" [Cox, p. 140].

Cox's text on the treatment of insanity, which contained considerable discussion of the chair and its therapeutic uses, was translated into German in 1811. It drew the attention of a number of German asylum physicians who either used the chair as described by Cox, or modified it for their own purposes.

The text also was studied by Joseph Guislain, chief physician at the asylums for the insane in Ghent, Belgium, and a significant force in his own right in the moral treatment movement [see **Moral Treatment**]. In that latter role, Guislain was an activist for the humane treatment of the insane, therefore he initially approached Cox's chair with some hesitance. Reasoning that the device might have a beneficial effect on the nervous system, he engaged in a series of trials, using thirteen of his patients as subjects. Guislain's careful observations provided a scientific rationale for the effect of the chair and other such devices that had been missing from the promotions and testimonials of its most enthusiastic users, and from the criticisms of its most ardent detractors. First, Guislain described the series of physiological effects the chair produced, beginning with disagreeable sensations in the forehead and epigastric region, followed by painfully labored respirations; squeamishness then set in, producing giddiness and vomiting. The voluntary muscles were then struck by an instantaneous palsy and the patient lost equilibrium, head dropping to chest, and all physical and mental sensation was lost. Second, Guislain disputed the claims that patients could tolerate the chair for several continuous minutes. Rather, he found considerable variation in the degree of tolerance: while young manic patients could bear it for several minutes, most patients could only tolerate two or three revolutions of the chair and there was no therapeutic advantage, he argued, in continuing beyond the point of tolerance. Guislain also observed that if the rare patient did tolerate the chair for five, eight or even fifteen minutes without violent vomiting or loss of consciousness, the chair had to be considered useless as a therapeutic in that particular case. Finally, Guislain called into question that the chair was equally effective in all types of insanity. Rather, he argued, its most effective use was demonstrated in cases of mania. In fact, he had been able to completely cure two of the thirteen patients upon whom these observations were made with the chair alone, both of them diagnosed with mania; halt the accession of manic symptoms in two, and repress the manic symptoms in three more. The chair had no appreciable therapeutic effect on the remaining patients who had been diagnosed with disorders other than mania.

## Gyrater, or Gyrator

A chair on which a patient was strapped and then spun at a rate of approximately one hundred rotations per minute, a force considerable enough to not only produce vomiting, purging and disorientation, but bleeding from the nose and eyes, and even unconsciousness.

The gyrater was designed by Benjamin Rush at the Pennsylvania Hospital and used for its ability to stimulate blood circulation. Rush had experimented with swings and seesaws to bring blood into the brains of melancholic patients, but found those were inadequate to the task. After reading Joseph Mason Cox's claim that he had cured melancholics with rotations in the chair he had designed, Rush endeavored to construct a device that would maximize the therapeutic effects of vertigo, nausea and increased pulse, all of which he took as evidence of the "centrifugal direction of the blood towards the brain" (Rush, p. 223).

Rush was dissatisfied with the gyrater, however, commenting that "it would be more perfect did it permit the head to be placed at a greater distance from the center of motion" (p. 223). Rush never redesigned the gyrater and seemed rather quickly to lose interest in it as a therapeutic. There was little evidence that it was used in other asylums.

## Hallaran's Circulating Swing

A wooden box in which the restrained patient sat; the box was spun via a windlass capable of producing one hundred complete rotations per minute. In the early nineteenth century, and inspired by the success of subduing the maniacal patient with Cox's chair, William Hallaran, medical superintendent of the County and City of Cork Lunatic Asylum in Ireland, designed the circulating swing as an enhanced "moral and medical" therapeutic for the cure of insanity (Hallaran, 1810, p. 59). He immediately claimed great success, stating that since he had started using it, he had "never been at a loss for a direct mode of establishing extreme authority over the most turbulent and unruly" (p. 60).

The circulating swing had several therapeutic advantages, according to Hallaran, in that it not only caused "a sufficiency of alarm to insure obedience" in the manic patient, but created "a natural interest in the affairs for life"

A replica of Hallaran's circulating swing, capable of spinning a patient 100 complete rotations per minute. Designed as an enhanced "moral and medical" therapeutic for the cure of insanity, Hallaran admitted that it also worked well as entertainment for bored asylum staff (courtesy of the St. Joseph Museums, Inc./Glore Psychiatric Museum, St. Joseph, Missouri).

in the melancholic patient (p. 64). It accomplished both of those outcomes by exciting the action of the bowels, stomach and bladder; producing a profound fatigue that eventually lapsed into a tranquil sleep; and causing such dread as to make the mere mention of it sufficient to bring about compliance and obedience. Hallaran found that these, and other, effects were enhanced by reversing the rotation of the circulating swing every six to eight minutes, and/or by occasionally, albeit abruptly, stopping its rotation altogether.

Unlike Cox's chair, in which a single patient was seated, the circulating swing could be easily modified to accommodate as many as four patients at a single time by dividing the box attached to the perpendicular shaft into separate compartments via the addition of partitions. Since the circulating swing had its strongest effects on the horizontal patient, the partitions could be removed so that the patient could lie down, rather than sit, in the wooden box. A few years after the construction of the circulating swing, and in recognition of the enhanced therapeutic effects of the horizontal position, Hallaran attached an open wooden platform to the perpendicular shaft; situated several feet above the box, this modification made it possible to simultaneously rotate both recumbent and sitting patients.

Despite the dread that the circulating swing caused for most patients, Hallaran encouraged its use for amusement, but only for the "idiot" patient who was thought incapable of experiencing either its negative physical or its positive psychological effects. He also thought it appropriate for the bored and tired attendant in need of occasional entertainment.

One of its most enthusiastic proponents, Paul Slade Knight, medical superintendent of the Lancaster County Lunatic Asylum in northwest England, provided the only account, brief and edited as it was, that can be found in the psychiatric literature, of a patient's experience with the circulating swing:

> Mary Sandiford, a very fine young woman, said to me on the 20th September 1823, "Putting me in the circular swing did me more good than any thing else; it threw all the sour stuff off my stomach." Shortly after this, she recovered, and was discharged well [Knight, pp. 61–62].

## Hallaran's Mat

A hammock suspended by two parallel ropes from the ceiling and supported at each end by cords hooked to the upright ropes. The mat was devised by William S. Hallaran, medical superintendent of the County and City of Cork Lunatic Asylum in Ireland in the early nineteenth century as another alternative to Cox's chair. The patient, who may or may not have been restrained, laid on the mat which was rocked back and forth in a gentle oscillatory motion by an attendant in a dark and quiet room. If the presence of the attendant was bothersome to the patient, a string was attached to the mat and passed through an aperture in the door to an adjoining room; from there, the attendant could continue rocking the mat by simply tugging on the string.

Hallaran touted the mat as particularly effective in subduing "furious maniacs" by rendering them utterly powerless. "They, by this contrivance, are completely enveloped, and kept sufficiently warm," he wrote, "and when the attendants will obey the injunction of silence, the disposition to a return of violence may again be restrained by the repetition of such gentle expedients" (Hallaran, 1818, p. 97).

The added feature of the mat was that it could be spun, rather than rocked, by twisting the parallel ropes to their full extent and then letting them unwind. The rotating movement produced the same nausea, dizziness, vomiting and bowel evacuations as the rotary chair or bed, and could be used in the absence of having either or both available.

Hallaran proudly declared that the mat, "never fails to overawe" (p. 98). It was used in many British asylums, and with some modifications in German asylums as well.

## Hollow Wheel, or Hayner's Wheel

An approximately eight by five foot empty wooden wheel which a patient entered through a small trapdoor. The interior of the wheel was padded and the patient was expected to walk or run forward or backward, thus rotating the wheel; a stationary patient was prodded into movement by an attendant who stood on the outside and moved the wheel by hand. As a rotary device, the hollow wheel was intended to:

> divert the patient from his aberrant course, to lead him back from the world of his dreams to the world of reality. It was to block the stream of erratic, fragmentary thoughts, direct his attention towards the attainment of a definite goal and to awaken and identify his self-consciousness [Kraepelin, p. 89].

Designed in the late nineteenth century by German physician Johann Reil, the hollow wheel was first constructed and used by Christian August Hayner, chief physician at the Colditz Asylum housed in an eleventh century castle in Saxony, Germany. Although Hayner used the hollow wheel with some therapeutic success, indeed for a time the device was so intimately associated with him that it was sometimes referred to as Hayner's Wheel, he later denounced it as cruel and unnecessary. Although it is not clear what caused this change in attitude, Hayner, who had trained under the tutelage of reformer Philippe Pinel at the Asylum de Bicêtre in Paris, was increasingly influenced by Enlightenment thought, and went on to become a leader in the German non-restraint movement.

The hollow wheel was never used widely in Germany or any other country's asylums, and soon was regarded a relic of a dark and shame-

A replica of the "squirrel cage" that was known as the hollow wheel, or Hayner's wheel, after its designer Christian August Hayner, chief physician at the Colditz Asylum in Germany. Hayner eventually denounced his own invention as cruel (courtesy of the St. Joseph Museums, Inc./Glore Psychiatric Museum, St. Joseph, Missouri).

ful past. In the late nineteenth century, Emil Kraepelin, the German physician who often is lauded as the founder of modern scientific psychiatry, acquired a hollow wheel for his psychiatric museum. A full-scale replica also can be seen at the Glore Psychiatric Museum in St. Joseph, Missouri.

## Horn's Rotary Bed, or Drehbett, or Whirling Bed

A canoe shaped bed turned by a crankshaft connected by ropes to a capstan. The patient was restrained face-up in the bed, with feet pointed towards the axis. The speed of rotation was regulated by several attendants who would tense a rope around a wheel near the ceiling. At its maximum speed of forty to sixty spins per minute, and with a rotation diameter of thirteen feet, it recently has been estimated that Horn's rotary bed was capable of producing a gravitational force (G-force) of four to five in the head region, resulting in shortness of breath, disorientation, nausea, fear and vertigo.

The rotary bed was designed by Ernst Horn at the Berlin Charité Hospital in Germany in the early nineteenth century after having read a translation of Joseph Mason Cox's text, *Practical Observations on Insanity* (1804), which cited Erasmus Darwin's design for a bed-shaped rotary device. Constructed by a local carpenter, the bed was first tried out by several Charité physicians, none of whom could tolerate it for more than two to three minutes. Although Horn speculated that insane patients were less sensitive to unpleasant encounters than refined physicians, his experience soon demonstrated that patients could endure the bed no longer or better than his colleagues had.

At the Charité the rotary bed was most often prescribed for the maniacal, demented or hysterical patient whose symptoms disturbed the order of the asylum and usurped the authoritarian control of the physician. Horn found that a single application of this therapeutic tended to produce fearful compliance, but that repeated applications tended to be counterproductive in that the patient apparently adapted to the experience.

## Horn's Rotary Chair, or Drehstuhl

A significantly modified version of Cox's chair designed by Ernst Horn at the Berlin Charité Hospital in Germany. The chair actually was a cylindrical wooden cage, approximately ten feet high, with a slatted front from its floor up to the waist of the sitting patient whose feet and arms were bound by leather straps to the slats. The chair was rotated at a speed of 125 rotations per minute by a single attendant via a lever that turned a wheel at the top of the cylindrical case.

A ninety second application of this device produced vertigo, nausea, vomiting and, like Cox's chair that had inspired its design, a fearful compliance. Horn prescribed the chair most often for those recalcitrant patients, quite regardless of diagnosis, whose compliance was necessary to maintain the order of the asylum.

## Nursery Yacht

A wooden cradle, shaped like a small boat, with seats at each end and in the middle, and mounted on rockers; three patients in synchronous movement were able to pitch the yacht back and forth. Several of these were placed in the airing court of Colney Hatch Lunatic Asylum in London, England, in the mid-nineteenth century and were used both for their calming effect and for out-of-doors entertainment.

## Rocking Chair

A chair set on curved supports so that the patient could rock back and forth. The hallways and porches of most American asylums in the mid-nineteenth century were lined with rocking chairs and because rocking was thought to be particularly therapeutic for demented patients, those asylums that had a large number of them were sometimes referred to as "rocking chair asylums."

## Rocking Horse

The figure of a horse, mounted on rockers, and large enough for five or six patients to ride. The rocking horses were suggested by John Conolly, medical superintendent of the Hanwell Lunatic Asylum in London, England, as an alternative to other rotational and oscillatory devices such as see-saws, swings and roundabouts which he feared could be used for "mischievous purposes" (Conolly, p. 54). The large rocking horses were placed on the airing courts of the asylum in the mid-nineteenth century and the gentle motion they provided both soothed and entertained patients, and had the added advantage of relieving the "irksomeness" of the daily duties of attendants (p. 54).

## Vibratory Chair, or Dancing Chair, or Jolting Chair, or Trembling Chair, or Trémoussoir, or Fauteuil Trépidant

A heavy armchair, fixed to a base, and jolted back and forth via an electrical or gas motor, or by compressed air. Invented to simulate a fast carriage ride over bumpy roads, the vibratory chair was designed by the influential French writer and political radical Charles-Irénée Castel de Saint-Pierre in the early eighteenth century. He, in turn, most likely was influenced by the earlier writings of Pierre

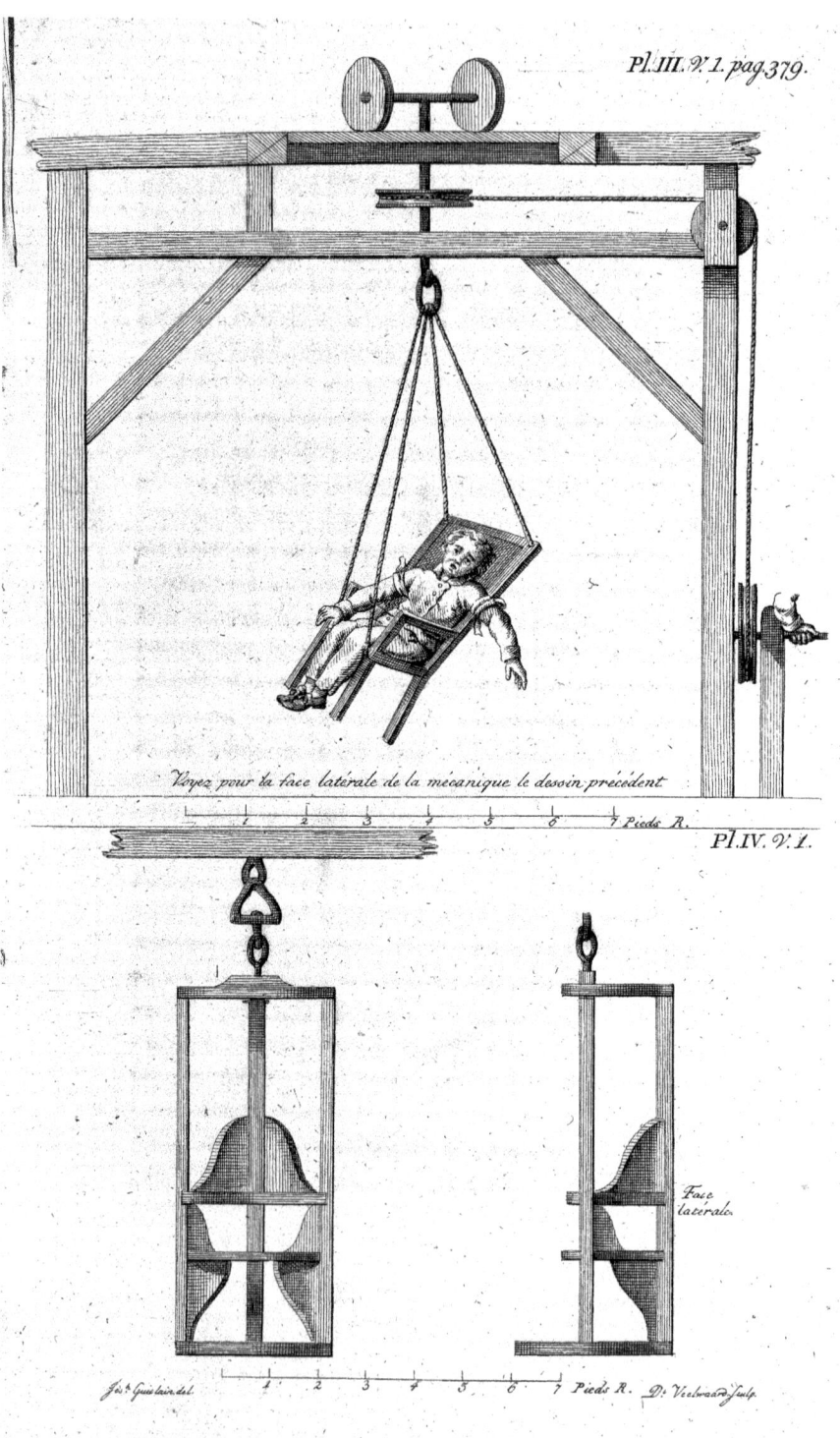

Two rotary devices used at the Berlin Charité Hospital in Germany. The top figure is of the rotary chair designed by Ernst Horn. It spun at a speed of 125 rotations per minute, producing nausea, vertigo and vomiting. The bottom figure is a modification of Horn's chair that spun the patient in a tight spiral, producing the same effects (courtesy of the Wellcome Library, London).

Chirac, physician to King Louis XV, who had asserted that any plethora of blood that collected in the body, sluggishness of the digestive system and of the bowels, or shallow respirations, all of which in the received medical wisdom of his era were thought to cause a variety of physical and mental illnesses, could be cured by several days of a rapid carriage ride over rough roads.

Aggressively marketed, the vibratory chair was advertised for the homes of the rich and sedentary and, because of its exorbitant cost, was not at first found outside of them or the offices of physicians. But as word spread, vibratory chairs were placed in apothecaries, among other places, and any member of the public could purchase an hour in it for three francs. A few also found their way into asylums in the early nineteenth century and it was at the Glasgow Lunatic Asylum in Scotland that the English physician George Mann Burrows, gave an account of his experience of trying one out:

> I placed myself for a few minutes in a vibratory chair of great strength and power, in which when a patient is seated, he experiences a far more violent jolting than from the roughest-trotting horse. Such tremendous motion being given to all the viscera, I should think, would conduce most effectually to correct habitual costiveness; and if persevered in as a punishment, it must also soon break the resolution of constrained constipation [Burrows, p. 638].

The vibratory chair was particularly popular in spas, sanitaria and homeopathic institutes around the world. It was advertised in the United States by Leach and Greene as an "unrivalled exercising apparatus," suited not just for the "corpulent," but the "insane" as well (Hoolihan, p. 450). John Harvey Kellogg, founder and director of the Battle Creek Sanitarium in Michigan, was an enthusiastic promoter who used the chair to stimulate intestinal peristalsis, tone the muscles, and increase the respirations of his high-society patrons. The clientele of establishments like his, however, tended to be more interested in improving or maintaining health, rather than in curing disorders or disease, so by the late nineteenth century the vibrating chair had to be specifically repurposed for medical and, to a lesser extent, psychiatric purposes.

That task was accomplished by the neurologist Jean-Martin Charcot, chief physician at the Salpêtrière Asylum in Paris. Drawing on a small corpus of medical literature on the relief of pain, stiffness and muscle contracture by vibratory devices that included a clock work percuteur that percussed a particular area of the body with an ivory-headed hammer, an electric percuteur to which either a hammer or brush could be attached, and a large diapason (tuning fork) mounted on a resounding box, Charcot oversaw the construction of a vibratory chair for the specific purpose of relieving the symptoms of *paralysis agitans* (Parkinson disease).

While he reported success with this therapeutic application of the vibratory chair, his assistant, Gilles de la Tourette experimented with its use in treating neurasthenic patients at the asylum. This nervous disorder was characterized by anxiety, depression and loss of memory; the relief of these symptoms by the vibratory chair was mixed and quite short-lived.

Outside of France, one or another model of the vibratory chair was used in asylums in Italy, Germany, England and Scotland for a variety of mental, physical and punitive purposes, and on a variety of patients. The therapeutic efficacy of the vibrating chair, however, was never firmly established and some asylum physicians, such as Enrico Morselli at the Royal Mental Hospital in Turin, Italy, who had been impressed with its potential, dismissed whatever brief and transitory positive effects it reportedly had on suggestion alone.

## *Vibratory Helmet, or* Le Casque Vibrant

A cylindrical nickel-plated cap that was fitted over the top of the head, with a small electric motor mounted on top. The revolving armature of the motor had small wheels that rapidly rotated, producing 2000 to 4000 revolutions, that is, vibrations, per minute to the entire circumference of the cranium, while also emitting a soothing purring sound. The helmet was designed by Gilles de la Tourette in the late nineteenth century at the Salpêtrière Asylum in Paris, France, where experiments with vibration therapy to treat a range of neurological disorders, from *paralysis agitans* (Parkinson's disease) to hysteria, were being conducted.

The helmet was not designed to treat a specific neurological disorder, but certain physical symptoms shared by various disorders, such as headache, numbness in the extremities, muscle contractures and neuralgia. Upon experimentation, however, it was discovered that its more psychological effect as a calmative, sedative and hypnotic, were nicely suited for the treatment of the melancholic, neurasthenic, hysterical or even psychotic patient who generally wore the helmet from five to fifteen minutes at a time, and from three to six times per week.

This "massage of the brain" was not used widely outside of the Salpêtrière Asylum, nor for long. Physicians were divided in their opinion of it; some speculated that its reported efficacy was due to its vibratory effects on the nerve cells; others that it was due to nothing more than suggestion.

## *Von Hirsch's Hammock, or Von Hirsch's Ship-Bed*

A sling of heavy cloth suspended from the ceiling in which the recumbent patient was rocked back and forth. The hammock was designed much in the fashion of Hallaran's mat, but with the unusual feature of cold water poured on the head through a trapdoor in the ceiling during the rocking. This combination of oscillatory movement and hydrotherapy [see **Hydrotherapy**] was described by its designer, C.F. Von Hirsch, at the asylum in Bayreuth, Germany, as particularly soothing and very effective in reducing mania, in particular, and inducing sleep in general.

# Salutary Fear

*The creation of fear by blows to the body, threats of physical injury or death, extreme physical discomfort, or humiliation for therapeutic purposes.*

The idea that the insane are like wild beasts, insensitive to pain and imbued with Herculean strength may be almost as old as history, itself. "Madmen, what ever they bear or suffer, are not hurt," the eminent late seventeenth century physician and Oxford scholar Thomas Willis declared, "but they bear cold, heat, watching, fasting, strokes, and wounds, without any sensible hurt" (Willis, p. 205). Although an expert on insanity, Willis had never worked in an asylum. Physicians who read and studied his canonical works, however, did—and they had little reason, at first, to question his proclamations. Many, but certainly not all, patients of the first asylums constructed in that era often had spent years, even decades, under the unreliable care of family and community. There is no doubt that some were treated with kindness and compassion; there is no doubt that others were not. Sometimes chained or contained in strong rooms, sometimes confined in lunatic cages in public squares, sometimes beaten and starved, many of the first asylum patients already had lived lives of torment and humiliation that had deprived them of the most rudimentary social acumen. Once in the asylum, their domestication required, first and foremost, mastery over them. Salutary fear, then, was considered a reliable therapeutic, as Benjamin Rush, the "Father of American Psychiatry," explained:

> I know it has been said in favour of madness being an ideal disease, or being seated primarily in the mind, that sudden impressions from

fear, terror, and even ridicule have sometimes cured it. This is true, but they produce their effects only by the healthy action they induce in the brain [Rush, p.15].

Over subsequent eras, asylums not only increased in number but were transformed into total institutions, that is, isolated and enclosed social systems that confined patients whose personal, demographic and diagnostic characteristics took back seat to the fact that they were considered "insane." Bureaucratically complex, with a hierarchical distribution of power, the modern asylum was unlike the old—except that, on occasion, it allowed, overlooked, hid and rationalized the use of salutary fear as a therapeutic.

Modern asylums may have been out of sight, but they were not out of mind. Details of scandals, deaths and maltreatment, government and grand jury investigations, criminal trials and civil law suits were commonly reported in the press. And while some of these sparked public outrage and promises of reform, most did not. The victims, after all, were insane. Even if they were considered credible in their complaints, they retained the vestiges of the historical idea that insanity was not only tantamount to unreason and irrationality, but to violence and impulse. Not matter how architecturally handsome the asylum, how well educated its physicians and staff, how theoretically sophisticated or technologically savvy its therapeutics, in the end and for the sake of themselves and others, insane patients had to be managed, controlled, even mastered within the confines of asylums.

## References

Andrews, J. (1997). *The history of Bethlem*. London: Routledge.
Bakewell, T. (1809). *The domestic guide in cases of insanity*. Newcastle, UK: C. Chester.
Battie, W. (1758). *A treatise on madness*. London: J. Whiston & B. White.
Bucknill, J.C., and Tuke, D.H. (1879). *A manual of psychological medicine, containing the lunacy laws*. London: J. & A. Churchill.
Burrows, G.M. (1828). *Commentaries on the causes, forms, symptoms, and treatment, moral and medical, of insanity*. London: Thomas and George Underwood.
Conolly, J. (1850). *Familiar views of lunacy and lunatic life*. London: John W. Parker.
Cullen, W. (1746). *First lines of the practice of physic*. Edinburgh: Bell & Bradfute, and William Creech.
"Ducking: How it has been practiced at the Columbus Insane Asylum" (1878, Nov. 15). *Cincinnati Daily Gazette*, p. 2.
Esquirol, J.E.D. (1838). *Mental maladies: A treatise on insanity*. Trans. E.K. Hunt. Philadelphia: Lea and Blanchard. 1845.
Farrar, C.B. (1909). Some origins in psychiatry. *American Journal of Insanity, 66*, 277–294.
"Flagellation in hysteria" (1892). *Lancet, 1*, 1162–1163.
Gaar, S.L. (1883). *Report of investigation, Lakeland, KY, Central Kentucky Lunatic Asylum*. Louisville, KY: The Gilbert & Mallory Publishing Co.
Galt, J.M. (1846). *The treatment of insanity*. New York: Harper & Brothers.
Gerard, D.L. (1997). Chiarugi and Pinel considered. *Journal of the History of the Behavioral Sciences, 33*, 381–403.
Gilman, S. (1982). *Seeing the insane*. New York: Wiley.
Goffman, E. (1961). *Asylums: Essays on the social situation of mental patients and other inmates*. New York: Anchor Books.
Guislain, J. (1826). *Traité sur l'aliénation mentale et sur les hospices des aliénés*. Amsterdam: J. Van Der Hay et Fils, & H. Gartman.
Hamre, B. (2010). Disciplinary power and the role of the subject at a nineteenth-century Danish asylum. *PhaenEx, 5*, 1–27.
Haskell, E. (1869). *The trial of Ebenezer Haskell*. Philadelphia: Author.
House Special Committee (1907). *Report of the special committee on investigation of government hospital for the insane*. Washington, D.C.: Government Printing Office.
Hunter, R., and Macalpine, I. (1963). *Three hundred years of psychiatry, 1535–1860*. London: Oxford University Press.
Hurd, H.M. (1883). Ducking in asylums—A refutation. *American Journal of Insanity, 39*, 506.
Hurd, H.M., Drewry, W.F., Dewey, R., Pilgrim, C.W., Blumer, G.A., and Burgess, T.J.W. (1917). *The institutional care of the insane in the United States and Canada*, Vol. 4. Baltimore, MD: Johns Hopkins University Press.
Kiernan, J.G. (1884). Report of the investigation of the Central Kentucky Lunatic Asylum. *Journal of Nervous and Mental Disease, 11*, 99–100.
Kraepelin, E. (1962). *One hundred years of psychiatry*. Trans. Wade Baskin. New York: Citadel Press.
Millingen, J.G. (1839). *Curiosities of medical experience*. London: Richard Bentley.
New York State Legislature (1877). *Documents of the Senate of the state of New York*. Albany, NY: Jerome Parmenter.
Pinel, P. (1806). *A treatise on insanity*. Sheffield, UK: W. Todd.
Pratt, A. (1860). *Seven months in a lunatic asylum, and

*what I saw there.* Kingston, Jamaica: George Henderson Savage & Co.

Qvarsell, R. (1985). Locked-up or put to bed: Psychiatry and the treatment of the mentally ill in Sweden, 1800–1920. In W.F. Bynum, R. Porter, & M. Shepherd (eds.), *The anatomy of madness,* Vol. 2, pp. 86–97. London: Tavistock.

"Recent discoveries in the treatment of the insane" (1884). *Medical Times and Gazette, 1,* 125–126.

Reil, J.C. (1803/2010). *Rhapsodieen Uber Die Anwendung Der Psychischen Curmethode Auf Geisteszerruttungen* [*Rhapsodies on the Use of Psychological Therapies for the Mentally Disturbed*]. Whitefish, MT: Kessinger Publishing.

Rush, B. (1830). *Medical inquiries and observations upon the diseases of the mind.* 4th ed. Philadelphia: John Grigg.

Shaw, G.B. (1977). Shaw on "Flagellomania": A lecture and a letter. *The Shaw Review, 20,* 89–93.

Tuke, S. (1813). *Description of the Retreat.* York, UK: W. Alexander.

"Whipping therapy cures depression and suicide cries" (2005, March 26). Retrieved at http://english.pravda.ru/health/26-03-2005/7950-whipping-0.

Wilbur, H.B. (1877). *Report on the management of the insane in Great Britain.* Albany, NY: Weed, Parsons, and Company.

Willis, T. (1684). *Practice of physick.* London: Dring, Harper, and Leigh.

## *Bath of Surprise, or Bain de Surprise, or Plunge Bath, or Dumping*

The plunging of an unsuspecting and often blindfolded patient through a trapdoor and into a vat of icy cold water. This method of producing shock *usque ad deliquum,* or to the brink of death, was introduced by Flemish physician and chemist Jean Baptiste vanHelmont, who had observed that at times an accidental near-drowning could restore the reason of an insane person by putting a stop to the "too violent and exorbitant operation of the fiery life" (Hunter & Macalpine, p. 256). His seventeenth century writings, as well as those of his son, Franciscus Mercurius vanHelmont, a physician and mystic philosopher, later influenced asylum physicians to recreate the near-drowning experience in more controlled circumstances.

The bath of surprise was used in asylums throughout Europe into the early nineteenth century when it was somewhat reluctantly relinquished as dangerous and even barbaric. Even the noted French asylum reformer Philippe Pinel as late as 1806 praised it for its ability to interrupt "a chain of delirious ideas" (Pinel, p. 265), but conceded that it should be used only as a last resort. His student, Jean-Étienne Esquirol, a noted reformer in his own right, later sardonically recommended that rather than subjecting a patient to the bath of surprise, asylum physicians should be advised "to precipitate the patient from the third story, because we have known some insane persons cured by falling on the head" (Esquirol, p. 84).

## *Bathing, or Towel Bath*

The pouring of water on the face of a gagged and bound patient, or, alternatively, the wrapping of a wet towel over the face of a bound patient. Bathing was used in asylums across the United States. In an 1883 investigation into alleged abuses at the Central Kentucky Lunatic Asylum in Lakeland, Kentucky, testimony from Superintendent Robert Gale affirmed that the purpose of bathing or the towel bath was to achieve the seemingly contradictory goals of therapy and punishment:

> *Gale:* The towel bath is nothing more than confining the hands of the patient, and the feet, to keep them from kicking or striking the patients or patients assisting. A towel is dipped in water and laid over the face. It produces a sense of suffocation, and the patient soon gives up and becomes tractable. The remedy is used in every institution in the United States.
> *Q.:* Is there anything cruel in it?
> *Gale:* Not a thing in the world [Gaar, p. 13].

After taking testimony from physicians, staff and patients, the investigating committee concluded that while bathing or the towel bath sometimes was used more for punishment than therapy by untrained attendants and in direct violation of printed rules of conduct, Gale and his chief physicians could not be faulted for ordering it be administered as a

The bath of surprise as it must have looked in the eighteenth and nineteenth centuries. Unsuspecting patients, often blindfolded, plummeted through a trap door and into a vat of cold water (courtesy of the St. Joseph Museums, Inc./Glore Psychiatric Museum, St. Joseph, Missouri).

treatment. The committee concluded in a letter to the Governor:

> After a careful consideration of the whole matter, we have reached the conclusion that there is no serious cause of complaint ... when proper allowances are made for the surroundings.... In regard to the kind or mode of restraint or punishment to be used with such unfortunates, we do not profess to be competent judges, and must content ourselves with leaving this vexed question to the discussion of medical men [Gaar, pp. 181–182].

A scathingly sarcastic editorial published in the British journal, *The Medical Times and Gazette,* reacted to the exoneration of the superintendent and medical staff of the Central Kentucky Lunatic Asylum for ordering the use of the bathing:

> [T]he Commissioners have certainly done a service to the community by showing, on the authority of this humane and benevolent superintendent, what practices are not cruel—do not even approach cruelty—and are not only legitimate, but absolutely necessary for the treatment of the insane.... The Central Kentucky Asylum is entitled to the entire and unquestioned credit of introducing a method of treating lunatics by having them half-suffocated.... The treatment is as economical as it is ingenious, dispensing in the first place with the cost of attendants, and doubtless, if it is carried out as thoroughly and continued long enough, with the cost of keeping patients also ["Recent Discoveries," pp. 125–126].

## *Beating*

Hitting or striking with the closed fist, or with a leather or rubber truncheon. The beating of the insane as discipline or punishment has a history as long as that of the asylum, and has been the subject of many investigations, inquiries and scandals over the centuries. The era of non-restraint [see **Mechanical Restraint**] challenged asylum physicians and attendants to interact with their patients in more psychological, as opposed to physical, ways, yet the need to keep order in what invariably were loud and chaotic institutions was no less pressing. In asylum iconography, the attendant to whom that responsibility fell, is not often represented. One notable exception is in Wilhelm von Kaulbach's 1835 painting, "The Mad House." While the primary images in the painting are those of unrestrained patients—the raving madman, the demented old woman, the hapless melancholic, among them—in the background stands an attendant whose duty it is to keep the order. In his left pocket is a truncheon, Kaulbach's reminder that even in the era of non-restraint, order is therapeutic in its own right, and has to be maintained.

The beating of the insane as treatment, however, both predated the asylum and provided the justification for its practice in the asylum. As early as the second century C.E. the Roman physician and encyclopedist Aulus Cornelius Celsus, for example, encouraged the therapeutic beating of the insane. William Cullen, the preeminent Scottish medical educator, asserted that blows often were necessary to maintain "a very constant impression of fear, and therefore to inspire [the insane] with the awe and dread of some particular persons" (Cullen, p. 163). And beatings were both prescribed and tolerated by the "psychic school" of European asylum physicians who found the cause of insanity in moral failings that had to be disciplined to be treated.

One of the devotees of that school was Johan Henrik Seidelin, the chief surgeon of the newly established Sankt Hans Hospital in Copenhagen, Denmark. Complaints against him for beating patients started being heard within weeks of his arrival in 1816. He successfully defended himself against this early wave of complaints by appealing to the therapeutic value of the fear the beatings engendered:

I have considered it my duty to tame evil by diverse means in keeping with its diverse nature, so far as I am able...[In regards to patients] in whom bad upbringing above all has gradually unfolded as an evil that often degenerates into rage, I believe, in the main, that the corporal punishment that the parents neglected at the time would prove the most powerful means for making them at least tolerable among their unhappy compatriots, and secure them from perfidious attacks. I have used this means on some five to six demented patients and have not yet seen any unfortunate effects therefrom; they are infused with fear, which is the only thing that can keep them from their harmful intent [Hamre, p. 9].

## *Chinese Temple*

An elaborately constructed cage, approximately ten feet high and situated over an arched bridge that spanned a small, deep pond. The interior of the temple contained a moveable lightweight iron enclosure into which the patient was placed; by means of pulleys and ropes, the enclosure descended rapidly on rails and plunged the patient into the water below.

This ornate version of the bath of surprise was designed by Joseph Guislain, a Belgian physician, as part of an 1821 competition sponsored by the Provincial Board of Medicinal Research and Supervision to design better methods of treating the insane. Guislain's competition entry, later published as *Traité sur l'Aliénation mentale et les Hospices des Aliénés*, led to his appointment as senior physician at the Manweeshuys and the Vrouwenweeshuys asylums in Ghent, Belgium. Although Guislain greatly improved the conditions at these asylums, he did not perceive the use of the temple as antithetical to his goal of moral treatment [see **Moral Treatment**]. Rather, he argued, the temple "considerably affects the patient, and its utility is based upon the fear which it inspires of impending suffocation [drowning]... The apparatus which I give appears to me to be better qualified to fulfill our purpose. To render ourselves master of the patient, and to

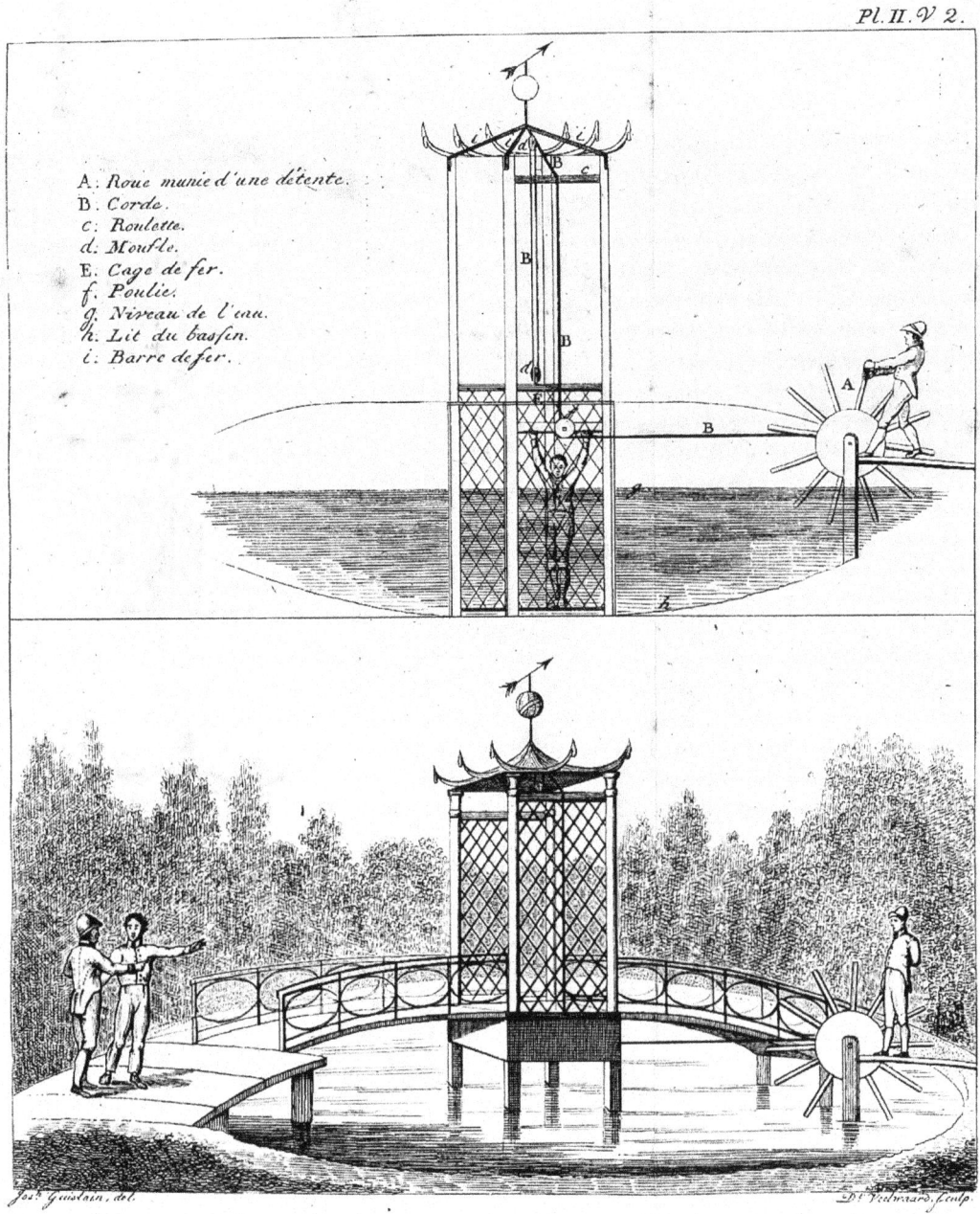

The Chinese Temple, an elaborate version of the bath of surprise that was designed by Joseph Guislain, senior physician of the asylums in Ghent, Belgium, who reasoned that the fear of drowning had salutary effects on patients (courtesy of the Wellcome Library, London).

shun suffocation [drowning] are the two measures which we must take" (Guislain, p. 166).

## *Ducking, or Tanking, or Cold Ducking*

A modification of the bath of surprise in which the patient's head repeatedly was pushed and held under water; if rendered unconscious, the patient was revived and the procedure was repeated. The shock and fear the treatment produced was thought not only to "suffocate mad ideas" (Hunter & Macalpine, p. 254), and "gather up the senses" (Conolly, p. 96), but punish recalcitrant behavior and prompt obedience.

Ducking had been recommended by seventeenth century physicians such as Jean Baptiste vanHelmont, Herman Boerhaave and Thomas Willis, the latter of whom once treated a "furious maid" by having her stripped, bound, and ducked into the river. The American physician Benjamin Rush, who believed that terror had therapeutic effects, ducked insane patients with some enthusiasm during his tenure from 1783 to 1813 at the Pennsylvania Hospital, and may have coined the term "ducking" to refer to the procedure.

Feared by patients and often abused by staff, ducking was the subject of a number of high profile scandals that not only tarnished the reputations of powerful asylum medical superintendents, but called into question the state of knowledge about insanity. One of those scandals occurred at the Kingston Lunatic Asylum in Jamaica where a self-published pamphlet distributed by a former patient named Anne Pratt, precipitated a major inquiry that spread to the British empire. Pratt, a "poor mulatto woman," as she described herself, had defied convention by cohabitating with a Jew who was the father of her two children. Although she believed herself to be sane upon admission to the asylum, she was diagnosed with mania alternating with melancholia and was ducked, or tanked, as it was referred to in Jamaica, several times during her seven month institutionalization. In her pamphlet, she described the experience:

> I was... seized by Antoinette, Julian Burke, assisted by lunatics, Rosa Lewis, Eliza Scott, and one called Mary. I was stripped; my arms held behind me, my legs extended and forcibly separated from each other I was plunged into the tank, and kept under the water till all resistance, on my part, ceased; their grasp was then relaxed; I rose to the surface and breathed as if it were my last. Scarcely, however, had I drawn my breath when I was again subjected to the same horrible treatment, with the addition of having my head hurt against the sides of the tank, and my poor body beaten and confused with blows, till the fear of murder prompted them to desist [Pratt, p. 9].

Pratt complained to the chief medical officer who made light of her grievance, and was tanked again by matron Judith Ryan in retaliation. It was a local physician, Lewis Quier Bowerbank, long a critic of the asylum, its staff and their practices, who learned of her complaint and sent her pamphlet to the British Lunacy Commissioners who launched an investigation. The Commissioners' five-volume report was filed in 1861; it specifically condemned the practice of tanking, and generally criticized the asylum for poor sanitation, overcrowding, understaffing and ineffective daily management. The Colonial government brought action against those named in Pratt's complaint and, as a result, the asylum's chief medical officer and his assistant were dismissed, as was matron Ryan and two of her nurses. As a note of interest, tanking appears to have been introduced in the Kingston Lunatic Asylum by matron Ryan and her husband, who had been dismissed as superintendent of the male section of the asylum years before for similar misconduct.

While the scandal resulted in legislation that regulated all colonial asylums, and in a new asylum building in Kingston, it also called into question the civilizing mission of British imperial rule. Moral treatment [see **Moral Treatment**] that was proving itself to be the most humane and effective method of treating the insane, and to which the British proudly laid claim as their own creation, was rarely used in colonial asylums, where the indigenous insane were still being subjected to abuse and neglect.

Ducking was at the heart of another scandal, this one at the Central State Asylum in Columbus, Ohio, in 1878. An investigation there into patient abuse found that a newly hired matron, Anna Brown, who had had extensive experience in Canadian asylums, had surreptitiously trained her nurses into the practice of ducking the chronically insane women of their ward, and then secured their silence through a system of favors and rewards. The pact of the "Ducking Society," as the nurses referred to themselves, was broken when a nurse who had been discharged by Brown exposed the practice. Although there was evidence that asylum administrators endeavored to quietly handle the situation and, that once it was made public, refused to name the nurses in order to protect their reputations, the ducking scandal was fodder for the national news.

The Ohio scandal certainly prompted medical superintendents to more closely scrutinize the overt and covert therapeutic practices in their own asylums. Thus their reaction to the assertion by one of their own that not only was ducking being used in virtually every asylum in the country, but that asylum superintendents had agreed that it was an effective remedy, was one of outrage. That assertion was made during an 1883 investigation of patient abuse at the Central Kentucky Lunatic Asylum by superintendent Robert Gale in his defense under questioning of the practice of ducking:

> Q.: You say that in ducking, the real object was to purge the patient's system, and that it was given as a dose of medicine?
>
> *Gale:* I say that was part of the treatment, and sometimes it was resorted to as a punishment for the refractory.
>
> Q.: How is this treatment regarded in other institutions?
>
> *Gale*: That question has been discussed between medical superintendents publicly and privately. I cannot give any reference to any publications at this time, but it has been frequently discussed at the meetings of the superintendents.
>
> Q.: Have you attended these meetings?
>
> *Gale:* Yes; I have attended them ever since I have been in charge of the institution, and I have *yet to meet* the *first* man who disagreed with me in my ideas on that subject [Kiernan, p. 99].

In fact, superintendents greatly disagreed. Writing on behalf of the Medical Superintendents of American Institutions for the Insane, Henry Hurd, superintendent of the Eastern Michigan Asylum, stated that Gale's assertions "do not represent the views or the practices" of the organization. I have yet to meet the first man," he continued, "who believes that refractory patients should be punished at all—much less by ... ducking—nor can I allow such a stigma to rest upon the good name of American asylum management" (Hurd, p. 506).

## *Flogging, or Flagellation*

Thrashing the body with a rod, cane or switch. The moral and indeed therapeutic use of the rod reaches back through history, and its acceptance as a form of therapeutic discipline, whether for the miscreant, the penitent, the sick, the cowardly soldier, the wayward school child, the lazy worker or the slave, is well documented. The distinguished playwright, George Bernard Shaw, in fact, once castigated late nineteenth century British society for its "flagellomania," that is, its lingering belief in the utility of flogging.

Flogging also was used in early asylums, and for the same moral and tutelary purposes. Although he dismissed it as a "degrading remedy," Benjamin Rush thought the bodily pain inflicted by the rod was, perhaps, the only remedy for the chronic lying he observed in his morally deranged patients at the Pennsylvania Hospital (Rush, p. 265). John Gideon Millingen, resident physician at the County of Middlesex Pauper Lunatic Asylum in Hanwell, England, who was opposed to flogging, nonetheless invested it with a medical rationale that competed with the moral and tutelary: flogging, he argued, reanimated the torpid circulation of the capillary and cutaneous blood vessels, increased muscular energy, and promoted absorption and secretion, although, he hastened to add, because of the sympathy between the nerves in the lower spine and other organs, it also had the capacity to increase erotic pleasure, even in the insane.

Although the practice of flogging disappeared from most asylums by the early nineteenth century, it persisted in many German asylums for decades longer. As late as 1845, the physicians at the Stralsund Asylum in Germany flogged "dirty" patients, that is, those who urinated and defecated on themselves, arguing that a few lashes of the birch rod "had a favorable influence on the sphincter muscles of the bladder and consequently of the anus" (Kraepelin, p. 145).

## Mental Cure Technique, or Psychic Cure

Using the sensory influence of fear to cure the sick soul. The mental cure technique was developed by Johan Henrik Seidelin, chief surgeon at the Sankt Hans Hospital in Copenhagen, Denmark in the early nineteenth century. Greatly influenced by the German physician Johann Christian August Heinroth and his "psychic school" of psychiatry that saw insanity as a moral failing that had to be disciplined, Seidelin made liberal use of fear in his treatment of patients. His treatment regime included beatings, the withdrawal of food, prolonged restraint and ridicule, all aimed at extinguishing the propensity for evil that had caused the insanity.

One of the Sankt Hans Hospital patients, Wilhelm Frydendahl, filed a complaint against Seidelin for his treatment of another patient, a simple-minded grocer by the name of Kofoed. The complaint exposed the mental cure technique to a country that had only just separated out the insane from the poor, the disabled and the physically ill, and placed them in a purpose-built asylum where it was expected that they would be the recipients of enlightened treatment. In his complaint, Frydendahl gave a detailed account of Seidelin's mental cure technique in the treatment of the grocer:

> One day, he ordered him to play chess and, when the foolish man made a wrong move, he seized him by the locks and dealt him light blows on the side of the head with his hand, while uttering these words, "Did he see that he moved like a stupid fool?" And when he lost the game, exclaimed, "Does he now grasp that he is a deluded cow?" Following this, he dealt him severe blows beneath the ears when the feeble-minded man contradicted him. He further assured him that he would invariably win the game, but when Kofoed would not take his paws from his ears, as Seidelin constantly shouted, he ordered the ward orderly to fetch the rod. This person thereupon dealt him blows to the back. Not satisfied with this, however, the Chief Surgeon himself in a fit of ill-temper, took hold of the rod, beat the unfortunate man on the back, thighs, and wherever he could reach, screaming continuously that he should shut up and stand still, until he had backed Kofoed against the wall and ordered him not to move a limb or twitch a muscle. Thereupon he took a step or two back to see whether the man was standing as he wanted, but when he saw that he was in convulsions, he rushed toward him and beat him anew [Hamre, p. 11].

The Chancellery, to whom the complaint was filed, completed a thorough investigation, taking testimony from asylum physicians as well as the chaplain. All confirmed Frydendahl's account. It also took testimony from Seidelin, whose rendition of the event in question illustrated that therapeutics and punishment were inextricably entwined in many early asylums. Seidelin recollected this about the event in question:

> About the game of chess, of which [Kofoed] boasted a perfect understanding, I found that he hardly knew of the moves of a single piece.

Therefore, after he lost the game, and I had called his attention to this fact in a way that I thought would best affect his lethargy, and he nevertheless showed himself ill-tempered towards me, I determined it a suitable moment to subdue these outbursts in him, which were closely connected to his disease and failing whose suppression he would never be restored. This was the true reason from meting out corporal punishment to him [Hamre, p. 11].

Persuaded by his argument that the mental cure technique was both therapeutic and punitive, and that the two aims were neither incommensurate nor contradictory, the Chancellery defended the technique as accepted in the current field of asylum medicine, but castigated Seidelin for administering the blows, flogging and ridicule without the appropriate sober-mindedness expected of a physician. He was dismissed from his post in 1831.

## *Nausea Treatment*

The induction of stomach distress with the urge to vomit. The sensation of nausea, usually induced by the administration of the poisonous efflorescent crystalline salt known as tartar emetic, was thought to stimulate the nerves of the stomach, creating a sympathetic reaction in the brain. Because it also diminished the power of the heart and retarded circulation, nausea was considered an ideal therapeutic, even curative, for the treatment of mania.

George Mann Burrows, proprietor and physician at a private asylum in the Chelsea area of London, England, described the curative effects of nausea treatment in the following manner:

> To the sensation [nausea] creates, the whole attention of a maniac is often directed. In this respect it acts like anything that excites local pain. While nausea lasts, hallucinations of long adherence will be suspended, and sometimes be perfectly removed, or perhaps exchanged for others; and the most furious will become tranquil and obedient [Burrows, p. 642].

German asylum physicians tended to disagree with Burrow's additional observation that nausea treatment was contraindicated for the melancholic patient whose hallucinations and delusions often were persecutory in nature. Such a patient, Burrows had argued, was likely to attribute the nausea to a deliberate act of poisoning perpetrated by the physician and, as a result, refuse to cooperate in future therapeutic interactions. Peter J. Schneider, an influential professor of medicine and expert on insanity, scoffed at the idea, and expounded on the psychologically transformative sensation of nausea. He stated that whether the patient is manic or melancholic,

> we can take for granted that the subjective personality is figuratively destroyed and that the psyche, freed from its physical husk and wafted to a higher plain, no longer recognizes its own personality. But nausea... introduces into the material organism a new sickness which is communicated to the whole sensorium directly through the plexus of nerves in the stomach and through the whole network of nerves in the abdominal region. But since the psyche always maintains certain ties with its material substratum, it is compelled to descend from its ethereal perch and to re-enter its husk and examine the changes that might have occurred in its absence. This act of reflecting is the *ancora sacra* of the distinct personality that makes its reappearance; the longer nausea persists, the more attentive the psyche becomes to the strange new process; it widens the gap between the psyche and its transcendental perch and brings into clearer focus the consciousness of the returning personality; sustained, it prevents the mental patient from becoming immersed in his own thoughts [Kraepelin, pp. 58–59].

Nausea treatment was used in many European asylums during the early nineteenth century, and although tartar emetic was the preferred agent of induction, it was not unusual for less pharmaceutical, but certainly more creative, methods to be used. William Battie, physician to St. Luke's Hospital for Lunatics in London, England, induced nausea by exposing the patient to the "oily and penetrating steams arising from skins and other soft parts of animals newly slain" (Battie, p. 75). At the Berlin Charité Hospital, nausea was induced in the unresponsive patient by a stinking rag tied tightly around the face, while at the Spring Vale Asylum in England, Thomas Bakewell paced the patient in a boat that was briskly agitated by attendants. And, of course, in many asylums the swings, rotary chairs, whirling beds and wheels [see **Rotation, Oscillation and Vibration**] that were all the rage for a brief time, nicely and efficiently induced stomach distress and the urge to vomit.

## Non-Injurious Torture

A term used by the eminent German physician Johann Christian Reil to indicate a variety of unpleasant and even painful therapeutics directed at the body of the patient. Displeasure, he argued in his 1803 text, *Rhapsodies on the Use of Psychological Therapies for the Mentally Disturbed*, not only was a cause of insanity, but a cure of it. Creating physical disgust, fear and/or anger, then, would make possible what Reil referred to as a "psychic cure."

The methods of non-injurious torture Reil discussed in his text ranged from tickling, to flogging with stinging nettles; and from dripping hot molten wax on the patient's palms, to burning the neck with a red hot iron. Although it is not certain how many of these and other specific methods of non-injurious torture actually were translated into asylum practice, there is evidence of Reil's regional influence. At the Marsberg Asylum in northern Germany red hot irons were brandished at patients; the mere sight of them reportedly had a more pronounced effect than their actual use.

## Paddling

Striking the patient's body with an oval piece of heavy sole leather riveted to a wooden handle. In some cases, the patient's body was first covered with a sheet that had been soaked in salt water; this served the dual purpose of preventing skin lacerations and of irritating those lacerations that did result from the beating. Paddling, which occurred routinely in American prisons in the nineteenth century was not at all a common practice in asylums, with the exception of asylums for insane prisoners or, less often, in those asylums that had prison wards. One of the former was the New York State Asylum for Insane Criminals in Auburn. Testimony given by an attendant in an 1877 State Senate investigation of prison conditions revealed that, just as it was in the prison system, paddling also was used in the asylum:

> *Q.*: Did you ever have occasion to use [paddling]?
> *A.*: I was ordered to, but I did not do it; I will tell you the circumstances of it; a year ago.... Dr. Wilkie [medical superintendent] sent for me; at that time there was a patient by the name of William Barr; he was a very abusive young man—very bad language and habits; the doctor says, "I want you to go right into the fourth ward and take any men you want with you, and paddle him good...." I took [William Barr] in and says I, "I am obliged to paddle you today ... have you anything to say before I commence?" At that time he dropped on his knees and said, "for God's sake don't kill me." ... He cried like a child and his tears rolled down his cheeks. I says to the young man who was with me, "I cannot paddle that man" [New York State Legislature, p. 669].

The New York State Asylum for Insane Criminals in Auburn, later known as Matteawan State Hospital, was the first asylum of its kind in the United States. Opened in 1859, it quickly was overcrowded with both males and females who had been convicted and were insane, or who had been found not guilty by reason of insanity. Although both the State Commissioner of Lunacy and a committee representing the Association of Medical Superintendents of American Institutions for the Insane had visited the asylum, they either had not learned of the practice of paddling or were not concerned about it. The latter committee, as a matter of fact, declared that at this asylum "even the most desperate convict, bereft of reason, is treated like fellow-men" (Wilbur, p. 18). The practice of paddling ceased under Carlos MacDonald who took over as superintendent in 1876.

## *Ridicule*

The subjection of a patient to mockery and derision. Like threat, ridicule sometimes was thought to be therapeutic in nature; although no early physician bothered to explain how and why it could be considered therapeutic, quite a few took the time to describe the kinds of situations and cases for which it was.

Vincenzo Chiarugi, medical director of the Ospedale di Bonifazio in Florence, Italy cautioned that ridicule should only be used with the patient who had delusions of grandeur and was "swollen with pride, with fancies of great wealth and power" (Gerard, p. 394). A ridiculing reminder of his or her fallibility, he asserted, deflated the power of the delusion.

It was, in fact, the power of the delusion that baffled asylum physicians and led to a spate of ruses, deceits and trickeries that were referred to as pious frauds [see **Pious Frauds**], many of which had the leitmotif of ridicule. It was the prominent late nineteenth century German physician, Johann Christian Reil, however, who provided the oft-repeated example of ridicule as both theme and method in an interaction he had with a patient who believed he was dead. Unable to convince the patient otherwise, Reil had him placed in a coffin and had his friends, who were party to the ruse, deliver scathingly nasty eulogies in his presence. Ridiculed and humiliated, the patient leapt from the coffin to defend his honor. Perhaps needless to say, upon doing so he also relinquished his delusion.

The reformer, Philippe Pinel of the Asylum de Bicêtre in Paris, France, used ridicule to a therapeutic advantage that was most admired by his colleagues around the world, if the number of times the case he used it in was repeated or cited in the psychiatric literature was any indication. This was the case of a celebrated watchmaker who had been so obsessed with the chimera of perpetual motion and with the disturbances of the French Revolution, that he had developed the delusion that he had lost his head to the guillotine, and that when the judges realized their error, they had ordered his head be returned to him. They, however, gave him the wrong head. So certain was he that he had been given the head of an ugly person that he was committed to the Asylum de Bicêtre. There, he became ferociously maniacal, but calmed considerably when Pinel set him up in a small workshop and encouraged him to continue to ponder the problem of perpetual motion. After several months, he briefly and elatedly imagined he had built a perpetual motion mechanism and, after realizing he had not, was overwhelmed with despair, believing his failure was due to the fact that he had the wrong head. Another patient was conscripted in what Pinel described as a "comedy" devised to ridicule the watchmaker into surrendering his delusion (Pinel, p. 72). That patient engaged the watchmaker in a conversation about the miracle of St. Denis, the patron saint of the French monarchy who was martyred by beheading in 250 C.E. As the legend went, St. Denis picked up his decapitated head, kissed it, and then with head in hand walked several miles to the place where he wanted to be buried. The watchmaker defended the possibility of such an event, and cited his own decapitation as evidence. The patient laughed derisively and replied, "Madman as thou art, how could Saint Denis kiss his own head? Was it with his heels?" (p. 72). Retreating from the ridicule, the watchmaker never again mentioned his head and after several months was cured and released.

## *Slapping, or Striking*

Hitting the face or the head with an open hand. Like beating, slapping as a mode of punishment occurred with some frequency in asylums around the world and, also like beating, was the subject of any number of investigations and inquiries into patient mistreatment. One of those, at the Government Hospital for the Insane, later and better known as St. Elizabeths, in Washington, D.C., concerned charges against an attendant who had slapped a number of patients in the course of their work in the asylum laundry. While the accused attendant did not deny the allegations, he did justify them in a manner that likely was repeated in other such investigations around the world. In a lengthy letter to the investigation committee, he wrote:

> I did not act any different there than anyone else in my place would have done. In the case of the patient becoming unruly it was someone's duty to restore order and try to quiet the excited ones, which I tried to do. I did not in any way abuse or mistreat any of them, as I was obliged to use whatever strength it required to overpower them or it would be hard to say what I would have received at the patients' hands [House Special Committee, p. 407].

While attendants could justify slapping by an appeal to their onerous responsibility of maintaining order, some asylum physicians rationalized it by an appeal to their even more onerous responsibility of curing the insane. The controversial and somewhat enigmatic Francis Willis, the keeper of a private madhouse who was called upon to treat King George III, was not at all opposed to hitting a patient, believing that it was one of the best methods for inculcating the salutary fear that was necessary to teach restraint and good judgment. The therapeutic use of slapping also was advocated by Johann Christian August Heinroth of Leipzig University in Germany. A follower of the "psychic school" he believed that insanity was the result of a "defection from God," and that its essence is "in the partnership of the human soul with the evil principle—and not merely in partnership, but rather in its entire subjection to the latter" (Farrar, p. 290). The asylum physician, he argued, had both the therapeutic and the moral duty to discipline to the norm and punish sinfulness.

## *Spread-Eagle Cure*

Practice in nineteenth century American asylums of holding an agitated patient on the floor in the spread-eagle position, while buckets of ice cold water were repeatedly poured on the patient's face from a height of seven or eight feet.

Ebenezer Haskell, a Philadelphia merchant who was involuntarily committed to the Pennsylvania Hospital for the Insane in 1866, witnessed the cure:

> The spread eagle cure is a term used in all asylums and prisons. A disorderly patient is stripped naked and thrown on his back, four men take hold of the limbs and stretch them out at right angles, then the doctor or one of the attendants stands up on a chair or table and pours a number of buckets full of cold water on his face until his life is nearly extinct, then the patient is removed to his dungeon cured of all diseases; the shock is so great it frequently produces death [Haskell, p. 43].

## *Standing Posture*

Standing with unrestrained arms to the side and unrestrained feet together for twenty-four continuous hours. The American physician Benjamin Rush found the treatment helpful for the reduction of mania because it "reduced excitement by the expenditure of excitability, from the constant exertion of the muscles which support the body" (Rush, pp. 190–191). Further, he argued, the tension in the muscles "attracted morbid excitement from the brain" (p. 191), therefore not only relieving mania but preventing outbursts of it.

Rush developed the therapeutic after coming to learn that a method of taming stubborn horses in England at the time was to keep them from lying down or sleeping for several days by thrusting sharp pointed nails into their bodies. He mused that the same advantages might be derived from keeping the insane patient standing and awake, but by "different and more lenient means" (p. 190).

## Strapping

Striking with a leather strap, or buckled belt. Strapping was often used in early asylums and was the subject of any number of inquiries and investigations into patient mistreatment. An 1894 investigation of the Asylum for the Insane in New Westminster, British Columbia found that strapping was often used to coerce patients into conformity with institutional rules; patients stated that the buckle end of the strap was sometimes used. Although the investigation found no proof that the superintendent I.I. Bentley approved of strapping or, for that matter knew it was occurring, he was forced to resign.

## Threat

A verbal statement of the intention to inflict pain, injury, harm or death. While threats certainly were, and are, made in circumstances of frustration and exasperation, the therapeutic use of threat was unabashedly promoted by early asylum physicians such as Richard Mead, physician to St. Thomas' Hospital in London in the early eighteenth century who insisted that hard words and threats, at time, were the only methods an asylum physician had to control a furiously maniacal patient. Joseph Guislain, senior physician at the two asylums in Ghent, Belgium, agreed, but with an important exception: threats should be issued by someone other than the treating physician who always must appear to the patient to be the protector.

Threat had the psychological advantage of frightening the patient into submitting to a therapeutic intervention, and the sociological advantage of reinforcing the power hierarchy within asylums. In his widely read treatise on insanity, Benjamin Rush illustrated the dual advantages of threat in his enthusiastic account of the interaction between one of the physicians he supervised at the Pennsylvania Hospital and a patient whose disruptive behavior had not been modified by more conventional forms of punishment:

> If all these modes of punishment should fail of their intended effects, it will be proper to resort to the fear of death. Mr. Higgins proved the efficacy of this fear, in completely subduing a certain Sarah T-----, whose profane and indecent conversation and loud vociferations offended and disturbed the whole hospital. He had attempted in vain by light punishments and threats, to put a stop to them. At length he went to her cell, from whence he conducted her, cursing and swearing as usual to a large bathing tub, in which he placed her. "Now, (said he) prepare for death. I will give you time enough to say your prayers, after which I intend to drown you, by plunging your head under this water." She immediately uttered a prayer, such as became a dying person. Upon discovering this sign of penitence, Mr. Higgins obtained from her a promise of amendment. From that time no profane or indecent language, nor noises of any kind, were heard from her cell [Rush, pp. 180–181].

For Rush and many of his colleagues, threat was a humane alternative to the whip and fetters and to the mechanical restraints [see **Mechanical Restraints**] still being used in most asylums. Indeed, the very threat of *being* whipped, or buckled into a straitjacket, often sufficiently altered the behavior of the patient so as to make those measures unnecessary. But in asylums where non-restraint was practiced and corporal punishment was eschewed, threats such as these were empty. William Tuke pondered that dilemma when he established the York Retreat in northern England as the paragon of moral treatment [see **Moral Treatment**]. He argued that the reliance on threat and fear to change behavior overlooked the more powerful "desire of esteem" that even the most obstreperous patient possessed (Tuke, p. 157). This desire:

> is found to have great influence, even over the conduct of the insane.... Though it has obvi-

ously not been sufficiently powerful, to enable them entirely to resist the strong irregular tendencies of their disease; yet when properly cultivated, it leads many to struggle to conceal and overcome their morbid propensities; and, at least, materially assists them in confining their deviations, within such bounds, as do not make them obnoxious to the family. This struggle is highly beneficial to the patient, by strengthening his mind, and conducing him to a salutary habit of self-restraint; an object which experience points out as of the greatest importance, in the cure of insanity, by moral means [pp. 157–158].

## *Whipping*

Lashing with a single-tailed whip of braided leather, often referred to as a bullwhip or a crop, or with a multi-tailed whip, often referred to as a cat o'nine tails whip. While whipping was used to some extent until the mid-nineteenth century in asylums around the world for disciplining, punishing and terrifying patients, its use should not be overestimated. As the harsh vagrancy laws that called for the lashing of the vagrant insane at public whipping posts were being repealed during the eighteenth century, many early physicians were loath to revive the practice in their own asylums. At London's Bethlem Hospital, better known as Bedlam, for example, physician John Monro declared in the that any type of corporal punishment, including whipping, was both cruel and unnecessary, and the grounds for the prompt dismissal of the offending physician or attendant. In Germany, Christian August Hayner, chief physician at the asylum in Waldheim, cursed any asylum physician who sanctioned its use.

The dark and occluded history of early asylums where chains and cages were *de rigueur* certainly tempts the conclusion that whipping must have been as well, and so does the fact that some early physicians unabashedly endorsed it, largely on the principle that bodily pain and fear had salutary effects. William Cullen, the preeminent Scottish professor of medicine, for example, argued in 1772 that in the case of the "angry maniac" it was necessary to "employ a very constant impression of fear" that, at times, could only be induced by "stripes [whipping] and blows" (Hunter & Macalpine, p. 478). Aton Müller, as another example, had achieved his considerable reputation for the orderly care of the insane at the Julius-spital in Würzberg, Germany, with the use of the whip. He boasted that thrashing "was almost a part of the daily routine" (Kraepelin, p. 14). For those asylum physicians who were opposed to adding whipping to the daily schedule, it was reserved for specific violations of comportment.

Cat o'nine tails whip, a particular favorite of asylum attendants for keeping recalcitrant patients in line. The whip may have been named after the claw-like marks it left on the skin. The English expression, "Not enough room to swing a cat," referred to this whip, not a feline. And the expression, "Letting the cat out of the bag," referred to the bag in which the whip was stored (courtesy of the Wellcome Library, London).

Johann Heinrich Ferdinand von Autenrieth, a highly respected medical educator and psychiatric innovator from the University of Tübingen, Germany, urged his colleagues to save the whip for the woman patient who persisted in wandering about the asylum naked, and Heinrich Neumann, director of a private psychiatric clinic in Breslau, Germany, recommended it for uncleanliness.

Curiously, even the occasional reformer who advocated non-restraint and moral treatment [see **Moral Treatment**] found the superannuated practice of whipping both sometimes necessary and almost always effective. Thomas Bakewell, proprietor of the Spring Vale Asylum in Staffordshire, England, found the whip to be the "most prompt, and least disagreeable" of punishments for the recalcitrant patient. To soften its blow in the milieu of moral treatment he advocated, he recommended its use always be prefaced with words to this effect: "I am extremely sorry to be under the necessity of using force, but my duty obliges me.... I wish not to hurt you, but I have no time to lose" (Bakewell, p. 40). Vincenzo Chiarugi, medical director of the Ospedale di Bonifazio in Florence, Italy, saw no need for an apology to introduce the use of the whip. Although he had forbade corporal punishment in his asylum, he thought whipping therapeutic, but only for "those arrogant maniacs with a certain residue of reason" (Gerard, p. 396). And in Germany, Johann Christian Reil, who had coined the term "psychiatry" and was a widely respected reformer, noted that the bullwhip at times was necessary for bringing the patient into line.

By the late nineteenth century whipping was such an uncommon occurrence in asylums around the world that the trial of Georg Moritz Wiederhold, the owner and director of a private asylum for nervous patients in Kassel, Germany, attracted international attention and revived what was a moribund debate about whipping. Wiederhold was charged with assaulting a middle-aged patient, the wife of a retired military officer, in the course of her treatment for hysteria which she allegedly had acquired after a surgical procedure had weakened her nerves. Her constant screaming, fits of uncontrollable rage and incessant crying not only disturbed the other asylum patients but, more critically, interfered with any of Wiederhold's attempts to kindly reason with her. He therefore turned to salutary fear to break through her resistance: he threatened to beat her, then later boxed her around the ears and when that did not get her attention, he struck her repeatedly on the buttock with a rod, and finally whipped her with a horsewhip. Although he denied none of this during his trial, he did deny that he had denounced her for being a "bitch" and a "slut" while doing so. Expert testimony from some of the leading asylum physicians of the day illustrated the contradictory attitudes about whipping that remained long after the most vigorous debates had wound down. One expert asserted that whipping was scientifically indefensible and that, except in largely apocryphal stories, it had no therapeutic value; another agreed, pointing out that whipping was forbidden by law in German asylums, but conceding at the same time that more than a few asylum physicians still approved of its use. Wiederhold was convicted of the charge against him, and sentenced to three months in prison.

The debate over whipping was resurrected briefly in 2005 when Sergei Speransky, a well-respected Russian scientists, proposed "whipping therapy" as a cure for substance abuse addiction. Speransky, who had successfully treated his own depression by self-flagellation, argued that addiction, like depression and suicidal ideation, was a marker of the loss of interest in life which, in turn, decreased the production of endorphins by the pituitary gland and hypothalamus. A course of thirty sessions of sixty lashings of the buttock, he contended, would stimulate the endorphin receptors and activate the release of what is idiomatically known as the "hormone of happiness." Speransky claimed "good results" in a trial involving a small group of institutionalized addicts, and pointed out that the best results occurred when the whipping was administered by a person of the opposite sex. Although Speransky uses the whip as well as spanking in his practice, it has not been adopted in Russian asylums.

# Shock Therapy (Convulsive Therapy)

*The therapeutic induction of convulsions or coma through the use of electrical current or drugs.*

The history of asylum therapeutics is, in a curious way, a history of shock. Whether startling patients from senselessness by sudden and unexpected drum rolls [see **Awakenings**], or plunging them blindfolded through a trapdoor and into a vat of cold water [see **Salutary Fear**] or copiously bleeding them into a stupor [see **Depletive Therapy**], shocking the mind or the body long was thought to be curative. Shocking the brain, however, was a different matter altogether and it would take a century beyond the drumrolls and bleedings before the procedures for doing so became an acceptable, indeed wildly popular, therapeutic practice in asylums around the world.

Credit for introducing the proposition that the brain could be shocked into normality has been given to Constance Pascal, a Romanian-born physician who was one of the first women to pass the demanding competitive examination to practice asylum medicine in France. Fired with a passion to reform the care of the insane, she was confronted by the same reality that had stifled the enthusiasm of so many of her male colleagues: an over-crowded, understaffed asylum teeming with disorientated, distressed and even dangerous patients. It was those patients with dementia praecox that concerned her most. And it was in regards to them that she refused to surrender to therapeutic nihilism. She wrote:

> To have to look on helplessly at the fatal advance of psychosis, to indifferently note demented immobility and the transition to chronicity, is just to endorse fate; accepting the predisposition to delusions and the fatal destiny of constitution also means renouncing the practical applications of the biological sciences that have modified the study of general pathology [Shorter & Healy, p. 10].

Pascal had an orthodox understanding of dementia praecox, informed by the theory of Emil Kraepelin who held that it was a steadily deteriorating, irreversible disorder that afflicted young people, men more often than women. Its onset was characterized by depression and confusion, delusions and hallucinations, incoherent speech and bizarre behaviors, and was followed by an inexorable cognitive deterioration. Although she constantly amended her theory of dementia praecox in the light of new theories, particularly that of Eugen Bleuler who had coined the alternative diagnostic label of schizophrenia, Pascal eventually settled on her own theory. This disorder, she posited, was caused by the sudden impact of emotional shocks on constitutionally sensitized individuals, setting off mental anaphylactic reactions, first in the form of reversible functional disorders such as hallucinations and disorientation, then irreversible organic disorders such as cognitive deterioration.

Aware of what even in the mid–1920s must have seemed the naïve "shock" therapy attempts of previous generations of asylum physicians, as well as the shocks induced by high fevers [**Fever Therapy**] that were being used by some of her contemporaries to cure neurosyphilis, Pascal set out to "reset" the brains and autonomic nervous systems of dementia praecox patients. She injected them with blood derivatives and vaccines, colloidal gold, milk and oil of turpentine, but with little notable therapeutic success. It is imperative to note that none of these substances resulted in convulsions or coma, in fact Pascal was adamant that they be avoided, but the persistence of the idea that an induced shock of some kind could restore the functioning of the brain entranced asylum physicians. And the hope that the bigger the shock, the greater the cure, loomed large.

## References

Abou-Saleh, M.T., and Christodoulou, G. (2009). The WPA position statement on the ethics of unmodified electroconvulsive therapy. *Arab Journal of Psychiatry, 20*, 57–65.

Accornero, F. (1988). An eyewitness account of the discovery of electroshock. *Convulsive Therapy, 4*, 40–49.

Alexander, G.H. (1953). Electroconvulsive therapy—a 5 year study of results. *Journal of Nervous and Mental Disease, 117*, 244–250.

Alper, T.G. (1948). Case reports: An electric shock patient tells his story. *Journal of Abnormal and Social Psychology, 43*, 201–210.

American Psychiatric Association (1978). *Report of the task force on electroconvulsive therapy*. Washington, D.C.: Author.

Andrade, C., Shah, N., and Venkatesh, B.K. (2010). The depiction of electroconvulsive therapy in Hindi cinema. *Journal of ECT, 26*, 16–22.

Anonymous (1940). Insulin and I. *American Journal of Orthopsychiatry, 10*, 810–814.

Barbier, J.M., Serra, G., Loas, G., and Breathnach, C.S. (1999). Constance Pascal: Pioneer of French psychiatry. *History of Psychiatry, 10*, 425–437.

Bender, L. (1947). One hundred cases of childhood schizophrenia cured with electric shock. *Transactions of the American Neurological Association, 72*, 165–169.

Bennett, A.E. (1938). Convulsive shock therapy in depressive psychoses. *American Journal of Medical Sciences, 196*, 420–428.

Bourne, H. (1953). The insulin myth. *Lancet, 262*, 964–988.

Braslow, J. (1997). *Mental ills and bodily cures*. Berkeley: University of California Press.

Cameron, D.E. (1960). Production of differential amnesia as a factor in the treatment of schizophrenia. *Comprehensive Psychiatry, 1*, 26–34.

Cameron, D.E. (1963). The process of remembering. *British Journal of Psychiatry, 109*, 325–340.

Cameron, D.E., Lohrenz, J.G., and Handcock, K.Z. (1962). The depatterning treatment of schizophrenia. *Comprehensive Psychiatry, 3*, 65–76.

Cameron, D.E., and Pandy, S.K. (1958). Treatment of the chronic paranoid schizophrenic patient. *Canadian Medical Association Journal, 78*, 92–96.

Cerletti, U. (1950). Old and new information about electroshock. *American Journal of Psychiatry, 107*, 87–94.

Chabasinsky, T. (n.d.). Personal stories. Retrieved at http://www.mindfreedom.org/personal-stories/chabasisnskited.

Clardy, E.R., and Rumpf, E.M. (1954). The effect of electro shock treatment on children having schizophrenic manifestations. *Psychiatric Quarterly, 28*, 616–623.

Collins, A. (1988). *In the sleep room*. Toronto, Ontario, Canada: Lester & Orpen Dennys.

Cooper, D. (1967). *Psychiatry and anti-psychiatry*. London: Tavistock.

Cottington, F. (1941). The treatment of childhood schizophrenia by metrazol shock modified by B-erythroidin. *American Journal of Psychiatry, 98*, 397–400.

Crossley, N. (1988). R.D. Laing and the British anti-psychiatry movement: A socio-historical analysis. *Social Science and Medicine, 47*, 877–899.

Culver, C.M., Ferrell, R.B., and Green, R.M. (1980). ECT and special problems of informed consent. *American Journal of Psychiatry, 137*, 586–591.

Dawson, W.S. (1924). *Aids to psychiatry*. New York: William Wood and Company.

"Dementia Praecox Curbed by Insulin" (1937, January 13). *New York Times*, p. 11.

Devine, H. (1929). *Recent advances in psychiatry*. Philadelphia: Churchill.

de Young, M. (2010). *Madness: An American history of mental illness and its treatment*. Jefferson, NC: McFarland.

Doroshow, D.B. (2006). Performing a cure for schizophrenia: Insulin coma therapy on the wards. *Journal of the History of Medicine and Allied Sciences, 62*, 213–243.

Dravet, C., and Roger, J. (1996). In Memoriam: Henri Gastaut, 1915–1995. *Epilepsia, 37*, 410–415.

Eghigian, G. (2010). *From madness to mental health*. New Brunswick, NJ: Rutgers University Press.

Farnsworth, C. (1992, November 19). "Canada Will Pay 50s Test Victims," *New York Times*, p. A9.

Fine, P. (1974). Women and shock treatment. *Radical Therapy, 2*, 9–11.

Fink, M. (1984). Meduna and the origins of convulsive therapy. *American Journal of Psychiatry, 141*, 1034–1041.

Frank, L.R. (1978). *The history of shock treatment*. San Francisco: Author.

Gastaut, H., and Cossa, P. (1949). Le choc cardisolique facilité par la stimulation lumineuse intermittente ou "photo-choc." *Semaine d. Hosp, Paris, 25*, 2738.

Gazdag, G., Bitter, I., Ungvari, G.S., Baran, and Fink, M. (2009). László Meduna's pilot studies with camphor inductions of seizures: The first 11 patients. *Journal of ECT, 25*, 3–11.

Glueck, B.C., Reiss, H., and Bernard, L.E. (1957). Regressive electric shock therapy: Preliminary report on 100 cases. *Psychiatry, 31*, 117–136.

Gordon, H.L. (1948). Fifty shock therapy theories. *Military Surgeon, 103*, 397–401.

Greaves, D.C., Regan, P.F., and West, L.J. (1955). An evaluation of sub-coma insulin therapy. *American Journal of Psychiatry, 112*, 135–139.

Hilton, C. (2007). An exploration of the patient's experience of electro-convulsive therapy in mid-20th century creative literature. *Journal of Affective Disorders, 97*, 5–12.

Hirshbein, L., and Sarvananda, S. (2008). History, power and electricity: American popular magazine accounts of electroconvulsive therapy, 1940–2000. *Journal of the History of the Behavioral Sciences, 44,* 1–18.

Horrock, M.N. (1977, August 2). "Private Institutions used in CIA Effort to Control Behavior," *New York Times,* pp. 1, 16.

Hotchner, A.E. (1967). *Papa Hemingway.* New York: Bantam.

Hunter, R., and Macalpine, I. (1963). *Three hundred years of psychiatry, 1535–1860.* London: Oxford University Press.

Impasto, D. (1960). The story of the first electroshock treatment. *American Journal of Psychiatry, 116,* 1113–1114.

"Insanity treated by electric shock" (1940, July 6). *New York Times,* p. 17.

James, B.O., Omoaregba, O.J., Igberae, O.O., and Oluto, S.O. (2009). Unmodified electroconvulsive therapy: Changes in knowledge and attitudes of Nigerian medical students. *African Health Sciences, 9,* 279–283.

Janis, I.L. (1948). Memory loss following electric convulsive treatments. *Journal of Personality, 17,* 29–32.

Kalinowsky, L.B., and Hoch, P.H. (1946). *Shock treatment and other somatic procedures in psychiatry.* New York: Grune & Stratton.

Kennedy, C.J.C, and Anchel, D. (1948). Regressive electric shock in schizophrenics refractory to other shock therapies. *Psychiatric Quarterly, 22,* 317–320.

Kesey, K. (1962). *One flew over the cuckoo's nest.* New York: Viking.

Kneeland, T.W., and Warren, C.A.B. (2002). *Push-button psychiatry.* Westport, CT: Praeger.

Kolb, L. (1941). *Shock therapy survey: U.S. Public Health Service Report.* Washington, D.C.: U.S. Government Printing Office.

Kragh, J.V. (2010). Shock therapy in Danish psychiatry. *Medical History, 54,* 341–364.

Leiknes, K.A., Jarosh-von-Schweder, L., and Høle, B. (2012). Contemporary use and practice of electroconvulsive therapy worldwide. *Brain and Behavior, 2,* 283–344.

Lydons, C. (1972, July 26). Eagleton tells of shock therapy on two occasions. *New York Times,* p. 1.

Malzberg, B. (1938). Outcome of insulin treatment of one thousand patients with dementia praecox. *Psychiatric Quarterly, 12,* 528–533.

Malzberg, B. (1939). A follow-up study of patients with dementia praecox treated with insulin in the New York State Civil State Hospitals. *Mental Hygiene, 23,* 641–651.

McCrea, N. (2006). "A violent thunderstorm": Cardiazol treatment in British mental hospitals. *History of Psychiatry, 17,* 69–70.

McDonald, A., and Walter, G. (2001). The portrayal of ECT in American movies. *Journal of ECT, 17,* 264–274.

Meduna, L. (1938). General discussion of cardiazol therapy. *American Journal of Psychiatry,* [Supplement], *94,* 40–49.

Meduna, L.J. (1950). *Carbon dioxide therapy: A neurophysiological treatment of nervous disorders.* Springfield, IL: Charles C. Thomas.

Mental Disability Rights International (2005). *Behind closed doors: Human rights abuses in the psychiatric facilities, orphanages and rehabilitation centers of Turkey.* Washington, D.C.: Author.

Milligan, W.D., and Atkin, I. (1946). Psychoneuroses treated with electrical convulsions: The intensive method. *Lancet, 248,* 516–520.

Moore, W. (1955). *The mind in chains.* New York: Exposition.

Nasar, S. (1998). *A beautiful mind.* New York: Simon & Schuster.

Nash. J.F. (1994). Autobiography. Retrieved at http://www.nobelprize.org/nobel_prizes/economics/laureates/1994/nash-autobio.html.

O'Shea B., and McGennis, A . (1983). ECT: Lay attitudes and experiences—a pilot study. *Irish Medical Journal 76,* 40–43.

Plath, S. (1963). *The bell jar.* New York: Bantam.

Rensberger, B. (1972, July 29). Psychiatrist explain medical facts in depression. *New York Times,* p. 11.

Reston, J. (1972, August 9). Psychology and politics. *New York Times,* p. 37.

Rivers, T.D., and Bond, E.D. (1941). Follow-up results of insulin shock therapy after one to three years. *American Journal of Psychiatry, 98,* 382–384.

Rosen, S.R., Cameron, D.E., and Ziegler, J.B. (1941). The prevention of metrazol fractures by beta-erythroidin hydrochloride. *Psychiatric Quarterly, 14,* 477–480.

Rothschild, D., VanGordon, D., and Varjabedian, A. (1951). Regressive shock therapy in schizophrenia. *Diseases of the Nervous System, 12,* 147–150.

Sakel, M. (1937). A new treatment of schizophrenia. *American Journal of Psychiatry, 93,* 829–841.

Schwartzman, A.E., and Termansen, P.E. (1967). Intensive electroconvulsive therapy: A follow-up study. *Canadian Psychiatric Association Journal, 12,* 217–218.

Shorter, E. (1997). *A history of psychiatry.* New York: John Wiley and Sons.

Shorter, E., and Healy, D. (2007). *Shock therapy: A history of electroconvulsive treatment in mental illness.* New Brunswick, NJ: Rutgers University Press.

Stafford, J. (1938, May 21). The shock that cures. *Science News Letter,* pp. 334–337.

Starks, H.A. (1938). Subjective experiences in patients incident to insulin and metrazol therapy. *Psychiatric Quarterly, 12,* 699–709.

Szasz, T.S. (1961). The myth of mental illness. London: Paladin.

Teh, S.P.C., Helmes, E., and Drake, D. (2007). A Western Australian survey on public attitudes toward and knowledge of electroconvulsive therapy. *International Journal of Social Psychiatry, 53,* 247–271.

Thompson, J., and Blaine, J.D. (1994). Use of ECT

in the United States in 1975, 1980 and 1986. *American Journal of Psychiatry, 151,* 1657–1661.

Tomlinson, P.J. (1948). Sub-coma insulin therapy: An analysis of 300 cases. *Psychiatric Quarterly, 22,* 609–620.

Tondo, L. (2011). Closer look: Interview with Lothar B. Kalinowsky. *Clinical Neuropsychiatry, 8,* 303–313.

"Transcript of Kitty Dukakis's interview on ABC-TV's *Good Morning America*" (2006, September 18). Retrieved at www.nami.org.

Tyler, E.A., and Löwenbach, H. (1947). Polydiurnal electric shock treatment in mental disorders. *North Carolina Medical Journal, 8,* 577–582.

Ulett, G.A. (1953). The use of photically activated EEG as a research tool in psychiatry. *Psychosomatic Medicine, 15,* 66–83.

Ulett, G.A., Gleser, G.C., Caldwell, B.M., and Smith, K. (1954). The use of matched groups in the evaluation of convulsive and subconvulsive photoshock. *Menninger Clinica Bulletin, 18,* 138–146.

Vallenstein, E.S. (1986). *Great and desperate cures.* New York: Basic Books.

Walter, G., McDonald, A., Rey, J.M., and Rosen, A. (2002). Medical student knowledge and attitudes regarding ECT prior to and after viewing ECT scenes from movies. *Journal of ECT, 18,* 43–46.

Weitz, D. (2006). "Personal Stories." Retrieved at http://www.mindfreedom.org/personal-stories/weitzdon.

Winslade, W.J., Liston, E.H., Ross, J.W., and Weber, K.D. (1984). Medical, judicial, and statutory regulation of ECT in the United States. *American Journal of Psychiatry, 141,* 1149–1155.

Wortis, J. (1958). In memoriam: Manfred Sakel, M.D., 1900–1957. *American Journal of Psychiatry, 115,* 287–288.

## *Depatterning*

The administration of intensive and repeated electroconvulsive shocks to patients who were in a state of continuous sleep. The therapeutic was developed by D. Ewen Cameron, director of the prestigious Allan Memorial Institute which housed the psychiatry department of McGill University's Royal Victoria Hospital in Montreal, Quebec Canada. Cameron had extensive experience in the use of continuous sleep therapy [see **Deep Sleep Therapy**] and in what was called "preventative" electroconvulsive shock treatment, so named because its continued use after therapeutic results were achieved was believed to minimize the risk of relapse. He conjectured that a combination of the two therapeutics would produce maximum positive results in the treatment of schizophrenia by producing the "required brain syndrome," and "controlling excitement and anxiety" (Cameron, Lorhenz, & Handcock, p. 66).

To that end, Cameron began in the mid–1950s inducing prolonged sleep in schizophrenic patients by administering a cocktail of three powerful barbiturates, Veronal, Seconal and Nembutal, along with Largactil, better known as Thorazine. The patients were awakened three times daily from their drug-induced sleep to eat and go to the toilet. After several continuous days of sleep, the Page-Russell electroconvulsive shock technique was administered twice daily; this involved the delivery of six separate shocks in such rapidity that convulsions did not begin until the termination of the last shock.

The result of this combination of therapeutics was what Cameron referred to as "depatterning," and it proceeded in three distinct stages. First, after approximately five continuous days of electroconvulsive shock treatment, patients experienced "disturbance of the space-time image" (p. 67), that is, they experienced marked memory deficits but were still well orientated to time and place. In the second stage, which occurred between the tenth and twentieth day of treatment, at which point they had received an average of thirty-five electroconvulsive shock treatments, the patients had lost the space-time image but not the sense that they should have one. As a result, they no longer knew where they were or how they came to be there, but they were anxious and concerned about why they did not know. In the third a final stage patients not only had lost their orientation to time and place, but any concerns about having done so. It was during this stage that schizophrenic symptoms disappeared. Patients were left able to respond appropriately to questions, although their replies were "in no way conditioned by recollections of the past or by anticipations of the future" (p. 67). Some could no longer walk without assistance or feed themselves; some were doubly incontinent. The complete obliteration of memory having been achieved, the patients then were observed while they passed in reverse order through the three stages, a progression from the third stage, to the second and finally to the first, that was referred to by Cameron as "reorganization."

That reverse progression from the third to the first stage of depatterning sometimes brought about "periods of turbulence" (p. 68), in which the patients became restless, anxious, belligerent and even delusional. Large doses of sodium amytal or the monoamine oxidase inhibitor RO4-1038 were given to ease the transition; psychotherapy, however, was not offered since previous experience had proved to Cameron that the results would be "positively calamitous" (p. 68).

The post-treatment protocol required that patients submit to monthly electroconvulsive shock treatments for two years. Now amnestic, their memories had to be reconstructed for them by family and friends who also had to be alert for any signs of relapse. In fact, approximately 30 percent of patients relapsed within the first year; most were successfully re-treated by another round or two of depatterning.

At the Allan Memorial Institute, thirty schizophrenic patients with an average age of thirty-six years were administered the depatterning treatment by Cameron and his associates. Only one of those patients, a female diagnosed with paranoid schizophrenia, went into complete recovery after a course of forty-eight electroconvulsive shock treatments with an additional twenty-four such treatments over the two years subsequent to her discharge. Cameron defined complete recovery in terms of restoration to a "best functioning self in the fullest meaning of the term" (p. 69). An additional nine patients socially recovered, that is, they became socially active despite some "residual subjective disturbances" (p. 69). One of that group of patients, a forty-two-year-old female diagnosed with paranoid schizophrenia, had undergone 150 electroconvulsive shock treatments during the depatterning regime, and an additional thirty-two over the two years subsequent to her discharge. Nineteen of the patients had improved in that they were no longer institutionalized and were able to meet some of their social and occupational demands. One patient, who at twenty years old was the youngest of this group, received seventy-five electroconvulsive shock treatments with an additional twenty-six over the two years after his initial discharge. He relapsed and had to be institutionalized.

Hailing depatterning as a successful treatment for schizophrenia, Cameron then formulated a working model of schizophrenia from the treatment results. Rather than analogizing schizophrenia to the progressive and often fatal disease of cancer, he argued, it would be better analogized to poliomyelitis—"a disease with a very acute phase followed by long-lasting sequelae which may become progressively worse if not treated" (p. 75). This kind of *post hoc* theorizing, or generating hypotheses and working models on the basis of data already observed, certainly was not uncommon among entrepreneurial asylum physicians. But to Cameron who had achieved considerable recognition and status in the field of psychiatry, the circular logic that justified and rationalized depatterning and that influenced the development of his most controversial therapeutic, psychic driving [see **Psychic Driving**], eventually became evident. In a 1963 Presidential address to the American Psychopathological Association, an organization devoted to the scientific investigation of disordered human behavior, he offered a *mea culpa,* saying that nothing he had done to treat schizophrenia had been successful in the end, but that was how science worked.

His revelation was somewhat unexpected. Depatterning had never caught on as a therapeutic, although it was just as controversially as cautiously used in a very few asylums in North America and Great Britain during the 1950s and early 1960s. And the devastating results of a follow-up study of seventy-nine patients in the third stage of depatterning at the Allan Memorial Institute had not yet been published. That study found that 23 percent of the patients had experienced mild to severe physical complications from the repeated electroconvulsive shock treatments; 60 percent reported a persistent retrograde amnesia for the previous six months to ten years; and 75 percent of the forty-seven patients who had been discharged as completely or socially recovered demonstrated unsatisfactory or impoverished social adjustment.

In the face of Cameron's considerable status, colleagues around the world were quietly critical of depatterning. Some found the research he published in top psychiatric journals to be conceptually flawed and lacking scientific rigor. Others questioned the ethics of so severely compromising patients' memory, which Cameron himself had rhapsodized as the "bastion" of being. "Without memory," he had asserted, "there is no personal identity, there is no continuity to the days of [their] lives. Memory provides the raw material for designs both great and small. Thus, governed and enriched by memory, all the enterprises of man go forward" (Cameron, 1963, p. 325).

Cameron's regret also was expressed years before it was discovered that depatterning and psychic driving treatments of patients at the Allan Memorial Institute had been secretly funded by the Canadian government and the United States Central Intelligence Agency through an organization called the Society for the Investigation of Human Ecology. The potential of both of Cameron's therapeutics to further top secret mind control initiatives, commenced after the Korean War and in reaction to the emergent concern about "brainwashing," had been noticed, and the majority of those who had been administered one or both of the treatments, in fact, were more the unwitting guinea pigs of a political agenda than patients of a therapeutic one. They were used to provide information on how to "crack the mental defenses of enemy agents—to be able to program them... to carry out any mission, even against their will and 'against such fundamental laws of nature as self-preservation'" (Horrock, p. 1).

That nefarious relationship was uncovered in 1977, a decade after Cameron's death, by *New York Times* journalists who had reviewed Central Intelligence Agency documents. Although Cameron always had vigorously asserted that he was unaware of the funding sources of his treatment regimes, a colleague who worked closely with him said otherwise. "It was directly related to brainwashing," Leonard Rubenstein stated. "They had investigated brainwashing among soldiers who had been in Korea. We in Montreal started using some of these techniques, brainwashing patients instead of using drugs" (Horrock, p. 16). Rubenstein added that he and Cameron had hoped that their brainwashing techniques would have the added benefit of accelerating the treatment of schizophrenic patients.

The *New York Times* investigation prompted a flurry of law suits. The first, filed by Velma Orlikow, the wife of a Member of Parliament, was settled out of court in 1981 for $41,000. A few years later, both the United States Justice Department and the Canadian government agreed to settle claims and law suits by Cameron's former patients of both depatterning and psychic driving.

## *Electroconvulsive Shock Therapy, or Electroshock Therapy, or ECT*

The induction of generalized seizures by passing an electrical current through the brain. Electroconvulsive shock therapy originated in Italy in the early twentieth century, the result of research on the hippocampus of the brain conducted by Ugo Cerletti and Lucio Bini. The hippocampus, or "Horn of Ammon," already was known to play a role in learning and memory, but also was suspected of playing a role in epilepsy. To test the received medical wisdom of the time that epilepsy and schizophrenia were antagonistic, Cerletti and Bini considered the possibility that electrically-induced convulsions would improve, or even cure, schizophrenia.

But how much of a voltage and for what duration? In their search for an answer Cerletti and Bini visited a Rome slaughterhouse where they learned that there was a wide margin between a convulsive jolt of electricity (120 volts) and a fatal one (400 volts), and that a one to two-and-half minute continuous charge of electricity was required to cause death, at least in pigs. Assured by that margin of error, Bini constructed a rudimentary apparatus that regulated both the voltage (80 to 100 volts) and the duration (fractions of second) of its administration and looked for a human subject with schizophrenia on which it could be tested.

The opportunity to do so presented itself in 1938 when the police commissioner sent a disoriented man who had been found wandering around the city to the Clinica delle Malattie Nervose e Mentali della Regia Università di Roma (Rome Royal University Clinic for Nervous and Mental Illnesses) that Cerletti headed. Speaking in a jargon of his own invention, and expressing delusions of being telepathically influenced, the man could not give any identifying information, and a subsequent investigation revealed none. "S.E.," as he was referred to, was assumed to be a chronic schizophrenic, and he became the first human subject of electroconvulsive shock treatment. Strapped to a table with electrodes fixed to his temples with rubber bands, "S.E." was given eighty volts of electricity for one-tenth of a second, causing his body to tremble slightly, but not producing unconsciousness. A second dose of ninety volts for one-tenth of a second was administered ten minutes later, causing a longer tonic spasm followed by stentorian breaths. And then "S.E." began singing. The tune was a salacious little ditty, and he sang it very much out of tune. But when he overheard Cerletti and Bini's heated discussion about whether they should try again with a higher voltage, "S.E." stopped singing and calmly interjected, "Not another one! It's deadly!" (Impasto, p. 1113). A third jolt, however, was administered, this one at 100 volts for a quarter of a second. "S.E." convulsed for more than a minute, then stopped breathing for a terrifying minute more before he finally emitted a deep breath. Bini described what followed:

> Thereupon we observed with the most intensely gratifying sensation, the characteristic gradual awakening of the patient "by steps." He rose to a sitting position and looked at us, calm and smiling, as though to inquire what we wanted of him. We asked: "What happened to you?" He answered: "I don't know. Maybe I was asleep." Thus occurred the first electrically produced convulsion in man, which I at once named electroshock [Valenstein, p. 51].

"S.E." improved steadily with nine more electroshock treatments over the subsequent month and accompanied Cerletti and Bini to a meeting at the Royal Academy of Medicine. There, he was shocked once again, this time in front of an incredulous audience. He then answered their questions and was so coherent and responsive that he left no doubts that his schizophrenia had been cured. While accolades began pouring down on Cerletti and Bini for finding the cure for that most vexing type of insanity, "S.E." was released from the clinic and returned home. Two years later he was committed to a Milan asylum, once again diagnosed with schizophrenia.

Meanwhile, electroconvulsive shock treatment became the treatment *du jour* at Cerletti's clinic. Each session was announced by the sound of a trumpet, played badly by all accounts by an eager assistant. Dozens of physicians rushed into the room not just to witness the administration of the therapeutic, but to measure its physiological outcome: respiration rate, blood pressure and temperature were taken for each patient; urine and blood were withdrawn and later analyzed; lumbar punctures were performed; eyes were examined for changes in retinal circulation; deep tendon reflexes were tested with a reflex hammer. The psychological, emotional and cognitive changes in the treated schizophrenic patients, however, were of considerable less interest. Upon publication of the physiological findings, and despite the absence of thorough discussions about the psychic consequences, Cerletti and

Bini's therapeutic innovation spread widely across Europe. In its wake, papers touting it as a remedy for both schizophrenia and major depression were delivered at medical conferences and published in leading psychiatric journals, and new machines were designed and patented to deliver higher currents of electricity. Behind the scenes, however, Cerletti found the violent thrashings of his patients more than a little disconcerting. He hoped that it was not the convulsion *per se* that accounted for symptom improvement, but the body's response to the shock of the convulsion. If that were true, he conjectured, then the brain was releasing some kind of a "vitalizing substance." If he could isolate this "acroagonine," or "acroamine," as he variously referred to it, from the brains of shocked animals, it could be injected directly into patients, thereby avoiding convulsions altogether. He had no success with that endeavor.

Interestingly, the outbreak of World War II in Europe facilitated the rapid spread and acceptance of electroconvulsive shock therapy. In order to aid the war effort, pharmacies had been emptied of drugs, and the insulin for insulin shock therapy, at the time the preferred treatment for schizophrenic patients, was almost impossible to source. Electroconvulsive shock therapy quickly became a reasonable substitute.

World War II also brought electroconvulsive shock therapy to the United States. A number of psychiatrists, such as Lothar Kalinowsky, a German Jew who had trained with Cerletti and Bini, fled the rising tide of fascism and took refuge in the United States. Although other American psychiatrists already had experimented with electroconvulsive shock therapy, it was Kalinowsky's use of it at the New York State Psychiatric Institute that captured the attention of the press which played a major role in popularizing the therapeutic:

> Although [it is emphasized] that hope for any "miracle cure" must not be pinned on the new method, as the experiments have been in progress only a few months and findings are inconclusive, it was reported that "considerable success" had resulted in treatment of certain types of insanity....Adherents of the electric-shock method contend that metrazol sometimes is an uncertain treatment, and that the process of injection of the chemical into the veins has disagreeable features that sometimes instill fear in the patient. The electric treatment, they say, at least is not unpleasant, so the patient may be more inclined to cooperate with the physician in future treatments ["Insanity Treated," p. 17].

Within a short time, asylum physicians from all over the United States were coming to New York to train with Kalinowsky. Their enthusiastic reaction to electroconvulsive shock therapy was evident: 129 of the 305 asylums polled in 1941 reported using it; just six years later, an unpublished survey found that nine out of every ten public and private asylums were using the therapeutic.

Its relatively low cost and ease of administration accounted, in part, for the popularity of electroconvulsive shock therapy. But the largest reason for its popularity had to do with its effectiveness and its efficacy. Asylum physicians and staff observed its success in relieving not so much the symptoms of schizophrenia, for which it had originally been intended, but those of major depression. Early studies showed that when compared to untreated patients, those patients who had undergone electroconvulsive shock therapy showed much more rapid and sustained improvement. The therapeutic certainly was not without its risks. Before the drug curare started being administered to block neuromuscular connections and eliminate the violent convulsions, the rate of fractures during electroconvulsive shock treatment occurred for nine out of every 1,000 patients, a rate, by the way, that was less than one-quarter of that for metrazol shock treatment. After the introduction of curare in the late 1940s, and later succinylcholine, the rate was negligible. And electroconvulsive shock treatment always produced amnesia, although the question remained unanswered as to whether it was the result of a psychological reaction to the therapeutic or a physiological change in the brain.

Asylum physicians often considered amnesia therapeutically advantageous in that patients, especially those who were depressed, were no longer able to ruminate on past failures and disappointments. For patients, however, memory loss often was much more problematic; it eclipsed personal identity and a sense of generational continuity, and that always tempered to some degree their sense of optimism when symptoms remediated. A twenty-four-year-old university student who had been institutionalized before taking his final exams, described his experience of memory loss in an essay he wrote for a psychology class upon returning to university a year later:

> I woke up sometime later feeling completely refreshed, not tired or logy, or drugged with sleep, just ready for a big day.... I began looking around. I was in a large cream colored room with fifteen or twenty beds neatly made, and covered with white counterpanes. It looked like a hospital, but why should I be in a hospital? I shut my eyes and tried to think. But nothing came.
> "What is the date?" I asked myself.
> "I haven't any idea."
> "What day of the week is it?"
> "Don't be silly."
> "What month is it?"
> "I don't know."
> "What year is it?"
> That shouldn't be hard. But I wasn't sure. It was later than 1941. I tried to outsmart myself by asking how old I was and then figuring one year. But I didn't know how old I was [Alper, p. 206].

In response to patients' concerns about memory loss, asylum physicians experimented with ways to reduce it. They decreased the dosage of electricity, tried passing a direct rather than an alternating current through the brain, and placed the electrodes on top of the skull rather than on either side of the head in order to spare the non-motor parts of the brain responsible for memory and sensation from a direct current of electricity. To some extent, each of these strategies was successful in preserving memory.

Its high efficacy rate aside, the question remained as to how electroconvulsive shock therapy actually worked. Cerletti's early acroamine theory remained unproven, as did the more than fifty other theories that had been advanced by the mid-twentieth century. Although each theory had its proponents who were just as ardent as its detractors, the prevailing consensus emerged that the curative mechanism of electroconvulsive shock therapy remained in the words of Kalinowsky and his co-author, "shrouded in mystery" (p. 243).

That obscurity invited speculation. Undoubtedly the most unsettling and contentious of the many theories about how electroconvulsive shock therapy worked was that it permanently damaged the brain. This theory in many ways had even more political than scientific implications. It was seized upon by the burgeoning anti-psychiatry movement in the United States, Great Britain, Western Europe and Scandinavia during the 1960s and 1970s and became the lynchpin of its critique of psychiatry as a tool of oppression and of the asylum as a tool of social control. Among other things, this movement raised disconcerting questions about the extent to which asylum patients were able to give informed consent for the treatment, were allowed to withdraw it, or were even asked to give consent in the first place. It proclaimed that certain groups of asylum patients—women, racial minorities, gays and lesbians, the poor and the young—whose roles in society were rapidly and to many, disturbingly, changing were disproportionately being subjected to electroconvulsive shock therapy. It presented case after case of asylum patients who were administered electroconvulsive shock therapy with no adjunctive treatment whatsoever; who laid strapped to beds in wards or even hallways, dreading their turns with the "buzz box," the "shock factory," the "power cocktail" and the "stun shop," some of them for treatment, others for punishment.

Representatives and self-identified "survivors" involved in the anti-psychiatry movement did a great deal to tarnish the appeal of electroconvulsive shock therapy. They circulated horror stories and political treatises through their various newsletters, held public demonstrations outside of asylums and psychiatric conferences, testified before governmental bodies, gave interviews to the media, filed law suits, and published a "shock doc roster" that named and shamed physicians who administered or authorized the controversial therapeutic as well as their institutional affiliations. As a result of the movement's efforts, electroconvulsive shock treatment came under increasing regulation.

Obscurity about how electroconvulsive shock treatment actually worked also invited representation. The 1949 film *The Snake Pit* was the public's first glimpse into overcrowded public asylums and what was being touted as the miracle cure that would empty them. For its time, the representation of electroconvulsive shock treatment was quite graphic, and raised questions for the viewing public as to whether the cure was worse than the insanity. Over subsequent years, the cinematic representations of electroconvulsive shock therapy returned to that question, but it was the quintessential anti-psychiatry film, *One Flew Over the Cuckoo's Nest*, based on the Ken Kesey novel by the same name, that swayed public opinion the most. The film depicted a ferociously rebellious protagonist who feigned madness to avoid a jail sentence, and was sent to a state asylum where he engaged in a constant battle of wills with the staff. After rousing his fellow patients to revolt, he was subdued and sent to the "shock shop" for punishment. A mouth-guard was stuck between his teeth and electrodes were placed on his temples. Fully conscious when the jolts were delivered, he convulsed horribly, and later returned to the ward in a zombie-like state that, in the end, was more feigned than real.

The effect of this film on public attitudes about electroconvulsive shock treatment was considerable. In post-screening surveys, the majority of audience members considered it barbaric and punitive, and declared that they would refuse to allow a family member or friend to undergo it. The attitudes of medical students also changed in a negative direction. After viewing the electroconvulsive shock therapy scene in "One Flew Over the Cuckoo's Nest," as well as scenes in three additional films, 33 percent of surveyed medical students, who had little accurate pre-test information about the therapeutic, decreased their support for it, and 25 percent of them indicated they would dissuade a family member or friend from undergoing it.

Cinematic representations after *One Flew Over the Cuckoo's Nest* generally continued its theme of electroconvulsive shock therapy as punitive rather than therapeutic, and damaging rather than curative This was evident not only in American and European films, but in Hindi films. Between 1967 and 2008, electroconvulsive shock therapy was depicted in thirteen Hindi films; in nearly all of them, it was punitively administered, and resulted in no clinical improvements in the treated characters.

Autobiographical accounts of electroconvulsive shock therapy by celebrities such as Judy Garland and Gene Tierney, writers such as Antonin Artaud and Janet Frame, and musicians such as Lou Reed and Vladimir Horowitz, also shifted public attitudes in a negative direction. *The Bell Jar,* a semi-autobiographical account of depression and its treatment by the American poet and novelist Sylvia Plath, was particularly influential in its depiction of the course of electroconvulsive shock therapy she underwent in the 1950s while a patient at McLean Hospital in Boston, Massachusetts:

> Doctor Gordon was unlocking the closet. He dragged out a table on wheels with a machine on it and rolled it behind the head of the bed. The nurse started swabbing my temples with something greasy.... "Don't worry," the nurse grinned down on me. "Their first time everybody's scared to death."
> I tried to smile, but my skin had gone stiff, like parchment.
> Doctor Gordon was fitting two metal plates on either side of my head. He buckled them in place with a strap that dented my forehead, and gave me a wire to bite.
> I shut my eyes. There was a brief silence, like an indrawn breath.

Then something bent down, and took hold of me, and shook me like the end of the world. Whee-ee-ee-ee-ee, it shrilled, through an air crackling with blue light, and with each flash a great jolt drubbed me till I thought my bones would break and the sap fly out of me like a split plant. I wondered what terrible thing it was that I had done [Plath, pp. 117–118].

Plath committed suicide soon after the publication of *The Bell Jar*. This apparent risk of suicide after the treatment, already suggested by the suicide of writer Ernest Hemingway who had shot himself in the head a few days after going through a second course of electroconvulsive shock treatments for depression, further darkened the public attitude about the treatment. "It was a brilliant cure," Hemingway had told his biographer just a short time before his suicide, "but they lost the patient" (Hotchner, p. 308).

It was the case of Thomas Eagleton that best illustrated public, political and psychiatric attitudes about electroconvulsive shock treatment. Nominated as the running mate of George McGovern, the Democratic nominee for president in the 1972 election, he publicly revealed that he had been hospitalized on three separate occasions for depression and had undergone two courses of electroconvulsive shock treatments. The revelation was unsettling: it exposed ignorance about depression, reified the stigma that always has surrounded it, uncovered the distrust not only in those who have been labeled depressed but in the professionals who treat them, and revealed the qualms about electroconvulsive shock as a therapeutic. Capitulating to public and political pressure, McGovern asked for, and received, Eagleton's resignation. While the American Psychiatric Association weighed into the Eagleton case by submitting a carefully worded public statement about the nature and extent of depression, it said nothing that redressed the qualms. It neither vigorously defended nor attacked electroconvulsive shock therapy. After carefully explaining how the treatment is administered, and that it has a high success rate in the remediation of depression, that statement went on to say that not all psychiatrists favor its use, and that some consider it "a drastic and barbaric procedure" (Rensberger, p. 11).

In the face of this controversy and in the context of rapidly liberalizing social and political attitudes and an emergent emphasis on civil rights in the United States, Great Britain and many countries in Europe, the use of electroconvulsive shock therapy in public asylums declined considerably from the 1960s well into the 1990s. In private asylums, however, its use continued, with demographic consequences: the typical electroconvulsive shock therapy patient was no longer the poor, marginalized patient of a public asylum, about whom antipsychiatry arguments about social control were most convincing, but the white, middle class, voluntary patient whose insurance covered the treatment.

In the United States, the controversy over electroconvulsive shock treatment prompted the American Psychiatric Association to issue a 1978 report that gave the mark of approval to the procedure by stating that it was appropriate for the treatment of suicidal depression, drug-resistant mania and catatonia, but interestingly, given its original use, not for chronic schizophrenia. The report set out the conditions of informed consent, pre- and post-assessments, adjunctive pharmacological and psychological therapies as well as maintenance courses of electroconvulsive shock therapy. Once its report was published, the American Psychiatric Association initiated a public relations campaign that created a generally favorable, albeit quite brief, media interest in the therapeutic. The report also stimulated a vigorous effort to scientize electroconvulsive shock treatment. Led by Max Fink and Harold Sackeim, the scientizing movement organized conferences, sought grants to fund research, formed an association and a new journal, all with one overweening goal: to place the controversial therapeutic "in a framework of a history of progression in science and medicine ... extol[ling] its place among modern psychiatric treatments" (Hirshbein & Sarvananda, p. 11).

The electroconvulsive shock therapy of contemporary times, as a matter of fact, barely resembles that of previous decades. With anesthetics and muscle relaxers, unilaterally placed electrodes and ultra-brief pulses of electricity, the brutal convulsive thrashings, dislocations, shattered teeth and fractured bones are distant memories. First-person accounts now more often extol its virtues than not. Kitty Dukakis, the wife of a former presidential candidate Michael Dukakis, as an example, used her considerable social capital to promote the therapeutic that had successfully treated her depression and alcoholism, as this interview on a national morning news show illustrated:

> *Dukakis:* I was frightened. We had a double reason to be frightened. Michael's brother had had shock treatment years before during what I call the Dark Ages of shock treatment. And it was a very difficult time. I don't know at this point whether it helped at all, but the process itself was almost barbaric.
> *Interviewer:* But your process was very different. First of all, you get a medication that makes you not remember it.
> *Dukakis:* Yes. Right. There's an anesthesia that puts one to sleep, I'm on oxygen, I mean, there are muscle relaxants. There are all kinds of things that happen as a result. And it is seconds, the current that goes in are seconds. I had unilateral ECT, so it's on one side. Oftentimes, bilateral on both sides can cause real memory loss.
> *Interviewer:* Did you have any memory loss?
> *Dukakis:* Yes. Yes.
> *Interviewer:* And what happens when you wake up?
> *Dukakis:* Well, when I wake up, I'm a bit groggy. And after anesthesia, even though it's, you know, within 15, 20 minutes, a half-hour, you're very much awake. I have a slight headache and I go about my business. Oftentimes, I'll sleep, the day, you know, in the morning, the day of my treatment. And then I go about my business. And for me, it's just, Michael calls it the miracle in my life. It's just made, you know, I'm not everybody.

> Lots of people have not been helped. But I have; one of the lucky ones ... I feel very blessed. I'm one of those people who has been helped. Large numbers of people are helped by this treatment. And I've been one of them ["Transcript," para. 29–35, 41].

Testimonials like this helped, but in the end it was the ideological agenda of Fink, Sackeim and others that went the greatest distance not just in scientizing, but in destigmatizing, the controversial therapeutic. Endorsements flowed in from the American Medical Association, the United States Surgeon General, the National Alliance on Mental Illness, and the World Psychiatric Association. Electroconvulsive shock therapy began making a respectable comeback. Of all of the so-called "great and desperate cures" that assailed the body in order to reach the mind, it and it alone is the one left standing as an asylum therapeutic.

The "unmodified" use of electroconvulsive shock treatment, that is, without anesthesia, oxygenation or muscle relaxers, however, remains controversial. It continues to be administered in many Asian, Latin American and African countries. In Japan, for example, 57 percent of all electroconvulsive shock treatments administered are unmodified; in Thailand that figure is 94 percent. More than 25 percent of all Latin American countries administer unmodified electroconvulsive shock treatment, largely, although not solely because of the cost of doing otherwise. Cost, in fact, was the primary reason for the unsuccessful attempt to introduce the modified form in Nigeria, where the lack of qualified anesthesiologists also impeded its introduction. In Turkey, where more than 15,000 institutionalized adults and children were subjected yearly to unmodified electroconvulsive shock treatment, the practice came under serious scrutiny by the Disability Rights International organization. Its scathing 2005 report that labeled the practice as a violation of the European Convention against Torture and called into question Turkey's application to the European Union, led to a sharp turnaround in practice. The use of electroconvulsive shock treatment in general quickly decreased, and the unmodified form of it in that country has all but disappeared.

## *Insulin Shock Therapy, or Insulin Coma Therapy, or Hypoglycemic Shock Therapy*

The administration of insulin, a pancreatic hormone that lowers the level of glucose (blood sugar) in the brain, in order to induce convulsions and coma. Insulin was discovered in the early twentieth century and quickly tested as a treatment, ultimately unsuccessful, for a variety of diseases other than diabetes, for which it originally was intended. It was the young Polish neurologist, Manfred Joshua Sakel, working at the Lichterfelde Hospital, a private asylum in Berlin, who first experimented with its use to ease the anxiety, tremors and agitation of opiate withdrawal. One of his addicted patients, who also was schizophrenic, slipped into a coma when Sakel inadvertently injected him with a high dose of insulin. Quickly administering glucose to reverse the coma, Sakel was quite startled to find that the patient's most agitated symptoms of schizophrenia had diminished upon his awakening. Sakel wondered if he had stumbled upon the cure for schizophrenia. After some rather unrefined animal experiments conducted in his own kitchen, he became increasingly convinced that despite its considerable risks, insulin shock indeed remediated the perplexing symptoms of schizophrenia. Returning to the asylum he induced insulin comas in fifty-eight patients diagnosed with acute schizophrenia and brought fifty of them to full or partial remission.

Sakel moved to Vienna to begin work in the University's psychiatric service under the tutelage of Otto Poetzl who was at first skeptical about insulin shock therapy, but after seeing his first case became a believer. "The first treated case I ever saw," he wrote, "convinced me that this method of treatment outclassed any other presently available" (Wortis, p. 287).

The imprimatur of that distinguished neurologist and psychiatrist relegated the criticisms by other physicians that there was no scientific rationale for *why* insulin coma therapy seemed to work to mere background noise. Soon, the treatment drew the attention of European asylum physicians and ushered in a long overdue tide of therapeutic optimism.

Sakel visited the United States several times in the 1930s to personally supervise insulin shock sessions. On one of those visits, he lectured to more than a thousand North American asylum physicians; so much of a success was the lecture that the following day the *New York Times* lauded insulin coma therapy as "one of the great milestones in the treatment of mental ills" ("Dementia Praecox," p. 11). In 1938 Sakel emigrated to the United States, opened a free private practice and took a position as an attending physician and researcher at Harlem Valley State Hospital in New York.

Sakel had his critics in his newly adopted country, just as he had had in Europe. It was his lack of scientific rigor in his insulin coma experiments that raised questions about the legitimacy of his claims for curing schizophrenia. To these criticisms Sakel defensively retorted:

> I have a high regard for strict scientific procedure and would be glad if we could follow the accustomed path in solving this special problem: it would have been preferable to have been able to trace the cause of the disease first, and then to follow the path by looking for a suitable treatment. But since it has so happened that we by chance hit upon the wrong end of the right path, shall we undertake to leave it before better alternatives present themselves? For even if the hypoglycemic treatment of psychoses accomplishes only a part of what it promises, it nevertheless has a value beyond its therapeutic claims, for it should perhaps now enable us to work backwards from it to the nature and cause of the schizophrenia itself [Sakel, p. 840].

The criticisms of colleagues about the scientific method were offset by often hyperbolic praise from the popular press for therapeutic outcomes. A medical journalist described how "the living dead" were being restored to sanity by what was widely known in Europe as "Sakel's Technique":

> In the special wards reserved at the [Harlem Valley] hospital ... for the newly-discovered insulin shock treatment I saw some 15 patients stretched in death-like coma on their beds. At 7 o'clock that morning each had received a huge dose, by hypodermic injection, of insulin.... For nearly five hours after that they lay unconscious, oblivious alike to their actual surroundings and, presumably, to the unreal world of their disordered minds.... At noon I saw the patients awakened. The sweet, life-saving insulin-counteracting solution of sugar and water was poured into the stomach through a rubber hose inserted in the nostril. The waking process was horrible to watch.... The patients retched and choked. They uttered terrifying, animal-like sounds. Some vomited the vital sugar.... There was not time to wipe up the vomitus, or to change soiled bedding. Attendants moved swiftly, tightening restraint sheets to keep the awakening patients from throwing themselves out of bed as they thrashed about. Arms, rigid as boards, were thrust into the air, fingers spread stiffly apart. Inhuman grimaces distorted the unconscious faces.... The scene I witnessed at Harlem Valley Hospital is being repeated daily in many public and private hospitals through the United States and foreign countries. Patiently, heroically, physicians and nurses and attendants are performing over and over again the deft, life-saving ministrations I watched [Stafford, pp. 334–335].

The journalist went on to report the results of the insulin coma therapy at Harlem Valley Hospital: of the fifty-two patients treated at the time of the report, six had completely recovered, fifteen were "much improved," twenty-two were "improved," and nine were "unimproved." None of those evaluative terms was defined by either the journalist or Sakel, himself. This was a lower improvement rate than he had boasted for his European patients, as was pointed out in the article, but Sakel clarified that most of the American patients were chronic, rather than acute schizophrenics, and therefore more resistant to treatment.

The therapeutic outcomes remained unquestioned by the press, if only because they justified the considerable distress the patients had to go through to achieve them. Insulin shock therapy not only was unpleasant but risky. It had a 2 percent mortality rate, with most patients dying from complications such as heart failure, aspiration pneumonia, cerebral hemorrhage and hypoglycemic encephalopathy. Although Sakel never really acknowledged its unpleasantness, he insisted the risk could be reduced by allegiance to the "Sakel Technique." Patients were to be slowly built up over weeks or even months to tolerate increasing doses of insulin until they finally lapsed into comas. This "coma dose" would continue, usually for hours, until asylum physicians concluded they had derived the greatest possible benefit from the depletion of glucose in the brain. The comas then were terminated with either injections of an intravenous glucose solution, or administrations of a sugar solution via a nasogastric tube. To maximize its therapeutic efficacy, Sakel insisted, it should be administered to each patients as many as fifty or sixty more times over the ensuing months.

The first-person account of William Moore, a patient at the Binghamton State Hospital in New York described both the unpleasantness and the risk of insulin shock therapy. Diagnosed as schizophrenic, Moore kept a detailed diary of his treatment which included fifty-five separate insulin shock treatments. A random sample of days described his experience:

> *Treatment 1:* D-day and H-hour came. This morning between 7:00 and 7:30, a group of us were taken to a side room and given our injection of insulin. I had previously asked other patients how they like this treatment. Answers varied from, "Not bad. You just die every morning," and "Sometimes it is hell," to "It isn't bad at all. You just lie down and go to sleep." I didn't really feel any strong emotion about the idea of treatment. It couldn't be avoided, so I was resigned...
> 
> *Treatment 2:* The head nurse-attendant asked to read my notes. He asked about the remark, "People may destroy my mind, but they cannot pervert it!" "You don't think they are

trying to pervert it, do you?" he asked. My answer, summed up, came to something like this: "To the extent that they are trying to make me conform to another's 'normal,' and not to my own 'normal,' it is perversion."...

*Treatment 16:* Everyone should take insulin treatment. Then they will know beforehand what all my life I have wondered about—how it feels to die, what it is like to pass from this life into the next. For the coma one goes into during treatment is just what happens when the insulin eats up the sugar in the blood or something; it is dying of starvation, kind of, the only real difference being that we are brought back to life, we are returned to the world we left....

*Treatment 40:* "If I should die before I wake, I pray the Lord my soul to take." I died. The Lord took my soul. Then, at the end of the treatment, He gave it back to me....

*Treatment 47:* When I came to, I asked the new doctor..."How many treatments do I have to take?" "As many as you think you need." "How many is that?" "Don't pin me down."

*Treatment 55:* Two sheet straps were fastened across my body. Someone was sitting on my legs. Someone was behind me, looking down in my face. A person was on each shoulder, holding it down. At least eight people were around the bed. I couldn't move a muscle. There was something nightmarish about the whole thing. Yet, when the one injecting the glucose asked how I was, I could only reply, "All right" [Moore, pp. 244–248].

Moore never attributed the remission of his schizophrenia to insulin shock therapy, but he improved enough to be discharged. Yet skepticism about how he defined improvement continued to bother both him and other asylum physicians who were using the therapeutic. Sakel had never been particularly precise in assessing his own results, and used evaluative terms such as "cured" and "improved" without bothering to operationally define them, let alone describe them. And there was skepticism, too, about the efficacy of the therapeutic, much of its arising from a treatment trial of 1,039 patients diagnosed with schizophrenia who were treated with insulin shock therapy in New York asylums in 1938. Using an unmatched comparison group comprised of patients who had been admitted to the asylum two to three years earlier when insulin shock therapy was not yet available, the findings of the study tempered the most immoderate of Sakel's claims but, in the end, certainly did not dismiss them. Overall, 65 percent of the schizophrenic patients treated with insulin shock therapy showed some degree of improvement, compared to only 22 percent of the untreated comparison group.

"Improvement," however defined, might not, in the end, have been the outcome of insulin shock treatment alone. In an essay titled "Insulin and I," a former asylum patient who had undergone the treatment offered an interesting perspective: "Insulin did make me well," she wrote, "but the hospital doctors and nurses connected with it are entirely responsible for my well-being" (Anonymous, p. 814). This interesting distinction between wellness and well-being not only tempered any conclusions about the efficacy of insulin shock therapy, but often put asylum physicians' enthusiasm for the therapeutic at odds with patients' assessments of it. Thus the study's results, especially in the absence of any other new therapeutics for schizophrenia, redirected critics who now wondered not only just what "improvement" really meant, but how long it actually lasted. On that point, long-term follow-up studies conducted in the United States, Great Britain and Europe, consistently showed that it was, in fact, not very long. At four years post-treatment, studies found, an average of only 17 percent of the patients had maintained improvement, a rate comparable to that for untreated controls.

It was disappointing long-term follow-up results such as these that fueled the decline of interest in insulin shock therapy. In hundreds of asylums the special units where it had been administered were converted for the use of other treatments, and the highly skilled nurses and attendants who had provided the close personal care that most likely contributed to the therapeutic's initial success, were reassigned.

Thus when Princeton University mathematician John Forbes Nash was committed to Trenton State Hospital in New Jersey in 1961, insulin shock treatment was on the wane. Diagnosed as schizophrenic, Nash nonetheless was subjected to a course of insulin shock treatment, after which he was assessed as in remission and then discharged. Although he had nothing good to say about it, referring to it as "torture," he did have an "interlude of enforced rationality," as he described it, upon his discharge (Nasar, p. 294). Unfortunately, and consistent with the findings of long-term studies, it did not last long. Two years later, Nash once again was involuntarily committed, this time to a private asylum; two years after his discharge from there, he was involuntarily committed once again. From that point on, as Nash wrote in his Nobel Prize autobiography:

> I became a person of delusionally influenced thinking but of relatively moderate behavior and thus tended to avoid hospitalization and the direct attention of psychiatrists.... So at the present time I seem to be thinking rationally again in the style that is characteristic of scientists. However this is not entirely a matter of joy as if someone returned from physical disability to good physical health. One aspect of this is that rationality of thought imposes a limit on a person's concept of his relation to the cosmos. For example, a non–Zoroastrian could think of Zarathustra as simply a madman who led millions of naïve followers to adopt a cult of ritual fire worship. But without his "madness" Zarathustra would necessarily have been only another of the millions or billions of human individuals who have lived and then been forgotten [Nash, para. 27–28].

## *Metrazol Shock Therapy, or Cardiazol Shock Therapy*

The administration of pentylenetetrazol. Known by its trade name metrazol and in Europe by its brand name cardiazol, pentylenetetrazol acted as a circulatory and respiratory stimulant and when administered in large doses produced convulsion and coma.

In the mid-eighteenth century the British physician Richard Mead proposed that insanity was incompatible with other major diseases. Although his theory, based on a single observation, waxed and waned over the subsequent century, it never completely disappeared. Thus, when László Meduna, an Hungarian neurologist, observed an apparent antagonism between schizophrenia and epilepsy, his observation was well within the bounds of received medical wisdom. It was the early 1920s and Meduna sought confirmation of his observation by conducting postmortem examinations of the brains of epileptic and schizophrenic patients at the Interacademic Brain Research Institute in Budapest. He found what he believed were subtle differences in the glial cells. Speculating that it must have been the convulsions that kept epileptics from developing schizophrenia, he hypothesized that if convulsions were induced in schizophrenics, they would have a curative effect. In a search for the most effective pharmacological agent to produce convulsions, Meduna engaged in a series of animal experiments, variously trying strychnine, coramin, and caffeine, before settling on camphor, an extract of the laurel bush.

Administering camphor to human patients, however, posed some risk to his career at the prestigious Institute where he was employed, so Meduna sought out an experimental subject at the Royal National Hungarian Institute of Psychiatry and Neurology at Budapest-Lipotmezö. There, he came across a thirty-three-year-old chronic schizophrenic patient who had deteriorated so much that all of his bodily needs had to be attended to by the asylum staff. Meduna administered five intramuscular injections of camphor over a short period, producing a convulsion each time. Upon the fifth convulsion the patient who had barely moved by his own volition in years, got out of bed, dressed himself and began talking with the asylum staff.

In his unpublished autobiography, Meduna identified his first patient as "Zoltán L.," and then cobbled together a story, as amazing as it was apocryphal, about him. What Meduna remembered was that although his improvement was astonishing, it was not enough to secure his discharge from the asylum. So, he escaped. He ran home, only to find his wife in bed with her lover. He gave both of them a good thrashing, threw the lover out of the house, and dramatically declared to his wife that he would rather live in an insane asylum than in this crazy world. It was that proclamation, according to Meduna, that convinced him that "Zoltán L." really had been cured after all. In fact, "Zoltán L." was not that first patient he treated with camphor—he was the tenth. There were no records of his having escaped from the asylum, and no mention of his having ever beaten up anyone. Somewhat ironically, the real "Zoltán L." had never responded favorably to the thirty-six camphor treatment sessions he underwent between 1933 and 1935. He died in the asylum a decade later.

After the administration of camphor to the first patient, whomever he may have been, Meduna experimented with an additional eleven schizophrenic patients, noting with some disappointment that the administration of camphor did not produce convulsions in all of them. Nonetheless, improvements were noted in those for whom it did: two improved well enough to be discharged, and one well enough to participate in the asylum's occupational therapy program.

Hoping to produce a higher rate of convulsions, Meduna then tried metrazol, a synthetic preparation known in Europe as cardiazol, a quick-acting and effective convulsant when administered in high doses. Against the advice of his mentor at the Institute, who dismissed him as a "swindler, humbug and cheat" for claiming he could cure schizophrenia (Fink, p. 1036), Meduna published his findings: ten of the twenty-six schizophrenic patients "recovered," three showed "good results," and thirteen showed "no improvement."

No other therapeutic for schizophrenia, the most baffling and intractable type of insanity, showed such promising results. Metrazol shock therapy quickly became the therapeutic of choice in Europe, largely as a consequence of Meduna's considerable entrepreneurial activities which included the telling and retelling of the specious "Zoltán L." success story. In Denmark, for example, cardiazol as metrazol was called, was administered to asylum patients as early as 1937 in its three state asylums. At one of those asylums, Vordingborg, cardiazol treatment started at seven each morning. Patients were placed on their backs, their limbs spread out, and administered fifty to seventy centigram doses of cardiazol in a 10 percent aqueous solution. Convulsions usually began within seconds and lasted as long as a minute; the limbs stiffened then jerked rapidly and rhythmically, until the patients, their faces often blue with exertion, passed out. The success rate of cardiazol treatment mirrored that found by Meduna: 19 percent of the 207 schizophrenic patients treated at the three Danish state asylum improved enough to be discharged, 33 percent improved somewhat and 48 percent showed no improvement. All of an additional thirty-nine patients diagnosed with the mood disorders of depression and/or mania went into full remission.

The results, replicated in asylums throughout Europe and Great Britain, caused one Danish asylum physician to proclaim that cardiazol was "like a miracle!" (Kragh, p. 350). But there was dark side to cardiazol treatment: patients loathed it and often had to be forcefully coerced into taking it. A Danish patient described his experience with cardiazol in a letter to his relatives that was confiscated by his treating physician:

> Lately I have had 5–7 injections with something called Cardiazol. It is injected in a vein in the right elbow joint. It is something new Dr. Hahnemann says. It has a very strong effect, completely different from anything else I have been injected with up until now. About 10 seconds after having received the injection, it is as if you are pulled out of yourself and into another world, but you can still see the persons around you as if in a limpid fog. It is utterly unbearable and quite impossible to get out of. Sometimes the effect is stronger, sometimes weaker; when it is strong you have hallucinations.... The room you are lying in begins to look like Hell, and it is as if you are burned

by an invisible fire. It is very scary. But luckily it is over now [Kragh, p. 351].

The patients' experiences with metrazol shock therapy were of much less interest to asylum physicians than the outcomes. Indeed, it was the most widely used somatic therapeutic in Europe in the 1930s, arming beleaguered asylum physicians with what appeared to be an effective and easy to administer treatment that promised to cure the schizophrenic patients who comprised half of nearly every asylum's census. It did not take long for word of its success in treating schizophrenia to reach asylum physicians in the United States. In 1938 the *American Journal of Psychiatry* published the proceedings of a Swiss symposium on shock therapies that included a paper by Meduna; a year later, he emigrated to the United States and was given a professorship in neurology at Loyola University in Chicago, Illinois. And by 1940 almost every public and private asylum in the country was using metrazol, not just for the treatment of schizophrenia but for mood disorders, especially depression, for which it was thought to be particularly efficacious, terminating severe depressive reactions in 90 percent of cases.

These outcomes did not go unnoticed, or unappreciated, by asylum patients, their loathing and fear of metrazol shock therapy aside. Thirty-seven patients to whom it had been administered at Rockland State Hospital in Orangeburg, New York, were interviewed about the experiences in 1938. All described it as unpleasant and many feared they were about to die, yet almost all of them reported feeling better upon its completion. One patient described feeling less discouraged and pessimistic. "I don't worry now," she explained. "I feel calm because I make the best of everything now" (Starks, p. 704). Another, who had been institutionalized for more than two years, said he had better control of his thoughts. "Impressions become more clear and distinct," he clarified. "One seems to observe things and judge. Before, impressions were not voluntary. Now, all the difference in the world. The impressions are fresher, not the same old things, and they are voluntary" (Starks, p. 705).

This early and rare look into the subjective experiences of treated patients seemed to indicate that the positive results of metrazol shock therapy outweighed the negative. There was some reason, however, to be skeptical of the first-person accounts. Metrazol shock therapy produced retrograde amnesia, so patients may have not remembered the latency period between the injection and the convulsion. It was during that time that they tended to become the most frightened, anxious and often difficult to manage.

There was another reasons to be concerned about metrazol shock therapy as well. Unlike insulin shock therapy, in which sugar or glucose served as a fast-acting antidote to the convulsions, there was no antidote for metrazol. Asylum physicians, therefore, had little if any control over the convulsions that often were so violent that they resulted in bone fractures, dislocations, and shattered teeth. At Bellevue Psychiatric Hospital in New York City, for example, the incidence of fractures for schizophrenic children who underwent the treatment was so alarmingly high that physicians were forced to administer beta-throidin hydrochloride to diminish the strength of muscle contractions, a practice that became widely prescribed for adult patients as well.

But the larger concern for asylum physicians in the United States, Europe and Great Britain was the pestering question of efficacy. Metrazol shock therapy seemed to produce improvements only in the short-run, and despite Meduna's insistence that it was a cure for schizophrenia, patients diagnosed with depression tended to show the most lasting positive effects. While that may have been considered an achievement in and of itself, a new type of shock therapy—electroconvulsive shock therapy—was proving itself easier to administer and with better long-term effects than either metrazol or insulin.

That did not seem to bother Meduna much. He had lost interest in metrazol after a while and had turned his attention, instead, to carbon dioxide therapy [see **Cerebral Stimulation**]. Without his continuing entrepreneurship, and with high risks and low long-term positive results, metrazol shock therapy all but disappeared from asylums by the mid-twentieth century.

## *Photoshock*

The generation of convulsions in sedated patients by means of exposure to intermittent photic stimulation in the form of fifteen flashes of intense light per second from a stroboscope. The photoshock treatment was developed in the mid-twentieth century by the French neurologist Henri Gastaud. Interested in the neurology, taxonomy and phenomenology of epilepsy, Gastaud took note of the fact that some of his patients experienced self-induced photosensitive seizures. He hypothesized that if he could produce the seizures with light, he will have found a viable alternative to electroconvulsive shock in the treatment of various types of insanity. Gastaud's preliminary research on what he was now calling "photoshock" produced mixed results and the therapeutic was not aggressively pursued.

In the United States, however, there was keen interest in photoshock among a handful of academics, researchers and asylum physicians. Most notable among them was George Ulett, affiliated with the Department of Neuropsychiatry of Washington University Medical School and the Malcolm Bliss Hospital, both in St. Louis, Missouri. Ulett and his colleagues set about to create a protocol for the administration of photoshock and a rigorous set of criteria for comparing its outcomes to those of more conventional shock treatments, most particularly electroconvulsive shock treatment.

In regards to protocol, Ulett and his colleagues determined that the drug Azozol produced a consistent and reproducible lowering of the convulsive threshold when it was administered in a single dose and at a constant rate of injection. Convulsions were not produced by the Azozol alone; rather, they were triggered by an intermittent light flashed fourteen to twenty times per second on the patients' closed eyelids. To assess the outcomes of photoshock treatment, Ulett and his colleagues administered a battery of psychological tests to patients who had been diagnosed with depression of the manic-depressive, involutional, senile or reactive types, as well as those with acute catatonic schizophrenic and schizoaffective reactions, and randomly assigned them to matched experimental and control groups. All of the experimental group patients were administered photoshock in the morning, three times per week, for a total of twelve to fifteen treatments. Upon completion of the treatments, the battery of psychological tests measuring intellectual functioning, ideomotor retardation, amount of depression of affect and contact with reality, was re-administered. The final evaluation of improvement was summarized with a numerical rating on a continuum from "worse" to "complete recovery." With its allegiance to the scientific method, this rigorous approach was an antidote to the uncontrolled and sometimes sloppy observations and measures that were then being used to evaluate the various shock treatments. The rigor also strengthened the validity of Ulett's findings. Photoshock was found to have the same therapeutic effect as electroconvulsive shock treatment and, in the bargain, had a milder onset and less severe course. The findings, in Ulett's opinion, gave validity to the observation that it was the convulsions that cured depression.

Photoshock, however, was not without its risks. The experiences of asylum physicians who used it, as well as of Ulett himself, showed that it had an alarming ability to reproduce previously experienced symptoms in asylum patients. Nine patients in a sample of sixteen who had been photoshocked by Ulett, had such an experience. One of them, a fifty-five-year-old female who had a history of astasia-abasia (inability to stand or walk) and glove anesthesia (loss of sensitivity in the hand and wrist), reported that the photoshock treatment made her feel "like when my spells starts—a sort of falling feeling" (Ulett, p. 72). During the treatment she would rub her upper lip at times, later stating that it would swell at the onset of one of her hysterical attacks. Another patient, a twenty-one-year-old female with a diagnosis of psychoneurosis with depression, re-experienced the constant choking sensation that had brought her to the asylum in the first place. During the photoshock treatment, she became restless and anxious and "rubbed her neck and shoulder in a slow, automatic fashion" (p. 72).

In the end, however, it was not so much the risks associated with photoshock that impeded its widespread therapeutic use; rather, it was the hegemony of electroconvulsive shock treatment. By the 1970s, photoshock had all but disappeared as an asylum therapeutic.

## *Regressive Electroconvulsive Shock Treatment, or R.E.S.T, or Intensive Electroconvulsive Shock Treatment, or Annihilation Therapy, or Polydiurnal Therapy*

The electrical induction of several grand mal convulsions per day over several days in succession, until clinical signs indicated that "regression" had been achieved. Those clinical signs, which were products of organic brain syndrome, included "memory loss, marked confusion, disorientation, lack of verbal spontaneity, slurring of speech to the point of complete dysarthria or muteness, and utter apathy" (Glueck, Reiss, & Bernard, p. 118). A patient who was in a state of regression also behaved "like a helpless infant, is incontinent in both bowel and bladder functions, requires spoon-feeding and, at times, tube-feeding" (p. 118). Upon cessation of the treatment, the organic symptoms would recede rather quickly and original symptomology would not immediately reappear.

Originally labeled "annihilation therapy,"

this therapeutic was promoted in the mid-twentieth century by Lucio Bini who, with Ugo Cerletti, had developed electroconvulsive shock treatment years before. Annihilation, Bini argued, produced a severe amnesic reaction that had therapeutic benefits for the patient in the throes of obsession, depression, neurasthenia or hysteria. Finding the word "annihilation" too provocative, the Swiss psychiatrist Oscar Forel renamed the procedure "intensive electroconvulsive shock treatment." The therapeutic, which maximized rather than minimized memory loss, was used with phenomenal success by W. Liddell Milligan who claimed to have cured or markedly improved ninety-seven of his 100 psychoneurotic patients at St. James Hospital in Portsmouth, England, and by Hans Löwenbach and Edward Tyler, who further softened the label by referring to it as "polydiurnal therapy" at Duke University Hospital and the North Carolina State Hospital in the United States.

Löwenbach and Tyler had observed that post-convulsion confusion seemed to be therapeutic and were eager to produce it in patients whose mental problems were more debilitating than those of the psychoneurotic patients who seemed to benefit from it most. To that end, they subjected thirty-two asylum patients, variously diagnosed with schizophrenia or some type or major depression, to several electroconvulsive shock treatments per day and for several days in succession. Fifteen of those patients showed no significant improvement and remained institutionalized; seven were released although none had improved well enough to work. Ten patients, however, who had received an average of ten treatments each, were discharged to their families and returned to work, no longer plagued by the symptoms that had brought them to the asylum in the first place. One of those patients was a thirty-five-year-old white married man whose "jittery" feelings had evolved into loss of appetite, sleeplessness, uncontrolled sexual thoughts, and a stubborn belief that his friend, who was very much alive, had been killed. In the throes of what he was calling a "nervous breakdown," he had attempted suicide by slashing his throat.

Committed to the asylum, he was given thirteen electroconvulsive shock treatments over three successive days. At the end of the first day he was still fully oriented to time, person and place, but could no longer recall his symptoms; at the end of the second day he was orientated only to person and believed he was a decade younger than he actually was, and that he was single and childless; at the end of the third and final day, he believed he was a teenager who was living on a farm. Over the next several days, evidence of what Löwenbach and Tyler posited were the therapeutic effects of extreme confusion were meticulously documented:

> The fourth day the patient was very much confused and was unable to understand even simple instructions. His speech was thick and slow, and frequently unintelligible. When given food or water he sat swishing it around his mouth without swallowing it. He resisted going to the toilet.... He began letting saliva drool from his mouth and he voided on the bathroom floor. The fifth day he said he felt better and talked a little spontaneously. He was unable to remember his name when asked, but responded to it when called. He ate well but slept poorly. The sixth day he got up early, went promptly to the bathroom and started washing his face and hair, but repeated this action until interrupted. He now thought he was in his twenties, unmarried and working in a grocery store. He began to complain of things whirling about him and would frequently say, "This elevator is going up too fast." The seventh day he wandered about the hall trying to unlock doors and spoke of getting ready to go to work in a few minutes. He now dressed spontaneously, but was slow in initiating each new action.... During the first part of the second week after shock therapy ... he gradually remembered being married, but not that he had a child. He was friendly and cooperative.... In the third week, the patient regained much of his memory except for a period extending almost one year. He was totally unable to remember having been sick.... In this condition he was discharged on the twenty-first day after the treatment had started [Tyler & Löwenbach, pp. 579–580].

Except for a lingering embarrassment that he could not always remember the faces and names of his friends, the patient showed steady improvement over several outpatient visits. Interestingly, and unexpectedly, the comparison of a battery of pre- and post-treatment assessments showed that he had gained sixteen points on his IQ score.

Within a short time span, not only had the names of this type of electroconvulsive shock treatment changed, but so had the target patient population. Originally labeled annihilation therapy, "one of the most unfortunate coinages of postwar medicine" (Shorter & Healy, p. 137) and then changed with as much rapidity as wisdom to "intensive electroconvulsive shock treatment," it was administered to the psychoneurotics who were the most recent additions to the census of asylums in Great Britain, Europe and the United States. Relabeled "polydiurnal therapy," it was used to treat schizophrenic patients, and in yet another rebranding it was called "regressive electroconvulsive shock treatment" or R.E.S.T., and was used to treat chronic schizophrenic patients who had not responded to other courses of treatment.

That iteration took place in the late 1940s when Cyril Kennedy and David Anchel targeted refractory schizophrenic patients at the Kings Park State Hospital in New York. They administered two to four electroconvulsive shocks daily from ten to fourteen successive days until a "desired degree" of regression had been created, that is, "when [the patient] wet and soiled, or acted and talked like a child of four" (Kennedy and Anchel, p. 318). In this state, the patients were cooperative and suggestible, their minds "like clean slates" upon which the asylum physicians could therapeutically write (p. 318). With the exception of one patient, the remaining twenty-four showed improvement, often to a considerable degree, although it might be noted that neither "improvement" nor "considerable degree" was defined in detail. Kennedy and Anchel concluded that the kind of "deep regression" they had produced with what they now referred to as "regressive electroconvulsive shock treatment" was a valuable technique for the treatment of refractory schizophrenic patients.

Regressive electroconvulsive shock treatment was used with some frequency well into the mid-twentieth century, perhaps as an attempt to ease the burden of horribly overcrowded, understaffed and underfunded public asylums. Under increasing professional, public and political scrutiny, asylum physicians also were eager to raise their profile as scientists and healers and, arguably, there was no type of patient who sullied both the asylums' and their physicians' reputations more than the chronic schizophrenic for whom other types of treatment had failed to produce results.

Bernard Glueck, Harry Reiss and Louis Bernard treated 100 such patients at the Stony Lodge Hospital in New York. They electrically induced three grand mal convulsions daily to each patient until regression, that is, behavior "like a helpless infant" (p. 118) had been achieved, requiring an average of thirty-four treatments per patient. Emergence from this regressed state occurred over seven to ten days post-treatment. Placid, benign and with significantly impaired memories, the patients were rendered particularly amenable to psychotherapy, especially because previously unconscious conflicts were likely to surface at that time. The results were encouraging, although they left the physicians somewhat confused as to whether it was the regressive electroconvulsive shock treatment, the intensive psychotherapy and attentive nursing care post-treatment, or some combination of both that actually produced them. Three months after treatment, forty-eight of the 100 patients had improved significantly enough to be released from the asylum; twenty-four more were considered improved, but not enough to be discharged. Only ten of the patients, however, still could be considered "recovered" after five years, although thirteen others showed continuing improvement over that period of time. Acknowledging that their results were somewhat atypical and that previous studies of its use, such as that by David Rothschild, Donald VanGordon and Anthony Varjabedian at Worcester State Hospital in Massachusetts, had led to a much more pessimistic conclusion, they nonetheless decided that regressive electroconvulsive shock treatment should be considered the "treatment of choice" for schizophrenic asylum patients.

It was not until the early twentieth century that child psychiatry emerged as a specialty in Great Britain, Europe and the United States and, as it did, asylums began creating separate children's units. During World War II and immediately after, the changing nature of the family, the increased case-finding functions of public education, social services, juvenile courts and child guidance centers, assured those facilities filled rapidly. Schizophrenia, always thought to have an adolescent or early adulthood onset, increasingly was being diagnosed in children—and it was being treated with regressive electroconvulsive shock treatment. What better way to inscribe the *tabula rasa* that were the minds of young children?

One practitioner of this controversial innovation was Lauretta Bender. Between 1942 and 1947, Bender administered at least three electroconvulsive shocks each day to ninety-eight children hospitalized in the Children's Ward of the Psychiatric Division of Bellevue Hospital in New York City. Ranging in age from four to eleven years, all of them had been diagnosed with schizophrenia.

Fear always was considered both a reasonable response to electroconvulsive shock treatment and a necessary "terror defense reaction," as Cerletti had termed it, for a successful outcome. The idea of terrorizing children, however, was unsettling. Bender, in effect, neutralized that fear by psychoanalytically interpreting their reactions:

> There was very little anxiety in relation to the treatment [although] some children showed preoccupation with the meaning of the shock experience. Girls clearly related it to sexual intercourse and fantasy. Boys concerned themselves with aggressive implications as with the

possibility that it was punishment or that they might not recover consciousness. Children in or near puberty showed the most marked anxiety. Some of the youngest mute children were negativistic and resistive sometimes to the point of panic. However, most of the children would lend themselves passively and actively to the treatment both physically and psychologically [Bender, p. 167].

The outcomes, however, were not promising. The disturbances in thought and language, social withdrawal and emotional ability which were the hallmark symptoms of childhood schizophrenia remained for the most part, unremediated. Half of the children, though, had improved enough to return home; the other half remained institutionalized. Bender, however, concluded,

> it is the opinion of all observers in the hospital, the school rooms, of the parents and other guardians that the children were always somewhat improved by the treatment inasmuch as they were less disturbed, less excitable, less withdrawn, and less anxious. They were better controlled, seemed better integrated and more mature and were better able to meet social situations in a realistic fashion. They were more composed, happier, and were better able to accept teaching or psychotherapy in groups or individually [Bender, p. 168].

A study by E.R. Clardy and Elizabeth Rumpf, however, called into question both the effects and the efficacy of regressive electroconvulsive shock therapy with schizophrenic children, not to mention the very diagnosis of childhood schizophrenia in the first place. Thirty children who had been treated in Bender's program were still institutionalized seven years later, this time in the children's ward in Rockland State Hospital in New York. They and two additional children were the subjects of a follow-up study that found that for four of the nine children for whom the diagnosis of schizophrenia was "definite," the regressive electroconvulsive shock therapy produced "much improvement"; for two it produced "improvement," and for the remaining three, "no improvement." For the twenty children in Bender's program for whom the original diagnosis of schizophrenia was questionable, most improved immediately after the regressive electroconvulsive shock treatments, but relapsed into considerably worsened states quite soon after. For the three remaining children rediagnosed as psychopathic, the treatment had significantly worsened their conditions, although other types of adjunctive therapies had improved two of them over subsequent years.

The experiences of the children with regressive electroconvulsive shock therapy were described in brief case studies:

> Ten year old boy with IQ of 122, who had been reared in "a disorganized, strife-torn home where he witnessed and was subjected to much physical violence," spoke of an intense desire to kill the doctor who treated him with ECT. He also was hostile to mom for committing him. Before admission to Rockland, he assaulted mom and then attempted to jump out of apartment window.
> 
> Eleven year old boy with IQ of 130 who at 7 "had been exposed to sexual experiences by an irresponsible, alcoholic father," described his reaction to ECT a year after treatment: "When I heard the word 'shock' I thought they would put me in something like an electric chair. I was scared to death of them! I thought maybe I'd die, but after I woke up I wasn't so scared any more. But I felt like a bunch of rocks were going around in my head; I mean I had a headache! I was just as tense as I was before, and I was mixed up about things as before. I don't think they did me any good, because when I came here I was just as bad as ever. I couldn't do any school work so good any more."
> 
> Nine year old girl with IQ of 107 who had felt severely rejected at home, and who at 7 had played truant and engaged in sexual practices with older boys, expressed "considerable resentment" for ECT five years before. "They are only for crazy people, and I hope I'm not crazy. I had awful headaches and then I went to sleep. Only when I woke up I didn't feel like I slept at all. I think I'd have gotten better without them" [Clardy & Rumpf, p. 621].

In their follow-up study, Clardy and Rumpf found that the effects of regressive electroconvulsive shock treatment "were temporary and resulted in no sustained improvement in the patterning of behavior. Relapses occurred in all cases, necessitating continued hospitalization" (p. 620), and any improvement seen in the children over subsequent months and years was due largely to "transference or attachment, giving the child contact with suitable parental substitutes" (p. 622). It concluded with a warning that drew a bright line along the schism between practitioners of standard electroconvulsive shock therapy, and those advocating it in its regressive form:

> It appears to the writers that one should be fearful of giving electric shock therapy to very young children—those four or five years old—for we have no good understanding of what pathology may take place in the child's brain or the later effect of shock treatment on the personality that is only in the developmental stage. It seems that one would be justified in giving this treatment when the child has remained in a chronic state, or is deteriorating, and when all other measures have failed. Important consideration must also be given to the psychological influence of shock experience on the long-range emotional and social maturation of youngsters treated in their formative years. Perhaps some clues have been given by the children's personal reactions and their interpretations as reported here [Clardy & Rumpf, pp. 622–623].

One of those children was Ted Chabasinski. Sent at the age of six to the Children's Ward of the Psychiatric Division of Bellevue Hospital by a social worker who was overseeing his foster home placement, he was diagnosed as schizophrenic and given a daily course of regressive electroconvulsive shock treatments. Chabasinski, now an attorney who is active in the psychiatric survivors' movement, recollected his experience:

> I wanted to die but I really didn't know what death was. I knew that it was something terrible. Maybe I'll be so tired after the next shock treatment I won't get up, I won't ever get up, and I'll be dead. But I always got up. Something in me beyond my wishes made me put myself together again. I memorized my name, I taught myself to say my name. Teddy, Teddy, I'm Teddy.... I'm here, I'm here, in this room, in this hospital. And my mommy's gone.... I would cry and realize how dizzy I was. The world was spinning around and coming back to it hurt too much. I want to go down, I want to go where the shock treatment is sending me, I want to stop fighting and die ... and something made me live, and to go on living. I had to remember never to let anyone near me again [Chabasinski, para. 5–7].

The practice of administering regressive electroconvulsive shocks to patients, whether children or adults, deeply divided asylum physicians. The efficacy of the therapeutic and, particularly, its ethics were debated until the mid-twentieth century when powerful medications that produced the same regressive states, were introduced into asylum medicine.

## Sub-Coma Insulin Treatment, or Sakel Borderline Insulin Treatment

The induction of repeated mild hypoglycemic shocks with doses of insulin sufficient enough to cloud consciousness for forty-five to sixty minutes, but not sufficient enough to produce coma. The treatment preserved the underlying therapeutic logic of insulin shock therapy while at the same time reduced the considerable risks associated with it.

Don Weitz, who had been diagnosed with schizophrenia when he was involuntarily committed by his parents to McLean Hospital in Boston, Massachusetts, after dropping out of university in 1951, described the treatment in detail. He had been started on five units of insulin three times a day which was increased by increments of five units daily over the following days. The effects of each treatment lasted three to four hours and were terminated with a drink of fruit juice laced with glucose or dextrose. Aside from weight gain (Weitz had gained 50 pounds over six weeks of treatment), the effects were described in the nurses' observations that were attached to his file. On selected days of the last three weeks of his treatment, these observations were made:

Day 23—Treatment 60: Some tremors, response poor, face very pale, some twitching of face, hands trembling, moderate to severe crying...

Day 24—Treatment 63: "Patient became drowsy about 4 pm and had to be awakened several times. ...perspiration, facial tremors & fits of crying...

Day 25—Treatment 66: Perspiring profusely, very slow response, skin cool. Patient remarked, " I can't take it."

Day 29—Treatment 77: Slow tongue-mouthing, grimacing, twitching of facial muscles and extremities.

Day 32—Treatment 84: Patient seeking reassurance. Says he's had enough of this insulin. Patient remarked this was the biggest reaction. Skin was moist. Response slow.

Day 33—Treatment 86: Apprehensive about going into coma—states he was very worried about his condition this AM.

Day 34—Treatment 90: Emotional outburst, shouting and sobbing up and down hall that he must get out of here, that he can't stand insulin any longer, etc.... Still sobbing frequently and unpredictably faint tremors, slight twitching of facial muscles in addition to above. Very confused.

Day 36—Treatment 98: Perspiring freely. Myoclonic twitching of the face. Tremor of the hand. Bizarre movements. Resistive to termination. Terminated with a great deal of resistance, using pure dextrose.

Day 40—Treatment 104: Stumbled twice on returning from bathroom ... jerky movements of arms & legs.

Day 45—Treatment 110 [last treatment]: No tremors. Delayed reaction. Recovery [Weitz, para. 14–23].

The notes of Weitz's treating physician indicated that the major symptom of his schizophrenia were the outbursts and tantrums his parents had reported upon his commitment, and that these were successfully eliminated by the sub-coma insulin treatment. Physicians at the Payne Whitney Psychiatric Clinic on the Upper East Side of Manhattan, New York, reported a similar success in removing or reducing the symptoms of excitability, anxiety and depression in 80 percent of the 133 schizophrenic patients they treated between 1942 and 1952. At the same time, they admitted that while symptoms were reduced, the underlying illness of schizophrenia could not be considered altered, let alone cured.

The report of these findings by Donald Greaves and his colleagues prompted a vigorous debate as to the efficacy of sub-coma insulin treatment and, tangentially, about insulin shock therapy which already was on the wane. While most agreed that the sub-coma variation reduced risks to the patients, made it easier to assure their cooperation, reduced personnel needs and was less expensive in the bargain, some asylum physicians argued that it was little more than a "symptom sedative" because in the absence of a coma, it could not nothing to affect the underlying illness. Others disagreed, arguing that it was not the coma, per se, that accounted for any reported successes of traditional insulin shock treatment, but the psychological aspects, most particularly the fear of death it created in patients.

While certainly not confined to the United States, sub-coma insulin therapy was most popular there as physicians struggled, in the face of professional and public cynicism, to transform asylum psychiatry into an authoritative medical specialty. Just as was the case of insulin shock therapy, sub-coma insulin treatment disappeared as a therapeutic in the mid-twentieth century when powerful antipsychotic medications came on the market.

# Surgery

*The treatment of insanity by operative procedures.*

In the late nineteenth and early twentieth centuries autointoxication theories held out promise for the treatment, even the cure, of the most intractable types of insanity. The eminent German physician Emil Kraepelin, regarded in his own lifetime as the founder of modern scientific psychiatry, declared that dementia praecox, the most obdurate of insanities, was caused by "an endogenous process of chronic autointoxication which led to a 'self poisoning (*Selbstvergiftung*)' of the body and, eventually, its brain" (Noll, 2007, p. 303). In so declaring a somatic cause, he suggested, even if he did not recommend, a remedy: surgical excision of the pathogenic site.

Kraepelin's conclusion was both a constituent and a consequence of a tangled skein of medical theories during that era about autointoxication. These, in turn, were derived from the new medical specialties of bacteriology, endocrinology, immunology and serology that had been spawned by that era's revolution in laboratory medicine. Each was adapted to asylum medicine and, in its own way, influenced asylum therapeutics. Bacteriology's germ theory, as an example, was based on the proposition that disease was caused by toxins secreted by bacterial organisms. The theory was serviceable as an explanation for insanity: it must be caused, some asylum physicians speculated, by toxins that had circulated to the brain. Because the teeth were thought to one particularly noxious site of bacteria and infection, their removal was considered an expedient remedy [see **Exodontia**]. Endocrinology, as another example, was based on the proposition that disease was caused by the under- or over-production of the secretions of the body's various glands. If that were also the cause of insanity, some asylum physicians reckoned, then the treatment was obvious: the injection of glandular extracts [see **Organotherapy**].

One of the most compelling of the autointoxication theories was that the toxins that caused disease were products of the putrefactive process of the intestines. In normal and healthy conditions the toxins so produced are filtered by other organs of the body, most particularly the liver and kidneys, but in some conditions of the over-production of such toxins, it was argued, the filtering organs were overwhelmed. The toxins then circulated through the bloodstream, adversely affecting the cells of the brain, causing that most puzzling and frustratingly incurable type of insanity, then called dementia praecox. The therapeutic intervention in these cases, then, was evident to some asylum physicians: surgical excisions of the sites of infection in the gastrointestinal system.

It is important to appreciate that in the era in question, autointoxication and its surgical cure were well within the bounds of both medical knowledge and acceptable medical practice. The controversy that eventually engulfed this surgical cure for dementia praecox and other types of insanity had less to do with the changing contours of medical knowledge than with its zealous use and the exaggerated claims of cure made by just a few asylum physicians.

Among them was Bayard Taylor Holmes. A surgeon and bacteriologist by specialty, Holmes had an intense and deeply personal interest in dementia praecox. His own son was suffering from it. Determined to find its cause and cure, Holmes engaged in meticulous laboratory research that brought him to the conclusion that focal sepsis, a localized site of infection in the colon, was the source of the autointoxication that caused dementia praecox. Although his research finding required careful follow-up and replication before it could be considered valid, Holmes was eager to act on it. In a Chicago, Illinois, hospital in 1916, he operated on his son. He performed an appendicostomy, a surgical opening of the tip of the diverticulum of the right colon to irrigate the bowel, followed by post-surgical irrigations of the colon with a mixture of water and magnesium sulfate. His son died four days later. His unfortunate death did not send Holmes back into the laboratory to re-examine his findings; instead, it hurried him into the surgery suite where he operated on two more dementia praecox patients. Buoyed by the fact that both were "apparently improved" (Holmes, p. 702), he then published his claim that he had found both the cause and the cure of dementia praecox.

Holmes and surgeons under his tutelage performed a total of twenty-two appendicostomies, but with mixed results. Holmes went on to found and edit *Dementia Praecox Studies: A Journal of Psychiatry of Adolescence*, compile an exhaustive bibliography on the results of laboratory studies on dementia praecox, and advocate for adding laboratory facilities to asylums. Yet he received neither the attention nor the notoriety for the surgical treatment of dementia praecox as Henry Cotton did.

At the turn into the twentieth century, Cotton was appointed the medical superintendent of Trenton State Hospital in New Jersey, the first state asylum built as the result of the advocatory efforts of reformer Dorothea Dix. He was appalled at what greeted him: deplorable conditions, a demoralized and sometimes brutal staff, hopeless and helpless patients. His reform efforts were immediate and laudable. He improved the physical facilities, hired and trained new staff, and then closely supervised their interactions with patients. To Cotton, these reforms were as strategic as they were necessary in that they paved the way for his most pressing initiative—the transformation of the already archaic asylum into a modern hospital where the insane would be cured by the best that medicine had to offer.

And that best was based on the theory of autointoxication. To Cotton, insanity was a disease of the body not of the mind, and it had a single cause that could be remedied with a single cure. Confirm the source of the infection that was spreading toxins to the brain, he reasoned, surgically remove it and insanity would be cured. He began by extracting the rotten teeth of fifty patients who languished in the asylum's backwards, and then later removed the tonsils of twenty-five of them; all but one improved so dramatically post-tonsillectomy that they were discharged as recovered.

Certain that he had indeed found the cure for insanity, Cotton began to hunt for all foci of chronic sepsis and to surgically remove them. Appendixes, gallbladders, uteri and thyroid glands were removed in the asylum's bespoke surgical suites, as were parts of stomachs, small intestines and, especially, colons.

Why the colon? Certainly there was a lingering influence of humoural theory in targeting this part of the digestive system. But there was also a growing body of medical literature that implicated infections of the colon, especially the proximal segment known as the right colon where ingested materials are absorbed, as the cause of dementia praecox. It was there that ingested materials could ferment, or the movement of fecal material out of the body could be slowed or even stopped, thus causing infection with resulting autointoxication.

Between 1918 and 1925, Cotton and his medical team performed 300 partial or full colectomies on asylum patients diagnosed with dementia praecox; 25 percent of the patients recovered, but an astonishing 33 percent died, most of them from peritonitis. Yet despite these low cure and high mortality rates, Cotton became a surgical enthusiast, seeking every opportunity to inform his colleagues, state politicians and the general public of his revolutionary cure for insanity. He published articles in prestigious medical journals, presented one paper after another in professional meetings, and gave talks to community groups, urging parents to consider colectomies for their children as prophylactics against insanity, as he himself had done for his own two sons.

It was neither the disturbingly high mortality rates nor any scientific refutation of autointoxication theory that brought an end to the surgical therapeutics at Trenton State Hospital. Rather, it was Cotton's unabashed pandering to politicians and the larger public, trying not just to sell them on the surgical cure but to secure funding for the transformation of the asylum into a modern hospital, that provoked his peers to urge an investigation into his surgical practices and outcome data. That investigation was conducted as part of the larger Bright Investigation into waste and fraud in state government. The committee held a series of hearings in 1925 that were voraciously reported by the press that had always been favorably inclined to Cotton and his work. It took testimony from what turned out to be "a parade of disgruntled employees, malicious ex-patients, and their families, testifying in damning detail about brutality, forced and botched surgery, debility and death" (Scull, p. 176). Although vigorously defended by a few of his peers, the hearings took a toll on Cotton. Becoming increasingly erratic and disorientated, he was quietly removed from his duties as the medical superintendent of Trenton State Hospital.

While recovering from his breakdown, Cotton missed the testimony of a young psychiatrist named Phyllis Greenacre who, at the request of Cotton's mentor, the eminent professor of psychiatry Adolf Meyer, had spent months reviewing patient files at Trenton State Hospital. She informed the investigating committee that Cotton's claims of having successfully cured dementia praecox with surgery were wildly exaggerated. To drive home that point she focused on sixty-two patients who had undergone the most aggressive surgical interventions. Seventeen had died immediately of post-operative shock or peritonitis, she reported, and several more who had lingered for months before dying were never counted as surgical mortality cases. Only five had recovered completely, an additional three were improved but still symptomatic, and the remainder were unimproved, leading Greenacre to conclude that "the lowest recovery rate and the highest death rate occurs among the functional cases who have been thoroughly treated ... the least treatment was found in the recovered cases and the most thorough treatment in the unimproved and dead groups" (Scull, p. 200). Suspicious that many patients who had been discharged as improved or cured were, in fact, neither, Greenacre hunted down ex-patients and interviewed them extensively. The interviews confirmed her suspicions.

All of these observations and data analysis were put into a report that, in the end, was all but ignored by the investigating committee that seemed distracted by the barrage of obfuscating data, learned opinions, and *ad feminam* attacks by Cotton's peers who were called to defend him and discredit Greenacre. What had begun with such rectitude ended with none at all. The Bright Investigating Committee simply declared that it no longer had reason for any interest in the therapeutics practiced by Cotton at the Trenton State Hospital.

The ruling gave Cotton *carte blanche* to continue his surgical interventions, lecture across the country, Great Britain and Europe, and continue to build a lucrative private practice from the most wealthy patients seeking admittance into the Trenton State Hospital. Yet controversy continued to follow him. A visiting Swiss psychiatrist was appalled at what he had observed at Cotton's asylum: hundreds of edentulous patients, aggressive surgical interventions upon the scantiest laboratory findings of focal infection, slipshod recordkeeping and grossly inflated recovery rates. Another investigation, this one at the behest of the hospital's board and conducted by the director of the New Jersey Department of Institutions and Agencies, examined the records of 645 patients who had undergone colectomies or pericolic membranotomies and compared those to the records of 407 patients who had not undergone these surgeries. His findings were unsettling: not only was the death rate high for both surgical procedures, but the recovery rate was higher for patients who had never undergone any surgery at all. This study, just like the one Greenacre had conducted years before, seemed to reveal the futility of trying to cure any type of insanity, let alone dementia praecox, through surgical techniques.

In the face of the scandals, bad publicity and internecine battles, surgical interventions all but stopped at Trenton State Hospital. Cotton's brief attempt to recharge enthusiasm was futile. He died in 1933, eulogized in the *Trenton Evening Times* as a "great pioneer whose humanitarian influence was, and will continue to be, of such monumental proportions" ("Death Notice," p. 6).

It may be tempting to extract Cotton from his historical and social context and treat him as nothing more than a "maniacal Trenton psychiatrist" (Shorter, p. 112). To do so, though, would elide the fact that he was well situated within the *zeitgeist* of the moment. Not only had autointoxication and focal sepsis theory achieved hegemonic status, but surgery *à la* Cotton was considered by many asylum physicians to be the theory's best practice. In fact, when at the 1922 meeting of the American Psychiatric Association findings were presented of carefully designed and controlled studies that had found no evidence that the surgical removal of focal sepsis, by itself, brought about recovery, calls for a thorough investigation of Cotton's claims were shouted down by his colleagues.

Even the prestigious Mayo Clinic gave its imprimatur to Cotton's surgical therapeutics, as did the British Medical Association. In fact, in England where autointoxication theory remained influential well into the mid-twentieth century, Cotton's friend and ally, Thomas Chivers Graves, the rather flamboyant superintendent of the Rubery Hill and Hollymoor asylums in Birmingham, was also performing colectomies. tonsillectomies, tooth extractions and sphenoidotomies, that is, the surgical opening of the sphenoid sinus, in an effort to cure insanity.

To dismiss Cotton as maniacal is to also overlook the fact that the national press lauded his work. It piqued public optimism that what heretofore had been impossible—the cure of dementia praecox—now was within easy reach. So enticing was this hope that not only did the desperate families and friends of the Trenton State Hospital patients agree to, or at least not disagree with, the surgeries performed, but wealthy people across the country brought their loved ones to Cotton for a surgical cure. The air of despair and hopelessness that had always surrounded dementia praecox in particular, seemed finally to be lifting and a *Trenton Evening Times* article mocked those who would suggest otherwise:

Dr. Henry A. Cotton ... can hardly ask for a better endorsement of his new methods of treating insane patients than is contained in the statement that within the past two years the discharge rate from the institution has overtaken the admission rate.... Jealous rivals may ridicule what they call the "tooth-pulling" treatment practiced by Dr. Cotton but results count, and when one can show that his methods have measurably increased the number of cures and made a noticeable decrease in the hospital population, which for years has shown a steady increase, he can afford to laugh at his critics and feel encouraged that he is pursuing his experiments in the right direction ["Treating the Insane," p. 6].

Politicians also lauded Cotton, not for the science of autointoxication theory, but for fiscal savings to the state that the resulting surgical therapeutics offered. Across the nation, the number of state asylum patients had increased 36 percent, from 187,791 to 255,245, between 1910 and 1923 alone, far outpacing the increase in the general population, thus leaving the distinct impression that insanity was epidemic. Overcrowded and understaffed, state asylums were increasingly expensive to maintain. Thus the prospect of checking the increase in insanity, emptying asylums, and surgically transforming those who had been incapacitated by insanity into productive citizens was particularly appealing to the fiscal bottom line.

Within that *zeitgeist,* though, were strains of discontent that eventually were heard. In the tactful language of asylum physicians of that era, the wisdom of Cotton's approach—if not its science and ethics—was being debated. William White, superintendent of St. Elizabeths Hospital, for example, disclosed in a 1919 letter to the superintendent of the Georgia State Sanitarium that Cotton's focus on infected teeth "is a most unfortunate one" since "anything that impairs the general health of the individual may be a factor in causing a mental break" (Grob, p. 109). In 1922, the associate editor of *Southern Medicine and Surgery,* prompted by a manuscript submitted by Cotton, wrote to a colleague that Cotton was "infected with red ants" in that he was "injudicious in his attitude and unsound in his reasoning" (Grob, p.110). He urged his colleague to send data about how the treatment of asylum patients has been contravened by inadequate state funding, rather than by ignorant physicians, so that he could counter Cotton's argument that only physicians schooled in the theory of focal sepsis and trained in advanced surgical therapeutics will be successful in treating the insane. Even Adolf Meyer, mentor and ardent defender of Cotton, was more circumspect in a 1927 letter to a Norwegian colleague, saying that his own assessment of Cotton's claims did not give him "the impression [that] his own figures could be anywhere near correct," that his claimed success in treating insanity may be "due to the atmosphere of action and helpfulness which pervade the place, and that the diagnosis and estimation of the condition in the discharged cases is strongly colored by a policy rather than a painstaking scrutiny of the cases." Finding it "deplorable" that there had not been more control over Cotton's surgical therapeutics, Meyer emphatically concluded, "such an experiment will hardly ever be possible again" (Grob, p. 115).

The autointoxication theory of madness lingered for some time after Cotton's death, but even at Trenton State Hospital the enthusiasm for surgical intervention had long since waned considerably. It had at other asylums across the country and in Great Britain as well.

REFERENCES

Cotton, H.A. (1923). The relation of chronic sepsis to the so-called functional mental disorders. *Journal of Mental Science, 69,* 434–465.

Cotton, H.A. (1932, November 20). Mental cases treated for physical defects. *New York Times,* p. 10.

"Death notice of Henry Cotton M.D." (1933, May 9). *Trenton Evening Times,* p. 6.

de Young, M. (2010). *Madness: An American history of mental illness and its treatment.* Jefferson, NC: McFarland.

Grob, G.N. (1985). *The inner world of American psychiatry, 1890–1940.* New Brunswick, NJ: Rutgers University Press.

Holmes, B.T. (1916). Dementia praecox studies: The treatment of the toxemia of dementia praecox. *American Medicine, 11,* 702–704.

Kopeloff, N., and Cheney, C.O. (1922). Studies in focal infection: Its presence and elimination in the functional psychoses. *American Journal of Psychiatry, 79,* 139–156.

Kopeloff, N., and Kirby (1923). Focal infection and mental disease. *American Journal of Psychiatry, 80,* 149–187.

Noll, R. (2006). Infectious insanities, surgical solutions: Bayard Taylor Holmes, dementia praecox, and laboratory science in early 20th century America. *History of Psychiatry, 17,* 183–204.

Noll, R. (2007). Kraepelin's "lost biological psychiatry"? Autointoxication, organotherapy and surgery for dementia praecox. *History of Psychiatry, 18,* 301–320.

Porter, R. (1997). *The greatest benefit to mankind: A medical history of humanity.* London: W.W. Norton.

Ramchandani, D. (2007). Fooling others or oneself? A history of therapeutic fads and its current relevance. *Psychiatric Quarterly, 78,* 287–293.

Scull, A.T. (2005). *Madhouse: A tragic tale of megalomania and modern medicine.* New Haven, CT: Yale University Press.

Shorter, E. (1997). *A history of psychiatry: From the era of the asylum to the age of Prozac.* New York: John Wiley & Sons.

Torrey, E.F., and Miller, J. (2001). *The invisible plague: The rise of mental illness from 1750 to the present.* New Brunswick, NJ: Rutgers University Press.

"Treating the insane" (1921, January 3). *Trenton Evening Times,* p. 6.

# Total Push

*The application of all available therapeutics in the treatment of the chronically insane.*

Total push was designed in the late 1930s by Kenneth Tillotson and Abraham Myerson of the McLean Hospital in Boston, Massachusetts. Frustrated by their failure to even therapeutically engage with what were known as "backwarders," that is, patients who were chronically and intractably insane and had been institutionalized for years or even decades, they decided to bring everything asylum medicine had to offer into the treatment protocol. Long overlooked by staff, infrequently visited by family and friends, and left to sit for hours, sometimes in their own bodily wastes, the patients were dressed neatly, taken on walks, given invigorating showers and massages, and encouraged to engage in sports activities. Usually left to eat meals in their own wards, they were taken to the patient dining room to eat, and their proper conduct in this, and all other, settings was rewarded with candy, cigarettes and praise. As supplements to their prescribed drugs, they were administered appetite stimulants and large doses of vitamins.

Total push was initiated with eleven McLean Asylum patients, ten of whom suffered from chronic schizophrenia, and most of whom had been institutionalized more than a decade. After three months of total push therapy, all had improved to some degree in that they demonstrated better contact with reality, increased sociability and activity, improved mood and overall physical health. While the improvement noted ranged from slight to marked, no patient in the original study seemed unaffected by the therapeutic, and none regressed in overall functioning.

Tillotson's discussion of the results of the initiative provided a description of total push as a therapeutic and of the range of improvement it brought about. It also revealed a great deal about the plight of backwarders and the frustration of asylum physicians in treating them.

*Patient 1*: male, 28, had 6 months of college, unemployed, catatonic schizophrenia for 4 years, in hospital 3.5 years. Had both insulin and metrazol shock therapy, improved, then relapsed. Seclusive and uncooperative, prone to fits of rage. Had quick response to total push, especially eager to be rewarded with cigarettes. Had to be rather forcibly coerced into activities and into the physical program of exercise, walking, badminton, bowling and swimming. Gradually worked up to 6 hours of activity per day. Also received medical baths and ultraviolet radiation. Now more interested in his physical appearance; less negativistic, less preoccupied, better contact with reality and physical health is improved [Tillotson, p. 1207].

*Patient 2*: male, 17, student. Hebephrenic schizophrenia 5 years, 3 different hospitals. Had insulin and metrazol shock therapy, improved, and regressed. Following total push, activities markedly increased. Allowed to play cards as a reward. Able to go home on weekends to parents' house with a nurse, and now by himself. Pays more attention to physical appearance; has improved contact with reality; and is now taking classes [p. 1208].

*Patient 8*: female, 41, grammar school grad and was taking classes in practical nursing. Hospitalized 18 years with hebephrenic schizophrenia. Before total push was considered completely deteriorated and demented because of her destructive tendencies and excitement. Spent 7 hours per day in continuous baths. Reward with total push is not taking baths. Goes to gym daily, plays simple games. On ward, dresses herself and conducts herself in socially acceptable manner. Plays simple music on the piano. Contact with reality is markedly improved, as is mood and general conduct [p. 1210].

*Patient 10:* female, 43, housewife with 3 years of college. Paranoid schizophrenia 11 years. Before total push, spent most of her time in seclusion; disturbed and combative. Now in seclusion less. Developed interest in playing piano and taking long walks in the garden. Her aestheticism has markedly increased; interested in use of cosmetic and facial creams given to her as reward. Takes meals in dining room; mood and sociability improved as well as general contact with reality [p. 1211].

Total push was administered to an additional twenty-two McLean Asylum patients, with a similar range of encouraging results. One result, equally encouraging, had been nonetheless wholly unanticipated: because total push depended on the coordinated efforts of physicians, nurses, physiotherapists, occupational therapists, and activities coordinators, "it stimulat[ed] the entire personnel and added much to the hospital morale" (Tillotson, p. 1213). It also changed the nature of the asylum as an institution. It had long been noted that asylums as total institutions were better suited for preparing patients to be patients rather than citizens of society. Total push problematized that institutional function and its underlying logic that the longer patients were institutionalized the less likely it was that they would ever be discharged. In doing so it injected a much needed optimism into the care of the chronically insane.

Physicians at other asylums were eager to try it. At the Fergus Falls State Hospital in Minnesota, fifty-four seclusive and unresponsive schizophrenic patients, all of whom had been institutionalized more than five years, were administered the total push program. All activities of the patients were prescribed, supervised and evaluated by a team of psychiatrists, psychologists, nurses, psychiatric aides and occupational and recreational therapists. Although the quantitative findings after six months of the total push program had only little if any statistical significance, the qualitative findings provided reasons for cautious optimism. At the end of the total push program, the number of patients in this cohort who were able to work in the asylum increased from four to twenty-two; those still unable to attend to their bodily needs decreased from thirty-six to twenty-three; those who remained mute decreased from thirty-two to nine; and, the number of patients who still were unable to dress themselves decreased from twenty-two to just five.

The use of total push at Fergus Fall State Hospital, however, tempered the expectation that chronically insane asylum patients would recover significantly enough to be discharged. Rather, it showed that "though the recovery of the patient was held as a highly desirable goal, the main aim of the program was to make for better hospital adjustment of the patients" (Sines, Lucero, & Kamman, p. 189). Indeed, observations and/or measured outcomes of the total push therapeutic in other asylums across the United States and Europe affirmed that it improved both the quality of life of severely insane patients and their adjustment to the asylum, but it did not produce improvements significant enough to assure discharge.

As total push was tried in other asylums, another caveat emerged: as a type of milieu therapy, it was very costly. Even at McLean Hospital that once boasted that it greeted its well-heeled patients with a "class of accommodations and a style of living more than simply comfortable, and in a degree luxurious" (Beam, p. 23), the cost of maintaining the one-to-two staff-patient ratio necessary for total push was considerable. Under other circumstances its most ardent entrepreneur, Kenneth Tillotson, may have had the necessary influence and connections to get McLean Hospital to reconsider its financial bottom line. But in 1948 he was embroiled in a humiliating sex scandal involving a nurse and was forced to resign from the prestigious hospital and from the faculty of Harvard University Medical School.

Although total push was still being administered to small groups of patients in a few asylums into the mid-twentieth century, for all intents and purposes the therapeutic faded from attention during the World War II era. The combination of cost, decrease in staffing levels due to the draft, and increase in patient census as psychologically traumatized soldiers returned from the war, rendered the therapeutic too expensive and too complicated to administer.

## References

Beam, A. (2001). *Gracefully insane: The rise and fall of America's premier mental hospital.* New York: PublicAffairs.

"Boston psychiatrist and nurse arraigned on adultery charges" (1948, December 1). *Chicago Daily Tribune*, p. 31.

Goffman, E. (1961). *Asylums.* New York: Doubleday Anchor.

Kamman, G.R., Lucero, R.J., Meyer, B.T., and Rechtschaffen, A. (1954). Critical evaluation of a total push program for regressed schizophrenics in a state hospital. *Psychiatric Quarterly, 28,* 650–667.

Myerson, A. (1939). Theory and principles of the total push method in the treatment of chronic schizophrenia. *American Journal of Psychiatry, 95,* 1197–1204.

Query, J.M.N. (1973). Total push and the open total institution. *Journal of Applied Behavioral Science, 9,* 294–303.

Sines, J.O., Lucero, R.J., and Kamman, G.K. (1952). A state hospital total push program for regressed schizophrenics. *Journal of Clinical Psychology, 8,* 189–193.

Tillotson, K.J. (1939). The practice of the total push method in the treatment of chronic schizophrenia. *American Journal of Psychiatry, 95,* 1205–1213.

# Index

Numbers in ***bold italics*** indicate pages with photographs.

Abbington Abbey 143
abreaction 17, 51, 276
Accra Psychiatric Hospital 74
acupuncture 38
addiction 46–47, 49, 125, 189, 321
Adelaide Lunatic Asylum 201
adrenalin 262
adrenochrome hypothesis (*aka* M-Hypothesis) 262; *see also* schizophrenia
"Adrienne Lecouvreur" 108
Aegineta, Paulus 297
aesthesiogen 240, 241
Alabama State Hospital for the Insane (*aka* Bryce Hospital) 91, 116; *The Meteor* 119
Albany Hospital 20
Aldini, Giovanni 89–90
Alexander, Frederick 20, 21
Alfieri, Vittorio 109–110
*All the King's Men* 294
Allan Memorial Institute of Psychiatry 45, 49, 275, 277, 325, 326, 327
Alleged Lunatics' Friend Society 251
Allen, B.W. 116
amber 24, 32, 82
amenorrhea 185, 232
American Art Therapy Association 105
American Dance Therapy Association 107
*American Journal of Insanity* 108
*American Journal of Psychiatry* 339
American Neurological Association 215
American Pediatric Association 263
American Psychiatric Association 25, 134, 263, 278, 332, 350
American Psychopathological Association 277, 326
amnesia 131, 327, 329, 330, 339; magnetic 240
Amnesty International 219, 237
amytal interviews 50–51
Anchel, David 342
anemia 39
anergic stupor 84
angiography 282

anorexia nervosa 142
anti-psychiatry movement 330–332
ants 5
anxiety 16, 17, 18, 19, 47, 135, 151, 155, 190, 269, 274, 281, 282, 305, 325, 334, 343, 344, 346
anxiety hierarchy 18
aphonia 87
arc-de-circle (*aka* arc-en-cercle) 108, 267; *see also* hysteria
Argentina 196–197
arsenic 22, 122, 261
art brut (*aka* outsider art) 105–106
Artaud, Antonin 331
*Artistry of the Mentally Ill* 105
Asclepiades 112
Askew, Joseph 105
Association of Medical Superintendents of American Institutions for the Insane 108, 112, 210, 236, 248, 316
astasia-abasia 340
Asylum de Bicêtre 69, 71, 77, 87, 221, 272, 301, 317
asylum food 72, 80; in colonial asylums 72, 77; food shortages 73–74, 77; *see also* diet
Asylum for Fife and Kinross 294
Asylum for the Insane 319
Asylum Workers Association 223
asylums 2, 3; attendants in 9, 48, 113, 141, 144, 148, 149, 151, 166, 172, 183, 196, 197, 200, 201, 205, 209, 215, 216, 220, 223, 224, 238, 243, 252, 273, 301, 302, 303, 308, 309, 310, 316, 318, ***320***, 335, 336; colonial 31, 59, 201, 221, 225, 312–313; deinstitutionalization 193, 200; geographic isolation 192; journals 118–***119***, 120; nurses in 9, 17, 48, 91, 282, 292, 312, 313, 335, 336, 345, 352, 353; official investigations into 67, 73, 172, 195, 197, 198, 207, 219, 224, 228, 237, 307, 308, 309, 312, 313, 314, 316, 318, 319, 327, 348–350; order in 8, 9, 45, 176, 179, 243, 244, 247, 248, 267, 303, 310, 318, 320; rocking

chair asylums 303; scandals in 45, 48–49, 95, 198, 203, 216, 228, 244, 307, 309–310, 312–313, 349, 353; surveillance wards (*aka* Wachabteilung) 8; as total institutions 7, 58, 102, 307, 352; visitors to 109, 141, 195, 197–198, 210, 215, ***218***, 273; *see also* by individual name; *see also* moral architecture
Athens State Hospital 182
Aubanel, Honoré 214
Autenrieth, Johann Heinrich Ferdinand 30, 199–200, 206, 217, 321
Autenrieth Ointment (*aka* unguentum antimonii tartarizati) 32
autism 172–173, 263
Autism Rights Watch 173
Avenbrugger, Leopold 170
Avicenna 62
awakenings 5, 322; ants 5; cannon shots 6; cat-piano (*aka* katzenclavier) ***6***; catapult 7; drumroll 6; eels, 6; firecracker 6; furmen 6; mice 6; salting feet 6; skeleton 6; snakes 7; *see also* German Romantic psychiatry; Reil, Johann Christian
Ayr District Asylum 11

Babinski, Joseph 94
backwarders 351–352
bacteriology 254, 347
Badger, Barber 118
Bailey, Harry 49
Baillarger, Jules 142, 146, 148
Bakewell, Thomas 65, 66, 316, 321
Balken, Eva R. 262
Ballet, Gilbert 266
Balmanno, John 143
barbiturates 45, 48, 49; Luminal 45; Nembutal 276, 325; Seconal 276, 325; Somnifaine 48; Somnifen 47; Veronal 325
Barnsley Hall Asylum 256
Barrett, Albert 278
Barrus, Clara 159–160
Bartholomew, William 105
Baruch, Simon 167, 185

355

# Index

Battey, Robert 157–158
Battie, William 30–31, 70, 315–316; *Treatise on Madness* 55
Battle Creek Sanitarium 305
Bayfield, Samuel 71
Bayle, Antoine Laurent Jessé 121–122
*bdellomètre* 64
Beard, George Miller 12, 82
Bechterev, Vladimir 288
bed therapy 7–**10**, 11–13, 81, 199, 202
Beers, Clifford 201, 227
Beethoven, Ludwig van 114
Bell, Luther V. 96–97
*The Bell Jar* 331, 332
belladonna 77, 96
Bellevue Psychiatric Hospital 339, 343, 345
Bender, Lauretta 343
Benger's liquor pancreaticus 150
Bennett, Abram E. 131
Bentley, I.I. 319
Berlin Charité Hospital 38, 42, 76, 122, 129, 176, 185, 186, **222**, 223, 237, 302, 303, **304**, 316; Horns' sack scandal 227–228
Berlin Medical Congress 288
Berlin University 228
Bernard, Louis 343
Bernhardt, Sarah 108
Bethlem Asylum (*aka* Bedlam) 5, 7, 43, 57, 79, 101, 104, 121, **139**, **146**, 151, 197, 205, 216, 227, 269, 295, 320; *Bethlehem Star* 120; depletive therapies in 30, 31, 55–56, 62, 70; licensed beggars 191; mechanical restraints in 220–**221**, 227, 229, 234; "Melancholy and Raving Mania" (*aka* "Brainless Brothers") 208, **209**; Norris case 220–**221**; *Over the Dome* 120; padded rooms in 200; *Under the Dome* 120
Betz, Frank 129
Bicêtre Asylum 69, 87, 141, 148, 272, 301, 317; depletive therapies in 71; expressive therapy in 115; food shortage in 77; hydrotherapy in 174–175, 180, 187; isolation in 194; mechanical restraints in 234; striking of chains at 221, 241, 243
Binghamton State Hospital 335
Bini, Lucio 327–329, 341
Binswanger, Otto 202
Bisgaard, Axel 134
Blackwell Island Asylum 113, 114, 215
Blalock, Joseph 135
Blanche, Emile 148
Bleckwenn, William Jefferson 50, 52
Bleuler, Eugen 125, 322
blood 31, **32**, 36, 76, 77, 78, 83, 115, 132, 134, 136, 163, 167, 171, 173, 174, 177, 179, 181, 182, 185, 187, 188, 235, 254, 261, 270, 291, 294, 299, 314, 322, 328; alcohol concentration level 79; blood brain barrier 122; blood type 133; as cause of inflammation (*aka* plethora, congestion, determination, excitation, irritation) of brain 14, 33, 34, 38, 39, 40, 41, 42, 52, 55, 56, 57, 60, 62, 65, 71, 80, 125, 173, 174, 176, 180, 188, 270, 305; corpuscular richness theory 59–60; humour 26, 32; of the insane 58–59; and sea water 183; tonics 12, 13, 59; *see also* depletive therapy, "heroic therapy," or antiphlogistic therapy, or "Rush's system"
Bloomingdale Asylum 60, 205, 235, 238, 250
Blumer, G. Adler 114–115, 217
Boerhaave, Herman 312
Bohnice Psychiatric Hospital 220
Bologna University 89
Bombarda Asylum 280
Bonaparte, Napoleon 108
Bonner, Clarence 269–270
*Borrelia recurrentis* (*aka Spirochaeta duttoni*) 136
Bosquillion, Édouard Françoise Marie 56
Boston Psychopathic Hospital 128, 130, 135
Boston State Hospital 269
"Le Bourgeois de Gand" 110
Bowerbank, Lewis Quier 312
brain 3, 12, 13, 15, 20, 26, 29, 31, 32, 33, 34, 36, 37, 39, 49, 52, 63, 64, 76, 77, 78, 83, 89, 91, **99**, 112, 121–122, 130, 156, 158, 159, 160, 163, 167, 171, 183, 184, 225, 235, 246, 254, 257, 260, 263, 266, 270, 271, 273, 277, 278, 283, 287, 291, 295, 299, 307, 315, 318, 322, 325, 327, 329, 330, 334, 335, 337, 345, 347, 348; arachnoid lining 121; blood-brain barrier 122; brainstem 16, 21; cerebellar cistern 16; cerebral convulsions 86; cerebral cortex 18, 161; cerebrum 22; choroid plexi 125; cingulate gyrus 281; common sensorium 244; cortex 22, 287; cortico-striato-thalamo-cortical circuitry 280; dura mater 294; extract (*aka* myelin, cerebrinin) 256–257; frontal lobes 278, 281, 282, 284, 290; functional specialization 287; hippocampus 327; humours and 55; inflammation (*aka* plethora, congestion, determination, excitation, irritation) 14, 33, 34, 38, 39, 40, 41, 42, 52, 55, 56, 57, 60, 62, 65, 71, 80, 125, 173, 174, 176, 180, 188, 270; lesion 57, 176, 265; locus of insanity 9, 32, 33, 62, 189, 245, 249, 255, 283, 288, 289; massage of 306; medulla oblongata 21; meninges 125; metabolism 13, 14, 15, 19, 21–22, 59, 255, 257; organic brain disease 122, 341; "psychic centers" 22; relationship to mind 41, 112; reflex irritability theory (*aka* reflex arc) 156, 157, 167; *see also* cerebral stimulation or psychic stimulation; electrotherapy; psychosurgery; shock therapy or convulsive therapy
Brain Anatomy Institute 125
brainwashing 49, 276–277, 327
brainworkers 12
Brandon Hospital for Mental Diseases (*aka* The Hill) 25
Brattleboro Retreat 119
Brehmner, Hermann 10
Brennan, Commissioner Thomas S. 114
Bridgewater State Hospital for the Criminally Insane 112
Brigham, Amariah 112, 214
Bright Investigation 348–349; *see also* Cotton, Henry
Brindley, James 295
Briquet, Pierre 181
Brislington House 251
British Association of Art Therapy 105
British Medical Association 294, 350
Brooklyn State Hospital 21, 285
Broussais, François-Joseph-Victor 62–63; *see also* physiological medicine
Brown, Anna 313
Brown, Isaac Baker 156–157; *On the Curability of Certain Forms of Insanity, Epilepsy, Catalepsy and Hysteria in Females* 157
Brown, Tilden 112, 214
Brown-Séquard, Charles-Édouard 161, 254
Brown-Séquard Elixir 161, 254
Browne, William A.F. 104–105, 110, 111, 120
Bruetsch, Walter 128
Brushfield, T.N. 207
Bryce, Peter 91, 119
Buchanan, Joseph R. 34
Bucke, Richard Maurice 163
Bucknill, John C. 188, 211, 273
Bukowski, Charles 95
bulimia 142
Burckhardt, Gottlieb 287–289
Burghölzli Clinic 45, 47, 155, 157
Burke, Edmund 138
Burq, Victor Jean-Marie 239–241
Burrows, George Mann 13, 33, 41–42, 43, 61, 66, 189, 305, 315
Burton, Robert 113, 164
Butler Hospital 97

Cabred, Domingo 9
Cachero, Jackie 225–226
Cairns, Sir Hugh William Bell 281
Cairo Lunatic Asylum 77, 201
Calmeil, Louis-Florentin 63, 235
calomel 41, 44, 65, 77, 208
Cameron, D. Ewen 277; deep sleep therapy 45, 325; depatterning 49, 276, 325–327; red-light cage 25; *see also* brainwashing; psychic driving
camphor 42, 43, 247, 337, 338
cardiac arrhythmia 21
Carroll, Robert 125–127
Casa Dei Matti Asylum (*aka* Royal Hospital for the Insane) 109, 273
catalepsy 87, 157
catatonia 51, 114, 332
*Catatonic Cases After Intravenous Sodium Amytal Injection* (film) 50
Celetka, Michel 219
Céline, Louis-Ferdinand 95
Celsus, Aulus Cornelius 164, 254, 297, 310
Center for Legal and Social Studies 197
Central Islip State Hospital 190
Central Kentucky Lunatic Asylum 308–309, 313
Central State Asylum 313
cerebral stimulation, or psychic stimulation 13–15; air pressure 15–16, 283; carbon dioxide inhalation therapy, or Meduna's mixture inhalation therapy, or carbogen inhalation therapy 16–18, 283, 340; carotid compression 13–14; continuous oxygen therapy 18–20; nitrogen inhalation therapy 20–21; nitrous oxide inhalation therapy 21; sodium cyanide therapy 21–22
Cerletti, Ugo 327–329, 341; acroagonine (*aka* acroamine) 329, 330; terror defense reaction 343
Chabasinski, Ted 345
Chace, Marian 107
Chambeyron, Antoine 114
Charcot, Jean-Martin 107, 181, 199, 239–241, 266–267, 305; aesthesiogens 240; Charcot douche 185–186; isolation therapy and 198; as Napoleon of Neurosis 198–199; Tuesday Lectures 108, 265; as "*visuel*" 199; *see also* hysteria; Salpêtrière Asylum; Wittmann, Blanche
Charenton Asylum 63, 101, 121, 230, 231, 235; theatrical productions in 108; *see also* de Sade, Marquis
Charlesworth, Edward Parker 219
Chase, L.H. 262
Chelmsford Private Hospital 49
Chemical Castration Statute 156
chemotherapy 131
Cheshire Lunatic Asylum 207
Chestnut Lodge Asylum 172
Chiarugi, Vincenzo 68, 245, 272, 317, 321; commitment regulations 244; cradle, swing or restraining cradle 297; maniac's bed 230, 244; moral treatment (*aka la cura morale*) 70, 243, 244, 248; non-restraint 209; ties and cuffs 235, 244
*Chicago Defender* 136
Chicago Medical College 47
Chinese water torture 177
Chirac, Pierre 304–305
chloroform 142, 151
Church, Archibald 47
Cibber, Cajus Gabriel 208
"circle of learning" 1, 2
City of London Mental Hospital 132
City Parochial Asylum 256
civil death 192
Civil War, U.S. 23, 91, 112, 215
clairvoyance 108
Clardy, E.R. 344–345
Clark, D.H. 17
Claybury Asylum 84, 161
Cleveland State Hospital 99
Clinic for Psychiatry and Nervous Diseases 94, 123, 132
Clinica delle Malattie Nervose e Mentali della Regia Università di Roma 328
*A Clockwork Orange* (film) 294
Cloetta, Max 125
Clouston, Thomas S. 259; gospel of fatness 75–76; and ovariomania (*aka* Old Maid's Insanity, uteromania) 158; and tuberculosis 10–11
Cobbett, William 61
Coga, Arthur 57–58
Cohen, Maurice 127
Cold War era 227
Colditz Asylum 301, **302**
Colney Hatch Asylum 187, 201, 303
Colonia Montes de Oca National Asylum 197
color cure, chromotherapy, or colorology 22–26, 195; blue glass craze 23–24; red-light cage 25; red-tinted spectacles 25
Columbia-Greystone Project (*aka* New York State Brain Research Project) 289–290; *see also* Freeman, Walter; Pool, J. Lawrence; psychosurgery
Columbia University Medical Center 289
Columbia University's College of Physicians and Surgeons 167, 185
combat neurosis 50
Committee on Lunacy of the Pennsylvania State Board of Charities 159
community-based care 193
*A Complete Concordance to the Holy Scriptures* 233
compound 606 (*aka* "magic bullet") 122
Connaught District Lunatic Asylum 76
Conolly, John 5, 7, 62, 71–72, 303, 312; non-restraint movement 72, 200, 209, **210**; use of padded rooms 200–201
consecutive oscillations 240
consent to treatment 134
Constantinovich, S.K. 79
constipation 37, 44, 66, 67, 177, 305
contagion theory of disease 121
Cornell University 278
Cott, Alan 78–79
Cotton, Henry **99**, 100, 125, 348–351; and Bright Commission Investigation 348–349; and New Jersey Department of Institutions and Agencies investigation 349; *see also* exodontia; focal sepsis (*aka* autointoxication) theory; Graves, Thomas Chivers; Greenacre, Phyllis; surgery; Trenton State Hospital (*aka* New Jersey State Hospital, New Jersey State Lunatic Asylum)
counterirritation 26–28; actual cautery **28**–29, 69, 316; artificial eruptions 29–30; blistering 30–31, 67, 138, 165, 245; cataplasm 31–33; dry cupping (*aka* cupping, or exhausting cupping) **32**, 33; dry friction 33; gum lancing 34; inoculation of small pox (*aka* variation) 34–35; inoculation of the itch (*aka* inoculation of psora) 35–36; issue 36; Junod's boot (*aka* Dr. Junod's exhausting apparatus, Junod's *grand ventouse*, Junod's hemospasic apparatus) 36–37; lacrimation 37–38; moxa (*aka* moxibustion) 38; mustard pack 39; nasal discharge 39–40; peas therapy 40; pediluvium 40; salivation (*aka* ptyalism) 40–42; seton (*aka* haarseil, setaceum, pus band) 42–43, 245; sweating (*aka* diaphoresis, transpiration) 43–44
County and City of Cork Lunatic Asylum 43, 296, 299, 301
Cox, Joseph Mason 35, 180, 186; Cox's chair (*aka* Cox's swing) 228, 249, 296, 297–298; **300**, 301, 303; criticism of Cox's chair 298–299; intoxication as therapeutic 79; pious frauds 271; *Practical Observations on Insanity* 302
creativity 101
cretinism 259–260
Crichton-Brown, Sir James 223

Index

Crichton Royal Asylum 104, 110, 120; *New Moon* 120
Cripps, Harrison 294
*crocus metallorum* 69
croton oil, or *oleum tiglii* 29, 65, 67, 163
Cruden, Alexander 233–234
Cruikshank, George 221
"A Cry for Humanity: The Life of Dorothea Dix" 107
Cullen, William 52, 59–60, 310, 320
Culmer, Helen 292
cult of curability 251
Cumming, William F. 186

Dachau Concentration Camp 190
Dadd, Richard 101
Damerow, Heinrich Philipp August 64, 147
dance 6, 76, 96, 101, 102, 106–107, 110, *111*, *113*, 115, 265; Lunatic Ball 106–107
Danvers State Hospital 269
Danvik Asylum 36
Darwin, Charles 295
Darwin, Erasmus 295, 296, 297, 298, 302; *Zoonomia* 295, 297
Dawson, William S. 260
de'Arsonval, Jacques-Arsène 87
Deas, P. Maury 232–233
deBoismont, Alexandre Brierre 147–148
deBry, Theodor 7
de Coulmier, François Simonnet 108
deep sleep therapy, prolonged narcosis, prolonged sleep, or continuous sleep 44–46; bromide sleep 46–47; deep sleep therapy (*aka* prolonged narcosis, *dauernarkose*) 47–49; sodium amytal sleep (*aka* narcoanalysis, narcosynthesis) 50–52
Delaware State Hospital 286
Delion, Pierre 172
delusions 21, 29, 40, 41, 43, 44, 47, 58, 64, 67, 81, 90, 96, 97, 110, 112, 126, 138, 142, 152, 188, 251, 258, 260, 261, 262, 270, 271, 272, 273, 274, 286, 287, 288, 291, 315, 317, 322, 328
de Marsiliis, Hippolytus 177
dementia paralytica 121–122; *see also* general paralysis of the insane; general paresis; neurosyphilis; syphilis
dementia praecox 84, 100, 126, 127, 161, 162, 183, 257, 260, 285, 286, 322, 347, 348, 349, 350; *see also* Kraepelin, Emil; schizophrenia
*Dementia Praecox Studies: A Journal of Psychiatry of Adolescence* 348
dentists 34, 98, 100
depletive therapy, "heroic therapy," antiphlogistic therapy, or "Rush's system" 52–54; bleeding (*aka* bloodletting, venesection) 30, 33, 34, 52, 54–57, 66, 80, 165, 244, 245, 246, 296; blood transfusion 57–59; copious bleeding 41, 59–61, 80, 245, 322; leech therapy (*aka* leeching, hirudotherapy) 34, 57, 62–*63*, 64–65; purging 30, 34, 41, 44, 52, 63, *65*–67, 80, 138, 165, 246, 296, 299; spermatic evacuation 67–70; vomiting 30, 34, 52, 69–71, 80, 138, 165, 246, 296; wet-cupping *32*, 57, 71
Depo-Provera (*aka* medroxyprogesterone acetate, or MPA) 156
depression 22, 23, 47, 49, 50, 82, 85, 87, 89, 97, 98, 100, 101, 138, 162, 172, 182, 184, 188, 259, 271, 281, 282, 284, 290, 305, 321, 322, 329, 331, 332, 333, 338, 339, 340, 341, 346
derivation 26
de Sade, Marquis 108–109
de Saint-Pierre, Charles-Irénée Castel 303
Deschamps, Jean-Baptiste 95, 96
desensitization 18
Deutsch, Albert 211
Devine, Henry 261
Devon County Asylum 188
Diamond, Hugh Welch 116–*117*
Dickens, Charles 10, 106, 109, 147, 237
diet 6, 45, 53, 55, 57, 61, 64, 66, 71–75, 95, 125, 141, 150, 163, 177, 181, 243, 245, 251, 258, 264; controlled fasting (*aka* controlled starvation, total food abstinence) 78–79; cooling diet 42; Gospel of Fatness 75–76; 72; hospital diet 76; hunger or famine cure 76–79; intoxication 79; low, or lowering, diet 79–80; milk diet, milk cure, milk regime, or nutritive cure 80–81; pellagra diet 81–82, 261–263; rest cure, or Mitchell's cure, or rest/fattening cure 11–13, 81, 199, 202
dining 73; social graces and 352
"dirty" insane 11, 314
Disability Rights International 193, 197, 333
District of Columbia Medical Society 284
divulsion 110
Dix, Dorothea Lynde 99, 107, 235–236, 248, 250, 348
Dixmont Asylum 195
Dobbins, Virginia 116
Dobřany Psychiatric Hospital 220
doctrine of associations 270–271
dogma of individualization 147
Doherty, Charles Edward 198
Dolley, Daniel 184
dollhouses 201
Dorothea Dix Hospital 160
Dover's Powder 43
*Down Syndrome and Vitamin Therapy* 263
Drake, Katherine 106
dramatic productions 132, 261, 107–112; *see also* expressive therapy
drumrolls 6, 322; *see also* awakenings
Duchenne, Guillaume-Benjamin-Armand 82, 87, 88–89, 92
Ducking Society 313
Dujardin-Beaumentz formula 150
Dukakis, Kitty 333
Dukakis, Michael 333
Duke University Hospital 341
Dullunda Asylum 31
Dumas, Alexandre 10, 109–110
Dumontpallier, Amédée 239, 240
Dundee Mental Hospital 258
Dutch East India Company 38
dysmenorrhea 37, 185

Eagleton, Thomas 332
Earle, Pliny 40, 42–43, 77, 116, 174, 222, 235, 238; on bleeding 57, 60–61; criticism of cure rate at the Narrenturm 181; on moral treatment cure rates 250–251
Easterbrook, Charles 11
Eastern Michigan Asylum 313
Eastern State Hospital (Oklahoma) 162
Eastern State Hospital (Virginia) 69, 207, 273
*L'eau de Mer Milieu Organique* 183
eels 5, 6, 82
Eguisier, Maurice 144
Ehrlich, Paul 122
electric chair 82, 344
electric fish 82
electrotherapy 82–84; electric air bath 84; electric bath 84–85; electronarcosis 85–86; electrosleep therapy 86; electrotherapeutic cage (*aka* d'Arsonval cage, autoconduction cage) 86–87; faradic brush 87; faradic moxa (*aka* faradic moxa, electric moxa) 87; faradization *88*–89; galvanization (*aka* localized galvanism, galvanotherapy) 89–91; Leyden jar (*aka* Leiden jar) 91–92; surprise attack shock treatment (*aka* Kaufmann's cure, electro-suggestive therapy, *Überrumpelungsmethode*) 92–94; torpillage 94–96
Elgar, Sir Edward 115
Elgin State Hospital 262
Ellis, William 163
Elsinore Hospital 229
Emancipation 112
Emerson, Ralph Waldo 96
encyclopedia 1, 2, 3; *see also* "circle of learning"

Endenich Asylum 101
endocrinology 254, 255, 347
Engström, Georg 5
Enlightenment 30, 59, 242, 245, 301; American 139; Midlands 295; Scottish 52
Epifanio, Giuseppe 45
epilepsy 37, 38, 59, 82, 84, 158, 183, 186, 254, 270, 294; as antagonistic to schizophrenia 327, 337; hysterical 156; self-induced photosensitive seizures 340; uterine 153
Epstein, Norman 127
Epstein, Samuel 128
Ernst, Max 105
errhines 39, 40
Esquirol, Jean-Étienne Dominique 29, 34, 35, 37, 38, 63, 65, 66, 73, 109, 113, 141, 170, 308; claim for professional care of the insane 65, 109; on isolation 203; on masturbation 68, 69, 163; moral treatment and 109–110; on the passions 107; pious frauds and 271
Estates-General 108
etherization 96–98
ethics 134, 141, 277, 294, 327, 345, 350
Ethiopian Extravaganzas 112
eugenics 153, 158, 161, 162; *see also* genital surgery
European Convention against Torture 333
exercise 6, *10*, 11, 12, 42, 45, 63, 93, 94, 110, 125, 169, 185, 245, 246, 251, 273, 352
exodontia 34, 98, *99*, 100–101, 125, 348; *see also* Cotton, Henry
expressive therapy 101–103; art (*aka* art therapy) 103–106; dance 106–107, *111*; drama (*aka* drama therapy) 107–112; music therapy (*aka* music cure, music remedy) 112–*113*, 114–116; photoTherapy 116–*117*, 118; writing and editing 118–*119*, 120

Fallowes, Thomas 32–33
Falret, Jean-Pierre 170
Farmer, Francis 182
*The Father and Daughter* (play) 108
fear 28, 37, 38, 41, 52, 53, 66, 86, 126, 138, 151, 160, 162, 167, 172, 174, 181, 235, 236, 284, 292, 302, 329, 339; and compliance 303; as cure 307, 314, 316; of dark 194–195, 298; of death 20, 127, 319, 339, 346; of drowning 310, *311*; of insanity epidemic 47; and moral treatment 244, 245; of pain 56; of soldier-patients 95; of suffocation 18; terror defense reaction 343; of unfit 153; *see also* salutary fear
Feist, Sister Theresa 263
Féré, Charles 87, 266

Ferenczi, Sándor 94
Fergus Falls State Hospital 353
Ferriar, John 43
Ferrus, Guillaume 148
fever 28, 31, 41, 48, 53, 55, 176, 295; erysipelas (*aka* St. Anthony's Fire) 123, 132; "feverish" symptoms of mania 171, 189; hay 90; malaria 94, 121; typhoid 61, 66, 137; yellow 61; *see also* fever therapy, pyrotherapy, pyretotherapy
Fever Research Project 131
fever therapy, pyrotherapy, pyretotherapy 44, 120–125, 322; aseptic meningitis 125–127; blanket method 127; diathermy (*aka* electropyresis) 127–129; fever cabinet (*aka* electric light bath cabinet, systemic heating box, hot box) 129; hot air bath (*aka* the oven) 129; hot bath therapy (*aka* hyperpyrexia bath therapy) 130; hypohyperthermia (*aka* the swing method) 130–131; inductotherm (*aka* electromagnetic induction) 131; Kettering hypertherm 131; malarial fever therapy 123, 131–134; radiothermy (*aka* ultra-high frequency oscillation) 135; rat-bite fever (*aka* sodoku) 135–136; relapsing fever 136–137
Fiamberti, Amarro 290
Filipi, Angelo 145–146
Fillon, François 173
Fink, Max 332, 333
Finsen, Niels 24
firecrackers 6
First and Second Psychiatric Hospitals 79
Fishponds Asylum 35, 79, 180, 271, 297
Fitzgerald, F. Scott 125
Fitzgerald, Zelda 125, 127
"fixed ideas" 282
fixing (*aka* the eye, catching the eye, the gaze, the clinical gaze) 107, 137–*139*, 140–141, 153; *see also* Foucault, Michael
Florimond, Ronger (*aka* Hervé) 115
focal sepsis (*aka* autointoxication) theory 34, 98, 99, 100, 270, 347, 350, 351
Fodéré, François Emmanuel 192
Fogel, E.J. 21
food refusal 11, 81, 142, 145, 149; *see also* forced feeding, forced alimentation, gavage; sitophobia
Forbes, Father Alexander 203–204
forced feeding (forced alimentation, gavage) 81, 98, 141–143, 237; Balmanno's feeding apparatus (*aka* Balmanno's syringe) 143; Eguisier's irrigateur 143–144; feeding spoon (*aka* forcing spoon) 98, 144–145; gag 98, 145; galvanic method 145–

146; Haslam's key *146*–147; manual force 147; mouth-opener 147; nasal tube 98, 147–148; nasogastric intubation 148; nose feeding 148; nose holding 149; Paley's feeder 149; rectal feeding (*aka* clyster, nutrient enema) 149–150; screw (*aka* screw-gag, screw key, fish tail gag) 150; spouting boat 150–*151*; stomach pump (*aka* stomach tube) 151–152; wedge 152; *see also* food-refusal (*aka* sitophobia)
Fordyee, O.O. 182, 183
Forel, Oscar 341
Foucault, Michel 5, 140; on clinical gaze 140; criticism of moral treatment 252–253
Fournier, Alfred-Jean 122
Foville, Achille-Louis-François 180
Fox, Edward Long 251
Frame, Janet 331
Frankenstein 82
Frankfurt Hospital 122
Franklin, Benjamin 82, 91–92
Franklin, T.M. 215
Freeman, Walter 15, 279, 281; and cerebral stimulation or psychic stimulation 15–16; criticism of diathermy 128; head-hunting trip 291; prefrontal lobotomy (*aka* leucotomy, Freeman-Watts Procedure) 281–287; transorbital lobotomy (*aka* ice pick lobotomy) *290*–291, *292*–294; *see also* Columbia-Greyston Project (*aka* New York State Brain Research Project); psychosurgery; Watts, James; West Virginia Lobotomy Project
French Revolution 77, 108, 272, 317
Freud, Sigmund 14, 105, 172; eulogy of Charcot 199; expert witness in Wagner-Jauregg trial 94; on hysteria 266; the unconscious 105; *see also* psychoanalysis
Friends Asylum 42, 235, 246
Frydendahl, Wilhelm 314
Fulton, John 278, 281, 282

Gale, Robert 308, 313
Galen 54, 82, 164
gallbladder 26, 98, 100, 125, 348
Galt, John Minson 69, 207, 273
Galvani, Luigi 82, 89
Garland, Judy 331
Garlands Asylum 58
Gartnavel Royal Hospital (*aka* Glasgow Lunatic Asylum, Glasgow Royal Asylum) 120, 143, 163, 237, 305; *Chronicles of the Cloister* 120; *Gartnavel Gazette* 120
Gastaud, Henri 340
Gaveaux, Pierre 101
gender ideology 152

# Index

General Electric Company 135
General Medical Society for Psychotherapy 202
General Motors 131
general paralysis of the insane 42, 121, 294; *see also* dementia paralytica; general paresis; neurosyphilis; syphilis
general paresis 23, 94, 121, 122, 129, 172, 294, 295; *see also* dementia paralytica; general paralysis of the insane; neurosyphilis; syphilis
genital surgery 68, 152–154; castration 68, 154–156; clitoridectomy (*aka* female circumcision) 156–157; oophorectomy (*aka* ovariectomy, "normal ovariotomy," Battey's operation, female castration) 157–179; tubal ligation (*aka* female sterilization) 159–160; vasectomy 160–162; wiring 68, 162–164; *see also* eugenics
Geoghegan, J.J. 85
George III, King 137, 318
George Washington University 283
Georget, Etienne-Jean 187
Georgia State Sanitarium 350
germ theory 121, 123, 347; *see also* bacteriology
German Research Institute for Psychiatry 137
German Romantic Psychiatry *5,* 7, 206, 207, 225, 249
Gheel Lunatic Colony 220
Ghent Lunatic Colony 237
Gieseing Asylum 222
Giliarovskii, Vasilii 86
Gilles, André 94–95
Gilmore, Patrick 114
Giraudy, Charles François Simon 230, 231
Glore Psychiatric Museum 302
glove anesthesia 340
Glueck, Bernard 243
Goldberger, Joseph 261
Goldman, Douglas 190
Grace Arthur Point Performance Scale 262
Gracie Square Hospital 78
Grand Duke of Tuscany 243
Grant-Smith, Rachel 67
Granville, John Moritmer 44, 210–211
Graves, Thomas Chivers 98, 99, 350
Great Pox 121; *see also* syphilis
Greaves, Donald 346
Greenacre, Phyllis 349
Griesinger, Wilhelm 8, 163, 204
Groos, Friedrich 236–237
Guantanamo Bay prisoners 142
Guggenbühl, Louis 259
Guislain, Joseph 30, 31, 43, 237, 272, 319; as "Belgian Pinel" 248; Chinese temple 310–*311*, 312; and moral treatment 195, 298; scientific test of Cox's Chair 298–299; *Traité sur l'Aliénation mentale et les Hospices des Aliénés* 310
Guy's Hospital 71
gynecology 156; *see also* Tait, Lawson

Haigh, Walter Abraham 43
Hallaran, William Sanders 104; Hallaran's belt 226; Hallaran's circulating swing 43–44, 299–*300*; Hallaran's mat 301, 306; on "mechanical anodynes" 296
Halle-Nietleben Asylum 64
hallucinations 17, 34, 40, 43, 47, 50, 75, 87, 96, 101, 110, 126, 135, 138, 174, 188, 189, 240, 257, 258, 260, 265, 270, 271, 273, 285, 286, 287, 288, 315, 322, 338
Hammatt, Alice Hood 283–284
Hammond, William 215
Hampshire County Lunatic Asylum (*aka* Hants County Lunatic Asylum) 148, 205
Hanwell Asylum (*aka* County of Middlesex Pauper Lunatic Asylum) 13, 29, 62, 71, 72, *111*, 163, 200, 209–210, 213, 216, 222, 266, 303, 314; *see also* Conolly, John; non-restraint movement
Harlem Valley State Hospital 334
Hartford Retreat for the Insane 118; *Retreat Gazette* 118
Harvard University Medical School 136, 353
Haskell, Ebeneezer 252, 318; *Astounding Disclosures! Three Years in a Mad House* 251
Haslam, John 31, 79, 104, *139*–140, 151; defense of use of handcuffs 229–230; description of general paresis (syphilis) 121; Haslam's belt (*aka* Haslam's girdle) 227, 229; Haslam's key *146*–147; *Observations on Madness and Melancholy* 139; Parliamentary Select Committee inquiry *221*; *see also* Bethlem Asylum (*aka* Bedlam); Norris, James (*aka* William)
Hastings State Hospital 131
Hawkins, J.R. 18
Hayner, Christian August 301–*302*, 320
*Healing Schizophrenia: Complementary Vitamin and Drug Treatment* 263
Heath, Robert Galbraith 59
Heidelberg's University Hospital 105
Heinroth, Johann Christian August hellebore 77; black 69; white 40
Hemingway, Ernest 332
hemodialysis 59
hemospasia 36–37
heredity 170

Hergt, Karl 147
Hershfield, Alex 136
Hesperia Hospital 86
Het Dolhuys 203
Higgens, Godfrey 226
Highland Hospital 125, 127
Hill, Robert Gardiner 209; non-restraint and 209–210, 219
Himmler, Heinrich 191
Himwich, Harold 20, 21
Hinsie, Leland 18–20, 133, 135
Hippocrates 33, 54, 69, 82, 113, 120, 164, 188, 254, 257
Hoen, Thomas 190
Hoffer, Abram 262, 263–264
Hoffman, Erich 122
Hoffman's Balsam of Life 32
Hölderlin, Johann Christian Friedrich 101, 206
Holmes, Bayard Taylor 347–348; *Dementia Praecox Studies: A Journal of Psychiatry of Adolescence* 348
Holmes, Oliver Wendell 122
Holloway Sanatorium (*aka* Holloway Asylum for the Insane) 224, 261
Hollymoor Asylum 350
homeopathic asylums and clinics 81, 84, 305
Homewood Retreat 85
homosexuality 17, 155
Hôpital de la Charité 181
Hôpital de la Pitié 239, 240
Hôpital Sainte-Anne 179, 232
Hôpital St. Louis 122
hormone 255, 259, 269; hormone of happiness 321; Hormotone 255; neurohormone 255
Horn, Ernst 42, *222*, 223, 237; and drenching 176; Horn's rotary bed (*aka* Drehbett, whirling bed) 302–303; Horn's rotary chair (*aka* Drehstuhl) 303–*304*; Horn's sack (*aka* Horn's bag) 227–228
Horowitz, Vladimir 331
Hospital Psiquiátrico do Juqueri 283
Hôtel-Dieu 56
Houdini, Harry 177
*How to Live with Schizophrenia* 263
Hudson River State Hospital for the Insane 262
Hufeland, Christoph Wilhelm 76
Human Betterment Society 162
human rights 142, 173, 192–193, 197, 219, 279
humours (*aka* vital spirits, vapors) 3, 26, 34, 36, 37, 38, 42, 43, 54–55, 65, 76, 187; black bile 26, 32, 55; blood 26, 36, 55; phlegm 26, 55; yellow bile (*aka* choler) 26, 55
hunger strikes 142
Hunt, Isaac 251–252
Hunter, William 98–99
Hurd, Henry 313
Hurst, Arthur 274

Hutton, Joanna 105
hydrotherapeutic clinics (*aka* hydros) 165; *see also* hydrotherapy or hydropathy
hydrotherapy or hydropathy 13, 43, 44, 53, 57, 66, 78, 84, 130, 164–169, 189, 206, 228, 273; beach bathing (*aka* strand bathing) 169–170; cold water ingestion 170, 189; cold water pour 170–171; cold wet pack (*aka* packing) 44, 171–173, 179, 189; continuous hot bath (*aka* refractory bath, or waterbed treatment) 44, 173–174, 352; continuous warm bath with application of cold to the head 174; douche 33, 174–*175*, 176, 189, 249, 252, 273; drenching 176; drip sheet 44, 176; dripping machine 176–177; fan douche 177, *178*; fomentation 177; liver spray 177; mustard bath 75, 177, 179, 247; needle spray 179, 189; Neptune's girdle (*aka* Neptune's belt) 179; nightcap (*aka* wet cap, ice cap) 179–180; pail douche (*aka* pail pour, *bain d'affusion*) 180; pelvic douche (*aka* perineal douche, ascending douche) 180–181; prolonged cold bath (*aka* the soak) 181–182, 244, 245, 252; salt glow bath 182; Scotch douche (*aka douche Écossaise*) 182–183; sea water injection (*aka* marine plasma injection, ocean plasma injection, Quinton plasma injection) 183–184; shower bath (*aka* rain bath, spray douche) *178*, 184–185, 252; sitz bath (*aka* hip bath, half bath) 185; spinal douche (*aka* Charcot douche) 185–186; tepid bath (*aka* warm bath) 35, 43, 63, 65, 186–187; Turkish bath (*aka* hot air bath) 44, 187–188; vapor bath (*aka* Russian bath, steam bath, cabinet bath) 188
hyperpnea 18
hypnotism 241, 276
hypochondriasis 33, 88, 89, 138, 166, 282
hysteria 25, 37, 43, 87, 87, 88, 89, 91, 107, 153, 158, 166, 171, 176, 180, 181, 186, 187, 198, 239, 306, 321, 341; *agents provocateur* 265; arc-de-circle (*aka* arc-en-cercle) 108, 267; aura 25, 266; Charcot's theory of 265; culturally idiomatic symptoms 264–265; "Golden Age" of 239, 241, 266; *grand hystérie* attack 266; hysterical paralysis 91; hysterogenic zones 265; and masturbation 157–158; and men 87, 181, 266–267; and reflex irritability (*aka* reflex arc) 156, 266; theories of 265; in Tuesday Lectures 108, 265; and womb 179, 181, 265; *see also* Charcot, Jean-Martin; metallotherapy, metalloscopy or Burquism; ovarian compression; Salpêtrière Asylum; Wittmann, Blanche

Ideler, Karl Wilhelm 38, 39, 185–186
Illenau Asylum 116, 147
Illinois Neuropsychiatric Institute 22
immigrants 250
immunology 254, 347
Imperial Provincial Lunatic Asylum 222, 235
Industrial Revolution 101, 296
industrialization 72
informed consent 22, 134, 142, 159, 330, 332
insane person, characterizations of 3, *117*; as children 201; deprived of reason 5, 28, 30, 52, 71, 79, 93, 101, 104, 105, 106, 107, 138, 182, 186, 192, 195, 209, 220, 225, 245, 248, 249, 252, 271, 280, 282, 298, 307, 308, 317, 321, 351; pre-asylum confinement 191, *218*; as sick 9; unique character of American insane 210, 211; as wild beast 73, 110, 141, 211, 220, 221, 242, 306
Interacademic Brain Research Institute 337
*The Invisible Man* 294
Ionesco, Sally "Ellen" 290–291
ipecac syrup 69
Irish Republican prisoners 142
isolation 141, 191–194, 206, 249; *basses-loges* (aka *la chapelle*) 194; dark chamber (*aka* dark room, dark cell) 194–197, 245; isolation therapy 197–199; oubliette (*aka* fool's pit) 199, 204; padded cell (*aka* padded room, rubber room) 47, 97, 199–202, 237; psychic abstinence treatment (*aka* deprivation therapy) 202–203; solitary cell (*aka* isolation cell) 141, 203–204; strong room 204–205, 306

Jackson, Charles Thomas 96–97
Jacobi, Mary Putnam 171
Jacobi, Maximilian 176, 181, 222
Jefferson, Thomas 61
Jenner, Edward 29, 30
Jepson, George 145
Jim Crow 112
Johns Hopkins University 278
Jones, Robert 84–85
*Journal of Convulsive Therapy* 16
*Journal of Schizophrenia* (later *Journal of Orthomolecular Medicine*) 264
*Journal of the American Medical Association* 159, 160, 292

*Juliette* 108
Julius-Maximilians University 270
Julius-Spital 30, 195, 271, 320
Jung, Carl Gustav 125
Junod, Victor-Théodore 36–37
Junod's Arm 37
Junod's Depurator 37
*Justine, or The Misfortunes of Virtue* 108
Jütland Asylum 170

Kalinowsky, Lothar 329
Kant, Immanuel 5
Kantorovich, N.V. 79
Karell, Phillip 81
Kassabian, Mihran Krikor 270
Kateřinky Lunatic Asylum 101, 116
Kauders, Lt. Walter 94
Kaulbach, Wilhelm von 310
Kellogg, John Harvey 305
Kennedy, Cyril 342
Kensington House 151
Kesey, Ken 331
Kettering, Charles Franklin 131
Kidder, Margot 263
Kings Park State Hospital 342
Kingston Lunatic Asylum 312
Kircher, Athanasius 7
Kirkbride, Thomas Story 70, 117, 192, 214–215, 246–248, 252; Kirkbride Plan 9, 111, 192, *247*, 248, 267; *see also* moral architecture; moral treatment, moral management, moral therapy
Klaesi, Jakob 45, 47–48
Klaus, Pres. Vaclav 219
Kleist, Karl 293
Knight, Paul Slade 226, *231*, 232, 233, 300
Kohlraush, Henrich 228
Korean War 327
Korem, Aya 95
Korsakoff, Sergei 9
Kozlowski, Michael 94
Kraepelin, Emile 105, 223, 288, 302; autointoxication theory 260, 347; and cretinism 259–260; dementia praecox 260, 322, 347; founder of modern scientific psychiatry 302, 347
Kretschmer, Ernst 202–203

*The Lady of the Camellias* 10
Lakin State Hospital 292
Lancaster County Lunatic Asylum 226, 232, 233, 301
lancet 55, 56, 60, 62
*Lancet* 142
Lancet Commission 210, 214
Landolt, Hans Heinrich 150
Langenheim, Frederick 117
Langenheim, William 117
Langermann, Johann 6, 228, 249
Lanzarini, Luigi 89–90

# Index

Lathrop, Clarissa Caldwell 181–182, 216
Lawrence, T.E. 281
learning disorders 263
LeBeau, Jacques 290
Leduc, Stéphane Armand Nicolas 85
Lehmann, J.H. 5
Leipzig University 207, 225, 318
Leksell, Lars 280
*lettres de cachet* 108
Leubus Asylum 9
Leuret, François 141, 142, 174–176, 180
Lichterfelde Hospital 334
Liebig's meat extract 150
Lima, Almeida 282
*Limbo* 294
Lincoln Lunatic Asylum (*aka* The Lawn) 219
Lindsay, W. Lauder 58, 216
Linguiti, Giovanni-Maria 237
Lipetz, Basile 20–21
liver 26, 55, 170, 177, 254, 347
Livingston, Alfred T. 90–91
Locke, John 270–271
Loevenhart, Arthur Solomon 16, 21, 22
Lomax, Montagu 67
Lombroso, Cesare 82
London Asylum 163
Longview State Hospital 190
Louis XV, King 305
Louis XVI, King 272
Löwenbach, Hans 341, 342
Lower, Richard 57
Loyola University 339
lucid intervals 50
Lujan Lunatic Asylum 9
Lunacy Commission 39, 172, 185, 204, 207, 216, 224, 312
Lunar Society 295
Luys, Jules Bernard 239, 240, 241

M-hypothesis (*aka* adrenochrome hypothesis) 262
MacBride, David 233–234
MacDonald, Alexander 170
MacDonald, Carlos 317
Macdonald, James 60
Macleod, Neil 46–47
Macphail, S Rutherford 58
Macpherson, John 295
"The Mad House" 310
Madden, Richard 77
magic lantern shows 101, 110, 117
*The Magic Mountain* 10
Maine Insane Hospital 251
Maisel, Alfred Q. 211
Maison Coloniale de Sante 237
Malcolm Bliss Hospital 340
Mangan, Valentin 232
mania 11, 13, 23, 26, 28, 29, 31, 34, 37, 39, 40, 41, 42, 43, 44, 46, 47, 50, 55, 57, 59, 60, 61, 69, 79, 80, 91, 96, 97, 104, 107, 110, 114, 116, 138, 139, 156, 157, 163, 166, 173, 178, 179, 180, 184, 186, 189, 195, 200, 201, 224, 225, 235, 244, 245, 250, 251, 256, 258, 290, 297, 299, 301, 303, 306, 312, 315, 317, 318, 319, 320, 321, 332, 338, 354; "feverish" symptoms of 171, 189; flagellomania 313; homicidal mania 223; hypomania 15; monomania 29, 121, 210; monomania with paralysis 63; nymphomania 153, 158, 203; ovariomania (*aka* Old Maid's Insanity, uteromania) 153, 158; puerperal mania 62; suicidal monomania 33, 170, 223
manic-depression 16, 137, 190, 269
Mann, Thomas 10
Manning, F. Norton 216
Manor House 251
Manteno State Hospital 183
Manweeshuys Asylum 310
"Marat/Sade" 109
Marcé, Louis-Victor 257
Mariaberg Asylum 203, 204
Marin-Foucher, M. 190–191
Marsberg Asylum 316
Marseille Lunatic Asylum 192
masks, gags and toggles 205–206; Autenrieth's mask (*aka* Autenrietische maske*) 206–207; brank (*aka* gossip's bridle, scold's bridle, witch's bridle) 207; cap of silence (*aka* helmet of silence) 207; gag 98, 145, 207; muffle 207; toggle (*aka* pear, bulb) 207–208; wire mask (*aka* net mask, grating mask, net cap) 208
massage 11, 12, 78, 169, 352; of the brain 306
masturbation 35, 67–68, 156, 157, 163, 164, 174, 227, 230, 232; *see also* masturbatory insanity
masturbatory insanity 68, 153, 163
Maudsley Hospital 17, 255, 260
Mayo Clinic 350
McCulloch, Warren Sturgis 17
McGill University 45, 49, 98, 275, 325; *see also* Cameron, D. Ewen; psychic driving
McGovern, George 332
McKissock, Sir Wylie 286
McLean Asylum 96, 97, 129, 179, 238, 246, 352
McLeod, Julius 292
Mead, Richard 319, 337
mechanical anodynes 296; *see also* rotation, oscillation and vibration
mechanical restraints 2, 24, 72, 97, 140, 165, 166, 181, 200, 201, 205, 208–210, 211–213, 242, 244, 297, 309, 310, 319, 335; arm-chair 213; Aubanel's restraining bed (*aka* Utica crib, protection bed, enclosed bed, safety bed, preservation bed, DeKalb crib) 112, 214–**215**, 216–217; Autenrieth's chamber (*aka* chamber of palisades) 217; ball and chain 217–218; Belgian cage (*aka* lunatic's cage, idiot's cage) **218**, 306, 320; boot hobbles (*aka* quarter boots) 218–219; cage bed (*aka* net bed, veil bed) 219–220; *la ceinture à bracelets mobiles* 220; chains (*aka* shackles, fetters) 63, 72, 166, 194, 195, 201, 203, 205, 217, 220–**221**, 222, 229, 234, 235, 242, 243, 248, 320; coercion chair (*aka* English chair, *Zwangstuhl*) 222; cruciform stance **222**–223; *cuirass* 223; dry pack 223–224; English clock case (*aka* English coffin, pen, lunatic box, box, press, isolation cell) **224**–225; enveloping bag (*aka* envelope bag) 225; five-point restraint 225–226; four-point restraint 226; gyve (*aka* leglock) 166, 211, 219, 220, 226; Hallaran's belt 226; hand-muffs (*aka* locked gloves, soft gloves) 211, 226–227, **231**; Haslam's belt (*aka* Haslam's girdle) 227; high collar 194, 227; Horn's sack (*aka* Horn's bag) 227–229; lacing 229; leather hobbles 229; locked jumpsuit 229; mad box (aka *Daarekiste,* or *Dollkasten*) 229; manacles (*aka* handcuffs, wrist shackles) 203, 208, 219, 220, **221**, 229–230, 235, 245; maniac's bed 230; monkey jacket 230; osier basket (*aka* osier cage, wicker basket, basket of force) 230; Perkins sexual armor 230–231; pillory wicker 231; pocket muffs **231**–232; posey vest (*aka* criss-cross vest) 232; restraining girdle 232; side-arm dress (*aka* maillot de bain*) 232–233; six-point restraint 233; sleeves **231**, 233, 247; spring straps 72, 182, 186, 211, 233; stock 233; straitjacket (*aka* camisole de force, strait-waistcoat, madd-shirt, polka) 2, 42, 114, 138, 166, 178, 181, 195, 198, 201, 202, 203, 206, 211, 214, 219, 224, 226, 227, 229, 232, 233–**234**, 235, 237, 243, 244, 245, 297, 319; strong dress/suit (*aka* locked dress/suit) 234; suspended sack 234–235; swaddling bed (*aka* swaddling basket) 235; ties and cuffs 235, 244; tranquilizing chair (*aka* restraint chair) 166, 222, 235–**236**, 237, 245; wall camisole 237; Wyman bed-strap (*aka* bed saddle) 238–239; *see also* non-restraint movement
*Medical Annals of the District of Columbia* 284
*The Medical Times and Gazette* 309

# Index

Meduna, László 337–338, 339; carbon dioxide inhalation therapy 16–18; as "father of shock therapy" 16; Meduna's Mixture 16; and metrazol (*aka* cardiozol) 338–340; sodium cyanide treatment 22
Meerenberg Asylum 9
Mehrtens, Henry 130
melancholy 24, 29, 34, 41, 60, 62, 71, 82, 87, 89, 92, 113, 139, 166, 172, 179, 244; hysterical 68; religious 79
"Melancholy and Raving Mania" (*aka* "Brainless Brothers") 208, **209**; *see also* Bethlem Asylum
Mellage, Heinrich 203
menstruation 37, 155, 157, 182, 185, 254, 258; menstrual insanity 158
mental defectives 162, 286
Mental Health Bell 222
Mental Treatment Act 67
*Merck Archives* 46–47
mercury 40–42, 122
mescaline 262
mesmerists 137, 241
metallotherapy, metalloscopy or Burquism 239; aesthiogens 240, 241; and Burq, Victor Jean-Marie 239–24; and Charcot, Jean-Martin 239, 241; consecutive oscillations 240; and Dumontpallier, Amédée 239, 240; internal ingestion of metals 240; and Luys, Jules Bernard 240; magnetic amnesia 240; magnetic crown 240; magnets 240; metals 239, 240, 241; psychic polarization 240; Société de Biologie investigation 239, 241; and Spiritualism 241; suggestion 241; transference 240; and Wittmann, Blanche 239–240; *see also* hysteria; Salpêtrière Asylum
metanarrative 1, 2
Meyer, Adolf 278, 349, 351; Dean of American Psychiatry 278
miasma theory of disease 121
mice 6
Michigan Asylum for the Insane 11, 152, 216
Michigan State Board of Corrections and Charities 196
Mickel's formula 150
Middlesex County Asylum (*aka* Hanwell Asylum) 13, 29, 62, 71, 72, **111**, 163, 200, 209, **210**, 213, 214, 216, 222, 266, 294, 303, 313–314
Middletown State Hospital 81, 159
Midland Hospital for Nervous Disease 18
milieu therapy 105, 353
milk 11, 72, 73, 75, 76, 78, 79, 80, 114, 121, 142, 145, 148, 149, 150, 199, 261, 282, 322; salted 81
Milligan, W. Liddell 85, 341

Millingen, John Gideon 13, 29, 266, 313
mind 3, 5, 14, 24, 32, 35, 37, 41, 44, 45, 50, 58, 59, 60, 66, 68, 70, 71, 72, 75, 80, 83, 86, 98, 100, 101, 102, 108, 110, 112, 113, 117, 120, 138, 139, 140, 141, 144, 146, 151, 152, 169, 170, 171, 172, 175, 187, 191, 192, 201, 211, 233, 245, 248–249, 251, 256, 259, 271, 272, 278, 279, 298, 306, 307, 320, 322, 333, 335, 342, 343, 348; feeble-mindedness 153, 160, 314; mind control 277, 327; *see also* brainwashing
Miraglia, Biagio 109–110
mirroring 107
Missouri State Hospital #4 258
Mitchell, Silas Weir 11–13, 81, 176, 199, 202
Monakow, Constantin von 125
Monakow Kränzli 125
Mongols 149
Moniz, Egas (*aka* António Caetano Abreu Freire) 278–279; and leucotomy 281–283; Nobel Prize 278
Monro, John 31, 55, 70, 320
Monro, Thomas 62
Monroe, Colonel James 277
Montagu, Lady Wortley 35
Moore, William 335–336
moral architecture 9, 70, 197, 245, **247**, 248, **249**, 267; *see also* Kirkbride, Thomas Story
moral contagion 104
moral treatment, moral management, or moral therapy 9, 53, 57, 62, 80, 117, 192, 197, 200, 203, 204, 205, **215**, 236, 242–253, 267, 268, 273, 296, 298; in colonial asylums 201, 225, 312–313; cult of curability 251; cure rate 250; disappearance of 105, 112, 196, 248–253; and expressive therapy 101, 102, 104, 105, 106, 108, 109, 110, 111, 112, 116, 118, 120; Foucault's criticism of 252–253; kindness and 118, 252, 253; not incompatible with depletive therapy 70–71; not incompatible with forced feeding 141, 145, 147; not incompatible with isolation 195, not incompatible with mechanical restraint 234, 242; not incompatible with pious frauds 272–273; not incompatible with salutary fear 310, 319, 321; not incompatible with somatic therapies 91, 155; physician and patient relationship 47, 140; professional vs. lay practitioners 109; view of insane person 73, 220; 242–254; *see also* Chiarugi, Vincenzo; Foucault, Michele; Guislain, Joseph; Kirkbride, Thomas Story; moral architecture; non-

restraint; Pinel, Philippe; reason; Rush, Benjamin; Tuke Samuel; Tuke, William
Morison, Sir Alexander 200
morphine 44, 46, 47, 206, 247
Morrison, Jim 95
Morselli, Enrico 305
Moscow Institute of Psychiatry 78
Mott, Frederic 161
Mount Vernon Hospital for the Colored Insane 82
Mount Zion Hospital 127
Moxey, D. Anderson 148–149
Müller, Anton 30, 77, 195, 271–272, 320
Müller, Charles 242
Murray, George Redmayne 259
Murray, Maynard 190
Murray Royal Asylum 120, 216; *Excelsior* 120
music 6, 101, 102, 106, 109, 112–**113**, 114–116, 132, 138, 192, 244, 246, 331, 352
Musilova, Vera 220
*Musurgia Universalis* 7
*Mycoderma aceti* 121
Myerson, Abraham 269, 351
myxedema (*aka* hypothyroidism) 259, 260

N., Friedrich August 288
*The Naked Lunch* 294
Napier, Richard 164
Napoleon III 121
narcotics 24, 96, 167, 177
Narrenturm Asylum (*aka* Fools' Tower) 181
Nash, John Forbes 337
National Alliance on Mental Illness 333
Neissen, Clemens 9
neosalvarsan 122; *see also* syphilis
nervine clinics 12, 82
Nervous Illness Station of the Reserve Infirmary 92
Neumann, Heinrich 321
Neumann, Karl 179
neurasthenia 11–12, 81, 87, 88, 91, 153, 158, 172, 176, 179, 255, 341; as fashionable disease and distinguished malady 13
neurosis (*aka* psychoneurosis) 14, 17, 176, 179, 276, 277, 341; Charcot as "Napoleon of Neurosis" 198; combat 50; compulsion 255; functional 183; obsessional 49; obsessive-compulsive 16; sexual 255; war neurosis 17; *see also* Charcot, Jean-Martin
neurosyphilis 23, 94, 295, 322; asylum admissions for 122–123; and fever therapy, pyrotherapy, pyretotherapy 123, 127, 128, 129, 130, 131, 132, 133–134, 135, 136, 137; *see also* syphilis

Neustadt, Rudolph 269
New York City Asylum for the Insane 188
New York State Asylum for Insane Criminals (*aka* Matteawan State Hospital) 316
New York State Lunatic Asylum (*aka* Utica) 90, 96, 112, 114, 115, 133, 182, 185, 295; Blackbird Minstrel shows 112; *Opal 119*; Utica crib 112, 214–*215*, 216–215
New York State Psychiatric Institute and Hospital 18, 133, 329
*New York Therapeutic Review* 254
*New York Times* 277, 327, 334
New York's Ninth Regiment Band 114
Newcastle-Upon-Borough Lunatic Asylum 204
Newington, Samuel 39, 178, 179
Neymann, Clarence 127–129
Nichols, C.H. 215
Nikolayev, Yuri Serge 78–79
Nistri, Santa 216
Nobel Prize 24, 94, 123, 132, 278, 282, 337
non-restraint movement 8, 172, 200, 209, 210, 211, 213, 225, 234, 242, 319, 321; affect on physician-patient relationship 310; *see also* Chiarugi, Vincenzo; Conolly, John; Hill, Robert Gardiner; mechanical restraints; Pinel, Philippe; Tuke, William
Norris, James (*aka* William) 220–*221*
Norristown State Hospital for the Insane 158
North Carolina State Hospital 341
Northampton General Lunatic Asylum 144
Northwestern University Medical School 127
Notkin, John 262
Nuremberg trials 190, 293
nymphomania 62, 153, 158, 203

Oberholzer, Emil 155
occupational therapy 105, 125, 132, 253, 338
ocular stigmata 25
Odense Hospital 229
Odessa Psychopathic Hospital 137
odor of the insane 165, 187, 204
Oebeke, Bernhard 149–150
Oleum Cephalicum 32–33
*One Flew Over the Cuckoo's Nest* (book) 294
*One Flew Over the Cuckoo's Nest* (film) 331
opium 37, 43, 44, 61, 66, 96, 114, 178, 206, 208, 247; *see also* narcotics
organotherapy, opotherapy, Séquardotherapy, histotherapy, zootherapy, or *Materia Medica Animalis* 254–255; brain extract (*aka* myelin, or cerebrinin) 256–257; ovarian extract (*aka* Oöphorin) 257–259; thyroid extract 259–260; thyroid shock therapy (*aka* hyperthyroid treatment) 260–261
Orlikow, Velma 327
orthomolecular therapy 261; adrenochine hypothesis (*aka* M Hypothesis) 262; and American Psychiatric Association task force 263; Hoffer, Abram 262, 263–264; *Journal of Orthomolecular Medicine* (*aka Journal of Schizophrenia*) 264; Pauling, Linus 262–263; popular books 263; *see also* pellagra; schizophrenia; vitamins
Osawatomie State Hospital 126
Osmond, Humphry 262
Ospedale di Bonifazio 68, 70, 235, 243, 272, 317, 321
Ospedale Psichiatrico S. Maria Maddalena (*aka* Aversa) 109, 110, 237
Ospedale San Lazzaro 207
ovarian compression 264–267; compressor belt 266; manual 266; *see also* hysteria
Oxenbridge, Daniel 164
Oxford University 43, 141
Oxo bouillon cube 150
oxygen 14, 15, 16, 18, 21, 333

Paine, Alfred 48
Palmer, Harold 48
Paraguay, asylum patients in 193
paralysis 34, 38, 63, 186, 239, 265; hysterical 89, 91, 239, 240; *paralysis agitans* (*aka* Parkinson's disease) 305, 306; sleep paralysis 85; *see also* dementia paralytica; general paralysis of the insane
Paré, Ambroise 34
Pargeter, William 272
Parliamentary Select Committee Inquiry 221, 226
Parry, Caleb Hiller 13
Pascal, Constance 322–323
passions 106, 107, 170, 175, 195, 203, 225, 242, 244, 249
Pasteur, Louis 121
pasteurization 121
Paterson, A. Spencer 85
"Patient Ball, held in the Kitchen of the Somerset County Asylum, England" 106
Pattison, John Nelson 114
Pauling, Linus 262–263
Payne, Arthur 225
Payne Whitney Psychiatric Clinic 346
Peckham House Asylum 26
Peeters, J.A. 220
pellagra 261; pellagra diet 81–82, 261–263; psychosis 261, 262, 263; vitamin B3 (*aka* niacin, nicotinic acid) 261, 262
penicillin 122, 129, 134
Pennsylvania Hospital 31, 37, 40, 41, 52, 53, 56, 59, 77, 80, 170, 195, 235, 245, 246, 299, 312, 313, 319; *see also* Rush, Benjamin
Pennsylvania Hospital for the Insane (*aka* Institute of Pennsylvania Hospital) 70, 117, 173, 192, 197, 214–215, 246, *247*, 248, 252, 285, 318; *see also* Haskell, Ebeneezer; Kirkbride, Thomas Story; moral treatment, moral management, or moral therapy
Peoria Asylum for the Insane 23, 24, 195, 295
Pepys, Samuel 58
Perceval, John Thomas 251
Perfect, William 42, 43, 194
Perkins, Ellen 230–231
Pescor, Michael 59
Peterson, Frederick 165, 166, 167
Pfeffer, Arnold 59
Pfeiffer, Jan 219
Philadelphia Hospital for Mental Disease 125–126
Philiatria 170
phobia 16, 17, 18, 86
phototherapy, or light therapy 267–268; heliotherapy (*aka* ultraviolet therapy) 268–269; infrared therapy (*aka* photothermal therapy) 269–270; X-ray therapy 270
phrenology 64
phthisical insanity 11; *see also* tuberculosis (*aka* consumption)
physiological medicine 63
Pienitz, Ernst 176
Pilgrim State Hospital 285, 286
Pimenta, Aloysio de Mattos 283
Pinel, Philippe 6, 62, 69, 70, 77, 104, 187, 192, 194, 246, 249, 301; in re bleeding (*aka* bloodletting, venesection) 56–57, 61; moral treatment (*aka* moral management, moral therapy) 70, 141, 242–244, 245, 248, 252, 273; and non-restraint 209; and pious frauds 272–273; and salutary fear 308, 317; statistical analysis of cure rates 250; striking chains 63, 234, 242; *Traité Médico-Philosophique sur l'aliénation Mentale, ou la Manie* 243; *A Treatise on Insanity* 234
pious frauds, salutary demonstrations, innocent ruses, curative ruses, or suggestive therapies 2, 5, 56, 107, 243, 270, 317; doctrine of associations 270–271; not incompatible with moral treatment 272–273; and soldier-patients 274–275;

*see also* Cox, Joseph Mason; Esquirol, Jean-Étienne Dominique; Pinel, Philippe; Rush, Benjamin
pipe smoker medic 66
Pisani, Baron Pietro 109, 273
Pitres, Albert 25
Plath, Sylvia 331–332; *The Bell Jar* 331, 332
Plaut, Felix 137
Pleasonton, Augustus J. 23–24
Pliny the Elder 69, 254
Poetzl, Otto 334
Poirier, Dr. 266
Poltava Asylum 177
"Pomp and Circumstances" 115
Ponza, G.L. 22–23, 24
Pool, J. Lawrence 289, 290
Pouppirt, Pearl 130
Power, Thomas 187
Powick Asylum (*aka* Worcester County Pauper and Lunatic Asylum) 115
Pratt, Anne 312
Prefargier Psychiatry Clinic 287
Preobrazhenski Mental Hospital 9
Prestwich Asylum 66–67
Price, Joseph 158–159
Prichard, James Cowles 40
Prichard, Thomas 143
Priessnitz, Vincent 164–165, 167, 171
Priestley, Joseph 82
Prinzhorn, Hans 105
Prinzhorn Collection 105
Proteus 69
Provincial Asylum for the Insane (Canada) 163
Provincial Board of Medicinal Research and Supervision (Belgium) 310
Provincial Lunatic Asylum (Austria) 222, 235
Provincial Lunatic Asylum (Germany) 80
psychiatry 5, 94, 98, 123, 172, 255, 257, 262, 277–278, 321, 326, 346; child 343; conflict with neurology 215; German Romantic (*aka* psychic) 56, 206, 207, 217, 225, 314; psychodynamic 98; racialized 221; scientific 8–9, 99, 100, 101, 302, 347; social problems and 278; Soviet 85; *see also* anti-psychiatry
psychic driving, accelerated psychotherapy, or automated psychotherapy 49, 275–277, 326, 327; Allan Memorial Institute of Psychiatry 275; Cerebrophone 275; cue communication (*aka* dynamic implant) 276; and deep sleep therapy 276; and electroconvulsive shock 276; "fire blizzard" 276; lysergic acid diethylamide (*aka* LSD) 276; sensory isolation 276; sodium amytal 276; *see also* brainwashing; Cameron, D. Ewen; depatterning; repatterning
psychic polarization 240
psychoanalysis 14, 50, 94, 104, 105, 173, 241, 265, 266; *see also* Freud, Sigmund
psychosurgery 15, 128, 277–280; capsulotomy 280–281; cingulectomy 281; prefrontal lobotomy (*aka* leucotomy, Freeman-Watts procedure) 281–287; topectomy (*aka* cortical ablation, frontal gyrectomy) 287–290; transorbital lobotomy (*aka* ice pick lobotomy) **290–292**, 293–294; trephining (*aka* trephinization, trepanning, trepanization) 294–295; *see also* August, N. Friedrich, Burckhardt, Gottleib; Columbia-Greystone Project (*aka* New York State Brain Research Project); Fiamberti, Ammaro; Freeman, Walter; Fulton, John; Hammatt, Alice Hood; Ionesco, Sally "Ellen"; Moniz, Egas; Watts, James; West Virginia Lobotomy Project
psychotherapy 18, 47, 48, 49, 102, 132, 326, 343, 344; torpillage 94–96; *see also* psychic driving, accelerated psychotherapy, or automated psychotherapy
Puccini, Giacomo 10
*Punch* 72
Pussin, Jean-Baptiste 243–244
Puusepp, Ludvig 288

quacks 37, 82, 91, 241
Quakers 246
"Quills" 109
quinine 12, 59, 132, 247, 261
Quinton, Réne 183–184; Quinton's Plasma 184

Racconigi Asylum 283
racialized psychiatry 201, 221
Rainhill Asylum 11, 90
"Raising the Wind" 110–111
*The Rake's Progress* (play) 108
Rawert, Ole Jørgen 229
Ray, Isaac 97–98, 108, 251
Reconstruction 112
Reed, John Foster 151
Reed, Lou 331
Rees, William 80
Reicha, Anton 114
Reil, Johann Christian 5–7, 301, 316, 317; coined "psychiatry" 321; as "Father of German Psychiatry" 69; *Rhapsodies on the Use of Psychological Therapies for the Mentally Disturbed* 5; *see also* awakenings; German Romantic Psychiatry
Reiss, Harry 343
repatterning 49; *see also* brainwashing
repetitive core 17
reproductive insanity 257, 258; climacteric 158, 258; lactation 257, 258; pregnancy 158, 257, 258; puerperal (*aka* parturition insanity) 59, 76, 257, 258
Research Institute for Cutaneous Disease 130
respiration 13–14, 16, 21–22, 66, 114, 171, 173, 265, 299, 305, 328
*Revue des Sciences Hypnotiques* 241
revulsion 26, 64
Richarz, Franz 149–150
rickets 267
Rider, Jane C. 64
Riga's formula 150
Riverview Sanitarium 259
Rizatti, Emilio 283
RO4–1038 326
Robert-Fleury, Tony 242
Robertson, Alexander 256
Robertson, C. Lockhart 171, 203
Robertson, George M. 201–202
Robinson, George 241
Rochester State Hospital 285
Rockefeller Foundation 262, 278, 285
Rockland State Hospital 339, 344
Roman College Astronomical Observatory 23
Romand, Hyppolite 210
Romanticism 101, 104; American 248; *see also* German Romantic Psychiatry
Röntgen, Wilhelm Conrad 270
Rosenblum, Alexander Samoilovich 137
rotation, oscillation and vibration 43, 44, 66, 79, 189, 228, 249, 273, 295–297; Chiarugi's cradle (*aka* Chiarugi's swing, restraining cradle) 297; Cox's chair (*aka* Cox's swing) 297–299; gyrater (*aka* gyrator) 299; Hallaran's circulating swing 299–**300**, 301; Hallaran's mat 301; hollow wheel (*aka* Hayner's wheel) 301–**302**; Horn's rotary bed (*aka* Drehbettt, whirling bed) 302–303; Horn's rotary chair (*aka* Drehstuhl) 303, **304**; nursery yacht 303; rocking chair 303; rocking horse 303; vibratory chair (*aka* dancing chair, jolting chair, trembling chair, *trémoussoir, fauteuil trépidant*) 303, 305; vibratory helmet (aka *Le Casque Vibrant*) 305–306; Von Hirsch's hammock (*aka* Von Hirsch's ship-bed) 306; *see also* Charcot, Jean-Martin; Chiarugi, Vincenzo; Cox, Joseph Mason; Guislain, Joseph; Hallaran, William; Hayner, August; Horn,

# Index

Ernst; Reil, Johann Christian; Rush, Benjamin
Rothman, Max 274
Rothschild, David 343
Roussy, Gustave 95–96
Rowling, J.K. 219
Royal Academy of Medicine 328
Royal Edinburgh Asylum (*aka* Morningside) 10, 75, 158, 163, 201, 241; *Morningside Mirror* 120
Royal Humane Society 66
Royal Medico-Psychological Association 161
Royal Mental Hospital 305
Royal National Hungarian Institute of Psychiatry and Neurology 337
Royal Society of Medicine 57, 58
Royal Victoria Hospital 275, 325
Royal Waterloo Hospital 49
Rubenstein, Leonard 275, 327
Rubery Hill Asylum 98, 100, 350
Rule, Anna 130
Rumpf, Elizabeth 344–345
rural idyll 170, 192
Rush, Benjamin 31, 37, 39, 40, 41, 53, 57, 77, 80, 272; and bleeding (*aka* bloodletting, venesection) 56; and cold water pour 170–171; and copious bleeding 59–61; on effect of dark on patients 195; Enlightenment and 139, 245; as "Father of American Psychiatry" 68, 104, 138, 171, 245, 306; on fixing (*aka* the eye, catching the eye, the gaze, the clinical gaze) 138–**139**; and gyrater (*aka* gyrator) 299; and masturbation 68; *Medical Inquiries and Observations Upon the Diseases of the Mind* 39, 60; and moral treatment 245–246; and salutary fear 306–307, 312, 313, 318–319; and tranquilizing chair (*aka* restraint chair) 235–**236**, 237; unitary theory of disease 52–53; *see also* Cullen, William; depletive therapy, "heroic therapy" antiphlogistic therapy, or "Rush's system"
Ruskin, John 101
Russell, John Fenn 105
Ryan, Judith 312
Ryder, Hugh 40

Sackeim, Harold 332, 333
St. Anne's Hill Hydropathic Establishment 187
St. Denis 317
St. Elizabeths Hospital (*aka* Government Hospital for the Insane) 15, 107, 128, 133, 179, 187, 215, 238, 283, 350
St. George Home 217
St. George's Asylum 237
St. Hans Asylum 169, 170
St. James Hospital 85, 341

St. Luke's Hospital 30, 55, 70, 106, 237, 315
Saint-Méen Asylum 114
St. Peters Asylum 225
St. Thomas' Hospital 319
Saint-Yon Asylum 180
Sakel, Manfred Joshua 334–336; Sakel's technique (*aka* Sakel's method) 335
Saks, Elyn 212
Saks Institute for Mental Health, Law, Policy and Ethics 212
Salmon, William 141
Salpêtrière Asylum 25, 29, 34, 35, 37, 38, 65, 107, 141, 146, 148, 163, 170, 181, 186, 187, 198, 271, 305; communal dining in 73; "cry of the hospital" 194; "museum of living pathology" 265; striking chains at 63; *see also* Charcot, Jean-Martin; Esquirol, Jean-Étienne Dominique; hysteria; Pinel, Philippe
salutary fear 5, 28, 38, 66, 138, 141, 164, 189, 244, 306–308, 322; bath of surprise (*aka* bain de surprise, plunge bath, dumping) 66, 166, 167, 308, **309**, 311; bathing (*aka* towel bath) 308–309; beating 141, 198, 309–310; Chinese temple 310–**311**, 312; ducking (*aka* tanking, cold ducking) 167, 312–313; flogging (*aka* flagellation) 249, 313–314, 316; mental cure technique (*aka* psychic cure) 314–315; nausea treatment 315–316; non-injurious torture 316; paddling 316–317; ridicule 107, 138, 270, 307, 317; slapping (*aka* striking) 317–318; spread eagle cure 318; standing posture 318–319; strapping 319; threat 251, 319–320; whipping 141, **320**–322; *see also* Guislain, Joseph; Rush, Benjamin
salvarsan (*aka*, compound 606, magic bullet) 122, 135, 136, 137; *see also* syphilis
San Hipólito Asylum for the Insane 165–166
Santo Orsola Hospital 89
Sargant, William 49, 291–292
Sarlandière, Jean-Baptiste 64
Savage, George Henry 30, 43, 234
scabies 35–36
Schager, Ludwig 23
Schelling, Wilhelm Joseph 5
schizophrenia 3, 14, 15, 16, 18, 25, 47, 48, 49, 85, 86, 100, 125, 126, 127, 129, 132, 133, 137, 160, 161, 189, 190, 260, 262, 263, 277, 285, 286, 293, 322, 325, 328, 329, 332, 334, 336, 338, 339, 341, 345, 346, 352; adrenochrome hypothesis (*aka* M-hypothesis) 262; antagonism with epilepsy 327, 337; and

bad mothering 19, 276; catatonic 15, 16, 19, 20, 22, 50, 52, 79, 189, 352; childhood 343–344; and controlled fasting 79; faulty metabolism of brain cells theory 59; hebephrenic 352; *Journal of Schizophrenia* (*aka Journal of Orthomolecular Medicine*) 264; paranoid 189, 326, 352; *"primäre Verrücktheit"* 287; spontaneous remission 21; tarxein 59; *see also* Bleuler, Eugen; dementia praecox
Schneider, Peter J. 315
Schüller, Max 171
Schumann, Robert 101
*Science* 262
Seabrook, William 172
Seale Hayne Military Hospital 274
Secchi, Father Pietro Angelo 23
Second and Third Great Awakenings 106
Second Annual Neurological Conference 278, 282
Seidelin, Johan Henrik 310, 314–315
self-consciousness 5, 6, 176, 285
Selmer, Harald 170
Senavra Asylum 296
senile testicles 161
sensory deprivation 49
Seppili, Giuseppi 288
serology 254, 347
sexual intercourse 6, 68, 69, 343
sexual psychopath 153; statutes 153, 155, 156
Shakespeare, William 3, 108, 130; *Hamlet* 62; *Macbeth* 3, 254; *Othello* 226; Shakesperean criticism and asylum physicians 108
Shamberg, Jay 130
Shaudinn, Fritz 122
Shaw, Claye 294, 295
Shaw, George Bernard 313
shell-shock 67, 87, 105, 132, 202, 274; deaf-muteness 274; deafness 274; disparaging terms for 202; psychic abstinence treatment (*aka* deprivation treatment) for 202; suggestive therapies 274; surprise attack shock treatment (*aka* Kaufmann's cure, electro-suggestive therapy, Überrumpelungsmethode) for 92–94; torpillage 94–96; wonder drug fraud 274; *see also* soldier-patients
Shepard, Charles 188
Sheppard, Edgar 187–188
shock therapy or convulsive therapy 5, 14, 16, 20, 25, 52, 86, 102, 107, 168, 278, 322–325; depatterning 276, 325–327; electroconvulsive shock therapy (*aka* electroshock therapy, ECT) 22, 48, 49, 85, 89, 262, 276, 284, 327–334; insulin shock therapy (*aka* insulin coma therapy, hypoglycemic shock ther-

apy) 20, 21, 48, 89, 261, 285, 334–337, 352; metrazol shock therapy (*aka* Cardiazol shock therapy) 16, 20, 22, 48, 86, 89, 285, 337–340, 352; photoshock 340–341; regressive electroconvulsive shock treatment (*aka* R.E.S.T, intensive electroconvulsive shock treatment, annihilation therapy, polydiurnal therapy) 341–345; sub-coma insulin treatment (*aka* Sakel borderline insulin treatment) 345–346; *see also* Cameron, D. Ewen; Meduna, László
Siegburg Asylum 176, 222, 225
Sillman, Leonard 21
Skae, David 158, 163
skeleton 6, 68
sleepwalking (*aka* somnambulism) 64, 265
smallpox 34–35; vaccine 29
Smetana, Bedřich 101
*Smiles and Tears, or the Widow's Stratagem* 108
Smith, Lydia 152, 216–217
Smith, Stephen 233
Smith, W. Maule 256–257
Smythies, John 262
snake pit 354
*The Snake Pit* (film) 331
Snape, Charles 184–185
Société de Biologie 239, 241, 254
Society for the Investigation of Human Ecology (SIHE) 277
soldier-patients 92, 93, 94, 95, 132, 202, 274
Solomon, Harry C. 130–131, 135–136
somatic school 176, 217
*sommeil à distance* 108
Sommer, Robert 274
Sonnenstein Asylum 116, 176, 204
Sonoma State Hospital 162
soul 6, 10, 108, 194, 249, 314, 318, 336
Southern Medical Association 284
*Southern Medicine and Surgery* 350
Spanish fly 30, 32
Spanish Inquisition 177
Spanish water torture 177
Speransky, Sergei 321–322
spermatic anemia 254
Spiritualism 241
spirituality 101
*Spirochaeta morsus-muris* (*aka* Spirillum minor) 135
Spitzka, Edward 215
Spradley, James 190–191
Spring Vale Asylum 316, 321
Spurzheim, Johann Gaspar 74
Stanford University Medical School 130
Starr, Moses Allan 288
State Hospital Lübeck 204
State Infirmary of Leros 74

State Mental Hospital of Umedalen 286
Steiner, G. 137
Steinhof Mental Hospital (*aka* Vienna Asylum) 23, 87
Stephansfeld Hospital for the Insane 40
Stiff, Phillip 114
Stirling District Asylum 295
Stockton State Hospital 160, 162
Stony Lodge Hospital 343
Stralsund Asylum 314
Strecker, Edward 285
stuttering 17
*Suddenly, Last Summer* 294
suffragettes 142
suggestion 18, 86, 93, 138, 241, 274, 305, 306
suicide 41, 49, 196, 232, 288, 332, 342
surgery 97, 270, 278, 347–351; appendicostomy 347; colectomy 348, 349, 350; pericolic membranotomy 349; sham 274; sphenoidotomy 350; tonsillectomy 348; *see also* Cotton, Henry; exodontia, genital surgery, psychosurgery
Surrealist artists 105
Surrey County Lunatic Asylum for Paupers 116, *117*, 184
Sussex Lunatic Asylum 171
Sutherland, Henry 145
Sydenham, Thomas 43
syphilis 42, 122, 129, 130, 132, 137, 172; Great Pox 121, 122; neosalvarsan 122; salvarsan (*aka*, compound 606, magic bullet) 122, 135, 136, 137; penicillin 129; *Treponema pallidum* 122; Wasserman test 122; *see also* dementia paralytica; general paralysis of the insane; general paresis; neurosyphilis

Taguet, Henri 23
Tait, Lawson 159
Tait's surgery 159
Talairach, Jean 280
Talbot, John 189
talking cure 102, 266; *see also* Freud, Sigmund; psychoanalysis
taraxein 59
tartar emetic 29, 30, 185, 315
Tarumianz, Mesrop 286
Templeton, W.L. 132
Terrence, Christopher 21
testosterone 156, 269
Théatre du Palais-Royal 115
Thiel, Luise 228
Thorazine (*aka* Chlorpromazine, Largactil) 168, 188, 196, 211, 276, 325
Thurnam, John 186
Ticehurst House Private Asylum 39, 178

Tierney, Gene 331
Tillotson, Kenneth 189, 351, 352, 353
*Time* magazine 136, 284
Tissot, Samuel Auguste Daniel 67, 163; *Onania* 67
"Titicut Follies" 112
tobacco 40, 66, 122; tobacco smoke enema 66
Todde, Carlo 160–161
*Tollhaus* 201
Toronto Temporary Asylum 80
total push 269, 351–353; *see also* Myerson, Abraham; Tillotson, Kenneth
Tourette, Gilles de la 305, 306
transference 240; as redirection of feelings 240, 345; as redirection of symptoms 240, 241
trauma 73, 93, 102, 107, 181, 265, 278, 288, 291, 353
traveling medicine shows 82
Traverse Colantha Walker 73
Traverse City State Hospital 73, **249**
Trenton State Hospital (*aka* New Jersey State Hospital; New Jersey State Lunatic Asylum) 73, **99**, 100, 125, 190, 348, 349, 350; *see also* Cotton, Henry; exodontia; Nash, John Forbes; surgery
Tschallener, Johann 235
tuberculosis (*aka* consumption) 9–11, 24, 123, 221, 268; tuberculin vaccine 123, 132; *see also* phthisical insanity
Tuke, Daniel Hack 30, 33, 150, 151, 170, 216, 217, 218, 230, 273
Tuke, Harrington 144, 148
Tuke, J. Batty 294
Tuke, Samuel 80, 245, 246; moral architecture 247; tenets of moral treatment 245; *see also* moral treatment, moral management, or moral therapy; York Retreat
Tuke, Thomas Harrington 251
Tuke, William 70, 248, 252; moral treatment 209, 244, 319; York Retreat 244–245
tuning fork (*aka* diapason) 240, 305
Tuskegee State Hospital 291–292
Tyler, Edward 341, 342

Ulett, George 340–341
unconscious 14, 94, 104, 105, 147, 241, 281, 343
*Une Visite à Bedlam* 108
unfit 153, 160
United Nations Convention on the Rights of Persons with Disabilities 197
United States Army Chemical Warfare Service 22
United States Central Intelligence Agency (CIA) 45, 49, 277, 327;

# Index

MKULTRA sub-project 68, 277; Society for the Investigation of Human Ecology 277, 327; *see also* Allan Memorial Institute of Psychiatry; brainwashing; Cameron, D. Ewen; Sargant, William
United States Surgeon General 333
United States Veterans Administration 292
Universal Declaration of Human Rights 219
university-based psychiatric clinics 8
University of Giessen 247
University of Heidelberg Hospital for the Insane 105
University of Jenna 202
University of Leipzig 56, 217
University of Nebraska College of Medicine 131
University of Paris 122
University of Tartu 288
University of Tübingen 30, 200, 206, 217, 321
University of Vienna 167
University Psychiatric Clinic 45
Upper Peninsula Hospital 196
Upson, Henry Swift 99
Urquhart, David 187
uterine epilepsy 153
uterine restlessness 179
Uwins, David 26

Vadstena Asylum 5
Valentin, Louis 28–29
van der Kolk, J. Shroeder 38, 40; as "Dutch Pinel" 249; as "Dutch Tuke" 249
Van Deusen, Edwin Holmes 11–12
vanDeventer, Jacob 9
Van Gellhorn, Arthur 80
VanGordon, Donald 343
van Helmont, Franciscus Mercurius 308
van Helmont, Jean Baptiste 167, 308
Varjabedian, Anthony 343
Västra Marks Hospital 173
Venetian Treacle, or Venice Treacle 43
ventricular arrhythmia 86
vesaniae 52; *see also* Cullen, William
Ville-Evrard Asylum 23
Vincent, Clovis 94–96
*vis medicatrix naturae* 53
Viszanik, Michael 181
vitamins 261, 262, 263, 352; A 262; B1 262; B2 262; B3 (*aka* niacin, nicotinic acid) 261, 262; C (*aka* ascorbic acid) 262; D 262, 267; megavitamin therapy 263; *see also* orthomolecular therapy
Volta, Alexander 82
voltaic pile 89, 145
Von Hirsch, C.F. 306
Vonnegut, Kurt 95
Vonnegut. Mark 263; *The Eden Express* 263
Vordingborg Asylum 338
*Voyage au Bout de la Nuit (Journey to the End of Night)* 95
Vrouwenweeshuys Asylum 310

Wagner, Charles Gray 295
Wagner-Jauregg, Julius 94; Kauders trial 94, 132; malaria-induced fever 123, 132, 134, 137; Nobel Prize 94, 123, 132
Wakefield, Edward 220, 221, 227
*The Wall (Le Mur)* 172
Wallace, David 295
Ward 5 sleep room 49
Wards Island Asylum (*aka* Manhattan State Hospital East) 11, 24, 195, 215
Warner, George 133
Warren Sate Hospital 21
Washington University Medical School 340
Watson, W.S. 259
Wattenberg, Oscar 204
Watts, James 283, 284, 285, 286; Freeman-Watts Procedure 281–287; terminating partnership with Freeman 291
*The Way Up from Down* 263
Weir, Thomas 224
Weitz, Don 345–346
Wesley, John 82
West Riding Pauper Lunatic Asylum 204
West Virginia Lobotomy Project 291–293; *see also* Freeman, Walter; psychosurgery
Western Washington State Hospital for the Insane (*aka* Western State Hospital) 182, 226, 291
Westminster Hospital 145
White, William Alanson 133–134, 173–174, 238, 350
Wickham, R.H.B. 204
Widroe, Harvey 183
Wiederhold, Georg Moritz 321
Wiglesworth, Joseph 11, 90
Williams, S.W.D. 144–145
Willis, Francis 6, 137–138, 318
Willis, Nathaniel Parker 109
Willis, Thomas 40, 113, 141, 220, 306, 312
Willmar State Hospital 285
Wilson, Milo 114
Wimmer, August 9
Winslow, Forbes 185
Winternitz, Wilhelm 167
Wisconsin Psychiatric Institute 50
Wiseman, Frederick 112
Wittmann, Blanche 240; Queen of the Hysterics 266
Wolpe, Joseph 17, 18
wonder drug fraud 274
Woodbury, Michael 172
Woodson, Marion Marle 162
Woodward, Samuel B. 44, 64, 250–251
Worcester Asylum 44, 64, 250, 251, 262, 343
World Association of Psychoanalysis 173
World Health Organization's Chain-Free Initiative 222
World Psychiatric Association 25, 333
World War I 45, 66, 87, 92, 93, 94, 95, 105, 132, 202, 223, 274, 275, 278; Treaty of Versailles 282
World War II 22, 48, 50, 52, 73, 153, 184, 190, 211, 286, 293, 329, 343, 353
Worthing, Henry 285
Wright, Doug 109
Württemberg Hospital 202
Wyman, Rufus 238

Yale University 278
Yankton State Hospital 291
Yellow House 201
Yellowlees, David 162–163
yin and yang 38
yoke 13
York Asylum 120, 226, 244; *York Star* 120
York Retreat 70, 80, 105, 145, 186, 195, 244, 246, 247, 248, 249, 319; cure rates 250; *see also* moral treatment, moral management, or moral therapy; Tuke, Samuel; Tuke, William

Zanzibar Psychiatric Hospital 74
Zeller, George 23–24, 195, 295

www.ingramcontent.com/pod-product-compliance
Ingram Content Group UK Ltd.
Pitfield, Milton Keynes, MK11 3LW, UK
UKHW051851210426
5322IPUK00025B/656